The Qing Dynasty
and Traditional
Chinese Culture

To Cynthia —
With best regards
and warmest wishes)
Richard Smith
November 10, 2016
Rice University

The Qing Dynasty
and Traditional
Chinese Culture

Richard J. Smith

ROWMAN & LITTLEFIELD
Lanham • Boulder • New York • London

Published by Rowman & Littlefield
A wholly owned subsidiary of The Rowman & Littlefield Publishing Group, Inc.
4501 Forbes Boulevard, Suite 200, Lanham, Maryland 20706
www.rowman.com

Unit A, Whitacre Mews, 26-34 Stannery Street, London SE11 4AB, United Kingdom

British Library Cataloguing in Publication Information Available

Library of Congress Cataloging-in-Publication Data

Smith, Richard J. (Richard Joseph), 1944-
  The Qing Dynasty and traditional Chinese culture / Richard J. Smith.
  pages   cm
  Includes bibliographical references and index.
  978-1-4422-2192-5 (cloth : alk. paper) — 978-1-4422-2193-2 (pbk. : alk. paper) —
  978-1-4422-2194-9 (electronic) 1. China—Civilization—1644-1912. I. Title
  DS754.14.S6 2015
  951/.03 – 23

                                                                2015001789

Printed in the United States of America

To Lisa and Tyler,
with gratitude, as always,
for the love, the help and the humor

And to my teachers and students,
for their continual inspiration

Contents

Preface

In the twenty or so years that have elapsed since a version of this book appeared in print under the title *China's Cultural Heritage: The Qing Dynasty, 1644–1912* (Westview Press, 1994), there has been an explosion of Western-language scholarship on China—the Manchu-dominated Qing dynasty (1636–1912) in particular. One reason, of course, is that new information has become available, much of it produced by Chinese scholars on Taiwan and the Chinese Mainland. Previously unavailable or undiscovered archival materials in Chinese, Manchu, Mongolian, and other relevant languages have come to light, vastly enhancing our knowledge of the multicultural world of the Manchus. At the same time, and in the same way, archaeological discoveries have enhanced our understanding of the ways that the Manchus established and ruled their vast empire.

This new information has not only advanced our knowledge of, and heightened our appreciation for, political, social, economic, intellectual, and cultural developments in the Qing period (now dated from the declaration of the dynasty by the Manchus in 1636, nearly a decade before the conquest of China in 1644, to the abdication of the last emperor in 1912). It has also produced new ways of looking at the relationship between the Manchus and their Chinese subjects, as well as the relationship between the Manchus and other Inner Asian peoples (including the Mongols, Tibetans, and Central Asians). One result has been the emergence of what has been called "The New Qing History." This scholarly approach is based on the idea that the Qing empire and "China" were not, in fact, the same thing—that the Manchus regarded China not so much as the "center" of their empire (although their primary capital became the Chinese city of Bejing after 1644), but rather as part (albeit an important part) of a much wider dominion that extended far into the Inner Asian territories of Mongolia, Tibet, the Northeast (often called Manchuria until comparatively recent times), and Xinjiang (also called Chinese Central Asia).

This broader and far less "sinocentric" (China-centered) approach to the Qing has prompted a fundamental reevaluation of the degree to which the success of the Manchus as alien conquerors can be attributed to their adoption of Chinese culture—a process often described as "sinicization." This nationalistically inspired notion has long dominated Chinese scholarship on the Qing (and other dynasties of conquest in China as well). Today, however, most China scholars in the West, and increasingly in China, accept the basic outlines of the New Qing History. There are still, however, lively debates over matters of degree: for instance, to what extent did "traditional Chinese culture" influence the political, social, economic, and cultural policies of the Manchus? Conversely, to what extent did the culture of the Manchus and other Inner Asian peoples affect Chinese patterns of perception, thought, and behavior, not only during the Qing period but also in earlier eras?

Previously, in what at least some advocates of the New Qing History must have seen as a capitulation to "traditional" Chinese scholarship, my perspective was one that placed primary emphasis on the ways the Manchus promoted and adopted Chinese culture. I have not abandoned my interest in the multifaceted role played by Chinese culture in the Qing period, but I have tried to locate this evolutionary process within a larger conceptual and analytical framework—one that includes not only the cultural heritage of the Manchus but also the world of Inner Asia more generally. By focusing on the elaborate cultural interaction between the Tungusic-speaking Manchus and the Han Chinese, whose inherited traditions were more than three thousand years in the making, I hope to identify the processes by which the alien conquerors and their domestic subjects negotiated their respective identities and at the same time came to share certain cultural assumptions.

I chose the cover illustration of this book with multiculturalism in mind. Dorgon (1612–1650) was the fourteenth son of Nurhaci (1559–1626), founder of what became the Qing dynasty. A highly respected warrior and an imperial prince, Dorgon played a crucial role in the Manchu conquest of China in 1644, and was also a powerful regent for the young Shunzhi emperor (r. 1643–1661). This official portrait nicely captures, I think, the interplay of Manchu and Chinese influences. The sword suggests the proud military heritage of the Manchus, and the inscription is written in Manchu. The full text (partially cropped out) reads: "Portrait at thirty-eight years of age, painted by younger brother Canghai." At the same time, however, the painting is clearly in the manner of Chinese imperial portraiture. Dorgon wears Chinese-style imperial regalia (modified according to Manchu fashions), and he is surrounded by Chinese artifacts, including painted "dragons," a book bound in the traditional Chinese manner, an antique Chinese bronze, and a table with Chinese decorative motifs. As the de facto ruler of China during the first decade of the Shunzhi emperor's reign, Dorgon championed Manchu military virtues, but also relied heavily on Chinese advisers as well as a Ming dynasty-style civil bureaucracy staffed by large numbers of Chinese officials.

What else is distinctive about this book? In addition to broadening the concept of Qing dynasty culture to include influences from Manchuria, Mongolia, Central Asia, and Tibet, I have, like many advocates of the New Qing History, placed the Qing empire in a truly "global" context—one that existed well before China's nineteenth-century encounter with Western imperialism. This historical perspective takes into account not only the regime's long-standing and ongoing engagement with the interconnected worlds of Inner Asia, East Asia, Southeast Asia, and South Asia, but also its more recent political, economic, and intellectual interactions with the larger international world that included Europe and the Americas.

Although my major emphasis in this study is on broad interpretive themes and general historical and cultural patterns, I will give a significant amount of attention to anomalies, contradictions, and especially debates—not only those that occurred among scholars during the Qing dynasty but also those that have engaged Asian and Western scholars ever since. Despite the apparent cultural unity of late imperial China, which Chinese intellectuals have long remarked on and generally celebrated, China's historical experience, as well as the scholarship focused on that experience, has been marked by a great deal of division and dissent. What I have tried to do in this work is to track the complex interplay between centrifugal and centripetal tendencies in Qing politics, society, and culture, and to identify certain important scholarly controversies surrounding Qing studies.

Another goal in this volume has been to give greater attention to several important cultural themes of the Qing period that received somewhat short shrift in the first two editions of *China's Cultural Heritage*—notably law, science and technology, gender, sexuality, and military affairs. These are all areas in which the scholarly literature over the past two decades has been especially rich. In this literature we can see, for example, that Qing political, social, and cultural policies made a decided difference in the lives of elite women empire-wide and, by the same token, women's activities made a difference to the ruling Manchus. The same basic point can be made for many other realms of culture, including those noted above.

Finally, the volume in hand addresses in a more direct and systematic way the relationship between elite and popular culture in Qing dynasty China than was evident in *China's Cultural Heritage*. My recent work on almanacs (*tongshu*, *lishu*, etc.) and especially topically organized encyclopedias of daily use (*riyong leishu*) has caused me to reflect more carefully on this complex and constantly evolving relationship. Such sources have also contributed to a more sophisticated discussion of a primary theme of the original book: culture as categorization.

The list of people to thank for assistance with this study is nearly as long as the selected bibliography, and virtually all of them are listed there, often with multiple citations. But I owe a special debt to the following people, who read parts of the manuscript in one form or another but who bear no responsibility for the final product: Mark Elliott and Stephen Wadley (for whom there is no doubt not enough on the Manchus in this book), Benjamin Elman (for whom there is no doubt not enough on science and technology), Jonathan Ocko (for whom there is no doubt not enough on law), Nanxiu Qian and Harriet Zurndorfer (for whom there is no doubt not enough on women and literature), Susan Shih-shan Huang (for whom there is no doubt not enough on art), and William Rowe and Kent Guy (for whom there is no doubt not enough of everything). All I can say is that my discussions of these topics are richer for their concrete suggestions and, above all, their excellent scholarship. Among the others who have assisted me at one or another stage in my writing and/ or thinking about this book are my colleagues at Rice University—including not only Susan Huang and Nanxiu Qian, as noted above, but also Lisa Balabanlilar, Anne Chao, Anne Klein, Jeffrey Kripal, and Allen Matusow. I would also like to thank Christopher Basso at Rowman and Littlefield for his patience and excellent editorial assistance. Above all, and as always, I am grateful to my wife, Lisa, and my son, Tyler, for their substantial help and invariable good humor.

Introduction

Traditional Chinese culture is hot in contemporary China. To be sure, "Let the past serve the present" (*Gu wei jin yong*) has been a prominent slogan in the People's Republic of China (PRC) since its founding in 1949, but the phrase has often rung hollow. During the Great Proletarian Cultural Revolution (1966–1976), for example, traditional Chinese values were officially and explicitly condemned as the core of the hated Four Olds: "Old thought, old culture, old customs, and old habits." Now, however, political figures and intellectuals alike are singing the praises of the past. Since his inauguration in 2012, the president of the PRC, Xi Jinping, has consistently promoted China's ancient values and traditions as a means by which to achieve a new "spiritual civilization." Vice Chairman Xu Jialu of the Standing Committee of the National People's Congress claims that the "worldviews, values, ethics, and aesthetics" of China can serve as an antidote to the corrosive effect of modern American culture, which, he avers, "poses a serious challenge to our traditional values."[1] Meanwhile, prominent writers on both sides of the Taiwan Strait have churned out hundreds of books in the last few years celebrating every aspect of traditional Chinese beliefs and behavior, from Confucianism, Buddhism, and Daoism to the practices of ancestor veneration and even *fengshui*.

But what, exactly, are "traditional" Chinese beliefs and values? The book in hand seeks to answer this question, focusing on features of language, patterns of behavior, beliefs, and values, systems of logic, symbolic structures, aesthetic preferences, material achievements, and institutions that came to be considered distinctively "Chinese" before "modern" Western values and ideas became viable cultural options in the late nineteenth century. The natural time frame for such a study is the Qing dynasty (1636–1912), the last imperial regime and a crucial bridge between traditional and modern life in

China. The Qing was the largest consolidated empire in Chinese history and by far the most successful dynasty of conquest. It has often been said that no dynasty was more "Confucian" in outlook or more self-consciously antiquarian in its promotion of traditional Chinese culture.[2]

But, as indicated in the preface to this book, these matters are the subjects of great debate in the scholarly community, particularly among advocates of the New Qing History. This revisionist view of the Qing dynasty has been championed by a number of able scholars such as Beatrice Bartlett, Pamela Crossley, Nicola di Cosmo, Mark Elliott, Johan Elverskog, James Millward, Carla Nappi, Peter Perdue, Evelyn Rawski, and others, who work comfortably with various Inner Asian languages in addition to Chinese and Japanese. These authors have taken pains to locate the Qing dynasty in its broader Inner Asian context, and to place special emphasis on Manchu as opposed to Chinese traditions.[3] Against this trend is Pei Huang's recent work, *Reorienting the Manchus: A Study of Sinicization, 1583–1795* (2011), which attacks the New Qing Historians and attempts to revive the 1960s argument of Chinese scholars, such as P. T. Ho and others, that the Manchus were thoroughly "sinicized"—that is, they fully assimilated Chinese traditions at the expense of their own. There is obviously a productive middle ground between these interpretive poles, and I intend to explore it systematically.[4]

Much can be said for the view that the key to the political success of the Manchus was their hierarchically conceived multiculturalism—specifically their ability to exploit cultural links with "the non-Han peoples of Inner Asia and to differentiate the administration of the non-Han regions from the administration of the former Ming provinces."[5] As Joanna Waley-Cohen has noted in a stimulating and insightful review article on the New Qing History, the Manchus judiciously and self-consciously combined "Inner Asian and Chinese traditions so as to simultaneously appeal to both constituencies," thus creating "a continuum between the sedentary agricultural world of China proper and the pastoral nomadic world . . . where once a strict line had been drawn."[6] What is more, advocates of the New Qing History have demonstrated that the Manchus kept far more of their ethnic identity than P. T. Ho's account of the sinicized Qing allowed. Indeed, Manchu identity grew stronger during the eighteenth century, particularly under the Qianlong emperor (r. 1735–1796), who, by emphasizing genealogy and not simply cultural affinity, helped to sharpen the distinction between who was Manchu and who was not.

Yet by all accounts the Qianlong emperor, like his accomplished grandfather the Kangxi emperor (r. 1661–1722), was a great patron of Chinese culture, well versed in the Chinese language, deeply wed to Confucian values (especially filial piety), conversant with Chinese art and literature, and willing to promote Chinese scholars at virtually all levels of his administration. Was he "sinicized" or not? Perhaps, as I have indicated elsewhere, this is the wrong question to ask. The important point, underscored by the title of a 2009 biography by Mark Elliott—*Emperor Qianlong: Son of Heaven, Man of the World*—is that for essentially pragmatic reasons, Qianlong and all subsequent Qing emperors presented a "Chinese" face to their subjects who lived south of the Great Wall while presenting other ethnic faces to their subjects in other parts of the empire. To be sure, as we shall see, there was much to admire about China's cultural heritage—its philosophies, its religious traditions, its art, its literature, and so forth. Indeed, all Manchu princes, and a great many other Manchu and Mongol elites as well, received a substantial education in these areas. But they also received a solid grounding in other cultural traditions, including, quite naturally, their own.

One of the most persistent critics of "sinicization," Pamela Crossley, has argued vehemently that this particular notion is "conceptually flawed, intellectually inert and impossible to apply," because Chinese culture has itself changed constantly in response to, among other things, the "challenging and differentiating effects of aboriginal, border and heterodox cultures." As she puts the matter, "historically it is surely true that the geographical and cultural entity of China is a totality of convergently and divergently related localisms."[7] No modern scholar would quarrel with this basic characterization. Yet simply to speak of aboriginal, border, and heterodox cultures is to implicitly acknowledge a hegemonic, "central," and "orthodox" culture in constant tension with them. What then, we may legitimately ask, were its most prominent and significant features during the Qing period—at least in China Proper?[8]

Somewhat surprisingly, at least to me, *China's Cultural Heritage* remains the only book in English (or any other Western language for that matter) to give systematic attention to all major facets of traditional Chinese culture in the Qing period. The best and most balanced overview of the Qing dynasty to date, William Rowe's *China's Last Empire: The Great Qing* (2009), focuses primarily on political, social, and economic events and institutions, devoting less than ten pages to Chinese philosophy, religion, art, and literature. Evelyn Rawski's *The Last Qing Emperors: A Social History of Qing Imperial Institutions* (1998) focuses primarily on the political, social, and ritual activities of the Manchu court, giving comparatively little attention to the arts and sciences. And even Pei Huang's *Reorienting the Manchus* (2011), for all its emphasis on the theme of sinicization, has comparatively little to say about most Chinese cultural practices beyond a single final chapter titled "Architecture, Religion and Confucianism."

How do we account for this comparative neglect of "culture" as a thematic focus among historians of China in the West? It is certainly not a problem for most scholars in Chinese environments, whether the People's Republic, Taiwan, or Hong Kong. One reason is that throughout the twentieth century and into the twenty-first, one of the most persistent topics of both scholarly and popular discourse has been the question of what place "traditional Chinese culture" should occupy in China's quest for "modernity." This question acquired special urgency after the fall of the Qing dynasty in 1912, and it continues to this day in the form of debates over "National Studies" (*Guoxue*) and the idea of a contemporary "Cultural Renaissance" (*Wenhua fuxing*) in the PRC. Not surprisingly, then, there are literally thousands of recent studies by Chinese scholars with titles that contain the phrase "China's traditional culture" (*Zhongguo/Zhonghua chuantong wenhua*).[9] These works identify, often with considerable precision, not only the general categories of Chinese cultural concern but also the specific "special characteristics" (*tezhi, tese, tezheng*, etc.) of traditional Chinese culture.

But the situation for Western scholars of China is somewhat different. Although they are well aware of the effort on the part of modern Chinese scholars to grapple with the legacy of their complex past, they also bear a special, self-imposed burden—one that comes with the responsibility of objectively and sensitively evaluating the outlook and experiences of the "other." The introduction to Paul Cohen's *China Unbound: Evolving Perspectives on the Chinese Past* (2003) suggests the weight of this intellectual obligation:

> When I initially advanced the notion of a China-centered approach [to the study of Chinese history], I observed that one of the approach's more important concomitants was a gradual shift away from *culture* and toward *history* as the dominant mode of structuring problems of the recent Chinese past (by which I meant chiefly the nineteenth and twentieth centuries). During the 1950s and 1960s, when the impact-response and tradition-modernity paradigms held sway in American scholarship, enormous explanatory power was invested in the *nature* of China's "traditional" society or culture—and, of course, in the ways in which this society-culture differed from that of the West (or Japan).[10]

Cohen's concern here is that an emphasis on "culture"—and particularly an emphasis on cultural differences between "China" and "the West"—will lead to cultural essentialism: "the radical reduction of a culture to a particular set of values or traits that other cultures are believed incapable of experiencing." Yet throughout Cohen's book he repeatedly speaks of "culture," and at one point even acknowledges the obvious fact that "there are important differences between the cultural traditions of China and the West."

The reason for this apparent inconsistency, as I have discussed elsewhere,[11] is that we have to generalize in order to make meaning, even as we recognize, at least proverbially, that "all generalizations are false, including this one." So what then is the difference between generalizing and essentializing? Perhaps it is a matter of motive. As Cohen and others have argued, in the past an emphasis on culture in Western scholarship has sometimes encouraged the "Orientalist" idea of a "stagnant and involuted China"—a notion that served to justify the Western invasions of the nineteenth century as a "necessary stimulus" to modernization.[12] In the view of critics such as Judith Farquhar and James Hevia, a "static" conception of culture allowed imperialism to be represented as "a salvation project."[13]

But the misuse of a term hardly justifies its abandonment. In fact, a moment's reflection tells us that culture, however defined, is never static; it constantly undergoes transformations in response to new stimuli, whether generated from within or introduced from without. Ideas, values, aesthetic standards, and customs change, as do institutions, laws, rituals, symbols, and even language. Moreover, there are always significant gaps between theories and practices. At any given time, however, a shared sense of meaning(s) within a particular group provides the necessary framework for cultural conversations, with respect not only to points of agreement but also, and importantly, points of disagreement. As Marshall Sahlins has observed, "In order for categories to be contested . . . there must be a common system of intelligibility, extending to the grounds, means, modes, and issues of disagreement." It would be difficult, he argues, "to understand how a society could function, let alone how any knowledge of it could be constituted, if there were not some meaningful order in the differences. If in regard to some given event or phenomenon the women of a community say one thing and the men another, is it not because men and women have different positions in, and experience of, the same social universe of discourse?"[14]

The conception of culture put forward in this book emphasizes the many and varied ways that groups of people, large and small, name, categorize, and interpret experiences and phenomena in order to create a coherent version of reality, and how, in turn, their understanding of this "reality" tends to influence their attitudes and behavior.[15] Seen in this light, "tradition"—by which I mean an inclination on the part of individuals and groups at a given time to draw on inherited wisdom and indigenous experience for guidance in dealing with the present and the future—is not a negative value, nor is it necessarily inimical to "modernization," whatever the latter term might mean. As my colleagues and I put the matter in our introduction to *Different Worlds of Discourse: Transformations of Gender and Genre in Late Qing and Early Republican China* (2008), "terms such as 'tradition' and 'modernity' can no longer be seen as mutually exclusive concepts with fixed characteristics but rather as fluid categories that existed in a vast crucible of cultural choices."[16]

Some cultural choices, however, are more attractive or meaningful than others at a particular time. Again, we may ask why. The fundamental reason is that they are rewarded in some way: politically, socially, financially—even psychologically. Childhood stories invariably reflect desired cultural attributes, as do the books assigned in more formal educational environments. Similarly, reference works of various kinds indicate important categories of cultural concern. Arts and crafts also convey symbolically significant and/or aesthetically satisfying messages. For these reasons, I have given particular attention in this book to the mechanisms by which politically and socially valued knowledge was transmitted, as well as the means by which it was reinforced in Qing dynasty China.

Among the most influential conduits for the transmission of useful cultural knowledge in the Qing period, at least in China Proper, were primers such as the *Sanzi jing* (Three character classic), anecdotes such as those contained in the *Ershisi xiao* (Twenty-four examples of filial piety), and popular religious tracts, plays, and short stories of all sorts. Also influential were topically organized handbooks, almanacs (*lishu, huangli, tongshu,* etc.), and "encyclopedias for daily use" (*riyong leishu*). Encyclopedias such as the *Wanbao quanshu* (Complete book of myriad treasures; hereafter WBQS) not only provided guidance to literate individuals regarding the management of their daily lives (lifecycle ceremonies, the instruction and care of children, agriculture, sericulture, animal husbandry, medicine, martial arts, and so forth), they also included sections on amusements, language, calligraphy, art, music, and poetic composition. In addition, they summarized information derived from far more complicated ritual regulations, penal statutes, commercial codes, and a wide range of other official and unofficial documents (see appendix E).[17]

In addition to encyclopedias, popular tracts, and performances designed for entertainment, public readings of imperial pronouncements such as the so-called Sacred Edict (*Shengyu*) disseminated culturally valued information, although with mixed results. And, of course, of crucial importance to Qing rulers and subjects alike were the philosophical, historical, and literary works on which the Chinese civil service examination system was based. As we shall see, the exam system in late imperial China was a particularly powerful instrument for reinforcing desired cultural values. But so were other aspects of Chinese culture: the legal system, clan rules that had the force of law, and a wide range of Chinese religious beliefs and practices, from the veneration of ancestors to notions of supernatural retribution in Buddhism and Religious Daoism.

By looking closely at the most important documents, structures, spaces, rituals, and artifacts of the period, we are in a position to outline the contours of what may be described as the "dominant culture" of Qing dynasty China—not the only culture, of course, but the one that virtually all Qing subjects who saw themselves as "Chinese" (the self-styled "Han people" or *Hanren,* comprising nearly 95 percent of the population in China Proper) identified with to a significant extent. Few, if any of them, would have disagreed in principle with the following fourteenth-century characterization of "China" (*Zhonghua*, the "Central [Cultural] Florescence"):

> Central Cultural Florescence is another term for Central Kingdom [*Zhongguo*]. When a people subjects itself to the Kingly Teachings [that is, Confucianism] and subordinates itself to the Central Kingdom; when in clothing it is dignified and decorous, and when its customs are marked by filial respect and brotherly submission; when conduct follows the accepted norms [of ritual] and the principle of righteousness, then one may consider them [part of the] Central Cultural Florescence.[18]

This was the evolving culture that was challenged by the "differentiating effects of aboriginal, border and heterodox cultures" discussed by Crossley (and a number of other New Qing historians as well). And its putative "special characteristics" are among the ones that Chinese scholars in Taiwan, Hong Kong, and the Mainland continue to identify as important markers of what they comfortably describe as "traditional Chinese culture."

Let us consider briefly the case of Wei Zhengtong, a prolific scholar from Taiwan, whose book *Zhongguo wenhua gailun* (An introduction to Chinese culture) has been extraordinarily influential to this day on both sides of the Taiwan Strait—not least in a number of college courses devoted to China's traditional culture. Originally written in 1968, it has been reprinted a number of times, most recently in 2008 on the Mainland. In it, Wei identifies the following "ten great special characteristics" of traditional Chinese culture: (1) Isolated creation (*duchuang xing*), (2) a long [and glorious] history (*youjiu xing*), (3) an absorptive capacity (*hanshe xing*), (4) unity (*tongyi xing*), (5) conservatism (*baocun xing*), (6) an esteem of peace and harmony (*chongshang heping*), (7) feelings of local affinity (*xiangtu qingyi*), (8) a humane cosmological outlook (*youqing di yuzhou guan*), (9) the fundamental position of the family and clan (*jiazu benwei*), and (10) an emphasis on moral spirit (*zhongde jingshen*).[19]

Wei naturally appreciates the difficulties of generalizing across space and time, as well as problems of theory and practice, and the very real differences in outlook arising from social variables such as class, gender, age, and so forth. It is clear, for example, that "China," however defined, has never been entirely isolated from outside influences, and that despite a deep cultural commitment to "peace" and "harmony" on the part of elites and commoners alike, Chinese history has often been marked by extraordinary violence.[20] Still, Wei sees value, as do I, in identifying certain broad patterns of belief and behavior that were not only part and parcel of Han identity during the

Qing period, but were also meaningful to the Manchus and other ethnic groups, both within China Proper and on the periphery.

We may take Wei's fourth "special characteristic," unity, as an example of his historically grounded approach. One important factor contributing to China's unity, Wei argues, was the standardization of the Chinese written script, which began during the Qin dynasty (221–206 BCE). From that time onward, into the twentieth century, any classically trained literate person could read anything written during that entire twenty-two-hundred-year period. Another factor, he claims, was the pervasiveness, longevity, and effectiveness of Confucianism as a ruling ideology after the establishment of the Han dynasty (206 BCE–220 CE). A third factor was the strength and tenacity of traditional Chinese cultural values. Foreign invaders, he writes, might periodically offer a military threat, and even conquer all of China—as they did during the Yuan/Mongol (1279–1368) and Qing/Manchu dynasties—but they did not offer a fundamental cultural challenge. This apparent domestication of foreign invaders also accounts, in Wei's view, for China's extraordinary longevity as a civilization.[21]

There were, of course, other factors that contributed to the unity of traditional Chinese culture—notably the civil service examination system, established in a rudimentary form during the second century BCE and extended empirewide in China during the Tang dynasty (618–907 CE). In the Ming (1368–1644) and Qing periods, this system produced a highly literate, culturally homogeneous social and bureaucratic elite, which served as a conscious model to be emulated by all levels of Chinese society. Because the mature examination system drew candidates from nearly every part of the empire and every major social class (including, on occasion, the peasantry), it encouraged a relatively high degree of both geographical and social mobility (see chapters 2, 3, and 10).

Furthermore, for several centuries China's government leaders had recognized the need for centrally supervised political and social control mechanisms that transcended kinship ties and helped to overcome local loyalties—devices such as the frequent transfer of officials, the rule of avoidance (which prohibited officials from serving in their home areas), and various systems of mutual responsibility in matters such as tax collection and the maintenance of order. All the while the imperial Chinese state, with its enormous authority and substantial coercive power, attempted to standardize conduct, regulate customs, maintain status distinctions, and promote ideological orthodoxy by means of carefully crafted systems of law, education, ritual, religion, and propaganda.[22]

There can be no doubt that during the Qing period China's alien Manchu rulers—outnumbered at times by as much as two hundred to one by the Han

Chinese majority—saw the practical value in patronizing and enhancing inherited forms of political, social, and ideological control, at least in the area south of the Great Wall. As a result of their vigorous and self-conscious promotion of Ming dynasty institutions and culture, together with the dramatic growth of agriculture, industry, commerce, and literacy during the sixteenth and early seventeenth centuries, the Qing dynasty witnessed the fullest development of traditional political, economic, and social institutions up to that time, as well as the greatest degree of regional integration within China Proper.[23]

Yet cultural integration in the Qing period was far from complete, and not simply because of the self-conscious and highly particularized multiculturalism of the Manchus—an approach to administration that involved not only a recognition of other "kings" and cultures within the vast Qing empire, but also efforts to preserve their own ethnic identity and a deliberate effort to separate themselves physically from their Chinese subjects. Even taken only on its own terms, Qing dynasty China's immense size, regional variety, and ethnic cleavages present a picture of staggering political, social, and economic complexity. As in the past, Qing China remained a sprawling patchwork of more or less discrete physiographic regions of varying sizes—all with different landforms, soils, climates, natural resources, marketing systems, communication networks, population densities, local dialects, non-Han ethnic groups (now referred to as minorities [*shaoshu minzu*]), and so forth.

Qing policymakers recognized the administrative problems attending this cultural diversity all too well. As caretakers of the largest consolidated empire in Chinese history, they oversaw (and tried to manage) a myriad of local cultures—each with its own distinctive styles of food, housing, clothing, speech, worship, entertainment, and so forth. Feelings of local affinity ran extremely deep in China (note Wei Zhengtong's seventh "special characteristic"), and regional peculiarities were expressed in the common saying: "Customs differ every ten *li* [several miles]" (*shili butong feng*). Qing propaganda efforts, such as the Yongzheng emperor's *Shengyu guangxun* (Amplified instructions on the Sacred Edict)—first promulgated in 1724 and designed to be read aloud to commoners by local officials or scholars throughout the empire on the first and fifteenth days of each month—openly acknowledged China's regional variety. One version stated, for example: "In some places people are kindly, in others, reserved; in some places they are extravagant and pompous, in others, frugal and simple. Because the customs of each place differed, the ancient sages created ceremonial practices [*li*] to standardize conduct."[24]

Regional stereotypes, which were deeply rooted in the consciousness of all Chinese, remained remarkably consistent throughout the Ming and Qing dynasties, and many persist to this day (see appendix C). Some focused on

fundamental differences between the north and south; others were based on
a few large geographical areas defined primarily by prominent river drainage
systems; and still others had a provincial foundation. Thus, for instance, the
people of north China were generally considered stronger, more diligent, honest, and conservative than their southern counterparts; the people of Yue (part
of the Xi River drainage system in the far south of China) were described as
"the most susceptible to a belief in ghosts and spirits" (*zui xin guishen*); and
the Kangxi emperor reflected widely prevailing attitudes in describing the
people of Jiangsu province as "prosperous but immoral."[25] The Qianlong emperor, for his part, considered the area of Jiangnan (basically southern Jiangsu
and northern Zhejiang) "the center of [Chinese] culture," and therefore the
area that was most resistant to direction from the Qing state.[26]

Not only did such stereotypes affect the way people from one area perceived (and treated) people from another, they also affected the self-image
of residents within each particular subculture. Moreover, because localism
was so powerful and ubiquitous a force in China Proper, sojourners and even
longtime residents in urban centers continued to identify strongly with their
"home" areas—hence the popularity of native-place guild halls (*huiguan*) and
other associations based on common geographical origins. Natives, for their
part, categorized "outsiders" hierarchically according to different gradations
of "Chineseness."[27]

As might be expected, urban and rural dwellers in China had different
viewpoints and lifestyles. But the cultural gap between them was perhaps not
as great as in many other agrarian societies, because only about 25 percent
of the traditional elite in Qing times had permanent urban residences, and
many of them played an active role in rural affairs within the structure of the
so-called standard marketing system. Nonetheless, Robert Redfield's famous
distinction between the "great tradition" of literate urban elites and the "little
tradition" of essentially nonliterate peasants has been highly influential as
a conceptual paradigm. And indeed, commoners and elites wore different
clothes, ate different foods, lived in different dwellings, and occupied different positions in the eyes of both society at large and the state. They even
received markedly different treatment under the law. Their beliefs also differed significantly. Arthur Wolf contends, for example, that "there has always
been a vast gulf between the religion of the [Chinese] elite and that of the
peasantry."[28]

Of course many scholars maintain that this dichotomy is too stark, that
it does not do justice to "complex historical and spatial patterns of cultural
interaction." Majorie Topley, for one, has emphasized the way "the scholar's
tradition acted on that of the ordinary man . . . [and] the latter's tradition
reflected back on him." In the same spirit, Maurice Freedman has castigated

those who distinguish too sharply between elite "rationality" and peasant "superstition." G. William Skinner's pioneering research on marketing communities shows that China has always been a multi-tiered society, not simply a two-leveled one; that instead of a single "little tradition" there were in fact many "little traditions." And Wolf himself argues that the most significant point to be made about Chinese religion is that "it mirrors the social landscape of its adherents. There are as many meanings as there are vantage points."[29]

David Johnson, co-editor of *Popular Culture in Late Imperial China* (1985), identifies at least nine different vantage points. In an effort to do justice to the complexity of traditional Chinese society, and to illustrate the ways in which consciousness is influenced by "relations of dominance and subordination," Johnson proposes a model of late imperial China based on three crucial variables: education, legal privilege, and economic position (either self-sufficiency or dependence). In his conceptual framework, the Chinese social spectrum ranges from the classically educated, legally privileged, and economically self-sufficient elite (the most dominant group) to illiterate and dependent commoners (the least influential). Intermediate groups reflect different combinations of these three variables—for instance, self-sufficient and literate but neither legally privileged nor classically educated; legally privileged and self-sufficient but not literate.[30]

The virtue of this scheme is that it provides a way to identify with greater precision the relationship between any given social or political strategy and any given system of thought—whether conveyed through symbols and myths, religious visions, or other products of the human "verbal imagination"—and China's hierarchy of dominance. At the same time, it alerts us to the various ways that ideas and strategies may have moved from one social group to another—a process that Johnson hypothesizes "must almost always have involved the mediation of some of the groups lying in between."[31] Johnson's model is not, however, particularly helpful in identifying differences in outlook and activity within any one of the nine groupings. After all, dominance in traditional China involved more than literacy, legal protection, and economic well-being. An elite woman could enjoy all three of these advantages and still experience discrimination. What about the problem of gender?

On the one hand, we know that in many respects women in Qing dynasty China were disadvantaged; their subordinate status was reflected in law and social customs, elite and popular literature, proverbs, handbooks on household ritual, and even medical texts. Yet despite these forms of discrimination, there were ways for women to establish a positive identity and to protect their interests in a male-dominated world. The narrative of women in the Qing period is much more than simply the story of subordination and discrimination.[32] Like disadvantaged men, women at all levels of Chinese society developed various strategies of empowerment, some of which simultaneously improved their lot and threatened the social status quo. Moreover, the Qing period witnessed an unprecedented surge of literary and artistic creativity on the part of Chinese (and Manchu) women. An enormous amount of research on these "writing women" over the past two decades has vastly enhanced (and complicated) our understanding of late imperial China.[33]

Of course the theme of diversity, like the theme of unity, has its limits. Taken to extremes, this kind of sociological "deconstruction"—like its counterpart in literary criticism—leads to the discomfiting conclusion that ultimately there can be no cultural meaning beyond individual experience and idiosyncratic interpretation. This will not do, for, as I have suggested earlier, the term "culture" itself implies shared frameworks of understanding, and I hold as an article of interpretive faith the assumption that cultural meanings can in fact be derived from a careful "reading" of various forms of social discourse and symbolic action, whether expressed in written texts (both classical and vernacular), art, architecture, music, the production and exchange of artifacts and commodities, rituals, dramatic performances, or in predictive activities such as science, economic speculation, medicine, and divination.[34]

To be sure, the historical record is vast, complex, and often contradictory, and we are far from understanding all we need to know about the Qing period, especially at the local level. But one thing is certain: the Qing was, by virtually any measure, one of the greatest of all dynasties in China, and it lasted for nearly three hundred years, despite enormous challenges from both within and without. How do we account for its remarkable success? As we shall see, part of the answer lies in the Inner Asian assumptions and cultural practices that the Manchus brought to China, including their distinctive notions of pan-Asian kingship and their strategic employment of a powerful political, social, and military organization that came to be known as the Eight Banners (*Baqi*). Part of the answer can also be found in the administrative institutions and bureaucratic practices that the Manchus inherited from the Ming dynasty and modified, often significantly, for their own purposes. Yet another reason for their success rests in their selective appropriation and/or patronage of certain Chinese cultural practices and constructions. These practices and constructions are my primary focus in the pages that follow.

So just to be perfectly clear: although I have tried to take into account the many ways that the Manchus and other Inner Asian peoples and cultures contributed to the special character of the Qing dynasty, my fundamental goal remains to identify and explain the basic features of Han culture in China Proper as it evolved during the Qing. Clearly this evolution was not simply a matter of "sinicizing" the Manchus, regardless of the degree to which the Qing court and/or the inhabitants of Banner garrisons in the provinces may have found certain features of Chinese culture attractive. Instead it was a complex process that worked in both directions.

Three related themes serve as the interpretive foundation of this book. As with Wei Zhengtong's somewhat more abstract and idealized "special characteristics," all three have loomed large in the Chinese documentary record for at least two thousand years, providing fundamental frameworks of understanding for Chinese and Manchus alike during the Qing period. The first might be described as cognition, the way the Chinese viewed the world around them. Despite the complexity of this outlook, with its intersecting Confucian, Buddhist, and Daoist elements and elaborate interplay between elite and popular conceptions of reality, we can identify at least one construct, or paradigm, that transcended ideology and class. Sometimes described as "complementary bipolarity," this viewpoint was expressed by the well-known but much-abused concepts of *yin* and *yang*. These terms and their equivalents appear everywhere in the Chinese language and literature, yet too often they are taken for granted by Chinese scholars and either misunderstood or underestimated by scholars in the West.

In traditional times, *yin* and *yang* were used in three main senses, each of which may be illustrated by the following excerpts from *Honglou meng* (Dream of the red chamber), China's greatest and most influential novel.[35] In a colorful conversation with her maidservant Kingfisher, Shi Xiangyun remarks: "Everything in the universe is produced by the forces of *yin* and *yang*. All the transformations that occur result from the interaction of *yin* and *yang*. When *yang* is exhausted, it becomes *yin*, and when *yin* is exhausted, it becomes *yang*. *Yinyang* is a kind of force in things that gives them their distinctive form. For example, Heaven is *yang* and Earth is *yin*; water is *yin*, fire is *yang*; the sun is *yang*, the moon is *yin*." "Ah yes," replies Kingfisher, "that's why astrologers call the sun the '*yang* star' and the moon the '*yin* star.'" After a lengthy discussion of several other such associations and correlations, Kingfisher ends the conversation by observing: "You're *yang* and I'm *yin*. That's what people always say: the master is *yang* and the servant is *yin*. Even I can understand that principle."[36]

Yin and *yang* were then (1) cosmic forces that produced and animated all natural phenomena; (2) terms used to identify recurrent, cyclical patterns of rise and decline, waxing and waning; and (3) comparative categories, describing dualistic relationships that were inherently unequal but almost invariably complementary. Virtually any aspect of Chinese experience could be explained in terms of these paired concepts, ranging from such mundane sensory perceptions as dark and light, wet and dry, to abstractions such as unreal and real, non-being and being. *Yinyang* relationships involved the notion of mutual dependence and harmony based on hierarchical difference.

Yin qualities were generally considered inferior to *yang* qualities, but unity of opposites was always the cultural ideal. Moreover, the logic of *yinyang* thinking included the important idea that something that was *yin* in one set of relationships could be *yang* in another. For instance, a wife might be considered *yin* to her husband but *yang* to their children.

Perhaps no other major civilization in world history has had such a pervasive, tenacious, and essentially naturalistic world view—an accommodating outlook contrasting sharply with the familiar religious dualisms of good and evil, God and the Devil, which are so prominent in the ancient Near Eastern and Western cultural traditions. The notion of *yinyang* complementarity, reinforced by certain Confucian intellectual predilections, no doubt contributed to the remarkable harmonizing tendencies of traditional Chinese thought—the obvious inclination on the part of Chinese scholars to value "similarity and convergence" over "difference and divergence."[37]

Much that is most distinctive about traditional Chinese culture can be explained by reference to *yinyang* conceptions and to the elaborate correlative thinking associated with these ideas. *Yinyang* polarities appear explicitly or implicitly in the description or evaluation of nearly every area of traditional Chinese life, from politics, cosmology, aesthetics, symbolism, and mythology to ancestor worship, divination, medicine, science, and sex. All classes of Chinese literature employ *yinyang* terminology and/or symbolism, from the exalted Confucian classics to popular proverbs. Steven Sangren's *History and Magical Power in a Chinese Community* (1987) provides an excellent example of how a full understanding of the hierarchical and asymmetrical "contrastive logic" of *yin* and *yang* provides valuable insights into the complex relationship between order and disorder in Chinese social life.[38]

The second major theme of this study is ethics, an abiding cultural concern, as a glance at any Chinese political, social, or philosophical tract will clearly indicate. Like the concepts of *yin* and *yang*, ethical terms pervade every area of traditional Chinese culture, including music and the arts. The modern Chinese philosopher Zhang Dongsun tells us that the most numerous terms in the Chinese language come from the related realms of kinship and ethics; and the index to Feng Youlan's well-known abridged history of Chinese philosophy states apologetically, "So much of Chinese philosophy is ethical that a complete list of 'ethical' references would be almost impossible."[39]

Yet it is not only the pervasiveness of ethical concerns in China that is striking. It is also the essentially nonreligious source of basic moral values. In sharp contrast to many other cultural traditions, the Chinese viewed their moral order as a human product. To be sure, Confucian philosophers perceived a fundamental "spiritual" unity between the mind of Heaven (*Tianxin*) and the mind of Man (*Renxin*), but the ethical system prevailing in China throughout the entire imperial era did not emanate from any supernatural authority. The major institutional religions of late imperial times—Buddhism and Religious Daoism—made no major contribution to the preexisting core of Confucian values, although they did play an extremely important role in reinforcing secular norms.[40]

The relationship between secular values and traditional Chinese religion is reflected in the following inscription taken from a stele in the temple of the Consort of Heaven (*Tianhou*) in Foshan, Guangdong:

> When administrative orders from the national and local capitals attain their objectives, and when there is the Way of Man to provide effective principles and discipline, it is not necessary that spirits and gods play an impressive and prominent role [in government]. But when [such orders and the Way of Man] fail to effect justice, spirits and gods will be brought to light. . . . As the ancients put it, in the age of perfect government, spirits became inefficacious. It is not that the spirits are inefficacious; it is that when rewards and punishments are just and clear, the *yang* [human elements] function effectively, and the *yin* [spiritual elements] retreat into the background . . . so there is no need for the efficaciousness [of spirits and gods].[41]

Supernatural authority might always be invoked in China, but in the ideal Confucian world it was considered unnecessary.

At the core of the orthodox Chinese ethical system in the Qing period were the so-called Three Bonds (*Sangang*), explicitly identified throughout most of the imperial era with the *yinyang* notion of complementary inequality. The Three Bonds were those between ruler and subject, father and son, and husband and wife. The nonreciprocal obligations owed by inferiors to superiors within this framework set the authoritarian tone of much of life in traditional China and gave concrete expression to two of the most powerful organizational symbols or metaphors in the Chinese sociopolitical vocabulary—the bureaucracy and the family. Undergirding both these symbols and these relations was an expansive, cosmologically based structure of ritual (*li*).

Ritual provides the third major theme of this book, in a sense uniting the other two themes with itself. Like art, ritual can be considered a kind of "language" that celebrates manmade meaning. It indicates the way a culture group represents its situation to itself, how it links "the world as lived and the world as imagined."[42] Of course, there are many different kinds and definitions of ritual, but in its broadest sense the term includes all forms of structured social behavior, from the etiquette of daily greetings to solemn state ceremonies and religious sacrifices.

Such a broad definition accords well with traditional Chinese usage. Although the term *li* never completely lost either its original religious and mystical connotations or its close association with music as a source of moral cultivation, by late imperial times *li* had come to embrace all forms of sacred and secular ritual, as well as the entire body of social institutions, rules, regulations, conventions, and norms that governed human relations in China. *Li* has been variously translated as standards of social usage, mores, politeness, propriety, and etiquette, but no single term does justice to the wide range of its meanings and manifestations.[43]

Testimony to the enduring value of *li* in traditional China may be found in the venerated classic texts known as the *Yili* (Etiquette and ritual), *Zhouli* (Rites of Zhou), and *Liji* (Record of ritual), which together exerted a profound influence on the Chinese elite from the Han period through the Qing. These three works alone provided hundreds of general principles and guidelines, as well as thousands of specific prescriptions for proper conduct in Chinese society. Furthermore, they inspired a huge number of supplementary ceremonial handbooks, which left few questions of ritual or etiquette to chance. For hundreds of years the Chinese commonly referred to China as "the land of ritual and righteousness" (*liyi zhi bang*), equating the values of *li* and *yi* with civilization itself.

One measure of esteem for ritual in the Qing dynasty may be found in the great imperially commissioned encyclopedia titled *Gujin tushu jicheng* (Complete collection of writings and illustrations, past and present, 1726; hereafter TSJC), which devotes nearly 350 of its 10,000 *juan* (volumes) to *li*. This figure does not include the 320 *juan* devoted to the subcategory on religion (which overlaps ritual in subject material to a significant degree), nor does it take into account the prominent place occupied by the teachings of ritual (*lijiao*) and ritual institutions (*lizhi*) in subcategories such as music, Confucian conduct, classical and noncanonical writings, human affairs, social intercourse, family relations, official careers, examinations, government service, and political divisions. Indeed, very few of the TSJC's thirty-two subcategories are devoid of references to *li*.

The observations of longtime Western residents in China provide yet another index of the importance of ritual in the Qing period. Even during the nineteenth century, when Chinese society seemed to be disintegrating in many areas, informed Westerners repeatedly remarked on the scrupulous attention still given to all forms of ritual by the Chinese. S. W. Williams spoke for many in asserting that "no nation has paid so much attention to [ceremonies] in the ordering of its government as the Chinese. The importance attached to them has elevated etiquette and ritualism into a kind of crystalizing force which has molded [the] Chinese character in many ways." Arthur H. Smith maintained that "ceremony is the very life of the Chinese," echoing John Nevius, who said "politeness [in China] is a science, and gracefulness of manners a study and a discipline."[44]

No major aspect of Chinese life was devoid of ritual significance, and ritual specialists were ubiquitous at all levels of society. Everyone from emperor to peasant recognized the importance of ritual in preserving status distinctions, promoting social cohesion, sanctifying ethical norms, and transmitting tradition. Closely linked to both cosmology and law, ritual in China performed the function Clifford Geertz assigns to "sacred symbols" in synthesizing moral values, aesthetics, and world view.[45] Perhaps no other single focus allows us to see so clearly the preoccupations of the Chinese people (and their Manchu overlords) in late imperial times.

Although this book is organized topically for clarity and convenience, it emphasizes the interrelationship of the parts of traditional Chinese culture to the whole. Therefore, in addition to weaving a web of significance around the distinctive unifying themes of cognition, ethics, and ritual, I have tried to build an integrated structure of meaning through the sequential presentation of the topical material. Unlike most of the book, the first two chapters are more or less chronologically organized. Their primary purpose is to provide a general sense of how China's leaders in the Ming and Qing dynasties responded to changing local, regional, and global circumstances, and how their leadership helped to shape the outlook and institutions of both the Manchus and the Chinese into the twentieth century. The next two chapters analyze Qing institutions in some detail, illustrating the various ways in which traditional political, social, and economic organizations simultaneously reflected and reinforced the Chinese sense of order and cultural unity. At the same time, these chapters highlight distinctively Manchu contributions to both state and society in Qing times, underscoring, among other things, the problems created by regional and ethnic differences in China and the larger empire.

The subsequent discussions of language, thought, and religion, taken together, should contribute to an understanding of the complex interplay between certain longstanding Chinese patterns of perception, expression, belief, and behavior. Again, we must keep in mind the multicultural heritage of the Manchus, which included the use of Manchu, Mongolian, and Tibetan as "official" languages and involved religious practices derived entirely from Manchu traditions. Similarly, the chapters on art, literature, and social customs are designed to show not only how Qing cultural policies varied under different emperors and historical conditions, but also how certain shared symbols, organizing principles, aesthetics, and ethical values were manifest in various important areas of Qing artistic and social life over time and across space. By the end of these discussions, the reader should have a clearer understanding of the internal "logic" of the hybrid Chinese cultural system and an appreciation for why it lasted so long and held together so well—despite many challenges.

The final chapter of this book explores the place of traditional Chinese culture in China's historical development from the mid-nineteenth century to the present. For most of this period—including both the Republican era (1912–1949) and the People's Republic of China (1949–present)—a prominent theme in both scholarly and popular discourse has been the disparagement of the Manchus. In particular, they have been blamed for the humiliations suffered by China at the hands of foreign imperialists in the last few decades of the Qing dynasty. But this is too narrow a view. As a number of late Qing (Chinese) patriots observed, China's problems predated the Manchus; they were the legacy of two thousand years of Chinese tradition.[46] And this, too, may be an overly narrow view because, as I suggested earlier, "tradition" and "modernity" are not mutually exclusive categories. In any case, this much is certain: although the dominant theme of Chinese history during the last century and a half has been dramatic, revolutionary change, it is clear that longstanding patterns of language and perception, as well as traditional attitudes toward politics, ritual, social organization, ethics, art, and literature, have played a significant role in the "search for modern China" (to play on a famous book title).[47]

Chapter One

The Ming Dynasty Legacy

As with all previous and subsequent regimes, the Ming or "Bright" dynasty (1368–1644) built on the institutional foundations established by its predecessor. Yet it also modified them in significant ways, and, of course, created new institutions as well. In the case of the Ming, the preceding regime was the Mongol-controlled Yuan dynasty (1271–1368), which, like the Manchu-dominated Qing less than three centuries later, created an administrative system that drew on the cultural traditions of the conquerors as well as those of the conquered. If we can speak of the "sinification" of the Qing, we can, perhaps, also speak of a certain "Mongolization" of the Ming.

The Ming was, by any standard, a great and glorious dynasty. Overall, the state was well organized and powerful, society was stable, and the regime's agrarian economy flourished. Law codes became regularized and legal texts served as educational tools. Urban networks expanded, reflecting and contributing to the growth of productivity and commercial exchange. The Chinese population doubled over the course of the dynasty, and literacy became ever more prevalent. Massive construction projects reflected the state's formidable political and economic strength, as did its military campaigns. The pacification of China Proper involved consolidation of areas in the far south and southwest that had been largely beyond imperial reach during the Yuan dynasty. Meanwhile, the more fully integrated southeastern provinces of China became the launching point for a vibrant maritime trade. By the late Ming period, China had become deeply involved, for better and for worse, in the world economy.[1]

Not surprisingly, the Ming was a period of great accomplishment in literature and the arts, not only in terms of elite culture but also "popular" culture. The Ming is known for its crafts (especially porcelain, but also gardens and architecture) and its vernacular literature (especially novels), as well as for its accomplished painters, essayists, and calligraphers. Ming religious life was robust and philosophy of all sorts flourished. What is more, although the Ming state generally championed a relatively rigid form of neo-Confucian orthodoxy known as the School of Principle (*Lixue*, also designated the Cheng-Zhu School, based on the family names of its two eleventh-century progenitors), a number of other schools of philosophy developed in the Ming, some of which offered radical challenges to orthodox Confucianism. A particularly distinctive feature of late Ming intellectual life was the presence of Jesuit missionaries at court and in the provinces, a development that had implications not only for Ming philosophy, but also for science and technology.

At no time in China's history—either before the Ming dynasty or after—was the so-called tributary system of Chinese foreign relations as highly developed and comprehensive as it was during Ming times. John Wills has noted, however, that only from about 1425 to 1550 were all facets of the regime's foreign relations "fitted into . . . a fully fledged 'tribute system.'" After 1550 or so, he maintains, "private overseas trade in Chinese shipping, the opening of Macau, Mongol trade at border markets, and regional military politics on the northeast frontier were among the many signs of an unraveling of the Ming tribute system."[2] Looking ahead to the Qing, however, we may ask whether the tributary system unraveled irrevocably.

A fair-minded assessment of the Ming dynasty and its legacy forces us to consider a number of issues that will also be relevant to our analysis of the Qing: What was the nature of imperial rule? To what extent did the early emperors shape the character and course of the dynasty? Was the government marked by effective centralized administration or was it one constrained by factional politics at court and vested interests in the provinces? How prevalent were Confucian ruling principles, and how effectively did they operate? What was the relationship between "foreign" influences and domestic culture?

One can argue that the early Ming emperors' desire to exert their will over all acts of governance was never as effectively institutionalized as they intended or perhaps supposed it to be. David Robinson writes, for example, that throughout the Ming period, even during the autocratic reign of the first emperor, the court was "an arena of competition and negotiation" in which "a large cast of actors pursued individual and corporate ends." Moreover, "Ming court culture underwent frequent interpretation and rearticulation, processes often driven by immediate and keenly felt personal imperatives, mediated through social, political, and cultural interaction, and producing sometimes unexpected results."[3]

Nonetheless, as Frederick Mote points out, "the aura of great power" on the part of the Ming cannot easily be dispelled: "For evidence," he writes, "one need only look at China's enhanced position in East Asia in Ming times." Mote goes on to assert that the Ming emperors were "the capstone in an authority structure that could not function without them. They were the ritual heads of state and society within a civilization in which ritual possessed a scope of functional significance scarcely comprehensible to us today." At the same time, they were "the executive officers of a system that required their daily participation in deciding and validating routine acts of governing." Because no actions or appointments were possible without the emperor's literal seal of approval, his workload was enormous, and his tasks were "operationally institutionalized in Ming times to a degree hitherto unknown."[4] Not all of the Ming emperors could shoulder this enormous burden, however, with the result that as the state administrative apparatus grew ever more expansive and sophisticated, there was a natural devolution of power holding from direct rule by a pair of extraordinarily powerful early autocratic emperors to a system of shared authority. Sometimes this authority was effectively delegated and at other times it was simply usurped.

One of the most important features of Ming government was the civil service examination system. As we shall see, this recruitment apparatus did not always yield officials who were properly prepared to undertake practical administrative tasks. But according to the deep-seated Confucian principles that served as justification for the exams, government was a matter of personal integrity and moral example, not technical expertise. Officials were not expected to be specialists, they were supposed to be moral leaders. Of course, there was always a gap between the theory and practice of Confucian government, but the Ming examination system assured that every decade or so a new group of highly educated individuals would enter the service of the state, bringing "freshness and energy" to the regime.[5]

Most scholars have favorably viewed the Ming founder's efforts to better the lot of the peasantry by improving rural conditions and curbing abuses in local government. Whether these efforts were motivated by altruism or a recognition of the state's political interests or both is impossible to state with certainty. But success in all such enterprises depended entirely on the cooperation of local bureaucrats and nonbureaucratic elites known as "gentry" (*shenshi*)—usually, but not always, examination degree holders. When these functionaries operated in concert and according to the dictates of the throne, much could be achieved. But resistance at the local level could, and did, thwart many an idealized plan. And so it was that in Ming administration, as it would later be under the Qing, imperial policymaking involved a wide array of actors, not all of whom had the same goals and interests, much less the same levels of integrity.

Timothy Brook has pointed out that although the Ming state "legitimately monopolized all authority, secular and spiritual," this formal monopoly did not mean that the state's authority was either "unencumbered or unchallenged." Officials might resist government policies that did not suit their political interests, and the gentry class, for its part, proved able to develop "horizontal strategies of control and competition," turning economic opportunity into social gain "without threatening the survival or legitimacy of the state." This bargain between political and social power, "paid for by trading wealth and autonomy for durable state tokens of status," held until the latter decades of the nineteenth century.[6]

THE ESTABLISHMENT OF THE MING

The founder of the Ming dynasty, Zhu Yuanzhang (known by his posthumous title Ming Taizu or "Grand Progenitor of the Ming," but more commonly by his reign name Hongwu, "Great Martial Power"), ruled China with an iron hand from 1368 to 1398. No account of the Ming can avoid reference to the personality and policies of this emperor, or those of his equally dynamic son, the Yongle ("Eternal Happiness") emperor. John Dardess describes the dynastic founder as "a grim and suspicious autodidact" who "inspired fear and respect, but no love or devotion," and whose "penal repressions were frequent and savage." Not a pleasant fellow, it seems. Having raised the standard of revolt against the Yuan dynasty using the vocabulary of Buddhist millenarianism, Zhu Yuanzhang recognized in the course of his anti-Mongol rebellion, and especially after coming to power, the need to attract Confucian scholars to his cause as a form of legitimization. By the early 1630s he had recruited several prominent Chinese intellectuals—notably Liu Ji (1311–1375) and Song Lian (1310–1381)—as his political advisers. Their advice to him was to become a "ruler-teacher" (*junshi*), and to emphasize the idea of "restoring antiquity" (*fugu*). These roles, they argued, would bring China back from the laxity, corruption, and oppression that had occurred under Mongol rule.[7]

One may question whether the Hongwu emperor exemplified the "Confucian" values he espoused, but there can be no doubt about the vigor with which he championed them. During the early years of his reign, the emperor churned out a great many rules, regulations, and especially moral admonitions, including his famous Six Sacred Maxims (*Shengyu liuyan*), drawn directly from the writings of the great Song neo-Confucian philosopher Zhu Xi (1130–1200). They were: (1) perform filial duties to your parents; (2) honor and respect your elders and superiors; (3) maintain harmonious relationships with your neighbors; (4) instruct and discipline your sons and grandsons; (5) let everyone work peacefully for his own livelihood; and (6) do not commit wrongful deeds.[8] These admonitions were distributed widely throughout the empire and were reportedly even recited to peasants in the field.

As steadfast as he was tireless, the Hongwu emperor transformed much of the Ming political, social, and economic landscape in the thirty years of his reign, leaving a concrete institutional legacy to his successors.[9] In the realm of government, he began by establishing a rudimentary Yuan-style bureaucratic structure in his southern capital at Nanjing (formerly known as Jiankang or Yingtian), and ordering leading scholars of the realm to draft ceremonial regulations, statutes, and ordinances. He embarked on a building campaign to erect imposing palace structures, as well as altars for imperial sacrifices to Heaven, Earth, and other state-approved spirits.[10] He commissioned educational institutions, including a new National University and a new Hanlin Academy for Confucian scholars who were charged with various literary and secretarial tasks. He also ordered the building of a shrine to his ancestors, and arranged for the preparation of a state calendar to be known as the *Datong li* (Calendar of the Great Unification).

All these measures were designed to bolster the new emperor's claim to have received the Mandate of Heaven (*Tianming*) from the Mongols. This legitimizing concept, which lay at the heart of Chinese dynastic politics from the early Zhou dynasty (c. 1050–256 BCE) into the twentieth century, was predicated on the idea that Heaven, variously conceived (as an impersonal deity or an abstract moral-spiritual force; see chapters 3, 6, and 7), bestowed the right to rule on the household of an ethically upright leader, but its "mandate" could be withdrawn if any ruler of the family line proved unworthy.

The accession of the Hongwu emperor took place on January 23, 1368. It began with sacrifices to Heaven and Earth at separate suburban altars, followed by ceremonies at the shrine of his ancestors, where he bestowed patents and seals conferring posthumous temple names on four generations of his forebears. The ceremonies ended at the imperial palace, where he received congratulations from civil and military officials. John Langlois summarizes the purpose of these activities:

> The accession ceremony blended the emperor's two roles in a formal ritual. The emperor was head of the imperial lineage, which he ruled by birthright in perpetuity. He thus performed sacrifices and acts of filial submission to his ancestors in a shrine constructed expressly for this purpose. He was also head of the bureaucracy and the representative of all the empire vis-a-vis the powers of Heaven and Earth. The ceremonies allowed the officials and the emperor to act out symbolically their respective relationships.[11]

Significantly, the emperor issued a "Proclamation of the Accession," which was not only circulated throughout the areas under direct Ming control, but also distributed to neighboring East Asian states. It is worth quoting at length:

> I am the ruler of the Middle Kingdom. When the dynastic fortune of the Song dynasty had reached an end, Heaven commanded the immortal [referring to Qubilai Khan] in the desert to enter the Middle Kingdom and become the lord of the empire. [The throne] was passed from son to grandson for more than a hundred years. But now [the Yuan] dynastic fortune also has ended. . . . Bearing the favor of Heaven and the spirits of the ancestors, . . . [I] repeatedly commanded my military officers to make a rigorous show of our might. The four quarters were suppressed and settled, and the people have come to rest secure in their fields and villages. Today the great civil and military officers, the numerous officials, and the masses join in urging me to ascend [the throne], revering me as August Ruler (*Huangdi*), thereby making me the lord of the black-haired people [the Han Chinese]. Reluctantly acceding to the requests of the multitude, on the fourth day of the first moon of the second year of Wu, I offered sacrifices to Heaven and Earth on the south side of Zhong Mountain and ascended the throne of the emperor at the southern suburban altar. The title of the empire has been set as Great Ming. The present year has been designated the first year of Hongwu [Great Martial Power]. Respectfully entering the Ancestral Temple, I have conferred posthumous titles of emperor and empress upon four generations of my ancestors. [I] have erected in the capital a great altar to the Spirit of the Land and a great altar to the Spirit of the Grain. The consort, née Ma, has been made [my] empress, and the eldest son has been made heir apparent. This shall be promulgated throughout the empire, and all shall be made to know of it.[12]

Here we see the Ming emperor performing his most important symbolic and substantive roles: as high priest, secular king, filial son, and protector of China's agrarian economy.

The Hongwu emperor was also commander in chief of the Ming military. Because several parts of China Proper were still in the hands of the Mongols or millenarian rebels, he sent his armies to "pacify" these areas to the north, west, and southwest. His most pressing goal was, of course, the capture of the Yuan capital of Khanbaliq (Chinese: Dadu). On September 14, 1368, his forces attacked the city, which soon fell. He renamed it Beiping ("Pacified North"). Further campaigns secured control over various strategic northern areas. Meanwhile, Ming troops extended the reach of the dynasty into the southern provinces of Guangxi, Fujian, and eventually remote Yunnan.

During the long reign of the Hongwu emperor, the Ming army came to be organized into outposts known as *weisuo*. Under this system, which had its direct origins in the Yuan, each prefecture had a garrison (*suo*) of about a thousand soldiers and each grouping of two or more prefectures had a military district (*wei*) consisting of about 5,600 troops. These forces were sustained by the so-called *tuntian* system, which provided each soldier in peacetime with from forty to fifty *mou* of agricultural land (c. six to eight acres). The result was that *weisuo* garrisons were largely self-sufficient. According to the official Ming History (*Mingshi*), about 70 percent of the soldiers in border areas took up farming while the remaining 30 percent were employed as guards. In the interior, the balance was about 80 to 20.[13] These soldiers were recruited primarily from three sources of manpower: Yuan dynasty remnants, the military forces that had brought Zhu Yuanzhang to power, and a system of conscription implemented after the conquest. All of these troops and their families were part of a hereditary class of warriors. This system operated with reasonable effectiveness until the 1430s.

The Hongwu emperor recognized from the outset that military power, although essential, was only part of the formula for effective dynastic rule. Within weeks of his accession to the throne in 1368, therefore, he made a concerted effort to bolster his religious authority, creating a pair of parallel agencies to control the two main religious orders of the realm. These agencies were known as the Buddhist Affairs Academy (*Shanshi yuan*) and the Daoist Affairs Academy (*Xuanjiao yuan*), each headed by a respected cleric. Later that year, while the emperor was campaigning in the north, the learned Buddhist monk Fanqi (1296–1370) conducted elaborate ceremonies outside of Nanjing designed to placate the spirits of the soldiers who had died in the Ming wars of conquest (monetary indemnities were also distributed to survivors).

In early 1369, the emperor further extended his religious reach by granting official titles to several hundred "spirits of walls and moats" in administrative centers from the county level to the capital. These deities were known popularly as City Gods (*chenghuang*), and they served as the otherworldly counterparts to local civil officials (see chapter 7). Somewhat later, the emperor brought Daoist clerics to Nanjing to give counsel on religious affairs and to assist in divination. Meanwhile, he banned all "unorthodox" sects, including the White Lotus Teachings (*Bailian jiao*) and the Manicheans (*Mingjiao*). Later (1382) the emperor would order the Confucian temples throughout the land to offer twice-yearly sacrifices to the Sage and his major disciples.[14]

One of the first official secular documents issued by the Hongwu emperor was the Great Ming Code (*Da Ming lüling*; later simply *Da Ming lü*), promulgated in 1368 and based on the Tang dynasty's legal code of 653. As with his administration more generally, the emperor tinkered with the Code substantially, making major revisions that were published in 1374, 1376, 1383, and 1389. The final version of 1389 became the law of the land for the rest of the Ming dynasty (it is sometimes described as the Ming "constitution"), as well as a concrete model for the Great Qing Code of the following regime. Yonglin Jiang has translated the Ming Code into English and, in a companion study, he has situated it in the broader context of the evolution of law in late imperial China. What he shows clearly is that although the Code was intended to be a tool of social engineering, designed to harmonize Ming society and assimilate non-Han peoples to Han culture, it was also a deeply metaphysical document, predicated on the idea that crime was nothing less than a violation of the cosmic order, which had to be rectified by state policy.[15]

During the early years of the Hongwu reign, the Ming bureaucracy followed the general administrative model of the Yuan. At the highest level it consisted of a Grand Secretariat (*Zhongshu sheng* and later *Neige*, led by a Prime Minister), a Censorate (*Ducha yuan*; later *Yushi tai*) and a Chief Military Commission (*Dudu fu*). Below these three major offices were the Six Boards (*Liubu*), in charge, respectively, of Civil Appointments, Revenue, Rites, War, Punishments, and Public Works. An office of transmission soon developed to handle written communications between the Six Boards and provincial officials who were known as "commissioners for the promulgation and dissemination of government policies" (*chengxuan buzheng shi*, later shortened to *buzheng shi*).

The thirteen provinces (*sheng*) of the Ming empire were subdivided into prefectures (*fu*), departments (*zhou*; also known as subprefectures), and counties (*xian*; often described as "districts"). These counties, administered by magistrates (*zhixian*) who were appointed directly by the throne, served as the key institutions of Ming local government. At the beginning of the dynasty, the state claimed jurisdiction over 887 counties, and by the end of the dynasty this number had risen to 1,159. These units, in turn, were divided into administrative subcategories known generally as *xiang* (sometimes translated as "cantons"), which were, in turn, subdivided into various smaller units. At the lowest level, villages were organized into essentially self-governing communities overseen by "elders" (*laoren*).[16]

In order to help staff his nascent bureaucracy, the Hongwu emperor ordered the reinstitution of the civil service examinations in mid-1370, based on Yuan models and Yuan neo-Confucian orthodoxy. The format did not, however, become regularized until 1384. From that time onward the exams consisted of three main parts: (1) explicating the meaning of the Confucian Classics and the Four Books (see chapter 6); (2) discourses (*lun*), including questions on law; and (3) policy questions (*ce*). The notorious "eight-legged" essay (*bagu wenzhang*), based on carefully balanced clauses (*duiju*) and equally well-chosen pairs of balanced characters (*shudui*), did not become the official style of the civil service examinations until 1487. This basic stylistic model prevailed in China until the late nineteenth century.[17]

A high priority of the new Ming government was naturally the reconstruction of the agrarian economy and the distribution of grain to war-ravaged parts of the country. As early as 1370, the emperor ordered the Board of Revenue to require all households (*hu*) throughout the land to register with the local government, listing the names of all adult males and all properties. Although taxes were comparatively low, the imperial granaries almost always had a surplus. Later, in the 1380s, after various experiments with different forms of tax collection, the Hongwu emperor instituted two new systems—the "Yellow Registers" (*huangce*) and the "Fish Scale Registers" (*yulin tuce*)—ostensibly in order to curb governmental fiscal abuses that had disadvantaged the peasant class, but also to curb tax evasion. He also embarked on campaigns to improve the state's economic infrastructure, opening up new land, planting trees, building roads and bridges, institutionalizing the courier system of communications, repairing irrigation systems, building dikes, and dredging waterways, including the Grand Canal—the economic lifeline between north and south China. In addition, he enrolled the population in a household registration system known as *lijia* ("communities organized by decimal units"), which provided labor and material for local government offices and projects, supplementing the land tax.

A turning point in the early history of the Ming was the emperor's personal attack on a number of his high-level administrators and their followers, beginning in 1380. Fearing that his Prime Minister was planning to assassinate him, the Hongwu emperor began a wide-ranging purge that lasted for nearly fifteen years. An estimated forty thousand individuals lost their lives as a result. From an institutional standpoint, the vendetta was also far-reaching. In the course of his purge, the emperor abolished all three of his highest-level administrative bodies—the Grand Secretariat, the Censorate, and the Chief Military Commission. From this point onward, the emperor acted as his own Prime Minister, the sole supervisor of about a dozen major organs of Ming government. Small wonder it has become common among historians of China to describe the early Ming dynasty as particularly "despotic."[18]

In foreign policy, the Hongwu emperor's priority remained the eradication of the Mongol threat in the north and the protection of other parts of the empire. After the Eastern Mongols had been defeated and a Tibetan invasion of Sichuan had been repelled, the emperor turned his attention to solidifying and regularizing China's relationships with its tributaries. Early in his reign he had proclaimed a noninterventionist policy toward tributary states on or near China's borders. In this proclamation he made it clear that these foreign entities were all equal to one another but not equal to the Middle Kingdom, and that China would not attack them unless compelled to do so for defensive purposes. He also sought to limit Ming contact with foreigners and to ban maritime trade—apparently because he feared that foreign alliances might threaten his regime. Naturally, however, the ban could not be effectively enforced.

The last two decades or so of the Hongwu emperor's reign were marked by further military campaigns, more tinkering with both the bureaucracy and the law, uneasy relations with the tributary state of Choson (Korea), and a number of brutal purges of real or suspected enemies, including scholars who had not even become officials yet. On occasion there were mass slaughters of officials and commoners alike. In December 1397, after dealing personally with several administrative problems, including the handling of some recalcitrant princes, the Hongwu emperor fell seriously ill, and on June 24, 1398, he died. In his last edict, promulgated posthumously, the emperor directed the entire Ming empire to acknowledge his teenage grandson, the bookish Zhu Yunwen, as his legitimate successor. Since Yunwen was part of the required lineage (the male issue of a principal consort), he was eligible to become the new Son of Heaven. But in an another edict issued by the Hongwu emperor not long before his death, he charged his "oldest and wisest" son, Zhu Di, prince of Yan, with the defense of the entire empire, writing: "For repelling foreign [threats] and keeping secure the interior, who is there but you?"[19]

Historians of the Ming may debate the legacy of the Hongwu emperor, but standard Chinese sources of the period sing his praises unequivocally. Consider, for example, the preface to a revised edition of the *Da Ming huidian* (Collected statutes of the great Ming dynasty), published in 1587, which states:

> Our Exalted Emperor Taizu, having attained the virtue of a sage, expelled the barbarian Yuan dynasty and came into possession of All under Heaven. In all events [desiring] to practice unified government and exercise unified authority, he would invariably summon the multitude of Confucian scholars and consult with them. While respecting the laws of antiquity, he gave careful consideration to what was appropriate in the immediate circumstances, leaving something out here or adding something there. Gloriously the principle of Heaven [*Tianli*] was applied [in his laws]. His divine plans and sage-like decisions excelled those of earlier ages, and he wholly purged the vulgar accretions of later times.[20]

THE EVOLUTION OF MING INSTITUTIONS

Zhu Yunwen ascended the throne on June 23, 1398, at the age of twenty-one, announcing that his reign title would be Jianwen ("The Establishment of Civil Virtue"). Unlike his grandfather, he was meek and moderate in temperament.[21] Tutored and advised by several outstanding Confucian scholars, including the legendary Fang Xiaoru (1357–1402), the Jianwen emperor, as his reign name suggests, sought to regularize and "civilize" Ming imperial administration. But the changes that he and his advisers attempted, which seemed to be departures from the policies of the Hongwu emperor, eventually gave the militant, aggressive, and ambitious Prince of Yan, Zhu Di, a pretext for usurping power. One change in particular—the tightening of imperial control over the adult Ming princes, who had become semi-autonomous power holders in their vast hereditary estates—gave Zhu Di the pretext he needed to move against his nephew. When the Jianwen emperor began to purge some of his brothers, the Prince of Yan acted decisively and raised the standard of revolt.

In July 1399, after a military official loyal to the Jianwen emperor seized two officials connected to Zhu Di's fief in the area now known as Hebei province, he retaliated, inaugurating a three-year civil war. Justifying his actions on the filial grounds that the Jianwen emperor had repudiated the policies of his (Zhu Di's) father, the Prince of Yan moved against the young emperor. At the outset of the rebellion, Zhu Di had about one hundred thousand men, including a crack contingent of surrendered Mongol cavalry. Aided by defectors from the Ming court and possessed of superior military skill, Zhu Di marched southward toward Nanjing and eventually reached the outskirts of the capital unopposed. Negotiations followed, and the rebellious forces entered the city without a fight. The imperial palace compound was then set ablaze and several badly burned bodies were discovered—reportedly those of the Jianwen emperor, his principal consort, and his eldest son. Their actual fate has never been decisively determined.

On July 17, 1402, after ritually declining a number of petitions urging him to become emperor, Zhu Di ascended the throne as the "rightful" successor to his father, declaring his reign name to be Yongle ("Eternal Happiness"). The remaining months of 1402, however, were designated the thirty-fifth year of the Hongwu reign, in effect denying the legitimacy of the Jianwen regime altogether. In an effort to underscore the theme of filial devotion, the Yongle emperor quickly restored all the laws and institutions of his father and ordered the destruction or proscription of all writings related to events of this period. He also executed a large number of the Jianwen emperor's supporters, along with their entire extended families. Fang Xiaoru was only one of many who suffered this cruel fate. By such means, the reign of the Yongle emperor's immediate predecessor was essentially effaced, except for documents, many of them fabricated, designed to justify Zhu Di's usurpation of the throne. Only in 1595 did the then-reigning emperor restore the Jianwen reign name.

Like his father, the Yongle emperor was intensely ambitious and wildly energetic. During his twenty-two-year reign, he revamped his father's civil bureaucracy; sponsored a number of important scholarly projects; conducted several major military campaigns against the Mongols; moved the primary capital of the Ming from Nanjing to Beiping (renaming it Beijing, the "Northern Capital"), where he built what is now known as the Forbidden City (*Zijin cheng*); ordered massive repairs to the Grand Canal; established diplomatic relations with several Inner Asian states, including Tibet; restored trade and tributary relations with Japan and Korea; annexed the state of Annam (part of present-day Vietnam); and sponsored a series of extraordinary naval expeditions. Let us look more closely at some of these endeavors and their consequences.

As a usurper, the Yongle emperor was somewhat paranoid and relied on an extensive secret police apparatus to root out potential enemies. But unlike his father, who disdained eunuchs, Yongle relied heavily on them as palace spies. By stages, the eunuch population, comprised not only of Han Chinese but also some Mongols, Central Asians, Jurchen, and Koreans, grew in numbers and responsibilities, becoming involved not only in espionage and matters of internal security, but also in politics, military and foreign affairs, taxation, tributary administration, and the operation of imperial monopolies. Their proliferation and abuse of power caused serious difficulties down the road for the Ming dynasty, as we shall see.

During the Yongle emperor's time, eunuchs were not the problem they would become. Although he was a military man by training and experience, the Yongle emperor also received a thorough classical education. He thus understood the need to bolster the civil side of Ming administration. So it was that in addition to reorganizing the military establishment and abundantly rewarding the military officers who had brought him to power, the Yongle emperor rebuilt the imperial bureaucracy. His justification came in an edict that read in part:

Giving and nourishing lives is the utmost virtue of Heaven. A humane ruler needs to learn from Heaven; hence, loving the people should become the principle of his rulership. The four seas are too broad to be government by one person. To rule requires the delegation of powers to the wise and able who can participate in government. That was the way followed by such sage kings as Yao, Shun, Yu, Tang, Wen and Wu. Throughout history there have been clear examples showing that when the government was run by wise and able ministers, the state was orderly. On the other hand, when the ruler failed to find the wise and able to help him, the state was chaotic. My late father, the Hongwu emperor, received the Mandate of Heaven and became the master of the world. During his rule there was peace and tranquility within the Four Seas. . . . His clear administration and disciplined population were not matched by any in the recent past. The way he accomplished these feats was by selecting the wisest persons of the world to help protect the people and run the government.[22]

One of the first administrative changes undertaken by the Yongle emperor was to gather together a group of seven high-ranking Hanlin Academy scholars known as "grand secretaries" (*da xueshi*), whose offices were located inside the palace compound. These scholars had personal access to the emperor and enjoyed his trust; they made important state decisions and assisted the throne in policymaking. They also came to exert considerable influence on the Six Boards and other metropolitan offices. Another major administrative step taken by the Yongle emperor was to regularize the civil service examination system. During the Hongwu period, the examinations had been somewhat sporadic, and there were times when they were suspended altogether. But empire-wide exams were revived in 1404 and soon they became routinized, providing the dynasty with a steady pool of highly literate talent.

As mentioned previously, the subject matter and evaluation of these tests was heavily weighted in favor of Cheng-Zhu neo-Confucian orthodoxy. Thus we find that in 1414, acting as a "sagely ruler" and the leading imperial patron of Chinese scholarship, the Yongle emperor ordered a team of Hanlin scholars to compile a definitive collection of the Five Classics and Four Books with commentaries written by Zhu Xi and like-minded Song dynasty scholars. This work, published in 1417, was intended as a summary of "all true learning," a Confucian guide for all the literati of the land. He also ordered the compilation of other reference works designed to provide guidance for examination candidates. Another reference work, completed somewhat earlier and intended for different purposes, was the gigantic *Yongle dadian* (Great [literary] repository of the Yongle era, more commonly known as the Yongle encyclopedia), bound in 11,095 large volumes. Although never printed, this comprehensive compendium later served as a vast repository of information for Qing dynasty encyclopedists.[23]

The Yongle emperor's foreign policy, which was far more sophisticated than that of his father, involved both the carrot and the stick. During the first few years of his reign, the situation on China's northern borders was relatively stable. Several Mongol tribes in northwestern Manchuria that had surrendered to the Ming became part of the dynasty's *weisuo* system and offered regular tribute. Other loyal Mongol tribes were resettled in the area of modern day Rehe. To the west, the Yongle emperor courted Muslim states and cities in Central Asia, offering them an opportunity to participate in the Chinese system of tributary trade. Many accepted. In July 1404, for instance, the ruler of Hami, Engke Temür, received the Ming title of "prince" (*wang*). Later that year, Tamerlane, the powerful ruler of the Timurid empire, embarked on a full-scale invasion of China, but he died en route in early 1405 and the planned campaign never materialized.

Meanwhile, to the west and north of the Mongol tribes in Manchuria, other powerful groups of Mongols refused to acknowledge Ming authority. In response to their recalcitrance and incursions into Chinese territory, the Yongle emperor launched five major campaigns in the period from 1410 to 1424. Unfortunately for the emperor, who often went into battle with his troops, these costly campaigns did not eliminate the Mongol threat. Indeed, from this time onward, Ming military strategy in the north remained basically defensive (except for a disastrous campaign against the Mongols in 1449). Ming military operations to the south of China were no more successful. Displeased over political developments in Annam, the Yongle emperor ignored the stated policy of his father and sent forces to "pacify" the region in 1406. Initially, Ming troops prevailed, and on July 5, 1407, Annam was incorporated into the Ming empire as the province Jiaozhi—the name it had been given during the Tang dynasty occupation of this same area. Soon, however, Annamese rebels rose up against the Ming and eventually, after twenty years of almost continual struggle and great expense, the Chinese forces withdrew.

The most spectacular achievements of the Yongle era came by sea. In the period from 1405 to 1421 the emperor launched six major maritime expeditions into the area that was then known as the Western Ocean (*Xiyang*). All were commanded by a Muslim eunuch named Zheng He, who had entered the Ming service after being captured during a military campaign in Yunnan. Subsequently castrated and placed in the service of the Prince of Yan, he became a confidant of the future emperor and went on several military missions with him. The motives behind Zheng's naval voyages are not entirely clear, but we can assume that at least one goal was to find new sources of wealth (the largest vessels, some reportedly over four hundred feet long, were called "treasure ships," or *baochuan*). Another goal was to extend the reach of the Ming tributary system, contributing to the glory of the empire. Still another may have been to gain information about the emperor's enemies to the west. Geoff Wade, for his part, argues that Zheng He's expeditions were part of a "proto-colonial" project, motivated by the Yongle emperor's desire to establish strategic footholds in Southeast Asia and elsewhere.[24]

Descriptions of Zheng He's voyages abound, and although some writers—notably Gavin Menzies—have made wild and unsustainable claims about them, we can say with assurance that they were impressive displays of China's advanced naval technology. Some of the expeditions involved as many as 250 ships and boasted nearly thirty thousand sailors at a time. These armadas not only penetrated the coastal waters of Southeast Asia, they also sailed through the Indian Ocean and at least one expedition reached the eastern coast of Africa. Yet soon after the death of the Yongle emperor in 1424 these maritime voyages were discontinued. Why?

In part, the reasons were financial; they were an enormous drain on the already strained Ming coffers, without yielding any significant economic gain. Moreover, after the death of the Yongle emperor there were no strong advocates of naval exploration. In fact, Confucian scholars increasingly criticized the idea of maritime expeditions as being antithetical to the tributary notion that foreigners would gravitate on their own to China and offer their submission. Aggressive measures, they argued, were not only costly but also unnecessary. Finally, the fact that Zheng He's expeditions reflected heightened eunuch influence in Chinese politics offended the sensibilities of Chinese scholar-officials. As a result, most records of Zheng He's naval voyages (and a subsequent one in 1433) were destroyed.

In the end, the Yongle emperor's efforts to extend his influence beyond China's immediate maritime frontiers, as with his attempts to stabilize the land areas beyond China's northern, western, and southern borders, had no lasting effect. Another one of his projects did, however: the establishment of the primary Ming capital at Beijing. This ambitious move, begun as early as 1403, made sense to the Yongle emperor. In the first place, the continued Mongol threat to China argued for a substantial and sustained Chinese presence in the north. Even the Hongwu emperor had at one time contemplated moving the capital northward for this reason. Also influencing the Yongle emperor's decision was the fact that the Beijing area had been his base of operations as Prince of Yan—the source of his initial power and support. Finally, in the first half of the fifteenth century, Beijing seemed to be the only major city near the northern frontier that could adequately support a large military garrison and a substantial civilian population.[25]

Between 1403 and 1420 the Yongle emperor effected the transfer. In February 1403 he formally designated the city his "Northern Capital" and soon sent his eldest son Zhu Gaochi (later to reign briefly as the Hongxi emperor, 1424–1425) to administer it. He also established a "branch ministry" (*xingbu*) to oversee branch offices of the Six Boards and other administrative organs at the capital. Significantly, he renamed the metropolitan prefecture Shuntian ("Obedient to Heaven"), echoing the designation given by his father to the metropolitan prefecture of Nanjing—(Yingtian "Responsive to Heaven").

In 1404 the emperor moved ten thousand households from nine prefectures in Shanxi province to increase the population of Beijing. Soon thereafter the city walls underwent repairs. Then, in 1407, preparations began for the building of a new imperial palace—the Forbidden City. Ming officials gathered together a huge work force—numbering hundreds of thousands of artisans, soldiers, and common laborers—including several thousand Annamese, who had been captured during the wars of annexation in the south. Meanwhile, repairs on the Grand Canal facilitated the movement of tribute grain and other commodities from the rich Yangzi River area to the new capital, supplementing the coastal transportation system of the Yuan. By 1418, most of the major palace buildings had been completed, and improvements to the city walls, moats, and bridges of Beijing were also made.

On October 28, 1420, Beijing became the new Ming capital. The next year, however, a fire destroyed the three main audience halls of the Forbidden City. Following precedent in the wake of such disasters, the emperor called for criticism of his rule. Several censors and some Hanlin scholars denounced the move to Beijing for the economic and other hardships it caused. One official by the name of Xiao Yi so offended the Ming monarch that he was executed. Thereafter, matters went forward without much further dissent.

A great many administrative changes took place in the next few years. Nanjing offices and agencies became auxiliary branches of their counterparts in Beijing. Frontier defenses came to be concentrated in garrisons south of the Great Wall rather than beyond it as in the Hongwu era. Meanwhile, most of the capital guards (*jingwei*) were transferred from Nanjing to the new capital and its environs, making them the largest single body of troops in the entire empire—a total of perhaps 250,000 soldiers. Military farms (*juntian*) in the Beijing area were enlarged, but substantial grain shipments by sea, inland waterways, and land were still necessary to meet the needs of both military men and civil employees.

In order to finance his ambitious civil and military projects and to prop up the tributary system (which often resulted in financial losses for the Ming state because tributary envoys regularly received lavish gifts), the Yongle emperor was constantly in the business of raising money. Financial austerity had been a priority for the father, but not for the son. A rough estimate is that the Yongle emperor's annual expenditures averaged about two or three times those of the first emperor. How did he meet these expenses? Ray Huang provides the basic answer:

> Although the details are not clear, the scattered evidence in many contemporary sources, when put together, suggests that taxation under the third emperor of the Ming was basically carried out by means of requisitions. Nominally, the tax rates were never increased; there were even select reductions. Yet, the service obligations of the populace were greatly extended. Taxpayers in the Yangtze delta were ordered to deliver their grain payments to Peking, which was over 1,000 miles away. Even when the army transportation corps took over some of the deliveries after the Grand Canal was opened for traffic, the surcharges collected from the taxpayers to cover the transportation costs equaled or exceeded the basic tax payments.[26]

The corvee labor system clearly felt the strain:

Statute laborers who normally had been required to perform unpaid services for thirty days a year were forced to work for considerably longer periods, sometimes for over a year. Furthermore, during the early Ming, surplus commodities in government granaries were not sold in the marketplace. They were distributed to pay for the materials and labor submitted by the populace beyond the statutory limits of taxation. . . . The compensation rendered for such goods comprised only a fraction of the actual market price. Such practices undermined the tax system. While ostensibly retaining the first emperor's fixed quotas for state income, extraordinary demands were placed on all fiscal units. The extra financial burden was not apportioned according to any plan, but was distributed on the basis of uncoordinated local ad hoc decisions.[27]

Tributary trade occasionally brought in some revenue for the state, but not enough to ease the burdens imposed by land taxes and corvee obligations.

The death of the Yongle emperor in the summer of 1424 marked the end of military expansion and a sharp inward turn in Ming policy. Not surprisingly, the emperor's successors, including his own son, "quietly retreated from his policies of unrestrained spending."[28] Institutional changes did take place, however: for instance, the establishment in the 1420s of a palace school for eunuchs (*nei shutang*), taught by Hanlin scholars and designed to give eunuchs the tools needed to handle documents and communicate formally with court officials. From this time onward, eunuch involvement in state affairs increased dramatically, as the Ming emperors charged them with ever-expanding responsibilities. Another important development at about the same time, which also enhanced the ability of emperors to work outside of established bureaucratic channels, was the expansion of censorial activities. Increasingly, censors served as a check on both the civil and military arms of the Ming government.

In the provinces, a significant change during the 1420s and 1430s was the establishment of a quasi-formal system of governorship known as *xunfu* (lit. "roaming pacifiers"). As with so many other Ming institutions and practices, this system had its origins in the Yuan dynasty. It was designed to coordinate the functions of the major civil, military, and censorial officials of each province, but it was not a recognized substantive position with a regular tenure. Most *xunfu* were metropolitan officials, often from one of the Six Boards, and their appointments were essentially ad hoc. They were, in effect, special imperial representatives with different responsibilities and different ranks. Eventually the *xunfu* system evolved into a type of governorship known as *zongdu* (lit. "general supervisor"). The upshot of this particular development was the imposition of an ever-greater degree of civil control over Ming military officials.

From an economic standpoint, the post-Yongle period was marked by a shift in fiscal assessment from discrete payments in labor and kind to unified payments in cash—a reform known as the "single-whip system" (*yitiaobian fa*). This development "moved the operation of state communications away from the ancient agrarian model of corvee in the direction of a more commercial model of hired labor." At the same time, "the monetization of the tax system induced more silver to enter the economy and to circulate at greater speed, thereby contributing to the conversion of goods into commodities and making it possible, and more economically rational, for a household to buy what it needed, rather than to grow it or to make it." [29]

On the foreign policy front, aside from the enormously expensive late-fifteenth- and early-sixteenth-century efforts to strengthen the Great Wall,[30] Ming emperors in the post-Yongle period continually sought to use the tributary system to minimize military threats on the Chinese periphery. The pattern was a familiar one. To the degree that foreigners found the status of "tribute-bearer" advantageous for political or economic reasons, they conformed to Chinese expectations, performing the appropriate rituals, offering local products as tribute, and receiving in return gifts, patents of authority, and trade privileges. Thus, for example, the "submissive" Mongol tribes in Manchuria periodically supplied the Ming throne with horses and other domestic animals and received in return paper money, silver, silk, and textiles. The chieftains and their "envoys" were granted official ranks and titles and the right to trade in certain specified locations. Similar arrangements prevailed with other Inner Asian peoples (including the Jurchen, precursors of the Manchus).

The Ming emperors made special efforts to enroll Korea, Japan, and the Liuqiu (Japanese: Ryūkyū) Islands as tributaries in an effort to protect the northeast, and they also tried to solidify tributary relationships with various Southeast Asian countries for the same strategic reason. But there was more to the matter than strategy. The Ming rulers also celebrated the symbolic dimensions of the system—in particular the idea that foreign peoples admired Chinese culture and were inclined to "turn toward civilization" (*xianghua*). As a result of these dual considerations—strategic interests and matters of dynastic prestige—the Ming dynasty sent an estimated 167,000 troops to Korea in order to help repel devastating Japanese military assaults in the period from 1592 to 1598. The Chinese incurred severe losses and spent millions of ounces of silver on what Kenneth Swope describes as the "first great East Asian war." In Swope's opinion, "modern scholars are mistaken to cynically underestimate the importance of the [Ming-Korean tributary] relationship and Ming feelings of obligation toward Korea."[31] Indeed, out of gratitude the Koreans would later send troops to help the Ming resist the Manchus.

A final point to make about Ming administration is the increased power of eunuchs during the Chenghua emperor's reign (1464–1487) and thereafter. The pattern was always the same: by virtue of their closeness to emperors, empresses, and concubines, eunuchs managed to gain the trust of the inner court, acquiring control over important offices, either directly or indirectly, and proceeding to patronize others of a similar disposition. Their involvement in Ming political and economic life took a variety of forms, even when strong rulers were on the throne—in part because they seemed to offer the emperor a check on civil service bureaucrats and even military leaders. As early as the Yongle period, for example, eunuchs had already become involved not only in espionage and internal security but also military affairs, foreign relations, taxation, tributary administration, and the operation of imperial monopolies, including the vital salt industry. In later periods, eunuchs also assumed prominent roles in the manufacture of silk and porcelain, flood control, the building of temples and shrines, and judicial affairs. Some were even able to draft edicts of appointment in the emperor's name, without his knowledge.

The less administratively engaged the emperor, the more likely eunuchs would arrogate power to themselves. And in the late Ming there was a great deal of imperial disengagement. According to one study, in the period from 1471 to 1497, the Chenghua and Hongzhi (r. 1487–1505) emperors held no audiences with their ministers. This was also reportedly true for the entire reign of the Zhengde emperor (r. 1505–1521). In the forty-five years of the Jiajing emperor's reign (1521–1567) he apparently held only one audience, and from 1589 to 1602, the Wanli emperor (1572–1620) also met his ministers only once. The result was that eunuchs such as Wang Zhi in the 1470s, Liu Jin in the early 1500s, and Wei Zhongxian in the 1620s virtually controlled Ming administration at the highest level.[32]

By 1644, there were an estimated seventy thousand eunuchs in the imperial city and another thirty thousand scattered throughout the rest of the empire. The more active the eunuchs became, the more opportunities arose to become embroiled in factional politics. As is well known, the abuse of power by eunuchs and factional strife proved to be enormous problems in the late Ming. Yet even in decline, Ming intellectual, artistic, and literary life remained remarkably vibrant. Indeed, as Jonathan Spence has written about the year 1600:

[At that time] China clearly appeared to [be] the largest and most sophisticated of all the unified realms on earth. The extent of its territorial domains was unparalleled . . . [and its] population of some 120 million was far larger than that of all the European countries combined. . . . The Chinese state was more effectively centralized than those elsewhere in the world . . . [and if] one points to the figures of exceptional brilliance or insight in late sixteenth-century European society, one will easily find their near equivalents in genius working away in China at just the same time. . . . Without pushing further for near parallels, within this same period in China, essayists, philosophers, nature poets, landscape painters, religious theorists, historians and medical scholars all produced a profusion of significant works, many of which are now regarded as classics of the civilization.[33]

MING CULTURE

The Ming period is generally regarded as a time of enormous cultural achievement. What were the reasons for its splendor, even when the dynasty seemed in decline? One important factor was continued economic development, in part a function of China's increasing involvement in global exchanges.[34] As Timothy Brook points out, from the standpoint of commodity production and circulation, the Ming dynasty

> marked a turning point in Chinese history, both in the scale at which goods were being produced for the market, and in the nature of the economic relations that governed commercial exchange. The improvements in transportation brought about by the Ming state and by individuals or groups were not of the same order; even so, the expansion of the state courier system [*yichuan*] and the reconstruction of the Grand Canal, plus the cumulative effect of mundane investments in canals and roads, were grand enough to contribute significantly to the movement of goods and people, and thus to facilitate the elaboration of commercial networks.[35]

The growth of commerce contributed to a blurring of class distinctions. To be sure, Ming China was by no means an egalitarian society. As the scholar Zhang Tao (fl. 1586) observed: "One man in a hundred is rich, while nine out of ten are impoverished. The poor cannot stand up to the rich who, though few in number, are able to control the majority. The Lord of Silver rules Heaven and the God of Copper Cash reigns over the earth."[36] Nonetheless, Ming commercial prosperity made it possible, at least in theory (and often in practice), for all classes of Chinese society to improve their respective situations. Assisting in the process was the emergence of a group of scribes, public lectors, and other village specialists who lowered the social barrier that separated those who could read from those who could not. Furthermore, there was a rise in general literacy. A Korean visitor to China in 1488 observed with some surprise that many Chinese could read, "even village children, ferrymen and sailors."[37]

The remarkable expansion of commercial printing in the Ming both reflected and contributed to this rise in literacy. As Brook, Benjamin Elman, Cynthia Brokaw, Lucille Chia, Kai-Wing Chow, Joseph McDermott, Wei Shang, Harriet Zurdorfer, and others have shown, the impact of printing on cultural production in the Ming (and Qing) dynasties cannot be overestimated. In the first place, commercialized printing facilitated the emergence of a distinctive new class of literary professionals—"writers, editors, compilers, commentators, critics, publishers and proofreaders"—whose professional life reflected the convergent careers of literati (*shi*) and merchant-businessmen (*shang*), hence the hybrid term *shishang*. Second, the expansion of the book market in Ming times created new forms of authority, new literary genres, and new readerships, whose interests went well beyond the boundaries of state orthodoxy.[38]

The emergence of new genres is especially significant. In addition to an unprecedented outpouring of scholarly works on the usual topics—language, philosophy, art, literature, belles lettres, and so forth—the Ming dynasty witnessed an explosion of "how-to" books on every conceivable subject, from sex to carpentry. There were primers for students, works to assist scholars in preparing for the examinations, guides to help literate artisans and peasants produce and market their goods more efficiently, and books designed to help merchants develop their businesses. There were also painting and calligraphy manuals, letter-writing guides, books about law and contracts, handbooks on ritual, works on the composition of verse, medical treatises, route books for travelers, and systematic tracts on connoisseurship, such as the famous *Gegu yaolun* (Essential criteria of antiquities, 1388). Printed almanacs provided valuable calendrical, divinatory, and other forms of practical information for all sectors of society, and morality books (*shanshu*) of various sorts transmitted information about Buddhism, Religious Daoism, and syncretic belief systems.

A particularly popular genre of "how-to" books in Ming dynasty China was the "encyclopedia for daily use" (*riyong leishu*). Works of this sort were designed to supply advice that might prove useful for literate commoners (*shumin*) who hoped to interact with members of the exalted "gentry" class, and much of their content clearly reflects this basic goal. Of all the encyclopedias for daily use that circulated in Ming times, the *Santai wanyong zhengzong* (Three platform orthodox instruction for myriad use) and the *Wanbao quanshu* (Complete book of myriad treasures; hereafter WBQS) seem to have been among the most popular. They were printed (and reprinted) in Fujian province, but distributed empire wide. A distinctive feature of these and related publications is that although they were produced locally, their content was designed to reflect forms of universal cultural knowledge—applicable and of value throughout the entire realm. For this reason, encyclopedias of daily use tended to have a similar system of categories and to draw on similar sources of information and authority.[39]

Let us look briefly at the content of a 1636 edition of the WBQS—putatively, but no doubt erroneously, attributed to the precocious and charismatic late Ming scholar Zhang Pu (1602–1641)—to get a sense of these categories (*men*).[40] In order they are: (1) the Heavens, (2) the Earth, (3) Human Relationships, (4) the Seasons, (5) Farming and Sericulture, (6) Correspondence, (7) Stylistic Models, (8) Exhortation, (9) Rank and Emoluments, (10) Tea Protocols, (11) Outer Barbarians, (12) Drinking Games, (13) Medicine, (14) Dream Interpretation, (15) Written Complaints, (16) Selection of Auspicious Dates, (17) Fortune-telling, (18) Physiognomy, (19) Fate Calculations (based on the "eight characters" of one's birth), (20) Chess (and other amusements), (21) Jokes (plus an unnumbered section on Playing the Zither), (22) Gestation, (23) Construction, (24) Geomancy, (25) Calligraphy, (26) Divination with Milfoil, (27) Couplets, (28) Calculations, (29) Painting, (30) Managing Illness, (31) Nourishing Life, (32) Divination with Arrowheads, (33), Oxen and Horses, and (34) Miscellaneous Matters (see appendix E).

Other Ming editions of the WBQS had special sections on marriage, mourning and sacrifices, the "immortal arts" (*xiuzhen*), infants, instructing children, mathematic calculations, and sexual adventures (*fengyue*). Many of these categories persisted in encyclopedias of daily use from the early seventeenth century to the mid-eighteenth century or later (see chapter 9), although the category on sexual adventures disappears in the WBQS with the fall of the Ming.

These encyclopedia categories provide an illuminating inventory of Chinese cultural concerns. The section on erotica, for example, is a veritable goldmine of information on Chinese sexual life in the late Ming, providing all kinds of practical advice, from sample letters for winning the hearts of courtesans to "marvelous recipes for thoughts of love" (*chunyi miaofang*). In addition to a wide range of prescriptions designed to provoke sexual arousal or increase male potency and stamina, there are various tips for men in the arts of seduction. They are told, for example, not to mention "the beauty of pale skin" to a woman with a dark complexion, and advised that giving napkins and fans as gifts to a courtesan is like "throwing out a brick to attract jade." Men also learned of the ways that courtesans and prostitutes might try to manipulate them, and the devices that they (men) could employ to manipulate women.[41] The significant point here is that popular encyclopedias like the WBQS not only played an important role in disseminating useful knowledge to literate commoners, they also served as a source of inspiration for other forms of cultural production, such as novels, in both the Ming and Qing periods.

The Ming was a time when short story writers and novelists had unprecedented influence.[42] Among other things, we can see in their works a new focus on the details of everyday life and greater attention to issues of gender, sex, and romantic love. Andrew Plaks argues that Ming novels reflect a self-conscious reevaluation of tradition on the part of the literati class, which can also be found in poetry and painting of the period.[43] But these works had multiple audiences, and even among elites there were a number of different opinions about how such forms of vernacular literature could and should be read. We may question, then, the degree to which at least some of these works actually subverted traditional views.

In two of the "four great masterworks" (*si daqishu*) of the Ming novel[44]—all four of which exist in excellent English-language translations—we find decidedly negative views of women that are not, I think, designed to be ironic. The popular historical narrative *Sanguo yanyi* (Romance of the Three Kingdoms period) is one; it depicts women as, among other things, devious subverters of male virtue. Reputedly written by Luo Guanzhong (c. 1330–1400), the novel is set in the Three Kingdoms period that followed the breakdown of the Han dynasty (206 BCE–220 CE). The novel is full of battle and intrigue, with prominent themes of brotherhood, loyalty, personal ambition, and righteous revenge. Among the many historical characters of the novel, several have become universally known in China as either noble heroes or arch villains: Zhang Fei, the symbol of reckless courage; Guan Yu, noteworthy for his unwavering loyalty; Zhuge Liang, the brilliant strategist; and Cao Cao, the selfish and evil tyrant.[45]

Like *Romance of the Three Kingdoms*, *Shuihu zhuan* (Water margin), is full of courageous deeds, with themes of friendship, loyalty, and revenge, as well as righteous revolt. But it, too, promotes negative female stereotypes. Although traditionally attributed to Luo Guanzhong (based, it would appear, on an earlier work by Shi Nai'an, 1296–1371), *Water Margin* is much more colloquial and less historical than *Romance of the Three Kingdoms*. It covers a shorter time span (during the Song dynasty) and consists of a sequence of cycles rather than an interweaving of narrative strands. Of the 108 "righteous brigands" of *Water Margin*—who represent a fascinating cross section of Chinese society—the faintly historical Song Jiang and the loyal and powerful Wu Song have become especially popular folk heroes. To this day, few Chinese are unfamiliar with the story of Wu Song's killing of a ferocious tiger with his bare hands.[46]

Xiyou ji (Journey to the west), as its title suggests, is a travel epic, full of adventure, magic, religious symbolism, and satire. The novel is based on the historic pilgrimage to India of the famous Buddhist monk Xuanzang (596–664), who made the trip by way of Central Asia between 629 and 645.

But instead of the sober travel account left by the historic Xuanzang, *Journey to the West* is a comic fantasy, written by the scholar Wu Cheng'en (c. 1506–1582). It revolves around the adventures of the humorless pilgrim Sanzang ("Tripitaka," a Buddhist pun on the name Xuanzang) and his traveling companions, including the well-known magical monkey named Sun Wukong and a sensual and slothful pig-like creature called Zhu Bajie ("Pigsy"). The novel can be approached from several angles—as allegory, social and political satire, comedy, and myth. At the level of allegory, and in the popular mind, Tripitaka represents selfishness and spiritual blindness; Pigsy, gross human appetite; and Monkey, intelligence, resourcefulness, and supernatural power. Monkey is, of course, the hero of the work. The novel is full of good-natured satire, and few subjects escape the author's barbs, including the "Monkey King" himself.[47]

Far different in subject matter from either the puritanical heroics of *Romance of the Three Kingdoms* and *Water Margin* or the delightful escapades of *Journey to the West* is the much-acclaimed Ming erotic novel *Jin Ping Mei* (Plum in the golden vase). This work has been aptly described by literary critics as inaugurating a "new era in the history of the Chinese novel"—not only because of its carefully constructed overall structure, but also because it captures in a vibrant fictional form the "rhythms, dynamics, and predicaments of the daily world."[48] The book consists of ten-chapter sets, each covering a major plot and a number of subplots. As many as four different authors have been credited with writing the novel, most notably the scholars Wang Shizhen (1526–1596) and Xu Wei (1521–1593).

Plum in the Golden Vase draws on many diverse literary sources, including *Water Margin*, vernacular short stories, classical works, plays, songs, and even popular encyclopedias. It is essentially a "novel of manners" set in the Song dynasty, which describes Chinese urban middle-class life in realistic detail and dwells at length on the sexual exploits of the merchant, Ximen Qing. The author shows a certain ambivalence toward his characters, displaying outward disapproval of their immoral behavior but covert sympathy for their physical and emotional frustrations. Yet ultimately he opts for morality: Ximen Qing dies of sexual overindulgence, and most of the other "evil" people in the novel are punished in one way or another. Ximen Qing's son redeems his father's sins by becoming a Buddhist monk. One especially noteworthy feature of the novel is its comparatively full and sympathetic treatment of women, a sharp contrast with the negative and stereotypical views projected in *Romance of the Three Kingdoms* and *Water Margin*.

As part of the process by which Ming society changed in response to economic transformations, elite women—especially those who lived in the rich area of Jiangnan and who enjoyed educational advantages—began to assume an ever greater role in Chinese literary life.[49] In the first place, they became readers of the new forms of vernacular and classical literature. But more importantly, they increasingly became writers themselves. The anthologies of Chinese women's poetry edited by scholarly teams such as Kang-i Sun Chang and Haun Saussy, Wilt Idema and Beata Grant, and Susan Mann and Yu-yin Cheng provide abundant and eloquent testimony to this point. Why the emphasis on poetry? Because, as Chang and Saussy point out, poetry has always been the most exalted literary form in China, whereas fiction seemed to be "a commercial venture engaged in by men who had failed in their pursuit of a literary career or who had stooped to putting their talent at the service of the market."[50] The fact that very few women wrote novels or even short stories in late imperial times is at least partly a reflection of their social status: they wrote verse because the elite men with whom they shared their lives did so.

The number of women poets in the Ming dynasty is enormous by comparison to earlier periods, not only because of their unprecedented access to printed books, but also because certain philosophical currents in the fifteenth and sixteenth centuries, such as the iconoclastic thought of Wang Yangming (1472–1529) and his disciples, conduced to it (see below). Another factor contributing to this surge of poetic creativity was the support of male scholars. At the same time, however, as Daria Berg demonstrates, many male literati in the Ming (and many of their early Qing counterparts as well) found the emergence of women writers to be an unsettling and even threatening development.[51]

In any case, the poetry of women writers such as Xia Yunying (1394–1418), Zhang Hongqiao (fl. c. 1400), Zhu Jing'an (fl. 1450), Chen Deyi (fl. 1476), Meng Shuqing (fl. 1476), Shen Qionglian (fl. 1488–1505), Zou Saizhen (fl. 1495), Wang Su'e (sixteenth century), Huang E (1498–1569, aka Huang Xiumei), Li Yuying (b. 1506), Wang Jiaoluan (sixteenth century), Yang Wenli (sixteenth century), Duan Shuqing (c. 1510–c. 1600), Dong Shaoyu (fl. 1545), Bo Shaojun (d. 1625), Xue Susu (c. 1564–c. 1637), Ma Shouzhen (1548–1604), Xu Yuan (fl. 1590), and Lu Qingzi (fl. 1590) reveals a high degree of achievement and a broad range of subject matter and style. The same can be said of talented women painters in the Ming, including not only Xue Susu (see immediately below), but also such celebrities as Ma Shouzhen (1548–1605), Xue Wu (c. 1573–1620), and Wen Shu (1595–1634)—the last, a descendent of the great poet and painter Wen Zhengming (1470–1559).[52]

Several of the above-mentioned writers deserve further mention. Lu Qingzi, for example, exceeded her talented husband in poetic skill and wrote with a flagrant disregard for social status, taking entertainers and servants as well as other gentry women as her audience. Xue Susu, a gifted courtesan, was a famous Ming dynasty painter and calligrapher, whose landscapes, orchids,

and bamboo elicited the highest praise from Dong Qichang (1555–1636)—
the foremost painter and art theoretician of his day (see below). Dong, it
may be added, also thought highly of Xue Wu's paintings and calligraphy.
Huang E is best known for her part in one of the most famous husband-wife
dialogues in all of Chinese literary history, and some critics believe that she
should be considered "the first woman of letters in the entire Ming period."
But many other women poets of the Ming were also highly accomplished.
Meng Shuqing, for instance, gained justifiable fame for her sociability, de-
bating skills, cleverness, literary talent, and discrimination. She is especially
well known for her ability to weave the lines of precursors seamlessly into
her own poetry (on this technique, see chapter 9).[53]

Male writers in the Ming are comparatively well known and much discussed. In the early years of the dynasty, four of the most famous authors
(three of whom were also highly regarded painters) were designated the "four
literary giants of Suzhou"—Gao Qi (1336–1374), Zhang Yu (1333–1385),
Yang Ji (c. 1334–1383), and Xu Ben (1335–1380).[54] All were gifted poets
and essayists, but they ran afoul of the Hongwu emperor for reasons related
to their hometown loyalties. Gao paid most dearly: he was executed by a punishment known as "slashing in half at the waist." Naturally enough, then, in
this early period there was a great deal of self-censorship on the part of Ming
writers. One of these authors was the child prodigy Qu You (1347–1433),
who is particularly well known for his collection of classical fiction, *Jiandeng
xinhua* (New tales told by lamplight). Zhu Youdun, a gifted playwright who
authored thirty-two short plays, seems to have been less restrained, perhaps
in part because he was a favored member of the royal household.

During the long fifteenth century, the city of Suzhou bounced back culturally from the devastation caused by the first Ming emperor. Among the
brightest lights of the period were Shen Zhou (1427–1509), Zhu Yunming
(1460–1526), Wen Zhengming, and Tang Yin (1470–1524). All four were
accomplished poets and extremely talented painters and calligraphers, who
earned a living primarily by selling their artwork. Touched by the vibrant
market forces at work in the Jiangnan area, money became a significant
theme in their writing—Shen's in particular. By contrast, at about the same
time, a group of young poets and prose stylists in north China developed what
came to be called the Revivalist School (*fugu xuepai*), inspired by great writers of the distant past. Like certain women poets and their male supporters in
the Ming, they were influenced by the freewheeling thought of Wang Yangming (see below), who was not only an enormously influential philosopher,
but also an excellent poet. These revivalist writers all started out as high court
officials, and so they had an unmasked disdain for the developing commercial
culture of the south.[55]

As in other realms of cultural life, the late Ming was a "great age" for theater, in particular a genre known as the "southern play" or Kunshan opera (*Kunqu*)—a creative blend of previously developed literary and musical forms. The most famous work of this sort in Ming times was *Mudan ting* (Peony Pavillion), written by Tang Xianzi (1550–1616). Tang's passionate love story revolves around a young woman, Du Liniang, who falls in love with a young man in an erotic dream. She dies pining for him, but not before she makes a self-portrait, which the young man, Liu Mengmei, later discovers. Naturally he falls in love with her, and through supernatural means they are united in life. Despite the difficulty of the play's language (a modern edition contains more than 1,700 explanatory notes), it was wildly popular, published in numerous private and commercial editions, performed onstage, and imitated by many playwrights. It appealed to both men and women and to elites and commoners alike.[56] Many authorities consider "Peony Pavillion" to be at the heart of the cult of romantic love (*qing*) that flourished in the late Ming.

Another late Ming development of a very different sort was the proliferation of literary societies (*wenshe*), which both reflected and contributed to the political factionalism that was endemic at the time.[57] Several renowned poets, including Chen Zilong (1608–1647) and Qian Qianyi (1582–1664), found themselves in the thick of it. Chen, along with such famous intellectuals as Huang Zongxi (1610–1695), Gu Yanwu (1613–1682), and Wu Weiye (1609–1672), was a member of the famous Revival Society (*Fushe*), which by the end of the Ming boasted members from all over China, including more than 15 percent of the successful examination candidates from the wealthiest provinces. Despite their political orientation, the members of the Revival Society did not suffer the fate of so many members of the Donglin ("Eastern Forest") Academy, whose direct involvement in late Ming politics during the Tianqi reign (1620–1627) resulted in a massive purge orchestrated by the powerful eunuch Wei Zhongxian (1568–1627).

The most important philosophical movement of the late Ming period was associated with the Learning of the Mind (*Xinxue*), championed by Wang Yangming and his disciples, Wang Gen (1483–1541), Wang Ji (1498–1583), and Li Zhi (1527–1602). This "intuitive" approach to moral knowledge—anticipated by Zhu Xi's intellectual rival in the Song, Lu Xiangshan (1139–1192)—emphasized the innate ability of all human beings to recognize goodness (*liangzhi*) without the need for formal study of the sort advocated so persistently and energetically by Master Zhu. In the hands of Wang Yangming and especially his disciples, the Learning of the Mind encouraged forms of relativism and skepticism that led, among other things, to a certain moral and even social egalitarianism. The irreverent polemicist Li Zhi, for example—one of the most influential figures in late Ming literature and arguably the most infamous of Wang Yangming's followers—offered many deliberately provocative and iconoclastic remarks in his wide-ranging writings. Thus, he once wrote: "It is fine to say that there are better and worse views—but can it be that men's are always better and women's always worse?"[58]

Li Zhi and several other prominent late Ming scholars were acquaintances of the famous Jesuit missionary, Matteo Ricci (1552–1610), architect of the Jesuit accommodation strategy in China from 1583 onward.[59] The Jesuit interlude, which extended well into the Qing, has been the subject of a great many scholarly studies. For our purposes, the salient point is that Ricci and his successors brought new religious, philosophical, mathematical, scientific, and technological knowledge to Ming (and Qing) dynasty China, which not only amplified the already vast Chinese cultural repertoire, but also stimulated research into indigenous Chinese traditions of learning in these areas. As Joanna Waley-Cohen, Benjamin Elman, Roger Hart, Harriet Zurndorfer, and others have pointed out, Chinese scholars borrowed European knowledge selectively during the late Ming and thereafter, just as previous Chinese regimes had drawn on Arabic and Indian knowledge. It is worth remembering that the Ming Directorate of Astronomy (*Qin Tian jian*) was often dominated by Muslims.

Contrary to the common stereotype that Chinese scholars in late imperial times were not curious about the natural world, a careful look at the literature reveals a long tradition of precisely such curiosity.[60] Encyclopedic works by late Ming scholars such as the *Bencao gangmu* (Compendium of materia medica; 1587–1596) by Li Shizhen (1518–1593) and the *Tiangong kaiwu* (Works of Heaven and the inception of things; 1637) by Song Yingxing (1587–1666) bear eloquent testimony to this sort of interest. Both of these individuals failed the Ming civil service examinations repeatedly, but both were first-rate intellectuals who read broadly and who carefully observed the world around them. They also engaged in lively and productive debate with their scholarly peers.

Li's work, which has been thoroughly and insightfully studied by Carla Nappi, took him thirty years to complete; it consisted of fifty-two volumes in its final form. Song's study, equally well examined by Dagmar Schafer, was more modest in scale; nonetheless it described the terms, configurations, and production stages for more than 130 different technologies and tools. The important point here is that late Ming scholarship of the sort conducted by Li and Song reflected a wave of literati interest in new approaches to knowledge "driven by the uncertainties of this era and a changing material and cultural world."[61] One might mention an additional late Ming work in this vein: the scholar-merchant Hu Wenhuan's set of books titled *Gezhi congshu* (Collectania for investigating things and extending knowledge), published in the 1590s. Although not as scholarly as the publications by Li and Song, it was more broad ranging, representing the interests of "low-brow literati" rather than elites, and reflecting traditions of "nourishing life" (*yangsheng*) that were central to Ming popular religious discussions about longevity and immortality.[62]

The introduction of Jesuit learning was part of this ongoing process of seeking scientific and technological knowledge. It may be true (and I believe it is) that the most valued knowledge in China remained moral knowledge,[63] but this did not prevent Chinese scholars of the Ming (and Qing) from reading and discussing scientific and technological ideas derived from the many Chinese-language tracts produced by the Jesuits and their amanuenses. When this information proved useful, as it did in the realms of astronomy, cartography, calendrics, and military affairs, it was eagerly embraced. If not, it was understandably rejected or ignored.[64]

Chapter Two

Conquest and Consolidation

The decline of the Ming dynasty in the 1630s and 1640s was obvious to all. Factionalism, neglect of public works and granaries, military bungling (pay in arrears, supply deficiencies, and forced conscription), abuses of power by eunuchs, overtaxation, and pervasive corruption on the part of officials at all levels compounded the misery caused by uncommonly cold weather (some have called it a "Little Ice Age"), floods, droughts, epidemics, and locust infestations. "Barbarians" on the northern frontier posed a growing threat, distracting Ming officials from domestic problems and depleting the regime's already strained military coffers. Monetary fluctuations and price instability, at least partially the product of China's involvement in the world economy (particularly the silver market), added to the dynasty's difficulties. Many contemporary observers in the late 1500s and early 1600s remarked on the corrosive effects of commerce and luxury consumption, which seemed to lead to a breakdown of civility and the degeneration of family ethics. But the most serious problems facing the dynasty were environmental.

Times were tough, even in resource-rich Jiangnan. A native of the once-thriving city of Suzhou wrote in 1642:

In the streets there are numerous beggars, very thin and worn. Moreover, since the new year, it has been cold and it has rained frequently. The spring has nearly come to an end, but the cold spell persists. After the full moon of the second month, it rained continuously for over ten days. The people are dying in great numbers through lack of food. I have seen with my own eyes several tens of [starved] corpses being buried daily in the property of the prince. . . . Most of the residences in the city are empty and they are falling into ruins. Fertile farms and beautiful estates are for sale but there is no one to buy them. Formerly the city of [Suzhou] was prosperous and its people tended to be extravagant. It is natural

48

that after a period of prosperity a period of depression should follow; but I never dreamed that I should have to witness these misfortunes in the days of my life.[1]

In the city of Huzhou in northern Zhejiang, a reported 30 percent of the population perished from "famine and disease" between 1640 and 1642. Some other urban centers apparently suffered an even higher percentage of loss of life—as much as 50 percent—the result, perhaps, of a virulent plague transmitted by northern invaders, who may have "introduced microbes for which the Chinese had no antibodies."[2]

Conditions in the countryside were abysmal for somewhat different reasons. Millions of displaced peasants roamed the land, looking desperately for food. Many found their way to urban areas, hoping to support themselves by begging or stealing. Whole rural districts in central China were reported to be deserted. In the province of Huguang, which bordered several other provinces, bandits held sway, moving freely and pillaging at will. During a famine in Henan province in 1640, as grain prices spiked, widespread cannibalism occurred.[3]

China was ripe for rebellion, which came in several forms. "Heterodox" religious sects inspired some uprisings. In 1622, for example, a member of what the Ming authorities described as an adherent of the outlawed White Lotus Teaching named Xu Hongru raised the standard of revolt in Shandong, an uprising that took a year to suppress. Many localized rebellions began with popular outrage over oppressive taxation by officials or resentment over gentry privileges. Regular *weisuo* soldiers from border areas increasingly became the leaders of popular rebellions, and in other parts of the country, irregular troops that had been mustered to suppress uprisings became insurgents themselves. There were also a number of insurrections by Muslim and other ethnic groups in the west and southwest of China, all motivated by discrimination and/or destitution.[4]

In 1628, during the early part of the Chongzhen emperor's reign (1627–1644), a great famine occurred in Shaanxi province, home to a pair of the most notorious rebels in all of Chinese history—Zhang Xianzhong (1606–1647) and Li Zicheng (1606–1645). The official history of the dynasty tells us: "Throughout the ages there has always been trouble from bandits, but there have never been so many disturbances as those caused by Li Zicheng and Zhang Xianzhong at the end of the Ming."[5] Both of these men had military experience, both were ambitious, and by 1630 both had become insurgents. Initially, Zhang established his own bandit group, while Li joined a much larger rebel force under his uncle, Gao Yingxiang. Gao's loose but destructive coalition of insurgents reportedly numbered two hundred thousand troops, and after Gao was captured and killed in 1636, Li replaced him and appropriated the title "Dashing General" (*Chuangjiang*). At times Li and

Zhang cooperated, as they roamed the plains of northern and central China, availing of widespread misery and causing it as well. But there was no love lost between the two men, and ultimately they went their separate ways.

After several changes of fortune, Zhang ended up in Sichuan with an army of some one hundred thousand men, declaring himself to be the "Western King" (*Xiwang*) of the province in 1644. But Zhang's reign was brutal. By some accounts, as many as a million people may have lost their lives in the campaign of deliberate terror that followed his occupation of Chengdu.[6] Meanwhile, Li had moved into the province of Henan, where a terrible drought in 1639 induced thousands of people to join his already swelled ranks, including two well-educated men who became his mentors. Niu Jin-xing (c. 1595–1692) proved to be a particularly valuable adviser. Although initially known for his unbridled cruelty, Li modified his approach somewhat under the influence of his scholar advisers and became more accommodating. He urged his troops to treat the people of surrendered cities fairly, and vowed exemption from taxes and equalization of land to the rural population. In 1641, Li—now known as the Dashing Prince (*Chuangwang*)—killed the Ming dynasty's Prince of Fu (Zhu Yousong, 1607–1646) in Luoyang, confiscated the prince's vast estate, and distributed his wealth to the poor and hungry. In 1643, Li set up his capital in Hebei province, calling himself the "New Prince of Submission" (*Xin Shunwang*). By the end of the year he had extended his rule to the adjacent provinces of Shaanxi and Shanxi, and had begun to march on the Ming capital.

THE FALL OF THE MING AND THE RISE OF THE QING

On February 16, 1644, Li Zicheng declared war on the Chongzhen emperor, but because of the dynasty's faulty intelligence system, the message failed to reach the throne until April 7. By this time the imperial court and Ming military forces at the capital were in near total disarray. On April 23, Li's vast army rode into the western suburbs of Beijing and advanced on the Xizhi gate of the city, meeting virtually no resistance. The eunuch Du Xun, who had assisted Li in his march toward the capital, brought a peace offer to the throne from the Prince of Submission: if the Chongzhen emperor would ennoble him, provide a reward of a million ounces of silver, and recognize his private kingdom in Shaanxi and Shanxi, he would not only destroy other rebel groups in China, but also defend the Ming from northern invaders. The emperor actually considered the matter, but eventually refused, and the next day, April 24, on the advice of his shamanic soothsayer Song Xiance, Li sent his troops to storm the capital—a task made easier by the complicity of yet another eunuch turncoat, Cao Huashun. In response to these events, on the morning of April 25, the Chongzhen emperor committed suicide on Coal Hill, just outside the towering northern walls of the Forbidden City. His body would not be found for three days.

At noon on April 25, Li Zicheng, self-declared emperor of the new Shun ("Submission") dynasty, entered the Forbidden City, escorted by three hundred palace eunuchs. A retinue of Shun civil officials followed him, bearing banners and placards comparing Li to the legendary sage rulers Yao and Shun. Soon thereafter he began staffing his civil and military offices with Ming scholars, along with a number of his own men. But despite his effort to acquire an imperial air, Li was no emperor and he was certainly no sage. We are told, for example, that Niu Jinxing wanted his master to offer sacrifices to Heaven on May 20 as a sign of legitimacy, and asked Li to set aside ten days in order to rehearse. But during the first rehearsal the rough-hewn former rebel rushed through the ceremony, making several critical mistakes. When informed that he would have to "take his timing from the ritual itself," he became furious and announced: "I am the horseback Son of Heaven (*mashang Tianzi*). How would I know how to perform the rites?" The all-important sacrifice was never performed.[7]

An even more serious problem turned out to be the behavior of Li's general Liu Zongmin, whom Li called his "big brother." Liu had a well-deserved reputation for cruelty, and after receiving orders to "kill the guilty and punish the greedy and covetous" in the capital, he embarked on an orgy of torture, extortion, death, and destruction. His first targets were former Ming officials, from whom he took vast sums of money, but soon the common people, too, began to suffer. Liu's soldiers ransacked homes, taking money, jewels, clothes, and even food. Women were sexually abused and men were callously beaten. When Li met with his military leaders in hopes of curbing their destructive and counterproductive behavior, they openly defied him, and so the depredations continued and popular resentment grew.

Meanwhile, in an effort to force the submission of Wu Sangui (1612–1678)—the most powerful Ming general in north China, with some forty thousand regular troops under his command on the northern border—Li Zicheng adopted a two-pronged approach: first he captured Wu's father and other family members, holding them hostage; second he sent a letter to Wu, accompanied by a reported ten thousand ounces of silver and one thousand ounces of gold, promising the Ming general not only the safety of his family, but also a patent of nobility, promoting him from earl (*bo*) to count (*hou*). Wu spurned the offer, however, whereupon Li Zicheng slaughtered the entire Wu household in the capital, nearly forty people in all, and reportedly displayed the severed head of General Wu's father on the Beijing city wall as a warning to all challengers. Moreover, on May 3, 1644, Li launched a campaign

Figure 2.1.   The Great Wall
Source: Beinecke Rare Book and Manuscript Library, Yale University.

against Wu Sangui's troops near the Shanhai Pass of the Great Wall. Li's forces under General Tang Tong were defeated. Another attack on May 10 was also repulsed. But when Wu Sangui heard reports that Li Zicheng was personally leading an army of sixty thousand troops against him, he decided to collaborate with the very forces he had been charged with holding at bay: the Manchus.

Let us now step backward briefly to trace the origins of this extraordinary and increasingly powerful ethnic group. During the late Ming they were known as the Jurchen (Chinese: *Nüzhen*), or, less politely, the Eastern Barbarians (*Dongyi*). They consisted of various tribal peoples living along the northeastern frontiers of the Ming empire. They came from a wide variety of genealogical stocks and cultural traditions, with not a few of their number fully or partly of Han Chinese ancestry. Chinese and Korean accounts of the sixteenth and early seventeenth centuries describe Jurchen soldiers as fierce warriors who valued strength and took death lightly. Ming almanacs and encyclopedias such as the WBQS and the *Sancai tuhui* (Illustrated compendium of the Three Powers; 1607) generally depict Jurchen men as heavily bearded, brandishing swords and/or bows and arrows, and wearing fur hats and collars, leather boots, breeches, and tunics.

The core institution of early Jurchen social life was the "clan" (Manchu: *mukūn*), bound together by a combination of ancestor worship and shamanism. Shamanism was the device through which the members of each Jurchen lineage "communicated with their individual spirits and sanctified their collective economic activities."[8] In the Jurchen homelands, clans were the organizations that governed hunting, gathering, farming, and warfare. They were also the medium through which all such activities were facilitated on the supernatural plane:

The clan headman (*mukūnda*) was in some cases a shaman (*saman*) himself, or moved close to the shaman, the better to invoke the needed communication with the spirits at the appropriate moment. . . . In accord with very ancient traditions, older sons were expected when grown to move downstream or over the hilltop, there to start a new homestead, initiate a new *mukūn*, and plan the new spirit pole [Manchu: *somo*; Chinese: *shenzhu*] that would be the clan's—and each member's—point of communication with the clan spirits and the sacred features of the terrain.[9]

There were thus two early forms of Jurchen shamanism. One has been described as "wild" (Chinese: *tiaoshen*; lit. "jumping spirits") shamanism, involving ecstatic trances, soul-travel, and healing on the part of an individual—usually a woman. This individualized type of shamanism persisted at all levels of Manchu society. The second type of shamanism, focused on the clan rather than the individual shaman, did not involve actual spirit possession or manipulation, and as suggested earlier, it provided a means by which clan members could summon spirits to receive offerings.[10]

Figure 2.2.　Map of Liaodong
Source: XNR Productions.

The story of the Jurchen rise to power begins in the 1580s with a man named Nurhaci (aka Nurgaci; 1559–1626), one of several brothers in a branch of the Gioro clan of a major Jurchen tribe that lived in the foothills between the middle Liao and Yalu rivers (see figure 2.2). In the internecine struggles that followed the death of his father and grandfather at the hands of a rival Jurchen chieftain, Nurhaci emerged in 1583 as the preeminent power holder in the area. At the time, he was twenty-four years old. From this revenge-fed beginning, Nurhaci and his heirs eventually brought most of the territory and population of eastern and central Asia under their domination. This empire at its fullest extent amounted to about 10 percent of the world's land mass and about 35 percent of the world's population.

In the earliest days of Nurhaci's ascendancy, while his political authority was confined to a relatively small area in east-central Liaodong, Nurhaci was a *beile* in the Jurchen tradition—that is, a lineage head/tribal leader who had assumed his position by "force or threat of force" and had thereby acquired the right to distribute and redistribute property among his subjects. This last right, according to Pamela Crossley, "was an extension of traditional shamanic rights," a process that suggested "either an amalgamation of political and spiritual functions, or a displacement of the latter by the former."[11] *Beiles* lived in fortified compounds within walled villages, and their status was dependent on their ability to gather and distribute resources and to provide protection. Naturally, then, they monopolized the production of bows and arrows and iron weapons. The most powerful among them sought to acquire exclusive trading privileges with the Chinese and/or Koreans in return for promises not to threaten their borders. Crossley writes: "Every *beile* who pursued a relationship with the imperial powers [that is, Ming China and Choson Korea] was also a master of spies, a geopolitical strategist, and a tempting target for assassination."[12]

Directly beholden to each *beile* was a relatively small elite group known as *irgen*, who owned a disproportionately large share of the community's resources. Below them stood the *jusen* class. The members of this latter group constituted the bulk of the Jurchen population and owed to their superiors various military and/or corvee obligations. There was also a class of slaves and bondservants (variously *aha, booi,* or *booi aha*) comprised of Jurchen people, Mongols, Koreans, and Chinese who, prior to 1616, were "held as chattel after being bought, taken captive, or condemned to servitude as a punishment."[13]

Unlike other prominent invaders and conquerors of China in previous eras—particularly the forebears of the Jurchen in the twelfth century and the Mongols in the thirteenth—Nurhaci's tribesmen were not primarily nomads. Their economy, located mainly in the Liao River valley, consisted of agriculture, hunting, and trade. Their principal agricultural export was ginseng (Chinese: *renshen*), a highly prized medicinal root. Much of Jurchen commerce was with Korea and Ming dynasty China. By some estimates as much as 25 percent of all the silver that found its way to China in the late sixteenth and early seventeenth centuries ended up in the hands of the various Jurchen tribes. Ming officials made the best of the situation by granting each of the major Jurchen groups separate patents that allowed them to participate in tribute missions. This enabled the Ming to use rivalry over patent acquisition as a means of playing the tribes against each other. But Nurhaci, eager to centralize his political power, eventually took control of all the patents himself, thus depriving the other tribes of access to tributary channels of trade. He personally led eight tributary missions to China before severing commercial and diplomatic relations with the Ming (see below).[14]

Nurhaci's campaign of conquest began in 1584. From that point onward, he rapidly expanded the territory under his control, making marriage alliances, conquering rival Jurchen and Mongol tribes, and refining his military machine, which eventually became known as the Eight Banners (Jurchen: *jakūn gūsa*; Chinese: *baqi*). The fundamental building block of the Banner forces was a "company" (Jurchen: *niru*; Chinese: *zuoling*), comprised of approximately three hundred soldiers. Some of these companies were based on preexisting lineage or tribal relationships, while others were designed expressly to overcome these particularistic identifications in order to create a more centralized military organization. In either case, the companies maintained their ethnic homogeneity. The Banner armies could thus incorporate several different ethnic groups into their organization—including Jurchen, Mongols, and Han Chinese—while still maintaining their cultural distinctiveness.[15]

Niru were social and economic units as well as military ones; they consisted not only of individual armored soldiers (both cavalry and infantry), but also their entire households—other adult males, women, children, and servants. When the hunt or battle was over, the fighting men returned to their families. Each soldier received a monthly wage and a tract of land once he was enrolled in a company; his family members either tilled the soil themselves or employed agricultural serfs for this purpose. When a woman in one Banner unit married a man in another, she changed her affiliation to his Banner. All matters relating to civil and military affairs fell under the direct supervision of an official known as a "company commander" (Manchu: *nirui ejen*; Chinese: *zuoling*).

By 1601 Nurhaci had more than forty companies under arms. In that year he inaugurated a series of reforms designed to formalize the structure of the Banner armies, some of which remained under his direct control and others of which he placed under the command of close relatives. Initially there were four "banners" of various colors. The uniforms of the soldiers in each banner bore the color of their respective identifying flags. Cavalrymen, each responsible for three horses, wore metal helmets adorned with red tassels. The bows of these soldiers were extremely powerful and the soldiers themselves were especially adept at firing their arrows at a full gallop. Their quivers contained thirty or more arrows—a formidable private arsenal for each soldier. Some Banner infantrymen were also archers, but a growing number of them used firearms, including both muskets and artillery.

During the late 1500s and early 1600s, Nurhaci took several additional measures in order to give a distinctive cast to his continually expanding regime. For instance, in 1599 he commissioned two of his translators to create a "Manchu alphabet" based on the Mongolian script that had been used previously to create written documents. In 1616 Nurhaci declared himself khan ("king") of the Aisin (Chinese: Jin or "Gold") dynasty, the same dynastic name that had been chosen by his ancestors in 1115. Two years later, he boldly issued a document titled "The Seven Grievances" (Manchu: *Nadan koro*; Chinese: *Qi dahen*), which blamed the Ming for the death of his father and grandfather and accused the dynasty of bad faith and abuse of power. In response, the Ming dynasty sent a large expeditionary force against him, which was defeated by a pan-Jurchen confederation under Nurhaci's leadership.[16]

Between 1618 and 1621, Nurhaci's armies assumed control over some eighty former Ming garrisons, which he used to defend the recently overrun Ming frontier province of Liaodong ("East of the Liao River"), an area beyond the Great Wall and immediately west of Korea (see figure 2.2). Nurhaci's capture of the city of Liaoyang in 1621 assured Jurchen control over most of the Liaodong area and laid the foundations for what would soon become the Qing dynasty. During this period, Nurhaci arranged for Chinese households that already enjoyed a certain economic status (measured in terms of grain) to be given land and houses, while those with less substantial resources were made into slaves. In some cases, enslavement took a paternal form, but in others individuals in the enslaved population became permanently indentured at hard labor. Under these conditions, a terminology of relative submission emerged—one that distinguished, for example, between "household slaves" (Manchu: *booi aha*) and "household persons" (*booi niyalma*). Individuals in the latter category sometimes came to be known as "bondservants" (*booi niru niyalma*, or *booi* for short), and, as we shall see, a number of them enjoyed extremely high status and influential positions.[17]

For a time, free Chinese and Jurchen Bannermen lived and worked together, as part of a stated policy of integration, cohabitation, and equality.

But economic distress and tensions between the Chinese and their Jurchen overlords led to an anti-Jurchen uprising in 1623. Nurhaci suppressed the insurrection easily, but thereafter his policy began to change from integration to segregation. For the first time, Bannermen were assigned separate quarters from the Chinese and were not even allowed to walk on Chinese streets. Manchus could carry arms, but the Chinese could not. By stages, Jurchen discrimination against the Han intensified, leading to another, more serious uprising in 1625. Again it was put down, but the upshot was the temporary imposition of a rigid system of surveillance and control involving the organization of thirteen Chinese households under a Chinese headman (Manchu: *jangturi*; Chinese: *zhuangtou*) who was responsible to Banner officials.

In 1625, despite the distraction of another Chinese insurrection and the threat of Ming military advances in the area, Nurhaci established a permanent capital at Shenyang (also called Mukden, or "Florescence"), which eventually became known as Shengjing (the "Flourishing Capital"). There he began construction on a palace that reflected Chinese as well as Jurchen architectural and decorative traditions. The next year, however, Nurhaci died, leaving completion of the project to his eighth son and heir, a man who came to be known as Hong Taiji (aka Huang Taiji; r. 1626–1643).

Hong Taiji came to power as one of the direct descendants of his paternal grandfather, Giocangga. His "primary line" included the sons of Giocangga's son, Taksi—that is, Hong Taiji and his three brothers, Daišan, Amin, and Manggultai. Initially, the four siblings shared power, but during the early 1630s Hong Taiji emerged as primus intra pares. In 1629 he had already demonstrated his military prowess by breaching the Great Wall and occupying four important Chinese cities to the south of it—Luanzhou, Qian'an, Zunhua, and Yongping. Two years later, using newly acquired Western cannon, Hong Taiji's forces captured the well-defended Ming garrison and commercial center of Dalinghe, defended at the time by about 14,000 battle-seasoned troops.[18] He also found ways to undermine the prestige of his brothers, beginning with Amin, whom he charged with cowardice after Amin abandoned the four cities that Hong Taiji had taken in 1629. By stages Hong Taiji also managed to disgrace or humiliate Manggultai and Daišan. By 1633 he had seized the armies of all three brothers, incorporating them into what were now called the "Three Superior Banners."

According to the Jurchen system of noble rank at the time, there were twelve principal titles for men and a similar set of titles for women. Titles were hereditary, but with the exception of some specially designated "perpetual rights of inheritance," they usually diminished by one or more ranks for the next generation. Nobles received regular subventions of silver and grain from the state, with amounts pegged to rank. They also enjoyed other privileges in the realms of housing, education, ritual displays, and access to civil and military positions. Another elite group was the Imperial Guard. This institution consisted of three separate entities: the Bodyguard (c. 15,000 men), the Vanguard (c. 1,500 men), and the Guard (c. 1,500 men). The Bodyguard, comprised only of Manchus, protected the ruler at all times, both within and outside the palace. The Vanguard, comprised of Manchu and Mongol Bannermen, led the way in battle and in escorting the emperor outside the palace. The Guard protected the palace itself.[19]

During the first decade of his reign, Hong Taiji consolidated the empire established by his father, which now included some one million Liaodong Chinese and large areas of what is now Inner Mongolia. Continuing most of the policies of his father but abandoning the thirteen-household supervision system, he employed literate Chinese and bilingual Jurchen as advisers, most of whom urged him to build a bureaucratic structure that drew on Ming dynasty institutions. These included the Six Boards, a Grand Secretariat, and a Censorate. Hong Taiji also created a rudimentary examination system and sponsored translations of the Confucian classics and other useful Chinese writings into the evolving Jurchen script. One of these translated works was a Wanli edition of the WBQS, rendered by the famous bilingual Bannerman Dahai (d. 1632). Dahai, who served in the newly created Literary Office (Chinese: *Wenguan*), also translated sections of the Collected Statutes of the Great Ming Dynasty, originally published in 1587.

In addition to drawing on Chinese cultural traditions, Hong Taiji developed utterly new Jurchen institutions, most notably a "Mongol Office" (*Monggo i jurgan*), which eventually became the Court of Colonial Affairs (Manchu: *Tulergi golo be dasara jurgan*, lit. "Ministry Ruling the Outer Provinces"; Chinese: *Lifan yuan*, lit. "Court for Managing Dependencies"). This was the first and only government institution in the history of China designed specifically to deal with Inner Asian peoples. The rituals of this administrative body—which were clearly distinct from, but in some cases related to, traditional Chinese ceremonies—included a pilgrimage to, and audience with, the Jurchen ruler; an imperial hunt; and a system of presenting tribute. The pilgrimage symbolized the supremacy of Hong Taiji over all Inner Asian peoples; the imperial hunt, which originated in Jurchen hunting customs, was designed primarily to appeal to the Mongols; and the presentation of tribute, although adopted from existing Ming practices, had a decidedly Inner Asian flavor.

Even before these administrative arrangements had been fully implemented, Hong Taiji had already determined that his people needed a new and special identity—one that would create the impression of political, social, and cultural unity, putting the Jurchen on the same formal standing as other prominent ethnic groups in the area, such as the "Mongols," the "Chinese," and the "Koreans." In 1635, therefore, he declared:

Originally, the name for our people [*gurun*] was Manju, Hada, Ula, Yehe, and Hoifa. Ignorant people call these "Jurchens." [But] the Jurchens are those of the same clan of Coo Mergen Sibe. What relation are they to us? Henceforth, everyone shall call [us] by our people's original name, Manju. Uttering "Jurchen" will be a crime.[20]

To add emphasis, he prohibited on pain of death the further use of the term "Jurchen" to describe his subjects. From this time onward, we may speak of this diverse yet politically unified ethnic group as the Manchus.

What were the markers of Manchu identity? One important and enduring sign was the hairstyle of males, who shaved off the front part of their hair and braided the back part into a long queue (Manchu: *soncoho*; Chinese: *bianzi*). Manchu women, for their part, had "natural" feet (as opposed to the bound feet of many of their Chinese neighbors). Another important marker for Manchu men and women alike was a deep interest in horsemanship and hunting with bows and arrows. The Manchus also had common legends and prominent shared symbols—notably the willow tree, crows, and magpies.[21]

A key feature of Manchu cultural identity was shamanism, which included not only the "individual" and "clan-based" varieties discussed above, but also a form of devotion focused on the *Tangse* (Chinese: *Tangzi*)—a ritual space containing a spirit pole for hoisting sacrifices to Heaven (similar to the ones in clan shamanism), a pavilion, and various ritual implements, including a spirit sword and/or a spirit arrow. The origin of the *Tangse* is unclear; our best guess is that it emerged as the various hunter-gatherer tribes in the area of Manchuria became more settled and increasingly looked to agriculture as the foundation of their local economy. But whereas ordinary clan-based shamanism involved specific territorial units, the rituals of *Tanse* shamanism asserted broader claims of rule by the imperial clan and involved greater numbers of both participants and observers (see chapter 7).[22]

Language was another marker of Manchu distinctiveness, for a great linguistic gulf separated spoken and written Manchu from spoken and written Chinese (see chapter 5). Throughout their long reign, the written script of the Manchus served as the "imperial language" of the Qing dynasty—the "fundamental medium of communications within the imperial family."[23] Early Qing policy required, for example, that selected civilians as well as Bannermen and nobles acquire literacy in Manchu. But Manchu was not the only written language of the Qing; classical Chinese and the Mongolian script also came into widespread use. Indeed, by 1635 the production of multilingual documentation in Manchu, Mongolian, and Chinese had become routine within the Manchu bureaucracy, and their use continued until the fall of the dynasty. These versions were not always exactly the same, however: mistakes in transcription, inadvertent omissions, and deliberate censorship all shaped the contours of this trilingual practice. As one example of deliberate distortion, the shamanistic context of Nurhaci's "Seven Grievances" was purposely obscured in the Chinese translation.

The year 1636 was a turning point in the history of the Manchus. Hong Taiji, having established the foundations of a serviceable bureaucracy, honed the skills of his Banner military forces, developed an effective system of multilingual communication, and created a distinctive Manchu cultural identity, was now ready to embark on a systematic campaign of empire building. As a prelude, in 1636 he boldly declared the establishment of the "Great Qing" (Manchu: *Daicing*; Chinese: *Da Qing*) dynasty.[24] By this time the Mongol Eight Banners had been formed. Some of these soldiers were Mongolian-speaking descendents of the Mongols who lived in the area of Manchuria during the Ming period. Others were descended from the Jurchen people who resided in northern Manchuria, but Nurhaci and his followers called them "Mongols" because they had organized themselves politically in the Mongol fashion. Still others were actually from the area we now know as Mongolia, who submitted to Nurhaci and his successors either before or after battles with the Jurchen.[25]

During the period from 1637 to 1642, the Han (Chinese) Eight Banners came into being. The origins of these "Chinese Martial Bannermen" (*Hanjun*), as distinct from the vast majority of Han people who were not part of the Banner system, were as diverse as those of the Mongol Bannermen. Some individuals had originally been inhabitants of North China who migrated to Liaodong; others were probably of Korean ancestry. But a large number were of Jurchen origin, who had assimilated elements of Chinese or Korean culture, including fluency in Chinese. In any case, all Chinese in the Manchu service, whether advisers or Bannermen, were required to shave their heads in the Manchu style and wear Manchu-style clothing as a sign of submission. But because they came late to the fold and because they were Han (as opposed to Inner Asian peoples), the Chinese Bannermen never received equal treatment within the Banner organization. This remained true even after the conquest of China Proper in 1644.[26]

In 1638 Hong Taiji's Manchu, Mongol, and Chinese Banner forces occupied much of Korea, forcing the king to renounce his loyalty to the Ming. Protected now on his eastern and western flanks and strengthened by ever greater numbers of defectors and surrendered Ming troops, the newly crowned emperor of the Qing turned his attention southward once again. In 1642 the strategic city of Jinzhou fell to the Manchus after a prolonged siege.

This event, coupled with a dramatic Qing victory at the fortress of Song-shan, demoralized the dynasty and put Ming forces stationed at the critical Shanhai Pass in jeopardy. But on September 21, 1643, Hong Taiji suddenly died, creating a temporary power vacuum. After some tense negotiations, the emperor's brother Dorgon (1612–1650), together with a famous general named Jirgalang (1599–1655), became co-regents for the new ruler—one of Hong Taiji's youngest children, a five-year-old boy named Fulin, who was enthroned on October 8, 1643, as the Shunzhi ("Compliant Rule") emperor.

During the next several months, the Manchus weighed their military options while their primary adversary, Wu Sangui, did the same. Prior to the fall of Bei-jing in April 1644, the Ming general had rejected an offer of enfeoffment by the Manchus, which had been conveyed by Wu's uncle, now a Qing official. But in the new situation, as the vaunted Ming warrior faced the prospect of engaging Li's possibly superior forces without additional military support, he decided to join forces with the Manchus and expel Li from the capital. In a letter to Dorgon that was addressed to the young Shunzhi emperor, he wrote:

I have long admired deeply Your Highness's majestic authority, but accord-ing to the obligations of the *Spring and Autumn Annals*, borders are not to be crossed, and I have therefore not communicated directly with you before now. . . . [But] roving bandits [that is, the forces of Li Zicheng] have revolted against Heaven and overthrown the emperor. How could such a disorderly mob of petty thieves be capable of carrying out such a matter?[27]

Wu went on to say that this sad situation in the former Ming capital caused him to "weep tears of blood in search of help." It was, he argued passionately, the Qing dynasty's moral responsibility to "obey Heaven's Mandate" and as-sist him in "rescuing the people from fire and water."

On May 27, 1644, Wu Sangui formally surrendered to Dorgon, along with more than a thousand civil and military officials. Moreover, Wu agreed to place his forces in front of the Qing armies in their attack on Li Zicheng's troops. In the initial confrontation, Wu's troops suffered serious losses and would have been defeated without the assistance of the Manchus. But Dor-gon's Banner armies outflanked Li's men at a critical moment and broke their ranks. "The retreat turned into a rout, and stragglers were cut down as the Shun army turned and fled toward the walls of Yongping."[28] After the de-feated Shun troops returned to Beijing in disarray on May 31, they proceeded to sack the offices and residences of former Ming officials. On June 3, in a pathetic last-ditch display of legitimizing ritual, Li Zicheng had himself en-throned in a hasty coronation ceremony. The next day he and his troops set the Forbidden City ablaze and headed westward, with Wu Sangui's forces in hot pursuit.

During the next several months, Qing forces gradually restored order to the capital, after convincing its skeptical population that a Manchu monarch, rather than Wu Sangui, had inherited the Mandate of Heaven. Dorgon's public proclamations, designed to restore confidence, emphasized the virtue and good intentions of the new regime, promising that those who submitted to the Qing would be given "rank and reward," while those who resisted would be slaughtered. He made a special appeal to "scholars of resolve" whom, he said, would "reap upright administration, meritorious fame, and the [unhindered] pursuit of their vocation" if they willingly joined the new dynasty. In this environment of conciliation, the young Shunzhi emperor officially ascended the throne on October 30, 1644. Qing official sources subsequently reported that "All [of the residents of Beijing] praised our dynasty as being humane and righteous." Its reputation, they maintained, "would resound for ten thousand generations."[29]

But while the Manchus sought to legitimize themselves as the protectors of China's cultural heritage in the midst of Li Zicheng's depredations, they also crystallized their image as "barbarian" conquerors in early 1645 by forcing the Chinese to adopt the Manchu-style queue (*bianzi*) as a sign of submission. This act occasioned serious resistance on the part of a great many Han people. In the first place, they considered their traditional hairstyle to be a fundamental feature of their Chinese cultural identity; secondly, they viewed shaving their hair as an unfilial act—the severance of something that had been bequeathed to them by their ancestors. In part because of resentment over the head-shaving decree, but also out of a strong sense of commitment to the Ming (particularly on the part of loyalist generals such as Shi Kefa, 1601–1645), some areas of China fought back against the Manchus with a vengeance, provoking Qing forces to massacre entire populations.[30] Accounts of the atrocities perpetrated at southern cities such as Yangzhou, Jiading, and Jiangyin—where Qing soldiers deliberately and brutally killed tens of thousands of often-innocent people—circulated underground for more than two centuries, feeding anti-Manchu sentiment and causing great damage to the dynasty when the stories surfaced in the late nineteenth and early twentieth centuries.[31]

THE QING EMPIRE AFTER 1644: A BRIEF OVERVIEW

As had been the case with the Ming, the Qing dynasty was shaped in profound ways not only by the institutional legacy of its immediate predecessor, but also by the aims and aspirations of its own talented and dynamic early rulers. Unlike the Ming emperors, however, the Qing monarchs had to grapple with problems of identity that came with their non-Chinese heritage. Moreover, they operated in an increasingly globalized world, which complicated their options and thus their political choices. On the whole the Manchus responded creatively and successfully to the challenges of their first two centuries on the throne. Thereafter, however, the complications and pressures, both internal and external, became too much for the alien regime to bear.

As with the Song-Yuan transition, the problem of foreign rule added an extra dimension to the perennial issue of fidelity to the fallen dynasty. In fact, the fierce resistance by Ming loyalists posed a much greater threat to the succeeding regime than that of their Song dynasty counterparts. Indeed, it took the Manchus nearly forty years after their occupation of Beijing in 1644 to consolidate their conquest. Moreover, a great many more people of prominence were involved in the resistance. For instance, the gigantic Qing encyclopedia known as the *Gujin tushu jicheng* (Complete collection of writings and illustrations, past and present, 1726; hereafter TSJC) contains over five thousand biographies of noteworthy Ming loyalists, as compared to less than seven hundred for the Song. On the other hand, even such famous Ming supporters as Gu Yanwu (1613–1682), Huang Zongxi (1610–1695), Wang Fuzhi (1619–1692), and Lü Liuliang (1629–1683)—all of whom steadfastly refused to serve the Qing—encouraged their children, relatives, and students to give their service to the new dynasty.[32]

In Beijing, meanwhile, the Jesuits proved remarkably adept at transferring their loyalties from the Ming to the Qing. Indeed, it was a version of the official state calendar created by the Jesuit father Adam Schall von Bell (1592–1666) that Dorgon chose as part of the elaborate ritual marking the ascension of the new Shunzhi emperor. This carefully crafted ceremony included a somewhat surprising imperial utterance to the effect that Dorgon, acting as regent for the youthful new emperor, had surpassed even the legendary Duke of Zhou in this essential administrative role. He was, the young Qing monarch purportedly said, conscientious, righteous, forthright, loyal, and virtuous—the very embodiment of the state (*ti guo*).[33]

Clearly the emperor's coronation speech was designed to enhance the political position of Dorgon, who was contending with rival Manchu princes for supreme power at the time. By stages, he was able to undercut their authority effectively. One concrete step undertaken, as always, in the name of the Shunzhi emperor, was to prohibit the other princes from interfering in state affairs. He also formalized the channels of command connecting the capital with the provinces. In an edict dated April 11, 1645, Dorgon announced that all government offices, large and small, would henceforth follow the Ming model for submitting memorials (that is, reports from subordinate officials to the throne). From that point onward, the Six Boards would serve as "the main clearinghouses" for such communications, which would be summarized by the appropriate Board and forwarded to the emperor to await his response.[34]

Although Dorgon was at pains to proclaim at the outset of Qing rule in China that there were "no distinctions between Manchus and Han" and that "the empire is a single whole," the Manchus were still primus inter pares. For instance, they always ranked higher than their counterparts in the top metropolitan offices, including the secretaries in the Grand Secretariat and the "presidents" of the Six Boards (see chapter 3). Administrative sanctions also differed by ethnic groups, with the advantage to the Manchus. Nonetheless, Dorgon took a number of Chinese officials into his confidence, such as Feng Quan (1595–1672) and Chen Mingxia (d. 1654), and he even began to be less suspicious of "corrupt Ming customs." He also started placing Han officials in ranking positions within the Six Boards. Chen, for example, became a full president of the Board of Civil Appointments in 1648, alongside the Manchu president, Tantai. Furthermore, Dorgon began to staff the lower Qing bureaucracy with candidates who had passed the newly instituted metropolitan-level (*jinshi*) exams. In order to accelerate this process, Dorgon arranged for competition to take place three times between 1646 and 1649, in contrast to the general Ming practice of holding the *jinshi* competition only once every three years. More than a thousand candidates passed these tests and most became civil officials.[35]

Military affairs were no less a priority than reform of the civil bureaucracy for Dorgon, who naturally recognized the need to establish Banner garrisons in strategic cities throughout China Proper. Estimates vary on the total number of Bannermen directly involved in the Qing invasion, but 120,000 to 150,000 seems to be reasonable enough. After the conquest, in the period between 1644 and 1669, the Qing authorities appropriated "well in excess of two million acres," mostly from the estates of Ming nobility and officials, in order to provide Banner companies with land for housing, stables, pastures, farmlands, and cemeteries. In all, a reported forty thousand Manchu Bannermen and their families "received approximately six acres each, with much larger estates being granted to senior Manchu officers."[36]

All of the original Qing subjects who were transferred from Liaodong to the Chinese provinces resided in walled enclaves called "Manchu cities" (Chinese: *Mancheng* or *Manzhou cheng*; Manchu: *Manju hoton*). The process began in Beijing, Xi'an, Nanjing, and Hangzhou (see figure 4.1). Eventually, Banner garrisons arose in nineteen locations, with by far the most substantial representation in Beijing (more than half of the total). Mark Elliott describes these garrisons in the following terms: "Part military bastion, part administrative center, and part ethnic ghetto, the Manchu city became the exclusive home of banner officers and soldiers, their families, and servants, giving the dynasty a high profile in major urban centers and functioning as anchors in the steady expansion of Qing control."[37] Initially, only Mongol and Manchu Bannermen occupied the metropolitan zone's defense perimeter. These troops were called the "capital Eight Banners," as distinct from soldiers in provincial locations who were known as "garrison Eight Banners."

For a few years after 1644, no sharp division existed between the living arrangements of Banner and Chinese households at the capital. But as in the case of Liaodong during the preconquest period, Manchu-Chinese tensions led to a "policy of separation." In October 1648, Dorgon mandated the segregation of Banner and Chinese residents in Beijing. The effect of this order, which greatly inconvenienced the non-Banner Chinese population, was to create a Banner cordon around the Imperial City and the Forbidden City nested within it (see figure 3.3). Yet despite this sharp physical division between an "inner" Manchu city in the north and an "outer" Chinese city in the south, Beijing as a whole became a "Sino-Manchu hybrid," where the Manchu written language was displayed over gates and on the streets along with Chinese characters; where Manchu food was available along with Chinese food; and where entertainment included Manchu performances. Han Chinese were permitted to enter the Inner City during the day, but they were officially forbidden to stay there overnight.[38]

At about the same time that the Manchus were establishing Banner garrisons at the capital and in the provinces, they also began transforming remnants of the old Ming *weisuo* system into a new Chinese fighting force known as the Army of the Green Standard (*Lüying bing*). By 1686, there were an estimated 578,000 Green Standard officers and soldiers in China according to the military historian Luo Ergang. These predominantly Han troops, scattered throughout the country in relatively small detachments, were designed as a means of "using the Han to control the Han" (*yi Han zhi Han*)—a nice domestic variation on the hoary Chinese foreign policy strategy known as "using barbarians to control barbarians" (*yi yi zhi yi*). Initially, the Manchus intended the Green Standard forces to function as a constabulary, charged with maintaining local order, supervising river conservancy, grain transport, and so forth—rather like the National Guard in the United States today. But following the suppression of the Revolt of the Three Feudatories in 1683 (see below), Green Standard forces began to assume military functions usually reserved for the Banner Armies.[39]

In the immediate aftermath of the Qing occupation of Beijing, Banner forces and Ming troops that had surrendered to the new dynasty (like those of Wu Sangui) set about eliminating the remaining military challenges to the state. There were many of them, large and small, with leaders of diverse backgrounds and varying economic interests. One noteworthy Ming loyalist, a woman named Qin Liangyu (1574–1648), was the wife of an enfeoffed native chieftain (*tusi*) in Sichuan province. Having received the same broad education afforded her brothers, she distinguished herself in military affairs and actually attained the exalted rank of brigade-general (*zongbing*) in the Ming army. She and her daughter-in-law Ma Fengyi both led loyalist troops against the Manchus, the former confronting the invaders in the vicinity of Beijing and the latter fighting to her death in Henan province.[40]

Somewhat surprisingly, the threats to the Qing posed by Li Zicheng and Zhang Xianzhong quickly dissipated; Li disappeared from view soon after his retreat from Beijing in 1644 (there are several different stories about his disappearance), and Banner forces killed Zhang in 1647 (assisted indirectly by Qin Liangyu). At about the same time, Qing armies put down Muslim revolts in Lanzhou and other frontier cities, and managed to keep the rebellious Khalka Mongols at bay. By 1650, Qing military power had been extended all the way south to Guangzhou (aka Canton), which fell on November 24, followed by a brutal massacre of the city's population ordered by General Kong Youde.

Meanwhile, the Prince of Fu at Nanjing had declared himself emperor of the Southern Ming dynasty on June 19, 1644, only to be captured and killed within a year. Subsequent Ming princes sought to maintain the dynasty in exile but to no avail. The last of these individuals, styled the Yongli ("Perpetual Calendar") emperor, traveled from place to place in south China, eventually ending up in Burma, where Wu Sangui's forces took him into custody. He was reportedly strangled to death in Wu's presence on June 11, 1662.

There remained, however, a formidable maritime challenge to the Qing in the person of Zheng Chenggong (aka Koxinga; 1624–1662), a degree-holding Ming loyalist and seasoned naval commander who managed in the 1650s to build an anti-Manchu fighting force of an estimated 250,000 men and more than two thousand ships. He set up his naval base in and around the city of Xiamen (aka Amoy), located on the coast of Fujian province—directly across the strait from the island of Taiwan (aka Formosa), where the Dutch had established a trading colony in 1624. Although Zheng's father, Zhilong, surrendered to the Manchus in 1646, his son continued to fight the northern invaders. In the summer of 1659, Chenggong sailed into the Yangzi River with hundreds of ships and between 50,000 and 100,000 troops, defeating Qing forces around Nanjing and laying siege to the recently recovered former Ming capital. He did not press his military advantage, however, and after experiencing a fierce Qing counterattack, he retreated to Xiamen.

Feeling vulnerable to further attacks by Qing forces, Zheng decided to dislodge the Dutch from their colonial foothold in Taiwan in order to establish his own maritime base on the island. He called it "the Ming Eastern Capital."

The expulsion of the Dutch colonialists made Zheng a modern-day hero to nationalistic Chinese, but his military actions at the time indirectly caused pain and misery to many. For example, in an effort to sever support to Zheng and other Ming loyalists in Fujian and Guangdong, the Qing government embarked on a drastic policy of evacuating much of the southern coastline and prohibiting maritime trade in the area. Many thousands of hapless farmers and fisherman in coastal areas died as a result of these draconian measures. Zheng Chenggong's premature death in 1662 diminished the immediate threat to the Qing, but his successors held the fort (literally) on Taiwan for several more years, and so the brutal policy remained in place until 1669.

Meanwhile, Dorgon had died unexpectedly on December 31, 1650. This naturally precipitated a power struggle, out of which General Jirgalang, the former co-regent for the Shunzhi emperor and conquering hero of recent campaigns against Ming loyalists in Hunan province, emerged the winner. Surprisingly, however, the youthful emperor, now twelve years old, began to assert his own personal authority—presumably having learned a great deal about governing from Dorgon before the prince-regent's demise. Somewhat ironically, one of the emperor's first political maneuvers was to encourage criticism of Dorgon and his closest followers in order to establish his own supremacy over certain Manchu princes. Denunciations of the prince-regent's arrogance and greed soon followed, and within weeks of Dorgon's magnificent funeral procession (on January 8), the Shuzhi emperor went public with these and other charges—to the surprise, we may assume, of most Chinese and Manchu residents of the capital.[41]

Having consolidated his power, the emperor proceeded to institute a series of bureaucratic reforms designed at least in part to burnish his image as a sagely, virtuous, and benevolent Confucian ruler. Most of these reforms were suggested by Ming holdovers in the Six Boards and approved by the throne. Many concerned the rectification of bad bureaucratic habits (corruption and extravagance) at both the capital and in the provinces, closer supervision of officials, changes in penal regulations and procedures, support of agriculture, better tax accounting, and so forth. Although the emperor enjoyed some success in reforming his administration, he also allowed factional politics, most based on regional affiliations, to emerge. One index of the importance of region affiliations in Qing political life during the Shuzhi emperor's reign is a comparison of the backgrounds of successful palace examination candidates, which shows a dramatic shift from the north to the south.[42]

For most of the period from 1652 to 1661 the Shunzhi emperor ruled diligently if not particularly forcefully, relying heavily on Chinese as opposed to Manchu officials. Continued military successes, orchestrated by Hong Chengchou, the Chinese governor-general of five southern provinces, buoyed the regime. But by 1659 the Shunzhi emperor had given himself over to cultural indulgences—especially Chinese literature, drama, and calligraphy—and Buddhist devotionalism. He also became infatuated with one of his junior consorts and increasingly surrendered power to court eunuchs and Buddhist priests. When he died, allegedly of smallpox, on February 5, 1661, another power struggle developed within the imperial court, one that involved accusations of a forged will and resulted in the execution of the emperor's favorite eunuch.

The Shunzhi emperor's seven-year-old third son (who had survived smallpox as a small boy) assumed the throne with four senior Manchus as regents. His personal name was Xuanye but he is best known by his auspicious reign name Kangxi ("Peaceful and Congenial"). During his extraordinarily long time on the throne, from 1662 to 1722, he achieved many remarkable things, all of which have been chronicled at length by historians east and west.

For our purposes, a few points about the Kangxi emperor are especially significant. The first is that almost immediately after he ascended the throne, his regents, led by the vaunted military commander Oboi (1610–1669), tried to effect fundamental changes in Qing government. Openly scornful of the Shunzhi emperor for departing from the martial ways of his Manchu forbears and for relying too heavily on eunuchs, these regents downgraded or abolished many eunuch offices and promoted Manchus to high bureaucratic positions. Perhaps their most important single achievement in these early years was to place the Imperial Household Department (Manchu: *Dorgi baita be kadalara yamun*; Chinese: *Neiwufu*) on a firm institutional footing. Although, as we have seen, this unique organ of Qing government had its origins in the preconquest period, it became an especially powerful tool of imperial policy after 1661, undercutting the influence of the palace eunuchs and carrying out a wide range of administrative responsibilities (see chapter 3).[43]

The regents also enhanced the power of the Court of Colonial Affairs and the Deliberative Council of Princes and Ministers (*Yizheng wang dachen huiyi*), downgraded the Censorate and the Hanlin Academy, barred Bannermen from taking the civil service exams (what could be more effete, after all?), and abolished the rigid eight-legged essay. In another power play, they severely punished members of the Jiangnan gentry for delinquency in tax payments (eighteen Han Chinese were executed). As part of their strategy to preserve and strengthen Manchu culture at the top, the regents apparently prevented the Kangxi emperor from formally studying Chinese. Although well educated in Manchu military arts and the Manchu written script, the emperor reportedly had to learn Chinese clandestinely with the assistance of two trusted court eunuchs. Later (1673), however, he began to pursue a more systematic program of Chinese-language instruction.

Not surprisingly, the Kangxi emperor resented the high-handed behavior of his princely overseers, and in the period between 1667 and 1669 he worked carefully and systematically to undermine their influence, assisted by a senior member of the Imperial Bodyguard and a number of other supporters, both Chinese and Manchus. During that time he was able to reverse some of their newly instituted policies, such as prohibiting Bannermen from taking the civil service examinations and abolishing the eight-legged essay. On June 14, 1669, the emperor moved directly against Oboi and his supporters, accusing them of arrogance and dishonesty, and placing them in prison. Some co-conspirators were executed or punished in less severe ways. Oboi died in prison. From this point onward, Kangxi took firm control of Qing political affairs. He was fifteen years old at the time.

Decisive and self-confident, the emperor first precipitated and then suppressed the famous "Revolt of the Three Feudatories" (1673–1681). This uprising involved three powerful individuals: Wu Sangui, who controlled a vast area embracing Yunnan, Guizhou, and parts of Hunan and Sichuan; Shang Zhixin (son of a surrendered Ming general), who held sway in Fujian; and Geng Jingzhong, who ruled Guangdong and parts of Guangxi. These men had been enfeoffed by the Qing with domains in these respective areas for their role (or, in the case of Shang, the role of his father) in suppressing Chinese resistance to the Manchus after 1644. Against the advice of a majority of the Deliberative Council of Princes and Ministers, and following instead the counsel of his Mongolian grandmother, the Kangxi emperor urged the three great fief holders to abandon their territories and return to Manchuria. Their refusal took the form of open rebellion, which required eight agonizing years to suppress and nearly cost the emperor his throne. Nicola Di Cosmo has ably translated the diary of a Banner soldier who fought in this prolonged campaign.[44]

Soon thereafter (1683), the Kangxi emperor brought Taiwan under direct Chinese control (to be administered as a part of Fujian province for the next century), and then turned his military attention to China's northern frontiers, where border clashes between Russian (Cossack) settlers and Manchu or Mongol residents had become more frequent. After a series of punitive expeditions launched against the Russian settlements, and with the help of Jesuit missionaries as negotiators, Qing representatives signed the Treaty of Nerchinsk in 1689, stabilizing and regularizing China's border relations with Russia. This facilitated the Kangxi emperor's later successful campaigns against the Western Mongol tribe known as the Zunghars (aka Dzungars or Ölöds), led by the brilliant military leader Galdan (1644–1697).

In the midst of near-constant warfare, the Kangxi emperor sought to bring Han Chinese elites more fully into the Qing political orbit. One such effort was a special examination for "great Confucians of broad learning" (*boxue hongru*) held at the capital in 1679. Of the 188 scholars invited to participate, more than thirty demurred. But of the remaining participants, fifty passed the exam, and all received official appointments. Significantly, the vast majority of the successful candidates were from Jiangnan—now divided administratively into the provinces of Jiangsu and Zhejiang. This was the area that had suffered from Oboi's harsh punishments for tax evasion in 1661. Eventually (1712) a civil service examination quota system developed, based on provincial affiliations and Banner privileges (see chapter 3).

As a mature ruler, Kangxi tended to be practical, frugal, tolerant, cautious, and conciliatory. Although notoriously disinclined to attack corruption (perhaps for fear of alienating a predominantly Chinese bureaucracy not yet fully reconciled to Manchu rule), he rewarded rectitude and tried to favor neither Manchus nor Chinese in official appointments. Increasingly reliant on "special commissioners" (*qinchai dachen*) to handle crisis situations, he also gave a significant amount of attention to the development of stable and efficient administrative institutions at the local level. Assisted by loyal eunuchs and bondservants, as well as Chinese, Mongol, and Manchu collaborators, he initiated a secret "palace memorial" (*zouzhe*) system, which enabled key civil and military officials at the capital and in the provinces to communicate with him directly, using their own confidential servants to transmit documents.[45]

In addition, the Kangxi emperor placed great value on a tool of government that had fallen into abeyance during the early Qing: imperial tours (*xunxing*). These elaborate events, dutifully recorded in magnificent paintings by court artists, provided the Qing ruler with opportunities for what Michael Chang has described as "ethno-dynastic aggrandizement"—that is, the creation of a careful balance between "legitimation by similarity (cultural assimilation) and domination by difference (ethnic differentiation)." These tours not only displayed the grandeur of the Qing state (and celebrated the specific military values of the Manchus), they also served as opportunities to promote in a very public way such virtues as the emulation of ancestors (*fazu*), diligence and activism (*wuyi, qinzheng, xilao*), and love for the people (*aimin*). Between 1681 and 1722, the Kangxi emperor embarked on a total of 128 imperial tours, an average of more than two in any given year. In twenty-four of these years he spent more than one hundred days traveling, and in eleven of these years he was on the road for more than two hundred days. His grandson, the Qianlong emperor (see below), was equally inclined to show that he could effectively "rule the empire by horseback."[46]

In all, the Kangxi emperor's reign after 1683 was peaceful and productive, notwithstanding a serious revolt by demobilized Green Standard forces in 1688, sparked by an effort on the part of the soldiers to recover arrears in pay. The emperor made no dramatic changes to the fiscal structure of the empire and abandoned the earlier pursuit of tax delinquent landowners in the Jiangnan area. Following the defeat of the Zheng family on Taiwan, he allowed the Chinese coastal population to return to their towns and villages and, as a result, overseas trade began to grow steadily. State services such as water conservancy and famine relief functioned reasonably well, although gross inequities in both income and services could still be found in various parts of the empire.

Chinese and Manchu bondservants, supervised by the Imperial Household Department, managed the state's monopolies in salt and ginseng, as well as major textile and porcelain industries. They also collected duties on certain kinds of foreign and domestic trade. Eventually, by the mid-nineteenth century, the number of bondservants working in and around Beijing would swell to a total of perhaps 20,000 individuals in addition to approximately 130,000 Banner officers and soldiers.

Unfortunately for subsequent emperors, the Kangxi emperor made one crucial fiscal mistake: in an effort to proclaim the prosperity of his realm, he froze the land tax (*di*) and labor tax (*ding*) in 1712, with the result that the Qing bureaucracy was stuck with tax assessments that took no account of population growth, internal migration, or changes in agricultural practice. Faced with shrinking revenues on a per capital basis, the Board of Revenue and Imperial Household Department became ever more reliant on irregular sources of income (see below). Also, perhaps inevitably, the financial situation in the Banner garrisons began to deteriorate.[47]

What do we know about the mental world of the Kangxi emperor? Jonathan Spence's *Emperor of China* (1974), which consists of translations of Kangxi's writings organized around the themes of traveling, ruling, thinking, growing old, and sons, has given us a fascinating look at the emperor's thoughts on a wide variety of personal and administrative topics; and Silas Wu, for his part, has provided us with an illuminating account of the Kangxi emperor's daily work schedules.[48] From these and other sources we can readily see that the Kangxi emperor was ambitious, energetic, broadminded, intelligent, and inquisitive—in fact, a person with a seemingly inexhaustible curiosity. Naturally, then, he took a great interest in the Western knowledge that the Jesuits made available during his long and distinguished reign.

As had been the case in late Ming times, Jesuit missionaries in the early Qing performed a great many important administrative, educational, technical, and advisory roles. Under the Kangxi emperor, Jesuit activity at the capital became even more substantial and significant than before: Jesuits served in the Directorate of Astronomy and other metropolitan offices, helped to map the growing Qing empire, produced paintings and engravings, cast cannon and made other mechanical devices, served as translators and negotiators, and tutored the emperor in subjects such as algebra, geometry, astronomy, cartography, anatomy, and pharmacology.[49] The emperor even learned to play the spinet from a Jesuit court musician.

For most of the Kangxi era, the throne enthusiastically supported the Jesuits, pleased with their scientific and technological contributions and satisfied with the strategy of religious accommodation inaugurated by Matteo Ricci during the Ming. But criticisms of the Jesuit approach by the Franciscans and Dominicans in the late seventeenth and early eighteenth centuries found its way to Rome, prompting Pope Clement XI to issue documents in 1704 and 1715 that prohibited the use of certain pragmatically inspired terms for "God" and insisted that Chinese Christians could not engage in ancestor worship or participate in other "pagan" rituals, including those conducted in Confucian temples (see chapters 1 and 7). In response, the outraged Kangxi emperor outlawed the propagation of Christianity altogether. The Jesuits were, however, allowed to continue serving the Qing court in purely technical and advisory capacities.[50]

Tibetan Buddhism, particularly the Dge lugs pa or "Yellow Hat" variety, represented another kind of "foreign" learning of interest to the Kangxi emperor. Since the Yuan dynasty, Tibet had been on the minds of the rulers of China, not only as a strategic area of enduring interest, but also as a source of religious inspiration. Not long after the Qing conquest of China Proper, the pious Shunzhi emperor invited the fifth Dalai Lama (1652–1682) to Beijing, continuing a tradition of court patronage of Tibetan Buddhism that began with Hong Taiji. The Kangxi emperor, who considered himself to be an incarnation of Qubilai Khan (r. 1260–1294), played an increasingly important role in Tibetan affairs. He may even have had a hand in the mysterious disappearance of the sixth Dalai Lama (1683–1706), as a prelude to the installment of the pro-Qing seventh Dalai Lama (1708–1757).[51] In any case, after Zunghar armies occupied Tibet in 1717, the Kangxi emperor sent troops to oust them and, after doing so, he left a Qing garrison in Lhasa. A few years later the Manchu court sent an *amban* (high official) to serve as a resident minister (Chinese: *Zhu Zang dachen*), overseeing Tibet as a protectorate under the Court of Colonial Affairs. These events inaugurated an extended period of direct Qing intervention in Tibetan life and politics.

Notwithstanding the Kangxi emperor's interest in Tibetan Buddhism and his ardent embrace of Western scientific and technical knowledge, he had a deep and abiding appreciation of traditional Chinese culture. This appreciation was manifest in a variety of ways. To be sure, he loved the hunt and other Manchu military practices. But the vast bulk of his Chinese-language writings—including his unedited valedictory edict of December 23, 1717 (as opposed to the heavily edited version issued after his death)—are liberally sprinkled with Confucian moral admonitions, classical quotations, references to great Chinese culture heroes, and other historical allusions. As a self-consciously Confucian-style ruler, he ardently embraced the teachings of the

Sage. He also patronized traditional style court painting, undertaken by the likes of Wang Hui (1632–1717; see chapter 8). In addition, he sponsored the compilation of a great many philosophical and literary works from China's past, including the *Quan Tangshi* (Complete collection of Tang poetry; 1704) and the *Zhouyi zhezong* (A balanced compendium on the *Zhou Changes*; 1715).

But by far his most ambitious effort to celebrate traditional Chinese culture was the commissioning of the *Gujin tushu jicheng* (Complete collection of writings and illustrations, past and present, 1726; hereafter TSJC). Begun in 1700, this massive (more than 100 million words) and well-organized encyclopedia, repository of "all that was best in the literature of the past, dealing with every branch of knowledge," was intended not only as a moral and practical guide for the Qing emperors and their officials, but also as an expression of the unity and totality of traditional Chinese culture (see the introduction and chapter 9).

Kangxi's death on December 20, 1722, precipitated a succession crisis from which his fourth son, Yinzhen, emerged as victor at the age of forty-five.[52] He reigned as the Yongzheng ("Harmonious and Upright") emperor from 1723 to 1735, and ruled in a rather feverish and sometimes unpredictable way. Relying on elaborate but generally informal networks of administration, he paid extraordinary attention to the smallest details of government, writing endless notes (in Manchu as well as Chinese) to his officials in a "surging tide of scribbling," allowing "no one group to monopolize a problem or manipulate information."[53] Sensitive to persistent rumors that he had usurped the throne, the emperor remained suspicious of all potential rivals, including his brothers—three of whom were arrested and died in prison. But if the Yongzheng reign was marked by harshness and the growth of imperial autocracy, it was also distinguished by a powerful moral vision and a genuine commitment to meaningful administrative reform.

This ethical orientation was evident everywhere. His communications with officials, for instance, are laced with moral admonitions. Similarly, his greatly amplified edition of the Kangxi emperor's Sixteen Maxims (known as the Sacred Edict, or *Shengyu*), designed to be read aloud by local officials as part of the "community compact" (*xiangyue*) security system, was intended as a device by which to achieve the moral transformation (*jiaohua*) of the general Chinese population.[54] Even the emperor's vaunted effort to "civilize" non-Han ethnic groups in remote areas of south China can be seen as motivated not only by a desire to integrate these groups more fully into the Chinese polity administratively, but also to assimilate them culturally as much as possible.[55]

Debates had always existed in the Confucian tradition about which institutions were best suited to good government; in fact, the early Qing period witnessed lively scholarly discussions on precisely this topic. But no one doubted the idea that there could not be good government without good men. The Yongzheng emperor understood this well, and was fanatical about choosing qualified officials to staff his administrative system, from the capital down to the counties. At court, the Yongzheng emperor relied primarily on his loyal brother, Yinxiang (1686–1730), and two especially able Chinese officials: Jiang Tingxi (1699–1732) and Jiang Tingyu (1672–1755). In the provinces, the emperor's strongest supporters included the distinguished Manchu Ortai (1677–1745) and the Chinese officials Yang Zongren (1661–1725), Tian Wenjing (1662–1732), and Li Wei (c. 1687–1738). Chen Hongmou (1669–1771), a more junior Chinese bureaucrat and the subject of a brilliant 2001 biography by William Rowe, served with distinction in both the Yongzheng and Qianlong reigns. With the assistance of these and other talented scholar-officials, the Yongzheng emperor pursued an energetic and largely successful program of fiscal reform that marked something of a turning point in Qing statecraft.[56]

One of the Yongzheng emperor's first priorities was a change in the Qing taxation system. In an effort to improve tax collection within the constraints imposed by his father, he focused immediately on the pervasive problem of corruption. What the emperor discovered in the course of his financial investigations was that the vast majority of local government expenses had no fixed budgetary category, and thus Qing officials had to find irregular sources of revenue to meet their administrative and personal needs. This naturally encouraged maladministration of one kind or another, from the widespread imposition of "customary fees" to the movement of monies from one budget category to another, a practice known as "shifting funds for public expenses." Madeline Zelin points out a major problem with the latter practice: "When a magistrate shifted funds meant to purchase relief grain to pay for the wages of workers building new dikes, he gambled that famine would not occur while he was in office and that the new dikes might fend it off for years to come."[57]

After much debate, both within the Qing court and outside of it, the Yongzheng emperor decided to allow local officials to collect an additional fixed percentage of the land and labor taxes, to be forwarded to the provincial financial commissioner (*buzheng shi*) and then redistributed to the various officials within his jurisdiction. These funds took two forms; one was a "salary supplement" (*yanglian*; lit. "to nourish integrity") and the other was a fund for "public expenses" (*gongfei*). An advantage to this redistribution system from the standpoint of fairness (an abiding concern of the Yongzheng emperor) was that some of the resources of a wealthy region in a given province could be redistributed to poorer ones. Another effort to make taxation somewhat more equitable was the merger of the labor service and land tax.

The Yongzheng emperor's approach to land reclamation differed from that of his Qing predecessors. Previously, most of the reclaimed land was in the economic heartland of China Proper. But during the Yongzheng reign, reclamation and land registration tended to be concentrated in more distant areas, which had a relatively low population density—for example, the remote provinces of Gansu, Guizhou, and Yunnan, and the mountainous regions of Guangxi and Guangdong. As a rule, persons who opened fields to cultivation were given a five-year grace period before any tax had to be paid, and land development loans did not have to be discharged for three years. Other policies designed to rectify the empire's fiscal system and/or to level the economic playing field included repeated efforts to diminish the privileges of landed elites, especially in the Jiangnan area.

The Yongzheng emperor steadfastly sought to protect the interests of commoners (especially those that had been abused by powerful landlords) and to eliminate longstanding hereditary categories that stigmatized certain social groups as "mean [lowly] people" (*jianmin*). He also tried to establish poorhouses, orphanages, and elementary schools in every county in China, and to place local grain reserves under central control for more equitable distribution. In all, these policies worked reasonably well, although elites continued to enjoy important privileges and prerogatives (see chapters 3 and 4).

In foreign policy, the Yongzheng emperor was somewhat less successful. He did manage to annex Eastern Tibet, administering it as Yazhou prefecture and placing it under the native chieftain (*tusi*) system. He also negotiated a treaty with Russia in 1727 (the Treaty of Kiakhta) that created two new trading towns and allowed for the presence of a Russian Orthodox church in Beijing. But efforts to chastise the Zunghars in Central Asia resulted in enormous expenditures (an estimated 130 million ounces of silver) and no significant victory. In fact, Qing forces were nearly wiped out in 1731–1732.

Despite his often-harsh administrative style, the Yongzheng emperor had a lifelong interest in Buddhism. He often associated with members of the Buddhist clergy and discussed Chan (Zen) studies with them (see chapter 7). He held Buddhist ceremonies in the imperial palace, bringing together highranking monks from throughout the empire, and he also arranged for a large number of Buddhist texts to be printed, for which he sometimes wrote calligraphic prefaces. One of these works was an anthology of quintessential Buddhist writings titled *Yuxuan yulu* (Imperially selected [Buddhist] sayings). As yet another indication of his piety, he adopted several Buddhist names for himself, such as "Layman of Aloofness from the Dusty World" and "Layman of Yuanming Garden." He also bestowed Buddhist names on his son Hongli ("Layman of Everlasting Spring") and some of his most trusted officials, including Ortai ("Layman of Composure") and Zhang Tingyu ("Layman of a Clear Mind").⁵⁸

The Yongzheng emperor's Buddhist beliefs may explain, at least in part, a fascinating series of fourteen paintings that he commissioned, which depict him in a variety of guises—as a Confucian scholar, a Buddhist monk, a Tibetan lama, a Daoist immortal, a Mongol nobleman, a Persian warrior, a Turkish prince, and even a tiger hunter wearing European-style clothing and a wig. Some scholars maintain that the emperor's fascination with the clothing and manners of exotic "others" was simply an expression of his desire to rule "All under Heaven" (my own view), but others have argued that these so-called masquerade portraits were designed as a Buddhist device to aid the emperor in "imagining his transformation into other beings" (presumably in future incarnations) and to metaphorically enact his "doubts about the nature of human existence."⁵⁹

One more point about the Yongzheng emperor's religious outlook is worth mentioning: he was deeply committed to practicing Daoist longevity techniques (see chapter 7). Indeed, some people believe that his sudden death in 1735 was the ironic result of an overdose of Daoist elixirs of immortality—one of several unsubstantiated rumors concerning his unanticipated demise.

The Qianlong ("Heavenly Eminence") emperor (1736–1796), who ascended the throne without incident at age twenty-five, deliberately sought to achieve a balance between what he saw as the excessive severity of his father and the overleniency of his grandfather.⁶⁰ By and large he succeeded, although his desire to be judged a benevolent Confucian ruler led him to approach his father's reforms with a certain detrimental hesitation.

According to Alexander Woodside, the Qianlong emperor "may well have been the strongest ruler in Chinese history."⁶¹ Yet he was far from omnipotent. One major problem was simply administrative overload. Beatrice Bartlett estimates that incoming provincial reports may have tripled over the course of his long reign and increased tenfold from the late Kangxi era.⁶² Moreover, to his periodic dismay, the Qianlong emperor found that bureaucrats might offer resistance to his policies. Perhaps the most dramatic instance of this occurred in 1768 with the so-called sorcery scare, which began in Jiangsu and Zhejiang and spread to other provinces. Without going into details of the case, the salient point is that when the emperor tried to intervene directly in the affair by bullying local officials with his powers of appointment and dismissal, the bureaucracy fought back passively, using delaying tactics. Meanwhile, at the capital his advisers managed to convince Qianlong that his unwarranted intervention in the affair not only damaged the throne's credibility, but also undermined judicial and other administrative processes at the local level. In the end, the mighty emperor had to abandon the campaign.⁶³

In financial affairs, the Qianlong emperor retreated from his father's land reclamation efforts as well as his attempt to centralize the "ever-normal granary" system. He also empowered the literati class, restoring many of the tax privileges and exemptions that the Yongzheng emperor had denied them. As a result of such policies, grave economic disparities began to reappear. The sharp line between the haves and have-nots did not cleave along ethnic lines, but it was readily apparent, even in the heyday of the dynasty. The emperor, who vigorously protected the interests of privileged groups, including salt monopoly merchants, was largely responsible.

Thus we find, on the one hand, reports of unprecedented numbers of extraordinarily wealthy people, including rich merchant households that could afford to spend 100,000 ounces of silver a day entertaining the Qianlong emperor on his imperial tours to the south (he, like his grandfather, made a fetish of these ritualized itinerant displays). On the other, there were massive numbers of poor people who sought, but often did not receive, financial relief. In 1740 the emperor expressed astonishment when he heard tales of "starving people" from Shandong who were traveling all the way to Fujian in hopes of improving their lot. In 1761 special punishments were imposed in order to deter indigent Manchu Bannermen in some southern cities from pawning their weapons, armor, flags, and other military equipment—perhaps to some of the very merchants that Qianlong supported.[64]

Unlike his father, who favored no-nonsense technocrats as advisers and officials, the Qianlong emperor preferred sophisticated aesthetes. More than any other Qing ruler before or after, his conception of the throne was a cosmopolitan one. Aesthetically speaking, his taste ran the gamut from Inner Asia sensibilities to those of the Middle Kingdom, from Manchu literature and Tibetan architecture to Chinese poetry and prose. Appreciative of traditional Chinese arts and crafts, he also admired Western painting techniques—especially those of the talented Jesuit court painter and architect Giuseppe Castiglione (Chinese: Lang Shining; 1688–1766). Castiglione, who had previously served both the Kangxi and Yongzheng emperors, found an especially appreciative patron in Qianlong. In this expansively eclectic court environment, Castiglione perfected a new style of courtly art, a hybrid combining Western realism (including linear perspective) with Chinese conventions of brushwork and composition. Most of his themes were traditional Chinese ones—portraits, flowers, landscapes, animals (especially horses, including tribute horses), etc.—but he also celebrated Manchu culture, recording military campaigns, individual Manchu warriors (including the emperor), and hunting expeditions.[65]

The great achievement of the Qianlong emperor, amply recorded by Castiglione and other Jesuit and Chinese painters at court (and also abundantly documented in print), was his expansive imperial vision: he sought to be not only the emperor of China, but also the ruler of a multicultural pan-Asian empire. His predecessors had already moved in this direction; for instance, they saw themselves as Inner Asian khans as well as Chinese emperors. But Qianlong vastly extended the area under Qing control, and administered it with a clear recognition and appreciation of its political, social, economic, and cultural diversity. The military actions that created this empire, doubling the previous territorial extent of the Qing domain, were known collectively as the "Ten Great Campaigns" (*Shi quan wu gong*). The most important of these involved the final destruction of the Zungars (1755–1757), and the "pacification," in the period from 1758 to 1759, of a large swath of Central Asia that would soon (1768) be renamed Xinjiang ("New Territories"). The other campaigns involved efforts to suppress domestic rebels (in Sichuan and Taiwan) and what amounted to police actions against border peoples to the south of China: the Burmese, the Vietnamese, and the Gurkhas in Nepal.[66]

These colonizing efforts, especially in the north, were not unlike those of the British in India, which "transcended ethnicity and camouflaged class," bringing together two important concepts of empire:

> One was the feudal principle of multiple centers and multiple powers in which the multiethnic, multilinguistic elements of the empire were held together by networks of hierarchical power that the emperor struggled to maintain as personal. The Qing emperor accepted and encouraged the existence of loyal lesser lordships under him, but "segmented" and "zoned" them by means of elaborate procedures and rituals in three different royal capitals. The other principle was the bureaucratic one of centralized written communications. It was affected, and even overwhelmed, by the political and literary magnetism of the tradition of civil service examinations. The examination system culture recognized only one ultimate capital: Beijing.[67]

To put the matter another way, administratively, a "feudal" principle prevailed in the wider Qing empire, held together by various combinations of civil and military institutions, marriage and other alliances, a system of native chieftains (*tusi*), commercial ties, and tributary relationships. But culturally, the examination principle triumphed, especially in China Proper. In an edict issued in 1779, the Qianlong emperor openly acknowledged this, noting that Manchu and Mongol interpreters who had grown up as Bannermen in Beijing had allowed their native languages to be corrupted by the city's "examination culture."

The two main functional capitals of the Manchus served, in a sense, as metaphors for their vast, somewhat bifurcated empire. Below the Great Wall, the city of Beijing, and particularly the Forbidden City within it, reflected features of Qing examination culture: they were formalized, regularized, rigid, and refined (*wen*). Both the larger city and the palace complex were built on a strict north-south axis, with a preponderance of Chinese-style buildings and classically derived inscriptions written primarily in Chinese (the inner court of the Forbidden City, however, had both Chinese and Manchu inscriptions). By contrast, the sprawling, asymmetrical Qing summer retreat at Chengde (Rehe), north of the Great Wall, was an undulating multicultural metropolis, begun in the Kangxi reign and completed under the Qianlong emperor. Although full of religious symbolism and certainly not bereft of classical Chinese inscriptions, it bespoke Manchu militarism (*wu*). In the words of Ruth Dunnell and James Millward, "strategically situated on China's northern frontier, Chengde became a practical and symbolic command center from which the Manchu rulers coordinated relations between China, an expanding Russian empire, and Inner Asia (i.e. the Manchurian homelands, Mongolia and Mongol-inhabited areas, Tibet and Xinjiang)."[68] As the essays in their co-edited volume indicate, the Manchus built Chengde to reflect and celebrate their expansion into Central and Inner Asia. As a result, its gardens, palaces, and pavilions replicated and brought together "key cultural monuments of China, Tibet, and Central Asia."

However comfortable the Qing rulers may have been with their hierarchically organized multicultural empire, they remained acutely aware of their position as alien conquerors of China—particularly in the face of critiques by Ming loyalists such as Lü Liuliang, who stridently asserted that the "barbarian" origins of the Manchus made them no better than animals, and therefore utterly unfit to rule China.[69] The issue of what constituted a "barbarian" was naturally, then, a matter of acute political concern to all Qing emperors. But they did not always agree on how to view the relationship between their "racial" heritage on the one hand and their "cultural" rule of China on the other. For example, the Yongzheng emperor believed that the Chinese cultural environment had helped to "refine" (*xiu*) the Manchus, and thereby enhanced their "holy virtue" (*shengde*), just as it had done for the "foreign" sage hero Shun and the "foreign" founder of the Zhou dynasty, King Wen. The Qianlong emperor maintained, however, that the Manchus had equal standing with China, and that its inheritors had no need to take on the civilization of others.[70] That they had done so was not in any way an indication of Manchu cultural inferiority, simply a pragmatic choice. But regardless of how the Manchu monarchs viewed their specific relationship to Chinese culture, all of them, Qianlong included, had a heightened sensitivity to any criticisms of "barbarians" on the part of Han Chinese that might be construed as an attack on the legitimacy of Qing rule.

One measure of this sensitivity was evident in the politics surrounding the monumental editorial project known as the *Siku quanshu* (Complete collection of the four treasuries, 1782; hereafter SKQS). This project, which began in 1772, took two decades to finish (see chapter 9). Intended as an imperial collection representing the best of China's magnificent literary heritage, the SKQS illustrates the ambivalence of the Qing rulers toward that inheritance. On the one hand, it was clearly designed by the Qianlong emperor as a monument to Manchu patronage of traditional Chinese culture. On the other, it became a device for ferreting out works that were deemed critical of the Manchus in particular and "barbarians" in general. In the course of the so-called Literary Inquisition that took place from the early 1770s to the early 1780s, over two thousand works were destroyed and many others suppressed or tampered with. A number of individual Chinese scholars were also punished for their allegedly "seditious" views.[71]

A parallel literary project of the Qianlong emperor involved a concerted attempt to celebrate his Manchu heritage by promoting the language of his ancestors, editing historical materials dealing with Manchu history, writing poems that glorified the Manchu homeland (especially "Ode to Mukden"), codifying Manchu religious rituals, and valorizing Manchu martial culture. Fearing that Bannermen had been seduced and softened by the attractions of Chinese urban life (see also chapter 4) and that their Manchu-language skills were declining along with their military capabilities, he sought to re-instill a sense of ethnic pride in them. As part of this effort, he furnished scholars with more and better tools for learning Manchu, such as dictionaries, and commissioned a Manchu-language version of early Qing history. He also sponsored a work titled *Manzhou yuanliu kao* (Research on Manchu origins; 1783), which sought to provide the Manchus with a grand historical narrative that would establish a concrete link with the Jin dynasty (1115–1234) and provide a historical justification for Qing rule. This account did not eliminate Song dynasty references to the "barbaric" behavior of the Jin people, but neither did it go so far as to include similarly unflattering descriptions of the Manchus in Ming sources.[72]

Other efforts by the Qianlong emperor to inscribe Manchu culture into historical memory and onto contemporary consciousness included a six-volume publication titled *Manzhou jishen ji tian dianli* (Manchu rites for sacrifices to the spirits and to Heaven; 1747 and 1783). In the preface to this work, the Qianlong emperor emphasized that his intent was to preserve and rectify native Manchu religious customs of the sort discussed earlier in this chapter. Significantly, the emperor expressed concerns that the spread of the Chinese language among Manchus had resulted in distorted shamanic chants that had altered meanings. Worse yet, in some shamanic rituals, Chinese had replaced Manchu incantations altogether.[73]

One of the most important literary projects of the Qianlong emperor had to do with the translation into Manchu of the monumental Tibetan Buddhist canon known as the Kanjur, which had previously been translated into Chinese. In his preface to this work the emperor wrote:

> Having . . . [the Sanskrit scriptures] translated from Chinese into Manchu will lead all people everywhere to study Manchu; even if they do not learn the Buddha's first truths, they will still learn to respect their lord and love their superiors, to abandon evil and pursue goodness. Is this not also worthy? Our primary intent in translating the Buddhist scriptures into Manchu is precisely this and nothing else.[74]

This statement suggests that bringing readers of Manchu to Buddhism was only a secondary concern of the emperor's. But we can be reasonably certain that the translation project, begun in 1771 and completed almost twenty years later, was motivated at least in part by genuine piety.

The Qianlong emperor's embrace of Tibetan Buddhism was not simply expedient. To be sure, it was unquestionably useful for the Qing monarch to be able to project (literally) an image of himself as a Tibetan deity to his lamaist subjects in Tibet and Mongolia, just as it was helpful to project a more domesticated image of himself as a Buddhist deity to his Chinese subjects. But as Patricia Berger and Johan Elverskog have both argued on the basis of different but complementary evidence, the Qianlong emperor was every bit as pious as his father (perhaps even more so), and he demonstrated his piety with much greater abandon. One cannot read accounts of the arrangements for the Panchen Lama's visit to the emperor's summer palace in Chengde (1779) without appreciating this point. The Panchen Lama's entourage consisted of five thousand monks escorted by one hundred soldiers and nearly a thousand servants and clerks. In support, the Qianlong emperor spared no expense. At each stop on the journey from Tibet to Chengde,

> The Qing court provided the entourage with two thousand new horses, one hundred camels, forty Mongol felt tents, one hundred cotton tents, chairs, cushions and other furniture, in addition to a large daily sum of money to pay for travelling expenses.[75]

When the Panchen Lama arrived at Chengde, he discovered that the emperor had ordered the construction there of replicas of the Dalai Lama's residence, the Potala, and the Panchen Lama's own residence, the Tashilhunpo (aka Bkra shis lhun po) monastery. Another index of the Qianlong emperor's piety (both religious and filial) was his gift of more than nine thousand images of Buddhist deities to his mother on her seventieth birthday.[76]

Still, as one authority has remarked, the Qianlong emperor was "at least as much a creature of Yangzhou, Suzhou and Hangzhou as he was of the Asia beyond the Great Wall."[77] In fact, his love of the gardens of the Yangzi River area was so great that he brought artists on his southern tours just to sketch them, so that they could then be reproduced in Beijing. As a patron of the arts, the Qianlong emperor had no Qing dynasty equal, even if both he and his courtiers exaggerated his personal accomplishments and taste.

For instance, the emperor once claimed to have produced over forty-two thousand poems, more than seven thousand of them in the last four years of his life. He is also credited with writing roughly a thousand prose pieces of various sorts and creating a large number of paintings and calligraphic inscriptions. Moreover, he

> had an omnivorous fondness for collecting art. This meant not just printing and calligraphy, but such things as Shang, Zhou, and Han dynasty bronze vessels and implements, Song, Yuan, and Ming porcelains, and even the inkslabs of various dynasties. Qianlong littered the antique paintings that he collected with his own obtrusive seal imprints and calligraphy, his duty being "to remain at the head of the arts even if, in the process, the art was destroyed."[78]

The costs of the Qianlong emperor's efforts to acquire great artworks, build expansive summer retreats, support enormous literary collections, and expand the Qing empire to an unprecedented extent eventually created severe fiscal problems for the state. Furthermore, in his later years Qianlong became increasingly careless, investing enormous power in a former imperial bodyguard named Heshen (Manchu: Hešen; d. 1799), who proceeded to embark on a monumental campaign of organized corruption. Although the full extent of Heshen's peculation remains to be determined, one Chinese historian, Li Jiannong, estimates the worth of his enormous personal estate as the equivalent of "ten times the seventy million tael annual income of the Chinese empire at the time."[79]

At this point the Qing dynasty was clearly in decline. Both the Banner forces and the Army of the Green Standard had deteriorated, nearly beyond redemption. As if to accentuate the security problem facing the dynasty, a large-scale rebellion broke out in 1796 and lasted for nearly a decade. This uprising, known as the White Lotus Rebellion (1796–1804), was suppressed largely by Green Standard forces, supplemented by local militias (*tuanlian*) and mercenaries known as "braves" (*yong*).[80]

The Qianlong emperor formally abdicated the throne in 1795, out of a filial desire not to exceed the reign of his illustrious grandfather. But his second son, the Jiaqing emperor (1796–1820), did not personally assume the reins of power until the death of his father in 1799. Jiaqing was an intelligent, well-educated, and energetic emperor, who immediately upon his accession to power at the age of thirty-nine initiated a series of reforms designed to rectify the administrative problems created by his father's late-reign dereliction of duty and his apparent protection of Heshen. As an essential first step, Jiaqing ordered Heshen to commit suicide. He then abolished the Secret Account Bureau (*Miji chu*), which Heshen had used to collect large fines (in some instances more than 100,000 *taels*) from servitors of the Imperial Household. A "drastic sweep" of top-level central government officials followed, along with various important reforms in the imperial communications system and especially border administration.[81]

Other efforts to reduce expenditures and curb corruption met with less success, however. By the early nineteenth century, population pressure, rising inflation, the increasing costs of river conservancy, and a myriad of other fiscal problems prompted the Jiaqing emperor to make his officials more closely accountable for cost overruns and to authorize deductions from their supplemental salaries (*yanglian*) in order to hold the line on administrative expenses. This only encouraged bureaucrats to seek other means to make ends meet. Madeleine Zelin summarizes some of the unfortunate consequences:

> Deprived in large measure of their own legitimate sources of income, . . . local officials began to resort to illegal surcharges, forced contributions, customary fees (*lougui*), manipulation of silver-copper ratios, and other devices for raising funds. Even the Jiaqing emperor was forced to admit that local officials had no choice but to rely on *lougui*. Rather than allow them to extort from the people as they pleased, the emperor made the extraordinary recommendation that *lougui* be legalized and set up for its collection.[82]

From this point onward, no chance existed for a more rational fiscal administration. Informal networks of funding became the hallmark of the Chinese bureaucracy, and the acceptance of *lougui* became the mark of even virtuous officials. Corruption remained a chronic problem, and the central government increasingly resorted to the sale of rank and even substantive offices to cover its costs.[83]

Although the dynasty was obviously in a downward spiral, it would be incorrect to claim, as some scholars have done, that the Qing state no longer had the capacity for effective action. Research by Jane Kate Leonard and others has shown that Jiaqing's successor, the Daoguang emperor (1821–1850), was, like his father, capable of dynamic and effective action—at least in those spheres of responsibility deemed essential to China's "national security." In late 1824, for instance, after flooding had destroyed the Grand Canal in northern Jiangsu and crippled the dynasty's grain transport system, the Daoguang emperor "undertook the disciplined supervision of canal-transport affairs," pursuing a flexible approach to crisis management that "was determined by changing realities in northern Jiangsu, rather than a mindless adherence to the regulations and traditions of the imperial ancestors."[84]

The Daoguang period also witnessed a shift in the focus of China's foreign relations. Matthew Mosca notes: "Seen in Eurasian perspective, the most striking feature of official Qing strategic thought between 1790 and the 1830s is that it remained unaltered by the rise of British power in Asia." But soon thereafter, networks of Han Chinese literati (as opposed to Qing bureaucrats) began to produce a relatively coherent vision of the threat posed by British imperialism, both by sea and by land, and they were able to devise a more or less coordinated strategy for dealing with it. The writings of these Chinese scholars, in Mosca's words, "began to corrode the three major pillars of [Qing] frontier policy"—the uncritical accumulation of local data, the loose link between geographic research and strategic policy proposals, and the tendency to focus on individual cases or "units of responsibility" rather than employing a broader perspective.[85]

Meanwhile, Qing control over Inner Asia, including Manchuria, had begun to crumble, and the area came increasingly under the influence of Han Chinese culture. This process had not originally been intended. Instead, as Joseph Fletcher puts the matter,

> The dynasty's need to make full use of Han Chinese talent, especially in the empire's non-Han territories, and to encourage Han Chinese settlers to people the Inner Asian frontiers, became evident to the Qing government only dimly and belatedly in the nineteenth century, after it was too late in Manchuria and Xinjiang to preserve the full territorial extent of the Qing realm. The Han Chinese expansion occurred in spite of the Qing government's efforts throughout the eighteenth century to prevent [it].[86]

Although in theory the Manchus expected their Inner Asian dependencies to be self-supporting, this proved difficult to achieve in practice.

By the Xianfeng era (1851–1861), the Qing dynasty was on its knees and the end appeared in sight. Foreign imperialism, domestic rebellion, and a series of succession crises over the next few decades combined to create unprecedented political and administrative problems for the imperial Chinese state. Yet as we shall see in chapter 11, the dynasty revitalized itself during the Tongzhi period (1862–1874) under the capable but conservative regency of the Empress Dowager, Cixi (1835–1908). Following the death of the Tongzhi emperor at the age of nineteen, she placed her four-year-old nephew on the throne to reign as the Guangxu emperor (1875–1908). Although often painted as a weak figure under the complete control of his domineering aunt, Guangxu seems to have been capable of bold, independent action, at least on occasion, during the later years of his reign. By this time, however, the dynasty was beyond redemption. When the Guangxu emperor died mysteriously in 1908 without issue, Cixi's infant grandnephew, Puyi, became the Xuantong emperor (1909–1912) under a conservative regent, Prince Qing. Three years later the dynasty fell.

Chapter Three

The Qing Political Order

The Qing empire was a realm of staggering size and complexity. At its height, this empire stretched latitudinally from Hainan Island in the south to the northern tip of Sakhalin Island (above Japan, near the mouth of the Amur River), and longitudinally from the Pacific Ocean to the Aral Sea—more than 12 million square kilometers (c. 4.6 million square miles). About half of this gigantic land mass was mountainous, however, and only about 10 percent of it was regularly under cultivation. Approximately 90 percent of the Chinese people lived on roughly 12 percent of the land. The diversity of this sprawling land mass posed one of the greatest challenges to administrators throughout the Qing period. In the words of Kent Guy:

> Stretching from the deserts of Mongolia to the subtropics, encompassing regions lightly and heavily cultivated, densely and sparsely populated, areas that could be held only with significant military presence and areas that responded best to light and distant government, the Qing empire was hardly a homogeneous land. Neither, of course, were its officials, who were originally men of different regional affiliation, capacity and political inclination. The task of central territorial administration was to incorporate regional difference into a single administrative structure, to manufacture homogeneity—or at least its image— out of diversity.[1]

Guy goes on to explain that the Qing emperors, each in his own way and for his own purposes, managed this impressive feat by dispatching different types of people to different types of posts.

Throughout most of the imperial era, China's population hovered between fifty and one hundred million. At the beginning of the Qing period, it probably stood at a little over 120 million. But during the extraordinary time of domestic peace and prosperity from the late Kangxi reign to the end of the

Figure 3.1. The Qing Empire
Source: XNR Productions

Qianlong emperor's reign, the Chinese population skyrocketed, until by 1850 when it reached an estimated 380 million people and quite possibly more. Ramon Myers and Yeh-Chien Wang briefly explain one of the ways that this may have happened:

Preliminary findings from a historical demographic study of the Liaoning provincial village of Daoyi reveal that, when [Banner] families experienced economic difficulties, they practiced female infanticide. When families began to prosper, as was the case in the eighteenth century, they stopped the practice, meaning that more females survived into adulthood and that more marriages occurred at earlier ages than in times of difficulty, such as the seventeenth century. In Daoyi village, between 1774 and 1804 the population grew at a rate of 1.1 percent a year. Life expectancy for Manchus also improved. In 1687 the Kangxi emperor established a pediatric clinic for the imperial lineage . . . [and] by 1750 most Manchu children were receiving these inoculations, so that some scholars claim that "over one-half the registered population of Beijing were regularly inoculated through state clinics."[2]

Needless to say, such developments were a good thing for many individuals, and not just for Banner men and women. But the exponential increase in people during the eighteenth century created an increasingly unfavorable population-to-land ratio, monumental economic and administrative problems, and severe social strains. The implications of this situation for China's historical development were profound and sustained.

For most of the Qing period, China's rulers did not even attempt to integrate their Inner Asian dependencies with China Proper. In fact, they made a conscious effort to maintain Manchuria as an exclusively Manchu tribal preserve and allowed considerable cultural and administrative leeway to the deliberately isolated colonized areas of Mongolia, Central Asia (Eastern Turkestan/Xinjiang), and Tibet. Although each of these three regions was overseen by Qing officials and supervised by the Court of Colonial Affairs in Beijing, the Qing government granted non-Han elites a large measure of political authority and allowed much of the indigenous governmental apparatus in these areas to remain intact. In Mongolia and Tibet, for example, Beijing supported the Buddhist religious hierarchy common to both regions, granted imperial titles to the hereditary ruling elites, and encouraged the preservation of their original tribal organizations and customs. Xinjiang was by far the most ethnically diverse territory in Inner Asia, and although governed like a huge garrison under the military governor in Yili and other civil and military officials, it too had native rulers and officials who enjoyed considerable cultural and administrative autonomy.[3]

Within China Proper, geography posed a different, but no less complex, set of problems. In addition to the basic north-south divide existing in China

Figure 3.2. China Proper
Source: XNR Productions.

Proper at about the middle of Jiangsu province, we can also identify several other regions, based either on more or less arbitrary provincial boundaries or on natural geographic configurations. One time-honored division of the latter sort has been into the northwest, northern China, southern China, the southeast, and the southwest. By and large, these designations correspond to major economic areas defined primarily by prominent river drainage systems.

A variety of models exist for analyzing China's regional diversity in late imperial times.[4] One of the most influential of these has been G. William

Skinner's notion of nine "macroregions" that, like the traditional Chinese regional divisions I have just mentioned, transcend provincial boundaries. According to Skinner's framework, the "Northeast" macroregion lies in an area that corresponds more or less with southern Manchuria. The north China macroregion embraces the provinces of Hebei and Shandong, while the northwest covers the area south of the great loop in the Yellow River and extends westward. The Lower Yangzi macroregion includes southern Jiangsu, eastern Anhui, and northern Zhejiang. The Middle Yangzi occupies much of Jiangxi, and virtually all of Hunan, Hubei, and Henan. The southeast coast extends from southern Zhejiang to northern Guangdong, while the Lingnan macroregion encompasses most of the rest of Guangdong and Guangxi. As its name suggests, the Yun-Gui macroregion consists of the provinces of Yunnan and Guizhou; and the Upper Yangzi macroregion focuses on Sichuan.[5]

Within these nine macroregions—usually in frontier provinces and in peripheral (as opposed to core) areas—there were dozens of ethnic groups, most of them quite distinct from the Han Chinese, who constituted nearly 95 percent of the total population of the realm. Among these groups, the most statistically (and therefore politically) significant were the Zhuang (in Guangxi and Yunnan), the Hui or Muslims (Gansu and Shaanxi), the Uighurs (Xinjiang), the Yi (Sichuan and Yunnan), and the Miao (also known as Hmong; Guizhou, Yunnan, and Hunan). Some of these groups were supervised by officials appointed by the Court of Colonial Affairs, while others—especially the smaller indigenous minorities of the southwest—fell under the administrative authority of their own hereditary local chieftains (*tusi*).[6]

At times these tribal leaders oversaw standard units of jurisdiction and received regular official titles preceded by the character *tu* (native or local). However, as with Qing policy toward ethnic groups in the dependencies of Inner Asia, the government's concern was more with control and stability than with cultural integration. As a result, the ethnic minorities under local chieftains in China Proper, like their Inner Asian counterparts, enjoyed a considerable degree of autonomy in their language, religious beliefs, customs, and government. Occasionally, however, non-Han peoples did suffer discrimination by both local Chinese and the state; and when they did, social conflict or outright rebellion sometimes ensued. Under these circumstances, Qing officials might more readily advocate "sinicization of the barbarians" through education and other means in order to encourage social stability.[7]

IMPERIAL RULE AND METROPOLITAN OFFICES

In its broad outlines, and in many specific respects, the government of the Manchus was patterned consciously on the Ming model. At the top stood the emperor, the Son of Heaven (*Tianzi*) and supreme executive of the Chinese state. He was the mediator between Heaven and Earth—less than a god, but more than a mere mortal—the arbiter of all human affairs. He served, in the well-chosen words of John Fairbank, as "conqueror and patriarch, theocratic ritualist, ethical exemplar, lawgiver and judge, commander-in-chief and patron of arts and letters, and all the time administrator of the empire."[8] To play all these roles effectively required a ruler of heroic talent and energy, and one of the most remarkable features of the Qing dynasty, as we have seen, is simply that several such individuals managed to materialize in the seventeenth and eighteenth centuries.

The Qing emperors were more than simply the stewards of the Middle Kingdom; they also boasted universalistic aspirations as the rulers of "all under Heaven." This self-image can be traced in part to a longstanding Chinese conceit: the idea of a sage king with all-encompassing moral authority holding sway over an "empire without neighbors." But it received powerful reinforcement in the Qing period from two more militant (and non-Chinese) conceptions of rulership, both of which shaped the identity and actions of China's Manchu monarchs to significant degrees. One was the idea of Inner Asian khanship—sustained historically by "fairly regular" engagements in battle; expressed in metaphors of slave ownership; and dependent on tribal or lineage leaders for corporate support. The other was the Buddhist concept of a cakravartin ("wheel-turning") king—that is, a religious leader who by his worldly activism (including militant expansion) "moves the wheel of time and brings the universe closer to the ages of salvation." These last two mutually reinforcing concepts invested Qing rule with a distinctive Inner Asian flavor.[9]

The Qing emperors, notably Kangxi, Yongzheng, and Qianlong, labored long hours from dawn to dusk. Memorials from high-ranking provincial and metropolitan officials, sometimes over a hundred a day, had to be read and acted upon. Emperors met every morning with officials and advisers to formulate domestic and foreign policies. During the rebellion of Wu Sangui in the 1670s, the Kangxi emperor reportedly handled as many as five hundred items of business a day and could not retire to bed until midnight. Both publicly and privately, the Qing rulers often spoke of the heavy burdens of their office and the enormous responsibilities involved in "giving life to people and killing people."[10]

Huge amounts of time were consumed by ceremonial activities, from mundane life-cycle rituals to solemn sacrifices of truly cosmic significance. The ritual role of the emperor was of special importance to the conduct of state affairs, for it was through his ritual responsibilities that the emperor legitimized his position, promoted confidence among his family members and within the bureaucracy, and inspired awe among the common people. He personally held countless inspections, audiences, and banquets; conferred titles on officials and gods; ratified agreements with foreign dignitaries; received tributary envoys from foreign states; sanctioned the Dalai Lama in Tibet and other religious figures within the realm; conducted state sacrifices to Heaven, Earth, and a host of lesser "deities"; prayed for relief from natural disasters; participated in the worship of his own and other imperial ancestors; oversaw the final stages of the civil and military examinations; and acted as the symbolic head of the imperial clan organization. These and other such ritual activities demanded painstaking and unwavering adherence to longstanding and carefully prescribed ceremonial requirements.[11]

Everything about the imperial institution was designed to foster a sense of awesome power and unapproachable remoteness. Ensconced in the walled, moated, and heavily guarded palace complex known as the Forbidden City, the Qing emperors carried out their daily tasks beyond the sight and sound of commoners. No buildings in the Inner (Manchu) or Outer (Chinese) cities of Beijing proper were permitted to rival those of the Forbidden City in size or splendor, just as no other individual in the entire empire was allowed to wear the special designs that graced the emperor's clothing and other items of personal use. The Forbidden City was itself a symbol of the emperor's unique position at the center of the universe and the apex of the world, at least from a Chinese perspective.[12] Chengde, as we have seen (chapter 2), was another story.

The Qing emperor wrote in red, whereas his officials wrote in black. In audience, he alone faced south, while they faced north. Only the emperor could use the special Chinese term *zhen*, meaning "I," "myself." The characters of his personal name were taboo throughout the land, and any reference to the emperor or the imperial will was always separated from, and elevated above, the rest of the lines of any document in which it appeared. Imperial edicts were received with incense and ritual prostrations, and temples were built for the worship of His Majesty. All subjects performed the traditional kowtow (three kneelings and nine prostrations) in the emperor's presence, but by design relatively few individuals saw him face to face. Contemporary accounts of the emperor's processions outside the Imperial City (that is, through the Inner and Outer cities of Beijing) and his tours of the provinces attest to the careful cultivation of an imperial aura of sacred splendor and dignified isolation. In fact, the term *sheng* (lit. "sacred") was conventionally and rather indiscriminately applied to nearly everything about the emperor, from his appearance and activities to his desires and personal attributes.

In the provinces, however, benign images of sacrality and dignity surrendered to more threatening images of severity and terror. Although the

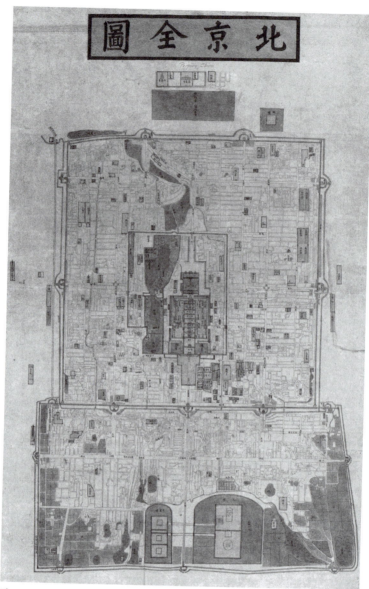

Figure 3.3. Beijing

This Chinese map, created sometime between 1880 and 1887, shows the square-shaped Inner City (for Bannermen and their families) to the north of the rectangular Outer City (for Chinese families). Inside the Inner City is the Imperial City (note the three artificial lakes on the west side), which surrounds the Forbidden City. The Chinese characters identify the major palaces, offices, and temples within the Forbidden City, as well as other important landmarks outside the palace area. For example, just south of the Forbidden City on the east side, we find the Six Boards, the Imperial Clan Court, the Hanlin Academy, the Court of Colonial Affairs, the Imperial Medical College, the Court of State Ceremonial, and the Imperial Board of Astronomy. At the southernmost part of the map we see the Temple of Heaven complex and the Temple of Agriculture complex. The large rectangle above the Inner City is designated "the Eight Banners training ground" (*Baqi jiaochang*). Source: Library of Congress "Map Division."

common expression "Heaven is high and the emperor is far away" (*Tian gao huangdi yuan*) generally referred to the absence of imperial intervention in most areas of Chinese everyday life, the potential for harsh and destructive action on the part of the emperor and his agents remained a persistent theme in local folklore. Legends such as the horrifying "Blood River" stories, which told of imperial retribution against arrogant lineage organizations, and tales concerning benevolent officials who were punished for interceding on behalf of local villagers in matters relating to imperial policy, perpetuated the idea of the emperor as a vengeful ruler, prepared to destroy any groups or individuals (including benevolent officials) foolish enough to challenge his authority.[13]

In theory, imperial power was absolute—as long as the emperor ruled by virtue. The Mandate of Heaven concept (see chapters 1 and 6) encouraged monarchs to be responsible to their subjects by giving the people the right to rebel against oppressive rule and by supporting an "ethics of remonstrance" on the part of Chinese officials. The emperor's sense of accountability to the people can be gauged by the tone of his prayers to Heaven in time of exigency. Consider the following excerpt from a long appeal for relief offered by the Daoguang emperor in the midst of a serious drought:

> Looking up, I consider that Heaven's heart is benevolence and love. The sole cause [of the drought] is the daily deeper atrocity of my sins. . . . Hence I have been unable to move Heaven's mind-heart and bring down abundant blessings. . . . [I ask myself whether] I have become remiss in attending to the affairs of government; . . . whether in the appointment of officers, I have failed to obtain fit persons; . . . whether punishments have been unjustly inflicted; . . . whether the oppressed have found no means of appeal; . . . whether in persecuting heterodox sects the innocent have been involved; . . . . whether in the successive military operations on the western frontiers there may have been the horrors of human slaughter for the sake of imperial rewards. . . . . Prostrate, I beg August Heaven to pardon my ignorance and stupidity, and to grant me self-renovation, for myriads of innocent people are involved [in this drought because of me].[14]

In addition to the emperor's general sense of accountability, his power was limited in practice by his workload and personal abilities, as well as by tradition, precedent, factionalism, and simple bureaucratic inertia (note the "sorcery scare" in chapter 2). Even the most energetic and intelligent of the Qing emperors needed help in running the show. This was true in the provinces, but it was especially true at the capital. Without able and efficient advisers at the top, the best-laid plans of rulers could easily become derailed. Beatrice Bartlett's careful study of imperial policymaking concludes that although China's eighteenth-century monarchs "retained all the powers that we ordinarily think of as imperial powers," they preferred to consult with their highest-ranking ministers and "tended not to exercise their decision-making authority alone." To be certain, the ministers remained dependent on imperial authorization of their objectives, but "ministerial cooperation was also essential to most imperial plans."[15]

Family obligations often exerted a profound influence on Qing government. Few emperors were inclined to alter the policies of their ancestors without careful consideration, and filial piety proved to be a formidable factor in imperial politics. The dedication of imperial sons to their mothers might simply take the form of extravagant and costly displays of indulgence, such as those of the Qianlong emperor, who took his mother on extended tours to south China and built lavish monuments to her.[16] But filial devotion might also allow empresses dowager to wield considerable influence in affairs of state.

The most dramatic illustration of this phenomenon in the Qing period was the rise to power of an imperial concubine titled Yi, from the Yehenala lineage, biological mother of the young boy who became the Tongzhi emperor. When the Xianfeng emperor died in late 1861, consort Yi became the Empress Dowager Cixi, and, with the support of the deceased emperor's brother, she engineered a coup d'état and assumed the reins of government, holding imperial audiences behind a diaphanous yellow silk screen. After the Tongzhi emperor's death, she manipulated the laws of dynastic succession in order to place her infant nephew on the throne and then adopted him as her son. This solidified Cixi's position by forcing the Guangxu emperor to treat her with filial respect and deference. Even after the emperor attained majority, Cixi continued to play an active role in court politics, using the demands of filial piety as a tool in her ongoing struggle with her adopted son.[17]

Although the Qing emperors (and empresses) fully accepted the ritual symbolism and traditional values undergirding the Chinese imperial institution, they never abandoned their ethnic identity as Manchus. Indeed, as the studies of scholars such as Beatrice Bartlett, Pamela Crossley, Mark Elliott, Evelyn Rawski, and others have made abundantly clear, Manchu rulers eagerly sought to preserve their cultural distinctiveness by discouraging the Chinese practice of foot binding among Manchu women, by banning intermarriage between Han civilian males and Manchu females, by isolating Banner families as much as possible from the general population, and by maintaining two capitals beyond the Great Wall (Shengjing and Chengde). They also modified Ming-style official dress to reflect Manchu fashions. In addition, the Qing rulers used Manchu as a specialized court language, promoted certain longstanding religious rituals (especially those associated with Tangse shamanism), encouraged Manchu-style education among members of the imperial clan, and gave Manchus preferential treatment in official appointments, under the law, in the examinations, and in many other areas (see chapter 4).[18]

Figure 3.4. Empress Dowager Cixi
Cixi (1835–1908) was the de facto ruler of China from 1861 to her death. The long string of honorific characters in the banner above her head represents her full official title; "*ci*" (kind) and "*xi*" (joyous) are the first two such words. *Source:* Beinecke Rare Book and Manuscript Library, Yale University.

In large measure, these efforts to remain culturally distinct were motivated precisely by fears that a "completely rationalized, civilized [Chinese] empire that treated all its subjects the same" would result in the eradication of all marks of Manchu identity.[19] This theme surfaces repeatedly in the writings of the early Qing emperors.

The effectiveness and rigor with which these policies of apartheid were pursued varied over time, but they served as a constant reminder to the Manchus of their precarious position as alien conquerors. This awareness, especially under pressure (for example, during the virulently anti-Manchu Taiping Rebellion, 1851–1864) encouraged at least some leaders—including the Empress Dowager Cixi—to ally with the most culturally conservative elements in Chinese society. The reason was that the Manchus had originally justified their rule by proclaiming themselves to be the defenders of Ming traditions and thus the protectors of China's cultural heritage. The alien origins of the Manchus and their cultural conservatism created serious, if not insurmountable, problems for the dynasty in the last decades of Qing rule (see chapter 11).

The day-to-day personal, administrative, and ritual needs of the Qing Inner Court were met by the Imperial Household Department (Chinese: *Neiwu fu*; Manchu: *Dorgi baita be uheri kadalara yamun*)—a kind of private mini-government within the Forbidden City, staffed primarily by imperial bond-servants (Manchu: *booi*; Chinese: *baoyi*). Established, as we have seen, by Hong Taiji, the Department grew substantially during the Kangxi period and attained its "final, definitive form" in the Qianlong era, employing a total of 1,623 officials by 1796. Evelyn Rawski has documented in exquisite detail the "bewildering variety of activities" it undertook, a few of which she summarizes in the following way:

> [The Imperial Household Department] was first and foremost the administrative unit in charge of palace affairs. It was in charge of the wardrobes, food, residences, and daily activities of the emperor and his family. It exercised jurisdiction over palace construction, security, rituals and palace staff. But its activities extended far beyond the walls of the Forbidden City and the imperial villas. . . . It held monopoly rights over the profitable jade and ginseng trades. It ran textile factories . . . and gathered precious objects such as sables, ermine, mink and fox from parts of Mongolia through the annual tribute system.[20]

Among the most important of the Imperial Household Department's numerous subdepartments were the Office of Ceremonial (*Zhangyi si*) and the Office of the Privy Purse (*Guangchu si*). The Office of Ceremonial, as its name suggests, regulated the sacrificial and other ritual observances of the Inner Court (see chapter 7). In addition, it managed the affairs of the imperial harem and controlled the eunuchs, who served within the harem and

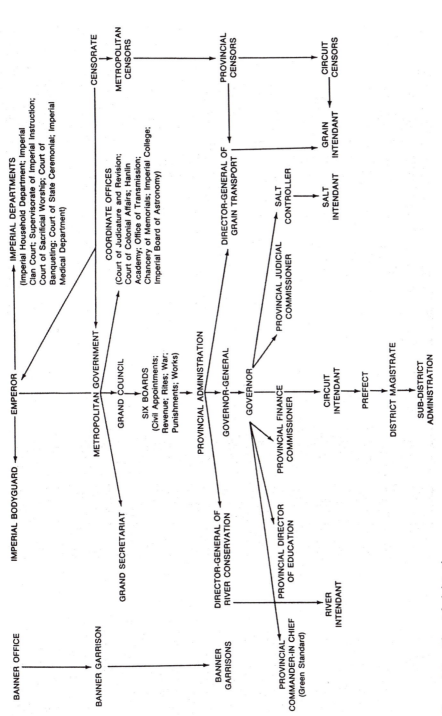

Figure 3.5. Qing Administration
Source: Adapted from Xiao Yishan 1962 and I. Hsu 2000.

elsewhere in the Forbidden City. Unlike the Ming emperors, who employed tens of thousands of eunuchs in various administrative capacities and who often surrendered substantial power to them, the Qing emperors retained between 1,500 and 3,000 eunuchs and kept them under close supervision. As the Kangxi emperor once remarked: "Eunuchs are basically *yin* in nature. They are quite different from ordinary people. . . . In my court I never let them get involved with government—even the few eunuchs-of-the-presence with whom I might chatter or exchange family jokes . . . [are] never allowed to discuss politics."[21] Still, by virtue of their closeness to the emperor and to imperial concubines, eunuchs in the Qing period, such as the notorious Li Lianying (d. 1911), might exert considerable political influence.[22]

The Office of the Privy Purse handled the Imperial Household Department's financial affairs. It derived revenue directly from the management of imperial estates in Manchuria and around Beijing, from the ginseng trade and other commercial operations, from the collection of customs revenue and foreign tribute, from loans to merchants, and from the expropriation of private property. These resources not only sustained the emperor, his family, and his entourage in proper imperial fashion, but also provided occasional funds for charitable purposes, such as disaster relief, and for rewards to meritorious officials. In addition, the Office of the Privy Purse supplied money for military campaigns and for public works projects. Its primary purpose, however, remained the maintenance of the imperial establishment and all its opulence.

Several other formal and informal Inner Court agencies attended to the emperor's personal, familial, and administrative needs. These included the Imperial Clan Court (*Zongren fu*), the Department of the Imperial Bodyguard (*Shiwei chu*), and the Banner Office (*Zhinian qi*). As a general rule, administrative responsibility for the affairs of the Manchu ruling house and the multi-ethnic Banner military organization lay outside of the regular bureaucratic apparatus, creating an extra echelon of imperial government.[23]

During the Qianlong reign and thereafter, the Grand Council (*Junji chu*) emerged as the most important advisory agency within the Inner Court. It was established in the late 1720s as an auxiliary office to assist the Yongzheng emperor in conducting military operations. The prestigious grand councilors, ranging anywhere from four to twelve officials but usually averaging about a half dozen, met at least once a day with the emperor to discuss all aspects of imperial administration. As the emperor's most trusted bureaucratic assistants, the grand councilors read secret palace memorials, recommended policies, drafted edicts, and carried out the imperial will by issuing orders to other governmental agencies within the regular bureaucracy.[24]

The Outer Court consisted of various bureaucratic agencies inherited from the Ming dynasty. Of these, the Grand Secretariat (*Neige*) occupied a position of paramount importance until the Grand Council eclipsed it as a formal advisory body after 1730. Although located far from the emperor in a distant southeastern corner of the palace complex, the grand secretaries of the pre-Qianlong era were high-ranking dignitaries who straddled the Outer and Inner Courts. From the Qianlong reign onward, however, they had power only by virtue of their concurrent appointments. The Grand Secretariat's functions then became highly routinized and relatively unimportant from the standpoint of imperial policymaking—even after the Jiaqing emperor attempted to limit the power and scope of the Grand Council in the aftermath of the Heshen affair (see chapter 2).

Below the Grand Secretariat stood the Six Boards: (1) Civil Appointments, (2) Revenue, (3) Rites, (4) War, (5) Punishments, and (6) Works, all based on the Ming model. These overlapping organs were responsible for the routine administration of the empire at the central governmental level, and each organization had its equivalent at lower bureaucratic echelons all the way down to the county (*xian*). Even the Qing law code was divided into these six categories. The heads of the Six Boards had no authority to issue direct orders, however, and the lines of communication between them were often hopelessly crossed.[25]

The Board of Civil Appointments stood first among the Six Boards. It was responsible for most matters relating to the appointment, evaluation, promotion, demotion, transfer, and dismissal of officials in the twenty-thousand-man metropolitan and provincial civil bureaucracy. Although Qing personnel administration was highly complex and not always bureaucratically "rational," on the whole the Board of Civil Appointments proved remarkably successful in establishing uniform standards for the appointment, evaluation, and discipline of both metropolitan and provincial officials. Particularly noteworthy as a control mechanism was the sophisticated Qing system of administrative sanctions embodied in the dynasty's *Chufen zeli* (Regulations on administrative punishment).[26]

The Board of Revenue, second in rank, held responsibility for empire-wide population and land registration; regulation of coinage; collection of duties, taxes, and grain tribute from the provinces; payment of salaries and stipends to officials and nobles; support of the military establishment; audits of central government and provincial treasuries and granaries; supervision of commerce, industry, state monopolies, and communications; and management of certain special administrative tasks relating to personnel and judicial affairs. Despite its wide-ranging bureaucratic scope and access to detailed economic information, the Board of Revenue—like the Qing government as a whole—confined its activities primarily to developing state revenue, promoting stabil-

Table 3.1. Approximate Central Government Revenues and Expenditures c. 1780

Revenues (Partial List)

Revenue	Millions of Ounces of Silver (Taels)
Land-poll (*diding*) tax	30.00
Wastage allowance (*huohao*)	4.60
Surtax on tribute grain*	2.00
Salt taxes	7.50
Customs	4.00
Land rents	0.26
Tea tax	0.07
Total	48.43

* Beijing received about four million *shi* (piculs; c. 133 pounds) of tribute grain from the south.

Central Government Expenditures (Partial List)

Expenditure	Millions of Ounces of Silver (Taels)
Salaries for princes, nobles, and officials	0.93
Military expenses (Banners and Green Standard)	6.00
Military expenses in Mukden and Rehe	1.40
Stipends for Mongolian and Muslim nobles	0.12
Office costs and food for metropolitan officials	0.11
Food allowances for Grand Secretariat, etc.	0.018
"Nourishing integrity" (*yanglian*) allowances for the Boards of Civil Appointments and Rites	0.015
Gifts to Mongolian and Korean tribute bearers	0.010
Miscellaneous	0.900
Total	9.503

Local Government Expenditures (Partial List)

Expenditure	Millions of Ounces of Silver (Taels)
Military expenses	15.00
Salaries of officials	1.00
"Nourishing integrity" (*yanglian*) allowances	4.22
Expense allowances	0.20
Upkeep of rivers and ponds	4.00
Miscellaneous	1.40
Total	25.82

Source: Adapted from Immanuel Hsü 2000, 61–63. For complete charts, covering many more categories, see Xiao Yishan 1962, 432–40. The above breakdown, and Xiao's as well, obviously includes sources of revenue and expenses that differed significantly over time. Prior to the nineteenth century, for example, the central government received a far smaller share of its revenue from foreign customs and none at all from the *lijin* transit tax. On the other hand, the central government did not have to pay for railways, customs services (such as lighthouses), foreign legations, or foreign loans.

ity, and maintaining political power and control. As E-tu Zen Sun has shown, the Board's limited ability to regulate and direct the private sectors of the Chinese economy determined its cooperative and conciliatory approach to the enterprises in which the state had a strategic stake.[27]

The Board of Rites, although ranked only third among the Six Boards, had extremely weighty responsibilities. Of its four major departments, the Department of Ceremonies (*Yizhi si*) handled regular court ritual, the examination system, regulations regarding official dress and other marks of status, forms of etiquette between various ranks, and forms of written communication. The Department of Sacrifices (*Ciji si*) oversaw state sacrifices, funerals, the dispensing of posthumous rewards, and the editing of the Imperial Calendar (*Shixian li* or *Shixian shu*) in conjunction with the Imperial Bureau of Astronomy (*Qin Tian jian*). The Reception Department (*Zhuke si*) managed the highly ritualized tributary system of China's foreign relations, as well as the giving of gifts to officials and other miscellaneous activities. The Banqueting Department (*Jingshan si*), as its name implies, was responsible for the preparation of food for banquets and sacrifices. Breaches of etiquette in any of these realms were usually punished severely.

Closely associated with the Board of Rites, and at times during the Qing period directly attached to it, were three "courts": the Court of Sacrificial Worship (*Taichang si*), in charge of all state sacrifices performed directly by the emperor or his appointed deputies; the Court of Banqueting (*Guanglu si*), responsible for providing food and drink for special ritual occasions, including tributary feasts; and the Court of State Ceremonial (*Honglu si*), charged with the task of instructing guests in proper observances at banquets. A Board of Music (*Yuebu*) also fell under the general direction of the Board of Rites, indicating the central importance of music to nearly all forms of Chinese ritual activity.[28]

The Board of War supervised various military rituals, but its major responsibilities were the instruction and maintenance of the Chinese constabulary known as the Army of the Green Standard (*Lüying*). It handled the majority of regular military appointments, dismissals and transfers, undertook the registration and periodic review of imperial troops, administered the military examinations, dispensed rewards and punishments, played a role in the making of military policy, and managed the dynasty's relay system of official communications. Although most matters relating directly to Banner administration were beyond its purview, the Board of War remained responsible for the allocation of about two-thirds of the central government's total expenditures and for the coordination of Green Standard and Banner forces in times of trouble.[29]

The Board of Punishments provided a symbolic counterpoint to the Board of Rites since law in traditional China was supposed to be invoked only after ritual had failed. The penal emphasis of Chinese law was reflected not only in the title of the Board of Punishments, but also in the contents of the *Da Qing lüli* (Legal code of the great Qing dynasty; hereafter Qing Code), which was incorporated into the massive *Da Qing huidian* (Collected statutes of the great Qing dynasty) and its supplements. The Qing Code was based largely on its Ming predecessor, with, as its early architects explained, "adjustments in accordance with the times"—that is, the elimination of certain "unsuitable" statutes (*lü*) and substatutes (*li*) and the inclusion of a few specifically Manchu regulations (for example, especially harsh punishments for those who harbored runaway bondservants and domestic slaves). The rationale for the adoption of the Ming Code offered by the Shunzhi emperor in a preface to the 1647 edition is quite fascinating. Because his administrative responsibilities now extended well beyond his homeland, the emperor argued that the old Manchu legal code was no longer suitable. His own people, he maintained, were fundamentally "honest" and therefore not in need of a complex code. But the Chinese were numerous and "full of guile," necessitating a more elaborate legal document.[30]

The Qing Code, as its preeminent translator William Jones points out, was predicated on the longstanding Chinese jurisprudential idea that the wise ruler "governs his officials, he does not govern the people."[31] In other words, the Code in its various incarnations was more concerned with the political and social interests of the state than with the interests of the emperor's individual subjects. This explains why the most severe penalty in the Code—"death by slicing" (*lingchi*)—was reserved for the so-called Ten Great Wrongs (*Shi'e*), crimes that threatened the social and/or political order (see chapter 10).[32] Jones suggests that one way to think about this approach to law is to imagine the Code as a directive to civil officials, telling them what punishments to impose in any circumstance viewed by the state as legally significant. Thus, Qing bureaucrats, particularly magistrates (see below), administered the Code and other legal documents in the same basic way that they undertook every other activity of government; they had no specialized training, but they were presumed to be upright Confucians, capable of making correct judgments, and mindful of the interests of the state.[33]

By the middle of the Qianlong reign the Manchus had accepted, at least in theory, the basic principles of Chinese law. From that time onward, court cases were adjudicated according to the principles of the Qing Code, although in practice Bannermen still enjoyed substantial privileges. Disputes between Manchus and Chinese, however, were generally resolved by local middle-ranking officials known as "civil commissioners" (Chinese: *lishi tongzhi* or *lishi tongpan*; Manchu: *tungjy, tungpan, weile beidere tungjy/tungpan* or *baita beidere tungjy/tungpan*), who eventually came to be posted in frontier areas as well as in China Proper. When the position was first created in the 1680s,

Han Chinese usually occupied it, but a decade or so later it became an exclusively Manchu position. Although civil commissioners were supposed to be impartial, it seems clear that more often than not they ended up defending the interests of Bannermen against the "encroachments" of Han Chinese.[34]

The Board of Punishments often undertook its more weighty responsibilities in consultation with representatives from the Court of Revision (*Dali si*) and the Censorate (*Ducha yuan*). Together, these three offices were known as the Three Courts of High Adjudicature (*Sanfa si*). Routine legal matters flowed through one of the eighteen major departments of the Board of Punishments. These, like the departments in the Board of Revenue, were organized along geographical lines but had responsibilities and jurisdictions that extended beyond provincial boundaries. Various other offices within the Board of Punishments dealt with matters such as judicial review, revision of the legal code, and management of prisons.[35] Although the Chinese legal system had no "due process" in the Western sense, no trial by jury, and no representation by counsel (aside from the employment of socially disesteemed and at times outlawed "litigation masters," discussed in chapter 4), it did at least provide convicted persons with recourse to appeal.

Indeed, the Qing period witnessed the fullest elaboration of the Chinese appellate system up to that time—including all-important capital appeals. Like so many other aspects of Qing administration, the system of appeals suffered from the pressures imposed by China's eighteenth-century population explosion; yet compared with other contemporary systems of justice, such as those of eighteenth- and nineteenth-century England and America, the Qing capital appeals system was, in Jonathan Ocko's words, "an admirable institution." And even in the late nineteenth century, a time of precipitous dynastic decline, the Chinese criminal justice system "encompassed a broad range of sophisticated procedural and administrative measures designed to convict the guilty and acquit the innocent."[36]

The Board of Works was the lowliest of the Six Boards, yet its functions were vital. In general, the Board of Works maintained all public shrines and temples, imperial tombs, official buildings, military and naval installations, city walls, granaries, treasuries, public timberlands, official communication routes, and government-sponsored dykes, dams, and irrigation systems. In addition it provided military stores and other essential supplies (including copper coins) to appropriate governmental agencies. During most of the eighteenth century, the Board of Works operated quite efficiently. A number of studies conclude, for example, that the Qing state played a significant role in feeding the Chinese population and that the power of the government to affect the movements of the population, to distribute resources among regions, to regulate the use of land and water, and to control the circulation of grain "was a critical factor in the presence or absence of food crises and famines." By the nineteenth century, however, the cumulative effects of population pressure "rendered ineffective the power of the state to perform the same functions of regulation, or at least intervention, that it had apparently done so well in the previous era."[37]

The Six Boards, like all other regular bureaucratic organs (with the noteworthy exception of the Grand Council), fell under the close and continual scrutiny of the Censorate. This longstanding Chinese institution served as the "eyes and the ears" of the emperor, providing him with secret information on the activities of civil and military officials at all levels. Although theoretically bound to guide and admonish even the emperor himself, in practice many censors became little more than imperial agents, tools of the autocracy. The dynastic record abounds with examples of noble and upright censors who sacrificed their careers and lives for their principles, but it also indicates that many censors became corrupted by power and ambition and embroiled in destructive factional politics. Moreover, the research of Adam Lui and others suggests that the Qing censorial system was not as active and independent outside the capital as in earlier periods of Chinese history.[38]

One last metropolitan institution merits brief discussion: the Court of Colonial Affairs (Chinese: *Lifan yuan*; Manchu: *Tulergi golo be dasara jurgan*), mentioned briefly in chapter 2. Designed initially (in 1636) to oversee Qing relations with the Mongols, its responsibilities grew along with the expansion of the Chinese empire to embrace the areas of Tibet, Mongolia, and Xinjiang. In addition, the Court of Colonial Affairs handled China's "special relationship" with Russia, which had the status of neither a colonial dependency nor a tributary state. Unlike most other metropolitan institutions, the officials of the Court of Colonial Affairs were always Manchu or Mongol Bannermen; to my knowledge no Chinese ever served in a high-level capacity in this organization. After 1860, under considerable duress, the Qing government established an office of foreign affairs known as the Zongli Yamen for the regular conduct of China's relations with Western nations, including Russia. But this body was basically an ad hoc graft on the existing administrative structure; it had no regular institutional status and was viewed by the Qing government as merely a subcommittee of the Grand Council—albeit an increasingly important one.[39]

ADMINISTRATIVE INTEGRATION

The relationship between the governmental organs at the capital and in the provinces was extremely complex and maintained by an unceasing flow of documents to and from the throne. Information from provincial officials arrived at Beijing via the imperial postal service in the form of rigidly formalized memorials and petitions. Routine memorials were received by the metropolitan Office of Transmission (*Tongzheng si*), which opened, checked, copied, and forwarded them to the agencies concerned and to the Grand Secretariat. The Grand Secretariat, in turn, drafted replies to these memorials for imperial approval. Special palace memorials, first used during the Kangxi reign, were transmitted directly to the emperor through the Chancery of Memorials (*Zoushi chu*) and were supposed to be initially for his eyes alone. Although the palace memorial system greatly increased the emperor's personal workload, it also provided him with information that could be used as a check on the regular bureaucracy, or as a means of circumventing it altogether.[40]

The emperor also received valuable data from his frequent "business" audiences (*bijian*) with metropolitan and provincial officials. These highly structured, face-to-face encounters not only resulted in the mutual exchange of information, but also enhanced the aura of the throne and reinforced bonds of loyalty. In any given interview the subject matter might range broadly. Typically the emperor began by asking about an official's family background and education. Often his questions revolved around examination experiences and scholastic issues. He might even ask officials to recite specific texts from memory—an exercise that usually revealed the prodigious mental powers of both parties. Although some conversations contained idle chit-chat, most focused squarely on administrative issues such as taxation, crops, local control, and especially the quality of other officials.

The following short excerpt from one of Governor Chen Bin's four audiences with the Kangxi emperor in late December 1715 and early January 1716 reveals something of the tone of *bijian* encounters:

[Emperor]: Do you have anything to say to me?

[Chen]: On account of Your Majesty's immense grace, I, incompetent as I was, received the appointment as governor of Hunan. Since the province is vast and the responsibility is heavy, I am afraid I have failed in my duty and the people have suffered because of me.

[Emperor]: How do you compare Hunan with Fujian?

[Chen]: The people of Hunan rely entirely on their farmland for living . . . [and their situation] is very difficult. Fujian province is very mountainous and its land is not sufficient for growing rice. People rely on fishing for their living. Neither province is easily governed . . .

[Emperor]: Who is the financial commissioner of Hunan?

[Chen]: Alin [a Manchu].

[Emperor]: How is his performance as an official?

[Chen]: He is very competent.

[Emperor]: He is competent, all right, but I am not sure about his heart [integrity].

Four days later, after receiving his new appointment as governor of Fujian, Chen Bin had his last audience with the emperor. Again, Kangxi asked him about provincial administration:

[Emperor]: Do you know any good official who doesn't take money?

[Chen]: Well, speaking of talent and ability, many officials possess such qualities. But offhand I don't dare mention anyone who doesn't take money. I will report to you in a palace memorial as soon as I discover any.

[Emperor]: All right, [I expect] you [to] report . . . on good ones as well as bad ones.[41]

The emperor added that he would not rely solely on Chen's opinions, but would make further inquiries in order "to find out the truth."

The large-scale ceremonial audiences known as *dachao* and *changchao*, which took place at the Hall of Supreme Harmony (*Taihe dian*) of the Forbidden City, lacked the intimacy of business audiences held in the Inner Court, but they performed another vital function—that of symbolically confirming a world view based on "notions of order, coherence, hierarchy, and the focal sacrality of the Chinese emperor." In a very real sense, these grand and elaborate rituals, like those of imperial worship (see chapter 7) contributed to what Angela Zito describes as "the symbolic construction of the King."[42]

Aside from the very general proclamations issued at large-scale audiences to announce joyous events, the imperial will was conveyed to the bureaucracy chiefly by means of edicts, court letters, oral instructions, rescripts, vermillion comments written by the emperor on memorials, and various general circulars. In analogous fashion, provincial officials sent down orders to their subordinates, commented on petitions and reports, and circulated rules and regulations. At the local level, imperial "yellow posters" and other public announcements informed gentry (*shenshi*) and literate commoners of official policy. Government business at all levels had to be validated by official seals, which varied according to the department that handled their manufacture, the material used to make them, their design and style of script, their size, designated name, and of course the office to which they were assigned. Some editions of the *Collected Statutes* list twenty-five different official seals for the emperor alone.

The so-called Beijing gazettes (*Jingbao*) and their provincial counterparts provided a valuable source of information on public policy. Although issued by various publishers under different names, the Beijing gazettes were alike in that they were supervised by the Communications Department of the Board of War and contained official documents released by the Grand Secretariat or the Grand Council. In the words of a well-informed foreign observer in nineteenth-century China, the Beijing gazettes were "very generally read and talked about by the gentry and educated people in the cities." In the provinces, thousands of individuals found employment copying and abridging the gazettes for readers who could not afford to purchase complete editions. Circulated both officially and privately, the Beijing gazettes provided a valuable means of horizontal communication in an empire in which vertical communications were generally emphasized.[43]

The most exalted figure in the regular provincial administrative hierarchy was the governor-general (*zongdu*, sometimes translated viceroy). This post was a Qing invention and it was usually occupied by a Bannerman. His jurisdiction encompassed at least one, usually two, and sometimes three provinces. Within this wide sphere he supervised and evaluated the work of civil and military officials, reported on provincial finances, and reviewed judicial cases. Below the governor-general stood the governor (*xunfu*), charged with the civil and military affairs of a single province. His responsibilities were similar to those of the governor-general, but he also held specific responsibility for overseeing the collection of customs duties, managing the salt administration, superintending the local examination system, and administering the grain tribute system. Kent Guy has insightfully remarked that much of the administrative effectiveness for which the Qing is known can be attributed to its innovative system of provincial governance. The ability to "secure borders, collect and transfer revenues, supervise local governments, manage grain stocks to provide relief in times of dearth, repair roads, dikes, and irrigation works, and to maintain local elite," he writes, was primarily the achievement of provincial governors.[44]

The provincial finance commissioner (*buzheng shi*, sometimes translated treasurer), served as a lieutenant governor, with primary responsibility for fiscal administration, the provincial census (taken every ten years), the promulgation of imperial commands, and a wide range of other administrative and judicial tasks. Most routine judicial responsibilities fell to the provincial judicial commissioner (*ancha shi*), who also helped manage the provincial postal system, evaluated officials, and assisted in supervising the local civil service examinations. The educational affairs of a province were generally supervised by a specially appointed officer from Beijing known as the director of education (*xuezheng*). His job was to travel around the province on a regular schedule, testing candidates and determining who would enter government academies for further schooling and who would go on to the provincial-level exams.[45]

The lower echelons of provincial administration were divided into a complex hierarchy of geographically based circuits (*dao*), prefectures (*fu*), independent departments (*zhili zhou*) or subprefectures (*zhili ting*), and counties (*xian*). Each circuit, consisting of two or three prefectures, covered from one-fifth to one-quarter the area of a province. The "intendant" (*daotai*) of each had administrative duties that were similar to those of the governor-general and governor. Some provincial capitals also had one or more intendants who performed specially designated functions in realms such as communications, waterworks, military affairs, customs collection, grain tribute, the salt monopoly, and so forth. After 1842, circuit intendants in newly established treaty port areas (see chapter 11) came to assume extremely important roles in diplomacy, intelligence gathering, military reform, and economic modernization.[46]

At the bottom of the Qing bureaucratic ladder stood the county magistrate (*zhixian*), who had direct responsibility for from 100,000 to well over 250,000 people. Horribly overburdened, the magistrate functioned as a kind of mini-emperor, playing the role of a "father-mother official" (*fumu guan*) to his constituents, undertaking religious and other ritual responsibilities, dispensing justice, maintaining order, sponsoring public works, patronizing local scholarship, and all the while collecting taxes for the state. In contrast to higher-level functionaries who "ruled other officials," magistrates "ruled the people." Reference works such as the *Fuhui quanshu* (Complete book on happiness and benevolence) by Huang Liuhong (b. 1633)—for which we have a useful English translation—show us how magistrates learned to do their arduous and multifaceted work.[47]

Magistrates, like virtually all other Qing officials, had no formal training in the law, despite their weighty responsibilities as judges. Handbooks such as the *Fuhui quanshu* and Wang Huizu's (1731–1807) *Zuozi yaoyan* (Prescriptions for assisting good government) provided a number of basic guidelines, but very little specific advice. A summary of the legal principles contained in these and other such works would consist of the following general points: (1) cultivate a mind that is fair and make the pursuit of justice a personal goal; (2) live a clean and meaningful life and preserve your personal integrity; (3) be strict but reasonable with subordinates; (4) be dedicated in your work and care for the people; (5) be thorough and compassionate; and (6) seek facts and don't rush to judgment.[48] Magistrates were naturally urged to read the Qing Code as well as various collections of official regulations, but they generally had to do this on their own time.

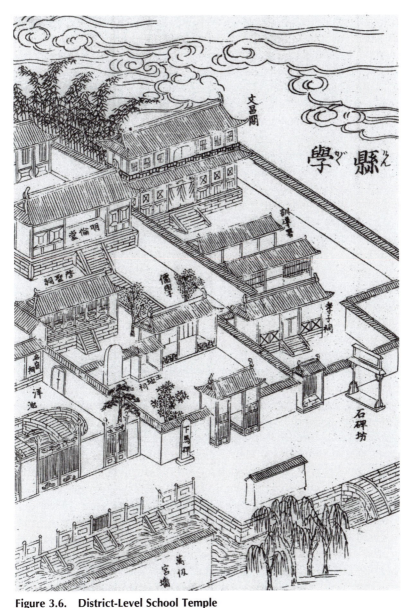

Figure 3.6.   District-Level School Temple
This image, drawn by a late eighteenth-century Japanese visitor to southeastern China, shows part of a Confucian temple complex, which includes not only instructional facilities, but also various religious shrines (for example, one honoring "Filial Sons" and another dedicated to the local "Lord of the Earth"). At the top of this partial view is a pavilion dedicated to the God of Literature (*Wenchang*). To the left of the pavilion is a Hall for Illuminating Human Relations (*Minglun tang*), a standard feature of all Confucian temples. *Source:* Nakagawa 1799.

The yamen (office) of the magistrate, which was always located within a walled city, served as both his residence and workplace. Within this large compound, hundreds of regular administrative personnel and other functionaries might operate: the assistant magistrate, county registrar, educational officials, jail wardens, clerks, and runners, as well as private secretaries, personal servants, and family retainers. None of these people, however, came close to matching the magistrate in prestige or power. Private secretaries (*muyou*) usually enjoyed high status because most were degree holders like the magistrate, but the majority of them did not hold formal bureaucratic positions and had to be content to act in an advisory capacity. Some *muyou* served as specialized "legal advisers" (*xingming* or *qiangu muyou*), having gained a certain amount of legal knowledge from other specialists. According to a recent article by Li Chen, a "substantial number of Qing legal advisors possessed the *shengyuan* status, and some boasted even a *juren* or *jinshi* degree."[49]

Clerks were usually commoners who had little hope of obtaining degrees or official rank; they handled routine documentation in each of the county yamen's six major departments corresponding to the Six Boards at the capital. Yamen runners were the lowest functionaries, socially disesteemed and at times officially classified as *jianmin* ("demeaned" people; see chapter 4). They served as court attendants, prison guards, policemen, and tax collectors. Although lacking in formal authority, they often enjoyed considerable local power; and because they relied on informal fees for their livelihood, they often found themselves in a position to gouge the local populace.[50]

Despite the hazards of extortion and what has been described as an "anti-litigation ideology" on the part of the Qing rulers, commoners and even some low-ranking elites proved willing to file suits at the county level. Some may have acquired a rudimentary knowledge of the law from popular encyclopedias such as the WBQS (see appendix E). As Guangyuan Zhou's research illustrates, among those who might decide to take their chances in court were "poor tenants, diffident and underprivileged daughters-in-law, powerless old widows, ascetic monks, and sanctimonious gentrymen." Their cases ranged from domestic disputes and gambling debts to broken contracts and accusations of sexual assault. According to Zhou, the litigants could be surprisingly unrestrained:

> [They] used devastating and destructive language to castigate their relatives and neighbors without much qualm; they combined powerful arguments with pathetic appeals as the norm of petitioning; they developed a series of strategies and tactics that made litigation an expensive, acrimonious, and messy game; they frequently resorted to collective actions and appellate appeals in legal battles; and they could pursue a lawsuit for years, decades, and even several generations without interruption or resignation. In short, litigants showed little

Figure 3.7.   Magistrate Hearing a Case
Here we see the district magistrate, flanked by his administrative assistants, dispensing justice to two individuals kneeling before him. *Source:* Nakagawa 1799.

court-shyness, but rather, toughness, audacity, tenacity, and [a] fierceness that could drive even the most staid judge to the brink of insanity.[51]

How and why did this happen? Part of the answer lies in the proliferation of "litigation masters" (*songgun* or *songshi*) from the late Ming onward, especially in the eighteenth and nineteenth centuries. Although these literate legal specialists had no formal institutional status and were utterly devoid of social prestige, they performed a useful function as advocates for their often poor and/or illiterate clients. Some operated as writers of routine legal documents while others took on more aggressive legal roles. Many were itinerants whose mobility made them difficult for the imperial authorities to control. Their fees were usually low, at least for their poorer clients, and they often performed other functions (like fortune telling) to bring in additional income. This explains why recourse to formal litigation in Qing times could be at once "economically and socially necessary and culturally abhorred."[52]

Subcounty administration in China rested with a variety of institutions that had no formal legal status. Each basic rural division (*xiang*), market town (*zhen*), and village (*cun*), for instance, had its own locally "elected" headman or headmen. In order to exert more effective bureaucratic control over these units, however, and to cut across clan lines and other natural divisions in Chinese society, the Qing government also attempted to impose its own artificial administrative order on subcounty urban and rural areas. These efforts included the tax collection and registration system known as *lichia* and the similar local security system called *baojia*—both based on decimal groupings of mutually responsible families. The heads of these organizations, usually commoners with some degree of local influence, reported to the magistrate periodically and could be punished by him for inattention to duty.

During the Qing period, the effectiveness of such tax collection and local control systems varied widely from place to place and from time to time. As a rule, however, from the eighteenth century onward, county magistrates increasingly assigned local commoners known as constables (*dibao* or *difang*) to urban wards and rural subdivisions within the formalized *lijia* and *baojia* networks to assist or supplant the local heads of these organizations. These unsalaried agents of the magistrate often combined the roles not only of *lijia* and *baojia* headmen, but also of yamen runners. They reported crimes, property disputes, fires, magical practices, and other suspicious activities; provided witnesses for inquests; assisted in public works projects; helped collect taxes; and played a role in the official registration of individual households. Like yamen runners, local constables made their living by levying informal fees and sometimes by outright extortion.[53] During and after the Taiping Rebellion (1851–1864), gentry-led militia organizations known as *tuanlian* (lit. "grouping and drilling") began functioning as quasi-official subcounty administrative organs, assuming not only *baojia* and *lijia* functions, but also judicial functions. This development only enhanced the already considerable power of the rural-based gentry class.[54]

For all the state's effort to dominate Chinese society from the county capital and above, successful administration—especially in the countryside—depended on an informal alliance between officialdom and the rural-based gentry (see also chapter 4). Because a county magistrate's bureaucratic reach could not possibly extend directly to the hundreds of villages under his immediate jurisdiction, even with the assistance of agents such as constables and runners, he had to rely on the prestige and authority of the local elite to maintain order and stability. A symbiotic relationship thus developed. Gentry members in rural areas helped assure public security and acted as buffers between the peasantry and officialdom, while urban-based bureaucrats helped to further gentry interests through direct patronage, favorable treatment in taxation and other matters, and by providing official access to higher provincial authority. Just as a balance existed within the county yamen between the state interests represented by the centrally appointed magistrate and his personal secretaries on the one hand, and the local interests represented by clerks, runners, and constables on the other, so a balance existed between the county magistrate and the local gentry class.

The cultural common denominator of both officials and the gentry, and the primary source of their social prestige, was preparation for, and success in, the civil service examinations. By Qing times the examination system had become, in Benjamin Elman's words, "a dominant force" in determining the character of traditional Chinese society.[55] To be sure, lower degrees and even substantive offices could be purchased, especially in periods of administrative decline. A recent survey of central government personnel files for approximately 1,600 Qing officials reveals, for instance, that in the nineteenth century upward of 50 percent of the sample used the purchase of office to enter the bureaucracy without direct certification through the examination system. Similarly, Elman has shown a dramatic increase in the purchase of offices during the Qing period. In 1764, for example, 22.4 percent of 2,071 local officials purchased their positions; in 1871, of a total of 1,790 local officials, 51.2 percent had purchased their positions.[56] Nonetheless, on the whole the Qing examination system provided the major means of social and bureaucratic mobility, and the primary avenue to wealth and power in China until the latter part of the nineteenth century. Women were not eligible for the exams, however, nor were Buddhist and Daoist clergy and certain other social groups (see chapter 4).

For most eligible Chinese of sufficient means, the Qing educational system was directed entirely toward success in the examinations. Family tutors, private schools (*sishu*), local academies (*shuyuan*), and Confucian school temples (*xuegong*) all sought to achieve this goal (see chapters 4 and 10). For Bannermen, the educational situation was more complex because the throne insisted on the preservation of their Manchu heritage, including riding and archery, in addition to training in the Confucian classics, the twenty-one official dynastic histories, and so forth (these subjects could be studied in either Manchu or Chinese). Over time, the Qing government established a number of special schools at the capital for Banner elites, including National Academies (*Guoxue*), Imperial Clan Academies (*Zongxue*), academies for members of the Aisin Gioro clan, and academies for members of the Imperial Household Department. There were also Banner Officer Schools (*Baqi guanxue*). Banner students in the provinces generally enrolled in private academies if they had the resources and charitable schools if they did not. A special examination for translators (*fanyi*) could be taken by Manchu, Mongol, and Chinese Bannermen who were not prepared well enough to take the regular exams. Their lack of adequate preparation, as Pamela Crossley points out, stemmed from the failure of the Qing state to devise a universal and effective means of providing elementary education for Bannermen.[57]

The regular Chinese civil examination system imposed rigid requirements on candidates for degrees. Success demanded diligent application on the part of males from the age of five on. Beginning with primers such as the *Sanzi jing* (Three character classic) and the *Qianzi wen* (Essay of a thousand characters), students went on to memorize the so-called Four Books and Five Classics—a total of some 430,000 characters. By the age of twelve or so a precocious child might accomplish this feat. Training in calligraphy, poetic composition, and the difficult "eight-legged essay" style followed. The several hundred word essay format, requiring strict adherence to the use of balanced clauses (*duiju*) and balanced pairs of characters (*shudui*; see chapter 5), consisted of: (1) a "breaking open" of the topic, (2) receipt of the topic, (3) a beginning discussion, (4) an initial "leg," (5) a transitional "leg," (6) a middle "leg," (7) a later "leg," and (8) a conclusion.[58] In addition to mastering these stylistic requirements, aspirants for degrees had to familiarize themselves with a huge body of classical commentaries, histories, and other essential literary works. Enterprising private publishers produced collections of examination essays designed as a shortcut to study, but few candidates could afford to place sole reliance on such aids for their future well-being.

The Chinese examination process consisted of an elaborate battery of tests at various levels. Success in the initial series of tests at the county level, held twice every three years, brought the *shengyuan* (government student) degree and eligibility for the triennial examinations at the provincial level. Successful candidates at this level received the *juren* ("recommended person")

Table 3.2. General Levels of Examination

Preliminary Examinations
  County-level (*xiankao*)
  Department-level (*zhoukao*)
  Prefectural-level (*fukao*)
County or Prefectural
  Examination for *shengyuan/xiucai* degree (*suishi* or *suikao*); county quotas
Provincial Examinations
  Examination for *juren* degree (*xiangshi* or *xiangkao*) after a preliminary qualifying
  test known as *keshi* or *kekao*; county quotas
Metropolitan Examinations
  Major examination known as *huishi* for *jinshi* degree; provincial quotas
Palace examination (*dianshi*)
  Optimus (*Zhuangyuan*)
  Further examination for specific official appointment (*zhaokao*)

Source: Based on Elman 2000, 659 (simplified).

degree and a chance at the coveted metropolitan *jinshi* ("advanced scholar") degree. Those who succeeded at the metropolitan level were ranked in order of excellence and invited to a special congratulatory banquet provided by the Board of Rites.

The last stage in the process was the more or less pro forma palace examination (*dianshi*), held for the top three classes of metropolitan graduates in the Hall of Preserving Harmony in the Forbidden City. The emperor generally presided over this affair with the assistance of various high-ranking civil officials who acted as "readers." In contrast to the brevity of the questions at lower examination levels, the emperor's questions were elaborate and florid in style. The responses of the candidates, in turn, were couched in the self-deprecating language and rigid form of a memorial to the throne. Following the announcement of the results of this examination, a series of banquets and ceremonies ensued, all of which enhanced the prestige of the *jinshi* graduates and served as reminders of status distinctions and obligations. The top *jinshi* were immediately appointed to the Hanlin Academy, where they performed various important editorial, pedagogical, and ritual functions for the emperor. Service in the Hanlin Academy virtually guaranteed metropolitan graduates rapid promotion in the regular bureaucracy.

The overall structure of the examinations varied over time. For most of the Qing period the testing process at the top two levels consisted of three sessions, each lasting a full day. One focused on classical texts; one emphasized certain types of discourse (*lun*); and one addressed policy questions (*ce*). Except for a brief two-year period during the Oboi regency, and another anomalous period from 1901 to 1905, by far the most important session (sometimes divided into two) was based on the Four Books and the Five Classics. Another important category, introduced in 1757 and continued until 1898, was poetic composition (eight-rhyme, five-character, Tang-style regulated verse). Although policy discussions always played a part in the formal Qing examination process, they generally counted for little. Moreover, "policy" was often broadly construed. The first policy question of the 1730 metropolitan exams, for instance, centered on the metaphysical attributes of the "Supreme Ultimate" (*Taiji*; see chapter 6).[59]

The evaluation process was expensive and labor intensive. For instance, the 1756 metropolitan exams cost more than four thousand ounces (*taels*) of silver to administer. For about a month, 706 copyists and 86 readers toiled at their task. Examination candidates, for their part, labored under difficult conditions. First, they had to arrive a week or so before the tests to present their credentials (identity, family lineage, and assurances that they were not in mourning for a parent) and to purchase supplies. Rice and gruel were provided for the candidates, but most preferred to buy their own food. Once inside the examination compound, they were completely cut off from the outside for three days and two nights. All were carefully searched and continually monitored. Some of the examination cells were close to public latrines and nearly unbearable; all were cramped and uncomfortable, with only a pair of moveable planks to serve as a seat, a desk, and a bed.[60]

Competition for degrees was ferocious as tight government quotas limited the number of successful candidates in each examination. At the metropolitan level, for example, only about three hundred individuals could pass at any given time. Most provinces were allowed a quota of from fifteen to twenty *jinshi* per examination, although some received fewer than ten slots and others had as many as twenty-five. A certain quota was also set aside for Manchu, Mongol, and Chinese Bannerman—usually in descending numbers for each group. At the lower levels of examination the quotas were less restrictive. About fifteen hundred *juren* degrees could be granted at one time, and as many as thirty thousand *shengyuan* degrees. Nonetheless, an aspirant for the lowest degree had only about one chance in sixty of success and only one chance in six thousand of ultimately attaining the *jinshi* degree. Candidates often took the examinations many times, and one could not normally hope to acquire the *shengyuan* degree before the age of twenty-four, the *juren* degree before the age of thirty, or the *jinshi* degree before the age of thirty-five.

Furthermore, the best minds of the empire were not always successful, as many frustrated Qing scholars were quick to point out. Although the examination system did create a highly literate, culturally homogeneous elite, it placed a heavy premium on tradition, rote memorization, calligraphic skill, and literary style at the expense of creative thought and independent

Table 3.3.   Successful *Jinshi* Candidates, 1890 (By Province)

Beijing	
Manchu Bannermen	9
Mongol Bannermen	4
Chinese Bannermen	7
The Provinces	
Jiangsu	26
Zhili	24
Shandong	22
Jiangxi	22
Fujian	20
Henan	17
Anhui	17
Guangdong	17
Hubei	15
Sichuan	14
Hunan	14
Shaanxi	14
Guangxi	13
Yunnan	12
Guizhou	10
Shanxi	10
Gansu	9
Taiwan	2
Total	328

Source: North China Herald, June 13, 1890; cf. Elman 2000, esp. 656–57. In 1702 a sliding scale of provincial *jinshi* quotas was instituted, based on the total of participants from each province in the three preceding examinations. This system became virtually frozen, with only minor adjustments during the latter half of the nineteenth century.

judgment. In addition, the examiners were often capricious and occasionally corrupt. Despite intense surveillance, cheating scandals plagued the system.[61]

As if this were not enough, Chinese scholars also faced the problem of limited bureaucratic opportunities once they had earned a degree. By design, only a small fraction of the empire's total number of degree holders (over a million during much of the Qing period) could expect to gain one of twenty thousand or so official civil government positions. *Jinshi* status almost automatically placed an individual in the middle stratum of the nine-rank bureaucracy, which ranged from metropolitan posts such as deputy commissioner in the Transmission Office (rank 4A) or reader in the Grand Secretariat (rank 4B), to local offices such as circuit intendant (rank 4A), prefect (rank 4B), and county magistrate (rank 7A). But *juren* degree holders could be assured of only the most minor posts, and *shengyuan* had very few opportunities for regular bureaucratic employment. The vast majority of *shengyuan* languished as "lower-gentry" (see chapter 4), enjoying certain gentry privileges to be sure, but forced to "plow with the writing brush" by teaching in local schools or serving as family tutors. Many of these individuals became small tradesmen or entered other "demeaning" occupations (including litigation masters) in order to sustain themselves.

Yet for all the frustrations of examination life, with its fierce competition and tightly controlled degree quotas, the lure of gentry status and the ultimate possibility of bureaucratic service—with its rich social and financial rewards—kept the vast majority of Qing scholars loyal to the system and the state. Officials, of course, had every reason to support the status quo. But the security-conscious Manchus, vastly outnumbered by the Chinese, made an unrelenting effort to ensure administrative control through an elaborate system of checks and balances inherited from the Ming and refined for their own purposes.

One check on the Qing bureaucracy was, of course, the despotic power of the emperor, which reached its apex in the eighteenth century only to sink to its nadir during the nineteenth. Philip Kuhn's absorbing account of the "sorcery scare" of 1768 provides an excellent case study of how the Qianlong emperor used reports of evildoing in the provinces, together with his powers of appointment and dismissal, to shake officials out of their administrative complacency and their longstanding patterns of cronyism and self-protection. Yet it also reveals the formidable bureaucratic inertia that rendered his victories at best temporary and incomplete. As Kuhn puts the matter, although bureaucrats "might be picked off one by one by an enraged sovereign, their position as a group was quite secure, and they knew it."[62]

Another feature of the Qing check-and-balance system was the appointment of more or less equal numbers of Manchus and Chinese to head most top-level organs of government, and the practice of appointing a careful mixture of Manchus and Chinese to oversee provincial administration. During the first few decades of Qing rule, the Manchus relied heavily on Chinese Bannermen (*Hanjun*) to play a leading role in provincial administration; but increasingly thereafter, regular Chinese civil officials and Manchus assumed their bureaucratic roles. Typically, a Chinese would serve as a governor, while a Manchu would occupy the position of governor-general. During the Qing period as a whole, only about one-quarter of the governor-generals were Han Chinese; of these, two-thirds had the *jinshi* degree, while less than one-third of the Manchus possessed it. [63]

A third check was the use of Banner forces to maintain military control at the capital and in the provinces. Although outnumbered at least two to one by

Figure 3.8.   Banner Soldiers
A Banner artillery unit in the late nineteenth century. *Source:* Beinecke Rare Book and Manuscript Library, Yale University.

the five-hundred-thousand-man Army of the Green Standard (an exclusively Chinese army), the multi-ethnic Eight Banners were carefully concentrated and positioned to assure them strategic superiority over Chinese forces in China Proper as well as in Inner Asia. Their principal task was, of course, the protection of Beijing and Manchuria and the main communication routes on the Grand Canal and the Yangzi River, but the Banners also served as a check on the Army of the Green Standard, greater in absolute numbers, but more fragmented in deployment.

Furthermore, military authority was carefully diffused. Although the governor-general and governor exercised administrative jurisdiction over regular provincial military forces, they had no authority over Banner garrisons in the provinces, which were commanded by generals (*jiangjun*)—functionaries who often had significant civilian authority. Governors-general and governors, for their part, shared responsibility for the Green Standard troops in the areas of their jurisdiction with a military officer titled the provincial commander in chief (*tidu*). As with the civil bureaucracy, the system of shared responsibilities and overlapping jurisdictions contributed to administrative stability, but often stifled initiative.[64]

Other Qing checks and balances included the effort to balance regular and irregular (purchased) bureaucratic appointments, the frequent transfer of officials (usually every three years or less), and rules prohibiting bureaucratic service in one's home area (that is, a county magistrate could not serve in his home county, etc.). Ironically, this "rule of avoidance" had somewhat opposite the intended effect because officials in unfamiliar areas often found it necessary to rely on clerks, runners, constables, and others who had precisely the kinds of local ties and loyalties that the avoidance rule was designed to overcome.

The problem of local ties and conflicting loyalties was evident at all levels of traditional Chinese government and in society at large. As Tom Metzger has noted:

> For all its stress on loyalty and hierarchy, Chinese society has been characterized by a remarkably fluid pattern of betrayal and intrigue. Individuals frequently oscillated between cooperation with the centralized state bureaucracy and support for smaller, often more ascriptive groupings, such as lineages, clubs, cliques, or secret societies, inhibiting political centralization.[65]

Enmeshed in a huge and impersonal bureaucracy, and lacking either institutional or legal protection from imperial caprice, Qing officials—like the rest of Chinese society—sought comfort and security in particularistic personal relationships known colloquially as *guanxi* ("connections").

Many different types of *guanxi* existed in Chinese political and social life. Sometimes they overlapped or intersected to create especially powerful affiliations. The most common relationships included those based on lineage (*qinshu guanxi*), in-law ties (*yinqin guanxi*), family friendships (*shiyi guanxi*), shared home area (*tongxiang guanxi*), educational ties (*shisheng guanxi* or *tongxue guanxi*), and bureaucratic linkages (*liaoshu guanxi* or *tongliao guanxi*). Sworn brothers (*jiebai xiongdi*) enjoyed a special sort of *guanxi*, and even people with the same family name felt a certain affinity with one another. Most forms of *guanxi* implied a superior-inferior relationship in which the "junior" person owed loyalty, obedience, and respect, while the "senior" owed protection and assistance in advancement. Gift giving from juniors to seniors, a reflection of the deep-seated Chinese social principle of "reciprocity" (*bao*), naturally solidified these bonds.

Andrew Nathan points out that *guanxi* facilitated cooperation between individuals in traditional China not only by delineating status relationships, but also by rendering the behavior of each party predictable, "both with regard to social formalities . . . and with regard to potentially critical questions such as what one person had to ask of the other."[66] Predictability and ease of intercourse, in turn, contributed to the establishment of trust. *Guanxi* as a system of "shared attributes" was thus highly formalized and extended well beyond what has been called the "old boy network" of acquaintances in the West. Furthermore, it implied a much stronger sense of responsibility, obligations, and indebtedness. No Qing official could afford to overlook *guanxi* in his political and social calculations, regardless of the issue at stake (see also chapter 4).

The particularism of traditional Chinese society also helps explain the system of "organized corruption" within the Qing bureaucracy. To be sure, in part the extraction of revenue in the form of "gifts" from subordinates can be attributed to unrealistically low official salaries and high administrative costs. The tenure of most bureaucrats was short, and there were many expenses involved in preparing for an official career. But another factor was assuredly the institutionalized gift-giving characteristic of individuals related by some form of *guanxi* or of those hoping to expand their network of useful acquaintances. Gift giving was essential to bureaucratic advancement, but the line between voluntary gifts and extortion was not always easy to draw. Even apparently honest officials derived much of their income from presents. According to the records of one late Qing metropolitan official, over 30 percent of the 16,836 *taels* he received from 1871 to 1889 was in the form of gifts.[67] And this was, of course, merely pocket change to someone like Heshen (see chapter 2). Small wonder, then, that even before the egregious excesses of the late Qianlong period, the Yongzheng emperor considered the pervasiveness of "favoritism and appeals to feelings [*renqing*]" to be particularly detrimental to good government.[68]

Corruption within the bureaucracy was also encouraged by the central government's chaotic fiscal system—as confused as "tangled silk" in the words of a late Qing encyclopedia. Although the central government knew whether or not its prescribed tax and tribute quotas had been received from the provinces, it had no precise way of determining what sums beyond the quota had been collected and retained by provincial officials. This situation, together with the pressing fiscal needs and inadequate budgets of locally minded officials, fostered the widespread practice of "tax farming" (collecting extra revenue to cover costs or make a profit), which often led to abuse. Efforts by the energetic Yongzheng emperor to reform the cumbersome and corrupt Qing tax system enjoyed a measure of temporary success, but ultimately he failed to overcome deeply entrenched patterns of *guanxi*. Meanwhile, the comparatively small amount of revenue received regularly by Beijing made the Qing government, in the words of Dwight Perkins, "an almost unbelievably weak [financial] instrument," especially in the nineteenth century.[69]

Another problem, common to all bureaucracies but especially acute in traditional China, was the double curse of massive paperwork and multifarious regulations. Officials could either drown in a sea of documents or be stran- gled by red tape. A bewildering variety of documents circulated within the Qing bureaucracy, each a reflection of the relative rank of the correspondents and the type of office involved. The requirements of bureaucratic protocol and the system of shared responsibilities and overlapping jurisdictions at all levels of government increased the volume of documents without facilitat- ing the flow. Meanwhile, literal and tedious adherence to a vast number of minutely prescribed administrative rules and regulations imposed a crushing burden on Chinese bureaucrats.

Yet despite the elaborate checks and balances, particularism, corruption, paperwork, and over-regulation of Qing administration, it would be wrong to dismiss the traditional Chinese state as nothing more than a ponderous, inflexible, and inefficient monolith. Notwithstanding the Manchu preoccupa- tion with administrative control, it is clear that in practice Beijing allowed considerable leeway to local officials in the handling of affairs within their jurisdictions. Moreover, as a matter of principle, many Qing officials dem- onstrated what has been aptly characterized by Tom Metzger as a "pervasive moral commitment to flexibility."[70]

Administrative adaptations were often conceived in terms of, and le- gitimized by, the classical notion of "making adjustments to meet changing conditions" (*biantong*). Respected writers in late imperial China repeatedly emphasized that the essence of statecraft was in making allowances for "hu- man situations." In the words of Wang Huizu (1731–1807), the well-known author of several extremely influential works on Chinese local government, "Law must distinguish between right and wrong, but the situation may allow moderation of the strict standard of right and wrong."[71] This meant that it was always possible for an official to bend regulations in the interest of justice and in the best interests of the state.

Confucian morality remained the paramount consideration in traditional Chinese government—more important than either abstract law or technical specialization in the eyes of most scholar-officials. But Qing administration was not merely a matter of mouthing moral platitudes. Administrative hand- books, encyclopedias, and compilations on statecraft provided much con- crete, practical, and valuable guidance for Chinese officials. What is more, in the evaluation of bureaucrats—whether through the annual process known as *kaocheng* or in the triennial reckonings known as *daji* (for provincial of- ficials) and *jingcha* (for metropolitan officials)—the criteria for achievement were also concrete and practical. Personal integrity (*shou*) was important, to be certain, but so were an official's ability (*cai*) and administrative skill (*zheng*). And for all the Chinese government's stress on moral suasion, it also placed a premium on impartiality (*xu*), attention to detail (*xiang*), and carefulness (*shen*).[72]

Even emperors were evaluated posthumously in terms of specific administrative categories. One index is the organization of each major division of the *Shichao shengxun* (Imperial injunctions of the ten reigns), which collected various important edicts and decrees of the Qing rulers up through the Tongzhi reign and categorized them according to about forty areas of imperial concern. Taking the imperial injunctions for the Daoguang reign (1821–1850) as illustration, we can see that while considerable space is given to categories such as imperial virtue (*shengde*), imperial filial piety (*shengxiao*), and improvement of moral customs (*hou fengsu*), far more attention is devoted to such categories as military exploits (*wugong*), fiscal administration (*licai*), strictness of law and discipline (*yan faji*), and frontier administration (*ji bianjiang*).[73]

In all, then, Qing government represented an effective balance between the emperor and the bureaucracy, civil and military rule, central control and local leeway, formal and informal authority, morality and law, idealism and realism, rigidity and flexibility, and personalism and impersonality. This balance gave Chinese government great strength and staying power, just as a similar set of balanced elements gave cohesiveness and continuity to Chinese social and economic life.

Chapter Four

Social and Economic Institutions

One of the most striking features of the Qing social and economic landscape during the heyday of the dynasty was the sharp distinction between Han Chinese and Bannermen (Manchus, Mongols, and Chinese). Mark Elliott aptly refers to the latter group as "resident aliens." Outnumbered at times by two hundred to one or more in China, the Banner population might well have been overwhelmed by the Han, one way or another, had the Manchus not given scrupulous attention to the establishment and maintenance of a carefully constructed physical and cultural space separating the conquerors from the conquered. Hence the prohibition of Chinese migration to Manchuria, stipulations forbidding the marriage of Han civilian males to Manchu females, and, above all, the establishment of separate "Manchu cities" (*Mancheng* or *Manzhou cheng*) at the capital and in the provinces (about twenty altogether). Over time, contact between the two groups, both in China Proper and even beyond the Great Wall, undermined the cultural barriers somewhat, but it never eradicated the ethnic distinctions entirely.[1]

The degree to which Bannermen in general and the Manchus in particular adopted Chinese social values is unclear (see also chapter 10). To the extent that they participated in civil examination culture it would certainly seem that they did, but the vast majority of Bannermen were not participants in that culture; indeed they were an integral part of what Joanna Waley-Cohen describes as a "militarized" High Qing culture. As late as the 1730s, for instance, Manchu was still the "primary medium of communications and of understanding" for Manchus serving in top civil posts at the capital and in the provinces.[2] But increasingly Chinese became the lingua franca not only for high-ranking officials but also for Bannermen at the lower levels of Qing society. By the middle of the nineteenth century, for example, some 15,000 Chinese shopkeeper families had moved into the once exclusively Manchu

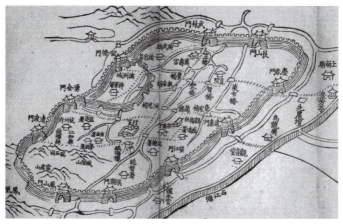

Figure 4.1. Hangzhou c. 1780
This eighteenth-century Chinese map of Hangzhou shows the walled Manchu City in the upper left, with an inscription indicating the yamen of the Banner General (*jiangjun*). The walled Chinese city surrounding it on three sides has inscriptions that indicate a number of important temples and shrines, as well as the yamens of the governor-general of Min-Zhe (Fujian and Zhejiang), the governor of Zhejiang, the provincial judicial commissioner, and several other important officials. *Source:* Library of Congress "Map Division."

Inner City of Beijing to conduct business, and by 1908 Manchus accounted for only 54 percent of the more than 400,000 residents in that part of the Qing capital.[3]

It is difficult to imagine that any social or economic interaction between Bannermen and Han Chinese, whether at the capital or in the provinces, would be devoid of personal connections (*guanxi*). I have discussed the political dimensions of this phenomenon at some length in chapter 3, but it deserves further treatment here as a feature of Qing social life. The famous Chinese anthropologist Fei Xiaotong once contrasted the "differential mode of association" (*chaxu geju*) in traditional China with the "organizational mode of association" (*tuanti geju*) in the modern West. The former, he maintains, is marked by "distinctive networks spreading out from each individual's personal connections." The latter involves the attachment of individuals to a preexisting structure, and then the formation of personal relationships through that structure.[4]

These two types of social organization reflect two different conceptions of morality according to Fei. In the West, he says, "people in the same organizations apply universal moral principles to themselves and so regard each other as equals"—at least in theory. In traditional China, however, where society tended to be viewed as "a web woven out of countless personal relationships," each knot in the web became attached to a specific, particularistic ethical principle. In this "self-centered" but not "individualistic" society, relationships "spread out gradually, from individual to individual, resulting in an accumulation of personal connections." The result was that Chinese social morality made sense "only in terms of these personal connections."[5] This was true for all levels of society.

A central principle of traditional Chinese social relations was the concept of *bao* or reciprocity. *Bao* covered all facets of social interaction and served as the rationale behind the highly refined system of gift giving in China. In the words of the *Record of Ritual*, "Reciprocity is what the rules of propriety value. If I give a gift and nothing comes in return, that is contrary to propriety; if the thing comes to me, and I give nothing in return, that is also contrary to propriety."[6] The object in Chinese life was thus to keep one's obligations in balance, to avoid "owing *renqing*" (lit. "human feelings") to another person.

Renqing covered more than mere sentiment. It referred to the concrete social expressions of "human feelings," such as the offering of congratulations and the giving of gifts on appropriate occasions. As a kind of "social capital" in Chinese interpersonal transactions, *renqing* occupied a position of crucial importance in the cultivation of *guanxi*. Favors dispensed (especially by superiors) required that gifts be given; gifts given implied that favors would be dispensed. The feelings of obligation in traditional Chinese society ran so deep that "even in a case of fulfillment of an official duty, if it happened to be beneficial to a particular person, he would be expected to cherish a sense of indebtedness to the person who was instrumental in the outcome."[7] Thus, for instance, an extremely close relationship was presumed to exist in Qing times between successful examination candidates and the examiners who passed them.

In Chinese economic life the cultivation of *guanxi*—particularly with officials—provided a significant measure of protection for merchants. But not all economic relationships in China involved *renqing*. To the extent that the terms of economic (as opposed to social) exchange were dictated by impersonal market forces, *renqing* had no place or purchase. In fact, Chinese businessmen often left their hometowns to do business far away precisely because it freed them from the particularistic pressures of *guanxi*. By the same cultural logic, villagers would walk miles to the local market town to do business in an impersonal setting, among "strangers," rather than exchange goods directly with their neighbors.

While the particularistic principles of Chinese daily life proved remarkably resistant to change in late imperial times, social and economic conditions most certainly did not. In fact, during the late Ming dynasty, as we have seen, a series of dramatic and far-reaching transformations began to take place in

China. These included a huge influx of silver from foreign trade; increased urbanization, especially of the lower Yangzi region of Jiangnan; the commutation of labor services into money payments; the growth of regional and long-distance trade; the emergence of a national market in bulk commodities; increased geographical mobility; the expansion of popular literacy; an increase in the size of the elite "gentry" class (*shenshi*); the growth of lineage structures in both size and complexity; the professionalization of local managerial activities; and so forth.[8]

These developments contributed to transformations in the style of local politics, in patterns of personal and intellectual affiliation, and ultimately in modes of thought (see chapter 6). They also created new opportunity structures that "altered the quality of gender relations and expanded the social roles actually assumed by women." By Qing times,

> The increasingly urbanized society, especially of Jiangnan, saw greater sexual mingling in workplaces such as textile manufactures, and in recreational sites such as teahouses and wineshops, where women appeared as both employees and customers. The cultural ideal of the sequestered women's quarters (*gui*) was ever more difficult to maintain in practice. Along with this, a new model of the worldly and refined professional courtesan arose . . . [and a] new ideal emerged of the "companionate marriage," a love match between men and women who were similarly cultivated and shared aesthetic tastes. This in turn reflected an actual rise in female (and society-wide) literacy rates. . . . The fiction consumed by this growing reading public exhibited a new sexual frankness, as well as the glorification of romantic attachments between men and women.[9]

Moreover, accelerated social mobility, a certain blurring of status distinctions, and the movement toward the relaxation of personal dependency bonds (symbolized and substantiated by the Yongzheng emperor's at least partially successful effort to emancipate various categories of "debased" peoples), "gave rise to urges both to reaffirm and reassess the moral imperatives implicit in social roles, especially those of gender."[10] The remarkable thing about these changes is not only that they occurred within an apparently rigid structure of political, social, and economic institutions. It is also that this structure remained fundamentally intact, despite these changes, during most of the Qing period.

SOCIAL CLASSES

Chinese society in late imperial times was highly stratified, with status distinctions that were carefully preserved in the vocabularies of both ritual and law. Nobles occupied the top of the Qing social pyramid. Below them were four main social classes: scholars ("gentry"), peasants, artisans, and merchants. Members of the clergy had a special status outside this four-class structure, as did a few other groups.

The Qing rulers recognized two main categories of hereditary nobles: (1) members of the Manchu imperial clan (the Aisin Gioro lineage) and (2) civil or military officials granted titles for conspicuous achievement. These high-status groups received special allowances of property, food, and money, in addition to certain other social and economic privileges, depending on their rank. Bannermen who were not members of the Imperial Household might also be considered "noble" in a certain sense by virtue of their hereditary status, special allowances, and substantial privileges.

As a rule, all Bannermen received a steady income provided by the Qing state, usually paid four times a year in silver and grain. In addition, they enjoyed a variety of practical advantages over the Han Chinese, including disability payments, pensions, frequent bonuses, free housing, and interest-free loans. Bannermen paid no taxes and were immune to prosecution by local Chinese civilian officials. Even if arrested they were held in separate jails, and when they were convicted of wrongdoing, they generally got off with lighter penalties, if they were punished at all. Moreover, their access to official positions, especially for those who lived in Beijing, where about half of the Banner population resided, was far easier than it was for Han Chinese because most Bannermen did not need to have examination degrees to fill posts in the imperial bureaucracy—particularly during the early Qing period.[11]

During the eighteenth century the advantages enjoyed by Banner families encouraged a number of Han Chinese to falsely claim a Banner identity—even though grants and stipends were allocated in a downward-sliding scale not only for different Banner ranks but also for Manchu, Mongol, and Chinese Bannermen of the same rank. Furthermore, as discussed in previous chapters, these grants and stipends diminished over time. Most importantly, the very fact of their hereditary position proved to be an impediment to the financial well-being of Banner families because they were not able to take full advantage of the dramatic economic changes occurring during most of the Qing period. With some exceptions, they were the captives of their status as a military caste.[12]

Civil bureaucrats enjoyed enormous prestige in Qing society, whether or not they possessed titular nobility. As indicated in chapter 3, the nine-rank bureaucracy was divided into three strata—an upper level (ranks one through three), a middle level (ranks four through seven), and a lower level (ranks eight and nine). Each of these ranks had two classes, conventionally designated "A" and "B," and each rank had its own official dress, colored

Figure 4.2. Wenxiang
Wenxiang (1818–1876) was a member of the Plain Red Banners, who received a classical education and earned the highest civil service degree (*jinshi*). He had a distinguished career as a Qing official, serving in a variety of important posts, and was posthumously granted hereditary rank for his service to the dynasty.
Source: Library of Congress "Prints and Photographs."

Figure 4.3. Banner-women
These women are distinguished by their Manchu-style clothing, their Manchu hairstyles, and their shoes with attachments designed to give the appearance and gait of bound feet. Source: Library of Congress "Prints and Photographs" (both images).

Table 4.1.

Post	Annual Salary (taels)	Rice Stipend (shi)
Prince of the Blood	10,000	5,000
Duke (First Grade)	700	350
Earl (First Grade)	610	305
Count (First Grade)	510	255
Viscount	410	205
Baron	310	155
Civil official, Grade 1A-B	180	90
Civil official, Grade 2A-B	155	77.5
Civil official, Grade 3A-B	130	65
Civil official, Grade 4A-B	105	52.5
Civil official, Grade 5A-B	80	40
Civil official, Grade 6A-B	60	30
Civil official, Grade 7A-B	45	22.5
Civil official, Grade 8A-B	40	20
Civil official, Grade 9A	33.1	16.5
Civil official, Grade 9B	31.5	15.8

Source: Immanuel Hsü 2000, 62, slightly modified. As indicated in chapter 2, from the early eighteenth century on, Qing officials received a supplementary salary known as *yanglian* (lit. to "nourish integrity"). Thus, a governor-general (grade 2A), whose salary was 155 taels, received in addition between 13,000 and 20,000 taels to encourage rectitude. Similarly, at the lower ends of the bureaucratic scale, a county magistrate (grade 7A), whose salary was about 45 taels, would receive a supplement of from 400 to over 2,000 taels, depending on the locality in which he served. Even so, unbudgeted administrative costs at all levels perpetuated the system of "customary fees" (*lougui*), a system that was regulated by local custom, but often led to abuses.

hat button, and other marks of status. Officials of the first rank, for example, wore a ruby button, a white crane embroidered on the breast and back of their official robes, and a jade girdle clasp set with rubies. At the other end of the bureaucratic scale, rank nine, officials wore a silver button, a white-tailed jay embroidery square, and a clasp of buffalo horn. In addition to official titles and ranks, which usually graced formal papers, family records, ancestral tablets, and tombstones, the state also granted a variety of distinctions of merit, including the right to ride horseback within the Forbidden City, the right to wear a decorative peacock feather, and the right to wear a yellow riding jacket (*huang magua*).[13]

Government statutes distinguished between ceremonial regulations appropriate for officials, for scholar-gentry, and for commoners. Although officials ranked above scholar-gentry on the Chinese social ladder, in fact the two groups overlapped significantly. In marriage and mourning ceremonies, for example, the ritual stipulations for the first group applied only to officials of the seventh rank and above; lower-ranking officials performed rituals appropriate to the second group, the gentry. Moreover, in public ceremonies at

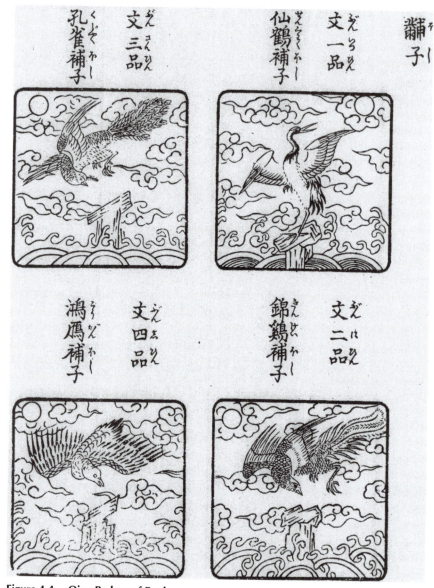

Figure 4.4. Qing Badges of Rank

These so-called mandarin squares (Chinese: *buzi*) display the animals that symbolize the top four civilian official ranks: the crane (upper right, grade 1); the golden pheasant (lower right, grade 2); the peacock (upper left, grade 3); and the wild goose (lower left, grade 4). *Source:* Nakagawa 1799.

Figure 4.5. Li Hongzhang
Li Hongzhang (1823–1901) was one of the most distinguished Han Chinese officials in the late Qing period. Like Wenxiang (figure 4.2), he earned the highest civil service degree and served in a number of important positions. Unlike Wenxiang, however, he gained his reputation in the provinces rather than at the capital (first as a governor and then as a governor-general), and he was notoriously corrupt.
Source: Beinecke Rare Book and Manuscript Library, Yale University.

Figure 4.6. The Yang Family of Beijing
This photo shows a late Qing official identified by the photographer (John Thomson) as a "Mr. Yang" and his extended family. His eldest son is standing next to him. Most of the women are dressed in Han Chinese style but one of them is wearing a Manchu-style headdress. The inscription at the top of the second story reads "Pavilion Amidst the Clouds." *Source:* Beinecke Rare Book and Manuscript Library, Yale University.

the local level, holders of the *jinshi* and *juren* degrees (the upper gentry) were generally considered equivalent in status to officials of the seventh rank and were therefore included in the first group.

As is apparent, upper-degree holders had a social status at least as exalted as that of lower officials. Even lowly *shengyuan* and holders of various purchased titles such as *jiansheng* (student of the Imperial College) enjoyed social prestige and substantial privilege. As a class, both upper and lower gentry members were entitled to special terms of address, special clothing, and other badges of rank. Degree holders wore gold or silver brocades and fancy embroidery; by statute no commoners were permitted to wear these items. Gentry members also received favorable legal treatment (including immunity from corporal punishment and exemption from being called as witnesses by commoners), official exemption from labor service or the labor service tax, and, above all, easy access to officialdom, which, of course, brought additional advantages and preferential treatment.

One did not need a degree to have influence, however. *Guanxi* could be of decisive importance. Frederic Wakeman has shown by means of a colorful parable how elite cultural common denominators gave access to officials and thus provided the key to power holding and power wielding in traditional China. He posits a land dispute between "Mr. Wang, a wealthy but untutored peasant of Jiangsu," and Mr. Chen, a scholar "whose great-grandfather had been a ministry official sixty years earlier." Although Mr. Chen held no official degrees and was therefore not officially a member of the gentry class, "he had been tutored in the Classics as a youth and still spent three hours a day in his small study making modest marginal comments on a text of the *Book of Changes* in his own, rather elegant hand." One afternoon a week, "he would meet eight close comrades at a temple near the county capital. Wine would be heated and served, philosophical papers presented, and—as dusk came on—poems exchanged or a friend's painted scroll admired."

Politically astute, Mr. Chen used his personal connections with these men to resolve the impending law case. His first step was to find the appropriate "middleman"—one of the members of his poetry club who had gotten his examination degree in the same year as the local county magistrate, and who thus enjoyed the relationship known as *tongnian* ("same year") *guanxi*. This friend was "most happy to introduce so cultivated a guest as Mr. Chen to the official the following day over tea." The two men hit it off well:

> The magistrate was also enamored of the *Book of Changes* and impressed by Mr. Chen's theories about that classic. As Mr. Chen was leaving, he asked if he might have the honor of presenting the magistrate with a small painting. "The antique-dealer claimed it's a Song scroll. It's not, of course. But it is quite a good forgery, and I thought Your Excellency might enjoy looking at such a trinket from so worthless a one as myself." The official was happy to accept, and the two men parted on the best of terms.

When Mr. Wang "discovered that his opponent in the coming lawsuit was an acceptable guest at the judge's own home, he realized how foolhardy he had been and dropped the matter altogether." Later, he paid his own visit to Mr. Chen, "apologizing for having disturbed His Honor," and obsequiously remarking "A great man does not remember the faults of a petty man" (*daren buji xiaoren guo*).[14]

The social life of the scholarly elite will be treated in greater detail in chapter 10. For now it is sufficient to note the substantial outlays of money required by the extravagant gentry lifestyle, which often included lavish parties, large numbers of servants, and expensive hobbies such as the collecting of books and art. Fortunately for most of the Chinese elite, adequate financial resources were within easy reach. Chung-li Chang estimates that at times the gentry class enjoyed a per capita income about sixteen times that of commoners, and other scholars have written about the "huge disparity of income" between degree holders and the masses.[15]

Contrary to stereotype, the gentry class was not simply a landed elite. Although a majority of degree holders did live in rural areas and many were indeed landlords, comfortably ensconced in country villas, by the early eighteenth century income derived from local managerial services (such as the mediation of legal disputes, supervision of schools and academies, management of public works and welfare projects, militia organization, and proxy remittance of peasant land and labor taxes to the county yamen clerks) began to replace landed wealth as the key economic underpinning of the gentry class—especially at the lower levels. At higher levels, gentry members also benefitted from commercial ventures with merchants (see below). For those gentry who were primarily landlords, collusion with officialdom usually enabled them to pay taxes at much lower rates than the rates applied to middle or poor peasants.

The wives and daughters of Qing elites were advantaged not only because they enjoyed the wealth, personal connections, and legal privileges afforded their high-status families, but also because frequently they were able to take advantage of educational opportunities that were not available to the vast majority of commoners. Although women were not eligible to take the civil service examinations, significant numbers were well educated in the classics and many learned to read, write and to paint (see chapters 8 and 9). Some women led Chinese troops against bandits, rebels, or foreign invaders, and at least a few—notably Lin Puqing (1821–1877)—played active administrative roles. A number of women assisted their husbands in business and others ran successful enterprises by themselves. As indicated in the introduction, recent research by a host of talented scholars has vastly enhanced our understanding of "women's culture" in late imperial China, including the ways that gender boundaries were constructed and contested over time.

Joan Judge identifies one major source of contestation—a perceived dichotomy between virtue (de) and talent (cai). She notes:

From the late sixteenth century, as increasing numbers of [Chinese] women became literate . . . this fundamental cultural construct was used to define the parameters of respectable womanhood. The saying "A man with virtue is a man of talent, a woman without talent is a woman of virtue" (nanzi youde bian shi cai, nüzi wucai bian shi de) was popularized at this time, defining male talent as the highest form of public service and essential to the reproduction of the political order, while female talent was a distraction from familial service and inimical to the reproduction of the social order. The virtue/talent binary continued to be used to structure disputes over the scope and objectives of women's learning from the late sixteenth through the early twentieth century, but the terms of the debates shifted over time. Initially, opponents of female education claimed that talent and virtue were mutually exclusive for women. By the eighteenth century, however, the debate was no longer focused on whether or not women should develop their talents but on how publicly they should be displayed.[16]

In chapters 10 and 11 we shall see some of the ways that this complex issue played itself out in Qing elite culture.

Unfortunately, we have far less information about the lives and achievements of women in the other strata of Chinese society during the Qing period. Even the fascinating tale of an eighteenth-century peasant woman poet named He Shuangqing cannot be fully verified. Her fame rests on an account written by an appreciative male literatus named Shi Zhenlin (1693–1779). We have examples of poems attributed to her, but there is no way to determine conclusively whether He Shuangqing actually existed; perhaps she was simply the product of Shi's fertile and somewhat iconoclastic mind.[17] In any case, we do know that in at least one area of China Proper, Jiangyong county in southwestern Hunan, non-elite women developed a unique women's script (*nüshu*), which they used to express in colorful verse their sophisticated and highly gendered thoughts about the world in which they lived (see chapter 5).

Below the scholar-gentry class in traditional China stood three broad classes of commoners. According to longstanding Chinese usage, they were ranked under scholars (*shi*) in the following order: (1) peasants (*nong*), (2) artisans (*gong*), and (3) merchants (*shang*). Their proportions in society varied according to time and place. One early twentieth-century survey of eighteen counties in north China, encompassing 4.5 million people, indicates that about 3 percent of the population were scholars, 2.5 percent were artisans, 4 percent were merchants, and the rest were peasants. On the other hand, a thriving commercial city like Hankou might have 30 percent merchants, 50 percent workers, 5 percent scholars, 5 percent peasants, and 10 percent "marginal elements."[18]

Within any given environment, individuals or families from each status group could be further subdivided according to specific occupation, income, lifestyle, and local prestige. Sometimes, for example, large property holders might be accorded polite terms of address and special privileges regardless of their education; and on occasion philanthropic commoners (*yimin*) came to be considered philanthropic officials (*yiguan*) because the government had accorded them certain privileges in acknowledgment of their generosity to the state. Similarly, upright elderly people might be officially recognized and socially honored as longevous commoners (*shoumin*) and eventually as longevous officials (*shouguan*). Thus, in certain local ceremonies, wealthy or

挿苗

Figure 4.7. Planting Rice
Source: Nakagawa 1799.

aged commoners could hold positions of honor and respect right along with the educated elite.[19]

Although rated second on the traditional Chinese social scale, peasants (some prefer the term "farmers," which is fine by me)—constituting at least 80 percent of the population in late imperial times—were often exploited and seldom well educated. Working long hours on the land at the mercy of the elements, their chances for meaningful social mobility were slim, and many lived on the barest margin of subsistence. In the absence of primogeniture, individual Chinese landholdings were constantly fragmented into small plots averaging at most twenty to thirty *mu* (c. three to five acres) per family in north China and perhaps twelve to fifteen *mu* (c. two to three acres) per family in the south. Holdings of this size, adequate to support a family of five, might be located in several different areas near a given village, making it difficult to farm efficiently. At any given time during the Qing period about 30 percent of China's peasant families were tenant farmers, and a further 20 percent or so were petty landowners who, in order to make ends meet, found it necessary to work rented land in addition to their own. In south China tenancy was especially common, but even in some northern areas during the prosperous Qianlong era at least one-quarter of the rural households were reportedly landless. Because of the relentless pressure on the land and a general shortage of capital, rents were high, and rural interest rates might approach 40 percent or more per year.[20]

Numerous local histories, official memoirs, and other accounts of the Qing period attest to the harshness and brutality of Chinese rural life. Listen to the residents of Tancheng, Shandong, describing conditions in their county during the early Qing: "Tancheng is only a tiny area, and it has long been destitute and ravaged. For thirty years now fields have lain under floodwater or weeds; we still cannot bear to speak of all the devastation. On top of this came the famine of 1665; and after the earthquake of 1668 not a single ear of grain was harvested, over half the people were dying of starvation, their homes were all destroyed and ten thousand men and women were crushed to death in the ruins." The county magistrate of the area later remarked, "When I was serving in Tancheng, many people held their lives to be of no value, for the area was so wasted and barren, the common people so poor and had suffered so much, that essentially they knew none of the joys of being alive."[21] Under these conditions, peasants often found it necessary to practice infanticide, and many were forced to sell themselves or members of their families into prostitution or slavery.

It is true, of course, that the times were not always so bad, and peasant welfare obviously varied from place to place, even in the same period. The extension of specialized cultivation into previously underdeveloped agricultural areas during the early Qing brought new economic opportunities to peasant households in these regions. The cultivation of mulberry leaves, for instance—initially concentrated in the silk-producing provinces of Zhejiang, Jiangsu, and Guangdong—expanded rapidly into the new agricultural frontiers of Sichuan, Hunan, and Hubei. Similarly, Sichuan and Taiwan joined Fujian and Guangdong as major sugar cane-producing regions; and tobacco growing moved northward from Jiangsu, Zhejiang, and Jiangxi to Shanxi, Shaanxi, and Sichuan. Meanwhile, more traditional agricultural products such as grain and cotton continued to flourish in the Lower Yangzi River region, one of China's richest and most productive farming areas.[22]

Whether out of ambition or exigency, growing numbers of small peasant producers turned to subsidiary occupations in order to supplement their family income. For them, it was a short and relatively easy step from producing raw materials for the growing handicraft sector to becoming a part of that sector. In fact, small rural workshops and peasant homes dominated the processing of many goods—from wine, oil, sugar, and tobacco to cotton cloth, leather products, iron utensils, and other items of daily use. Cottage industry was also responsible for most of China's silk and tea production. To the degree that peasant women played significant roles in home industry and field labor, they enhanced their economic importance and presumably their status within the family.[23]

The term "peasant" thus covered a wide spectrum of rural inhabitants. Local conditions and individual economic circumstances obviously affected the outlook of farm laborers and determined in large measure the extent to which they participated in the ritualized activities and everyday indulgences of the elite. Peasants could seldom afford the luxury of close adherence to gentry values, much less a gentry style of life.[24] Nonetheless, it is evident that many characteristic features of the elite viewpoint were closely mirrored in the rituals of Chinese peasant life. One striking indication is the general willingness of peasants to go deeply in debt in order to fulfill the ceremonial requirements of marriage and mourning. These performances "firmly linked China's common people to a national culture through their emulation of local elites."[25]

Artisans—or more generally workers—ranked third on the traditional Chinese social scale. Although lower in theoretical status than peasants, they often earned as much, or more, income per capita. In the words of a late Ming scholar (quoted by Gu Yanwu), "Agriculture gives a one-fold return on capital and needs the most labor of all, therefore fools do it. Manufacture provides a two-fold profit and requires a great deal of labor; clever fingers do it."[26] Sidney Gamble's pioneering study of wages for artisans in the Bejing area from 1807 to 1902 indicates an enormous variation in rates of pay, but as a rule, the daily income for unskilled laborers seems to have been between

1.5 times and twice the cost of their food. Thus, for example, the daily payment for unskilled carpenters and masons in the period from 1877 to 1887 was 160 cash, 100 of which went for food (see appendix B). Skilled laborers naturally earned more.

A wide variety of occupational groups fell under the general designation *gong*: craftsmen such as carpenters, masons, potters, metalworkers, coffin makers, tailors, and jewelers; manufacturers of commodities such as silk, cotton, tea, paper, cooking oil, furniture, and candles; and service persons such as butchers, barbers, doctors, fortune tellers, tool sharpeners, cooks, maids, and marriage brokers. Transport laborers were also considered *gong* because even peasants avoided, if possible, this "degrading" form of manual activity. Artisans and laborers could be either independent operatives or regular employees of gentry families, merchant families, or the state. Most independent artisans and laborers joined occupational groupings known as "guilds" (see below), but these organizations had little in common with their namesakes in the West. Although designed to provide a sense of solidarity and various

Figure 4.8. Street Scene
This photograph depicts common activities such as fortune telling and head shaving. The sign in front of the diviner's table indicates that he specializes in telling the future with the hexagrams of the *Yijing* (Classic of Changes; see chapter 5) as well as the interpretation of written characters (*cezi*). Notice the bound feet of his client. This appears to be a "staged" photograph. *Source:* Beinecke Rare Book and Manuscript Library, Yale University.

forms of mutual assistance for their members, they had virtually no political independence.

A remarkable book edited by Christine Moll-Murata, Jianze Song, and Hans Ulrich Vogel, titled *Chinese Handicraft Regulations of the Qing Dynasty* (2005), provides an illuminating bureaucratic perspective on the labors of Qing artisans, focusing in particular on the official rules (*jiangzuo zeli*) that stipulated the "techniques, materials, and funds for the production of utility goods."[27] These rules also addressed issues such as working hours and wages. The projects discussed by the contributors range from repairs on the Forbidden City after major fires to routine renovations of the Summer Palace, religious temples, and city walls. Other activities addressed in the essays include printing, river hydraulics, the maintenance of military weapons, minting, coastal shipping, and inland transport. Taken together, these detailed studies reveal yet another level of Qing bureaucratic practice and provide us with an appreciation not only of the conditions under which artisans worked, but also the mechanisms by which they sought to further their respective interests.

Merchants occupied the lowest position in the formal four-class structure of traditional China, at least in theory. Stigmatized in the official literature as unscrupulous and parasitic, most Chinese merchants were chronically insecure. As a class they lacked the power to command bureaucratic obedience and had little prospect of operating large-scale business without official support. Qing writers generally identified three main types of merchants: simple traders (*zuogu*), brokers (*yaseng*), and wealthy consignment merchants (*keshang*). Lowly street peddlers at one extreme of the commercial spectrum might barely make ends meet, but at the other end the great families of silk, tea, and salt merchants in the late imperial period often amassed huge fortunes and wielded substantial influence.[28]

Qing policies toward commerce were not as oppressive and intrusive as many scholars have claimed. For the most part, the Chinese government left local markets alone, encouraging self-regulation on the part of merchants. In the early Qing period, this approach took the form of brokerage licenses issued to individuals who assisted the state in regulating trade and tapping commercial wealth. These brokers also provided services for the merchants and used their licenses to control local resources for private gain. Later on, as the Chinese economy expanded, local elites assumed responsibility for collecting taxes in return for the authority to oversee the operation of local "benevolent markets"—once again out of economic self-interest. This was one of several ways that elites became more directly involved in the financial management of local communities. During the mid-nineteenth century, the Qing government's fiscal crisis compelled it to rely more heavily on commercial levies (notably the infamous *likin* [*lijin*] tax) than in the past; yet once again the throne's response was to look to local merchant organizations for a way to manage the problem.[29]

As should be apparent, the line between scholars and merchants, so clean and clear in theory, became increasingly difficult to draw in practice. Throughout the Qing period, and especially during the nineteenth century, official and gentry families readily engaged in warehousing, money lending, pawn broking, and various lucrative wholesale and retail enterprises. Commercialization thus increasingly fused merchants and gentry into what Mary Rankin describes as "a vigorous, numerically expanding elite whose power rested on varying combinations of landownership, trade, usury, and degree holding." Ping-ti Ho writes that during the Qing "the social distinction between officials and rich merchants was more blurred than at any time in Chinese history except for the Mongol Yuan period."[30]

Moreover, rich merchants could always use their wealth to acquire exalted academic-bureaucratic status, either by purchasing degrees (and sometimes substantive positions) or by educating themselves (or their sons) to take the civil service examinations. Commenting on the access to examination degrees available to merchants in Ming-Qing times, one Chinese scholar, Shen Yao (1798–1840), wrote somewhat hyperbolically: "While in the old days sons of scholars forever remained as scholars, in later times only sons of merchants could become scholars. . . . China's center of gravity has tilted towards commerce, and consequently heroes and men of intelligence mostly belong to the merchant class."[31]

In the absence of effective barriers to elite status, merchants had no incentive to challenge the existing Confucian social order. On the contrary, they upheld it, drawn by the maxim: "Commerce for profit and scholarship for personal reputation" (*gu wei louli ru wei minggao*). Frederic Wakeman writes:

Emulating the gentry's status manner on a colossal scale, they [rich merchants] consumed their capital conspicuously, dissipating the possibility of more productive investments and reaffirming the hegemony of the literati's high culture. There was a uniquely mad and millionarish quality to the "salt fools" . . . who lavished fortunes on mechanized toys, Lake Tai rock decorations, and exotic pets, but this was just a magnified perversion of gentry fashion. And for all the squander, families like the Ma clan of salt merchants not only presided over one of the most famous literary salons of the eighteenth century and patronized many of the noted artists of the day, they also amassed private libraries of rare editions which were the envy of the Qianlong Emperor.[32]

Through association and especially education, social mobility for all classes remained a possibility in Qing China—certainly more so than in, say, Tokugawa Japan. Ping-ti Ho has estimated that in the Qing period as a whole, nearly 40 percent of the highest degree holders (*jinshi*) came from families that had not produced an office holder or upper degree holder in the preceding three generations. But as Benjamin Elman indicates, Ho's figures "overlook or undervalue the number of commoners who had officials as relatives from collateral lines in a lineage or from affinal ties to other families."[33] In other words, great advantages redounded to commoners with the right kind of kinship and other connections. Nonetheless, representatives of all social classes in China continued to be attracted by the lure of the examinations until their abolition in 1905.

Even peasants and artisans hungered after the carrot of social mobility offered by the examination system. The vast majority, of course, had no real possibility of attaining the necessary formal education, which was overwhelmingly private in traditional China and beyond the financial reach of most of the population. As indicated briefly in chapter 3, private schools, local academies, and Confucian school temples were all closely associated with elite education, and they were normally sustained either by private tuition, private subscriptions, or official subsidies. The families of scholar-officials and rich merchants were naturally the principal beneficiaries of these educational institutions.[34]

At the same time, however, some educational opportunities did exist for the poor and disadvantaged in Qing China—notably charitable schools (*yixue*) and community schools (*shexue*) established by philanthropic individuals or local groups, and sometimes by the government. Although designed in part as a device for the ideological indoctrination of the lower classes (including ethnic minorities), such schools also provided the chance for latent academic talent to blossom. Apparently there were just enough Chinese-style Horatio Alger success stories to perpetuate a compelling social myth. In the somewhat idealistic formulation of Frederick Mote, "The belief in the active possibility of social mobility—perhaps even more than the actual statistical incidence of it—kept the different levels of cultural life coherent and congruent, if not truly identical in quality and character for each level of life was an active model to be imitated by the one below it."[35] In this view at least, the examinations served as a powerful vehicle for the preservation and transmission of China's Confucian cultural heritage.

In addition to the four major classes discussed earlier, several other social groups warrant mention. One was the regular Buddhist and Daoist clergy, reported to number in the hundreds of thousands. By late imperial times, Buddhism and Religious Daoism had lost virtually all of the economic and institutional power they had once possessed; only a few prominent monasteries still claimed substantial landholdings and large numbers of monks (four to five hundred). The great majority of the religious establishments in China Proper during the Qing period were small, poor, and weak.

Lacking adequate financial resources, Buddhist monasteries and Daoist temples provided few social services, aside from sponsoring occasional religious fairs and feasts and putting up pilgrims for the night. Although a number of monasteries and temples boasted libraries and even printing facilities, they played no significant role in the Chinese educational system. In fact, Buddhist books were not even used in the regular curriculum of Chinese schools. The primary function of Buddhist priests and nuns in Chinese society was to undertake various ceremonies and sacrifices connected with ancestor worship and to attend to certain other religious and personal needs of males and females, respectively. Fees for these services, together with solicited and unsolicited donations from pilgrims and lay people, sustained the Buddhist and Daoist establishment. The larger monasteries and temples also derived food and rent from their private landholdings.

In China Proper—as opposed to the situation in Tibet, Mongolia, and Manchuria (see chapter 7)—monks, priests, and nuns had little social standing and even less formal political influence.[36] Aside from a few comparatively well-educated abbots (*fangzhang*), most Chinese clergy seem to have been illiterate and uninformed. The majority came from lowly origins. Not a few had originally been sold or given to monasteries as children. An edict issued by the Qianlong emperor in 1739 conveys the throne's low opinion of most Chinese clerics:

> The ruling princes of old often issued decrees calling for the screening of [Buddhist] monks and Daoist priests. Certainly this was because there was indiscriminate mixture of the good and bad among the Buddhists and Daoists. Those among them who shut themselves [off] from the world to practice secretly the monastic discipline probably number but one or two in a hundred, while those who are idlers and loafers, joining the sangha [monastic community] under false pretenses just to seek for food and clothing, and those who are criminals . . . fearing punishment and concealing themselves to escape the clutches of the law, are probably countless.[37]

Monastic rules were often strict and detailed, but apparently seldom followed. And if monastic discipline became intolerable, priests and nuns found it very easy to return to lay life. Given the social composition and protective environment of monasteries and temples, it is not surprising that they occasionally became havens for gamblers, thieves, and vagabonds, as well as rallying points for disaffected members of Chinese society. The colorful history of Baoming temple, on the outskirts of Beijing in the Western Hills,

Figure 4.9.   Buddhist Monks
Source: Beinecke Rare Book and Manuscript Library, Yale University.

illustrates the way that heterodox beliefs and practices could survive in "or-thodox" institutional forms.[38]

   Although ideologically willing to tolerate Buddhism and Religious Daoism as doctrines that "encourage what is good and reprove what is evil" (in the words of the Jiaqing emperor), the Qing government greatly feared the po-tential political power of organized religion within China Proper. As a result, it imposed a number of restrictions on Chinese monastic life. Limitations were placed on the size of the clergy, the number of officially sanctioned monasteries and temples, and the scope of their religious activities. Abbots, monks, priests, and nuns were licensed by the Board of Rites and subject to indirect state supervision. The Qing government's administrative statutes contained a complete scheme of ecclesiastical gradations of rank and author-ity that conferred a kind of legitimacy on the religious establishment, but at the same time subordinated the church to the state and officialdom. The prin-cipal supervisory officials of the church, chosen by the local Qing authorities from among the leading abbots of each county and prefecture, were known as religious superiors (*Seng lu si* for Buddhists and *Dao lu si* for Daoists). These individuals provided the major link between China's secular authorities and the formal priesthood.

   Another prominent but disesteemed social group in Qing China was the hereditary Army of the Green Standard. Unlike the Banners, which the Manchus originally intended solely as a fighting machine, the Army of the Green Standard undertook a variety of diverse and often nonmilitary responsibilities. In addition to meeting the needs of national defense and internal security, soldiers from the Army of the Green Standard provided an escort service for state funds, provisions, and prisoners; guarded granaries, tombs, and city gates; carried out government postal functions; and stood ready to undertake other designated tasks, such as providing labor for public works projects. Unfortunately for the troops and the dynasty, the levels of pay, training, and general morale were low for common soldiers. Although officers of the middle grade and above were transferred regularly in the fashion of civil bureaucrats, the rank and file lived in designated garrison areas with their families for life. This arrangement had the advantage of placing soldiers in an environment in which social restraints might operate to keep the men under control, but it was precisely such a situation that bred vested interests and made it possible for underpaid and exploited soldiers to seek nonmilitary occupations in order to support their families.

Officers for the Army of the Green Standard were supposed to be chosen from successful candidates in the military examination system, which paralleled the civil service examinations in both levels and degrees. But the military examinations tested physical prowess and required almost no literary ability. Although military degrees brought official gentry status, they were disesteemed by scholars and not necessary for promotion within the army itself. In fact, most officers in the Qing military were not products of the military examination system, but rather men who had come up through the ranks. They, like their more esteemed counterparts in the civil bureaucracy, were divided into nine ranks, each distinguished by colored hat buttons, embroidered "mandarin squares," and other official regalia.

With the decline of both the Banner and the Green Standard armies by the end of the eighteenth century, mercenary armies known as *yong* (lit. braves) or *yongying* ("brave battalions") began to shoulder the dynasty's principal military burdens. These armies were organized along highly personalistic lines and usually commanded at the top by Qing civil officials. Comparatively well trained and well paid, *yong* and *yongying* recruits were heavily indoctrinated with Confucian morality. In the management and financing of such mercenary forces, local officials and their gentry advisers enjoyed considerable administrative leeway, but they were never beyond Beijing's reach. The throne's undiminished power of appointment and manipulation of empire-wide finances prevented the emergence of "warlordism" during the Qing period.[39]

At the very bottom of the social ladder, at least in the early Qing, were several groups of "demeaned people" (*jianmin*), as distinguished from respectable commoners or "good people" (*liangmin*). Included in this lowly and statistically rather insignificant category (at least in terms of the dominant Han culture)[40] were various slaves and indentured servants (such as the "tenant/servants" of Huizhou), entertainers, prostitutes, criminals, government runners, and certain regionally defined groups such as the Subei people of Shanghai, the shed people of the Yangzi Highlands (*bengmin*), the beggars of Jiangsu and Anhui (*gaihu*), the lazy or "fallen" people (*duomin*) of Zhejiang, and the boat people (*danhu*) of Guangdong. Members of these and related social groups suffered various forms of discrimination, from simple prejudice to unfavorable legal treatment. Until their partial "liberation" in the Yongzheng period, these demeaned people and their descendants could not take the civil service examinations or intermarry freely with ordinary commoners.[41]

As a rule, the Qing Code considered demeaned people (those of "low degree") to be subordinate as a class to ordinary commoners, just as commoners were subordinate to degree holders. It followed, then, that a crime committed by a demeaned person against a commoner had to be punished more severely than the same crime by a commoner against a demeaned person—just as a crime by a commoner against a degree holder brought more severe punishment than the same crime committed by a degree holder against a commoner. These stipulations applied to all kinds of relationships, in all sorts of circumstances, from the inflicting of bodily harm (including death) to theft, cursing, fornication, and marriage across class lines. In the case of demeaned people, for instance, there were carefully elaborated punishments in the Qing Code for such crimes as "Marriage between an Honorable and a Base Person" (article 115), "The Exchange of Blows between a Person of Honorable Degree and One of Low Degree" (article 313), "A Slave Striking the Head of a Household" (article 314), "A Slave Who Curses the Head of His Household" (article 327), and fornication between "Persons of Honorable and Base Condition" (article 373).[42] In accordance with the spirit of *li* (ritual), the relative class status of offender and victim was almost always a factor in determining penalties.

Yet despite the depressed legal status of *jianmin* and other servile status groups during much of the Qing period, a few opportunities for personal advancement did exist. Like lowly eunuchs at court, certain kinds of slaves and indentured servants came to acquire substantial power. This was certainly the case with imperial bondservants (Manchu: *booi*; Chinese: *baoyi*), such as the rich and famous Cao Yin (1658–1712), reading companion and trusted informant of the Kangxi emperor. But it was also true of some indentured servants (*jiaren*) and permanent attendants (*changsui*) attached to Chinese officials, who, like yamen runners, used their close association with government authority to protect personal investments or peddle influence. Some such servants acquired so much illicit power that they became known as "officials" (*tangguan*) themselves.

FORMS OF CHINESE SOCIOECONOMIC ORGANIZATION

The social groups described in the preceding section operated day to day within a complex network of relationships. The context of these relationships ranged from the formal structure of the state and the informal structure of various nonadministrative urban and rural systems to the clan and the nuclear family. The Qing government's attitude toward these informal institutions was characteristically ambivalent—at once supportive and suspicious—and always oriented strongly toward the concept of collective responsibility.

Theoretically, the state had nothing to fear from the family (*jia*), which it touted as the model for Chinese society at large. After all, the emperor acted as the father (*fu*) of his subjects (*zi*, lit. children); county magistrates were designated "father-mother officials" (*fumu guan*); and the Chinese people as a whole were considered to be one "large family" (*dajia*). The problem with the family system from the Qing government's point of view was that it tended to compete with the state for the loyalties of its members, and that it affected in fundamental ways the conduct of political as well as social and economic relationships.

The philosophical and religious assumptions that lay behind the Chinese family system will be discussed more fully in subsequent chapters. For now, it should suffice to outline the fundamental features of the system. The organization of the Chinese family was hierarchical, authoritarian, and patrilineal:

> Among the characteristic roles were those of the family head (*jiazhang*)—the senior male and the family's formal representative to the outside world—and the family manager (*dangjia*), who was in charge of the family work and earnings. Although there was a clear distinction between these two roles, in small families the father would have both; with his advancing age and increasing family size the position of family manager was frequently taken over by one of his sons. Brothers had equal rights to family property, the dominant form of ownership, but were also obligated to pool their earnings as long as the family remained intact. The distribution of this property among them was a key element in family division (*fenjia*), which also involved the setting up of separate kitchens for each of the new and now economically independent families.[43]

The theme of Chinese family life (and social life generally) was subordination: the individual to the group, the young to the old, and females to males. Kinship terminology, which reflected specific status rights and nonreciprocal

Table 4.2.   The Five Degrees of Mourning

Degree and Duration	Representative Relationships
1. *Zhancui* (3 years)	Mourning by a man for his parents By a wife for her husband and husband's parents By a concubine for her "husband" (master)
2. *Zicui* (1 year or less)	By a man for his grandparents, uncle, uncle's wife, spinster aunt, brother, spinster sister, wife, son, daughter-in-law (wife of firstborn), nephew, spinster niece, grandson (firstborn son of firstborn) By a wife for her spinster niece, husband's nephew, and husband's spinster niece By a married woman for her parents and grandparents By a concubine for her "husband's" principal wife, his parents, his sons (by the principal wife or other concubines), and her own sons Lesser period of mourning for great-great grandparents within the second degree
3. *Dagong* (9 months)	By a man for his married aunt, married sister, brother's wife, first cousin, daughter-in-law (wife of a younger son or son of a concubine), nephew's wife, married niece, and grandson By a wife for her husband's grandparents, husband's uncle, husband's daughter-in-law, husband's nephew's wife, husband's married niece, and grandson By a married woman for her uncle, uncle's wife, spinster aunt, brother, sister, nephew, spinster niece By a concubine for her grandson
4. *Xiaogong* (5 months)	Includes mourning by a man for his grand-uncle, grand-uncle's wife, spinster grand-aunt, father's first cousin, etc.
5. *Sima* (3 months)	Includes mourning by a man for his great grand-uncle, great grand-uncle's wife, spinster great grand-aunt, married grand-aunt, first cousin, grandfather's first cousin's wife, spinster first cousin of grandfather, etc.

Source: Adapted from Chai and Chai 1967. The last two degrees are especially complex and have been considerably abbreviated in the above chart. In all categories, the linkage is through the male line, so that "cousin" means only a father's brother's son, not a father's sister's son or daughter. Also, in practice the actual wearing of mourning clothes was generally considered a duty juniors owed seniors, rather than the reverse.

status obligations, was highly refined, with nearly eighty major kinship terms in general usage. The five basic degrees of mourning relationships (*wufu*), which extended outward in ever-widening circles, dictated ritual responsibilities within the family and also affected the legal decisions of the state.

In the absence of a well-developed system of protective civil or commercial law,[44] kinship bonds of blood, marriage, or adoption were the closest and most reliable ties in traditional Chinese society, even when the relationships were rather far removed from the nuclear family. For this reason, among others, nepotism was a common phenomenon in many urban and rural economic enterprises. We should not assume, however, that financial decisions were predicated only on good faith and benevolent paternalism. Even within the family, economic realities, including the diversification of family labor in response to ever greater competition for land, often made it necessary for households to draw up elaborate written agreements in order to provide for the smooth and efficient administration of family estates. The use of such documents within the family paralleled the employment of oral and written contracts in many other realms of Chinese social and economic life (see below). Significantly, popular encyclopedias such as the WBQS give considerable attention to various kinds of written contracts, including those for buying, selling, and renting land, animals, and other commodities.

Ideally, the Chinese nuclear family, which averaged a little over five persons in the Qing period, was a self-contained and self-sufficient social and economic unit. Extended families of three or more generations under one roof were comparatively rare in traditional China and confined almost exclusively to the well-to-do gentry class and rich merchants, who could afford to support a number of nonproductive family members and a large retinue of servants. Families with four or five generations living together enjoyed a great deal of social prestige and sometimes received ritual recognition from the state in the form of impressive memorial arches.

In both nuclear families and extended families, relatives were expected to live together in harmony. Responsibility for the care of the aged and infirm fell primarily on the family unit, which also disciplined and controlled its members. Social values were transmitted and reinforced by informal "family instructions" (*jiaxun*) of the following sort:

Follow parents
Unite with brothers
Love kinsmen
Teach sons
Provide for marriage
Maintain the dignity of the women's apartments
Punish malicious litigation
Be warned against prostitutes and gamblers
Establish a household head
Repair the ancestral temple
Establish ritual fields
Preserve ancestral graves.[45]

真　え
容　よう
圖　づ

Figure 4.10. Ancestral Portrait

Here we see a man worshipping a portrait of his ancestor. Notice the candle and flowers as well as the offerings of food. *Source:* Nakagawa 1799.

Figure 4.11.   Ancestral Display
Here, a father takes his son to inspect the elaborate offerings for a collective sacrifice on some special occasion. The ancestral tablets are housed in a cabinet at the top of the picture. The incense sticks have not yet been placed in the container situated immediately in front of the tablets. *Source:* Nakagawa 1799.

More formal family rituals (*jiali*)—which the state encouraged elites and commoners alike to follow—reinforced these social values. The enormous strength of the Chinese family system lay precisely in its multifaceted relationship with both religious and secular life.

One illustration of the complexity of this relationship can be seen in the practice of ancestor worship (also called "ancestor veneration;" for details see chapter 7). By late imperial times, domestic ancestor worship had become virtually a cultural universal in China. Even kinship-renouncing Buddhist monks were required by law to observe mourning rites for their parents. Enriched by Confucian, Buddhist, and Religious Daoist ideas, ancestor worship buttressed the Chinese family system not only by cementing social relationships and reinforcing status obligations, but also by fostering a profoundly conservative precedent mindedness at all levels of society. Important decisions within the family, whether made by peasants or by the emperor himself, required the "consent" of the ancestors, and all major social events were symbolically "shared" with them.

The policies of the Qing government were closely linked to the practice of ancestor worship. On the one hand, the state used negative sanctions to maintain order by addressing the most compelling concerns of the ancestral cult. Rebel leaders, for example, stood the chance of having their entire families wiped out and their ancestral tombs destroyed. Punishments such as mutilation of the body (a gift from one's ancestors) and banishment (detachment from the family and natal community) were clearly designed as deterrents to the filial minded. On the other hand, the state actively supported ancestor worship as a matter of Confucian conviction. Chinese officials were required to withdraw from duty for up to three years of mourning on the death of a parent (the requirement for Bannermen was far less stringent), and the Qing legal code even stipulated that criminals convicted of capital offenses might be allowed to receive a greatly reduced penalty and remain at home in order to continue family sacrifices if they were the sole male heirs of deceased parents.

Confucian family values mitigated the law in other significant ways. Punishments, for example, were meted out within the family system according to the five degrees of mourning. These relationships were based on the superiority of the senior generation over the junior generation and of the male over the female. Thus, a son who struck or beat a parent (degree 1 relationship) was liable to decapitation, irrespective of whether or not injury resulted, but no penalty applied to a parent who beat a son (degree 2b), unless the son died. Likewise, a wife who struck her husband (degree 1) received a hundred blows of heavy bamboo, but a husband who struck his wife (degree 2a) was punished only if he inflicted a significant injury—and then only if the wife personally lodged a complaint with the authorities. Perhaps the most astonishing feature of the Qing Code was its stipulation that accusations—even if true—by subordinate members of a family against their superiors would entail legal punishment for the reporter. The false accusation of a father by his son was punished by strangulation, but a true report (except in the case of treason or rebellion) still brought a penalty of three years' penal servitude plus one hundred blows of the heavy bamboo.[46]

Jonathan Spence's vivid reconstruction of the "Death of Woman Wang" illustrates some of the social variables that affected legal decisions in Qing dynasty China. In this celebrated case, a man named Ren killed his wife (née Wang) after she had an affair with another man and ran away from home. Ren then tried to blame the murder on a neighbor named Gao, who had earlier struck him in the face at a temple during an argument about Woman Wang. Spence summarizes the disposition of the case by county magistrate Huang Liuhong:

> By Qing law, both Ren and his father should have received the death penalty for falsely accusing an innocent person of a capital crime. But Huang found massive mitigating circumstances. In the first place, the father had known nothing about the crime; second, he was over seventy and Ren was his only son; third, Ren himself had no children, so the family line would certainly die out if he was executed; fourth, woman Wang had not followed the *dao* of a wife—she had betrayed her husband and had deserved to die; fifth, Ren had indeed been provoked in the temple by Gao, who should never have hit him.

The result was that Ren's father was exonerated, and Ren, instead of being executed, was sentenced to be beaten with heavy bamboo and forced to wear a portable stock or cangue (*jia*) around his neck for a long (and humiliating) period of time. Gao was ordered to pay for woman Wang's funeral expenses in order to placate her spirit and teach him "not to hit people in the face when he lost his temper."[47]

The family relationships expressed in Chinese ritual and law naturally extended into the lineage (*zong*) or, more generally, clan (*zu*), both of which reflected the social assumptions and organizational principles of the Chinese nuclear family. A lineage may be defined as an agnatic (patrilinear) descent group with an especially strong corporate character; the less precise term "clan" refers generally to a corporate organization composed of descent groups in which the agnatic links between the constituent units are "extremely remote and most likely fictionalized."[48] For the sake of simplicity, however, I have chosen here to use the more general term "clan" to refer to both types of corporate kinship.

Chinese clans varied widely in size, structure, and influence, but the largest might number as many as ten thousand members and possess enormous corporate wealth. Clan organizations tended to be largest and most highly developed in the southeast; well organized and widely distributed in the lower and central Yangzi provinces; and rather underdeveloped and thinly distributed in the northern provinces (see appendix C). Naturally enough, the social role of the clan differed substantially from place to place, but in both single-clan and multi-clan villages, kinship structures invariably affected the leadership and general tenor of village life.[49]

Clan organizations, dominated in the main by prestigious gentry families but composed of all social classes, undertook social responsibilities that lay beyond the capacity of the nuclear or simple extended family. These responsibilities included providing welfare services, maintaining local order, encouraging economic cooperation, and securing educational opportunities for clan members. The educational role of the clan was particularly important, both in perpetuating the notion of social mobility and in encouraging orthodox social values.

Clan charitable schools, sustained by revenue derived from clan property, gave poor but promising members the chance to acquire formal education. Part of the motive may have been Confucian altruism and the desire to give meaning to the Confucian dictum that "in education there are no class distinctions." More often than not, however, the motive was probably corporate self-interest. Success in the civil service examinations did, after all, bring prestige and usually wealth to the clan as a whole, making the investment in worthy candidates from any social class a wise one. Significantly, a number of clans expressly stipulated that educational priority be given to orphans and other poor clan members. In all, charitable schools provided one of the best opportunities in traditional Chinese society for disadvantaged individuals to acquire a formal education (see also chapter 10).

Clans did more than simply provide formal educational opportunities. They were also an important means of transmitting elite values to all classes of society within the clan. The principal device was clan rules (*zonggui*) compiled by the elite for the edification of all clan members. In the main they were Confucian in content, emphasizing family values, community harmony, ritual, respect, and self-control. Most clan rules included quotations from the classics, neo-Confucian writings, imperial injunctions (*shengyu*), and other inspirational sources. Although the Qing government officially charged bureaucrats, gentry, and "virtuous and reliable" community elders with the task of periodically lecturing to the Chinese populace on the imperial injunctions as part of its *xiangyue* or "community compact" system, it is clear that such exercises were often formalistic and ineffective, especially in the nineteenth century. Undoubtedly, regular lectures on the clan rules in clan meetings provided a much more effective channel for the communication of orthodox values to commoners, at least within the clan itself.

Hui-chen Wang Liu has shown that orthodox Confucian values were often adjusted in clan rules to conform more closely to the realities of Chinese everyday life, especially the outlook of commoners. She finds, for example, that many clan rules represented a creative blend of Confucianism, Buddhism, Daoism, and folk religion. Some rules advised members to read Buddhist or Daoist religious tracts, others cited Buddhist authority for sanction, and still others went so far as to allow Buddhist images to be placed next to ancestral tablets in the clan shrine. Through such forms of accommodation, the clan rules—like vernacular literature—provided a convenient meeting point between elite and popular culture.[50]

Clan solidarity and adherence to clan rules were based in part on the clan's ability to impose on its members punishments ranging from reprimands, fines, and suspension of privileges to corporal punishment, expulsion, and even death (although only the state could legally execute individuals). Clan heads (*zuzhang*) used the public format of clan meetings to exert enormous social pressure on members, censuring deviant behavior and rewarding adherence to group norms. Meritorious deeds might be publicly announced, recorded in special "books of virtuous clansmen," or commemorated by clan petitions to the government for honorary plaques or arches. Such plaques and other honors were displayed conspicuously in the ancestral temple, where clan meetings generally took place.

Collective ancestor worship unquestionably provided a strong sense of tradition, group cohesiveness, and conformity within the clan. The ancestral temple, which was usually the largest and most impressive clan building, was more than a mere meeting place; it also served as a constant and powerful reminder of the link between the dead and the living, the past and the present. Tiered rows of spirit tablets, sometimes numbering over a thousand, were organized by generations on the clan ancestral altar. Around them were the honorific plaques and moral exhortations left by clan forefathers that inspired moral behavior and promoted positive ambition among their posterity. In this environment many collective clan sacrifices and ceremonies took place on important occasions, such as the birth or marriage of clan sons, and on major festival days. These rites, and the clan feasts that followed, helped, in the words of C. K. Yang, "to perpetuate the memory of the traditions and historical sentiments of the group, sustain its moral beliefs, and revivify group consciousness. Through these rites and the presence of the group in its full numerical strength, the clan periodically renewed its sentiments of pride, loyalty, and unity."[51]

The state recognized the positive role of the clan in promoting orthodox values, providing social services, and maintaining local control. At the same time, however, it feared well-organized but nonofficial corporate entities. Thus, on the one hand, the Qing government willingly rewarded meritorious

clansmen and exhorted clans to compile genealogies and to establish ancestral shrines, clan schools, and charitable lands (*yitian*). On the other hand, it
sought whenever possible to make the clan system an adjunct of the official
baojia local control apparatus by requiring officially sanctioned clan officers
known as *zuzheng* (not to be confused with clan heads) to report on the affairs
of their respective clans to the county authorities.

Ultimately, the Qing government was as unsuccessful in imposing direct
control over Chinese clans as it was in exerting control over Chinese villages. This is not surprising because clans and villages were closely related
and held together with ties and loyalties that were not totally susceptible to
bureaucratic manipulation. Nonetheless, the throne and local bureaucrats
never abandoned their effort to limit the political and economic power of
clans and to closely supervise their social activities. For all the advantages of
clan organization as a self-regulating control mechanism, the particularism
of Chinese blood relationships could cause formidable political problems for
the state. The massive Taiping Rebellion in the mid-nineteenth century, for
example, which resulted in the loss of perhaps twenty million lives, had its
origins precisely in the endemic clan conflict of south China (see chapter 11).

Many disputes between clans, and social tensions more generally, stemmed
from economic causes. Often at issue were questions of land ownership, water rights, and related agricultural concerns. Arable land remained a scarce
and precious commodity in traditional China, and competition for it was
fierce. Qing official land records distinguished several kinds of land, including private land, banner land, military colony land, imperial estates, ritual
land, and so forth. In practice, most of the land in China was privately owned
and graded for tax purposes into over twenty separate classes. The Qing system of land tenure, based on a general freedom to buy and sell land, varied
from place to place, depending primarily on productivity. Factors such as
soil and climate, transportation facilities, and proximity to markets affected
terms of tenure, cropping practices, and the degree of reliance on subsidiary
occupations.

As indicated earlier, because the tendency of the state was to leave governance of the economy as much as possible to the private sector—and because
county magistrates generally proved willing to uphold written agreements—
contracts delineating economic and social responsibilities usually assumed
a written form in Qing dynasty China. Even in remote villages, written
documents governed matters such as the sale and rental of property, the
distribution of land rights, the hiring of labor, the pooling and redistribution
of resources, and the sale and indenture of human beings. Thus, despite the
weakness of the notion in China of "rule of law," there was still a respect for
certain kinds of legal instruments. In the words of Myron Cohen, throughout

the empire people "created, maintained, or severed relationships through contract, which was operative in family life . . . as well as in the wider social setting. The use of contract for instrumental purposes must therefore be seen as a fundamental feature of Chinese behavior in general." To the degree that Bannermen interacted with Chinese elites, merchants, artisans, and peasants, they, too, became part of the pervasive "contract culture" of China.[52]

Landlordism was especially prevalent in south China—not only because the land was more productive, but also because wealthy clans corporately owned so much property. As we have seen, in the absence of primogeniture in China, private landownings were often quickly broken up (contracts governed this process as well), but wealth derived from corporately owned property permitted many clans to acquire and maintain their economic power. Naturally enough, this power could generate intense rivalries. Thus, the Qianlong emperor remarked in 1766:

> The ritual land attached to the ancestral halls in the eastern part of Guangdong has frequently caused armed feuds [between clans]. . . . Ancestral halls are built and ritual land instituted normally for the purpose of financing the sacrificial rites and supplying the needs of the clansmen. If the land is used lawfully to consolidate and harmonize [kinship relations] . . . it is not a bad practice at all. But if [it induces people] to rely on numerical strength or financial power of their clans, to oppress their fellow villagers, or even worse, to assemble mobs and fight with weapons, . . . [such a practice] surely should not be allowed to spread.[53]

The Qing government's response to such abuses of power was to tighten bureaucratic supervision of clans, to punish clan leaders, and even to redistribute clan land.

Chinese landlords, whether individuals, clans, or other corporate entities, extracted rents in money or in kind (see table 4.3). These rents could amount to well over 50 percent of the yield, while official land taxes averaged only about 5 to 10 percent of the yield. In south China, fixed rents and generally longer leases encouraged farm improvements by tenants, but even in the north, increased inputs of labor allowed agricultural productivity to keep pace with population growth over the long run.[54] Landlord exploitation varied according to place and time, but as a rule it was most acute in periods of dynastic decline and in areas in which competition for land was most severe. Throughout most of the Qing period, absentee landlords were a distinct minority, and the physical proximity of peasants and elites, tenants and landlords, encouraged a certain qualified rapport (*ganqing*) between them.[55]

Although direct social contact between elites and commoners was minimal, both groups operated day to day within the shared context of a flourishing

Table 4.3. Some Estimates of Land Tenancy

Province	1880s Owners (%)	Tenants (%)	1920s/1930s Tenant households as a percentage of peasant households
Zhili	70	30	11
Henan			20
Shandong	60–90	10–40	16
Shanxi	70	30	16
Shaanxi			18
Gansu	70	30	18
Jiangsu	30–90	10–70	30
Anhui			43
Zhejiang	50	50	41
Hunan			41
Hubei	10–30	70–90	37
Jiangxi			39
Fujian	50	50	42
Guangdong			49
Guangxi			26
Sichuan			53
Guizhou	70	30	44
Yunnan			35
China as a Whole			32.1

Sources: C. L. Chang 1962 and Esherick 1981. For some estimates of the purchase price of land in Zhili and land rents in Henan during the 1810s, consult Naquin 1976, appendix B.

rural market system centered on one of forty thousand or more market towns (*zhen*) distributed throughout China Proper. These market towns were linked, in turn, to higher-level markets and finally to major commercial cities. Each basic market town served as the nucleus of a marketing "cell" that typically included between fifteen and twenty-five villages, averaging perhaps one hundred households (about five hundred persons) each. This "standard marketing community," comprising an area of perhaps twenty square miles, allowed all villagers within two or three miles of the town easy access to its periodic markets held every three days or so. In contrast to officially registered, licensed, and taxed markets at higher levels, lower-level markets generally supported only unlicensed petty brokers, who were self-regulated and self-taxed. Although most sellers (including peasants) at any standard market were likely to be itinerants, the standard market town normally possessed certain permanent facilities, including eating places, teahouses, wine shops, and at least a few shops selling basic items such as oil, incense and candles, looms, needles and thread, and brooms. Normally the town also supported a number of craftsmen and perhaps a few crude workshops for processing local raw materials.[56]

According to the economic historian Xu Tan, as early as 1800 there were already twice as many market towns in China as there had been in the mid-Ming period. The largest of these commercial centers during the High Qing had populations in excess of thirty thousand people, where great numbers of merchants, brokers, and shopkeepers "conducted business and used the large service sector, which consisted of tea and wine shops, money exchanges, tax payment offices, inns and hotels, pawnshops, and other mercantile establishments." As many as two hundred different kinds of commodities circulated in these large and vibrant commercial venues. In certain areas of China, such as the Jiangnan region, small towns that were only slightly larger than villages proliferated. These sites "had permanent markets attracting brokers and merchants from other areas who bought products and transshipped them to more distant markets."[57]

Standard marketing communities were, in the words of G. William Skinner, "the chief tradition-creating and culture-bearing units of rural China." Every few days, "the periodically convened local market drew to the center of social action representatives of households from villages throughout the system, and in so doing facilitated the homogenization of culture within the inter-village community." The standard market town was the major rural focus of extra-domestic religious life, recreation, social interaction, and conflict resolution. The marketing community contributed to the integration of local social groups, the standardization of local weights and measures, and linguistic unity. In some respects this only reinforced China's inveterate localism, but in others, as Skinner demonstrates, it promoted the spread of elite culture throughout much of Chinese society.[58]

One important reason was the cultural predominance of the gentry in nearly every market town. Landlords (or their agents) regularly dealt with tenant farmers in market towns, and on market days various gentry leaders and aspirants to local leadership "held court" in their favorite teahouses, publicly dispensing wisdom and solving local problems, such as disputes among peasants from different villages. In Skinner's words, the gentry class provided "*de facto* leadership within the marketing community *qua* political system" to which virtually every peasant, petty craftsman, and petty trader in traditional Chinese society belonged. Local villages might well be administratively self-sufficient, as James Hayes and others have ably shown, but to the extent that villagers participated in the traditional standard market system, they could scarcely avoid exposure to gentry cultural influences.[59]

In higher-level commercial centers, and especially walled cities, the urban ecology seems to have been characterized by two principal spheres of activity—one for merchants and the other for officials and gentry. Gentry and officials tended to reside and work in or near government yamens, Confucian school temples, and other educational centers, whereas merchants tended to be situated on or near major communication routes—locations determined more by transport costs than by convenience for consumers. It is difficult to know the full extent of Manchu–Chinese commercial interactions in the twenty or so urban centers where Banner garrisons were located. Generally speaking, however, the existence of a sizeable "Banner market" in these cities seems to have been a "positive factor in the local economy."[60]

But from the standpoint of the Manchus, there were two major problems. One was that in providing goods and services to Banner families, Chinese merchants often took financial advantage of them. The other was both economic and cultural: according to Manchu sources, Chinese entrepreneurs lured Bannermen into a lifestyle of decadence and debt. Listen to one outspoken critic:

> From all directions come Chinese drifting, looking to make a profit; they open all kinds of shops at places where the soldiers gather daily, on streets both large and small; they entice naïve Bannermen into their shops, and give them wine and liquor to drink, meat and victuals to eat, all on credit. Even if they are too afraid to go to brothels, they leave their women and children at home and go out with no-good servants looking to please their palates.[61]

This account goes on to state that when Chinese "businessmen" came to collect on the debts of Bannermen, they harassed and embarrassed them, "screaming and raging." And if the hapless Bannermen happened to come up short, the Chinese were not above setting upon them, stripping away their clothes, and stealing their weapons and gear.

Of course there was another side to the story, for Bannermen could also cause problems. In 1729, for instance, the Manchu lieutenant general at Xi'an, Cimbu, reported that the Bannermen there were "always grabbing more than they had paid for, cheating on the scales, squabbling and making threats [against the Chinese]."[62] Naturally enough, gentry and officials sought to distance themselves from all such disruptive activities and influences, whether caused by Han Chinese or Bannermen.

Sharpening the theoretical distinction between merchant and scholar-official spheres of activity in Qing cities was the general government prohibition that merchant shops should not be located too near to the local yamen lest they "spoil its dignity." In fact, however, the mutual commercial and cultural interests of well-to-do merchants and scholar-officials lessened the gap between the two spheres of activity in urban centers. Furthermore, although the style of life and range of diversions in Chinese cities could not possibly be matched in standard market towns, a striking feature of Chinese culture

Figure 4.12.   A Central Street in Beijing
Some of the people on this street are engaging in small-scale commercial activities, but most of them seem to be chatting, relaxing, sleeping, or watching games (probably chess). A few of them are beggars. Source: Beinecke Rare Book and Manuscript Library, Yale University.

in late imperial times was the lack of a sharp urban-rural dichotomy. Even at the beginning of the twentieth century, "The integrative features of [China's] late imperial polity and society were still present . . . and social changes had not yet produced an unbridgeable gap between modern urban centers and the countryside."[63] Of course William Rowe has a valid point in asserting that the Qing dynasty port city of Hankou was in many ways more like an early modern European city than a traditional Chinese one, and that differences in lifestyle between it and surrounding rural areas were therefore comparatively great. Moreover, he argues that Hankou shared "many social characteristics . . . [with other] important commercial cities throughout the [Chinese] empire." Yet as Rowe himself acknowledges, Hankou had no place in the dynasty's regular administrative hierarchy and was unique (or at least unusual) in a number of other respects.[64]

Comparatively speaking, most Chinese cities bore little resemblance to urban centers in the early modern West. One difference was certainly their cosmological symbolism, based solidly on *yinyang* and five agents correlations (see chapters 6 and 7). Another was the absence in China of religious structures comparable in size and importance to those in Western cities. Yet another was the general lack of class divisions in Chinese neighborhoods.

Furthermore, it appears that unlike early modern Europe, China's population growth occurred primarily in the countryside, not its cities. Also significant is the fact that no Chinese building was obviously datable by a particular period style. "Time did not challenge time in the eyes of a wanderer in a city street in traditional China. . . . No traditional Chinese city ever had a Romanesque or a Gothic past to be overlaid in a burst of classical renascence, or a Victorian nightmare to be scorned in an age of aggressive functionalism."[65]

During the Qing period as a whole, only about 25 percent of the gentry had permanent urban residences. Although in their capacity as officials members of the scholarly elite necessarily resided in urban areas, the majority came from the countryside and returned to the countryside upon retirement. With the exception of only a few commercial cities, such as Yangzhou, Hankou, and eventually Shanghai, no fundamental differences existed between urban and rural elites regarding basic family structure, housing, dress, eating and drinking habits, transport, and general cultural style. Many famous centers of learning were located in rural areas, as were great libraries and art collections. Just as there was no major gulf between the capital and the provinces in the cultural life of the Chinese elite, so there was no glaring cultural distance between the city and the countryside on the whole. Differences that did exist were primarily differences in degree or intensity rather than kind.

We do see, however, a distinct set of contrasting elite attitudes toward urban-rural relations. In office, Chinese scholars tended to emphasize the civilizing functions of the city; out of office, they esteemed the purity of the rural sector. Institutionally, the elite served predominantly public interests in one capacity and primarily private interests in another. Thus a gentry member might become an upright and incorruptible county magistrate outside his native place, but then return home to the countryside to use his bureaucratic influence and social status to obtain preferential treatment in taxation and to protect kinship interests. As Frederic Wakeman remarks,

> Local social organization . . . embodied contrary principles: integration into the imperial system and autonomy from it. The dynamic oscillation between these poles created the unity of Chinese society, not by eliminating the contradictions but by balancing them in such a way as to favor overall order. The balance was expressed in ideal terms as a Confucian compromise between Legalist intervention and complete laissez-faire.[66]

We can observe a similar balance in the Qing government's approach toward corporate organization in urban areas. Clan ties in Chinese cities were comparatively weak because many, if not most, influential urban residents were sojourners. There were, however, other social entities that embodied similar organizational principles, performed similar services, and posed similar problems to the state. Quite naturally the Qing government tried to control them, but predictably with less than complete success—especially as its power waned dramatically in the nineteenth century.

The most important of these organizations were guilds and religious temple associations.[67] Guilds went by a bewildering variety of names: *hang* (lit. lanes), *huiguan* (local lodges or *Landsmannschaften*), *gongsuo* (public associations), *bang* (cliques or subguilds), and so on. Some were simply units of professional affiliation (trade, crafts, or services); others were business organizations based on geographical affinity (*tongxiang*); still others were primarily hostels for sojourning scholars, officials, or merchants from the same areas. There were even local lodges (*huiguan*) for sojourning Bannermen. What studies of Chinese cities in the Qing period reveal, time and again, is not only the great variety of associational arrangements that existed within these urban centers, but also the public (*gong*)—as opposed to either bureaucratic (*guan*) or private (*si*)—functions that they increasingly assumed in the nineteenth century.

Guilds operated as self-governing corporate organizations, analogous in many respects to clans. Commercial guilds, for example, disciplined their members (individuals or businesses) through normative sanctions, fines, and the threat of expulsion; they sponsored business activity and regulated business practices; they mediated disputes among members; and they attempted, when possible, to resist excessive official pressure. Significantly, guild rules were often designed to preserve a stable economic environment by keeping outsiders out and limiting competition through control of prices and even regulation of quality. Guild revenues might be derived from contributions from corporately owned land and houses, rental income, interest from bank deposits, fines, dues, and levies.

Guilds performed a variety of important social functions. Some services were extended only to members, who joined the guild as a contractual act. These services included financial support for individuals and families that had fallen on hard times, family-style burial services and cemeteries for those who died away from home, and sponsorship of feasts and other celebrations. In addition, guilds and other associations—sometimes in combination—often provided services for the wider urban community, such as local policing, fire fighting, disaster relief, welfare (for orphans, the aged, and the poor), health care, education, and local defense. Their efforts paralleled and complemented clan-supported and independent gentry-supported social services in both rural and urban areas—services that were more extensive than generally supposed.[68]

The Qing government naturally applauded and encouraged the self-regulation and social service of guild organizations. At the same time, however, it made every effort to limit the scope of their power. One means was by supervising and attempting to directly control certain spheres of Chinese economic activity. The principal device was a system of formal and informal licensing, which allowed Qing bureaucrats to extend monopoly rights to individual entrepreneurs or to guilds for a fee. Sometimes these monopolies were official and comprehensive in scope, such as the so-called Co-hong [*Gonghang*] monopoly on foreign trade at Canton; other arrangements were local and contingent on personal ties and informal agreements. The monopoly mentality was widespread in Chinese economic life. In John Fairbank's memorable words, "The incentive for innovative enterprise, to win a market for new products, had been less than the incentive . . . to control a market by paying for an official license to do so. The tradition in China had not been to build a better mousetrap but to get the official mouse monopoly."[69]

The Qing government relied on guild cooperation for the collection of commercial taxes, but guilds depended on official support for commercial success. Although the detailed regulation of much of Chinese trade and industry, as well as the adjustment of disputes within these spheres, fell to organizations of merchants and craftsmen, the guilds were licensed by the state, subject to bureaucratic supervision, and always susceptible to official exploitation. Even in the absence of official pressures, guilds frequently called on the local Qing authorities to validate their rules and occasionally to assist in enforcing them. Undoubtedly urban gentry members involved in trade acted periodically as intermediaries between merchants and officials, helping to bridge the gap between commercial and bureaucratic points of view.

Religious temples in cities and towns were often closely linked with guilds and other common-interest organizations such as *hui* (associations) and *tang* (lodges). These societies—whether bound by ties of kinship, surname, home area, profession, scholarly interest, religious outlook, or simply mutual aid—patronized a particular deity, or deities, that protected their own special interests and also promoted the general welfare of people living and working in the sphere of the deity's specific "jurisdiction" (see chapter 7). One common focus for such religious patronage was the local Lord of the Earth (*Tudi gong*). Devotion to this deity involved a degree of community participation as well as special interest: neighborhood guilds, associations, and lodges often shared responsibility not only for local sacrifices and general upkeep of his temple or shrine, but also for local security, neighborhood cleanup and ritual purity, and occasional entertainment such as dramatic presentations and feasts. Religious activity in these urban organizations transcended the particularism of Chinese society more effectively than did ancestor worship in clan organizations, but it was not free from risks.

The state paid close attention to the religious activities of *hui* and *tang*. From the Qing government's standpoint (and often in fact), a thin line separated "legitimate" associations and lodges from the subversive secret societies that often went by the same generic names. In Qing times there was no Chinese equivalent for the Western term "secret society." Traditionally, the expressions *jiaomen* ("sects") and *huitang* ("association lodges") were used to refer to potentially threatening politico-religious cults. In such usage, sects were identified primarily with peasant-based religious organizations in north China, while association lodges were linked more closely with politically oriented organizations in the south based on declassed elements from both urban areas and the countryside.

In general, Chinese secret societies may be defined as associations whose policies were characterized by some form of religious, political, or social dissent from the established order. When dissent became disloyalty, members of such organizations were condemned as heretical (*xie*) and branded bandits (*fei*). The Qing Code (article 162) specified that leaders of "heretical organizations" were to be strangled and their accomplices to receive one hundred blows of heavy bamboo and banishment to a distance of three thousand *li* (about one thousand miles). Although some groups, such as the millenarian, anti-Manchu White Lotus sect (which is mentioned expressly in article 162), seemed especially threatening, heresy was a relative concept—in practice defined by the Qing government more in political and ritual terms than in ideological or theological terms (see also chapter 7).[70]

It would certainly be a mistake to underestimate the subversive character of certain sectarian associations, notably those of the Triad and White Lotus type. Yet in traditional China, even the most heterodox organizations were susceptible to domestication. Philip Kuhn warns against distinguishing "too sharply between . . . [orthodox and heterodox organizations] on grounds of supposed ideological differences"; and as if to underscore Kuhn's point, Frederic Wakeman suggests that the transformation of Zhu Yuanzhang from sectarian leader into founder and first emperor of the Ming dynasty may well have been "eased by certain ideological similarities between rebel heterodoxy and Confucian orthodoxy."[71] Perhaps such ideological affinities, including shared ritual symbols and assumptions, may help explain the endurance of the dynastic system in the face of frequent sectarian uprisings.

In any case, during the heyday of the dynasty, Qing social institutions operated efficiently on the whole. To be sure, not everyone benefitted equally from these institutions. Even during the "High Qing," commoners often petitioned the government for famine relief. There were also a great number of complaints about arbitrary and excessive state interventions against "illicit activities."[72] But overall there seems to have been considerable geographic and social mobility as well as a substantial amount of elite-commoner rapport within the traditional land system and market structure. The markets and fairs that brought merchants from dispersed places to a common center "fostered cultural exchange among local systems within the trading area in question," while the travels of successful scholars to far-flung places "increased their social and cultural versatility and enlarged the cultural repertoire from which they could draw upon their return home." Within their wider local market community, peasants were exposed to customs, values, and exogenous norms originating not only in other villages like their own but also in cities—cultural elements "drawn not only from other little traditions but also from the great tradition of the imperial elite." In contrast to many other traditional "peasant communities," local systems in rural China were wide open when the dynasty was at its peak. Social and cultural integration in both the rural and urban sectors was substantial.[73]

But in periods of dynastic decline, local communities in China began to close up. Resistance to exogenous cultural influences arose, and economic closure ensued. Local society became increasingly militarized, and tensions increased between elites and commoners. A *sauve qui peut* mentality prevailed. Urban-rural and gentry-peasant friction increased as gentry power grew, and landlords began to flee the countryside for the relative security of the cities, leaving rent collection in the hands of impersonal bursaries (*zuzhan*). The rapport that had existed between landlords and tenants in better times could not possibly be maintained under such circumstances. Social services probably declined in quality and number. The state used its coercive power more ruthlessly and perhaps more arbitrarily. This was the unhappy situation that Westerners encountered and described in nineteenth- and early twentieth-century China. It had not always been so.[74]

Chapter Five

Language and Symbolic Reference

The "official" languages of the Qing dynasty—Manchu, Chinese, and Mongolian (and to a degree, Tibetan)—reflect the deliberate multiculturalism of the regime. Pragmatically speaking, each language became a political tool, a means of administering different parts of a vast and variegated empire. But there was more to the matter than this. The use of multiple languages also enabled the Qing rulers to gain access to different cultural traditions and to consider different ways of thinking about their world, thus enhancing their cultural repertoire without diminishing their own strong sense of ethnic identity. This is where arguments about "sinicization" often go wrong. The Manchus did not become "Chinese" in any simple sense. Indeed, they relentlessly championed their martial heritage and remained highly critical of the "softness" of Chinese "civil" culture.[1] They did, however, draw on aspects of Chinese tradition that they found useful and/or interesting, in the same basic way that people in the contemporary world tap into global cultural currents. Culture is not a zero sum game.

It is true, of course, that over time most Manchus in Banner garrisons lost their ability to speak or write Manchu; this, in fact, had been a constantly reiterated fear of the first several Qing rulers—the Qianlong emperor in particular. And yet, as we have seen (and shall see again), Qianlong was an enthusiastic patron and practitioner of the Chinese arts, including painting, calligraphy, and poetry. What is often forgotten is that the emperor also appreciated a wide variety of Inner Asian cultural traditions as well, and not just those stemming from his own Manchu heritage. He enjoyed, for example, Tibetan art and architecture, and embraced Tibetan Buddhism. Furthermore, he was fluent not only in spoken and written Chinese, but also in spoken and written Manchu and Mongolian, and he knew some Tibetan and Central

Asian languages as well. Multilingualism, as with other forms of multiculturalism, did not deprive the emperor of his identity as a Manchu.

Although the primary focus of this chapter is on the use of the Chinese
language in China Proper, we should bear in mind that all the languages of
the Qing—including Chinese—were constantly interacting and evolving,
borrowing from one another in interesting and complicated ways.[2] James
Millward provides a fascinating example of how the four main languages of
the empire intersected and overlapped with respect to a commonly employed
ancient Chinese phrase, *huairou yuanren* 懷柔遠人, which referred generally
to China's treatment of foreigners who came to China from distant places.
As Millward's analysis makes clear, the term *huairou* was understood—with
intentional ambiguity perhaps—by the multilingual Manchus as the act of
"cherishing," "caressing," and "taming" people from afar.[3]

Comparatively little research has been done on exactly how Chinese and
the other languages of the empire evolved under the Qing, but we do know
that, as in earlier (and later) periods of Chinese history, the Han people under
the Manchus appropriated a number of words and expressions from other
languages, both within and outside of China's borders. For instance, several
Manchu terms, such as *sacima* (Chinese: *saqima* 薩其馬; a pastry made of
fried noodles, honey, and butter), found their way into the Chinese spoken
and written language via transliteration. There is also evidence to suggest
that the Manchu language may have influenced the development of certain
grammatical forms in Chinese.[4] Although the Chinese and the Manchus used
very different principles in naming their young, we know that a number of
Chinese Bannermen adopted Manchu names—even in the face of predictable
criticism by the Qing authorities.[5]

A good number of non-Banner civil and military officials learned Manchu,
as did many Jesuits and other missionaries in Qing times. Furthermore, nineteenth-century versions of Chinese encyclopedias such as the WBQS include
special sections (*men*) on Manchu terms, organized topically by conventional
categories. For instance, under the category "Heavenly Patterns" (*Tianwen
men*) in an 1828 edition, we find Chinese characters for the sky, sun, moon,
stars, clouds, and such, followed by their equivalents in the phonetic Manchu
script. Similar entries appear in categories such as "Earthly Configurations"
(*Dili men*), "Seasonal Terms" (*Shiling men*), "Clothing" (*Yifu men*), "The
Body" (*Shenti men*), "Buildings" (*Guanshi men*), "Implements" (*Qiyong
men*), "Food and Drink" (*Yinshi men*), "Fruits" (*Guopin men*), "Military
Stores" (*Junqi men*), etc. The WBQS gives no reason for including this information, but we can safely assume that the compiler(s) believed that it had
some value in Sino-Manchu social and economic interactions.

By the same token, transliterations of Chinese words and terms became a
part of spoken and written Manchu, especially in places affected by Chinese

commerce and/or settlement.[6] Prior to the Qing conquest of China, the famous translator Dahai (d. 1632) modified the evolving Manchu written script in order to take into account certain important Chinese sounds. This made it easier for the Manchus to appropriate loanwords from the Chinese. Some of these borrowed sounds were derived from the Chinese names for titles, weights and measures, proper names, administrative terms, and so forth. For instance, the Chinese character pronounced *gong* 公 ("duke") became the word *gung* in Manchu, just as the character pronounced *fuzi* 夫子 ("master") became *fudzy*.

The same process was used in the borrowing of Chinese philosophical terms. For example, one of the common Chinese expressions for devotion to parents and elders, *xiaoshun* 孝順, became the Manchu root word *hiyoosun* ("filial piety"). As in the case of Chinese terms borrowed by the Koreans, Japanese, and Vietnamese, we can usually assume that when we encounter sounds in Manchu that are based on Chinese pronunciations, the appropriated word(s) had no satisfactory counterpart in the indigenous language.[7] At times during the Qing period—especially under the Qianlong emperor—the court tried to purge the Manchu language of words borrowed from Chinese, but this effort failed.[8]

The development in China Proper of a unique "women's script" (*nüshu* 女書), mentioned briefly in chapter 4, provides another indication of creative linguistic adaptation. This predominantly phonetic form of writing, which included a great many non-Han lexical items in its basic syllabary of about one thousand characters, reflects a local form of speech known as "southern Hunanese" (*Xiangnan tuhua*). About half of the "characters" in this script are derived from Chinese—several dozen of which have remained essentially unchanged. But the vast majority of these borrowed words are used for their phonetic value, not their semantic meaning (see below). The emergence of this written language in the nineteenth century provided southern Hunanese women with a unique vehicle for the expression of their thoughts and feelings in a form that was completely inaccessible to men, and not surprisingly, many of the protagonists in these ballads are strong and capable women.[9] One might add that *nüshu* bears certain resemblances to other written scripts developed by ethnic groups in various parts of China—for example, the colorful hybrid writing of the Shui people in Guizhou province.[10]

By far the most significant way in which the Chinese language influenced Manchu culture was through translation. As indicated briefly in chapter 2, even before the Qing conquest, Nurhaci and Hong Taiji had already recognized the need to render certain Chinese works into Manchu. This was one of the early functions of the offices known as Translation Bureaus.[11] Among the most important documents rendered into Manchu were the Four Books and the Five Classics, including, of course, the hallowed *Yijing* 易經 or

Classic of Changes. The *Changes* had long been considered "the first of the [Confucian] classics," and no Qing scholar—Manchu, Mongol or Chinese—could hope to have any significant intellectual standing in China without a command of this cryptic and challenging work. No doubt one of the reasons that the Jesuit missionary Joachim Bouvet (1656–1730) became such a close and trusted adviser to the Kangxi emperor was, in fact, their shared interest in the *Changes*.[12]

The *Yijing*'s system of sixty-four six-line symbols (generally known as hexagrams; *gua*)—although not a language in the formal sense—nonetheless exerted a profound influence on Chinese thought and discourse throughout the imperial era. It explicated meaning through devices such as numerical symbolism, colorful metaphors, and words that were "indirect but hit the mark" (*qu er zhong*). During the Qing period a great many Chinese (and Manchu) scholars wrote tracts on the *Changes*, and a number of Manchu-language copies of this work, some with extensive handwritten annotations, are still extant. Scholars argued endlessly over every aspect of the text, scrutinizing each word and each graphic symbol in search of ever-deeper meanings. Although interpretations of the work tended to follow scholarly fashions (see chapter 6), the aim of most Qing intellectuals was not merely philological, for they all believed to some extent that the *Yijing* held the key to an understanding of the entire universe. For this reason they unquestioningly accepted the notion that Confucius had broken the bindings of his copy three times in assiduous study.

DISTINCTIVE FEATURES OF THE CHINESE LANGUAGE

As with Qing political and social institutions, the Chinese language exemplifies both the diversity and the unity of traditional Chinese culture. On the one hand, the spoken language was fragmented into at least a half dozen mutually unintelligible regional dialects (*diqu fangyan*), each of which had any number of local variants (*difang hua or tuhua*). On the other hand, the standard written language could be understood by anyone who had mastered it, regardless of the dialect he or she spoke. Over time, and on balance, the unifying features of the language outweighed the divisive ones. Of the various regional dialects in Qing China, the most widespread and significant was Mandarin or *guanhua* (lit. the speech of officials). In Qing times at least 70 percent of the population spoke some version of this "official" dialect as their native tongue, as is still the case today. For this reason, among others, the Chinese words transliterated in this book have been rendered according to their Mandarin pronunciation. The other major regional dialects of the Qing period were (and are), in descending order of numerical incidence: Wu (spoken in the provinces of Jiangsu and Zhejiang), Yue (also known as Cantonese), Xiang (Hunan dialect), Kejia (Hakka, spoken primarily in Guangdong, Guangxi, and southern Fujian), Southern Min (Amoy dialect; also known in more recent times as "native Taiwanese"), Gan (Jiangxi dialect), and Northern Min (Fuzhou dialect). According to an article by the linguist Xu Shirong, the differences among these dialects, taken as a whole, are roughly 20 percent in grammar, 40 percent in vocabulary, and 80 percent in pronunciation.[13] In addition, they vary in their use of tones (*shengdiao*) from four in Mandarin to almost a dozen in Cantonese.

In the Qing period, native speakers of Mandarin predominated in most of north, west, and southwest China. But even in non-Mandarin speaking areas (primarily the provinces of Zhejiang, Fujian, Guangdong, and Guangxi), scholars had every incentive to learn the Mandarin dialect because it served as the lingua franca of Chinese administrators. During the Kangxi period, the emperor ordered the governors of Guangdong and Fujian to establish schools for instruction in Mandarin so that officials coming from these areas would be able to communicate more effectively in audience, and eventually the entire Qing system of official schools was limited to candidates already fluent in Mandarin. But neither these measures nor any others eliminated the problem of verbal communication at the local level. Because the rule of avoidance prohibited officials from serving in their home areas, they often did not speak the dialect of the region in which they served. Legal proceedings were thus conducted empire-wide in Mandarin, with the awkward result that the remarks of Qing magistrates often had to be rendered by "translators" into the local dialect, and local testimony, in turn, into Mandarin.

Despite some regional peculiarities, the grammatical principles of spoken Chinese were (and are) the same, regardless of dialect. The basic semantic units (morphemes) of spoken Chinese are monosyllabic sounds, some of which have meaning by themselves and others of which have meaning only in combination with other monosyllables. For each syllable (with only a few exceptions), a written character exists, but knowledge of the character is not, of course, necessary for comprehension of everyday speech. The common feature of all major Chinese dialects is that they are not inflected for person, tense, or number. Many words can function unchanged as nouns, verbs, or adjectives, depending on their position in a sentence. Thus, context and word order are of crucial importance.

In Mandarin, there are only a little more than four hundred individual sounds, resulting in a great number of homophones. Even with the use of four separate tones as a means of differentiation, there are still many words with precisely the same pronunciation and tone. One playful Chinese linguist, Zhao Yuanren (Yuen Ren Chao), has written an entire short story of more than ninety characters using only words pronounced *shi* ("A history of the lion eater named Mr. Shi" 施氏食獅史). Although perfectly clear in writing, it makes absolutely no sense when read aloud. Through the use of various linguistic devices, including the joining of related morphemes (such as *yi* 衣 and *fu* 服, both of which mean clothing) to form the standard compound for clothes (*yifu* 衣服), Chinese—like any mature spoken language—can express virtually any idea with full clarity. Nonetheless, the Chinese have long prized the ambiguity of their language, its musical rhythm and tone, and its marvelous capacity for rhymes and puns.

Not surprisingly, Chinese scholars have traditionally devoted much attention to phonology. During the Qing period, phonological research flourished, beginning with the study of rhymes in classics such as the *Shijing* (Classic of poetry) and *Yijing*, but progressing to the study of phonetic changes in the Chinese language over time and in different regions, and eventually extending to an analysis of the human voice itself. Most of the great phonological achievements of the Qing period were made by exponents of the school of learning associated with Dai Zhen (1724–1777) and Duan Yucai (1735–1815), but the critical questioning and careful scholarship of this school had its Qing intellectual antecedents in the scholarship of Gu Yanwu (1613–1682), whose valuable writings include an extremely influential collection titled *Yinxue wushu* (Five books on phonology).

The study of phonology was only part of a broader scholarly interest in linguistics during the Qing. Although some noteworthy studies, such as Dai Zhen's *Fangyu shuzheng* (Commentary on the *Dialects*), were concerned primarily with speech and sounds, the major focus of Qing scholarship was on the classical written language, known as *wenyan wen* 文言文 ("patterned words"). From Zhou times to the Qing, this literary language served as the primary vehicle for the transmission of China's entire cultural tradition. Throughout the imperial era, familiarity with the classical language in effect defined the Chinese elite. No attribute was more highly prized, none brought greater prestige or social rewards, and none was more closely linked with moral cultivation and personal refinement. In the minds of most Chinese intellectuals, "writing" was "culture."

The term *wenyan wen* refers to an extremely terse and evocative style of writing found in the great philosophical texts of the Zhou dynasty—notably the Four Books and Five Classics of Confucianism, but also a number of other highly influential works; hence the term "classical Chinese." Considerable debate exists over the precise relationship between this ancient written language and the patterns of early Chinese speech, but it is safe to say that by Han times at the latest, and from that point onward into the twentieth century, a significant social gap separated the "elegant" (*ya*) classical language from the "vulgar" (*su*) written forms of "plain" vernacular speech (*baihua wen* 白話文).[14]

Although vernacular writing and classical Chinese both drew on the same basic repository of characters (*zi* 字; written words), they employed them in very different ways. Derk Bodde provides an apt illustration (see "Mencius Meets King Hui"). He compares a famous classical passage from the Confucian philosopher Mencius with a standard vernacular equivalent in order to show the great syntactical and stylistic differences that separate the two types of media. The classical text, for example, requires only twenty-four characters to express what the vernacular version says in thirty-eight. Moreover, these two versions have a mere thirteen characters in common—five of which occur in proper names. Aside from these names, all the rest of the classical characters are monosyllables. By contrast, the vernacular equivalent employs five dissyllabic compounds to provide the clarity necessary for communicating the meaning in actual speech.[15] The great prestige of the classical language during imperial times derived in part from the fact that it was not accessible through everyday speech.

MENCIUS MEETS KING HUI

Classical original from Mencius: 孟子見梁惠王。惠王曰：叟不遠千里而來。亦將有以利吾國乎？ Mencius had an interview with King Hui of [the state of] Liang. King Hui said: Venerable sir, you did not find a thousand *li* a far distance to come. Do you also have something of benefit to my country?

A vernacular rendering of the same: 孟子謁見梁惠王。惠王說。老先生，您不辭千里長途的幸勞前來；那對我的國家會有很大利益吧？

In the Qing, as in earlier periods, Chinese characters had a magical, mystical quality, presumably deriving from their ancient use as inscriptions on oracle bones and on bronze sacrificial vessels. Many Qing scholars traced Chinese writing to the revered *Yijing*. So venerated was the written word that anything with writing on it could not simply be thrown away but had to be ritually burned. One well-informed foreign observer during the late Qing wrote:

They [the Chinese] literally worship their letters [that is, characters]. When letters were invented, they say, heaven rejoiced and hell trembled. Not for any consideration will they tread on a piece of lettered paper; and to foster this reverence, literary associations employ agents to go about the street, collect waste paper, and burn it on an altar with the solemnity of a sacrifice.[16]

These altars, known as *xizi ta* 惜字塔 (pagodas for cherishing the written word), could be found in virtually every city, town, and village in traditional China. Today only a few exist—one of them in the town of Xitan in northern Taiwan.

The special reverence attached to Chinese writing may be illustrated in a variety of other ways. During the Qing period an official could be degraded for miswriting a single character in a memorial to the throne, and stories of the political and personal consequences of using taboo or even vaguely suggestive characters are legion. During the Yongzheng reign, for instance, an official named Zha Siting (1664–1727) was imprisoned for selecting a classical phrase for the provincial examinations in Jiangxi province that contained two characters similar in appearance to those of the emperor's reign title if the top portions had been cut off (雍正 was the emperor's reign name, and 維 and 止 were the first and last characters of the classical phrase 維民所止). The choice of this line (from the *Classic of Poetry*; see chapter 6) was interpreted as expressing the wish that the emperor would be decapitated. Zha died in prison, and orders were given for his body to be dismembered.[17]

In Qing popular culture, written characters had a special kind of magical potency. Prayers were often written and then burned as the most efficacious way of communicating with the gods. Protective charms, designed to be hung inside the home or workplace, often consisted only of a single character (or group of characters) with positive associations, such as "advance" 進, "peace" 安, "wealth" 富, "blessings" 福, etc. Auspicious "spring couplets" (*chunlian* 春聯), printed on red paper and displayed on the outside of virtually all Chinese households and businesses during the lunar New Year, had the same basic purpose. On the other hand, many Chinese believed that a piece of paper with the character "to kill" 殺 on it, or one that bore the word for a poison, a disease, a destructive animal, or an evil spirit actually had the capacity to harm another person.[18]

The prestige of calligraphy as an art form (see chapter 8) enhanced the value of the written word in China. Quite apart from "spring couplets," calligraphic inscriptions of one sort or another appeared everywhere in traditional Chinese society—from the outside of official buildings, temples, and commercial establishments to homes and landscape gardens. Deceased ancestors were usually remembered with written tablets rather than images, and calligraphic scrolls adorned every gentry study. Esteem for the written word may even help explain the extraordinary reliance placed on written contracts of all sorts in Qing dynasty China, from agreements over the hiring of labor and the distribution of land rights to negotiations surrounding marriage, concubinage, and adoption (see chapters 4 and 10).

From a scholarly standpoint, Qing intellectuals looked on the literary language as "a gateway to the classics," and they were profoundly devoted to it. In addition to works on phonology, the Qing period witnessed a proliferation of linguistic studies on ancient lexicons such as the *Shuowen jiezi* 說文解字 (Analysis of characters as an explanation of writing), as well as the creation of new dictionaries and other etymological and philological research aids. One outstanding achievement was the imperially commissioned *Kangxi zidian* 康熙字典 (Kangxi dictionary), ordered in 1710 and completed about five years later. This work, which became the standard Chinese dictionary for the next two and a half centuries, begins with a quotation from the *Yijing*: "The Great Commentary says, 'In ancient times people knotted cords in order to govern. The sages of a later age used written documents instead to govern officials and supervise the people.'"[19] This quotation testifies to the political importance attached to the written word in China from time immemorial.

Chinese scholars have generally distinguished six major types of Chinese characters: (1) representations of objects (*xiangxing* 象形); (2) indicative characters (*zhishi* 指事), whose forms indicate meaning; (3) grouped elements (*huiyi* 會意) that suggest meaning through the relationship of concepts; (4) semantic and phonetic combinations (*xingsheng* 形聲); (5) "borrowed" words (*jiajie* 假借); and (6) "turned" or "transformed" characters (*zhuanzhu* 轉注). (For examples of each, see below.) H. G. Creel points out that many of the characters designated *jiajie* or *zhuanzhu* may also belong to one or more other word classes and that these two groups are themselves "so obscure that nearly two thousand years of discussion have not produced an agreement, among Chinese scholars, even as to the fundamentals of their application."[20] Chung-ying Cheng contends, however, that the principles of phonetic borrowing and semantic extension expressed in these two categories reflect the inherent capacity of the Chinese written language for expressing deep, multidimensional philosophical meaning.[21]

TYPES OF CHINESE CHARACTERS

1. Representations of objects (*xiangxing*): 人 ("person") 口 ("mouth") 口 ("enclosure") 日 ("sun") 月 ("moon") 子 ("child") 宀 ("roof") 手 (hand)
2. Indicative characters (*zhishi*): 上 ("up") 下 ("down") 至 ("arrive"; an arrow hitting a target) 高 ("tall"; the picture of a building)
3. Grouped characters (*huiyi*): 木 ("wood"), together with 斤 ("axe"), becomes 析 ("to split" or "to analyze")

4. Semantic-phonetic combinations (*xingsheng*): 言 ("words," the semantic element), together with 公 ("public," used here only for its phonetic value, pronounced *gong*), becomes 訟 ("litigation" or "contention," pronounced *song*)

5. Borrowed" words (*jiajie*): 萬 ("scorpion," used for the word "ten thousand" because it had the same sound, *wan*)

6. "Transformed" characters (*zhuanzhu*): 布 ("cloth," used by extension to mean "money" because it was a unit of exchange)

By far the largest class of Chinese characters is that of semantic and phonetic combinations, sometimes called phonograms. Perhaps 90 percent of the lexical items in the *Kangxi Dictionary* are characters of this type. Each has a semantic indicator or "radical" (*bushou* 部首; often originally the representation of an object) and a phonetic element, which can usually stand alone as an individual character with its own set of meanings. The phonetic element indicates the way a written word is probably pronounced, while the radical suggests the category of phenomena to which the word belongs. These categories include animals (humans and other mammals, reptiles, birds, fish, and mythical beasts such as dragons); parts of animals; minerals; natural phenomena and physical formations; structures; utensils; descriptives (colors, shapes, smells, and so on); and actions.[22]

SOME COMMON RADICALS

一 *yi* (one) 二 *er* (two) 大 *da* (great) 女 *nü* (woman) 山 *shan* (mountain) 弓 *gong* (bow) 心 *xin* (heart/mind) 木 *mu* (wood) 水 *shui* (water) 火 *huo* (fire) 玉 *yu* (jade) 目 *mu* (eye) 竹 *zhu* (bamboo) 糸 *si* (silk) 羊 *yang* (sheep) 肉 *rou* (meat) 色 *se* (color) 艸 *cao* (grass) 衣 *yi* (clothing) 虎 *hu* (tiger) 行 *xing* (moving) 言 *yan* (speech) 車 *che* (cart) 門 *men* (door) 雨 *yu* (rain) 青 *qing* (green) 飛 *fei* (flying) 食 *shi* (food) 首 *shou* (head) 馬 *ma* (horse) 鳥 *niao* (bird) 魚 *yu* (fish) 鼎 *ding* (vessel) 龍 *long* (dragon)

Not all 214 radicals are equally helpful in indicating the basic orientation of a given Chinese character, but most provide fairly reliable and sometimes quite revealing clues. We find, for instance, that the "boat" radical (*zhou* 舟), together with the phonetic element *fang* 方 (lit. "square"), represents the idea of a "barge" or "galley" (舫; pronounced *fang* in the third tone). The same phonetic joined with the "speech" radical (*yan* 言) means "to ask" or "to invite" (訪; pronounced *fang* in the third tone). Together with the "door" or "household" radical (*hu* 戶), the phonetic 方 yields the character for a "room" or "house" (房; pronounced *fang* in the second tone). Dozens of other examples using the same phonetic element could easily be adduced.

All sectors of Chinese society were attuned to the composition of written characters. Simply to look up a word in a dictionary like the *Kangxi zidian* required a knowledge of its radical because all entries were categorized by radicals and listed by the number of strokes they contained in addition to the radical. Even in everyday speech an ambiguous-sounding name or concept might be clarified by reference to its constituent visual elements—for example, *shuangmu* 雙木 ("a pair of wood radicals") to indicate the family name Lin 林. In the case of Qing scholars, this sensitivity to the makeup of characters was heightened by their active interest in philology. Although most radicals and phonetics no longer looked like actual objects, the etymologies provided by ancient lexicons such as the *Shuowen jiezi* often encouraged scholars to think of them in this way. So did more "popular" etymologies, which served as mnemonic devices.

The common denominator of scholarly and more popular forms of word analysis was the technique known as "dissecting characters" (*chaizi* 拆字). This process, which involved breaking characters down into their constituent elements, had a variety of applications in addition to philology. Fortune tellers, for instance, commonly used *chaizi* as a means of "fathoming" the future. Clients would either select a character from a preexisting menu of possibilities or write one themselves, whereupon the diviner would derive an interpretation based on the relationship between the radical and phonetic of the chosen character, or between that character and other characters with similar shapes and sounds, or those with common radicals.[23]

Word analysis of this sort also found expression in games and riddles. For instance: "What raises its head in embarrassment and lowers it in wealth [contrary to expectations]?" Answer: The character *tian* 田 ("field"), which is at the bottom of the word for "wealth" (*fu* 富) and at the top of the word for "embarrassment" (*lei* 累). Nicknames also grew from this fertile linguistic soil. The famous scholar Yuan Mei (1716–1797), for instance, came to be called "monkey" because his family name, Yuan 袁, looked and sounded like the word for a certain kind of ape (*yuan* 猿).

Novelists, for their part, often paid close attention to the radicals and phonetic elements that comprised the names of the people and places they wrote about. Thus, we find writers of "how to read" (*dufa* 讀法) books on vernacular fiction resorting to the technique of "dissecting characters" in order to explain the meaning of personal or family names. One example would be Wang Ban'er, grandson of Liu Laolao ("Grannie" Liu), in the novel *Honglou meng* (Dream of the red chamber). The late Qing commentator Zhang Xinzhi tells us that the character *ban* 板 in his personal name expresses the idea of "springtime" because it is composed of the radical *mu* 木 (wood) and the phonetic element *fan* 反 (to return), which together suggest the "return of the season of wood [that is, spring]."[24]

Word analysis was even employed as a form of argumentation in late impe-rial China. Thus we find the social distinction between a scholar (*shi* 士) and an artisan (*gong* 工) explained in terms of the formation of their respective written characters. "The [person represented by the character] *gong*," we are told, "merely prepares human devices; therefore [the vertical stroke of the character] extends out neither above nor below [as in the character for 'tal-ent' (*cai* 才)]"; whereas "one who has set his will on the *dao* . . . [that is, an 'exemplary person' or *junzi* 君子] extends out at the top [like the vertical line on the character for talent]."[25] The persuasive power of such formulations cannot be appreciated without an understanding of the unique nature of the Chinese written script.

Although the *Kangxi Dictionary* boasts about fifty thousand characters, only a tenth or so had to be mastered for substantial literacy in Qing times. In fact, the major paradigmatic writings of the Zhou period are based on a core vocabulary of only about twenty-five hundred separate characters. Although the Four Books and Five Classics total well over four hundred thousand characters, the *Lunyu* (Analects) of Confucius, one of the Four Books, has only twenty-two hundred different lexical items and the classic known as the *Chunqiu* (Spring and Autumn Annals) only about a thousand.

Facility in classical Chinese has never been simply a matter of recognizing large numbers of characters; instead it has been a matter of fully understand-ing the wealth of accumulated meanings and associations a given term has acquired over time. Unfortunately for students of the language, some of the most common words in classical Chinese have the widest range of possible meanings. *Jing* 經, for example, can mean (among other things) "warp" (as opposed to "woof"); "longitude"; "vessels in a body"; "to manage, plan, ar-range, regulate, or rule"; "to pass through, experience, or suffer"; "constant or standard"; "classical canon"; and even "suicide by hanging." *Shang* 尚 can mean "still or yet"; "in addition to or to add"; "to honor"; "to surpass"; "to proceed"; "to be in charge of"; and so on. Philosophical terms are particularly rich in shades of meaning.

Complicating matters is the fact that in classical Chinese a great many words function in at least two, and often more, grammatical roles (nouns, verbs, adverbs, adjectives, etc.), depending on syntax. The expression *shangma* 上馬, for instance, might mean "to get up on a horse" or "a supe-rior horse (or horses)," whereas the reverse expression, *mashang* 馬上, could mean "on top of a horse" or, by extension, "immediately." The classical phrase *ming mingde* 明明德, "to illustrate (or exemplify) illustrious virtue," employs the character *ming* (lit. bright) in two different grammatical forms, first as a verb and then as an adjective. Similarly, in the Confucian admoni-tion *jun jun chen chen fu fu zi zi* 君君臣臣父父子子 ("Let the sovereign be [that is, act in the manner befitting] a sovereign; let the minister be a minister; let the father be a father; let the son be a son"), the first, third, fifth, and seventh characters function as nouns, while the identical characters in the second, fourth, sixth, and eighth places serve as verbs.

This range of grammatical functions is by no means arbitrary, however. Classical Chinese depends on rules of word order that are in several respects similar to those governing English. The standard sentence structure is: subject-verb-object. Adjectives generally precede the nouns they modify, and adverbs precede the verbs they modify. Even the lack of inflection in classical Chinese creates no special grammatical problems as long as the context is clear. Unfortunately for the uninitiated reader, this is often not the case. Although grammatical devices exist in the classical language to indicate verb mood, noun number, and so forth, their use, in the words of one authority, "is not a matter of prescribed necessity."

Furthermore, classical Chinese texts were not normally punctuated. Certain characters could be employed to indicate partial or full stops, questions, exclamations, and so on, but even they were sometimes ambiguous and not always used consistently and systematically. In the absence of clear-cut punctuation, the inherent ambiguity of written Chinese was amplified, with the result that even standard classical texts were often subject to a wide variety of possible grammatical readings. This necessitated heavy reliance on commentaries and lexicons. Such works were also useful in identifying and explaining the wealth of recondite historical and literary allusions in classical-style writing, as well as the huge number of specialized meanings acquired by certain characters in different philosophical or other contexts.

In all, there was no real alternative to rote memorization and intensive tutorial assistance as a means of mastering the classical script. Beginning with specially designed Confucian primers (see chapter 10), students recited passages aloud in rhythmic fashion with no initial appreciation of meaning. By stages, these texts were carefully explained, and students then advanced to more complicated materials. By memorizing vast amounts of diverse classical literature in this way, students internalized specific patterns of characters contained in a wide variety of paradigmatic sources—patterns that became indelibly etched in their consciousness. The same painstaking approach applied to the writing of Chinese characters. Over a long period of time, and with Herculean effort, the aspiring scholar eventually attained the necessary skills to chart his or her own scholarly path.

The memorization of Chinese texts was facilitated by the rhythm and balance of the classical script. Each character, when pronounced, was monosyllabic, and each occupied the same amount of space in a text, regardless of the number of strokes it contained. Thus each character became a convenient rhythmic unit. This naturally encouraged the Chinese, perhaps more than any other culture group, to think and write in terms of polarities. In the words of the world-famous linguist Y. R. Chao, "I venture to think that if the Chinese language had words of such incommensurable rhythm as *male* and *female*, *heaven* and *earth*, *rational* and *[ab]surd*, there would never be such far-reaching conceptions as *yinyang*, [and] *qian kun*."[26]

But *yinyang* (陰陽) and Qian Kun (乾坤; the symbolic equivalents of *yang* and *yin* in the hexagrams of the *Yijing*; see below) were only two of a huge number of such polarities. Many, if not most, of these polarities can be correlated directly with *yin* and *yang*—an expression of the central Chinese notion that ideas are complemented and completed by their opposites. Thus we find that the *Shuowen jiezi* defines *chu* 出 (going out) in terms of *jin* 進 (coming in) and *luan* 亂 (disorder) in terms of *zhi* 治 (order). Distance is *yuanjin* 遠近 (far-near); quantity, *duoshao* 多少 (much-little); weight, *qingzhong* 輕重 (light-heavy); length, *changduan* 長短 (long-short); and so forth. Possession (or existence) is expressed by the terms *youwu* 有無 (lit. have-not have, presence-absence), and in Chinese discourse of all kinds it is common to find juxtapositions such as ancient and modern (*gujin* 古今), beginning and end (*benmo* 本末), difference and similarity (*yitong* 異同), gain and loss (*deshi* 得失), and continuity and change (*yan'ge* 沿革). In these and other dualistic expressions we find a characteristic concern with the "relation of opposites" rather than with Western-style (Aristotelian) separate qualities and the "law of identity."[27]

Two things seem significant. The first is that for most polarities in Chinese, descriptions such as antithesis, contradiction, and dichotomy are misleading because the terms involved usually imply either complementary opposition or cyclical alternation. The second is that the widespread use of such polarities—especially in classical prose and formal philosophy—suggests a distinctive attitude toward abstraction—one in which abstract ideas tend to be expressed in concrete terms ("instantiated"), without dialectical resolution into a new abstract term as in the Indo-European linguistic tradition. I shall return to this point later in the chapter.

One index of the prevalence of polarities in Chinese writing is their frequent use in the classical literature. In the first eighty characters of the Great Commentary of the *Yijing*, for instance, there are nearly a dozen prominent *yinyang*-style juxtapositions, ranging from man and woman (*nannü* 男女), sun and moon (*riyue* 日月), and Heaven and Earth (*tiandi* 天地) to honorable and lowly (*zunbei* 尊卑), activity and quiescence (*dongjing* 動靜), and fortune and misfortune (*jixiong* 吉凶). A great many other such polarities are scattered throughout the classic, and indeed throughout all major works in the Chinese literary tradition. In imperial times, lists of polarities were compiled for ease of reference in composition, and Qing documents sometimes contain as many as six sets of polarities strung together for effect.

Another indication of the importance of polarities is their frequent use as subject headings in encyclopedias such as the TSJC. In the subcategories on human affairs and social intercourse, for example, we find many headings such as love and hate (*haoe* 好惡), guest and host (*binzhu* 賓主), teacher and pupil (*shidi* 師弟), misfortune and good fortune (*huofu* 禍福), and high and humble (*guijian* 貴賤). In the subcategory on Confucian conduct there are literally dozens of common polarities, including righteousness and profit (*yili* 義利), good and bad (*shan'e* 善惡), influence and response (*ganying* 感應), substance and function (*tiyong* 體用), knowledge and action (*zhixing* 知行), names and realities (*mingshi* 名實), and hard and soft (*gangrou* 剛柔).[28]

Such polarities were not only semantically significant, they were also aesthetically attractive. Good prose demanded them. Consider the following three examples taken from the enormously influential compilation titled *Jinsi lu* (Reflections on things at hand):

> In the changes and transformations of *yin* and *yang*, the growth and maturity of things, the interaction of sincerity and insincerity, and the beginning and ending of events, one is the influence and the other, the response, succeeding each other in a cycle.
>
> By calmness of nature we mean that one's nature is calm whether it is in a state of activity or a state of tranquility. One does not lean forward or backward to accommodate things, nor does he make any distinction between the internal and the external.
>
> The difference between righteousness and profit is only that between impartiality and selfishness. As soon as we depart from righteousness, we will be talking about profit. Merely to calculate is to be concerned with advantage and disadvantage.[31]

Significantly, in the last example cited, the term righteousness (*yi* 義) replaced the original term humaneness (*ren* 仁) in order to employ a more satisfactory juxtaposition of ideas, namely, *yili* 義利 (righteousness and profit). In translation, formulations such as those cited above often appear unsubstantial and unsatisfying, but to the Chinese reader, completely conversant with the full range of meanings and associations of a given word, term, or phrase, they were not only beautiful but also compelling.

The same emphasis on rhythm and balance that is manifest in the use of polarities may be found in entire phrases of classical Chinese. In the *Wenxin diaolong* (The literary mind and the carving of dragons), considered by the great Qing scholar Ruan Yuan (1764–1849) to be the very foundation of

China's "literary laws," we find the following passage in the section on parallelism:

> The "Wenyan" and "Xici" [Commentaries] of the *Book of Changes* embody the profound thought of the Sage. In the narration of the four virtues of the hexagram *qian* [that is, *yang*], the sentences are matched in couplets, and in the description of the kinds of responses evoked by the dragon and the tiger, the words are all paralleled in pairs. When describing the hexagrams of *qian* and *kun* [that is, *yin*] as easy and simple respectively, the passage winds and turns, with lines smoothly woven into one another; and in depicting the going and coming of the sun and moon, the alternate lines form couplets. Occasionally there may be some variation in the structure of a sentence, or some change in word order, but parallelism is always the aim.[32]

This parallelism, in the view of the author, Liu Xie (c. AD 465–562), was as natural as the endowment of living things with paired limbs.

Of the four types of parallelism distinguished by Liu Xie, the most esteemed was the couplet of contrast. Liu provides an example: "Zhong Yi, the humble, played the music of Chu; Zhuang Xi, the prominent, groaned in the manner of Yue." Both parts of the contrasted couplet refer to spontaneous expressions of homesickness, and each requires familiarity with a historical background naturally assumed by the author.[33] Virtually all of the most influential forms of Chinese writing, from simple primers to the most sophisticated poetry and prose, employed some type of linguistic parallelism, and a good "eight-legged essay" for the civil service examinations could not, of course, be written without it. Four-character phrases were especially common. The great majority of Chinese fixed expressions, or aphorisms (*chengyu* 成語), whether derived from the classics, poetry, or popular literature, consist of four characters. Such expressions are particularly prevalent in classics such as the *Shijing* and *Yijing*, but they also are employed in many Chinese folk sayings. Indeed, the succinctness, balance, and rhythm of the classical Chinese language made it eminently well suited for popular proverbs, which helped bridge the gap between the mental world of the Confucian elite and the Chinese masses.

The brevity and grammatical flexibility of classical Chinese have sometimes been compared to modern telegrams and newspaper headlines, but the parallel can be taken no further. Rhythm, poetic suggestiveness, and economy of expression were not simply convenient means in China, but literary ends. Chinese authors regularly and happily sacrificed precision for style, encouraging an intuitive as well as an intellectual approach to their work. Although Qing scholars distinguished between learning (*xue* 學) and thinking (*si* 思) and between erudition (*bo* 博) and grasping the essence (*yue* 約), neo-Confucian "rationalism" did not on the whole involve a conscious exaltation of reason over intuition. Indeed, Chinese thinkers often showed a marked preference for the latter—perhaps in part because the brevity, subtlety, and suggestiveness of the classical language encouraged an intuitive approach to the most profound understanding. A. C. Graham rightly observes that the Chinese have generally been most impressed by "the aphoristic genius which guides thought of the maximum complexity with the minimum of words, of which the *Daode jing* [see chapter 6] presents one of the world's supreme examples."[34]

LANGUAGE AND CULTURE

What else does the classical language tell us about traditional Chinese patterns of perception and thought? Certainly it provides important clues regarding elite social attitudes. We see, for example, that the classical language is extraordinarily rich in kinship terminology, indicating an intense and pervasive concern with family relationships. The early Chinese lexicon known as the *Erya*, which dates from the first century BCE, contains over one hundred specialized kinship terms, most of which have no counterpart in English. Later works of a similar nature, including those by Qian Daxin (1727–1804), Liang Zhangju (1775–1849), and Zheng Zhen (1806–1864) in the Qing period, continued to place special emphasis on the highly refined nomenclature of family relationships. Even the works on local dialects by scholars such as Hang Shijun (1696–1773) and Qian Dian (1744–1806) devote extraordinary attention to kinship terms and their variants. The great Qing encyclopedia TSJC includes two large subcategories—one on clan and family names and one on family relationships—that together account for 756 of the encyclopedia's total of ten thousand *juan*. Although not all of this material is related directly to kinship nomenclature, it does indicate the central significance of the family in traditional Chinese society.

Chinese kinship terminology underscores the importance of social distinctions based on age and gender. A Chinese writer in traditional times (and in fact more recently) could never, for example, simply refer to another person as "cousin." He or she would have to employ a much more specific term that distinguished between male and female, between paternal and maternal affinity, and relative age. Thus, a male cousin on the father's side older than oneself would be referred to as *tangxiong* 堂兄, a male cousin on the father's side younger than oneself as *tangdi* 堂弟, a male cousin on the mother's side older than oneself as *biaoxiong* 表兄, and so on for five other types of cousins.

Similar distinctions were obligatory for other members of both the male line, or *neiqin* 內親 (lit. inner relationship), and the female line, or *waiqin*

外親 (lit. outer relationship). This latter category was further divided into the subcategories of mother's kin (*mudang* 母黨), wife's kin (*qidang* 妻黨), and daughter's kin (*nüdang* 女黨). These and other status distinctions were carefully preserved and expressed in the ritual vocabulary of the five mourning relationships discussed briefly in chapter 4. In practice, of course, the ritual requirements of mourning might be modified or ignored, especially if they involved distant relatives or mourning for junior family members by their seniors. But while the rituals might not always be strictly observed, the relationships were seldom forgotten.

Other linguistic evidence may be adduced for the special importance of kinship identifications in Chinese society, as well as for the principle of the subordination of the individual to the larger social group. Derk Bodde writes, for example, that "the Westerner asserts his ego by placing his personal name first, then his family name" (John Jones rather than Jones John), whereas the Chinese does just the reverse (Sun Yat-sen rather than Yat-sen Sun). Further, Bodde notes, "The Westerner unthinkingly speaks and writes in terms of 'I' and 'you.'" The Chinese (in the past, much less now) tended to avoid such direct address by using instead indirect locutions in the third person, such as "humble person" (referring to oneself) and "sir" or "gentleman" (referring to the other person).[35] Among the major honorific terms in traditional China—used both within and outside the family—were *ling* 令 ("excellent" or "illustrious"), *zun* 尊 ("honorable"), *xian* 賢 ("virtuous"), *gui* 貴 ("exalted"), and *da* 大 ("great"). *Yu* 愚 ("simple" or "stupid") and *xiao* 小 ("small" or "inferior") were commonly used in self-deprecation. Naturally enough, usage varied according to the relationship. Thus, while a man might speak of his wife as "the demeaned one of the inner apartments" (*jiannei* 賤內), a guest of the household would refer to her as "the honorable one of the inner apartments" (*zunnei* 尊內).

I will discuss gender issues more fully in chapters 8, 9, and 10, but it is worthy of note here that a relatively large number of Chinese characters with the "female" radical (*nü* 女) have decidedly pejorative connotations, including *jian* 奸 (villainous or traitorous), *fang* 妨 (to hinder), *du* 妒 (to be jealous), *nu* 奴 (slave), *mei* 媚 (to flatter), and *jian* 姦 (licentious). Of course, a number of very positive terms in Chinese also contain the *nü* radical, but most of these have to do with traditional female physical attributes, roles, and relationships. In speech these associations would not be apparent, as they are with, say, the English word "sissy," but as I have tried to indicate, Chinese culture as a whole paid far greater attention to the constituent elements of written words than did Western culture. Thus, such associations, both positive and negative, were never far from consciousness—at least not for the literate members of Qing society.

There are other ways in which the Chinese written language seems to reflect basic cultural attitudes. Zhang Dongsun has pointed out, for example, that the language is extraordinarily rich in ethical terms and concepts, indicating China's longstanding preoccupation with moral values. Feng Youlan, for his part, suggests that traditional expressions for the world, such as *tianxia* 天下 ("all under Heaven") and *sihai zhi nei* 四海之內 ("all within the four seas"), reflect a decidedly continental orientation very much unlike the outlook of, say, the ancient maritime Greeks. And Kwang-chih Chang has employed a sophisticated analysis of early Chinese texts and terminology to support his contention that the Chinese are "probably among the peoples of the world most preoccupied with eating." Overall, however, the study of the Chinese language and its cultural implications is still in its infancy, especially in the West.[36]

On the other hand, the relationship between the classical Chinese language and formal philosophy has been much discussed (and vigorously debated) by both Western and Chinese scholars. Clearly Chinese language and thought enjoyed a mutually supporting, mutually enriching relationship. Yet one may argue that classical Chinese had an especially significant impact on the development of Chinese philosophy, not only because it endured so long as a living language, but also perhaps because of the striking visual properties of the characters themselves.[37]

While the ambiguity of the Chinese language may have encouraged an intuitive approach to understanding, it is possible that the ideographic origins of the script encouraged a preference for the concrete and descriptive over the abstract—at least in formal philosophical discourse. Although this hypothesis has been hotly contested, many scholars have observed that classical Chinese is relatively weak in resources for expressing abstractions.[38] Thus, a word such as *zhen* 真 ("true" as opposed to "false," *jia* 假) tended to be construed as "that which is true," rather than the abstract concept "Truth." (A. C. Graham aptly remarks, "Chinese philosophising centres on the Way rather than the Truth.") Similarly, *ren* 人 ("human being[s]") tended to acquire the meaning of "a person" or "people" (general), rather than Man (abstract). "Hope" was difficult to abstract from the notion of "a series of expectations directed toward specific objects."[39]

Yet it certainly cannot be said that the Chinese lacked the capacity to think abstractly. What can be said, I think, is that Chinese philosophers tended to express the abstract and general in terms of the concrete and the particular. The *Yijing*, as Chung-ying Cheng has observed, is an especially apt illustration of this particular attitude or orientation. In the highly refined symbolic system of the *Changes*, philosophical principles are "embodied in concrete instances of things and their relations." Viewing the matter from a somewhat different perspective, we might say that universal or abstract principles have been most significant to the Chinese when realized or revealed in concrete things and particular contexts. This observation—which conforms to Chad Hansen's argument that Chinese theories of language, unlike those of the West, emphasize prescription rather than description—would help account for the practical orientation of so much of Chinese philosophy and for the general lack of speculation for speculation's sake in China.[40]

Another prominent feature of Chinese philosophy, already alluded to, may also be explained by reference to the classical language: the strong emphasis on what has been variously called relational, associational, analogical, or correlative thinking. Traditionally, Chinese thinkers have been less concerned with Western-style ontological categories (that is, Platonic universals and Aristotelian essences) than with an analysis of relations among and between things, events, and concepts. Yu-kuang Chu believes that the emphasis on word relations in Chinese is "probably correlated with relational thinking in many areas of Chinese life and culture." We have already noted Chung-ying Cheng's use of the *Yijing* as an illustration of Chinese relational thinking; other Chinese and Western scholars, such as Zhang Dongsun and Joseph Needham, have also used the ancient classic to make the same basic point.[41]

China's *yinyang*-oriented "logic of correlative duality" (to borrow Zhang Dongsun's felicitous phrase) certainly differed from classical Aristotelian logic in the West. This does not, however, mean that the Chinese lacked the capacity to reason "logically." Many authorities—Westerners as well as Chinese—have demonstrated with abundant documentary evidence that logical rigor was possible, and even prominent, in certain types of Chinese philosophical discourse.[42] Nonetheless, it is true that the structure of the Chinese language, the aesthetics associated with it, and the penchant for relational thinking among the Chinese, made some forms of argumentation far more appealing and persuasive than others. This helps to explain, for example, the powerful Chinese preference for argument by analogy and the widespread use of numerical categories and correlations in all kinds of philosophical writing.

Although *yinyang* dualism lay at the heart of Chinese relational thinking, most Chinese numerical categories involved groups of more than two. Most of these were odd (*yang*) numbers—notably threes, fives, and nines. Thus, we find in Chinese philosophical writing (and in daily discourse) repeated references to the "three sovereigns" (Fu Xi, Shen Nong, and Huangdi, in one common configuration), the "three teachings" (Confucianism, Buddhism, and Daoism), the "three obediences" (subject to sovereign, son to father, and wife to husband), the "three powers" (Heaven, Earth, and Man), the "three [types of womanly] dependence" (on father, husband, and son), and so forth.

In all, over three hundred different numerical correlations or associations were current in Qing times, ranging from groups of two or three (there were about seventy for the number three alone) to groups of one hundred or more. Such categories not only identified certain important relationships, but also served as a convenient philosophical "shorthand." Like the concepts *yin* and *yang*, with which they were often correlated, numbers indicated hierarchy and precedence, expressed in a highly formalistic style.[43]

Correlational thinking, together with an emphasis on balance and rhythm (and the attractiveness of puns) in the Chinese language, helps to explain the popularity of four-character philosophical "definitions" of the following sort: *ren zhe ren ye* 仁者人也 ("*ren* [humaneness] means to be human [*ren*]"); *yi zhe yi ye* 義者宜也 ("*yi* [righteousness or duty] means that which is appropriate [*yi*]"); and *zheng zhe zheng ye* 政者正也 ("*zheng* [government] means that which is correct [*zheng*]"). Henry Rosemont argues that the advantage of such formulations is that they allowed a Chinese thinker to "maintain the semantic richness of his general terms and their relational representations yet unpack them when necessary—with or without logical explicitness—to elaborate one of their specific significations."[44]

This relational or associational process, so prominent in the classical language, was central to the way that the *Yijing* encouraged "the detection of analogous precepts, concepts and ideas in interrelated symbols, and a synthesis of them into more elaborate metaphysical or ethical notions."[45] In the following chapters we will take up the place of the *Changes* in Chinese cosmology, ethics, divination, and popular religion, but here we are concerned with the classic as a supplementary system of Chinese language, or to use Alfred North Whitehead's term, of "symbolic reference."[46]

The authority of the *Yijing* in late imperial China is seldom fully appreciated. Consider, however, the following quotation from the famous *Jinsi lu*, described by one scholar as "unquestionably the most important single work of philosophy produced in the Far East during the second millennium A.D." "[The *Yijing*] is comprehensive, great and perfect. It is intended to bring about accord with the principle of [human] nature and destiny, to penetrate the causes of the hidden and the manifest, to reveal completely the nature of things and affairs, and to show the way to open up resources and to accomplish great undertakings."[47] In a similar vein, the great Qing scholar Wang Fuzhi (1619–1692) wrote:

[The *Yijing*] is the manifestation of the Heavenly Way, the unexpressed form of nature, and the showcase for sagely achievement. *Yin* and *yang*, movement and stillness, darkness and brightness, withdrawing and extending—all these are inherent in it. Spirit operates within it; the refined subtlety of ritual and music is stored in it; the transformative capacity of ghosts and spirits emerges from it.

The great utility of humaneness and righteousness issues forth from it; and the calculation of order or disorder, good or bad luck, life or death is in accordance with it.[48]

Throughout the Qing period the *Yijing* remained a sacred work of nearly unchallenged scriptural authority, serving not only as a moral guide to action but also as a rich source of concepts and symbols.

According to Confucius (as cited in the Great Commentary of the *Yijing*), "Writing does not exhaust words, and words do not exhaust ideas. . . . The sages [therefore] established images in order to express their ideas exhaustively . . . [and] established the hexagrams in order to treat exhaustively the true innate tendencies of things."[49] To put the matter another way, the six-line hexagrams of the *Yijing* symbolically represented the images or structure(s) of changing situations in the universe, and as such were believed to have explanatory value, if correctly interpreted. Like Chinese characters, these hexagrams were a distinctly visual medium of communication, concrete but ambiguous, with several possible levels of meaning as well as a great many accumulated allusions and associations. To a greater extent than most Chinese characters, however, the hexagrams came to acquire abstract significations.

The basic text of the *Yijing* consists of sixty-four hexagrams (*gua* 卦), each with a name designed to indicate its basic symbolic significance. Most hexagram names (*guaming* 卦名) refer to a thing, an activity, a state, a situation, a quality, an emotion, or a relationship—for example, "Well," "Cauldron," "Marrying Maid," "Treading," "Following," "Viewing," "Juvenile Ignorance," "Peace," "Obstruction," "Waiting," "Contention," "Ills to be Cured," "Modesty," "Elegance," "Great Strength," "Contentment," "Inner Trust," "Joy," "Closeness," "Fellowship," "Reciprocity."[50] Each hexagram is composed of six solid (*yang*, _____) or broken (*yin*, __ __) lines in various combinations. Every hexagram also has a "judgment" (*tuan* 彖; aka "hexagram statement," "decision," or "tag") and an "appended statement" (*xici* 繫辭 or *yaoci* 爻辭) for each line.

The judgments are short explanations of the overall symbolic situation represented by a given hexagram. The appended statements (also called "line readings") characterize each of the six lines in turn and usually indicate a process leading from a beginning stage (line one, at the bottom of the hexagram), to a developmental stage (lines two through five), and on to an ending or transitional stage (line six). These lines also form a pair of individually named three-line trigrams (also *gua* 卦) juxtaposed within each hexagram. There are eight possible primary trigram configurations. According to the theory of the *Yijing*, the interpretation of various interrelated lines, trigrams, and hexagrams, and an appreciation of the changes they undergo and represent in

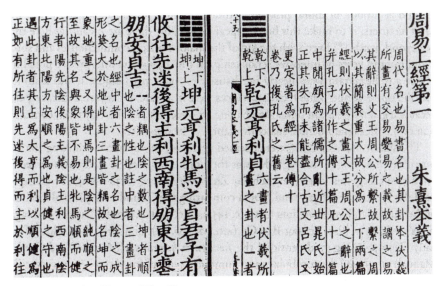

Figure 5.1. The Qian and Kun Hexagrams
Two separate pages from a Qing dynasty edition of the *Yijing*, with commentary by Zhu Xi (1130–1200). The first part of the page on the right-hand side explains the early evolution of the text. The Qian hexagram follows, with its name and its short judgment in four large characters directly below the hexagram name. The smaller characters that follow provide the first few words of Zhu Xi's long commentary. The page on the left-hand side introduces the Kun hexagram, followed by its name and its much longer judgment (twenty-seven characters). Again, the smaller characters that follow are part of Zhu Xi's extended commentary. The same combination of large characters and commentary in smaller characters applies to each of the six line statements as well as to the "Ten Wings." Source: Zhu Xi 1893.

certain concrete circumstances, will clarify the structure of human experience and, in the process of divination, illumine the future.

The so-called Ten Wings (*Shiyi* 十翼) of the *Yijing*, traditionally but erroneously attributed to Confucius, amplify the basic text and invest it with additional symbolism and multiple layers of meaning. Together, through the use of colorful analogies, metaphors, and other forms of imagery, these poetic commentaries elucidate the structure and significance of the hexagrams in terms of their individual lines and constituent trigrams as well as their relation to other hexagrams. Further, they provide a moral dimension to the *Yijing* and a solid metaphysical foundation based on *yinyang*/five-agents principles and

Qian	Dui	Li	Zhen	Sun	Kan	Gen	Kun
Heaven	Lake	Fire	Thunder	Wind	Water	Mountain	Earth

Figure 5.2. The Eight Trigrams

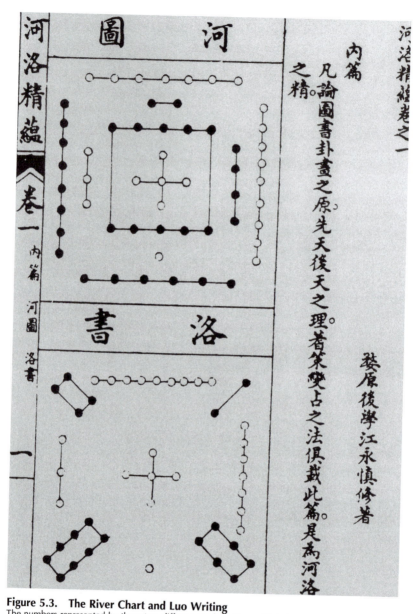

Figure 5.3. The River Chart and Luo Writing

The numbers represented by these two different configurations of light (*yang*) and dark (*yin*) circles were correlated with a large number of cosmic variables, including the five agents and the eight trigrams. To many (but not all) Qing scholars, these two documents represented the foundation for numerical explanations of all phenomena. *Source:* Jiang Yong 1774.

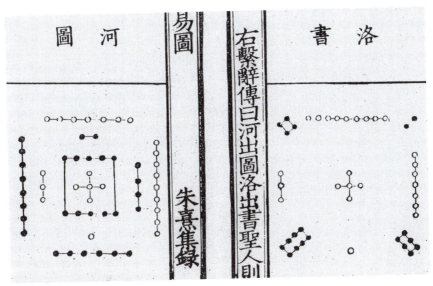

Figure 5.3. (*continued*)
Another version. Source: Zhu Xi 1893.

an elaborate numerology (see chapter 6). The metaphysics and numerology of the *Changes* were communicated to all levels of society during the Qing period by means of fortune tellers, almanacs, and schematic numerical devices such as the *Hetu* (River Chart) and *Luoshu* (Luo Writing).

Although a fundamental assumption of the *Yijing* has always been the mutual interaction or interrelationship of all of its constituent hexagrams, the two most important points of symbolic reference in the classic were clearly the first two hexagrams in the received order, Qian 乾 ("Creative") and Kun 坤 ("Receptive") (see figure 5.1). At the most basic level of symbolism, Qian and Kun represented Heaven and Earth in microcosm, as well as the generative power and potential of *yang* and *yin*, respectively. As *yinyang* conceptual categories, these hexagrams automatically assumed all of the attributes associated with these two sets of complementary opposites, including dark and light, female and male, quiescence and movement, and the numerical correlations of even and odd (see chapter 6). In addition, Qian and Kun acquired the associations of their constituent trigrams. Among Qian's various attributes were thus roundness, spirituality, straightness, the color red, and the cutting quality of metal. By contrast, Kun came to be associated with squareness, sagacity, levelness, the color black, and the transport capacity of a large wagon.[52]

Over time, Qian and Kun, and to a somewhat lesser extent the other sixty-two hexagrams derived from them, became rich repositories of diverse symbols, similar to variables in symbolic logic. As substitutes for various classes of objects, the hexagrams, individual trigrams, and even single lines had wide-ranging explanatory value. Feng Youlan writes, for example, "Everything that satisfies the condition of being virile [*yang*] can fit into a formula in which the symbol Qian occurs, and everything that satisfies the condition of being docile [*yin*] can fit into one in which the symbol of Kun appears." At the most rudimentary level, this meant that if a man sought an understanding of the role of, say, a ruler or a father (a *yang* relationship), he consulted the hexagram Qian and its associated commentaries, and if he sought an understanding of the role or place of a subject or a son (a *yin* relationship), he consulted the hexagram Kun and its commentaries.[53]

Of course, as I have discussed at length elsewhere, the process of consulting the *Yijing* for insight and guidance, whether in divination or in the course of general study, was usually far more complex than this. The very structure of the *Changes*, with its *yinyang* style reconciliation of opposites, cryptic language, multiple symbols, layers of meaning, and elaborate patterns of relationship among lines, trigrams, and hexagrams, militated against facile explanations, except by the simple minded. As the Kangxi emperor once remarked, "I have never tired of the *Classic of Changes*, and have used it in fortune-telling and as a book of moral principles; the only thing you must not do, I told my court lecturers, is to make this book appear simple, for there are meanings here that lie beyond words."[54] Even with the aid of the major classical commentaries and some two thousand years of intensive scholarship on the *Yijing*, the interpretive possibilities of any hexagram were nearly infinite.

The cultural significance of the *Changes* extended into virtually every area of traditional Chinese life. In the first place, it provided a seemingly inexhaustible repository of symbols with which to represent and explain nearly every realm of human experience, from artistic, musical, and literary criticism to science, medicine, and technology. Second, from the standpoint of philosophy, it established the conceptual underpinnings for much of traditional Chinese cosmogony and cosmology, as well as the point of departure for most discussions of space and time. It also contributed significantly to an enduring emphasis in traditional Chinese thought on "becoming" over "being," "events" over "things," and "relations" over "essences."[55]

The *Changes* supplied an indispensable vocabulary for a wide range of Chinese thinkers, from Confucians and Legalists to Buddhists and Daoists. Zhang Dainian's *Key Concepts in Chinese Philosophy* (2002), originally published in Chinese in 1989, devotes a substantial section to philosophical concepts derived from the *Yijing*, almost all of which we will encounter in chapter 6 and/or subsequent chapters. These concepts include: Taiji 太極 (the Supreme Ultimate), *shenhua* 神化 (spiritual transformation), *yi* 易 (change), *bianhua* 變化 (transformation), *dongjing* 動靜 (movement and stillness), *ji* 機 (incipience), and *xiang* 象 (image). Moreover, much of the rest of Zhang's book focuses on terms that are central to the *Yijing*—not least *Tian* 天 (Heaven), *Dao* 道 (the Way), *li* 理 (principle), *qi* 氣 (material force, etc.), *yin* and *yang* 陰陽, *wuxing* 五行 (the five agents), *sheng* 生 (life, genera-tion), *fan* 反 (return), *ming* 命 (destiny), *jingshen* 精神 (essence and spirit), *xingshang* 形上 and *xingxia* 形下 ("before form" and "after form" [that is, metaphysics]), *tongyi* 同異 (identity and difference), *he* 和 (harmony), and a whole range of additional moral and epistemological notions.[56]

The importance of the *Yijing* to Chinese aesthetic life is evident in several related realms. Artistically speaking, the *Changes* encouraged a preoccupa-tion with nature and natural processes, and provided a symbolic and ana-lytical vocabulary that proved as serviceable in art and literature as it was in philosophy. The author of the early Qing painting guide titled the *Jiezi yuan huazhuan* (Mustard Seed Garden manual), for example, employs the vocabu-lary and numerical symbolism of the *Yijing* in describing the composition of plum trees. "The blossoms," he tells us, "are of the *yang* principle . . . [and the] wood of its branches is of the *yin* principle. Its basic number is five, and its various parts and aspects are based on odd and even numbers [like the *Yijing*]. . . . [The] branches symbolize the six lines [of the hexagrams] . . . and the tips of the branches have eight knots or forks, symbolizing the Eight Trigrams."[57] We can also find many examples of Chinese paintings and line drawings that represent the idea of scholars contemplating the *Yijing*. Fur-thermore, the classic influenced a wide range of other aesthetically satisfying social activities and occupations, from music and dance to architecture and flower arranging.

Changes symbolism informed a great deal of Chinese literary criticism. The hexagram Bi (#22), for example, stood for beauty, grace, and simplicity of form, while Yu (#16) indicated energy, enthusiasm, and emotion. Guai (#43) symbolized resolute, critical judgment, and Li (#30) logical clarity. Qian (#1) generally denoted creativity and spirituality, while Kun (#2) sug-gested passive intelligence. Thus, we find the great Qing poet Yuan Mei jus-tifying his preoccupation with landscape gardens by reference to "the grace of hills and gardens," and Zhang Xuecheng (1738–1801), in a much-admired critique of Han dynasty historical scholarship, describing the writing of Sima Qian as "round and spiritual" and that of his successor, Ban Gu, as "square and sagacious."[58] In both cases, the critical vocabulary employed by these scholars is drawn verbatim from the *Changes*.

Qing scholars also used the *Yijing* to interpret some of China's greatest novels (see chapters 1 and 9). The Daoist priest Liu Yiming (1734–1820), for instance, felt that *Xiyou ji* (Journey to the west) could not be appreciated fully without an understanding of the way different meanings attached to the same apparent hexagram symbolism in various parts of the novel. Wentong, a late Qing Bannerman, developed the theory that several of the main characters in *Shuihu zhuan* (Water margin) were related directly to hexagram images derived from the *Yijing*. And Zhang Xinzhi's well-known exegesis of *Honglou meng* (Dream of the red chamber) placed special emphasis on hexagram relationships in its analysis of personalities, as we can see plainly in the following passage on the four "sisters" of Jia Baoyu:

> Yuanchun corresponds to the hexagram Tai [#11] the hexagram of the first month, so she is the eldest sibling. Yingchun corresponds to the hexagram Dazhuang [#34], the hexagram of the second month, so she is the second oldest daughter. Tanchun corresponds to the hexagram Guai [#43], the hexagram of the third month, so she is the third oldest daughter. Xichun corresponds to the hexagram Qian [#1], which is the hexagram of the fourth month, so she is the fourth oldest daughter. But since all . . . are female, their *yang* lines are transformed into *yin* lines. Thus Yuanchun's Tai is transformed into Pi [#12], Yingchun's Dazhuang is transformed into Guan [#20] Tanchun's Guai is transformed into Bo [#23] and Xichun's Qian is transformed into Kun [#2] This is one of the most important messages in the book, and I make comment on this in turn during the biographies of each of them.[59]

The *Yijing* served as a source of direct literary inspiration as well. The famous critic Liu Xie tells us, for example, that the *Changes* not only provided a model for the linguistic parallelism that was invariably prized in traditional Chinese writing, especially poetry, but that it also was the specific origin of several major types of prose, including *lun* (discussions), *shuo* (argumentation), *ci* (oracular pronouncements), and *xu* (prefatory statements). Chinese scholars wrote literally thousands of essays on the *Yijing* from the Han period through the Qing, many of which, along with various inscriptions, memorials, eulogies, and works of rhyme-prose focusing on the classic, found a place in the TSJC's massive section on the *Changes*. In addition, the editors of the TSJC brought together in this compendium a total of thirty-four poems on the *Changes* by some of the most prominent scholars in imperial China, ranging in time from the third century into the seventeenth (see chapter 9).[60]

In Chinese social life, the *Yijing* was particularly influential, quite apart from its widespread use in divination. As Chinese diaries, memoirs, correspondence, and reference books reveal, nearly all of the sixty-four hexagrams had potential application to human affairs. Among the most relevant seem to have been Qian (#1), conventionally signifying male dominance; Kun (#2), female compliance; Song (#6), litigation; Shi (#7), military affairs; Bi (#8), union and accord; Li (#10), circumspect behavior; Qian (#15), modesty; Yu (#16), comfort or satisfaction; Gu (#18), decay; Shihe (#21), criminal law; Fu (#24), return; Wuwang (#25), absence of falsehood; Dachu (#26), great ac-

cumulation; Daguo (#28), excess; Kan (#29), danger; Heng (#32), perseverance; Tun (#33), retreat; Jin (#35), advance in rank; Mingyi (#36), failure to
be appreciated; Kui (#38), separation or alienation; Guai (#43), breakthrough;
Gou (#44) social intercourse; Cui (#45), people gathered around a good ruler;
Sheng (#46), the career of an able official; Kun (#47), difficulty; Ding (#50),
nourishment of talents; Jian (#53), slow and steady advance; Feng (#55),
prosperity; Lü (#56), travel and strangers; Huan (#59), dispersion; Jie (#60),
restraint; Zhongfu (#61), kingly sway; Jiji (#63), accomplishment; and Weiji
(#64), something not yet completed.[61]

For guidance in making life choices, one needed only to consult the relevant hexagram(s) of the *Yijing* and then take both the text and its commentaries to heart. As a brief example, let us take a passage from the enormously
influential neo-Confucian compilation known as the *Jinsi lu* (Reflections on
things at hand), which employs about fifty different hexagrams, including
most of the above mentioned, to illustrate various social and political themes.
In the chapter on "The Investigation of Things," for example, we read:

> The fundamental method of studying the *Changes* is to know times and cir-
> cumstances. . . . In the Dachu hexagram ["Great Accumulation," #26], the two
> undivided [*yang*] lines at the bottom, being the substance of the Qian [Heaven]
> trigram, are strong and firm and yet not sufficient to advance. The fourth and
> fifth lines from the bottom are feminine and weak [*yin*] and yet can stop the
> advance. Students of the *Changes* should know thoroughly whether the time is
> high or low and whether the conditions are strong or weak.[62]

In other words, anyone contemplating a policy decision involving "accumulation" should consider carefully the strength of the forces opposing it,
represented by the fourth and fifth *yin* lines. A close metaphorical reading of
the appropriate line statements (which refer, respectively, to ox horns and boar
tusks) will provide further clarification of the situation—both its pitfalls and
its possibilities.

The *Yijing* also played a role in Chinese law. Although hexagrams never
featured prominently in the specific statutes of any particular dynasty, several of them were considered applicable to legal affairs. The Judgment of
Shihe (#21), for example, underscores the penal emphasis of Chinese law:
"Bite Together means prevalence [success], for here it is fitting to use the
force of criminal punishment." But the trigram symbolism for this particular
hexagram suggests at least a degree of flexibility: "Thunder and Lightning:
this constitutes the image of Bite Together. In the same way, the former kings
clarified punishments and adjusted laws." The Commentary on the Images of
Zhongfu (#61) counsels caution: "Above the Lake there is Wind: this constitutes the image of Inner Trust. In the same way, the superior man evalu-
ates criminal punishments and mitigates [or delays] the death penalty." The

Judgment of Song (#6), a hexagram that refers primarily to civil conflicts and bureaucratic problems, states in part "Exercise prudence in handling obstruction," and the Commentary on the Images of the Song hexagram notes that "Contention cannot be protracted forever."[63]

Even Chinese sexual life came to be described and analyzed by reference to the *Yijing*. According to R. H. van Gulik's pioneering *Sexual Life in Ancient China* (first published in 1961 but updated in 2003), Chinese handbooks on sex (*fangshu*) and collections of erotic paintings often cite the following passage from the Great Commentary of the *Changes* to indicate the naturalness of the sex act: "Heaven and Earth mesh together, and the myriad things develop and reach perfect maturity; male and female blend essences together, and the myriad creatures are formed and come to life."[64] The hexagram most emblematic of sexual union was Jiji (#63). It consists of the Li trigram (symbolizing "fire," "light," and "man") below, and the Kan trigram (symbolizing "water," "clouds," and "woman") above. Other hexagrams have also been interpreted in sexual terms, such as Bo (#23), with its reiterated bed imagery, and Xian (#31), which Wang Ming, a contemporary expert in Daoism, believes refers to foreplay. Wang notes that the Commentary on the Judgment for Xian refers not only to "stimulation" but also to the interaction of the "soft and yielding" and the "hard and strong," and to "joining together." He also points to references in the line statements that indicate a clear progression from the feet, to the calves, to the thighs, to the upper back, and to the "jowls, cheeks and tongue."[65]

The question of the *Yijing*'s place in the history of Chinese science is a vexed one. Joseph Needham, the acclaimed British historian of the subject, unhesitatingly blames the *Changes* for inhibiting the development of Chinese science (by which he means a Western model of historical development):

> I fear that we shall have to say that while the five-element [*wuxing*] and two-force [*yinyang*] theories were favourable rather than inimical to the development of scientific thought in China, the elaborated symbolic system of the *Book of Changes* was almost from the start a mischievous handicap. It tempted those who were interested in Nature to rest in explanations which were no explanations at all. The *Book of Changes* was a system for *pigeon-holing novelty* and then doing nothing about it. . . . It led to a stylisation of concepts almost analogous to the stylisations which have in some ages occurred in art forms and which finally prevented painters from looking at Nature at all.[66]

In a similar vein, Peng-Yoke Ho, another distinguished historian of Chinese science, has written that if the Chinese "were fully satisfied with an explanation they could find from the system of the *Book of Changes* they would not go further to look for mathematical formulations and experimental verifications in their scientific studies." Thus, he says, "Looking at the system of the *Book of Changes* in this light, one may regard it as one of the inhibiting factors in the development of scientific ideas in China."[67]

It is easy enough to see why Needham and Ho might hold these views. There was, in fact, very little about the natural world for which the *Yijing* did not provide some sort of explanation, as a glance at the index to any one of the many volumes in Needham's monumental *Science and Civilisation in China* (under the heading "I Ching") will reveal.[68] The terrain covered by the *Changes* included not only the fields we now know as mathematics, biology, chemistry, physics, and medicine, but also other areas of scientific knowledge such as geography, topography, and cartography. The color and flow of blood, the anatomy of crustaceans, the physical constitution of people from different areas of China, acupuncture and pulse points, chemical and alchemical reactions, the nature of earthquakes, musical tonality, and a great deal more were all explained by reference to trigrams, hexagrams, or both.[69]

Sometimes *Yijing*-grounded explanations consisted primarily of established correlations or relationships. Thus, for example, the early Ming scholar Wang Kui could state confidently: "The upper eyelid of human beings moves, and the lower one keeps still. This is because the symbolism of the hexagram Guan (#20) embodies the idea of vision. The trigram Sun (Wind) is moving above, and the trigram Kun (Earth) is immobile below." Employing a similar associational logic, it is easy to see why the hexagram Jiji (#63) came to be employed to describe the physiology of sex: the constituent trigrams of Li (Fire) and Kan (Water) referred, respectively, to the sexual responses of men (quick to heat; quick to cool) and women (slow to heat; slow to cool).[70]

But trigrams and hexagrams did more than simply symbolize correlative functions; they also "controlled" time, phenomena, and situations in concrete ways, rather like "force fields." Some hexagrams were considered donators, others receptors; some involved movement; others, immobility; some encouraged aggregation, others disaggregation; some entailed progression, others retrogression. Trigrams possessed similar attributes, whether paired as opposites in the "Former Heaven" (*Xian Tian*) sequence, or arranged developmentally in the "Later Heaven" (*Hou Tian*) sequence.[71] Symbol and substance were indistinguishable in this view. To take one simple example, in figure 5.4 we see part of a 1721 map of the cosmos in which the trigrams are arranged in the Later Heaven sequence on the outside of a circle. The circle represents the Heavens while Earth is depicted as a square. Respectively, the trigrams exert tangible power in the eight major directional spaces that they occupy.

At a micro-level, the Qing dynasty physician Li Yanshi (1628–1697) explains how such cosmic correlations work on the human body. Here he is discussing the way certain trigrams, arranged fundamentally in the Later

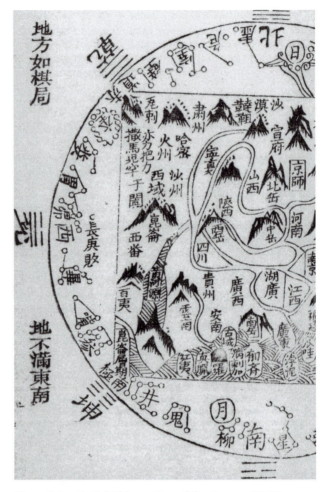

Figure 5.4. Partial Chinese Map of the Cosmos (1721)
In addition to showing five of the eight trigrams, this section of a larger cosmological map depicts the influence exerted by certain constellations known as "lodges" (*xiu*). The portion shown here represents the entire world west of Beijing. In the lower left corner are inscriptions that refer to groups of people such as the "Red [Haired] Barbarians" (Europeans) and a generic category, "The Hundred Barbarians." Source: Reproduced with permission from the British Library Board, the Oriental and India Office Collections of the British Library (#15257 a 24).

Heaven sequence but correlated with the five agents, need to be taken into account in the evaluation of pulse sites (*xue*) on the hands:

> North is Kan, the site of water. South is Li, the site of fire. East is Zhen, the site of wood. West is Dui, the site of metal. The center is Kun, the site of earth. Try facing south and looking at the sites in the two hands. The heart belongs to fire and resides in the *cun* [inch] site. This is also in the south. The kidneys belong

to water. They reside in the *chi* [foot] site. This is also in the north. The liver belongs to wood. It resides in the left. This is also in the east. The lungs belong to metal. They reside in the right. This is also in the west. The spleen belongs to earth. It resides in the *guan* [pass] site. This is also in the center.[72]

Li's assumption is that each site on the body is enmeshed in a specific network of stimulus and response, dictated in this case by position and marked by the directional power of one or another of the eight trigrams. Similar correlative assumptions operated in a great number of related realms, from alchemy and acupuncture to therapeutic calisthenics and meditative practices (see chapters 7 and 10).[73]

Let us return now to the question of whether the *Yijing* should be blamed for standing in the way of Chinese science. Nathan Sivin has launched a vigorous attack on the above-mentioned views of Needham and Ho, showing the fallacies that surround their reasoning. One of these fallacies has to do with confusing for a "cause" or a "necessary condition" a description of "an earlier state of a culture or a culture's way of doing something"—in other words, "blaming the earlier state for the later state." The other, its complement, assumes inhibition in the absence of a subsequent state, that is, "using the absence of something modern at one point to explain the unattainability of modernity later."[74] Sivin explains:

One . . . looks in vain for a habit among Chinese scientists of constructing mathematical formulations and experimental verifications; if one cannot prove that this tendency was evolving steadily to a certain point, if there is no tangible evidence that without the *Book of Changes* they would have "gone further," there seems no warrant for introducing from modern biology the metaphor of inhibition.[75]

Sivin goes on to remark, "It is unfortunate to see that the remarkably interesting technical language of the *Book of Changes*, so powerful in systematically relating broader ranges of human experience than modern science attempts to encompass, written off as an obstacle before anyone has taken the trouble to comprehend it thoroughly."

I would like to give a bit more attention to Sivin's observations, beginning with his indictment of efforts to "turn the history of world science into a saga of Europe's success and everyone else's failure, or at best . . . [their] flawed and transitory success, until the advent of redemption through modernization."[76] The limitations of this sort of praise-and-blame approach are obvious, although comparisons of one sort or another are practically inevitable. Indeed, Sivin himself argues that in the seventeenth century, China experienced a genuine "scientific revolution," comparable in certain respects to the Scientific Revolution that began in the West at about the same time. He writes:

Western mathematics and mathematical astronomy were introduced to China beginning around 1630—in a form that before long would be obsolete in those parts of Europe where readers were permitted access to current knowledge. Several Chinese scholars quickly responded and began reshaping the way astronomy was done in China. They radically and permanently reoriented the sense of how one goes about comprehending the celestial motions. They changed the sense of which concepts, tools, and methods are centrally important, so that geometry and trigonometry largely replaced traditional numerical or algebraic procedures. . . . Chinese astronomers came to believe for the first time that mathematical models can explain the phenomena as well as predict them. These changes amount to a conceptual revolution in astronomy.[77]

He points out, however, that China's "scientific revolution"

did not generate the same pitch of tension as the one going on in Europe at the same time. It did not burst forth in as fundamental a reorientation of thought about Nature. It did not cast doubt on all the traditional ideas of what constitutes an astronomical problem. It did not narrow people's views of what meaning astronomical prediction can have for the ultimate understanding of Nature and of man's relation to it. Most important, it did not extend the domain of number and measure in astronomy until it embraced every terrestrial phenomenon. . . . Rather than replacing traditional values, the new values implicit in the foreign astronomical writings were used to perpetuate traditional values.[78]

Sivin goes on to say:

Revolutions in science as well as in politics take place at the margins of society, but the people who made the one in seventeenth-century China were firmly attached to the dominant values of their culture. . . . If we seek in China those for whom science was not a means to conservative ends, those for whom a proven fact outweighed values that had evolved for thousands of years, we do not find them until the late nineteenth century. Then it was people with little or no stake in the old society who became the first modern scientists.

Sivin's point, as I understand it, is an important one. Science in Europe during the sixteenth and seventeenth centuries developed increasingly beyond the institutional control of either church or state. But in imperial China, the state's potential for intervention in all areas of Chinese life, and its existing reward structure (most notably the examination system), went essentially unchallenged. Thus, until the late Qing period, when the weakness and ineffectiveness of the government had become obvious to all, the incentive to use science (or any other branch of knowledge) for revolutionary purposes was basically absent in China. Jesuit science and technology served the interests of the state, and the state alone.

Similarly, but in the realm of domestically generated knowledge, the contents of Song Yingxing's late Ming book on technology, *Tiangong kaiwu* (The works of Heaven and the inception of things; 1637), discussed briefly in chapter 1, were either forgotten or turned to the interests of the Qing government. The compilers of the TSJC and other imperially sponsored reference works "cannibalized" the book rather than canonizing it. They ignored, for the most part, Song's *qi*-based metaphysics as well as his brother's Ming loyalism and Song's own muted criticism of northern "barbarians." As Dagmar Schafer has noted in her insightful study of the *Tiangong kaiwu*, "Eighteenth-century Chinese scholars approached *Works of Heaven* intellectually and politically quite selectively, either adjusting its structure to fit traditional lines of knowledge categorization, or purposefully employing its contents to fit their needs."[79]

The title of Benjamin Elman's 2005 book *On Their Own Terms: Science in China, 1550–1900* reflects his (and Shafer's) fruitful interpretive stance: scientifically minded Chinese scholars were not trying to imitate European science in the seventeenth and eighteenth centuries; they had their own agenda, and it yielded impressive results in terms of both the recovery and amplification of "lost" Chinese traditions in fields such as astronomy, mathematics, and geography. Scholars of the period also produced an enormous amount of useful literature on natural science, including plants, animals, and people.[80] But as Nathan Sivin has indicated, this new information did not produce any sort of political, social, or economic transformation, nor was it likely to. This explains why, despite the significant progress in Chinese astronomical science during the seventeenth and eighteenth centuries, the knowledge gained had virtually no impact on state-sponsored astrology.

Let us return now to the *Yijing* for suggestions as to why the history of Chinese science unfolded in the way that it did. As should already be readily apparent, the structure and symbolism of the *Changes* lent itself to a wide range of epistemological options; indeed, it presented a field of virtually limitless interpretive possibilities. The fact that Chinese scholars did not take the *Yijing* in directions that conformed to Western hopes or expectations should come as no surprise to us. It is true that Western-style mathematics appealed to a number of Chinese scholars in Ming and Qing times—but not, for the most part, as a way of explaining natural phenomena in the Newtonian fashion.[81] And, of course, Newton's science was not available to them anyway, for the suppression of the Jesuit order in 1773 "delayed for almost a century the relaying of information from Europe about the role of calculus for engineering and mechanics for physics."[82]

As Sivin, Elman, Schafer, and others have emphasized, the late Ming period witnessed a burst of interest in scientific inquiry, which continued into the Qing. Scholars such as Huang Zongxi (1610–1695), Wang Fuzhi (1619–1692), Fang Yizhi (1611–1671), and Jiang Yong (1681–1762) investigated a wide range of technical topics that included medicine, mathematics, light and sound, magnetism, and hydraulics. They championed the idea of physical experimentation (*zhi ce*) and developed sophisticated methodologies of argumentation. Fang and Jiang proved to be particularly interested in the role of numbers in explaining natural relationships and processes. Moreover, both men had a substantial knowledge of Western mathematics. At the same time, however, their understanding of the natural world was profoundly influenced by inherited numerological ideas as reflected in the *Hetu* and *Luoshu*. Indeed, Fang tells us explicitly that "the images and numbers of the *Hetu* and *Luoshu* manifest the rules governing everything [in nature]."[83] Jiang held the same basic view. Yet these thinkers are often held out as paragons of late Ming and early Qing "evidential scholarship" (*kaozheng xue*; see chapter 6).

Other factors were at work in shaping the course of scientific inquiry in Qing dynasty China. For instance, Chinese scholars in the seventeenth and eighteenth centuries had neither a religious belief in "order" of the sort that inspired their European contemporaries, nor did they hold the conviction that in time all phenomena would yield their ultimate secrets. The typical Chinese belief, as Sivin puts the matter, was that "natural processes wove a pattern of constant relations too subtle and too multivariant to be understood completely by what we would call empirical investigation or mathematical analysis. Scientific explanation merely expressed, for finite and practical human purposes, partial and indirect views of that fabric."[84]

This intellectual disposition was reinforced by the Chinese civil service examination system, with its emphasis on the idealistic and highly metaphysical interpretations of the classics put forward by Zhu Xi. Zhu's scholarship, as Yung Sik Kim makes abundantly clear, was extraordinarily broad ranging, but not of a sort that prized methodological rigor, consistency, experimentation, or even direct and sustained observation. Zhu read extensively, but he was not interested in theoretical speculations about space, time, matter, motion, and so forth. As a result, his "science" was "a thoroughly 'common-sense' natural knowledge," which "covered everything in the world" but explained comparatively little.[85]

To be sure, as Benjamin Elman has recently noted, by the late eighteenth century the Chinese examination curriculum had begun to reflect the preoccupations of the schools of Han Learning and "evidential research," with their rigorous scientific analysis of ancient texts, their hostility toward Song learning, and their assault on certain elements of the inherited cosmology. But as Elman himself acknowledges, scholars of the period remained steadfast "moral generalists," who continued to believe that the *Changes* and other classics were the repositories of the most profound and ultimately valuable knowledge.[86] Although certain designated scientific subjects ("natural studies" or *ziran zhi xue*)—including astronomy and mathematical harmonics—had a significant place in the examination system at certain times, on the whole it was morality and statecraft that preoccupied most Chinese scholars and loomed largest in the exams.

In the twentieth century, and continuing up to the present, a number of Chinese scholars have identified features of the *Yijing* that seem compatible with "modern" science. Thus, we have contemporary individuals such as Yang Li arguing in the same basic vein as Fang Yizhi and Jiang Yong in the Qing period, that the numbers of the Yellow River Chart and the Luo River Writing are the "deriving coefficient" of everything in the cosmos. Tang Mingbang, for his part, asserts that the forms of atomic structure in nuclear physics, the genetic code in molecular biology, and the eight-tier matrix in linear algebra all seem to be related to the logic of the *Changes*.[87] Although this sort of thinking remains essentially correlative, it has nonetheless served as a source of satisfaction for Chinese scholars who have long been accustomed to the view that modern science had somehow passed China by (see chapter 11).

But the fact remains that science in pre-twentieth-century China never passed through a Newtonian phase of classical mechanics, with its emphasis on both direct observation and the mathematization of hypothesis. Although the binary structure of the *Yijing* entranced and inspired the great philosopher-mathematician G. W. Leibniz (1646–1716) when he learned of it through a Jesuit missionary to China in the late seventeenth century, the Chinese themselves did not develop the idea of using hexagrams as computational numbers. As a result, the number symbolism of the *Changes* in imperial times remained numerological and, with the possible exception of the work of a few remarkable *Yijing* scholars like Jiao Xun (1763–1820), never truly mathematical.[88]

One final point: a number of scholars have claimed that the classical Chinese language had a negative effect on the development of Chinese scientific thought.[89] Needham believes that this argument lacks merit, although he has remarked on the "unfortunate" tendency of the Chinese in pre-modern times to employ ancient words for scientific concepts rather than to develop a new scientific terminology. Part of the problem, he suggests, was undoubtedly China's inability to draw on Greek, Latin, and Arabic roots in the manner of Western (European) scientists.[90]

Another language-related factor shaping the contours of Chinese science may have been the tendency of scholars to create texts by amassing quotations from preexisting sources of authority and then organizing them in some sort of chronological or topical, but not necessarily analytical, order. This approach was not only a feature of most Chinese reference works, it was also characteristic of many philosophical and even "scientific" tracts. Prominent examples from late imperial times include Shen Gua's *Mengqi pitan* (Brush talks from Dream Brook) and Gu Yanwu's famous *Rizhi lu* (Record of daily [acquired] knowledge). Although this traditional approach to the accumulation and dissemination of scholarly learning certainly did not prevent Shen,

Gu, and others from developing creative ideas, on the whole it seems to have discouraged the intellectual habits of generalization and hypothesis.[91]

Robert Hartwell, in discussing traditional Chinese economic thought, reaches a similar conclusion. He remarks on the "amazing" propensity of writers in late imperial times to give equal treatment to statements of widely varying orders of abstraction and analytical significance. In his words:

> The Chinese normally did not distinguish . . . between the relative worth of alternative modes of logical presentation. . . . The failure to distinguish different orders of conceptualization severely limited the possibilities for integrating the separate ideas of economic doctrine into an explanatory system and precluded the broadening of abstraction essential to the progress of science. This was partly owing to the habitual use of the historical-analogical method . . . [but] primarily the result of neglecting to search consciously for general hypotheses.[92]

Arthur Wright, for his part, has discussed in detail the many problems of translation that faced proponents of foreign concepts in China, from the Buddhist missionaries in the Six Dynasties period to the Jesuits and other Christian missionaries during the Qing. Time and again, factors such as the semantic "weight" of Chinese characters—whether used as conceptual equivalents or merely in transliteration—tended to affect the meaning of the original foreign ideas (see chapter 11). In his view, the classical Chinese script did not provide a particularly fertile environment for the independent growth of foreign ideas. It did, however, contribute to the cohesiveness and continuity of Chinese civilization by helping to "domesticate" alien and potentially disruptive doctrines.[93]

The classical language contributed to cultural continuity and cohesiveness in two other important ways. First, it established a direct linguistic link between the Chinese present and a distant, but not forgotten, Chinese past. Because the ancient classics and contemporary documents were all written in the same basic script, a Qing scholar had immediate intellectual access to anything written in China during the past two thousand years. The language remained alive and well, part of a longstanding and still vital literary tradition and cultural heritage. Second, the script gave tremendous cultural unity to China across space. Because each Chinese character had the same basic set of meanings and associations, regardless of how it may have been pronounced, the literary language transcended local dialects, many of which were otherwise mutually unintelligible. There was thus no development in China comparable to the decline of Latin and the rise of national vernaculars in Europe. There was only the glaring fact that until well into the nineteenth century the Japanese, the Koreans, and the Vietnamese all continued to use classical Chinese as the principal means of written communication. This, of course, only fed China's already well-nourished sense of cultural superiority.

Chapter Six

Patterns of Thought

One of the most prominent features of Chinese thought in late imperial times was its extraordinary eclecticism, its ability to tolerate diverse and sometimes seemingly incompatible notions with little sense of conflict or contradiction. This syncretic capacity was vividly expressed in the Ming and Qing periods by the phrase *sanjiao heyi* ("the three teachings [of Confucianism, Daoism, and Buddhism] are united into one"). Thus, although the chapters on thought and religion in this book have been separated for convenience and clarity, in fact the two are inextricably related.

We should not, however, overestimate the fit among divergent strains of thought in Qing dynasty China. Even if we put "religion" aside for the moment and focus solely on Confucian philosophy,[1] it is clear that intellectual fashions changed significantly during the two and a half centuries of Manchu rule. These fashions, manifest in various separate "schools" of Confucianism, often invited powerful commitments based on regional identifications as well as patron-client and lineage ties. Benjamin Elman notes that in some cases, "a school was little more than a vague logical category whose members shared a textual tradition, or geographical proximity, or personal association, or philosophic agreement, or stylistic similarities, or combinations of these." But in many other cases, the definition of a school "legitimated the organizations that prepared its genealogy or provided rationalizations for the focus of scholarly activities peculiar to a particular region."[2]

Although the boundaries of Chinese intellectual life constantly shifted during the Qing period, we can identify several basic patterns of affiliation within which these shifts took place. As had been the case during much of the Ming dynasty, the Qing rulers generally supported Zhu Xi's School of Principle (*Lixue*)—also known as the Cheng-Zhu School—as their official orthodoxy. Emphasizing loyalty to the sovereign, moral cultivation, and the power of positive example, Cheng-Zhu Learning was distilled in the highly influential examination syllabus known as the *Xingli jingyi* (Essential Ideas of the School of Nature and Principle), commissioned by the Kangxi emperor in the early eighteenth century. Contrary to the view that this variety of Confucianism was merely "a philosophy of narrow metaphysical speculation," On-cho Ng has shown that it remained a vital intellectual force throughout most of the Qing period—one that provided room for both growth and contestation—even on the part of its most ardent advocates, such as the powerful court official Li Guangdi (1642–1718).[3]

The so-called Tongcheng School, centered on a county by this name in Anhui province, embraced Zhu Xi's moral idealism, but placed particular emphasis on ancient prose literature as a "vehicle of Confucian faith."[4] Proponents of this approach, like other less literarily inclined advocates of Cheng-Zhu Confucianism, were suspicious of, if not actively hostile to, the School of Evidential Research (*kaozheng xue*), whose iconoclastic advocates emerged as a "national elite" from the prosperous Yangzi River delta during the latter half of the seventeenth century. These creative *kaozheng* scholars—armed with sophisticated philological techniques and passionately committed to "seeking truth from facts" (*shishi qiu shi*)—devoted themselves primarily to textual criticism, although, as we have seen in chapter 5, a number of them engaged in scientific inquiry as well. Their research challenged certain orthodox interpretations of the Confucian classics, and even called into question the authenticity of some received texts. Although the overall "subversive" effect of *kaozheng* scholarship is a matter of debate, there can be no doubt that this school influenced Qing intellectual life in significant ways.[5]

During the eighteenth century, Qing scholars routinely identified the School of Evidential Research with Han Learning, so named because its intellectual progenitors, Gu Yanwu and Yan Ruoju (1636–1704), rejected Song-Ming sources in favor of earlier materials dating from the Han dynasty (206 BCE–220 CE). These writings from the Song and Ming eras—identified by most Western scholars as "neo-Confucian"—included not only the Cheng-Zhu School of Principle, but also the far more intuitive School of the Mind (*Xinxue*), associated with Lu Xiangshan (1139–1192) and Wang Yangming (1472–1529). Strictly speaking, however, Han Learning refers to a separate intellectual movement identified with the followers of Hui Dong (1697–1758) in Suzhou, individuals who focused primarily on materials from the latter part of the Han. Those who gravitated to sources from the earlier Han came to be identified as members of the New Text School (*Jinwen xue*).

The New Text School, also called the Gongyang School, stood on the intellectual frontier between Song and Han Learning. It grew out of a late eighteenth-century revival of a much earlier controversy over the authenticity of certain versions of the Confucian classics written in an ancient form of Chinese characters known as *guwen* ("old-style script"). These "old text" versions had been considered orthodox since the Later Han dynasty, when they replaced the set of classics written in the "new-style script" (*jinwen*) of the Early Han. But Qing *kaozheng* scholars such as Yan Ruoju began to uncover systematic evidence of forgeries in some of these Old Text versions, leading to a fierce debate over issues such as the place of Confucius in Chinese history and the role of institutional change within the Confucian tradition.

The School of Statecraft (*Jingshi xue*), as its name implies, took practical administration as its central concern, avoiding the moralistic extremes of Song Learning as well as the scholastic extremes of Han Learning. Although already an active intellectual force in the eighteenth century, Statecraft Learning rapidly gained momentum in the nineteenth, as dynastic decline underscored the need for practical solutions to China's pressing problems. One of several prominent centers of statecraft scholarship in the Qing was the famous state-sponsored Yuelu Academy in Hunan, a thousand-year-old institution whose distinguished nineteenth-century alumni included such stellar figures as He Changling (1785–1848), Tao Zhu (1779–1839), Wei Yuan (1794–1856), Zeng Guofan (1811–1872), Hu Linyi (1812–1861), and Guo Songtao (1818–1891).[6]

Some statecraft-oriented scholars, including Wei Yuan and Gong Zizhen (1792–1841), had a deep and abiding interest in New Text scholarship. But it was not until the late nineteenth century that the progressive potential of New Text Confucianism became fully apparent. At that time, reform-minded exponents of New Text learning—notably Kang Youwei (1858–1927) and his able student Liang Qichao (1873–1929)—moved to center stage in Qing political and intellectual life (see chapter 11). A central feature of Kang's spiritually inspired New Text approach was a "socio-moral pragmatism," which favored a free "ideological" interpretation of Confucianism over a literal and prosaic understanding.[7]

Many other schools of Confucian thought arose during the Qing dynasty. Some were inspired by idiosyncratic individualists such as the avowedly anti-scholastic Yan Yuan (1635–1704) and his famous disciple Li Gong (1659–1733). Other schools developed from the eclectic thought of renowned scholars such as Ruan Yuan (1764–1848) and Zeng Guofan. The syncretic tendencies of Chinese thought made it possible for a scholar-official like Zeng to esteem the literary and moral concerns of the Tongcheng School, and yet at the same time to recognize the merits of Han Learning, to gravitate toward the School of Statecraft in seeking solutions to the dynasty's administrative problems, and even to employ essentially Legalist methods in order to achieve idealistic Mencian aims. A distinctive feature of Zeng's thought, like that of many *kaozheng* scholars of his time and earlier, was an emphasis on *li*—by which he meant not only rules of social usage, rituals, and ceremonies, but also laws and institutions—as the common denominator of China's complex Confucian tradition.[8]

Yet for all this intellectual diversity, there were still significant common denominators existing among Qing scholars, in large part because the overwhelming majority of them were successful civil service degree candidates. In preparing for the exams, they read the same basic works, studied in the same basic way, and used the same set of evaluative terms and conceptual categories to express their ideas. The emphasis in private academies might differ somewhat from the curriculum in official schools, but, as we have seen, the practical aim of elite education in Qing times remained success in the examinations, and the early patterns of rote learning directed to this goal left a deep impression on most scholarly minds.

Further, as Yu Yingshi, Du Weiming, and others have indicated, the differences between certain schools of Confucian thought have often been overemphasized. There were, for example, important affinities between Song Learning and Han Learning in the area of philology, between Song Learning and the School of Statecraft in the management of practical affairs, and even between Song Learning and Wang Yangming's intuitive School of the Mind in the areas of both mental discipline and the relationship between knowledge and action. New Text scholars, for their part, shared many of the same administrative concerns as the School of Statecraft, although their proposals for governmental reform were generally more radical.[9] In all, as W. T. de Bary has suggested, the major polarities that existed in Confucianism between scholarship and public service, academic pursuits and self-cultivation, contemplation and activity, and aesthetics (or metaphysics) and practical concerns should be seen not as conflicting imperatives, but as "dynamic unities," a source of both vitality and adaptability in Chinese intellectual life.[10]

THE CHINESE INTELLECTUAL WORLD

Before proceeding to a detailed discussion of Confucian and Daoist philosophy, we may pause to review some general features of traditional Chinese thought—bearing in mind, once again, that at no time was there total agreement among scholars on any one of these points. On the whole, however, Chinese thinkers in the Qing period evinced an abiding concern with ethics and human relations; an interest in nature and natural processes; a deep sense of cultural distinctiveness and superiority; a profound awareness of and respect for tradition; a general preference for suggestiveness over articulation in philosophical discourse; an emphasis on the concrete over the purely abstract; and a heavy reliance on bureaucratic classification, analogy, and the "logic of correlative duality" as a means of organizing and understanding the vast whole of human experience.

Attunement to natural processes in China encouraged an organismic view of the universe, in which the cosmic forces of *yin* and *yang* continually interacted to produce the so-called five agents (*wuxing*)—qualities associated with wood (flourishing), fire (heat), earth (stability), metal (sharpness or durability), and water (coolness). These agents, in various combinations under various circumstances, became manifest in the material force (*qi*) of which all things, animate and inanimate, were constituted. Like *yin* and *yang*, the five agents not only influenced the production and composition of *qi*; they also dominated phases of time, succeeding each other in endless patterns of mutual interaction and cyclical alternation.

The Chinese viewed the universe as a regular, self-contained, self-operating whole, spontaneously generated and perpetually in motion. Everything within the cosmos existed as part of an orderly and harmonious hierarchy of interrelated objects and forces, in which "things of the same type" (*tonglei*) had a penchant for corresponding, resonating, and otherwise interacting with one another. Synchronicity (the coincidence of events in space and time) thus came to be stressed over simple causality as an explanatory principle. The harmonious cooperation and synchronic interaction of all things in the universe did not, however, arise from the commands of an external supreme will or authority. Instead, it proceeded out of a natural unified cosmic pattern or process (the Way, or *Dao*), which mandated that all things follow the internal dictates of their own natures. Thus we find that even Pan Gu, the legendary "creator" in Chinese folklore, was never viewed as a Logos or demiurge, much less as the omniscient, omnipowerful creator of the Semitic, Christian, and Islamic traditions.

Lacking the idea of a personalistic creator external to the cosmos, the Chinese developed an approach to religious life that led to the rejection of both monotheism and theological absolutism; the weakness of institutional religion; the strength of diffused religions (such as ancestor worship, the worship of Heaven by the state, and the worship of patron gods in associations such as guilds); and the failure to develop a concept of evil as an active force in the personified Western sense. The introduction of Buddhism and other alien belief systems in China, and the later development of an elaborate neo-Confucian metaphysics, did nothing to alter these basic features of Chinese religious life (see chapter 7). Neo-Confucianism (see below) did, however, contribute the idea of an eternal prime mover, or Supreme Ultimate (*Taiji*), which spontaneously and continually generated the cosmic forces of *yin* and *yang* and also served as the source (and sum) of the ideal forms, or principles (*li*), around which *qi* coalesced to comprise all things. By late imperial times elite interest in the metaphysical notion of *Taiji* had waned considerably, but the concept remained an integral feature of official Qing ideology and was also solidly imbedded in the popular mind.

Moreover, the use of *yinyang* as a conceptual paradigm continued unabated in all realms of traditional Chinese life. The idea of *yinyang* interaction generally sufficed as an explanation of cosmic creativity and change, and the specific evaluative terms *yang* and *yin* continued to be used to accommodate nearly any set of dual coordinates, from abstruse Buddhist or neo-Confucian concepts such as "perceived reality and emptiness" (*sekong*), "principle and material force" (*liqi*), and "substance and function" (*tiyong*) to such mundane but important polarities as light and dark, hot and cold, dry and wet, hard and soft, firm and yielding, active and passive, and male and female. It was a natural Chinese tendency to divide phenomena into two unequal but complementary parts (see also the introduction and chapter 5).

The important point to keep in mind is that *yin* and *yang* were always viewed as relative concepts. As creative forces they were continually in flux, each growing out of the other and each in turn "controlling" situations or activities. And even as specific evaluative categories, they were never viewed as absolutes. The *Daode jing* (The Way and its power) underscores this basic point: "Being [lit. having] and non-being [lit. not-having] produce each other; difficult and easy complete each other. Long and short contrast each other; high and low distinguish each other. Sound and voice harmonize with each other; front and back follow each other."[11] In the main, then, *yin* and *yang* were not things, but classifications of relations. Any given object or phenomenon might be designated *yin* in one set of relations and *yang* in another. Thus, in the vocabulary of painting and calligraphy, the brush was considered *yang* because it was the active instrument using ink (*yin*). Yet the brush could be considered *yin* in relation to the *yang* of the artist (or, for that matter, the artist's subject material); and although the ink was dark (*yin*) on the light paper or silk, it showed a *yang* aspect when applied to the "passive" paper or silk.

One's philosophical outlook also affected the perception of *yinyang* relationships, for what one thinker saw as positive, another might see as negative. Zhang Boxing's (1652–1725) commentary on a passage concerning the Fu hexagram in the *Jinsi lu* states, for example: "The way of the exemplary person [*junzi*] is the same as the way of *yang* [that is, strong and assertive]." But Daoists held the opposite view, arguing "to yield is to be preserved whole" and "the sage never strives for the great, and thereby the great is achieved."[12] To an extent, of course, Zhang is correct in contrasting Confucian activism

Table 6.1.

Yin *and* Yang *Correlations*			
Yang	*Yin*	*Yang*	*Yin*
Light	Dark	Activity	Quiescence
Hot	Cold	Life	Death
Dry	Moist	Advance	Retreat
Fire	Water	Expand	Contract
Red	Black	Full	Empty
Day	Night	Straight	Crooked
Sun	Moon	Hard	Soft
Spring-Summer	Autumn-Winter	Round	Square
Male	Female	South	North

Five-Agents (Wuxing) *Correlations*					
Correlation	*Wood*	*Fire*	*Earth*	*Metal*	*Water*
Animal	dog	goat	ox	chicken	pig
Organ system	liver	heart	spleen	lungs	kidneys
Number	3, 8	2, 7	5, 10	4, 9	1, 6
Color	green	red	yellow	white	black
Direction	east	south	center	west	north
Emotion	anger	joy	desire	sorrow	fear
Taste	sour	bitter	sweet	acrid	salty
State of yinyang	yin in yang (or lesser yang)	yang (or greater yang)	yinyang balance	yang in yin (or lesser yin)	yin (or greater yin)

Note: Like *yin* and *yang*, the five agents were used in Chinese thought to indicate both cosmic activities and conceptual categories. In either case, as with *yin* and *yang*, the pattern of movement was one of ceaseless alteration and cyclical change. The order of the agents and the process by which one displaced another varied according to different schemes, however.

with Daoist passivity. But his stark statement obscures two important points. The first is that Confucians often placed a premium on "yielding" in social situations and promoted a view of government by moral example that was in many ways quite passive (*yin*). The second point is that circumstances were continually changing, and despite Zhang's assumption that strength would always prevail, most Chinese—Confucians and Daoists alike—accepted the *Yijing*'s basic premise that change was a matter of *yinyang* alternation. Inevitably, the "hard" (*gang*) would surrender to the "soft" (*rou*), even if only temporarily.

The idea of *yinyang* alternation was central to the traditional Chinese conception of time, which, following the usage of the *Yijing*, came to be seen as a kind of field or receptacle for human events. Indeed, the *yinyang* paradigm itself developed out of an early appreciation of the rhythms and regularities of cyclical change in nature—notably the twenty-four-hour cycle of light and dark and the seasonal fluctuation between the two poles of summer heat and winter cold. The Chinese word for time (*shi*) originally meant "the period of sowing," and it never totally lost its specific seasonal and cyclical connotations.

"Timeliness" was of central significance to the Chinese in all facets of daily life, at all levels. Two of the most important ritual acts of a new dynasty were to "regulate the calendar" and to "fix the time." Control of time, like control of space, was a crucial index of imperial legitimacy. State calendars (*shixian li, shixian shu*) gave concrete guidance to Qing officials regarding auspicious and inauspicious times for a wide range of activities, both secular and sacred, and popular almanacs (*tongshu, liben, huangli,* etc.) did the same for the rest of Chinese society (see chapters 7 and 10). And, of course, the universal practice of divination was all about proper timing. In everyday matters, the water clock divided the day and night into two-hour segments, while the lunar calendar marked the twelve months of the year (with intercalary adjustments to compensate for the eleven-day difference between the lunar period of 354 days and the solar period of 365 days). Longer spans of time were conventionally measured in linear order by dynastic periods and by imperial reign names (*nianhao*) within each dynasty.

Overall, time in traditional China was usually viewed in cyclical rather than in strictly linear terms. Cycles might be as long as four Buddhist kalpas (each calculated in millions, billions and even trillions of years) or as short as the common sixty-year and sixty-day cycles of the native Chinese tradition. Even dynastic periods were seen as macrocosms of the natural lifecycle of birth, growth, decline, and death—comparable to the fourfold Buddhist cycle of formative growth, organized existence, disintegration, and annihilation alluded to above. In contrast with the Christian, Islamic, and Judaic traditions, the world had no fixed starting point, although in Chinese popular tradition human events were sometimes dated in successive years from the accession of the mythical Yellow Emperor in 2698 BCE.

Shao Yong's (1011–1077) widespread theory of recurrent and eternal 129,600-year cycles, originally inspired by Buddhism, provided one convenient means by which to reconcile a cyclical view of human experience with the pervasive idea of a golden age in China's past. According to Shao, the present cycle began at a date corresponding to 67,017 BCE, reaching its peak at about 2330 BCE during the reign of the legendary sage-ruler Yao. Human society was now in decline, however, and would continue to decline until the extinction of living creatures about CE 46,000. In CE 62,583 the world would end, and a new cycle would then begin. Because dynastic history, as part of the total cosmic process, moved in a cyclical pattern, it followed that an identifiable *yinyang* alternation between order and disorder, prosperity and decline, was both natural and inevitable. Each situation contained the seeds of the other.

But the Chinese also believed that historical circumstances depended on human action, and that dynastic decline could thus be at least temporarily arrested by the concerted efforts of moral individuals. Such a phenomenon was known as a restoration (*zhongxing*; lit. rising at mid-course). Only a few such restorations had been recorded in Chinese history, but one did occur in the late Qing period, during the strife-torn reign of the Tongzhi emperor (see chapter 11). Although most Chinese thinkers rejected the idea of historical change in the sense of progressive improvement, they continued to be moved by a strong impulse to improve society by hearkening back to earlier historical models and moral exemplars. Even non-elites were well aware of these paragons of the past. Popular encyclopedias like the WBQS commonly provided dynasty-by-dynasty summaries of Chinese history, usually under the category of "Human Relationships" (see appendix E). These concise chronological outlines focused primarily on emperors and other major historical figures, including mythical sage heroes of the distant past who were not assumed to be mythical at all.

In elite circles there were two main kinds of historians. One kind consisted of individuals who wrote about history as a matter of personal interest (virtually all Chinese scholars did some of this), but who were not "official" historians. A few such individuals, notably Zhang Xuecheng (1738–1801) in the Qing, became justifiably famous for their mastery of the historian's craft. Zhang is especially worthy of mention, not only because of his scholarly acumen, but also because—unlike most scholars of his time—he believed that women were as capable of writing proper history as men. In his view, the famous woman historian Ban Zhao (45–c. 114), who played a major role in compiling the much-admired official *Hanshu* (History of the [former] Han), was not at all an anomaly.[13] The other kind of elite historian operated as an employee of the state, working in the Bureau of National History (*Guoxue yuan*) under the prestigious Hanlin Academy or in related offices at the capital. Employment of this sort was one of the many ways that the Manchu rulers eventually brought reluctant Chinese scholars such as Wan Sitong (1638–1702) into the Qing fold.[14]

Theoretically, all history in China was viewed as a morality tale, reflecting Confucian value judgments of "praise and blame" (*baobian*). This was supposed to be true in particular for the official dynastic histories, each of which was written by the succeeding regime. History was more than just a narrative of the past, then; it was also a guide to proper conduct for the present and the future. The Qing scholar Zhao Yi (1727–1814) put the matter this way in the preface to his famous *Nianer shi zhayi* (Notes on the twenty-two dynastic histories): "The [Confucian] Classics are the principles of government; the histories are the evidences [lit. traces] of government."[15] The idea was that rulers and officials could, and should, learn from past events and personalities. In China, therefore, historical precedent acquired something of the power attached to law and formal logic in the West.

The traditional Chinese dynastic histories followed a general model provided by the great Han historian Sima Qian (c. 145–c. 86 BCE). Although no two of the twenty-six formal histories (including the draft history of the Qing) are exactly the same, most consist of four major divisions: the imperial annals, chronological tables, monographs, and biographies. Of these, the monographs and biographies are especially helpful in indicating traditional categories of historical concern. Let us examine briefly the *Mingshi* (compiled 1678–1739) and the *Qingshi gao* (Draft history of the Qing; compiled 1914–1927)—the last two traditional dynastic histories—with these concerns in mind.

Among the most significant monographs in each multivolume history are those on ritual, music, the calendar, astronomy, rivers and canals, food and commodities, law and punishments, the five agents, geography, literature, officials, chariots and costumes, the civil service, and the army. Among the most important shared categories of biography are those of dutiful officials, Confucian scholars, empresses, doctors, hermits, literary persons, eminent women, filial persons, and loyal subjects. Some differences are obvious—notably the special attention given to eunuchs, imperial relatives, and traitors in the *Mingshi* biographies and the new categories of monographs in the *Qingshi gao* relating to communications and foreign relations. These differences can be explained, of course, by the differing historical circumstances of the two dynastic periods.[16]

As we have already seen, the *Mingshi* omits any significant discussion of the dynasty's relations with the Jurchen ethnic group that would later be called the Manchus, especially in their subservient role as tributaries. Sources such as the Veritable Records (*Shilu*) of the Ming contain much information on interactions between the Jurchen and the Ming, including conflicts dating from the Wanli era (1572–1620), but they were not used in the compilation of the *Mingshi*; instead the Qing dynasty compilers drew on early Manchu documents. Furthermore, despite the avowed moral emphasis of the official dynastic histories, pragmatic politics often informed their specific content.[17]

Traditionally, China's foreign relations did not occupy a special place in the dynastic histories, although discussions of "barbarians" could be found sprinkled liberally throughout the various major divisions, notably the biographies.[18] For the most part, foreigners were viewed by the Chinese in terms of military security and/or trade—not as objects of independent ethnographic interest. Throughout most of the Qing period, as in previous eras, Chinese knowledge of outsiders was fragmentary and imprecise. This led to what Matthew Mosca describes as "geographic agnosticism"—the idea that "Some claims [about the outside world] might be preferred and others doubted, but none could be absolutely endorsed or eliminated."[19] As a result, although some Qing geographers and ethnographers made a concerted effort to acquire an accurate understanding of foreign lands and peoples,[20] few intellectuals, including most officials, had a realistic grasp of the world beyond the Qing empire until the mid-nineteenth century. Indeed, one prominent feature of both elite and popular encyclopedias in late imperial times was a more or less indiscriminate mingling of the "real" and the obviously fantastic in depictions and descriptions of "barbarians."[21]

The Chinese world view, which evolved over many centuries of extensive contact with foreigners within China, on China's borders, and beyond, was based on the essentially unchallenged idea of China's cultural superiority to all other states. As Benjamin Schwartz has remarked, "A random perusal of discussions of barbarians in the various [Chinese] encyclopedias and other sources reveals again and again the degree of emphasis on the five relationships, the 'three bonds' . . . and the whole body of *li* [ritual] as providing the absolute criteria dividing barbarians from the men of the Middle Kingdom."[22] Generally speaking, then, the further removed from the "civilizing influence" of Chinese culture, the more likely foreigners would be described as dogs and sheep, who were amenable only to policies such as beating, throwing them bones or food, and keeping them under a "loose rein." It is important to emphasize, however, that throughout the imperial era, Chinese foreign policy was highly sophisticated, varying according to China's strategic and administrative needs, the perception of an alien threat, the attitudes and activities of the "barbarians" themselves, and, of course, the desires of the emperor.

In theory, the Chinese world view was passive: foreigners were expected to gravitate to China solely out of admiration for Chinese culture. And indeed, the historical record abounds with praise for groups of foreigners as well as individuals who "admired right behavior and turned toward [Chinese] civilization" (*muyi xianghua*). Force was to be used only as a last resort in the conduct of China's foreign relations. As we have seen, however, foreign policy in the Qing, as in other dynamic periods of Chinese history such as the Han and the Tang, was openly aggressive. Moreover, as we have also seen, concerted efforts were made at various times to "civilize" non-Han ethnic groups in China Proper.

The gap between theory and practice in China's treatment of foreigners was especially evident in the so-called tributary system. Much debate surrounds this concept, and some scholars have suggested its abandonment—largely on the grounds that certain individuals have overgeneralized its historical significance. But for many hundred of years there *was* a tributary system in China, with its own highly refined vocabulary, institutions, rituals, and representations. Tributary rhetoric, regulations, and policies are evident in a great many official Qing documents, including the dynasty's Collected Statutes (*huidian*), its Comprehensive Rituals (*tongli*), and its Veritable Records (*shilu*).

The fundamental features of the tributary system were also reflected in a wide variety of visual media, ranging from maps, encyclopedias, and almanacs to the imperially commissioned ten-volume compendium titled *Huang Qing zhigong tu* (Illustrations of the tribute-bearing people of the imperial Qing; 1761). The Qing tributary system was also celebrated in a number of court-sponsored paintings, including the large and beautifully executed "Wanguo laichao tu" (Illustration of the myriad countries coming to [pay tribute at] court), produced by two of the Qianlong emperor's talented Chinese painters—Yao Wenhan (dates unknown) and Zhang Tingyan (1735–1794). Much of this visual and documentary material is now easily accessible, both in print and online.[23]

The importance of the tributary system to the throne naturally varied according to circumstances, and in any case it was never the sole mechanism for the conduct of Chinese foreign relations. Nonetheless, it remained an extremely important frame of reference for policymakers throughout the Qing period, reflecting an attitude toward foreigners and foreign relations that is especially interesting in the light of the "alien" origins of the Manchus (many Koreans and Japanese considered them to be "barbarians," even after 1644). What seems clear is that in keeping with their remarkable multiculturalism, the Qing rulers saw no conflict between their self-image as Inner Asian khans, Buddhist cakravartin kings, and stewards of the age-old Chinese tributary system—the most visible manifestation of the emperor's claim to rule "All under Heaven."

Historically, the Chinese viewed the tributary system as an extension of the ancient social and political order of the early Zhou dynasty (c. 1050–256 BCE). It rested on the assumption of a hierarchical structure of foreign relations, with China at both the top and center. Relationships were based on feudal principles of investiture and loyalty, with China serving as the lord and other states as vassals. According to the tributary regulations of the Qing period, non-Chinese rulers were given a patent of appointment, noble rank, and an official seal for use in correspondence. They, in turn, presented symbolic tribute, sent periodic memorials of congratulation or condolence, dated their communications by the Qing calendar, and performed the appropriate rituals required by the Qing court. Loyal tributaries received imperial gifts and protection in return, and were granted certain privileges of trade at the frontier and/or the capital.[24]

This was the basic theory of the tributary system and, in fact, the way it often operated in practice. But as indicated earlier, the system was flexible and Qing policymakers, like their predecessors for some two thousand years, were pragmatic. In times of military weakness the Chinese were often obliged to buy off "barbarians" with tributary gifts, and to make other compromises with the theoretical assumptions of the Chinese world order. In making peace with the foreign-ruled Jin dynasty in 1138, for example, the founder of the Southern Song had to accept the humiliating status of a vassal (*chen*). And even in periods of Chinese strength, the tributary system proved to be quite flexible.

John Wills has shown, for instance, that during the Kangxi emperor's reign, the Qing authorities were able to make pragmatic decisions based on domestic politics and strategic interests in dealing with foreign embassies from the Netherlands and Portugal—although significantly he emphasizes that the façade of imperial authority over "strangers from afar" had to remain intact. In 1793, the Qianlong emperor displayed a similar flexibility in allowing Great Britain's special envoy, Lord George Macartney, to have an imperial audience, despite Macartney's refusal to perform the ritually required full kowtow (three kneelings and nine prostrations, known in Chinese as *sangui jiukou*). Throughout the entire period of the Macartney visit, the Qing authorities continued to view the embassy as a tributary mission and treated it as such. They accepted British "tributary gifts" and offered presents in return, but they also refused British requests for regular diplomatic representation and the expansion of trade.[25]

In all, Chinese thinkers were not overly concerned with the gap between theory and practice in foreign relations. Zhao Yi, for one, maintained that the practice of "true principle" in foreign affairs necessarily involved adjustments. "The teachings of true principle," he wrote, "cannot always be reconciled with the circumstances of the times. If one cannot entirely maintain the demands of true principle, then true principle must be adjusted to the circumstances of the time, and only then do we have the practice of true principle."[26]

THE CONFUCIAN MORAL ORDER

Ping-ti Ho writes of the Qing: "In no earlier period of Chinese history do we find a deeper permeation and wider acceptance of the norms, mores, and values which modern students regard as Confucian." The Qing emperors ardently patronized Confucian scholarship and paid unprecedented homage to Confucius in official ceremonies, including two kneelings and six prostrations in Beijing, and the full kowtow in Qufu, the birthplace of the Sage. The education of Manchu princes followed carefully constructed Confucian lines, and the examination system was, of course, based solidly on the Confucian classics and commentaries. Lawrence Kessler tells us that by the end of the Kangxi emperor's reign in the early eighteenth century, "the Manchu-controlled state and the Chinese-guarded Confucian value system were harmoniously joined . . . [and the] Confucian ideal of the unity of state and knowledge, under the rule of a sage-king, seemed near realization."[27]

During the Qing period, as in earlier times, one's intellectual posture was ordinarily a function of several major variables: (1) personality and family background, (2) educational experience, (3) personal and dynastic fortunes, and (4) career concerns. Political factors were especially important in determining the popularity of a certain school of thought at a particular time, but the attachment of any individual to a given point of view might well hinge on career concerns. Thus, for example, young students and gentry awaiting official appointment could be expected to emphasize Song idealism, if only because a mastery of Zhu Xi's thought brought the possibility of personal advancement. Officials, on the other hand, might publicly espouse neo-Confucian moral principles only to seek administrative guidance from the School of Statecraft. And retired officials might find satisfaction in pure scholarship and the contemplative life, studying the *Yijing* and perhaps also investigating the officially disparaged but still attractive ideas of Wang Yangming, the Daoists, and even the Buddhists.

Despite the broad spectrum of Confucian thought that existed during the Qing period, we can identify certain general features that apply, more or less, to all major "schools": (1) a comparative lack of interest in metaphysics; (2) a rationalistic outlook, predicated on a belief in the intelligibility of the universe; (3) a great reverence for the past; (4) a humanistic concern with "man in society"; (5) an emphasis on morality in government and a link between personal and political values; (6) a belief in the moral perfectibility of all human beings; (7) the supreme authority of fundamental Confucian principles; and (8) a general disesteem of law. Frederick Mote explains the significance of the last point:

> In a civilization like the Chinese where there are only human sources (or among Daoists, "natural sources") of normative ideas, law could scarcely be expected to achieve the significance it possessed in other civilizations. For in all other civilizations it was based on the supra-rational and unchallengeable law of God, which commanded all creatures, and states as well, to enforce its literal prohibitions. Nor in China could there be any priestly enforcers of divine commandment, or even governors enforcing divine law or civil law armed with the analogy between man and God's law.[28]

In Qing China, the ideal emphasis was on *li* (ritual or, more generally, standards of social usage) rather than law. As Confucius once remarked: "If the people are led by laws, and an attempt made to give them uniformity by means of punishments, they will try to avoid the punishment, but have no sense of shame. If [however] they are led by virtue, and an attempt is made to give them uniformity by means of ritual, they will have a sense of shame and become good."[29]

The Confucian tradition drew on a vast corpus of classical literature and commentaries, with a particular emphasis on the Five Classics, the Four Books, and several additional works. The Five Classics were: (1) the *Yijing* (Classic of changes), (2) the *Shijing* (Classic of poetry or Classic of songs), (3) the *Shujing* (Classic of documents or Classic of history), (4) the *Chunqiu* (Spring and autumn annals), and (5) the *Liji* (Record of ritual). The Four Books were: (1) the *Lunyu* (Analects of Confucius), (2) the *Mengzi* (Book of Mencius), (3) the *Daxue* (Great learning), and (4) the *Zhongyong* (Doctrine of the mean). The other major texts included two works on ritual, the *Zhouli* (Rites of Zhou) and the *Yili* (Etiquette and ritual), and two on the *Spring and Autumn Annals*: the *Zuozhuan* (Commentary of Zuo) and the *Gongyang zhuan* (Commentary of Gongyang).[30]

Different schools of Confucianism emphasized different classics and/or commentaries. Scholars of Song Learning, for example, derived their understanding of the *Spring and Autumn Annals* from the "orthodox" *Zuo Commentary*, while those of the New Text persuasion looked to the *Gongyang Commentary* for inspiration and guidance (primarily because it was the only *jinwen* commentary that had survived intact from the Former Han dynasty). At the same time, "purist" *kaozheng* scholars, enamored of ritual (*li*) as an antidote to what they viewed as the "corrupt" and "debased" teachings of Song-style neo-Confucianism, favored the *Record of Ritual* and the work titled *Etiquette and Ritual*. Some intellectuals even explored the officially discouraged ideas of Xunzi, whose theory of man's innately "evil" nature stood in sharp contrast to the widely if not universally shared notion of Mencius, that all human beings were fundamentally good.

Works such as the *Classic of Changes* invited an especially wide range of interpretations. In addition to commentaries based on every major "school" of Confucianism described above, there were also different interpretive traditions within the special field of *Yijing* studies (*Yixue*). The two most prominent of these were the metaphysically oriented School of Images and Numbers (*xiangshu*) and the morally oriented School of Meanings and Principles (*yili*). And there were even more hermeneutical possibilities. As the renowned Qing scholar Huang Zongxi pointed out: "The nine traditions of philosophy and the hundred schools of thought have all drawn upon [the *Yijing*] to promote their own theories." These intellectual traditions included not only various schools of Confucianism, but also Buddhist and Religious Daoist traditions. According to the editors of the SKQS, interpreting the *Classic of Changes* was like playing chess: no two games were alike, and there were infinite hermeneutical possibilities.[31]

Although the Five Classics were all concerned with Confucian morality, they approached it from different angles. At the risk of overgeneralizing, the *Classic of Changes* offered a cosmically oriented vision of situation-based ethics; the *Classic of History* and the *Spring and Autumn Annals* focused primarily on issues of "praise and blame"; and the *Classic of Poetry* and the *Record of Ritual* contained prescriptions for proper behavior. The Four Books focused primarily on the idea of developing one's inner moral life. To be sure, all four of them contained a certain amount of spiritual wisdom, some examples of historical heroes and villains, and a number of prescriptions for proper behavior. But they spoke most fundamentally to problems of self-knowledge and self-cultivation. These were the themes that Zhu Xi and his followers had in mind when they brought the Four Books together as a special repository of classical teaching in the Song dynasty. From 1384 onward these four works generally took precedence over the Five Classics in the examination system.

The values contained in the Four Books were closely related. As Chung-ying Cheng has aptly remarked, the major Confucian virtues must all "be understood in relative definitions of each other . . . for each supposes the rest." A careful reading of the Four Books confirms the correctness of this view. Although the relationships are not always spelled out clearly, they are no less important for their lack of systematic exposition. At the same time, however, we should remember that, as with the Five Classics, Cheng-Zhu orthodoxy did not prevent Qing scholars from offering significantly divergent opinions about one or another of the Four Books.[32]

At the heart of the Confucian value system in late imperial times lay the Three Bonds (*Sangang*): between ruler and minister (or, more broadly, subject); between father and son; and between husband and wife. These were the first three of the so-called Five Relationships, which also included the relationship between older (brother) and younger (brother) and friend to friend. The concept of the Three Bonds may be traced to the influential Han scholar Dong Zhongshu, who wrote: "the relationships between sovereign and subject, father and son, and husband and wife, are all derived from the principles of *yin* and *yang*. The sovereign is *yang*, the subject is *yin*; the father is *yang*, the son is *yin*; the husband is *yang*, the wife is *yin*. . . . The three bonds of the Way of the [True] King may be sought in Heaven."[33]

Of these three relationships, the tie between husband and wife was considered most basic. "That male and female should dwell together is the greatest of human relations," asserted Mencius. The "Orderly Sequence of the Hexagrams" of the *Yijing* indicates that all other human relationships grow out of the relationship between man and wife:

Following the existence of Heaven and Earth came the existence of all things. Following the existence of all things came the existence of male and female.

Following the existence of male and female came the relationship between husband and wife. And following the relationship of husband and wife came the relationship between father and son. Following the relationship between father and son came the relationship between ruler and subject. Following the relationship between the ruler and subject came the general distinction between superior and inferior. Following the distinction between superior and inferior came the arrangements of ritual and righteousness.[34]

The entire Confucian social and moral order was thus based on the "natural" relationship of husband and wife, with its assumptions of inequality, subordination, and service. As Mencius once stated, "to look upon compliance as their correct course is the rule [*dao*] for women."[35]

Some Qing scholars, notably Qian Daxin (1728–1804), believed that marriage was a human artifact rather than a natural bond, and therefore mutable. It followed, then, that divorce was not necessarily improper. Taking a similar tack, Huang Zongxi challenged the idea of "cosmological kingship" as an integral part of the Three Bonds on the grounds that the ruler-subject relationship was secular and functional, and could thus be altered, depending on circumstances.[36] But neither Qian nor Huang, nor any other major Confucian thinker, could conceive of a mutable relationship between parents and children.

Filial piety (*xiao*) and its corollary, fraternal submission (*di*), lay at the very heart of Confucianism. Mencius tells us that devotion to one's parents is the greatest service and the foundation of every other service. The *Great Learning* remarks, "if one is not obedient to his parents, he will not be true to his friends," and "if one is not trusted by his friends, he will not get the confidence of his sovereign." The *Xiaojing* (Classic of filial piety) goes so far as to claim that the ancient Chinese sages "brought order to the world through filial piety." And the *Analects* state explicitly that *xiao* and *di* are the root of humaneness (*ren*)—the most exalted of the "Five Constant Virtues" of Confucianism: *ren*, *li* (ritual, propriety, or norms of social usage), *yi* (duty, or righteousness), *zhi* (humane wisdom), and *xin* (faithfulness).[37]

Let us examine these five cardinal virtues in greater detail, giving particular attention to the concept of *ren*. Qing Confucians considered *ren* to be a universal cosmic virtue that, in effect, generated and encompassed all the other virtues. Wing-tsit Chan's careful study of the evolution of *ren* leaves no doubt that by late imperial times the term had become all-important. *Ren*, he tells us, "precludes all evil and underlies as well as embraces all possible virtues, so much so that 'if you set your mind on *ren*, you will be free from evil.'" Confucius tells us that *ren* means to "love human beings" (*airen*); and Mencius equates *ren* with the innate goodness of man's nature, manifest in the feeling of commiseration: the inability to bear the suffering of others. *Ren*, in the view of most Qing scholars, was the "single thread" unifying the teachings of Confucius—the one moral principle for all human actions.[38]

Much has been made of the negative thrust of the famous Confucian dictum "Do not do to others what you would not want others to do to you." But it is clear that virtually all Confucian scholars understood this "Golden Rule" as having both a positive and negative aspect. The Qing commentator Liu Baonan (1791–1855) spoke for many in maintaining that if it is true that we must not do to others what we do not want done to ourselves, then it must also be true that "we must do to others what we want them to do to us." Further, Liu concurs with Zhu Xi and most other late imperial thinkers in equating the principles of *zhong* (usually translated "loyalty") and *shu* ("reciprocity") as referring, respectively, to the full development of one's mind and the extension of that mind to others, thus giving a positive cast to Confucian responsibility. As the *Analects* state: "The man of *ren*, wishing to establish his own character, seeks also to establish the character of others."[39]

This did not mean, however, that all people should be treated equally. Instead, the Confucian idea of *ren* was "love with distinctions" (*ai you chadeng*), that is, love graded outward from the family and focused particularly on the virtuous. From a Confucian standpoint, it was impossible to love all people equally (*jian'ai*) as the ancient philosopher Mozi had urged, for all people were not equal, either in closeness or in social station. According to Confucians, different values were appropriate to different relationships. Thus, Mencius informs us that "between father and son, there should be affection; between sovereign and minister, righteousness; between husband and wife, attention to their separate functions; between elder and younger, proper order; and between friends, faithfulness."[40]

Ren, in the orthodox view, was the key to good government. The *Great Learning* asserts: "Yao and Shun led the kingdom with benevolence [*ren*] and the people followed them," and again, "Never has there been a case of the sovereign loving benevolence, and the people not loving righteousness. Never has there been a case where the people have loved righteousness, and the affairs of the sovereign have not been carried to completion." Confucian government was never meant to be *by* the people, but it certainly was *for* the people, and the assumption remained that the moral cultivation of the ruler would bring peace and harmony to "all under Heaven." In the words of the *Record of Ritual*,

By honoring men of virtue and talent, the sovereign is preserved from errors of judgment. By showing affection to his relatives, there is no grumbling and resentment among his uncles and brethren. By respecting the great ministers, he is kept from errors in the practice of government. By kind and considerate treatment of the whole body of officers, they are led to make the most grateful return for his courtesies. By dealing with the mass of people as his children, they are led to exhort one another to what is good. . . . By indulgent treatment of men from afar, they resort to him from all quarters.[41]

There was also, however, a more "realistic" wing of Confucian political theory, which sought administrative inspiration in less idealistic works, such as the writings of Xunzi and the *Rites of Zhou*. This latter work, which had often been cited by radical reformers in China's past, provided classical precedents for systems of equitable land distribution, public security, famine relief, arbitration, and even criminal justice. When it became necessary to reconcile the idealistic Mencian emphasis on *ren* with the harsh realities of Qing political life, scholar-officials like Yuan Shouding (1705–1872) could argue that the Qing penal code was based on the concepts of the *Rites of Zhou*, but that its aim was to implement the Mencian values of humaneness and righteousness.[42] In any case, we find many examples of Qing scholars whose idealistic Confucian values were tempered by an un-Confucian emphasis on law, rewards, and punishments.

Standing between rule by moral example and rule by law, closer to the former than the latter, was rule by ritual and propriety. The *Record of Ritual* informs us that "Ceremonies [*li*] form a great instrument in the hands of the ruler. They provide the means by which to resolve what is doubtful, clarify what is abstruse, receive the spirits, examine regulations, and distinguish humaneness from righteousness. . . . To govern a state without ritual would be like plowing a field without a plowshare." The seventeenth-century censor Chen Cizhi spoke for many Qing officials in asserting that "for managing the world and pacifying the people there is nothing greater than ritual." Wei Xiangshu (1617–1687) advised the early Manchu rulers: "The moral transformation of the people is the dynasty's first task, and the regulations of ritual constitute the great beginning of moral transformation."[43] Through proper ritual, the emperor not only affirmed his position as Son of Heaven and ruler of all earthly domains, but he and his officials also promoted social harmony within the realm through moral example. This, at least, was the theory of Confucian government.

In Chinese ethical life, *ren* and *li* existed in a kind of creative tension, each contributing to the meaning or manifestation of the other. Du Weiming considers *li* to be the "externalization" of *ren* in concrete social circumstances. Confucius once said, "If a man is not humane, what has he to do with *li*?" But in another context, the Master remarked, "To conquer the self and return to *li* is humaneness." When asked how one could achieve this object, Confucius replied, "Do not look at what is contrary to *li*; do not listen to what is contrary to *li*; do not say what is contrary to *li*; and do not make any movement contrary to *li*." The three major Chinese classics on ritual prescribed—often in minute detail—the behavior appropriate to an exemplary person (*junzi*). Ritual handbooks of the Qing dynasty did the same.[44]

The massive compendium by Qin Huitian (1702–1764) titled *Wuli tongkao* (Comprehensive study of the five rituals) provides an indication of the standard categories of Chinese ceremonial practice: auspicious sacrifices, ceremonies of celebration, ceremonies of visitation, military ritual, and ceremonies of sadness.[45] Qin devotes most of his compendium (127 *juan* and 92 *juan*, respectively) to auspicious ritual (state sacrifices, commemoration of temples, clan and family sacrifices, and so on) and ceremonies of celebration (events such as imperial weddings and state banquets down to local festivals and the marriage of commoners). Military rituals, including imperial expeditions, hunts, and formal inspections, account for only thirteen *juan*—the same amount of space allotted to ceremonies of visitation, from tributary missions and audiences to daily social intercourse. Ceremonies of sadness, notably mourning ritual, account for seventeen *juan* in the *Wuli tongkao*. A similar emphasis can be found in other compilations on Qing ritual, including the Collected Statutes of the empire.

As a reading of the Four Books and other sources indicates clearly, the Chinese considered ritual and propriety to be essential to the performance of filial duties and to the overall harmony of the household. Together with music, poetry, and other forms of refinement, *li* contributed to self-cultivation and the establishment of character. Employed by the ruler and other exemplary people, it encouraged respect, reverence, and right behavior at all levels of society; followed as a standard of proper conduct, it imposed restraints on individuals and preserved social distinctions. Mencius asserts, "Without the rules of propriety and distinctions of righteousness, the high and low will be thrown into confusion." The *Record of Ritual* states expansively:

> The rules of propriety furnish the means of determining the observances toward relatives, as near and remote; of settling points which may cause suspicion or doubt; of distinguishing where there should be agreement, and where difference; and of making clear what is right and what is wrong. . . . To cultivate one's person and fulfill one's words is called good conduct. When conduct is ordered and words are in accordance with the *Dao*, we have the substance of the rules of propriety.[46]

Ren represented the idealistic thrust of Confucianism, with its emphasis on altruism, compassion, and reciprocity, but *li* gave structure and concrete expression to *ren*.

The virtue of *yi*, usually rendered duty, righteousness, or right behavior, can only be understood in light of the preceding two Confucian values. In the most general terms it served as a unifying and ordering principle, as well as a standard for moral judgment. *Yi* may be defined as appropriate behavior according to circumstance. Like *li*, it presupposed objective and external standards of correct behavior, but like *ren*, it had a subjective, internal component. To employ a rather mundane mechanical metaphor, *yi* served as a spring controlling the tension between *ren* and *li*. It was at once a universal and particular virtue, expressing the substance of *ren* and the form of *li*. The *Analects* state that the "superior person considers righteousness to be essential. He performs it according to the rules of propriety, he brings it forth in humility, and he completes it with faithfulness." But *yi* also allows for the occasional abandonment of the rules of propriety under special circumstances. In a famous illustration, Mencius remarks that although propriety demands that men and women not touch hands in public, if a man's sister-in-law were drowning, the man who would not extend his hand to save her is a "wolf." In this instance, *yi* mitigates *li*, but makes manifest *ren*.[47]

The Four Books define *yi* in a variety of ways. Mencius, who often discusses the term together with *ren*, contrasts *yi* and *li* (profit), defines courage (*yong*) as acting according to *yi*, and describes respect for elders as "the working of *yi*." Where *ren* is associated in the Four Books with filial piety, *yi* is associated with loyalty to the ruler or fraternal submission. Where *ren* is associated with a feeling of commiseration, *yi* is associated with feelings of shame and dislike. In many respects, *yi* comes close to the idea of Confucian "conscience." Simply stated, *yi* is knowing what to do and what not to do. Mencius repeatedly emphasizes the importance of a sense of shame (*chi*) in providing moral guidance.[48]

Humane wisdom (*zhi*), the fourth of the Five Constant Virtues, was essential to the full expression of *yi*. From an orthodox Confucian standpoint, it was the only kind of knowledge worth having. In various contexts, *zhi* is defined in the Four Books as the knowledge of filial piety and fraternal submission, as a feeling of approving and disapproving, and as the ability to recognize human talent. Mencius indicates that without humaneness and wisdom there can be no ritual and right behavior (*buren buzhi wuli wuyi*), which suggests that like *ren*, *zhi* is an internal virtue made manifest in other (external) virtues. Although to Mencius all these virtues were innate in man, the *Great Learning* indicates—and Song neo-Confucian metaphysics affirm—that some men are born with moral knowledge and others have to learn it. "Only the wise of the highest class and the stupid of the lowest class cannot be changed," the Master once said.[49]

The fifth virtue of faithfulness (*xin*) receives prominent exposure in the Four Books, often in combination with other values such as loyalty, reciprocity, and sincerity (*cheng*). Of these, the last deserves special mention. Described in the *Great Learning* as "the way of Heaven," sincerity may best be defined as being true to oneself, consistent in word and deed, fully developing one's own nature, and extending that development to others. In this respect, *cheng* is closely akin to the concepts of loyalty (*zhong*) and reciprocity (*shu*) discussed above. The *Doctrine of the Mean* tells us that "Sincerity is [the way of] self-completion. . . . [It] is the beginning and ending of all things; without sincerity there would be nothing. For this reason, the superior person regards the attainment of sincerity as the most exalted thing." Further, it states, "The individual possessed of the most complete sincerity is like a spirit."[50]

How did the exemplary person achieve sincerity and self-completion? The process began with the extension of knowledge and the "investigation of things." The *Great Learning* states:

> The ancients who wished to illustrate illustrious virtue throughout the world, first put their principalities in order. Wishing to regulate their families, they first cultivated themselves. Wishing to cultivate themselves, they first rectified their hearts and minds. Wishing to rectify their hearts and minds, they first sought to be sincere in their thoughts. Wishing to be sincere in their thoughts, they first extended to the utmost their knowledge. Such extensions of knowledge lay in the investigation of things [*gewu*].[51]

The "investigation of things" was variously interpreted by Confucian scholars. Zhu Xi naturally saw it primarily as "investigating principle" (*li*); Wang Yangming viewed it as an effort to "rectify the mind"; Ling Tingkan (1757–1809), a *kaozheng* scholar, concluded that it meant the study of ritual; and Yan Yuan considered it to be "learning from actual experience and solving practical problems." But regardless of the interpretation attached to the term *gewu*, the ultimate aim of any Confucian was to develop his or her innate potential and extend it to others. Self-improvement involved self-examination and the achievement of a balance between book study (*dushu*), meditative quiet sitting (*jingzuo*), and indulgence in ritual and the arts—especially music, poetry, painting, and calligraphy. The blend varied, of course, from school to school and from individual to individual.[52]

An examination of the Qing encyclopedia TSJC's subcategory on Confucian conduct yields a wealth of information on how Confucians approached the problem of self-cultivation. In addition to the basic techniques outlined above, self-improvement could be achieved through means such as "investigating principle to the utmost," "nourishing the mind," "paying attention to fundamentals," "regulating desires," "correcting faults," and "abiding in reverence." Confucians also placed emphasis on "proper timing," the value of "personal experience" in the quest for truth, and the importance of "unifying knowledge and action."

The Four Books provide numerous examples of the personal attributes of the "exemplary person" (*junzi*; aka "true gentleman," "superior person," etc.). He (conventionally—although a woman could also be a *junzi*) is described as virtuous, industrious, intelligent, learned, thoughtful, open-minded, impartial, kind, just, generous, reverent, respectful, cultured, solid, straightforward, cautious, slow in speech, dignified, modest, courageous, and eager to teach as well as learn. He "does what is proper to his station, and does not desire to go beyond this." Confucius even supplies a rough blueprint for the moral development of the sage. "At fifteen," he informs us, "I had my mind set on learning. At thirty I stood firm. At forty, I had no doubts. At fifty I knew the decrees of Heaven [*Tianming*]. At sixty, my ear was an obedient organ [for the reception of the *Dao*]. At seventy, I could follow what my heart desired, without transgressing what was right."[53]

Confucius demonstrated an abiding concern with the "mean"—the middle path of perfect harmony and equilibrium in thought, emotions, and conduct. "The exemplary person [*junzi*] embodies the course of the mean," said Confucius; "the petty person [*xiaoren*] acts contrary to the course of the mean." The *Doctrine of the Mean* states: "The exemplary person cultivates a [friendly] harmony without being weak. How firm is his strength! He stands erect in the middle, without inclining to either side." And how might the exemplary person determine the mean? The sage-ruler Shun provided the model. Shun questioned others, studied their words, concealed what was bad in them, and displayed what was good. "He took hold of their extremes, determined the mean, and employed it in governing the people."[54]

This reminds us that in the Confucian view, personal sagehood was never enough. Just as the internal, subjective value of *ren* required objective manifestation in *li*, so self-cultivation required manifestation in public service. Because the goal of Confucianism was social harmony rather than personal salvation, self-realization could never be divorced from service to humanity. The Confucian imperative was "internal sagehood and external kingship" (*neisheng waiwang*). If the exemplary person could achieve complete sincerity and an undisturbed mind, he might, like Confucius himself, become an uncrowned king and extend his good influence far and wide.

Despite a general lack of interest in metaphysics, Qing Confucians could hardly avoid considering the relationship between the moral order on earth and the great scheme, or *Dao*, of the cosmos. According to orthodox neo-Confucianism, the two were one. Zhu Xi's basic assumption, in other words, was that the principle (*li*) of man's nature was his original goodness (*ren*). The *li* for all men, then, was the same. What made them different in both appearance and morality was their dissimilar endowment of "material force" (*qi*). Zhu tells us: "Those who receive a *qi* that is clear, are the sages in whom the nature is like a pearl lying in clear, cold water. But those who receive a *qi* that is turbid, are the foolish and degenerate in whom the nature is like a pearl lying in muddy water." Long ago, Confucius had stated that "by nature, men are nearly alike, but by practice they get to be far apart"; and somewhat later, Mencius made the penetrating observation that men's innately good minds could be "injured by hunger and thirst." Xunzi, as we have seen, held that man's nature was basically evil.[55]

Orthodox neo-Confucianism, however, explained evil (*e*) as arising from selfish desires and other deviant impulses inherent in one's own physical endowment. Evil was thus a kind of moral imbalance in individuals that came with the specific conditions of their birth. The purpose of neo-Confucian self-cultivation, from this perspective, was to correct this imbalance by refining one's *qi* through book study and self-examination, allowing the luster of one's *li* to shine through. Neo-Confucians believed that the mind had this transformative capacity.

A number of Qing thinkers—ranging from Wang Fuzhi, Gu Yanwu, and Huang Zongxi to Yan Yuan, Li Gong, and Dai Zhen (1723–1777)—rejected the idea of a *liqi* duality, arguing that there was no "principle" apart from material force and thus no evil inherent in *qi*. They deplored Zhu Xi's attempt to distinguish man's heavenly conferred nature from his physical endowment, and the way he pitted "human desires" against "heavenly principle." Li Yong articulated his position this way: "The *Dao* is fully realized with empathies and feelings." Dai Zhen remarked in the same basic spirit: "To equate [the self [*ji*]) with selfish desires is . . . a notion the sages totally lacked." In short, to these thinkers, the metaphysical reality of nature (the *Dao*) and concrete things was one. Evil arose not from man's physical endowment per se, but rather from "outside" influences, such as selfishness and ignorance. To overcome evil required assiduous self-cultivation and the elimination of destructive desires.[56]

Although concepts such as *yin* and *yang*, principle and material force, and nature and concrete things continually crop up in Chinese philosophical discussions, they are by no means the only dualistic terms employed by Confucian thinkers. Neo-Confucians in particular were attracted by the terms *ti* (substance) and *yong* (function) to explain their ideas—including the basic notion that "principle is one, but the manifestations are many" (*li yi fen shu*). *Ti* signifies the inherent, enduring, and fundamental qualities of a thing or situation, while *yong* refers to its functional, fluctuating, and secondary manifestations.

The *tiyong* formula, like the *yinyang* paradigm, could be used in a great variety of ways, and like *yin* and *yang*, the two terms generally implied mutual dependence and the superiority or precedence of one quality (*ti*) over the other (*yong*). Although *kaozheng* scholars traced the *tiyong* concept directly to Chan (Zen) Buddhism (see chapter 7), Confucians of many different intellectual orientations continued to employ it freely. At a mundane level, the *tiyong* formula might be used to distinguish between the root of a problem and its manifestations. Thus, a bureaucrat would ask, "Which is the proper means of ridding an area of robbery: rigorous police measures or sound economic measures so that the people 'find it unnecessary to rob for a living?'" In the realm of ethics, the *ti* of a person's humaneness might be distinguished from the *yong* of his or her righteousness, or the *ti* of Confucian morality in general distinguished from the *yong* of government and institutions. At a higher metaphysical plane, *ti* might be equated with principle and *yong* with material force, or Heaven with *ti* and fate with *yong*.[57]

The place of Heaven (*Tian*) in Chinese philosophy is a central one. In Chinese discourse the term has at least five different meanings: (1) a material or physical sky, opposite the earth; (2) an anthropomorphic deity presiding over the heavens; (3) an impersonal dispenser of fate; (4) the equivalent of the English word nature; and (5) an amorphous ethical entity embracing moral principles and responding to the morality of men. In neo-Confucian discourse, the term Heaven is used in several senses, but it is generally devoid of any personality or anthropomorphism.

To most Confucians in late imperial times, Heaven represented "fullness of being and goodness," a concept equivalent to the way (*Dao*) of the universe, or to the idea of the Supreme Ultimate (*Taiji*) in Zhu Xi's neo-Confucianism. In the orthodox view, Heaven was a self-existent moral entity that endowed all living creatures with their natures. Heaven's will was that these creatures would all act in accordance with their respective natures. Heaven had the power to express its displeasure over the actions of men by visiting upon them natural disasters and other signs; and it could even withdraw its mandate to rule if the emperor should prove immoral and thus unworthy of the throne. "Heaven sees as the people see, and Heaven hears as the people hear," said Mencius. The idea that the people had the right to rebel against oppressive rule remained at the heart of Chinese dynastic politics until the twentieth century, and echoes of it could still be heard even after the fall of the Qing dynasty in 1912.[58]

Qing Confucians, like their predecessors for centuries, saw an essential unity between Heaven, Earth, and Man. The *Doctrine of the Mean* states that he who is possessed of complete sincerity can "assist in the transforming and nourishing powers of Heaven and Earth" and thus form a triad with them. The Great Commentary of the *Yijing* remarks, "The *Changes* is a book vast and great, in which everything is completely contained. The *Dao* of Heaven is in it, the *Dao* of Earth is in it, and the *Dao* of Man is in it." By using the *Yijing*, "Man comes to resemble Heaven and Earth, [and] . . . is not in conflict with them. His wisdom embraces all things, and his *Dao* brings order to the whole world; therefore he does not err. . . . He rejoices in Heaven and has knowledge of fate, therefore he is free from care."[59]

The key concept here is fate (*ming*). Although the term sometimes means Heaven's mandate, nature, or man's natural endowment, Confucian "fate" is best thought of as a series, or set, of predestined situations evolving out of the natural processes of eternal cosmic change. As we have seen, these situations were represented by the sixty-four hexagrams of the *Yijing* and their constituent lines. By consulting the *Changes* and establishing a spiritual link with Heaven, a scholar could not only determine the nature and direction of universal change, but also devise an appropriate Confucian strategy for coping with any situation. A person could therefore not only "know fate" (*zhiming*), but also "establish fate" (*liming*). In the words of the great Qing scholar Tang Jian (1776–1861), "He who knows fate will cultivate the Way; he who [merely] relies on fate will do harm to the Way."[60] The Confucian belief in predestination thus did not lead to a crippling of self-reliance, although it was sometimes used to explain personal failure and adversity.

All levels of traditional Chinese society evinced a concern with predestination, but not all had the luxury of time and money for leisurely study of the *Yijing* and the metaphysical principles that lay behind it. Nor did most have the education or the inclination to appreciate all the refinements of Confucian ethics. To the degree that economics allowed, commoners in Qing China tried to adhere to basic elite values in areas such as marriage, family life, and ancestor worship (see chapter 10). It is doubtful, however, that the vast majority of them were much attracted to philosophical Daoism, for as Joseph Levenson has remarked, "The pleasure of a flight from civilization is open only to civilized man."[61] Chinese peasants were perhaps too close to the land, too close to nature's cruel caprice.

DAOIST FLIGHT AND FANCY

For the elite, at least, the *yang* of Confucian social responsibility was balanced by the *yin* of Daoist escape into nature. Unlike Confucianism, which for virtually all Qing scholars was a way of life, if not a living faith, Daoism—at least in its philosophical form (see below)—was essentially a state of mind. It provided an emotional and intellectual escape valve for world-weary Confucians, trammeled by social responsibility. The writings of Daoist philosophers such as Laozi (tradit. sixth century BCE) and Zhuangzi (tradit. fourth century BCE) were fresh and poetic, often playful, and almost always paradoxical. They admired the weak, accepted the relativity of things, advocated spiritual release, and above all sought communion with nature. The concrete symbols of Daoism were *yin*: water, the female, the child, the emptiness of the valley, and the uncarved block of wood (*pu*).

During the last two decades there has been an explosion of research on Daoism, based not only on the discovery and analysis of new textual materials, but also on a fundamental rethinking of the entire Chinese philosophical tradition. This research has produced some extraordinarily interesting and diverse scholarly studies, such as Chad Hansen's *A Daoist Theory of Chinese Thought* (1992). We should not, of course, be surprised to find a Daoist-inspired reevaluation of traditional Chinese philosophy because a primary impulse of Daoism has always been to defy authority and question conventional wisdom. On the other hand, we should keep in mind that during Qing times the prevailing understanding of Daoism was precisely of the "authoritative" sort that Hansen decries.[62]

For the most part, Chinese scholars have distinguished sharply between "philosophical" Daoism (*Daojia*) and "religious" Daoism (*Daojiao*). A number of Western scholars have resisted this dichotomy, arguing that Daoist thought is part of a continuum that encompasses both orientations, and there is, of course, a point to their arguments.[63] Certainly the corpus of "Daoist" texts known as the *Daozang* (Repository of the *Dao*) makes no clear distinctions of this sort. Moreover, practices such as Daoist "alchemy" (see chapters 5 and 7), which were directed toward achieving longevity and immortality, have antecedents in early Daoist philosophical texts. These alchemical works pay much attention to what might be described as "magic," but they also involve meditation and moral cultivation—not unlike Confucian and Buddhist traditions. Nonetheless, there are, I believe, valid heuristic reasons for separating "philosophy" (as thought) and "religion" (as practice) in this book, as long as we recognize that religion embodies thought and philosophy may entail practice.

The essence of philosophical Daoism is reflected in two famous early works: the *Daode jing* (The Way and its power) and the *Zhuangzi* ([The words of] Master Zhuang). The basic Daoist idea is simply to do what comes naturally—no striving and no overexerting (*wuwei*; lit. "doing nothing"). "No action is taken," Laozi asserts, "and yet nothing is left undone."[64] Sustained by this viewpoint, the Daoist "sage" declares:

I take no action and the people of themselves are transformed. I love tranquility and the people themselves become correct. I engage in no activity and the people of themselves become prosperous. I have no desires and the people of themselves become simple.[65]

This "sage" was not, however, a Confucian-style exemplar, operating in concert with a "moral" Heaven and Earth. Indeed, the *Daode jing*, traditionally attributed to Laozi, states explicitly: "Heaven and Earth are not benevolent [*ren*]; they treat all things like straw dogs."[66] Nature, in this view, played no favorites; it did not discriminate in the Confucian manner.

Laozi's cosmogony and ontology were as simple as his ethics: "Reversion is the action of the *Dao*. Weakness is the function of the *Dao*. All things in the world come into being from being; and being comes into being from nonbeing." Zhuangzi elaborates on this point with his usual paradoxical playfulness:

There was a beginning. There was a no-beginning [before the beginning]. There was a no-no-beginning [previous to the no-beginning before the beginning]. There was being. [Similarly,] there was nonbeing [before there was being]; and there was no-nonbeing [before there was nonbeing]. There was no-no-nonbeing [before there was no-nonbeing]. Suddenly being and nonbeing appeared. And yet, between being and nonbeing, I do not know which is really being and which is really nonbeing. Just now I have said something, and yet I do not know whether what I have said really means something, or does not mean anything at all.[67]

Perhaps the most famous instance of Zhuangzi's playfulness and paradox involves a dream:

Once I, Zhuang Zhou, dreamed that I was a butterfly, and was happy as a butterfly. I was conscious that I was quite pleased with myself, but I did not know that I was Zhuang Zhou. Suddenly I awoke, and there I was, visibly Zhuang Zhou. I do not know whether it was Zhuang Zhou dreaming that he was a butterfly or the butterfly dreaming that it was Zhuang Zhou. Between Zhuang Zhou and the butterfly there must be some distinction [but one may, in fact, be the other]. This is called the transformation of things.[68]

Here, then, Zhuangzi pointedly rejects the distinction between subject and object and between reality and unreality.

Daoist relativity precluded absolute values of the sort embraced by Confucians. Listen, for example, to Zhuangzi discussing "right" and "wrong":

From the standpoint of preference, if we approve of anyone who is approved of by someone else [at least himself], then there is no one who may not be approved of. If we condemn anyone who is condemned by someone else, then there is no one who may not be condemned. To know that [sage-king] Yao and [tyrant] Jie would each approve of himself and condemn the other, then we have a clear realization of human preference. . . . Therefore it has been said, one who wishes to uphold the right and eliminate the wrong, or uphold order and eliminate disorder, must be ignorant of the great principles of the universe as well as the nature of things. One might as well try to uphold Heaven and eliminate the earth, or uphold the *yin* and eliminate the *yang*, which is clearly absurd.[69]

Such views gave Confucians fits; yet they could not help but admire Zhuangzi's insightfulness and the power of his arguments. For instance:

Whereby is the *Dao* vitiated that there should be a distinction of true and false? Whereby is speech vitiated that there should be a distinction between right and wrong? . . . Everything is its own self; everything is something else's other. Things do not know that they are other things' other; they only know that they are themselves. Thus it is said, the other arises out of the self, just as the self arises out of the other.[70]

And again:

It is because there is right, that there is wrong; it is because there is wrong, that there is right. . . . According to the other, there is one kind of right and wrong. According to the self there is another kind of right and wrong. But really are there such distinctions as the self and the other, or are there no such distinctions? When the self and the other [or the "this" and the "that"] lose their contrariness [mutually exclusive opposition] we have the very essence of the *Dao*.[71]

Zhuangzi goes on to say:

The possible is possible; the impossible is impossible. The *Dao* operates and things follow. Things are what they are called. What are they? They are what they are. What are they not? They are not what they are not. Everything is what it is, and everything can be what it can be. There is nothing that is not something, and there is nothing that cannot be something.

Laozi reveled in play and paradox, but he remained a child of the world, concerned with government and human affairs as well as the enjoyment and preservation of life. Thus he tells us, "in the government of the sage, he keeps their hearts empty [peaceful, pure, and free from both worry and selfish desires], fills their bellies, weakens their ambitions, and strengthens their bones." Above all, he embraces the doctrine of *wuwei*:

The more taboos and prohibitions there are in the world, the poorer the people will be. The more sharp weapons the people have, the more troubled the state will be. The more cunning and skill man possesses, the more vicious things will appear. The more laws and orders are made prominent, the more thieves and robbers there will be.[72]

Zhuangzi apparently lacked even the muted reformism of Laozi. In the words of Zhu Xi, "Laozi still wanted to do something, but Zhuangzi did not want to do anything at all. He even said that he knew what to do but just did not want to do it."[73] Predictably, Confucian commentators have excoriated him for advocating the pursuit of complete freedom. But Wang Shumin's critical study of the *Zhuangzi* argues that Zhuangzi was in fact neither egocentric nor an advocate of escapism and "libertine values." His ideal was simply the "pure man," who alone associates with Heaven and Earth and spirit, without abandoning or despising things of the world. He does not quarrel over right or wrong and mingles with conventional society. . . . Above he roams with the Creator [*zaowu zhe*, that is, Nature], and below he makes friends with those who transcend life and death and beginning and end. In regard to the essential, he is broad and comprehensive, profound and unrestrained. In regard to the fundamental, he may be said to have harmonized all things and penetrated the highest level.[74]

Another of Zhuangzi's alluring visions pictured the Daoist sage as

Leaning against the sun and the moon and carrying the universe under his arm, . . . [blending] everything into a harmonious whole. He is unmindful of the confusion and the gloom, and equalizes the humble and the honorable. The multitude strive and toil; the sage is primitive and without knowledge. He comprehends ten thousand years as one unity, whole and simple. All things are what they are, and are thus brought together.[75]

Daoism was, then, preeminently a philosophy of "naturalness." Where Confucianism stressed others, Daoism tended to stress self. Where Confucians sought wisdom, Daoists sought blissful ignorance. Where Confucians esteemed ritual and self-control, Daoists valued spontaneity and freedom from artificial constraints. Where Confucianism stressed hierarchy, Daoists emphasized equality. And where Confucians valued refinement (*wen*), Daoists prized primitivity. What to Confucians were cosmic virtues were to Daoists simply arbitrary labels.

Laozi highlighted the essential difference between Confucianism and Daoism in claiming

It was when the great *Dao* declined that there appeared humanity and righteousness. It was when knowledge and intelligence arose that there appeared much hypocrisy. It was when the six relations [father, son, elder brother, younger brother, husband, and wife] lost their harmony that there was talk of filial piety and paternal affection. It was when the country fell into chaos and confusion that there was talk of loyalty and trustworthiness. Banish sageliness, discard wisdom, and the people will be benefitted a hundredfold. Banish humanity, discard righteousness, and the people will return to filial piety and paternal affection. . . . See the simple, embrace primitivity; reduce the self, lessen the desires.[76]

This, in brief, was the Daoist message.

In the hands of political dissidents, this message could be extremely threatening (see chapter 7).[77] But on the whole, there was just enough affinity between Confucianism and Daoism to ensure an enduring philosophical partnership. Both schools of thought sought inspiration and guidance in the *Yijing*, both employed *yinyang* concepts to explain their ideas, and both cherished the ideal of harmony and oneness with nature (although one posited a moral universe and the other an amoral one). Each shared a sense of the interrelatedness of all things, and each, in its own way, advocated humility, passivity, simplicity, and, above all, the avoidance of selfish desires. Furthermore, although philosophical Daoism had no prominent proponents in late imperial times, Confucians found at least some Daoist concepts congenial to their own ideas. The *Jinsi lu*, for example, approvingly cites Zhuangzi's remark that "those who indulge in many desires have very little of the secret of Nature." Also, a number of phrases from the *Zhuangzi*, such as "not leaning forward or backward," were appropriated by neo-Confucians as a way of expressing their esteem for notions of spontaneity, naturalness, and impartiality.[78]

In all, then, Confucianism and Daoism could easily coexist. The former gave Chinese life structure and purpose, while the latter encouraged freedom of expression and artistic creativity. Most Qing scholars had a healthy schizophrenia. As W. T. de Bary points out, many Confucians recognized that man's response to Heaven and the fulfillment of his nature were not limited to social service. He writes that in the midst of social and political engagement, there was

> a need to keep some part of . . . [oneself] not subservient to the demands of state or society. To the neo-Confucian, the aesthetic and spiritual, or "supermoral" concerns [in the words of Tang Junyi] represent this area of freedom. Much of it was expressed in journals, lyrical poetry, prose-poetry, travel diaries written in a contemplative frame of mind, painting and calligraphy, and the appreciation of art expressed in poetic inscriptions.[79]

The inspiration of these activities was thus predominantly Daoist, even if the fruits of such labors were ultimately believed by Confucians to reflect moral worth.

Chapter Seven

Religious Life

Religious life in the Qing period was especially rich and varied, owing in no small measure to the multiculturalism of the Manchus. Probably at no other time since the Mongol Yuan dynasty had China's rulers evinced such a wide-open and tolerant attitude toward religion. To be sure, the Qing emperors would brook no challenge to their political authority, but as long as religious activities offered no tangible threat, they could be tolerated and perhaps also patronized. This was true even of Islam, which, at least in theory, held adherents to a loyalty above the emperor. We have seen in chapter 2 that Manchu shamanism played a significant role in Banner life at all levels, particularly after Nurhaci's creation of shamanic state rituals. So did patronage of Tibetan Buddhism, also on Nurhaci's initiative. After the conquest of China, his successors expanded their religious reach, not unlike the early emperors of the Ming dynasty, who sought at once to bolster their religious authority and to exert control over the preexisting religious establishment.

Evelyn Rawski has discussed at length the various forms of religious activity engaged in by the Manchus, from imperially sponsored state shamanism and patronage of Tibetan and Chinese Buddhism, to "private rituals" within the Qing Inner Court, which combined "shamanic, Daoist, Chinese Buddhist, Tibetan Buddhist, and popular religious traditions." These three forms of worship had different but related purposes. In Rawski's apt formulation: "If sacrifices at the state altars were about rulership, and Qing religious patronage was about politics, the private rituals were about the court as a household, a family writ large."[1]

The most distinctive form of Manchu religious practice was shamanism— in particular, sacrifices to Heaven (Manchu: *dergi abkai han*, lit. "Highest Heaven Khan"). This type of worship was based on Jin and Yuan dynasty precedents, although Han Chinese influences found their way into the ritu-

238

als as they evolved over time. The main ceremony focused on a *tangzi* (see chapter 2). In Shenyang the *tangzi* was located to the east of the imperial palace, while in Bejing it was located to the southeast. The participants in these shamanic state rituals were Manchu imperial princes and various high-ranking Manchu civil and military functionaries. The shamanic performances themselves were orchestrated by the Office of Shamanism (*Shenfang*), a division of the Imperial Household Department. This office employed 183 shamans—all of them women—who performed their rituals daily, in addition to participating in periodic calendrical performances that involved dancing, singing, and animal sacrifices. These female shamans were all selected from the wives of high officials of the Aisin Gioro clan.[2]

Qing patronage of Tibetan Buddhism proceeded from different motives. The Tibetan idea of "reincarnate lineages" enabled the Manchu rulers, like the Mongols before them, to claim not only to be "emanations" of a particular Buddhist deity, but also to be the reincarnations of a great leader from the past, such as the Mongol warrior and Chinese emperor Qubilai Khan. By this means the Qing emperors were able to bring the peoples of Northeast and Inner Asia more fully and comfortably into their multicultural empire. It bears repeating, however, that Manchu patronage of the Dge lugs pa (or "Yellow Hat") sect was a matter of genuine religious commitment as well as practical imperial politics. This is clear from the ritual schedules of the Qing rulers, which included a great many Buddhist devotions that took place within the towering walls of the Forbidden City.[3]

In China Proper, elite and popular religious beliefs and practices intertwined to produce a vast, multicolored fabric of institutional and individual worship. A French sinologist, Henri Maspero, once described Chinese religion as encompassing "an unheard-of swarm of gods and spirits of every kind, an innumerable rabble." But Maurice Freedman, a British anthropologist, saw order behind the chaos. He asserted that "all religious argument and ritual differentiation [in China] were conducted within a common language of basic conceptions, symbols, and ritual forms." In response, a number of more recent China scholars have reiterated some version of Maspero's position. David Johnson, for example, maintains that, "any unities among Chinese religious practices would be so abstract as to be meaningless."[4]

In an effort to reconcile these two seemingly antithetical views, James Watson has argued that Chinese religion allowed for "a high degree of variation within an overall structure of unity." According to Watson,

> The Chinese cultural system . . . allowed for what outsiders might perceive to be chaotic local diversity. The domain of ritual, in particular, gave great scope to regional and subethnic cultural displays. The system was so flexible that those who called themselves Chinese could have their cake and eat it too: They

could participate in a unified culture yet at the same time celebrate their local or regional distinctiveness."[5]

But the question of whether these ritual displays have ever reflected the high degree of cultural unity that Watson claims remains an open one, subject to intense debate.[6]

In considering issues of unity and diversity, we should bear in mind that there have also been significant transformations in religious practices in China over time. At the top, for example, state ceremonies, including both Manchu shamanistic rituals and Chinese-style official sacrifices, changed in accordance with the shifting attitudes and political priorities of individual emperors.[7] The same was true with respect to imperial policy not only toward established religions such as Chinese Buddhism and Religious Daoism, but also less entrenched belief systems, including Tibetan Buddhism, Islam, Judaism, and Christianity.[8] At the same time, the outlook and actions of foreign religious leaders—whether Chinese Muslim begs (local chieftains) in the northwest, the Dalai Lama in Lhasa, or the pope in Rome—often played a crucial role in the formation of imperial attitudes toward religion. We have seen, for instance, that the early Qing emperors were prepared to tolerate Western Christianity until papal interference made the Confucian rites a political issue (chapter 2).

At various local levels of organization, from massive "macroregions" to individual towns and villages, changing political, social, and economic conditions naturally affected the development of ritual forms and popular religious practices. For instance, gentry efforts to bolster their declining position through support of local lineage structures during the Ming-Qing transition had important implications for the conduct of Buddhist funerary rites in different parts of the country. Similarly, but with different effects, social changes, together with shifts in both popular piety and official religious policy, influenced (adversely) the longstanding Ma Yuan cult later on in the Qing period.[9]

Historical circumstances also affected the writing of religious texts. Cynthia Brokaw has shown, for instance, how the content of "morality books," and the conditions of authorship of such works, changed during the seventeenth and eighteenth centuries in response to new elite concerns, such as the regulation and even containment of social mobility. She describes shifts in religious ideology that "roughly followed the major developments in contemporary elite interests" during the Ming-Qing transition and into the eighteenth century; and although her study does not extend into the late Qing era, it seems evident that religion and intellectual life continued to follow intersecting routes. We find, for instance, that the unsettled state of China's domestic and foreign affairs during the nineteenth century gave rise to a burst of interest in "literati Buddhism"—championed by a number of leading statecraft and New Text scholars, including Gong Zizhen, Wei Yuan, and Kang Youwei.[10]

But for all this undeniable diversity over space and time, Freedman and Watson still have a point. There was indeed a "common language" in Chinese religious life, which included vocabularies laced with *yinyang* formulations and their equivalents, the widespread use of bureaucratic metaphors and models (including ritual fields), common forms of worship (bowing, the use of incense, and the burning of prayers), the widespread employment of written charms, shared symbolism (notably the auspicious color red), philosophical eclecticism, and much more.

STATE SACRIFICES

Arthur Wolf has written: "Assessed in terms of its long-range impact on the people, . . . [the Chinese government] appears to have been one of the most potent governments ever known, for it created a religion in its own image. Its firm grip on the popular imagination may be one reason the imperial government survived so long despite its failings." There is much to commend this view. To a remarkable extent, the organization of traditional Chinese religion mirrored the fundamental assumptions of Chinese bureaucratic behavior. This was true not only of official state ceremonies and sacrifices, as might well be expected, but also of institutional Buddhism, Religious Daoism, and even popular religion. It should come as no surprise, then, that the Manchus were as quick to adopt the basic religious rituals of the Ming dynasty as they were to adopt Ming administrative institutions and practices. At the same time, however, they modified some of these rituals, institutions, and practices to suit their own evolving political needs.[11]

The Qing government, like its Ming predecessor, periodically promoted and demoted various gods within its own supernatural bureaucratic establishment, called on Buddhist and Daoist clergy to say prayers and perform sacrifices as religious agents of the state, appropriated deities from the vast pantheon of popular religion into the structure of official religion, and canonized former mortals who were either exemplars of orthodox values or whose acknowledged supernatural powers made them potentially valuable to the state. Stephen Feuchtwang has identified a kind of dialectic operating in Chinese religious life in which

officials adopted deities from popular religion and bureaucratized them, while the [common] people worshipped gods that were like magic officials or that were magic official deities. Gods that in popular religion were fluid, whose identities flowed into one another, whose functions were potentially universal, and who were magic in their ability to metamorphose and to fuse man and nature in themselves, were in the official religion standardized and classed, minute distinctions and the separation of rites and cults keeping them apart.[12]

Qing official religion recognized three main levels of state sacrifice, aside from the exclusively Manchu shamanistic observances undertaken by the Imperial Household Department: (1) great sacrifices (*dasi*), (2) middle sacrifices (*zhongsi*), and (3) common sacrifices (*qunsi* or *xiaosi*). At each administrative level, designated officials performed elaborate ceremonies in accordance with longstanding ritual prescriptions. Divinations and deliberations involving the Imperial Bureau of Astronomy, the Board of Rites, the Court of Sacrificial Worship, and sometimes the emperor himself yielded auspicious dates for such ceremonies. A similar process resulted in the selection of auspicious and inauspicious days for the official Qing calendar, which was distributed to civil and military officials at the capital and in the provinces. The officials involved in state sacrifices also received guidance in the form of special ceremonial handbooks.

State worship at the various levels generally required ritual bathing, fasting, prostrations, prayers, and thanksgiving offerings of incense, lighted candles, precious objects, fruits, and food and wine together with music and ritual posturing. These activities were believed to purify the mind and body and to please the gods. Women did not participate in state worship with one exception: the sacrifice to the Goddess of Sericulture, Leizu (aka Canshen, the Silkworm Spirit), conducted by the reigning empress herself. According to the Qing Collected Statutes, official religious ceremonies had several specific purposes. Some deities were worshipped for the simple purpose of expressing gratitude and veneration; others for the beneficial or protective influences the deities were supposed to exert; still others for their outstanding civil virtues and/or military services. Some spirits were worshipped for fear that they would bring calamities to the people if not suitably appeased.

But behind these rather specific purposes lay more general considerations. One of these was to exemplify the cosmic order and to affirm the emperor's place within it. Another was to reinforce status distinctions and thus protect the social order. Yet another was to undergird the prestige and political authority of the state. Official religious ceremonies—undertaken by secular bureaucrats rather than a separate priestly class—were thus seen as powerful instruments of ideological control. The preface to one ceremonial handbook of the nineteenth century well illustrates the mixture of motives surrounding official religious practice: "Incense and vessels . . . [that is, ritual sacrifices] can control the gods and spirits. Jade, silk, bells and drums can reveal the rites and music. . . . Awe of virtue and the passing on of merit [through worship] civilize the people and form customs."[13] Official religion, in other words, manipulated both the gods and the people. Some officials downplayed the spiritual aspects of the rituals they performed, but they performed them nonetheless.

The most awe inspiring of the great sacrifices was the emperor's personal worship of Heaven, which took place during the winter solstice and on New Year's Day (from 1742 on). In the words of the *Record of Ritual*, "The sacrifice to Heaven [lit. *Di* or *Shangdi*] is the highest expression of reverence." As with most other Chinese ceremonies, great symbolic emphasis was placed on color, form, number, position, music, and sacrificial objects. The color of the jade and silk offerings to Heaven was blue-green, the altar was circular (*yang*) in shape, and the associated number was nine (also *yang*). Appropriately, nine pieces of music were played at the sacrifice. The emperor faced north, reversing his usual orientation. Contemporary accounts of the elaborate ritual—preceded by a dramatic imperial procession from the Forbidden City to the Temple of Heaven complex the night before—describe a solemn spectacle of awesome splendor.[14] Attended by an entourage of imperial princes, high officials, and other state functionaries, and flanked by the spirit tablets of his ancestors and various deities of nature, the emperor paid his respects to the tablet of Heaven with prayers and offerings—all accompanied by hymns, instrumental music, and ritual posturing undertaken by literally hundreds of performers.

The great sacrifice to Earth, also undertaken personally by the emperor, and similar in most respects to the sacrifice to Heaven, took place at a square

Figure 7.1. The Altar of Heaven
The round shape of this altar symbolizes Heaven, the three levels represent the interconnectedness of Heaven, Earth, and Man, and other elements, such as balusters and steps, involve configurations of nine, the highest single digit *yang* number. Source: Beinecke Rare Book and Manuscript Library, Yale University.

Figure 7.2.   The Emperor at the Altar of Heaven
This is a vastly simplified picture of the worship of Heaven from an unnamed Chinese source. In fact, the imperial retinue was huge. In this illustration, the emperor is kneeling before a spirit tablet inscribed in both Chinese and Manchu with the words "Supreme Lord of August Heaven." On either side of the main shrine are buildings that house the spirit tablets of a great many deities, representing previous emperors, imperial ancestors, and a wide range of natural spirits (the five agents, the sun, the moon, the wind, rain, mountains, and rivers and so forth). *Source:* S. W. Williams 1883.

(*yin*) altar during the summer solstice. In this ceremony, the jade and silk offerings were yellow, eight musical pieces were played, and the emperor faced south. Although the sacrifices to Heaven and Earth reflect an obvious *yinyang* symbolism, the use of the number three in the construction of the altars and in various aspects of imperial ritual, together with the importance attached to the emperor's worship of his ancestors and other notables at the Great Temple (*Taimiao*), indicates the symbolic unity of the three powers (*sancai*): Heaven, Earth, and Man. Another important great sacrifice at Beijing was to the Spirits of Land and Grain (*Sheji*). Here, too, the symbolism of number and color played a significant role; the number was five, and the colors were those associated with the five agents (*wuxing*).

Middle-level sacrifices at the capital included those for local spirits of Land and Grain; the Sun; the Moon; the spirits of Wind, Rain, Thunder, Clouds, Mountains, and Rivers; the emperors of previous dynasties; the patron deity of agriculture (*Xiannong*); and various sages, meritorious officials, wise men, and virtuous women. Confucius was worshiped at this middle level until 1907, when his ceremonies were elevated to the first level of great sacrifices.

Provincial-level middle sacrifices included all of the spirits noted above with the exception of previous emperors and naturalistic deities. Sacrifices to Confucius and other virtuous and wise individuals took place in Temples of Civil Virtue (*Wenmiao*), also referred to as school temples.

Common sacrifices, conducted at every capital city from Beijing down to the county level, included ceremonies dedicated primarily to local protective deities, the most common of which were the so-called God of War (*Guandi*), the God of Literature (*Wenchang*), the Three Sovereigns (*Sanhuang*), the Fire God (*Huoshen*), the Dragon God (*Longshen*), and the City God (*Chenghuang*). Common sacrifices also were undertaken for the unworshipped dead (*li*), whose wandering spirits were presumed to be a potential threat to the community unless placated. Significantly, these "neglected spirits" were supposed to report any immoral or illegal activities to the City God, who would in turn relay this information to his Qing bureaucratic counterpart at the appropriate level for official investigation and punishment.

According to the Qing Collected Statutes, the deities in official religion operated in a hierarchy that exactly paralleled the administrative structure of the empire. County-level cults were subdivisions of prefectural-level cults and so on up to the imperial capital. Tablets of local spirits such as those of Land and Grain were inscribed not only with their names, but also with bureaucratic designations appropriate to their respective administrative levels. Some received imperially bestowed titles of nobility or other marks of distinction.

Of all the deities in the official pantheon, the City God occupied a position of particular importance at the county level. As a rule, each newly appointed magistrate, before assuming his official duties, secluded himself in the local City God temple overnight, reporting to the local deity and offering a sacrifice, which usually included an oath that he would be honest and upright. "If I govern disrespectfully," read one such sacrificial oath, "am crafty, avaricious, get my colleagues in trouble, or oppress the people, may you send down retribution upon me for three years." Other similar oaths asked for assistance in administration and for the power to fortify personal virtue.[15]

As the otherworldly equivalent of the county magistrate, the City God not only had responsibility for all the spirits of the local dead (including the unworshipped dead), but he was also expected to cooperate with his bureaucratic counterpart in bringing peace and prosperity to his county. The following inscription on a late Ming stele expresses this charge unambiguously:

Chenghuang temples are universally established, from the national capital to the prefectures and counties. While it is the magistrates who rule in the world of light [*yang*], it is the gods who govern in the world of shadows [*yin*]. There is close cooperation between the two authorities. When Emperor Taizu of the Ming dynasty conferred titles on the City Gods throughout the empire [in 1370],

Figure 7.3. A City God Altar
This illustration, which represents only a portion of the City God temple complex, shows official devotions in which only degree holders and officials could participate. *Source:* Nakagawa 1799.

there were ranks of emperors, princes, dukes, lords and marquises. . . . The god's power is effective everywhere, rewarding the good with blessing and punishing the evil with calamity, . . . thus extending great benefit to man. Man prays to him for good harvests and for the avoidance of floods, droughts and pestilence.[16]

When trouble came, magistrates sought relief from the City God in the same spirit, as in this impassioned appeal during the early Qing:

> O City God, both of us have duties to perform in this county: resisting disasters that may occur, offering protection in times of trouble, such things are part of the City God's spiritual realm and are part of the official's responsibilities. This year, while the workers were out in the fields but the grain had not matured, the eggs that had been laid by last year's locusts hatched out in the soil, causing almost half the wheat crops in the countryside to suffer this affliction. . . . The people could not repel this calamity, so they appealed to the officials for help. The officials could not repel this calamity for the people, so they [now] pray to the City God.[17]

The prayer ends with the suggestion that because the City God anticipates the needs of the people and officials and because he sympathizes with them, could he not, then, transmit the prayers of the people and the officials to Heaven in the form of a petition? Like any other administrator, the City God could be appealed to by equals and inferiors, just as he could appeal to (or in fact be commanded by) a bureaucratic superior.

The bureaucratic character of the City God found expression not only in his administrative responsibilities and his role as a transmitter of messages to higher supernatural authorities; it was also reflected in his physical image and surroundings. Although represented by a tablet at the open altars of official religious ceremonies, the City God was represented by an image when worshipped in his own temple. The temple itself was modeled closely along the lines of a magistrate's yamen, and the image of the City God was dressed in official robes and usually flanked by fierce-looking secretaries and yamen runners. Furthermore, the position of City God was almost invariably occupied by the spirit of a deceased former official, appointed by the emperor for a limited term, usually three years, in regular bureaucratic fashion. As a general rule, the lower the deity in the spiritual hierarchy of official religion, the more "human" it was assumed to be.

Spirits such as the City God were considered powerful but not omnipotent; they had specific spheres of administrative responsibility, and like their human counterparts, they were neither infallible nor incorruptible. They could be "bribed" by mortals and punished by their superiors in either the regular or the supernatural hierarchy. It was also commonly believed that spiritual officials such as the City God had their own families, including parents, wives, concubines, and children. As with most other major religious traditions (with the exception, perhaps, of Manchu shamanism), Chinese religion in its various orthodox forms tended to reinforce traditional gender roles and distinctions.[18]

The City God cult represented a kind of symbolic meeting point between official religion and popular religion. Official worship of the deity involved solemn, dignified ceremonies in which only officials and degree holders could participate. These activities helped legitimize the state in the eyes of the common people and preserved local status distinctions. But popular worship of the City God had no such purpose and involved no such explicit distinctions. Individuals prayed to him for any and all kinds of favors (especially good health), and the ceremonies for the City God on his "birthday" and during his thrice-yearly tours of the city were among the largest, most impressive, and most widely observed public activities in traditional Chinese community life. On these occasions, the City God temple and its environs bustled with all kinds of activity: markets; theatrical performances; the selling of food; huge crowds; the noise of firecrackers, gongs, and drums; and the burning of incense. Most of these features were not to be found in the austere rituals of official religion.

It is tempting, and I think at least partially justified, to consider certain deities associated with popular religion—notably local Lords of the Earth (*Tudi gong*)—as supernatural subcounty administrators. Just as town or village leaders and *baojia* or *lijiia* headmen supervised subcounty administrative units but were ultimately answerable to county magistrates, so in the supernatural sub-bureaucracy local Lords of the Earth oversaw discrete administrative areas but were ultimately responsible to City Gods. Like regular subcounty administrators, these Lords of the Earth served localities rather than kinship groups, and although the vast majority of them were not based on decimal units, there is evidence to suggest that at least in some cases the subcounty spiritual world could be organized along the same lines and designed for the same purposes as *baojia*. A gazetteer for the market town of Foshan in Guangdong states, for example:

> Every one hundred households constitute a neighborhood [*li*]. In each neighborhood is established an altar for the gods of land and grain, where annual sacrifices are offered in the spring and fall, with the head of the neighborhood officiating. . . . Before the feast that follows the sacrifice, one person reads a written oath: "All persons in this neighborhood agree to observe the rituals, and the strong refrain from oppressing the weak. . . . Those who fail to observe the common agreement, and those committing rape, robbery, falsification, and other misdemeanors will be excluded from this organization."[19]

Figure 7.4. A City God Procession
One of the City God's thrice-yearly tours of the city. He is transported by a sedan chair and accompanied by musicians, lantern bearers, flag bearers, and other attendants. *Source:* Nakagawa 1799.

This oath, and the sacrifice that followed, established a concrete link between the neighborhood social and moral order and the local spiritual establishment, illustrating the use of spiritual sanctions to enforce secular norms.

The responsibilities of local Lords of the Earth, whether they were in charge of city wards, towns, villages, or subunits of these divisions, included "policing" the spirits of that area and reporting to the City God on human activities within the scope of their jurisdiction. The Lord of the Earth's human charges, for their part, appealed to him for protection and blessings, and dutifully conveyed to him information regarding recent births, marriages, deaths, and other important events. Not surprisingly, Lords of the Earth were often distinguished by status within the larger community, some being regarded as designated representatives of others.

In pursuing the idea of an analogy between Qing sociopolitical institutions and the supernatural order, it may not be too farfetched to suggest that certain deities stood in relation to the local City God as the gentry class in Chinese society stood to the bureaucracy. Arthur Wolf points out, for example, that in modern Taiwan, where many traditional religious practices still persist, ritual specialists and close observers of temple affairs commonly distinguish two types of deities: officials (*shi*), notably the City God and the Lord of the Earth, and wise persons (*fu*), a category represented in the Sanxia area of the Taibei basin by several deities, including the Holy Mother in Heaven (*Tianshang shengmu*), also known by her imperially bestowed title Tianhou (Consort of Heaven) and her popular name Mazu, which means "grandmother."[20] While the comparison is not perfect, it suggests a kind of status similarity between low-ranking deities in official religion, such as the City God, and unofficial deities who performed important social roles. And just as capable gentry members might eventually find positions in the regular bureaucracy, so might wise persons in the supernatural social order become adopted into the official pantheon. The Holy Mother in Heaven was so worshipped in Qing times.

County magistrates often found it necessary to worship a wide range of both official and "unofficial" deities. According to the Qing legal code, a magistrate could be punished with eighty strokes of bamboo for sacrificing to a deity not included in the dynasty's book of official sacrifices; but when calamity struck, the local populace often demanded that the county magistrate offer sacrifices to any god who might be of assistance. Wang Huizu, an insightful eighteenth-century scholar-official, informs us that during his tenure as a Qing magistrate, concerned residents of his county once brought more than twenty images to his yamen, demanding that he pray to them for rain. He refused on the grounds that worship of these gods was unorthodox, but he maintains that his refusal might have led to a disturbance had he not already won the people's confidence.[21]

Jeffrey Snyder-Reinke's cleverly titled book *Dry Spells: State Rainmaking and Local Governance in Late Imperial China* (2009) suggests that Wang's refusal to propitiate "unorthodox" gods was more the exception than the rule. In fact, he argues, rainmaking rituals were as much a part of a local official's responsibility during times of drought as the management of state-run granaries was in periods of famine (see chapter 3). But whereas the bureaucratic mechanisms of the Qing state introduced a significant amount of standardization in matters such as grain distribution, it could do little to unify rainmaking practices. In Snyder-Reinke's words, rainmaking rituals that were some two thousand years in the making "predated the founding of the Qing dynasty and, in many ways, superseded its authority." The result was a proliferation of strategies designed to propitiate the gods and placate the people that ranged from community fasting and official prayers to decidedly unorthodox rituals such as "throwing tiger bones into dragon holes, burying frogs, collecting snakes, and constructing dragons out of clay."[22] Officials were even known to exhume bodies believed to be responsible for absorbing moisture from an area.

In short, at every turn Qing officials were drawn into a supernatural world for which their classical Confucian training offered little concrete guidance.

Recall the inscription in the temple of the Consort of Heaven at Foshan that I cited in the introduction to this book:

> When administrative orders from the national and local capitals attain their objectives, and when there is the Way of Man to provide effective principles and discipline, it is not necessary that spirits and gods play an impressive and prominent role [in government]. But when [such orders and the Way of Man] fail to effect justice, spirits and gods will be brought to light.

It appears that in many cases, there was simply not enough perceived justice in the world of Qing bureaucrats to keep the spirits and gods at bay. In fact, as Paul Katz argues persuasively, religion actually played a significant role in shaping certain features of the Chinese legal system.[23]

As a general rule, a god's bureaucratic position, or at least his or her relationship to officials within the natural or supernatural hierarchy, meant more to most Chinese than any sectarian identification he or she might possess. But sectarian identifications were not insignificant, especially in the realm of nonofficial institutional religion. Before turning to the syncretism of Chinese popular religion, let us examine briefly the major features of "orthodox" Buddhism and Religious Daoism during the Qing.

BUDDHISM AND RELIGIOUS DAOISM

Of the two liturgical teachings, Buddhism had by far the greater intellectual appeal, as well as a greater institutional visibility and a larger number of both clerics and identifiable lay adherents. Although Religious Daoism enjoyed substantial imperial patronage in the late Ming period, it suffered some discrimination at the hands of the Qing emperors, who, as we have seen in chapter 2, were ardent advocates of Tibetan Buddhism in addition to traditional Chinese Buddhism. Under the aggressive patronage of the Kangxi, Yongzheng, and Qianlong emperors, a total of thirty-two Tibetan Buddhist temples were renovated or built in Beijing, and, in other parts of the empire, dozens of Chinese Buddhist monasteries were converted into Tibetan Buddhist monasteries. In 1744 the princely residence of the Yongzheng emperor became a Lamaist temple—the Yonghe gong—which served as a teaching center for the "Yellow Sect" of Tibetan Buddhism in Beijing. From the eighteenth century into the mid-nineteenth, it housed between five hundred and six hundred Manchu, Mongol, and Tibetan monks.[24]

The Qing emperors also built eleven Lamaist temples in Chengde, and developed a large Tibetan Buddhist complex at the pilgrimage site of Wutai Mountain in Shanxi province. Most importantly, at least from the standpoint of their Inner Asian administrative strategy, the Manchus established more than one thousand monasteries and temples in Mongolia, Xinjiang, and other areas on the Chinese periphery. These religious sites became "the de facto centralized state institution" of a decentralized nomadic society. According to some estimates, more than 30 percent of the males in Mongolia during the Qianlong reign were lamas living in monasteries. Significantly, seven of the largest and most powerful of these monasteries were designated as Banner units, distinct from the "secular" Banners who were garrisoned in various parts of Inner Asia. The heads of these monasteries, known as *jasagh da lama*, wielded both administrative and judicial power in the fashion of their secular counterparts.[25]

Qing control of the inherited Buddhist (and Daoist) establishment in China Proper (some 80,000 monasteries and temples at the beginning of the dynasty) was a matter of adopting and adapting Ming mechanisms of oversight, and, as indicated in chapter 4, these control mechanisms were on the whole quite effective. Moreover, Buddhism had already made compromises with the Chinese state. One illustration of its successful adaptation to the political environment in Ming-Qing times was the frequent use of names such as the Monastery for Honoring Loyalty [to the State] (*Baozhong si*) or the Monastery for the Protection of the State (*Huguo si*). Another illustration—particularly striking in view of the kinship-renouncing doctrine of Buddhism—was the designation Monastery for the Glorification of Filial Piety (*Guangxiao si*). Lay Buddhism, meanwhile, proved remarkably adaptable to the Chinese social and intellectual environment. It flourished during the Qing dynasty precisely because, in Kristin Yü Greenblatt's words, it "did not demand a radical break from the social system in which it existed." It was, she maintains, "more activist than contemplative, more moralistic than theological, more world affirming than world rejecting."[26]

Although the Qing government continually worried about the seditious potential of heterodox religious sects (see below), it was relatively unconcerned with the intellectual attractiveness of Buddhist philosophy and theology. To be sure, officially endorsed neo-Confucian works such as *Reflections on Things at Hand* emphasized that "a student should forthwith get as far away from Buddhist doctrines as from licentious songs and beautiful women. Otherwise they will infiltrate him."[27] But most Qing scholars did not reject Confucianism in favor of Buddhism, especially in their active years. Only in old age, or in times of severe social unrest and uncertainty, did significant numbers of intellectuals gravitate wholeheartedly toward Buddhist doctrines.

It is true that the well-known scholar Peng Shaosheng (1740–1796) abandoned a promising Confucian career in his late twenties, during the heyday of the Qing empire, to become a lay monk. Although he lived in a hotbed of anti-Buddhist *kaozheng* scholarship and had passed the *jinshi* degree before he was twenty, Peng grew ever more attracted to Buddhism, and became a disciple of the renowned cleric Shiding (1712–1778). Eventually he earned a reputation as the foremost Qing scholar in popularizing Buddhism among the laity. Yet Peng was interested not in establishing Buddhism at the expense of Confucianism, but rather in reconciling the two. As Richard Shek puts the matter, Peng dressed the Confucian sages in Buddhist garb, "portraying them as bodhisattvas with a message of salvation."[28]

Other Qing scholars found it possible to accommodate Buddhist ideas by viewing them in a Confucian light. Zhang Xuecheng, for example, advanced the rather common (and psychologically satisfying) argument that the origins of Buddhism could be found in the teachings of the *Yijing*. Further, he maintained that Buddhist mythology should not be taken lightly simply because it failed to make literal sense. "The Buddhists' description of Buddha as sixteen feet high with richly adorned, golden colored body, and their strange imaginings that no one has ever seen—the splendors of heaven, the torments of hell, the heavenly goddess scattering flowers, yakshas covered with hair—these things the Confucians criticize as absurd." But Zhang insisted that the Buddhists were simply presenting their teachings symbolically, just as the *Yijing* did in discussing things such as "dragons with dark and yellow blood." In the end, Zhang asserted, the best Buddhist writing came close to being "superior to that of the [Confucian] philosophers."[29]

A more down-to-earth illustration of the effort to interpret Buddhist concepts in a Confucian fashion appears in the following excerpt from a set of late Qing clan rules:

> The Buddhists say that if you want to know about previous lives, look at the sufferings of this life. If you want to know about the next life, look at what is being done in this life. This is an excellent statement. However, what the Buddhists refer to as previous lives and the lives to come stems from their theory of rebirth and transmigration of souls. I think what has happened before yesterday—the father and the ancestors—are really the previous lives, and that what will happen after today—the sons and the grandsons—are really the lives to come.[30]

In this view, at least, Buddhism and Confucianism were but two sides of the same coin of ethical conduct.

What, then, were the basic ideas of Buddhism? Buddhist teachings began with the Four Noble Truths: (1) life is painful (unsatisfactory), an endless cycle of births and deaths in a transient, sorrowful world; (2) the origin of pain and sorrow is selfish desire; (3) the elimination of pain and sorrow comes with the elimination of selfish desire; and (4) the elimination of selfish desire comes with following the Eightfold Noble Path. Buddhism thus shared with both Confucianism and Daoism an abiding concern with the reduction of harmful desires.[31]

The Eightfold Noble Path led from correct views to correct attitudes, correct speech, correct conduct, correct occupation, correct effort, correct perception and consciousness (alertness or self-examination), and correct concentration (meditation). By following Buddhist teachings as set forth in the huge corpus known as the *Tripitaka* (Chinese: *Sanzang* [Three repositories]) and derivative works, adherents could acquire the moral and mental discipline required to achieve Enlightenment. For the most part, Buddhist morality was based on concrete social values such as love, charity, courage, forbearance, and self-control, as well as respect for all living things; but Buddhist mental discipline was designed to demonstrate that in the end, all conceptions and distinctions were meaningless.

Buddhist Enlightenment implied a kind of transcendent understanding that permitted the perception of Ultimate Reality behind the "veil of illusion" (that is, the false idea that a permanent or "essential" ego exists). When this perception occurs, "the ties of false sensory discrimination and of the passions (greed, envy, etc.) are broken, so that we are no longer carried along in the stream of phenomenal existence." This stream of existence and continual flux, known popularly as the wheel of life and death, was based on the idea of karmic retribution (Chinese: *yeyin* or *yinguo*). Karma literally means "act," but the concept includes both thoughts and deeds and implies causality. According to Buddhist doctrine (vastly simplified), the accumulated karma of each sentient being in the present as well as past existences determines the future existence of that being. Rebirths are believed to take place on several different planes (divine, human, animal, insect, etc.) depending on the net balance of "good" and "bad" karma (that is, good or bad thoughts and deeds).

Enlightenment, then, brought a state of oneness with Ultimate Reality (Sanskrit: *paramamārtha-satya*; Chinese: *zhenti*), a break in the painful and sorrowful chain of causation that drives the everyday world of "conventional reality" (Sanskrit: *samvrti-satya*; Chinese: *suti*). In Sanskrit this state was termed Nirvana (Chinese: *Niepan*), which literally means "extinction." Likened to the blowing out of a flame or the merging of a drop of water in an endless sea, the state (or one might say non-state) of Nirvana was originally considered to be "incomprehensible, indescribable, inconceivable, unutterable." In the popular mind, however, it became equated with the idea of a heavenly repose. This was particularly the point of view encouraged by Mahayana Buddhism, a school of Indian Buddhism that developed in reaction to the austere and rather exclusive school known as Theravada, the Way of the Elders (pejoratively referred to as Hinayana, the "Lesser Vehicle," by Mahayanists).

Although the Mahayana school considered itself to be the Greater Vehicle (Chinese: *Dasheng* or *Dacheng*) of Buddhist truth, it could tolerate other belief systems, including Theravada, as "lesser truths," valid in some sense but ultimately inferior. This relativistic emphasis, a matter of expedience, made allowance for different levels of understanding both within Mahayana Buddhism and outside of its wide doctrinal sphere. Emphasizing salvation by faith and good works, Mahayana was more compassionate and other-oriented than Theravada. It involved more ritual and had a more elaborate metaphysics. Mahayana posited a universe consisting of an infinite number of spheres or realms going through an infinite number of cosmic periods. Within these realms were a myriad of heavens, hells, and assorted deities (all manifestations of the Buddha spirit or nature), which could be more easily comprehended by the common people. Nirvana was beyond all this. Given Mahayana Buddhism's eclectic spirit, ritualism, and polytheism, it is hardly surprising that it took firm root in China and peripheral areas such as Tibet, Mongolia, Korea, Japan, and Vietnam.

There were four main Mahayanist schools in late imperial China: the Tiantai or Lotus (*Fahua*) School; the Huayan (lit. Flowery Splendor) School; the Pure Land School (*Jingtu*); and the Chan or Meditation School, known commonly as Zen, the Japanese pronunciation of the Chinese character *chan* (meditation).[32] Indicative of both the syncretic capacity of traditional Chinese thought and the accommodating outlook of Mahayana Buddhism, the Chinese had a common saying: "The Tiantai and Huayan Schools for [metaphysical] doctrine and the Jingtu and Chan Schools for practice."[33] The scriptural common denominator of these and most other Chinese Buddhist schools was the so-called Lotus Sutra (*Miaofa lianhua jing*), a fascinating dramatic work blending elements of philosophy, theology, pageantry, and popular fable. In the fashion of the *Yijing*, the ideas of the Lotus Sutra were presented not in abstract terms but in concrete images and living symbols.

The Tiantai School, which called the Lotus Sutra its own but could claim no real monopoly on it, distinguished three levels of "truth," each of which centered on the idea of *dharmas* (Chinese: *fa*), or psychosomatic "elements of existence." One level was the Truth of Emptiness—the idea that all *dharmas* are empty because they have no independent nature of their own. Another level was that of Temporary Truth, or "relative reality," in which *dharmas* had a temporary and dependent existence. In this realm, there were ten types of manifest existence, ranging from deities such as Buddhas ("enlightened ones") and bodhisattvas ("enlightened ones" who have postponed Nirvana to help others achieve Enlightenment) down to humans, beasts, and insects. The third level of truth was the Truth of the Mean—that *dharmas* are both empty and temporary, that the only reality was the Mind of Pure Nature, of which all phenomena were merely transient manifestations.

The Huayan School represented the highest development of Buddhist metaphysics in China. Its central cosmological notion was that all things are "coexistent, interwoven, interrelated, interpenetrating, [and] mutually inclusive." This view was basically in accordance with the outlook of Tiantai Buddhism and was also congenial with the organic character of Chinese philosophy as a whole. In fact, the Huayan School contributed substantially to the development of neo-Confucian metaphysics in the Song period. According to Huayan theory, each *dharma* possesses six characteristics in three complementary pairs: (1) universality and speciality, (2) similarity and difference, and (3) integration and disintegration. In *yinyang* fashion, each opposing characteristic implied the other. As explained in the famous Chinese Buddhist analogy of the Golden Lion,

> The lion represents the character of universality. The five sense organs, being various and different, represent the character of speciality. The fact that they all arise from one single cause represents the character of similarity. The fact that its eyes, ears, and so forth do not exceed their bounds represents the character of difference. Since the combination of the various organs becomes the lion, this is the character of integration. And as each of the several organs remain in its own position, this is the character of disintegration.[34]

Yet finally, when feelings have been eliminated and "true substance" revealed, everything becomes an undifferentiated whole. No longer does a distinction exist between subject and object: the deceptive "self-nature" (*zixing*) of things in the conventional world yields to a recognition that there is in the end no self-nature. To quote again from the *Jinshizi zhang* (Essay on the golden lion),

> When we look [clearly] at the lion and the gold, the two characters both perish and afflictions resulting from passions will no longer be produced. Although beauty and ugliness are displayed before the eye, the mind is as calm as the sea. Erroneous thoughts all cease, and there are no compulsions. One gets out of bondage and is free from hindrances, and forever cuts off the course of suffering. This is called entry into Nirvana.

Chan Buddhism had much interest in Enlightenment, but little concern with metaphysical speculation. Chan was a distinctively Chinese brand of Buddhism, which had great appeal to artists and intellectuals—in part, no doubt, because of its strong affinities with philosophical Daoism. Chan Buddhism stressed the "Buddha-nature" within one's own mind and regarded the regular Buddhist apparatus of scriptures, offerings, recitation of the Buddha's name, and so forth as unnecessary. Instead, it favored an intuitive approach to Enlightenment. This emphasis on a direct apprehension of Ultimate Reality through meditation can be found in Confucian terms in the thought of the great Ming scholar Wang Yangming (see chapters 1 and 6), whose intellectual enemies considered him "a Buddhist in disguise."

Meditation appealed to virtually all members of the Chinese leisured class—Confucians, Daoists, and Buddhists alike. But Chan Buddhism normally required the discipline of a Chan master—which, as Beata Grant points out, could be a woman. The role of the master was not primarily to instruct in academic fashion, but rather to prepare the mind of the disciple to intuit Ultimate Reality. Various means were employed, notably physical shock—such as shouting or beatings—and the use of puzzling sayings, stories, or conversations known as *gong'an* (Japanese: *koan*; lit. "public cases"). The most famous *gong'an* is no doubt "Listen to the sound of one hand [clapping]." Sayings of this sort were designed to jar the mind loose from its conventional moorings, to bring a recognition that Ultimate Reality cannot be conceptualized or articulated. Such techniques set the stage for fruitful meditation.[35]

Although the basic goal of Chan was direct intuition of the Buddha-mind, meditation could also involve deliberations of intellect. Enlightenment might come instantly or gradually. In general, the so-called Southern School of Chan Buddhism emphasized the former approach; the Northern School, the latter. Paradoxically, in late imperial times the "wordless doctrine" of Chan gave rise to an extensive literature, with commentaries and subcommentaries explaining the cryptic sayings of past Chan masters in equally cryptic terms. During the Qing, this rather academic and somewhat fossilized form of Chan still enjoyed some influence, but in many cases it functioned more as an intellectual game of the Chinese elite than as a serious quest for Enlightenment.

The most popular school of Chinese Buddhism in Qing times was the Pure Land School. On the whole, this eclectic teaching avoided both the intense mental discipline of Chan and the scriptural and doctrinal emphasis of Tiantai and Huayan.[36] The central focus of the Pure Land School was on salvation through faith and good works. The reward was rebirth in the Western Paradise, also known as the World of Supreme Bliss, presided over by Amitabha (Chinese: *Amituo Fo*)—the "Buddha of Immeasurable Radiance." Chinese descriptions of this beautiful, enchanting, and serene land are as enticing as the descriptions of the bureaucratic purgatory known as the Courts of Judgment (*Diyu*) are terrifying. These "courts" are sometimes described as "hells" because the "soul" of the departed is subject to various tortures before being reborn, depending on the sins committed in the previous life (for instance, lack of filial piety and/or lack of respect for elders).[37]

In the view of Pure Land adherents, faith might be expressed by the mere repetition of Amitabha's name, while good works included conventional Buddhist virtues as well as the avoidance of the so-called ten evils—murder, stealing, adultery, lying, duplicity, slander, foul language, lust, anger, and false views. In the popular conception, faith in Amitabha not only offered the hope of salvation, but also protection from evil spirits, wild beasts, fire, bandits, and other threats on earth. Amitabha's principal agent, the female bodhisattva Guanyin (originally a male deity, Avalokitesvara, the "Lord Who Looks Down"), proved especially popular in China as a source of protection and blessings (including fertility) for women. Significantly, the late Qing Empress Dowager Cixi actively promoted an image of herself as an avatar of Guanyin—even going to the extent of being photographed at the imperial court in her own version of the goddesses' attire.[38]

Other major deities in the vast Chinese Buddhist pantheon included Yaoshi Fo (the God of Medicine, identified with Bhaisajyaguru), Mile Fo (Sanskrit: *Maitreya*, the Buddha of the Future), Wenshu (Sanskrit: *Manjusri*, a bodhisattva), Puxian (Sanskrit: *Samantabhadra*, also a bodhisattva), and Yanwang (Sanskrit: *Yama*, Judge and King of Hell [that is, the Courts of Judgment]). These, however, represented only a fraction of the Buddhas, bodhisattvas, *arhats* (Chinese: *lohan*; disciples of Buddha), and other deities who operated in the limitless Mahayana universes.[39]

It is worthy of note that in Qing times, a number of monasteries carried on the joint practice of Chan and Pure Land Buddhism. This usually meant that these establishments had both a meditation hall and a hall for reciting the Buddha's name. But monasteries might also permit a special form of joint practice in one hall. Holmes Welch explains: "In both sects the goal was to reduce attachment to ego. The Pure Land method of 'no stirrings in the whole mind' (*yixin buluan*) did not differ essentially from the Chan method of 'meditating to the point of perfect concentration' (*chanding*)." The eminent Chan abbot Xuyun (1840–1959) is said to have remarked, "All the Buddhas in every universe, past, present, and future, preach the same *dharma* [here meaning 'doctrine']. There is no real difference between the methods advocated by Sakyamuni [the historic Buddha] and Amitabha." For this reason, Xuyun advised some of his disciples who would have found Chan meditation too difficult to recite the Buddha's name instead.[40]

Before moving to a discussion of Religious Daoism, a few words about Dge lugs pa ("Yellow Hat") Buddhism are in order. As indicated previously, all major sects of Tibetan Buddhism were based on Mahayana beliefs. The Dge lugs pa sect, which developed in Tibet during the fifteenth century, focused in particular on Mādhyamika or "Middle Doctrine" teachings.[41] Philosophically speaking, the goal of this school was to reconcile notions of "conventional reality" and "ultimate reality" by denying, in a highly developed and sophisticated metaphysics, any meaningful distinction between them. In other words, to adherents of this particular sect the phenomena of the world were neither ultimately existent nor conventionally non-existent.[42]

In practice, Tibetan Buddhism involved not only the worship of deities in shrines, but also the use of esoteric Vajrayāna (Tantric) rituals. These exercises, which involved meditation and deity-visualization techniques, were designed to allow adherents to gain access to cosmic powers, and to achieve mental and physical transformation, thus providing a route to Nirvana beyond Mahayana and Theravada.[43] Under Qing imperial sponsorship, elements of Mongol and Chinese religious practice were added to Tibetan Buddhism over time; thus, for instance, the Chinese God of War (the deified historical hero known as Guan Yu) came to be added to Tibetan Buddhist altars during the Jiaqing and Daoguang reigns.[44]

As is well known, Religious Daoism owed much to institutional Buddhism. Wing-tsit Chan goes so far as to describe it as "a wholesale imitation of Buddhism, notably in its clergy, temples, images, ceremonies and canon." But despite Religious Daoism's profound cultural debt to Buddhism, it was not simply a pale reflection of the "sinicized" Indian import. Not only did formal Daoist ritual and symbolism differ significantly from that of institutional Buddhism, but the major thrust of Daoist religion ran counter to the conventional Buddhist emphasis on reincarnation. For all the diversity of Religious Daoist beliefs and practices, the aim was not primarily to break the chain of causation through the elimination of consciousness, but rather to achieve a special kind of transcendence, manifest in the ability to know and manipulate the supernatural environment. Although Religious Daoism shared with philosophical Daoism an organic view of man and the universe, the goal of Religious Daoist ritual and personal regimen (meditative, dietary, pharmacological, gymnastic, and sexual) was not merely to find one's niche in the cosmic order, but to acquire a form of cosmic power. Religious Daoism offered more than psychic release; it held the promise of longevity, invulnerability, and perhaps immortality.[45]

Two main schools of Religious Daoism flourished in late imperial times: the so-called Northern School, or Quanzhen (Complete Reality) Sect, and the Southern School, or Zhengyi (True Unity) Sect. The Complete Reality Sect arose during the Song dynasty in response to Chan Buddhism. Like devotees of Chan, members of this Northern School preferred the rigors of monastic discipline. Theirs was a life of celibacy, vegetarianism, and abstention from alcoholic drinks. The spiritual headquarters of the Complete Reality sect were located in Beijing, at the White Cloud Monastery. The True Unity Sect, which traced its spiritual origins to the late Han period, had its headquarters in Longhu ("Dragon-tiger") Mountain, Jiangxi province. The hereditary Heavenly Master (Tianshi) of this Southern School, sometimes erroneously termed the Daoist "Pope," had considerable religious authority in late Ming and early Qing times, but his power was considerably curtailed thereafter. Nonetheless, the True Unity Sect enjoyed what amounted to "liturgical hegemony" among the various schools of Religious Daoism in late imperial times, and continued to receive a measure of support from the Qing court until the mid-nineteenth century.[46]

True Unity adherents lived a very different life from that of their spiritual brethren in the Complete Reality Sect. True Unity priests were married, they lived at home among the people, they were not subject to monastic discipline (except by choice), and they were allowed to eat meat and drink alcoholic beverages, except during special fasts. They relied primarily on charms and magic rather than diet for self-preservation, and their principal function in traditional Chinese society was to sell charms, tell fortunes, and perform various religious ceremonies for the popular masses (see next section). As the True Unity Sect declined under the Manchus, the Complete Reality Sect experienced something of a revival, and it remains the dominant tradition of Daoism in China to this day.[47]

Religious Daoism, like Buddhism, had a wide variety of subsects that were at least tangentially related to one or another of the major schools. Despite some liturgical and ritual differences, most Religious Daoists embraced the same basic ideas. These were distilled from the huge Daoist canon known as the *Daozang* (Repository of the *Dao*)—the Daoist counterpart to the Buddhist *Tripitaka* (*Sanzang*). Among the most commonly recited official scriptures in this vast and varied corpus were the *Yuhuang jing* (Jade Emperor's classic) and the *Sanguan jing* (Three Officials' classic), both of which were used in Complete Reality and True Unity devotions. Although most of the scriptural, scholastic, and historical writings in the *Daozang* dealt with matters such as religious doctrine, liturgy, charms, magic, hymns, and lore, the collection also included the works of the great classical Daoist philosophers.

The world view of the Religious Daoists as expressed in the *Daozang* was based in a much more explicit way than that of the Buddhists on notions of *yinyang*/five-agents cosmogony and cosmology. According to one well-known formulation, derived from the *Daode jing* and clearly an inspiration for neo-Confucian cosmological ideas, the nameless, unmoved Prime Mover (*Dao*) gives birth to the One (*Taiji*, the Supreme Ultimate; or *Huntun*, Primordial Chaos). This One, in turn, gives birth to the Two (the *yang* force), and the Two gives birth to the Three (the *yin* force). These three forces are personified in Religious Daoism by the so-called Three Pure Ones (*Sanqing*): (1) the Primordial Heavenly Worthy, symbol of life-giving primordial breath (*qi*); (2) the Lingbao Heavenly Worthy, symbolizing the spirit (*shen*) of human beings; and (3) the Daode Heavenly Worthy, symbol of the "vital essence" (*jing*) in people. The Three Pure Ones generate the five agents (personified in the Five Rulers of traditional Chinese mythology); and from these come the myriad things of nature.

A knowledge of *yinyang*, five-agents, and *Yijing* symbolism is essential to an understanding of Daoist "alchemy," which aimed not at changing base metals into gold as in the West, but at producing physical benefits, such as strength and longevity. Since the Religious Daoists viewed the human body as a microcosm of the universe, both their meditative "internal alchemy" (*neidan*)—which included breathing exercises, sexual activity, and other forms of physical self-cultivation—and their "external alchemy" (*waidan*)—which involved the use of chemicals, drugs, and herbal medicines—were based on *yinyang*, five-agents, trigram, and hexagram correlations. So, in fact, was traditional Chinese medicine. Doctors and Daoists alike sought to achieve a harmonious balance of these cosmological influences within the body, and both assumed an integral relationship between the parts of the body and the whole. The basic principles and purposes of alchemy and acupuncture were thus essentially the same (see also chapter 10).

One of the most famous exponents of Daoist alchemy in the Qing period was Liu Yiming (1734–1821), an adherent of the Complete Reality sect and an eleventh-generation master of the Longmen (Dragon Gate) lineage. Liu had studied the Confucian classics when he was young, but he turned toward Daoism after a succession of serious illnesses, and eventually became not only a renowned master of Daoist alchemy, but also an expert in Chinese medicine. Liu was a prolific scholar whose highly regarded writings included a Daoist interpretation of the *Yijing* titled *Zhouyi chanzhen* (Elucidating the truth of the *Zhou Changes*; 1796). He also wrote a highly influential book on Daoist internal alchemy, the *Xiuzhen houbian* (Further discriminations in cultivating reality; 1798), which has been ably translated by Fabrizio Pregadio.[48] This latter work provides an excellent introduction to Daoist moral and meditative practice, framed as a series of questions and answers involving Liu and a disciple. Despite his self-image and reputation as a Daoist, Liu sought to unify the Three Teachings, using the *Doctrine of the Mean* (see chapter 6) as a foundational text. In his mind, unification was expressed in Confucianism primarily by the idea of centrality and commonality (*zhongyong*; "the mean"); in Buddhism by the notion of the "One Vehicle" (*Yicheng*); and in Daoism by the idea of the "Golden Elixir" (*Jindan*).

As was the case with Mahayana Buddhism, the value system of Religious Daoism reflected heavy Confucian influence. Indeed, all orthodox religious sects in China, and a good number of countercultural groups as well, admired the Confucian virtues of loyalty, faithfulness, integrity, duty, and filial piety. The curriculum in Buddhist and Daoist monasteries often included works from the classical canon, and Confucian values found their way to the popular masses in the form of vernacular religious tracts such as *shanshu* ("morality books") and *baojuan* ("precious scrolls"). Wilt Idema has translated two such tracts from the nineteenth century, both of which take as their focus the life of Guanyin, the Goddess of Mercy. The introduction to this excellent translation highlights the similarities and differences between the longer of the two Chinese works and the lives of female saints in medieval Europe.[49]

In keeping with its obsessive interest in longevity, but inspired by the Buddhist idea of karmic retribution, Religious Daoism developed an accounting system of merits (*gong*) and demerits (*guo*) that rewarded good behavior with extended life and subtracted years for evil deeds. By Ming-Qing times this system, which esteemed Confucian virtues but also took into account Buddhist concern for all living creatures, became deeply embedded in Religious Daoist thought and practice. Like the Buddhists, the Daoists worshipped a vast number of protective deities, including not only the Three Pure Ones and the Five Rulers, but also such popular gods and genies as the Jade Emperor (*Yuhuang*), the God of Literature (*Wenchang*), the Royal Mother of the West (*Xiwang mu*), the Eight Immortals (*Baxian*), and a host of spirits associated with stars and other natural objects, as well as historical figures and even parts of the body.

POPULAR RELIGION

These Daoist gods—like those of Buddhism and the official state cult—were the common property of the Chinese masses. Although some deities were clearly identified in the popular mind with either Buddhism or Daoism (or both) and others were patronized heavily by the elitist system of official religion, they all remained part of a gigantic, fluid network of national, regional, and local gods, each of whom could be supplicated by lay worshippers with no sense of disloyalty to the others.

Popular Chinese divinities were known by the generic term *shen*, or "spirit." These spirits, represented by images or tablets and sometimes by both, were deified individuals, objects, or forces of nature. All possessed magical power (*ling*). Some deities had their own private shrines, while others were worshipped together in temples. The significant feature of this expansive religious world, in addition to its obvious eclecticism, was its organization along functional lines. In the words of C. K. Yang,

> In popular religious life it was the moral and magical functions of the cults, and not the delineation of the boundary of religious faiths, that dominated people's consciousness. Even priests in some country temples were unable to reveal the identity of the religion to which they belonged. Centuries of mixing gods from different faiths into a common pantheon had produced a functionally oriented religious view that relegated the question of religious identity to a secondary place.[50]

Religious Daoists claimed, for instance, that the City God was their own creation, whereas frescoes depicting the Ten Courts of Judgment in the City God's temple testified to Buddhist influence. But the important point to both officials and the common people was that the City God was a local administrator, with vitally important bureaucratic responsibilities.

Yang has documented in detail the functional character of popular temple cults in traditional China. His survey of nearly eighteen hundred major temples in eight representative localities, although reflecting data drawn from sources published in the 1920s and 1930s, suggests patterns of distribution that probably prevailed in Qing times. Dividing these temples into five functional categories, Yang's survey yields the following information: 33.7 percent of the temples were devoted to deities associated with the well-being of the social and political order (kinship groups, local communities, and the state); 22.7 percent were devoted to the general moral order (heavenly deities and underworld authorities); 8.1 percent were devoted to economic functions (patron deities of occupational groups, etc.); 1.1 percent were devoted to the preservation of health; and 3.8 percent were devoted to general and personal welfare (including "devil dispellers," "blessing deities," and unspecified gods). The remainder of the temples (30.6 percent) were monasteries and nunneries, the overwhelming majority of which (nearly 90 percent) were Buddhist.[51]

Yang emphasizes that this functional breakdown is somewhat misleading because Chinese gods undertook a wide range of responsibilities and could be appealed to for many diverse purposes. Thus, the low percentage of temples specifically devoted to health-giving deities does not reflect lack of concern with good health. Quite the reverse was true. But the fact that most Chinese deities were believed to have the power to bestow or restore good health made functional specificity less important in this particular instance. On the other hand, specific functions might be very important in individual localities. The Sea God (*Haishen*) and the Consort of Heaven (*Tianhou*), for example, had special significance in coastal areas. The community of Foshan, near Guangzhou (Canton), which was well known for its firecracker industry, had nearly a dozen temples devoted to the Fire God.

Overall, the most popular deities countrywide tended to be those identified with institutional religion of one kind or another. But whether patronized institutionally or not, most deities were viewed in bureaucratic terms, for this was by far the most natural way for nearly everyone in Chinese society to conceive of meaningful power. The higher the god's bureaucratic status, the more powerful, although lines of authority and responsibility were not drawn as clearly in the huge popular pantheon as they were in the more orderly hierarchy of official religion. Moreover, as Benjamin Schwartz reminds us,

"The application of the bureaucratic metaphor to the numinous world did not *necessarily* lead to the view that the divine bureaucracy would invariably support its human counterpart."[52]

In the popular conception, as in the elite view, all gods were subordinate to, and servants of, Heaven. Characteristically, however, Heaven was personalized in the popular religious vocabulary by terms such as the Heavenly Emperor (*Tiandi*), the Heavenly Noble (*Tiangong*), and the Jade Emperor. Although popular religion was permeated with concepts and terms derived from elite culture, it was only a version of that culture, not a direct replica. Not only were abstractions such as Heaven generally personalized, but other concepts were also manipulated to conform more closely to the social outlook of commoners. Thus, whereas the elite version of nature and the cosmos emphasized harmony and order, the popular emphasis was far more on conflict and chaos. Whereas elite cosmology focused on the interaction and alternation of *yin* and *yang*, popular religion saw a constant struggle between *yang* spirits (that is, *shen*) and malevolent *yin* spirits known as *gui* ("ghosts" or "demons").

This struggle was viewed as natural and inevitable. According to a popular proverb, "Just as all things consist of *yin* and *yang*, and *yin* and *yang* are everywhere, so *shen* and *gui* are omnipresent." The struggle between *shen* and *gui* did not normally represent a titanic battle between the cosmic forces of good and evil, however. Instead, the relationship between *shen* and *gui* came to be viewed as analogous to that existing between the Qing government and disruptive elements in society such as bandits and beggars. From a popular perspective, the goal of most Chinese religious practices—whether state sacrifices or more localized rituals—was to enlist *shen* in controlling or neutralizing *gui*. The Daoist rite of "cosmic renewal" (*jiao*), for instance, was explicitly designed to restore *yang*—light and life—and to expel the forces of *yin*—darkness and death.[53]

Gui were held responsible for all kinds of misfortune and afflictions, from accidents, illness, and death to barrenness, crop failures, and birth defects. They were believed to possess or kidnap people, to steal things, and to play tricks on people. They could remain invisible or assume a human or animal form. Although *gui* existed in seemingly endless profusion, they were associated primarily with the realm of *yin*: darkness, the ground, water, and lonely places. Many were believed to be unplaced spirits of the dead; others were considered to be inimical forces of nature. None were friendly. The supernatural world of the Chinese peasant, like the real one, could be a frightening place.

Gui could be appeased by offerings of incense, food, money, or goods. They could also be repelled by various means, including the written names or images of "demon-dispelling" deities such as Zhong Kui and Jiang Taigong, amulets made of peach wood or other potent materials, paper strips with the eight trigrams or the characters Heaven and Earth and *yin* and *yang* written on them, weapons such as swords, daggers, clubs, and spears, and various other *yang* symbols, such as loud noises, fire, blood, mirrors, and so on. Many protective objects were closely identified with the scholarly life of the Chinese elite: copies or pages from the Confucian classics or imperial calendar, written characters, calligraphy brushes, official seals, and such.

Rituals of exorcism employed numerous objects such as those mentioned above, as well as spells (*jie* or *zhu*) and written charms (*fu*). Some of these rituals could be undertaken individually or collectively by laypersons, but most involved "professional" religious agents—Buddhist and Daoist clergy, spirit mediums, sorcerers, magicians, and soothsayers—sometimes in combination. These individuals were believed to possess the special skills required to identify the source of *gui*-related problems and to devise successful strategies for their eradication.

The primary means for expelling *gui* were charms written in the form of commands from superiors (*shen*) to inferiors (*gui*). Henri Doré describes these magical devices in the following terms:

> A charm is an official document, a mandate, an injunction, emanating from the god and setting to work superhuman powers who carry out the orders of the divinity. . . . The charm being an official document, . . . terminates in much the same manner as Chinese imperial edicts: "let the law be obeyed, let this order be respected and executed forthwith." . . . The effect of the charm, as well as that of any other decree or command, depends principally on the power of him who has issued it.[54]

Although charms were generally associated with Daoist religious activity, Buddhist priests also employed them and sold them for profit in monasteries and temples. Charms could be used not only to drive away *gui* in every conceivable circumstance, but also to right wrongs (such as unjust lawsuits) and to provide for the needs and interests of the deceased.

There are many colorful accounts of the activation and utilization of charms by religious agents of various sorts, but not all "spiritual" activities involved high drama. Public divination, for example—based on the *Yijing*, astrology, physiognomy, the dissection of characters, the casting of lots, the reading of omens, and numerous other techniques—tended to be a more somber and subdued ritual. The same was true of the popular form of geomantic divination known as *fengshui* (lit. "wind and water") or "siting." *Fengshui* was predicated on the belief that *yinyang* currents of cosmic breath (*qi*), which flowed in every geographic area, influenced human fortunes. These currents, subject to various astrological influences, including "star spirits," manifested themselves in local topography. The task of a geomancer (*fengshui xiansheng*) was to calculate, on the basis of an enormous number of topographical and astrological variables, the most favorable position to locate residences for both the living (homes, temples, businesses, official buildings, etc.) and the dead (graves).

Fengshui specialists operated at every level of Chinese society, from the Qing imperial household down to the peasantry. They played an important role in city planning, influenced military strategy, and were particularly important in making burial arrangements.[55] The most propitious site for any purpose was at the proper junction of *yin* and *yang* currents of *qi*. In the words of a knowledgeable nineteenth-century Western student of *fengshui*,

> The azure dragon [*yang*] must always be to the left [looking southward], and the white tiger [*yin*] to the right of any place supposed to contain a luck-bringing site. . . . In the angle formed by dragon and tiger . . . the luck-bringing site, the place for a tomb or dwelling, may be found. I say it *may* be found there, because, besides the conjunction of dragon and tiger, there must be there also a tranquil harmony of all the heavenly and terrestrial elements which influence that particular spot, and which is to be determined by observing the compass and its indication of the numerical proportions, and by examining the direction of the water courses.[56]

The "compass" in question was the *luopan*, an elaborate instrument about four to eight inches in diameter, with a magnetic needle pointing south and a series of concentric circles arranged in symbolic sets. Jeffrey Meyer describes the prototype:

> Schematically the circles of the compass begin with an inner set which deals with the center, then a group dealing with earth, then the Prior Heavens, and finally the Posterior Heavens. Represented among the circles are nearly all the Chinese symbols which are used in dealing with space and time: the trigrams and hexagrams in both the Prior and Posterior Heaven sequences, the ten stems and twelve branches, . . . the five agents, yin and yang, the twenty-four directions, the nine moving stars, the six constellations, the twenty-eight asterisms, . . . the four seasons and directions, the . . . twenty-four fifteen-day periods of the solar year, and the seventy-two five-day divisions of the year. All these are interrelated in various combinations and thus repeated frequently in the thirty-eight circles.[57]

Geomantic compasses were not always so complex, but all assumed an integral relationship between topography and astrological configurations. The *luopan* was often used in conjunction with popular almanacs (see chapters 1, 9, and 10) because the fundamental assumption of both was that certain stars and groupings of stars, in phase with *yin* and *yang*, the five-agents, the eight trigrams, and other cosmic variables, played a crucial role in earthly affairs. This assumption was shared by all levels of Chinese society and expressed in a variety of rituals, from the worship of Heaven in official sacrifices to the ceremonies of Religious Daoism and *fengshui* divination. Thus, in practice, popular astrology—not to mention Buddhist notions of karmic retribution, Religious Daoist ideas of merits and demerits, and concepts such as the mysterious, slow-moving cosmic force known as *qiyun* ("rhythms of fate")—complicated the essentially naturalistic interpretation of fate embraced by orthodox Confucians (see chapter 6).

Fengshui specialists had comparatively high status in traditional Chinese society, despite persistent criticisms from officials and gentry. These criticisms were not, however, directed against the general theory of *fengshui*, for, as indicated above, all levels of society accepted its basic assumptions, and all employed it in a wide variety of ways. Instead, scholars and officials objected to certain specific practices of geomancy that generated social tensions (competition for favorable *fengshui*) or led to delayed burials (a serious breach of mourning ritual). Above all, they decried the manipulation of the Chinese masses by religious agents who were not part of the orthodox elite. This fear motivated much elite criticism of popular religious practice in China.

Traditional Chinese homes reflected the complex religious world outlined above. They were served by religious agents such as priests and geomancers, and protected by a host of deities and guardian figures. The majority, at least in south China, had an altar to the household Lord of the Earth on the floor outside the door, a niche for the Heavenly Official (*Tianguan*) above it, and a place for the God of the Hearth (*Zaoshen*; aka Kitchen God) near the cooking stove. Wealth gods might be located in the hall or the main room of the house, along with Guanyin or another patron deity. Even the Qing emperors worshipped some of these deities. For instance, imperial devotions to the God of the Hearth took place in the Kunning Palace, with rituals closely approximating those of the Han Chinese.[58]

But the focal point of religious life in virtually every home in China was the ancestral altar, located by definition in the principal room. In Chinese society, ancestor worship was primary; individual or communal worship, only secondary. This became increasingly true of the Manchus as well as the Han. As Eveyln Rawski points out, not only did the Qing emperors devote ever more attention to official displays of filial piety at the Grand Ancestral Temple (*Taimiao*) and the less formal "family" ancestral hall known as the Fengxian Palace, they also carried out forms of domestic ancestor worship in more intimate surroundings, such as the Yangxin Palace, the Chengqian Palace, the Yuqing Palace, and the Qianqing Palace. Here, they burned incense in front of the portraits and/or spirit tablets of deceased ancestors in the

Chinese fashion. Special sacrificial offerings and the chanting of Buddhist sutras marked the birthdays and death dates of these departed spirits.[59]

From the standpoint of both the Qing rulers and their Han subjects, no ritual or institution did more to reinforce the solidarity of the family system, and thus the social order, than ancestor worship. The basic premise of the practice was that the soul of a departed family member consisted of two main elements, a *yin* component known as *po* (associated with the grave), and a *yang* component known as *hun* (associated with the ancestral tablet). According to one popular conception, these basic components became three separate "souls," each demanding ritual attention: one that went to the grave with the body, one that went to the Ten Courts of Judgment and was eventually reborn, and one that remained near the ancestral tablet on the family altar. *Po* had the potential of becoming *gui* if unplacated by sacrifices, but the spirits of one's own ancestors were not generally considered to be *gui*. One's own naturally became *shen*, assuming they received proper ritual attention.

There were two universal aspects of ancestor worship in traditional China, mortuary rites (*sangli*) and sacrificial rites (*jili*). Mortuary rites involved elaborate mourning practices that differed in particulars from region to region but shared certain major features. These were, in the order they usually occurred: (1) public notification of the death through wailing and other expressions of grief; (2) the wearing of white mourning clothing by members of the bereaved family, ideally according to the five degrees of relationship (see chapter 4); (3) ritualized bathing of the corpse; (4) the transfer of food, money, and other symbolic goods from the living to the dead; (5) the preparation and installation of a spirit tablet for the deceased; (6) the payment of ritual specialists, including Buddhist monks and Daoist priests; (7) music to accompany the corpse and settle the spirit; (8) the sealing of the corpse in an airtight coffin; and (9) the expulsion of the coffin from the community. These basic practices applied to Qing imperial burials as well.[60]

In most regions of China a funeral procession for the body and spirit tablet, followed by a feast for family members, marked the formal conclusion of the mourning process. Burial did not always take place immediately after death, however. High-status families—including the Qing imperial household—often kept the coffin in the domestic realm for several months or even longer as a mark of respect for the deceased (and perhaps to await an especially propitious time for interment according to *fengshui* calculations).[61] In all cases, regardless of when the funeral procession and feast took place, families strained their financial resources to the limit in order to exhibit the proper measure of filial devotion (and community status) in their ritual display. Deceased children were not usually so honored, however, for their premature death was itself considered an unfilial act.

Sacrificial rites were of two main sorts: daily or bimonthly devotions and anniversary services. Incense was burned regularly on the domestic ancestral altar, which housed the family spirit tablets in hierarchical order. In front of these tablets often glowed an eternal flame, symbol of the ancestor's abiding presence within the household (see figures 4.10 and 4.11). Anniversary rites took place on the death date of each major deceased member of the family. Sacrificial food was offered, and living members of the family participated in the ceremony in ritual order based on age and generation. Sacrifices were also made to the ancestors during major festival periods and on important family occasions such as births and weddings (see chapter 10). Analogous rituals took place in the sacrificial hall of each Qing imperial tomb, some of which were located in an area about eighty miles northeast of Beijing (the *Dongling* or Eastern Tombs) and others of which were located about ninety miles southwest of the capital (the *Xiling* or Western Tombs).

In the eyes of orthodox Confucians, ancestor worship was considered to be essentially a secular rite, with no religious implications. Deemed to be nothing more than the "expression of human feelings," mourning and other ritual observances expressed love and respect for the dead, at the same time cultivating the virtues of filial piety, loyalty, and faithfulness. Ancestor worship was a standard means of "honoring virtue and repaying merit" (*chongde baogong*) in the stock Chinese phrase. The Confucian gentleman sacrificed to his ancestors because it was the proper thing to do; lesser men did so to "serve the spirits."

This attitude was consistent with the general neo-Confucian tendency to encourage rational and secular interpretations of otherworldly phenomena. In neo-Confucian literature, for example, the popular religious terms *gui* and *shen* became expressly identified as the abstract forces of *yin* and *yang*. Official religion was justified at least in part as a means of motivating the masses to perform acts of Confucian piety. Sections on religion in local gazetteers often quoted the following remark attributed to Confucius: "The sages devised guidance in the name of the gods, and [the people of] the land became obedient." Even the employment of priests, geomancers, and other religious agents by elite households could be explained away as matters of habit, female indulgence, or a kind of filial insurance for ancestors in case the popular Buddhist version of the afterlife happened to be correct.[62]

But where did neo-Confucian "rationalism" end and popular "superstition" begin? Although popular religion reflected the social landscape of its adherents, it was still in many ways "a variation of the same [elite] understanding of the world." The "Heaven" of the Chinese literati may have been remote and impersonal, but it could reward Confucian virtue and punish vice in the same spirit, if not the same basic way, as the Jade Emperor and his agents.

The omens and avenging ghosts of popular vernacular literature had their supernatural counterparts in the official dynastic histories. The cosmological principles of astrology and divination—not to mention many specific religious beliefs and practices—were the same for all classes of Chinese society, as was the tendency to view the spirit world in bureaucratic terms.

Furthermore, the evidence suggests strongly that in the mind of the elite, *shen* and *gui* were not always identified simply as the abstract forces of *yin* and *yang*. It may even be suggested that the ceremonial observances for official sacrifices, community religion, and domestic worship evoked many of the same emotions in the elite that they did among the common people, although the evidence is largely impressionistic. At least the sense of interlocking rituals—reinforced by common symbolic elements (architecture, written characters, colors, numbers, plants, animals, deities, and culture heroes, etc.) as well as common practices (the use of music, the burning of incense and prayers, bowing and kneeling, etc.)—gave all sectors of Chinese society a sense of shared interest and common cultural purpose.

There was, of course, a heterodox tradition of popular religion that was far less compatible with the outlook of the Qing elite. Sworn brotherhood associations of the Triad type in southern China, and Buddhist-oriented folk religious sects of the White Lotus variety in the north, challenged Chinese social conventions, and were marked by a strong millenarian emphasis. Monotheistic religious teachings such as Islam and Christianity also contained millenarian elements and posed a threat to the Confucian order by their devotion to a religious authority higher than the state. Uprisings by groups with these and other religious affiliations caused enormous difficulties to the Qing state, as we have seen briefly in chapters 2 and 4. And while it is important to remember that large-scale insurrections such as the White Lotus Rebellion (1794–1804), the so-called Panthay Rebellion (1856–1873), and the Taiping Rebellion (1851–1864) had multiple causes, most of them socioeconomic, the millenarian appeal of certain sects of Daoism, Buddhism, Islam, and Christianity in Qing China should not be underestimated.[63]

Millenarianism in its quasi-Christian form proved to be particularly threatening in the case of the Taipings. They worshipped a non-Chinese God, looked to Jesus for succor and salvation, promoted Christian values, attacked Confucianism, Buddhism, and Daoism, advocated communalism and equality between men and women, and sought to eliminate longstanding social practices such as concubinage, foot binding, and ancestor worship.[64] But they also made many concessions to Chinese tradition in the realms of both theory and practice. For instance, they used concepts, phrases, and allusions from Confucian, Buddhist, and Daoist sources, held traditional views on the place of ritual in preserving status distinctions, honored Confucian views on matters such as name taboos, and employed conventional symbols of imperial legitimacy in their political institutions and public ceremonies. Even their private devotions to God (*Shangdi* or *Tian*)—the Heavenly Father (*Tianfu*)—bore a striking resemblance to ancestor worship down to the burning of incense before a spirit tablet in homes and offices.[65]

Undoubtedly the use of such time-honored terms and concepts, sources of authority, ceremonial forms, and political symbols somewhat diminished the revolutionary impact of heterodox movements—particularly in the popular mind. It is true, of course, that even in orthodox society a tension always existed between the "ordered" realm of elite ritual (*li*) and the "disorder" of popular (*su*) religious practices.[66] But the dialectic operating between the two favored order overall, as did shared ethical attitudes, philosophical concepts, and specific ritual practices. Similar cultural common denominators existed in the areas of Chinese art, literature, music, and drama, as we shall see.

Chapter Eight

Arts and Crafts

One of the most important themes in the history of Qing visual and material culture is the role of the state. In the first place, the Manchus saw patronage of Chinese art as a means of demonstrating their cultural legitimacy, and as a way to "glorify" the dynasty. Hence, most Qing emperors became avid collectors of Chinese-style arts and crafts (according to one estimate the Qianlong emperor owned "more than a million objects"), as well as practitioners of traditionally esteemed Chinese artistic activities such as painting and calligraphy. They also used Buddhist art and architecture to sustain their image as cakravartin universal rulers, and commissioned an enormous number of art works and craft productions to decorate their palaces and to present as gifts to officials, loyal subjects, and foreign emissaries. Furthermore, they employed court painters to produce impressive imperial portraits, and to document their court-sponsored civil and military activities—from campaigns against rebels and other enemies to imperial tours and the receipt of tributary envoys and products.[1] And, to the degree that maps were artistic productions (and many of them certainly were), the Qing rulers encouraged the creation of an unprecedented number of strikingly beautiful and symbolically redolent cartographic products, some produced by Chinese and Manchu artists, and others produced in concert with foreign collaborators, including the Jesuits.[2]

Traditionally, Chinese scholars considered two types of art worthwhile: that which they enjoyed but did not create, and that which they created and therefore esteemed most. The former included the work of skilled craftsmen, from elegant ancient bronzes to colorful contemporary ceramics; the latter embraced the refined arts of the brush—painting and calligraphy. Occupying a fluid middle ground were decorative textiles, often executed in exquisite detail by talented elite women. Popular art—from temple paintings and religious icons to folk crafts such as basketwork, fans, umbrellas, toys, and paper cuts—flourished throughout the Qing period, but Chinese connoisseurs seldom took it seriously.[3]

Although early Qing intellectuals stigmatized the decadent consumer society of the late Ming as a "culturally exquisite bloom, which was nevertheless in some sense rotten inside" (in the words of Craig Clunas), Chinese attitudes toward connoisseurship continued to be shaped by Ming models. It may indeed have become "unfashionable," as Clunas and others have suggested, for Qing intellectuals to consume conspicuously in the Ming style, or even to talk about superfluous "things" the way Ming aesthetes did, but works on connoisseurship such as Cao Zhao's fourteenth-century *Gegu yaolun* (Essential criteria of antiquities) remained highly influential as repositories of information on Chinese art, archaeology, and authenticity throughout the Qing period.[4] Moreover, the genre of "beautiful women paintings" (*meiren hua*) that proved so appealing to the Qing court deliberately exoticized Chinese women as representatives of Ming-style courtesan culture. By design, these paintings implicitly accentuated the Manchu conquest, which subjugated the Chinese—men and women alike—along with their "exquisite," but also "decadent and weak," culture.[5]

The Qing dynasty has been characterized as "an antiquarian age when, as never before, men looked back into the past." But during the first century and a half of Manchu rule there was considerable experimentation in the arts. Part of the impetus may have been the traumatic effect of the Qing conquest, which provided loyalist painters such as Gong Xian (1620–1689) with the tortured artistic theme of "a world gone corrupt." Another factor, unsettling in a different way but also encouraging innovation, was the rapid growth of commercial wealth, particularly in the Lower Yangzi region. There, the blending of literati and merchant culture produced new artistic fashions. The result was an enormous demand among consumers for innovative forms, colors, styles, and textures. Finally, there was the expanding foreign market for Chinese arts and crafts, especially porcelain. Although many of these goods came to be designed explicitly for export to the West, their production unquestionably influenced Chinese tastes.[6]

The Qing court's patronage of painters, calligraphers, and craftsmen naturally affected Chinese artistic developments. The Kangxi emperor began the process in earnest, but it was his grandson, the Qianlong emperor, who exerted the most profound influence. Michael Sullivan describes him rather unflatteringly as

a voracious art collector, a niggardly and opinionated connoisseur, an unstoppable writer of inscriptions and stamper of seals who was determined, as a function of his imperial role, to leave his indelible mark upon China's artistic legacy. His seals obliterate some of the finest paintings in the imperial collection, which

... grew to such enormous size that there were few ancient masterpieces that were not gathered behind the high walls of the Forbidden City, shut away forever from the painters who might still have studied them had they remained in private hands.[7]

Financial strains during the latter part of the Qianlong reign caused the emperor to cut back on his sponsorship of the arts, however; and by the end of the eighteenth century at the latest, the dominant influence on Chinese art was private patronage, together with the ever greater commercialization of production.

Meanwhile, "vernacular art" flourished. James Cahill's *Pictures for Use and Pleasure: Vernacular Painting in High Qing China* (2010) makes a strong case for expanding the boundaries of Chinese art appreciation to include works by urban-based painters "who produced pictures as required for diverse everyday domestic and other uses." These paintings, including the new genre of *meiren hua* mentioned earlier, were "executed in the polished 'academic' manner of fine-line drawing and colors, usually on silk, and were valued for their elegant imagery and their lively and often moving depictions of subjects." In Cahill's well-considered opinion, such paintings, which often drew on Western elements of style and "devices of representation," have been misguidedly underappreciated by Chinese connoisseurs and collectors, both now and in the past.[8]

During the nineteenth century, Qing painting seems to have lost a considerable amount of its vigor and vitality. Part of the problem was lack of direct inspiration, an unfortunate consequence of the Qianlong emperor's aggressive campaign to acquire local artworks for his imperial collection. Another difficulty was financial exigency, which diminished the court's support for painting, calligraphy, and craft production. Meanwhile, many "independent" Chinese artists went to one of two extremes—either they surrendered to the demands of patrons and other customers for hastily produced paintings, or they became overly academic in their artistic approach. Increasingly, we find late Qing works that were simply paintings about painting, "art-historical art." Too often, so the criticism goes, the artists' inspiration "was not nature but the very tradition itself."[9]

Nonetheless, there is evidence to suggest that the late Qing was not nearly as artistically sterile as it has often been portrayed. Although labor-intensive crafts such as cloisonné never achieved the same heights under private patrons that they had reached under court patronage during the eighteenth century, certain kinds of creative painting emerged among scholar-officials at the fringes of the court, as well as in the provinces. During the nineteenth century several bold regional styles either emerged for the first time or acquired new life, and cities such as Shanghai and Guangzhou (Canton) became centers of vibrant artistic activity.

ATTITUDES TOWARD ART

Connoisseurship in traditional China required wealth, leisure, and education. As amateur artists and devoted calligraphers, gentry and officials were expected to have a discriminating eye and to possess attractive art works, but they were not always the most famous or successful collectors. The salt merchant An Qi (born c. 1683), for example, was the envy of all literati in the area of Tianjin. Having purchased a number of paintings and calligraphic scrolls from well-known Ming and early Qing connoisseurs, in time An became a connoisseur himself. His annotated catalog of paintings and calligraphy, completed in 1742, was highly prized by Qing collectors for its detailed descriptions of outstanding artwork. In fact, the noted Manchu antique collector and art patron Duanfang (1861–1911) reprinted it twice. Duanfang, for his part, used his celebrated connoisseurship to cultivate important political and social relationships in the late Qing.[10]

Chinese art has long been characterized by a remarkable feeling for natural beauty, perfection of form, grace, and refinement. It is also noteworthy for its optimism, love of nature, and organic quality. As indicated in chapter 5, much of the formal aesthetics of the Chinese elite developed out of a longstanding cognitive emphasis on *yinyang* principles and relationships. As with music, ritual, and poetry, the most exalted forms of artistic achievement in China tended to display lyrical patterns of dualistic balance, periodic rhythms, and cyclical sequences.

These aesthetics had more than simply a linguistic foundation; by late imperial times they also had a cosmological one. Chinese art reflected life, which in turn reflected the order of the universe. Liu Xie's *Wenxin diaolong* (The literary mind and the carving of dragons) expresses this artistic relationship in the following way:

> *Wen*, or pattern, is a very great power indeed. It is born together with Heaven and Earth. Why do we say this? Because all color-patterns are mixed of black and yellow [the colors of Heaven and Earth], and all shape patterns are differentiated by round and square [that is, the shapes of Heaven and Earth]. The sun and moon, like two pieces of jade, manifest the pattern of Heaven; mountains and rivers in their beauty display the pattern of Earth. These are, in fact, the *wen* of the *Dao* itself. . . . Man, and man alone, forms with these the "three powers" [Heaven, Earth, and Man], and he does so because he alone is endowed with spirituality [*ling*]. He is the refined essence of the five agents—indeed, the mind of the universe.[11]

In praise of the great late Ming painter Dong Qichang (1555–1636), the *Wusheng shi shi* (History of silent poetry) states, "He [Dong] held the creative power of nature in his hand and was nourished by the mists and clouds.

. . . [It] may be said that everything in his paintings, whether clouds, peaks or stones, was made as by the power of Heaven, his brushwork being quite unrestrained like the working of nature."[12]
Michael Sullivan has aptly remarked that

> Just as ritual, and its extension through music, poetry, and the shape and decoration of the objects used in it, was the gentleman's means of demonstrating that he was attuned to the Will of Heaven, so was aesthetic beauty felt to be what results when the artist gives sincere expression to his intuitive awareness of natural order. Beauty, therefore, is what conduces to order, harmony, [and] tranquility.[13]

In the words of the *Record of Ritual*: "Music is [an echo of] the harmony between Heaven and Earth; ceremonies reflect the orderly distinctions [in the operations of] Heaven and Earth. From that harmony all things receive their being; to those orderly distinctions they owe the differences between them. Music has its origin in Heaven."[14] The goal of all elite artistic, literary, musical, and ritual activity in traditional China was thus to promote and display social and cosmic harmony.

Because the *dao* of art, literature, music, and ritual was inseparable from the cosmic *Dao* and the *dao* of human affairs, it followed that Chinese creative endeavor was never far removed from tradition. Like the Confucian classics, ancient artistic models were believed to have universal and transcendent value. As Frederick Mote reminds us, in traditional China

> neither individuals nor the state could claim any theoretical authority higher or more binding than men's rational minds and the civilizing norms that those human minds had created. That is a tenuous basis of authority, and since it could not easily be buttressed by endowing it with nonrational or suprarational qualities, it had to be buttressed by the weight granted to historical experience.[15]

This meant that in Chinese art, as in Chinese life, "the defining criteria for value were inescapably governed by past models, not by present experience or by future states of existence."

The relationship between past and present in Chinese art (and other areas of Chinese aesthetic and intellectual life as well) may be viewed in terms of a creative tension between the polarities of tradition and innovation, orthodoxy and aesthetics. Different individuals responded in different ways to these competing impulses. But however such tensions were conceived, and however they were resolved, the past in Chinese imaginative endeavor remained an integral part of the Chinese present.

How was the link established? Creative individuals sought the restoration of antiquity (*fugu*), a fundamental neo-Confucian concern and an obsession with many Qing intellectuals. But the restoration of the past did not simply mean the slavish imitation of early literary and artistic models. Instead, it involved "spiritual communication" (*shenhui*) with the ancient masters, a state in which the past and present became one in the mind of the creative individual. The greater the aesthetic or technical achievement of a Chinese writer or artist, the more he or she was thought to be in touch with the past—at once under its command and in command of it. Such spiritual communication required a total commitment on the part of the individual, body and mind.[16]

Chinese tradition thus suggested pattern, but it did not impose despotic rule. The result was a remarkable continuity of cultural style without the sacrifice of creative potential. In the words of Wen Fong, "in *fugu* the Chinese saw history not as a long fall from grace, but as an enduring crusade to restore life and truth to art."[17] That crusade gave vitality to Chinese culture in every period, including the Qing.

Naturally enough, tradition influenced not only the artist and craftsman, but also the collector and connoisseur:

When his eye falls on the miniature porcelain tripod standing on his desk, not only does . . . [he] savour the perfection of its form and glaze, but a whole train of associations are set moving in his mind. For him, his tripod is treasured not simply for its antiquity or rarity, but because it is a receptacle of ideas, and a visible emblem of the ideals by which he lives. Indeed, although he would be gratified to know that it was the genuine Song dynasty piece it purports to be, it would not be robbed of all its value to him if he subsequently found that it was in fact a clever imitation of the Qianlong period—particularly if it bore an appropriate inscription cut in archaic characters.[18]

Even a fragment of the past was sufficient to conjure up the right kind of cultural image. The Qing collector Lu Shihua notes in his fascinating *Shuhua shuoling* (Collector's scrapbook) that members of his circle of acquaintances would be quite content with one or two lines from a Song inscription, for "as soon as one has come to know the brush technique and the spirit of the work of the ancient artists, one can derive the rest by analogy."[19]

Books on connoisseurship, such as Cao Zhao's influential *Essential Criteria of Antiquities*, advised readers on how to determine artistic worth and detect forgeries, but they did not encourage in Qing collectors a passion for mere authenticity. Nor did they promote an inordinate attachment to individual art objects. A characteristic feature of Chinese connoisseurship in late imperial times was the trading of cultural artifacts—a Ming scroll for a Qing album, a Shang bronze for a Song ceramic. In this way, personal collections were invigorated by aesthetic variety and at the same time enriched by the scholarly associations that attached to newly acquired objects. In traditional

China, prior ownership of a work of art could be almost as important to the collector as the work itself.[20]

The unity of cultural style in Qing China was evident not only in shared aesthetics and attitudes toward the past, but also in the vocabulary of artistic, literary, and musical criticism. Terms such as *yin* and *yang*, *qi* (life spirit or force), *gu* ("bone" or structure), and *shenyun* (spirit and tone, spiritual resonance, or inspired harmony) were longstanding and indispensable in the evaluation of creative work of all kinds—although each expression might have several connotations in different contexts. These critical terms suggest the thematic importance in Chinese art of life, vitality, and natural process, as well as the structural importance of rhythm and balance.

Chinese symbolism, too, reflected a certain unity of cultural style. Closely linked with literary symbolism, artistic symbols were drawn from several rich sources of traditional inspiration—language (including puns and stylized characters), philosophy, religion, history, popular mythology, and, of course, nature itself. Some symbols that were once meaningful had lost their original connotations by Qing times and were considered largely decorative by all but the most sophisticated connoisseurs. Other symbols, like Chinese characters themselves, held different meanings depending on context. But despite these differences (and certain regional variations), the most potent abstract and concrete symbols in Chinese art and literature tended to be shared by all levels of society and to reflect common cultural concerns. Even non-Han peoples, the Manchus included, employed many of these symbols in their arts, crafts, and architecture.[21]

The overwhelming majority of Chinese artistic symbols were positive. Abstract designs tended to express the harmonious patterns and processes of nature, while concrete symbols generally indicated auspicious themes of happiness and good fortune. Although most of the spiral and angular designs on ancient bronzes and pottery (and later copies) no longer had specific symbolic value by Qing times, Chinese artists continued to represent natural processes through abstract symbolism. Square-circle motifs, for example, depicted in both art and architecture the cosmic relationship between Heaven (circle, *yang*) and Earth (square, *yin*). Also popular as a cosmic symbol was the Diagram of the Supreme Ultimate (*Taiji tu*)—a motif dating from Song times that adorned a wide variety of Chinese artwork, from paintings and carved jade to primitive ceramics intended for daily use in commoner households. It consisted of a circle composed of two equal parts—one light (*yang*) and one dark (*yin*)—separated by an S-shaped line. Often this diagram was surrounded by the eight trigrams and/or other cosmological symbols.

Animal symbolism figured prominently in Chinese artwork of all kinds. The most powerful and positive of all animals, whether actual or mythical, was the so-called dragon (*long*), a composite creature with the supposed ability to change size and render itself visible or invisible at will. Associated with the east and spring, the dragon was believed to inhabit mountains and to be capable of both ascending into the heavens and living in the water. Unlike its rough (very rough) European counterpart, the Chinese dragon symbolized benevolence, longevity, prosperity, and the renewal of life. It also served as a token of imperial majesty, especially when depicted with five claws on each of its four feet.

The so-called phoenix (*fenghuang*) was the *yin* equivalent of the dragon. Associated with the south and summer, it had some *yang* qualities, just as the dragon had some *yin* attributes. Like the dragon, it was a composite animal, with distinctly positive connotations. Symbolizing peace and joy, it was commonly used as the mark of an empress in imperial China.

The unicorn (*qilin*) was associated with the west and autumn. It symbolized good luck and prosperity and was believed to herald the birth of a hero or a sage. According to legend, a *qilin* was seen when Confucius came into the world. Like the dragon and the phoenix, the unicorn was a composite creature, sometimes depicted with one horn, but often with two. Its predominant characteristic was goodwill and benevolence to all living things.

The tortoise (*gui*), although not a purely mythical beast in the sense of the dragon, phoenix, and the unicorn, was nonetheless viewed as a supernatural animal. Associated with the north and winter, its outstanding attributes were strength, endurance, and longevity. Its symbolic importance stemmed not only from the Chinese preoccupation with longevity, but also from its legendary (and historical) connection with divination. As an imperial symbol, prominently displayed, for instance, on the grounds of the Forbidden City, the tortoise was often depicted with the head of a dragon.

Among more conventional creatures, the tiger was king. In general, it symbolized military prowess. The lion was viewed as the protector of all that was sacred and was particularly popular as a Buddhist symbol. Bronze, stone, and ceramic lions often stood in male-female pairs as guardians on either side of the entrance to important Chinese buildings, both secular and religious. Other large animals, such as horses and elephants (both symbolizing strength and wisdom), were also popular as guardian figures.

The deer symbolized immortality (because of its supposed ability to find a magical life-giving fungus known as *lingzhi*) and also official emoluments (because the character for deer, *lu*, sounds like another character meaning "salary"). A similar pun on the sound *yu* invested the fish with the symbolic meaning of "abundance." Yet another pun made bats (*fu*) the symbol for good luck and prosperity. The link between Chinese characters and sounds quite naturally yielded what Wolfram Eberhard calls a "rebus-mentality" (see chapter 5).

Among flying animals and other fowl, cranes symbolized longevity; swallows, success; and the quail, courage in adversity. Mandarin ducks indicated conjugal affection, whereas the wild goose conjured up feelings of sadness or longing. Roosters, hens, and chickens symbolized family prosperity. In the insect world, the cicada stood as a common symbol of fertility and rebirth. The butterfly signified joy and warmth (and also longevity, by virtue of a pun); the dragonfly, weakness and instability.

Plant symbolism was extremely popular in late imperial China. Without doubt the most prominent symbol in this category was bamboo. Quite apart from its inherent aesthetic appeal and multifunctional role in Chinese daily life (abundantly documented in the TSJC), bamboo symbolized the Confucian scholar—upright, strong, and resilient, yet gentle, graceful, and refined. The pine tree suggested longevity and solitude; the plum tree, fortitude and respect for old age. The willow, like the wild goose, indicated parting and sorrow, while the cassia tree, like the carp, connoted literary success.

Of various popular fruits, the peach had wide-ranging significance. It symbolized marriage, spring, justice, and especially Daoist immortality. The apple signified peace (a pun on the sound *ping*); the persimmon, joy; the pomegranate, fertility. Popular flower symbols included the chrysanthemum (happiness, longevity, and integrity), the peony (love and good fortune), the plum blossom (courage and hope), the wild orchid (humility and refinement), and the lotus (purity and detachment from worldly cares—a predominantly Buddhist symbol).

Religious symbolism was, of course, most evident in explicitly Buddhist and Religious Daoist arts and crafts. Virtually all of the major Buddhas, bodhisattvas, gods, genies, and other spirits of the popular pantheon were portrayed in paintings, sculpture, carvings, ceramics, and other temple art forms. An elaborate symbolism of hand gestures (Sanskrit: *mudra*; Chinese: *shoushi*) came to be associated with Buddhist images, in addition to the wide range of signs and objects related to specific aspects of Buddhist teaching. One of the most powerful of these signs was the swastika (*wan*), which symbolized the Buddha's heart and mind and served as a general indication of happiness, blessings, and sometimes immortality. Swords and other weapons denoted protection and wisdom; the conch shell, the universality of Buddhist law (*dharma*); and jewels or scepters, the granting of wishes. Similar symbols existed for Religious Daoism. For example, the Eight Immortals—all signifying longevity and good fortune—were represented by the Eight Precious Things: fans, swords, bottle gourds, castanets, flower baskets, bamboo canes, flutes, and lotus flowers.

Confucian art symbolism drew its primary inspiration from history and the classics, as well as from more "popular" stories of virtuous individuals, such as the famous "Twenty-Four Examples of Filial Piety" (*Ershisi xiao*; see chapter 10). In addition to common plant and animal symbols like the quail and bamboo, diverse objects such as pearls, coins, books, paintings, and the rhinoceros horn represented scholars. Also popular as symbols of scholarly refinement were the Chinese "lute" (*guqin*) and the so-called Four Treasures of Literature—writing brush, ink stick, grinding stone, and paper.

Indicative of both Chinese eclecticism and a penchant for combining elements into numerical categories, many artistic symbols were grouped together. Combinations of two of the same symbol often indicated conjugal affection or friendship, but such pairings also reflected *yinyang* juxtapositions—aesthetic patterns in which one element was clearly "superior" to the other. Thus quail were almost invariably depicted in pairs, one with its head turned upward (*yang*) and the other with its head facing the ground (*yin*). The pairing, which in Qing craft productions might connote a mother-child relationship, derives from a famous line in the *Classic of Poetry*. But the positioning of the two reflects a longstanding aesthetic of unequal balance.

Plants and animals were often grouped together—the phoenix and the peony, for example, to indicate opulence; the chrysanthemum and the grouse, to connote good fortune; the heron and the lotus, to symbolize integrity. Larger groupings were common as well. As the Three Friends of Winter (*Suihan sanyou*), the bamboo, plum, and pine signified perseverance and solidarity in the face of adversity. The plum, wild orchid, bamboo, and chrysanthemum were known as the Four Gentlemen and beloved by gardeners, poets, artists, scholars, and craftsmen. The dragon, phoenix, unicorn, and tortoise were grouped together as the Four Spiritual Animals (*Siling*).

The Four Spiritual Animals were not the only symbols reflecting seasonal or astrological correlations. The months of the year, for example, came to be represented by flora as well as fauna. The twelve animals of the Chinese zodiac, and sometimes even the twenty-eight astral animals, were also portrayed on art objects. Popular groupings of eight included not only the Buddhist Lucky Signs and the Daoist Immortals mentioned above, but also Eight Creatures corresponding to the eight trigrams. The Twelve Imperial Emblems, as the name suggests, adorned items for the emperor's personal use, including clothing. Initially the Manchu rulers outlawed them because they were associated too closely with the Ming, but the Qianlong emperor reintroduced them in 1759. The largest category of Chinese symbols was known simply as the Hundred Ancient Things, a generic designation for an indefinite number of auspicious signs and objects. In general, Confucian symbolism dominated this motif, but Buddhist, Daoist, and naturalistic symbols also figured prominently in it. Like most larger groupings of symbols, the Hundred Ancient Things appeared most commonly on Chinese craft productions.

CRAFTS

Chinese craftsmen in Qing times excelled at nearly every kind of technical art—textiles (including, of course, silk), wood and ivory carving, metalwork, lacquer ware, stone sculpture, ceramics, enamels, bronzes, jades, jewelry, and glassware. The Qing was also a period of technical accomplishments in areas such as architecture and landscape gardening.[22] Not surprisingly, much of the best craftsmanship of the period was done under imperial patronage. As early as 1680 or so, the Kangxi emperor had already established workshops in the imperial palace precincts for the manufacture of silk products, porcelains, lacquer ware, glass, enamel, jade, furniture, and other prized objects for court use. His grandson, the Qianlong emperor, was especially well known for his employment of skilled imperial artisans in the production of magnificent works of traditional craftsmanship.[23]

Of the many types of Chinese crafts, four may be singled out for particular attention: bronzes, jades, porcelains, and landscape gardens. All four gave special satisfaction to members of the Chinese elite, and each in its own way exhibited the major aesthetic features and symbolic elements of Chinese art discussed in the previous section.

The most highly prized bronzes in the Qing period, as in more recent times, were ancient ritual vessels of Shang and Zhou vintage. They were valued not only for their natural color and exquisite design, but also for their powerful historical and ritual associations.[24] The well-known Qing connoisseur Ruan Yuan (1764–1849) once identified three successive stages in the evolution of Chinese attitudes toward bronze vessels: before the Han, they were symbols of privilege and power; from Han to Song times, their discovery was hailed as a portent; and from the Song dynasty onward, "freed from superstition," they became the toys of collectors and the quarry of philologists and antiquarians. But the *Essential Criteria of Antiquities* suggests that even in late imperial times at least some members of the Chinese elite, probably a large number, considered ancient ritual vessels to provide a measure of protection against evil spirits—a function not unlike that of the more mundane charms of the so-called unenlightened masses.[25]

As indicated by Ruan Yuan, the inscriptions on ancient bronzes, together with early stone inscriptions, were of great interest to Qing antique collectors, who studied them systematically as a special class of Chinese scholarship. Some collectors, such as Chen Jieqi (1813–1884), possessed hundreds of bronzes and literally thousands of rubbings from stone inscriptions, not to mention a large number of ancient coins and other metal artifacts. Literati such as Liu Xihai (d. 1853) wrote numerous tracts on these and other antiquities, contributing to a general burst of antiquarian scholarship in the late Qing period.

Qing craftsmen often sought to imitate the shape and design of Shang and Zhou bronzes, either to conform to Qing ritual specifications in the case of ceramics, or out of sheer admiration for their form and style. The decorative motifs of these ancient models—particularly abstract designs such as the spiraling or curvilinear "thunder pattern" and "whorl circle"—endured in various types of Chinese art for thousands of years. The original piece-mold technique that produced them involved the transference of carved designs from one surface to another, a procedure also followed in Chinese seal carving, the carving of calligraphy in stone or wood, and, of course, the carving of printing blocks. In all these crafts, the artisan had to possess, in Wen Fong's words, "a highly refined sensitivity for the silhouetted form and a lively familiarity with, and love for, the interplay between the positive and negative design patterns."[26] Both the zoomorphic and abstract designs of classic-style bronzes reflect a complex *yinyang* interaction between solid and void, raised and recessed, relief and intaglio that proved invariably appealing to Chinese aesthetic sensibilities.

Some Qing copies of early Chinese bronzes were deliberate forgeries, but many made no pretense of antiquity and provided the actual date of casting on the vessel. Other bronzes produced in the Qing period did not even try to approximate ancient models. Containers for practical use, decorative bells, and ornaments, as well as small religious statues, came in a wide variety of styles and shapes that often reflected more "modern" tastes. Yet the aesthetic appeal of ancient bronzes, as well as their presumed protective value and their historical associations, made them highly prized throughout the ages, including the Qing period.

Ancient jades were viewed in much the same way. The Qing connoisseur Lu Shihua tells us:

Present-day people want jades of the Three Dynasties [Xia, Shang, and Zhou] only, and require that their color be pure white, "sweet yellow," or "sweet green." Even then they are not satisfied, and insist that the "blood spots" be spread evenly over the entire surface and that the object be large and in perfect condition. If one sets his standard as high as this, he had better have a jade object newly made, and submit it to the oil treatment [*tihong you*].[27]

For most Chinese connoisseurs it was satisfying enough if jade objects were of high quality and traditional design, but there can be no doubt that antique jade was considered more valuable than new jade, not only for its use in antiquarian studies, but also because it was believed to possess a much larger supply of "life force" (*qi*) or "virtue" (*de*).

From neolithic times through the Qing, jade was always highly regarded. The Chinese language is rich in words with the "jade" (*yu*) radical—words that often convey notions of beauty, preciousness, hardness, and purity. Confucius is said to have remarked,

> The sages of old beheld in jade the reflections of every virtue. In its luster, bright yet warm, humaneness; in its compactness and strength, wisdom; in its sharp and clean edges which cause no injury, righteousness; in its use as pendants, seeming as if they would drop to the ground, propriety; in the note it emits when struck, clear and prolonged, music; by its flaws neither concealing its beauty nor its beauty concealing its flaws; loyalty; by its radiance issuing forth from within on every side, faithfulness.[28]

Jade, in other words, united in itself moral and aesthetic beauty.

In various forms, jade was used in ceremonial sacrifices, buried with the dead, displayed in homes and palaces, and worn for both decoration and protection. For official ritual purposes, it was modeled into various symbolic shapes such as the disc (*bi*) and the squared tube (*cong*)—both of which had been employed in Shang and Zhou dynasty ceremonies. Jade amulets provided personal protection from evil spirits and conveyed "life force," while jade musical instruments were highly esteemed both in ritual life and daily affairs for their clear and uplifting sound. Scholars often fondled specially "carved" pieces of jade called *bawan*, both for the sensual pleasure it afforded and in order to refine their touch for the appreciation of fine porcelain.[29]

The Qianlong reign represented the high point of jade carving ("grinding" would be a more appropriate term) in late imperial China, in part because it was a period of great prosperity, but also because vast areas of Central Asia, where much precious jade is found, were brought under imperial sway at that time. During the long and illustrious rule of the Qianlong emperor, thousands of magnificent carved jades were added to the imperial collection, some of which bore poetic inscriptions in characters that imitated the emperor's calligraphy. In the words of S. Howard Hansford, during the Qianlong period "jade was applied to countless new uses in the Forbidden City and the stately homes of nobles and officials. Though the inspiration of the designers of two thousand years earlier was rarely attained, the execution and finish left nothing to be desired and much larger works were attempted."[30] Some of these monumental jade sculptures, still on display in the Forbidden City today, stand taller than a full-grown man (well, taller than I am anyway).

The heyday of Qing porcelain manufacture was somewhat earlier than that of jade carving, from about 1683 to 1750, during the reign of the Kangxi emperor in particular. Of all the Chinese ceramic arts, porcelain (*ci*) stood at the apex of achievement: it was universally admired, the subject of countless essays, and a fitting topic for poetry as well. It was also used to make colored ritual vessels for Qing state sacrifices.[31] Imperial patronage was enormously important to the successful production of high-quality porcelains. Soame Jenyns has written:

> The history of Qing porcelain is in effect the history of the town of Jingde zhen, which in turn was dominated by the presence of the imperial porcelain factory, which was situated there. Over 80 percent of the porcelains of China during the Qing period were made at this great ceramic metropolis in Jiangxi, or in its immediate neighborhood; the provincial porcelain factories, with the single exception of Dehua in Fujian, producing porcelain of poor quality and negligible importance during this period.[32]

This statement perhaps undervalues local production in Qing China, but it certainly testifies to the dominant position occupied by the imperial factory.

As with bronzes and jades, Qing connoisseurs greatly admired porcelain antiques, which had a kind of dull shine, or "receded luster" (*tuiguang*). Among the most esteemed of these early porcelains, in addition to official ware (*guanyao*), was the legendary sky-blue *chai* ware, *ru* ware, and crackled *ge* ware. Qing potters excelled in the imitation of these and other types of early ceramics, and expert forgers produced "receded luster" by rubbing new porcelain first with a grindstone, then with a mixture of paste and fine sand, and finally with a straw pad to obliterate the scratches. The Kangxi emperor is known to have sent to the imperial kilns at Jingde zhen rare pieces of Song dynasty *guan*, *chai*, and *ru* ware to be meticulously copied for imperial pleasure. The imperial kilns also continued to produce Ming-style porcelains, some of which, like the beautiful white "eggshell" bowls of the Yongle period, were executed by Qing craftsmen more flawlessly than the Ming originals.

Qing potters also excelled in producing the striking multicolored Ming-style porcelains known as *sancai*, *wucai*, and *doucai*. The significant feature of these three types of porcelain, in addition to their vivid use of rich blues, greens, and yellows in the fashion of much architectural decoration, is their amalgamation of popular religious and imperial symbolism, their seemingly inexhaustible range of shapes and colors (including reproductions of ancient bronzes), and their self-conscious *yinyang* juxtapositions. As with other porcelains, Qing craftsmen often inscribed *sancai*, *wucai*, and *doucai* pieces with reign marks other than those of the period in which they were produced, making positive identification of good copies extremely difficult.[33]

European influences found their way into the decoration of Qing porcelains for two principal reasons. One was the fact that a considerable amount of Chinese porcelain was intended for European markets in the latter half of the seventeenth century and most of the eighteenth. The other was the general receptiveness of the imperial court to Western artistic influences during the late Ming and most of the Qing period. These influences can be seen not only in porcelain and other ceramics, but also, as indicated both above and below, in court paintings and imperial architecture (notably the European-style buildings in the Summer Palace known as the *Yuanming yuan* or "Garden of Perfect Brightness").

Overall, however, Chinese crafts followed traditional models, and although some porcelains functioned as convenient vehicles for the transmission of foreign artistic influences, most conveyed a rich indigenous decorative tradition that in a real sense transcended class. Many of the highest-quality Qing porcelains were decorated with folk symbols and the bright colors of folk and religious art. It is true, however, that in several respects porcelains had a closer affinity with elite art than with the simple ceramics of commoner households. Like jades and bronzes, they were of antiquarian interest and appreciated both for their surface "feel" and melodious ring when struck. Furthermore, like paintings, many porcelains were carefully decorated with the brush and categorized according to a similar system of classification. But whereas in painting, landscape was the most popular and prestigious classification (see next section), in porcelain it was a relatively minor category.

Landscape gardening, on the other hand, sought precisely to capture the mood of a landscape painting. Although often overlooked as an art form, Chinese gardens in fact embodied the best principles of artistic expression in China, combining superb craftsmanship, complex symbolism, and the careful arrangement of aesthetic elements. During the Qing period, gardens ranged in size from the huge (seventy-mile walled perimeter) Yuanming yuan—largely destroyed during the Anglo-French hostilities with China in 1860—to tiny, cramped urban gardens only a few square feet in area, and even to miniature gardens in porcelain dishes.[34] Members of the Chinese elite and rich merchants, of course, took special pride in constructing individualized gardens, notably Yuan Mei's famous Suiyuan in the area of Nanjing (see below).

Chinese gardens were often viewed as Daoist retreats. In the words of the Qianlong emperor, "Every . . . ruler, when he has returned from audience, and has finished his public duties, must have a garden in which he may stroll, look around and relax his heart. If he has a suitable place for this it will refresh his mind and regulate his emotions, but if he has not, he will become engrossed in sensual pleasures and lose his will power."[35] Access to the extensive gardens of the Forbidden City and the western section of the Imperial City in Beijing did not always distract Qing emperors from sensual indulgence, but landscape gardens generally did provide a retreat for world-weary Confucians—and a fitting place of rest for those of a Buddhist or Daoist inclination as well.

Gardens were not always resting places, however. As we have seen in chapter 2, the garden-filled Qing "retreat" at Chengde was often the center of intense political and religious activity. And even private gardens served regularly as the sites for elite social interactions of various sorts. Yuan Mei's Suiyuan, for example, is well known for providing an environment in which he instructed a number of female disciples (*nü dizi*)—a reflection of his ardent support of women's literary education (see chapter 9).[36] Gardens also provided an ideal environment for entertaining friends and colleagues, composing verse, and admiring art. Small wonder, then, that the expansive Prospect Garden (*Daguan yuan*) of the Jia family provides the setting for much of the action in the great Qing novel *Dream of the Red Chamber* (see chapter 9). Andrew Plaks has brilliantly analyzed Cao Xueqin's use of this garden as a microcosm of the Chinese cultural world, and indeed of the entire universe. It is true, of course, that Chinese cities—Beijing in particular—were also viewed as microcosms of the universe, but whereas the cosmological symbolism of the capital was expressed in formal patterns of geometric symmetry, in the garden it was expressed in delightful informality and irregularity. The garden recreated nature in an idealized form, but not a geometrical one.

Aesthetic components of traditional Chinese gardens bore the unmistakable imprint of conscious *yinyang* duality. Manmade buildings were deliberately interspersed with natural features; rock formations ("mountains") stood juxtaposed to water ("rivers"); light areas alternated with dark; rounded lines with angular ones; empty spaces with solids. The small led to the large, the low to the high. The Qing scholar Shen Fu, a well-known connoisseur of gardens, expressed the garden aesthetic in the following way:

> In laying out garden pavilions and towers, suites of rooms and covered walkways, piling up rocks into mountains, or planting flowers to form a desired shape, the aim is to see the small in the large, to see the large in the small, to see the real in the illusory, and to see the illusory in the real. Sometimes you conceal, sometimes you reveal, sometimes you work on the surface, sometimes in depth.[37]

Chinese gardens thus had a kind of endless, rhythmic quality. Wing-tsit Chan writes, "Almost every part [of the traditional Chinese garden] is rhythmic in expression. The winding walks, the round gate, the zigzag paths, the melody-like walls, the rockeries which are frozen music in themselves, and flowers and trees and birds are all echoes and counterpoints of rhythm." Significantly, this rhythmic quality—and often a sense of endlessness as well—can be found not only in landscape gardens, but also in the structure of Chinese poetry and narrative prose (see chapter 9), the flow of melody in music, the movement and sound of Chinese drama, the curved roof and other architectural elements in Chinese buildings, and, of course, in the composition of landscape paintings.[38]

The decorative symbolism of Chinese gardens followed convention. The design of gates and doorways, for example, reflected the perfection of the circle or the shape of a jar—the latter a pun on the word "peace" (*ping*). Window grilles and other woodwork often carried stylized Chinese characters for "blessings" (*fu*), "emoluments" (*lu*), and "long life" (*shou*), as well as designs echoing ancient bronze motifs such as the "thunder pattern" and "whorl circle." Common animal symbols included the dragon, phoenix, deer, crane, and bat. Confucian symbolism was most evident in the books contained in garden buildings and often in the names given to specific pleasure spots. Religious symbolism was comparatively muted. Buddhist or Religious Daoist statues were rare, and there was no Chinese "garden god." *Fengshui* considerations obviously affected the design of Chinese gardens, but there was an aesthetic "logic" to this geomantic system that gave it significance beyond religion.[39]

In short, the major symbolism of the landscape garden was in its natural elements and in their arrangement. Rocks were chosen primarily for their fantastic shapes (those from Lake Tai, near Suzhou, were especially admired), while flowers, shrubs, and trees reflected the basic plant symbolism noted in the previous section. Among the most common floral elements in the landscape garden were the peony, orchid, magnolia, lotus, chrysanthemum, and gardenia. Bamboo was, of course, extremely popular, as were trees such as the willow, pine, peach, plum, and pomegranate. Most plants were identified with specific seasons and arranged with these identifications in mind.

A sharp distinction existed between the "naturalism" of the landscape garden and the rigid functionalism of the house to which it was connected. As the garden mirrored nature, the house mirrored society. Maggie Keswick writes, "In domestic architecture the orderly succession of rooms and courtyards that make up a Chinese house have often been seen as an expression of the Chinese ideal of harmonious social relationships: formal, decorous, regular and clearly defined."[40] This rigid symmetry—and, one might add, that of other Chinese architectural structures from temples to the imperial palace itself—stood in sharp contrast to the irregularity of the landscape garden.

But despite the structural distinction between house and garden in traditional China, the two were integrally related, for the structure of the former would have been considered intolerable without the latter, and the latter would have been deemed superfluous without the former. In all, the garden was a kind of "liminal zone" linking the spiritual and earthly concerns of man. Nelson Wu puts the matter poetically: "In . . . eternally negative space, between reason and untarnished emotion, between the correctness of the straight lines and the effortlessness of the curve, between the measurable and the romantic infinity, lies the Chinese garden which is between architecture and landscape painting."[41]

PAINTING AND CALLIGRAPHY

Although Qing connoisseurs regarded landscapes as the most exalted form of traditional Chinese painting, they were by no means the only type of admired brushwork. In addition to calligraphy—which was in a special class along with landscape painting—the Chinese also esteemed paintings of religious and secular figures, buildings and palaces, birds and animals, flowers and plants, and even antique objects such as bronzes and porcelains. According to the *Essential Criteria of Antiquities*, the artists of late imperial times were especially accomplished in the painting of landscapes, trees, rocks, flowers, bamboos, birds, and fish, but less skilled than their predecessors in the rendering of human figures and large animals. Folk painting in the Qing included murals in temples and other buildings, but it was generally considered to be the work of mere technicians, not true art. Significantly, even in religious temples, secular symbolism (including examples of filial piety, historical scenes, and depictions from works of fiction) often appeared prominently.

On the whole, Qing painting remained delicate and decorous. The gruesome scenes of rape and destruction so prevalent in the West would have horrified most Chinese artists. Figure painters in China shunned the nude; still-life painters found dead objects repulsive; and landscape painters usually ignored the artistic possibilities of deserts, swamps, and other desolate places. It is true, of course, that the Qing court commissioned a great number of battle paintings that commemorated important military victories, but they are not gruesome—at least not the ones that I have seen. Far more gruesome are the painted murals in Chinese temples that depicted in graphic detail the tortures of the Courts of Judgment. Although most Chinese artists avoided explicitly sexual scenes, "beautiful women paintings" were often quite suggestive, and there was also a long and well-developed tradition of erotic art (*chunhua* or *chunkong*) in China.[42] Finally, we should note that some Qing painters—like the "Yangzhou eccentric" Luo Ping (d. 1799)—went so far as to paint ghosts, skeletons, and even raging forest fires.[43] But overall the subject material of Chinese painting was uplifting, if not also expressly didactic.

One important function of painting throughout much of the imperial era had been moral instruction. Zhang Yanyuan, the ninth-century author of the influential *Lidai minghua ji* (Record of famous painters of successive dynasties), tells us, for example, that paintings should serve as models to the virtuous and warnings to the evil. He cites the Han scholar Cao Zhi, who describes how people seeing pictures of noble rulers "look up in reverence," while those who see pictures of degenerate rulers "are moved to sadness." As late as the Ming dynasty, we find examples of normative judgments impinging on standards of realism. The *Essential Criteria of Antiquities* states, for instance:

> Portraits of Buddhists should show benevolence and mercy; those of Daoists, moral cultivation and salvation; those of emperors and kings, the magnificence of imperial symbols such as the sun, the dragon and the phoenix; those of barbarians, their admiration of China and their obedience; those of Confucian worthies, loyalty, sincerity, civilized behavior and righteousness.[44]

Yet in the main, by late imperial times it was less subject matter than style that inspired and uplifted the viewer of Chinese paintings. During the Qing—and in fact well before—artistic achievement came to be seen as a reflection of the artist's inner morality. Like writing and musical compositions, paintings were considered to be "prints of the heart/mind [*xin*]"—not merely a means of Confucian cultivation, but also a measure of it. No critic of any consequence judged a painting solely on what he or she knew about the moral worth of the artist; but a scholar-critic certainly would be inclined to consider the admirable (aesthetic) qualities of a painting as an index of the artist's own admirable (Confucian) qualities. Thus, as James Cahill has remarked, "The notion of 'the man revealed in the painting' was used . . . [by Chinese critics] to account for excellence in art, not to determine it." Further, Cahill indicates that the creative impulses of naturalness, spontaneity, and intuition usually attributed to Daoism and Chan Buddhism in Chinese art and literature were also part of the late imperial Confucian tradition—central, in fact, to the *wenren* (literati) aesthetic.[45]

Confucianism shaped the interpretive contours of traditional Chinese painting in yet another sense. In Song and post-Song times, neo-Confucian metaphysics provided the concept of *li* (principle), which came to be used in Chinese art criticism as both a standard for realism and as a general metaphor for the creative process. Painting, in the neo-Confucian view, was tantamount to an act of cosmic creation and therefore governed by the natural principles inherent in all things. The task of the painter was to attune himself with the moral mind of the universe, and in so doing, convey the *li* of his subject material, giving it life and vitality. The gift of the ancient masters, in the view of Wang Hui (1632–1717), was precisely their ability to "harmonize their works with those of nature."[46]

The "life" of a Chinese painting was expressed by the term *qi*. *Qi* may be translated as "breath," but like *li* (principle) it acquired a metaphysical meaning ("material force") in neo-Confucianism. The constituent matter of all things, *qi* animated even "inanimate" objects. As a critical term, however, it predated neo-Confucianism by several centuries. Although no one term conveys the wide range and richness of its meanings, perhaps the best single translation of *qi* in the realm of art is "spirit"—as in Xie He's famous "First Law" of painting: "spirit resonance creates life movement" (*qiyun sheng-dong*). Employed in this fashion, *qi* suggests the breath of Heaven, which stirs all things to life and sustains the eternal process of cosmic change. This motive power, in the words of Zhang Geng (1685–1760), was something "beyond the feeling of the brush and the effect of the ink."[47]

As early as the fifth century CE, Chinese art critics had already begun to equate painting with the symbols of the *Yijing* as representations of nature, and by late imperial times morality and metaphysics had become inextricably linked. In the words of the Qing critic Wang Yu: "Everybody knows that principles [*li*] and vitality [*qi*] are necessary in painting, yet they are much neglected. The important point is that the heart and character of the man should be developed; then he can express high principles and a pure vital breath. . . . Although painting is only one of the fine arts, it contains the *Dao*."[48]

As an expression of the fundamental order of the universe, Chinese paintings clearly had to appear "natural," and works on connoisseurship suggested numerous guidelines for artistic realism.

A portrait should look as though [the person depicted] were about to speak. The folds of his wearing apparel, the trees and the rocks, should be painted with strokes similar to those in calligraphy. The folds of dresses should be large, but their rhythm subtle, and the strength of their execution gives the impression that they are fluttering and raised [by the wind]. Trees, with their wrinkled bark and their twists and knots, should show their age. Rocks should be three-dimensional and shading lines used in their depiction should produce a rugged yet mellow effect. A landscape with mountains, water, and woods and springs should present an atmosphere of placidity and vastness and should clearly show the season, the time of day, and [prevailing] weather. Rising or subsiding mists and clouds should also be depicted. The source whence a river flows as well as its destination should be clearly defined, and the water in it should appear fluent. Bridges and roads should show the way by which people come and go, as narrow paths wind through wildernesses. Houses should face in different directions in order to avoid monotony, fish swim hither and thither, and dragons ascend or descend. Flowers and fruit should bear dewdrops on all surfaces and should also indicate in which direction the wind blows. Birds and animals, poised to drink water, to pick food, to move, or to remain still, are captured in spirit, as well as form.[49]

Painting guides such as Wang Gai's (1645–1770) popular handbook *Jiezi yuan huazhuan* (Mustard Seed Garden manual) provided elaborate instructions on exactly how to paint such subject material—trees, rocks, people, buildings, flowers, bamboo, grass, insects, animals, and, of course, land-scapes (see figures 8.1, 8.2, and 8.3). The starting point, as in calligraphy (and, in fact, all of Chinese life) was self-discipline. "You must learn first to observe the rules faithfully," wrote the author-compiler of the *Mustard Seed Garden Manual*; then "afterwards modify them according to your intelligence and capacity. The end of all method is to seem to have no method." And again, "If you aim to dispense with method, learn method. If you aim at facility, work hard. If you aim for simplicity, master complexity." One began with the correct mental attitude, learned basic brushstrokes (sixteen, at first), and then progressed to more sophisticated painting techniques.[50]

An essential part of the artist's training was the study of the ancient masters. Zhang Geng advised students not to "throw out scattered thoughts in an incoherent fashion or to make strange things in accordance with the impulses of the heart." Instead, they should "carefully follow the rules of the ancients without losing the smallest detail." After some time, they will "understand why one must be in accordance with nature," and after some more time, "why things are as they are." Local collections of paintings by great masters were of tremendous importance to painters as a source of inspiration. We know, for example, that Wang Hui's mastery of so many different artistic styles was at least in part a product of his extended trips to art centers, which enabled him to study the masterpieces of well-known collectors. Unfortunately, as we have seen, the insatiable desire of the Qing rulers to enhance the holdings of the imperial collection in Beijing took many of these masterpieces out of the hands of private collectors, denying local artists an important source of education and inspiration.[51]

In addition to viewing great works of art, aspiring students were encouraged to copy them. There were three main avenues of approach: (1) exact reproduction by tracing (*mu*); (2) direct copying (*lin*); and (3) freely interpreting in the manner of the master (*fang*). The ultimate purpose of this artistic progression was not merely to produce outer form, but to capture inner essence. In the words of Fang Xun (1736–1801):

> When copying ancient paintings, the foremost concern must be to grasp the ancient master's spirit of life. Testing the flavor of the work and exploring it, you will get some understanding. Then you may begin to copy. . . . If it is done merely for the sake of similarity [however], you had better roll up the picture and forget it at once. You may copy the whole day, yet your work will have nothing whatsoever to do with the ancient master.[52]

The eighteenth-century Qing critic Shen Zongqian wrote in a similar vein:

> A student of painting must copy ancient works, just as a man learning to write must study good writing that has come down through the ages. He should put

Figure 8.1.   Illustrations from the Mustard Seed Garden Manual (A)
Note the *yinyang* elements of light and dark, high and low, "host" and "guest," large and small. Source:
Wang Gai 1888.

Figure 8.2. Illustrations from the Mustard Seed Garden Manual (B)
Source: Wang Gai 1888.

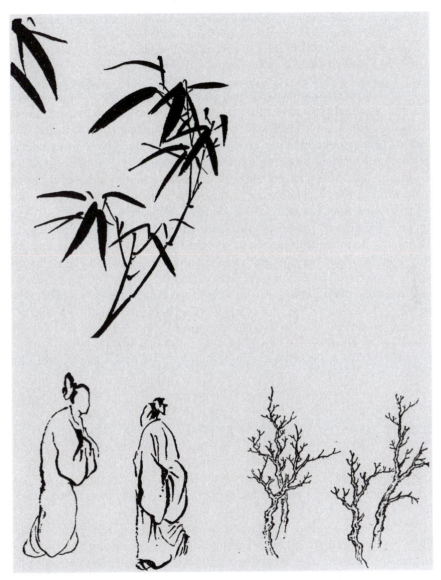

Figure 8.3. Illustrations from the Mustard Seed Garden Manual (C)
Source: Wang Gai 1888.

himself in a state of mind to feel as if he were doing the same painting himself.
. . . First he should copy one artist, then branch out to copy others, and, what is
more important, he should feel as if he were breathing through the work himself
and should identify himself with what the artist was trying to say.[53]

Fang and Shen are discussing here an effort on the part of the painter to
achieve "spiritual communication" (*shenhui*) with the ancient masters. *Shenhui* necessarily involved self-realization. Shen Zongqian puts the matter this
way: "The important thing in copying the ancients is that I have my own temperament. If I should forget myself to copy the ancients, I would be doing a
disservice to both the ancients and myself. . . . The painter's concern is how to
make the art of the brush his own. If this is done, then what I express is only
myself, a self which is akin to the ancients." Fang Xun counseled, "When
copying the ancients, you may first only worry about a lack of similarity;
afterward you ought to worry about too much similarity. For, when lacking
similarity, you have failed to get to the bottom of the model's style; being too
similar, you have failed to achieve your own style."[54]

Discipline was a prerequisite to artistic freedom. The early nineteenth-
century painter-critic Fan Ji asserted: "The beginner should imitate the
ancients constantly, . . . [but] he must then empty himself from what he has
relied on. Meanwhile, that which has fermented in him must flow out unin-
tentionally—and for the first time he will experience the joyous sensation of
freedom." On this basis, it was possible for a Qing painter like Wang Shimin
(1592–1680) to produce an "original" landscape following the Ming master
Dong Qichang in imitating Wang Meng's (Yuan dynasty) interpretation of
the Dong Yuan (Five Dynasties-Song) manner. Imitation (*fang*) in the hands
of an individual who had achieved "spiritual communication" with the great
masters became "creative metamorphosis" (*bian*), not simple plagiarism.
Fan Ji informs us, "If a *lin* copy shows the copyist's own manner, then it has
lost the truth; if a *fang* copy fails to show one's own manner, it becomes a
fake."[55]

Apart from preliminary sketches, Chinese painters seldom painted from
life. They preferred instead to seek inspiration in other works or to conjure up
and convey a mental image that bore no necessary relationship to a single objective reality. Meditation played a role in the creative process, as did external
stimuli. Wang Yu advised preliminary concentration and nourishment by

looking at clouds and springs, contemplating birds and flowers, strolling about
humming songs, burning incense, or sipping tea. . . . When the inspiration rises,
spread the paper and move the brush, but stop as soon as it is exhausted; only
when it rises again should you continue and complete the work. If you do it this
way, the work will become alive with the moving power of Heaven.[56]

The Chinese painter was a captive of his or her media, but it was a creative form of bondage. Unlike Western-style oil painting, Chinese black or colored ink applied to a paper or silk surface allowed little room for trial and error; once the artist put the brush down, he or she made an irretrievable commitment—especially when using ink on paper. Thus,

> when the brush touches paper, there are only differences in touch, speed, angle and direction. Too light a touch results in weakness while too heavy a touch causes clumsiness. Too much speed results in a slippery effect, too little speed drags; too much slant [of the tip of the brush] results in thinness; too perpendicular an approach in flatness; a curve may result in ragged edges and a straight line may look like one made with a ruler.[57]

Brushwork was extraordinarily important in Chinese painting, especially in late imperial times. Wen Fong writes, for example, that throughout the Ming and Qing periods, the brushwork of Chinese painting "assumed an increasingly expressive quality, eventually dominating the representational form."[58] This expressive quality, known as *xieyi* or the "writing of ideas," was a technique closely linked with calligraphy and quite distinct from the precise form of brushwork designated *gongbi* (see below). *Xieyi* required the appearance of spontaneity, but it was deliberate, preconceived, and, in fact, the product of intensive book study and calligraphic discipline. Wang Yuanqi's (1642–1715) advice to painters, in its essence, would apply to calligraphers as well: "When . . . [one] takes up the brush he must be absolutely quiet, serene, peaceful, and collected, and shut out all vulgar emotions. He must sit down in silence before the white silk scroll, concentrate his soul and control his vital energy. He must look at the high and low, examine right and left, inside and outside the scroll, the road to enter and the road to leave."[59]

In other words, the Chinese artist had to have a fairly complete vision of the painting before beginning. Modifications could be made, of course, as the painting developed, but a unified vision was essential. Shen Zongqian wrote:

> It would be a great fault to begin a picture without a preconceived plan, and then add and adjust as one goes along, with the result that the different parts do not have an organic unity. One should rather have a general idea of where the masses and connections, the light and the dark areas will be, then proceed so that one part grows out of another and the light and dark areas cooperate to build a picture. Examined closely, each section is interesting in itself; taken together, there is an organic unity.[60]

This idea of organic unity was expressed in the Chinese term *kaihe* (opening and closing or expanding and contracting). *Kaihe* may refer to the overall layout of a painting, to the relationship of individual elements within the painting, or to the composition of the elements themselves. In each part of the painting, including every individual object, the artist had to consider beginning, ending, and beginning again. Shen Zongqian explains:

> The combined work of brush and ink depends on force of movement [*shi*, a longstanding technical term in calligraphy, sometimes translated "kinesthetic movement"]. This force refers to the movement of the brush back and forth on the paper, which carries with it and in it the opening [*kai*] and closing [*he*] movements. Where something is starting up, that is the opening movement, but with every opening movement the artist must be thinking how it will be gathered up at the end. . . . The gathering up is called the closing movement, and with each closing movement the artist is already thinking where the next growth is going to arise. Thus there is always the suggestion of further development.[61]

Yinyang ideas such as *kaihe*, *xushi* (void and solid), *xiangbei* (front and back), and *qifu* (rising and falling) are essential to an understanding of traditional Chinese painting. Qing handbooks and critical works repeatedly drew on these and other concepts of complementarity and alternation to explain composition and brushstroke. Artists were encouraged to dip downward before coming up; to turn upward before going down; to intersperse sparse with dense and dark with light; to relieve thick ink with thin; to counteract the convex with the concave; and so forth. For example, in describing the method by which to paint tree trunks and branches, the *Mustard Seed Garden Manual* advises: "Pay attention to the way the branches dispose themselves, the *yin* and *yang* of them, which are in front and which are in back, which are on the left and which are on the right; consider also the tensions created by some branches pushing forward while others seem to withdraw." In landscape we find that "host" mountains required "guest" mountains, exalted trees required humble ones, and luxuriant foliage required at least some dead branches. In its most extreme form, the notion of *yinyang* complementarity was expressed in a kind of Daoist paradox: "When in your eyes you have mountains, only then can you make trees; when in your mind there is water, only then can you make mountains."[62] The term for landscape itself (*shanshui*, lit. mountains and water) suggests a basic *yinyang* relationship.

The point of *yinyang* juxtaposition in Chinese painting was not merely to create contrast, however. Primarily it was to indicate "life movement," nature's rhythm (*yun*). In their brushwork, Chinese artists attempted to recreate the endlessly alternating rise and fall, expansion and contraction, activity and quiescence of *yin* and *yang*, and in so doing come into closer harmony with the rhythmic cycles of life itself. This was especially true in landscape painting. Heaven dominated Earth, voids dominated solids, mountains dominated water, and movement dominated stillness, but all were integrated into a single

Figure 8.4.
Detail from Zhu Da's (c. 1626–1705) handscroll titled "Fish and Rocks" (mid- to late 1600s, ink on paper, 29.2 x 157.4 cm). Note the contrasting *yinyang* elements involving lightness and darkness, relative size, relative elevation, direction of movement (as with the two fish), and activity and quiescence. *Source:* Reproduced with permission from the Cleveland Museum of Art, John L. Severance Fund 1953.247.

philosophical statement reflecting the dynamism, grandeur, and limitlessness of nature.

Small wonder, then, that Chinese landscape painters refused to restrict themselves (or the viewers of their works) by the use of Western-style scientific perspective. It was not that they lacked the intellectual sophistication to employ it, but true perspective involved a fixed point of view that was completely inimical to the purposes of the painter of "mountains and water." An essential element of the dynamism of a Chinese landscape was the movement of both artist and viewer. Thus, "the painter . . . paints and the spectator views the results from many points, never from a single position or at any one moment of time." In a similar way, and for similar reasons, Chinese poets added new dimensions to the world directly perceived in their poems, and in so doing evoked a mood of infiniteness. Wang Shizhen (1634–1711) in particular was a master of the poetic "ending which doesn't end." Significantly, this "endless" quality can also be found in the best Chinese narrative literature (see chapter 9).[63]

In the critical writing of the Qing period, scholars drew a sharp distinction between the so-called Northern School of professional and court painting (*gongbi*) and the Southern School of nonprofessional literati painting (*xieyi*). The former has been characterized as academic, representational, precise, and decorative, painted mainly in polychrome ink and on silk. The latter has been described as spontaneous, free, calligraphic, personal, and subjective, painted mainly in monochrome on paper. In the late Ming period, the great artist and critic Dong Qichang drew these distinctions—which had nothing to do with geography—and they continued to dominate Chinese art criticism for the next three hundred years. Although based on genuine stylistic differences, Dong's system of classification was arbitrary and inconsistent, not only because it was based on certain "moral" criteria, Dong's personal preferences, and the assumed superiority of literati painting over that of professionals, but also because in a very real sense all the painting of the Ming and Qing periods was academic. Furthermore, during the Qing period there were many court painters who painted beautifully in the Southern School style, and many "amateur" literati who were well paid for their artistic efforts—some by the throne itself.[64]

Among the most accomplished painters of the early Qing were the so-called Six Great Masters: the Four Wangs (Wang Shihmin; Wang Hui; Wang Jian [1598–1677]; and Wang Yuanqi), Wu Li (1632–1718), and Yun Shou-ping (1633–1690). The works of each are "academic in the best sense: skillful, decorous, and knowledgeable about both the subject and the complex history of the *wenren* tradition." Although the Kangxi emperor patronized two of these painters—Wang Hui and Wang Yuanqi—the others remained loyal to the memory of the Ming dynasty and refused to serve the throne. In any case, identification with the "orthodoxy" of the Qing imperial court did not stifle creativity. Indeed, Wang Yuanqi was probably the most original of the Six Masters. His brilliant interpretations of past models and styles and his "passion for pure form" put Wang on a plane with the best "Individualist" painters of the Qing period.

The most famous and creative of the early "Individualist" painters were Zhu Da (also known as Bada Shanren, 1626–c. 1705), Kuncan (also known as Shiqi, c. 1610–c. 1670), Shitao (also known as Daoji or Yuanji, 1641–c. 1710), and Gong Xian. Sherman Lee summarizes the distinctiveness of their work:

> Kuncan's hairy and tangled landscapes; Zhu Da's abbreviated but firm brush-work recalling that of another, earlier eccentric, Xu Wei; Yuanji's brilliant us-age of wash, unusual compositions, and directly observed images, recalling the approach of Zhang Hong; and Gong Xian's deep and somber ink-play of light and shade; all justify their unusually high place in Chinese art history. The most various of the four was certainly Yuanji and that variety endears him particu-larly to modern critics and collectors.[65]

These "free spirits"—like the Six Great Masters and virtually all other Qing painters—acknowledged a debt to tradition. Shitao, for example, in his *Huayu lu* (Record of talks on painting) admits that for many years he had painted and written, declaring his independence of orthodox methods, only to discover that the way he thought was his own was actually "the *dao* of the ancients."[66]

Although Qing painting lost a certain amount of creative energy in the eighteenth century, the so-called Eight Eccentrics of Yangzhou managed to keep the Chinese art world tantalizingly off balance. Different critics have compiled variant lists of the eight, with the result that more than a dozen painters can be considered viable candidates. Among their number we may count such talented individuals as Jin Nong (1687–1764), Hua Yan (1682–c. 1755), Huang Shen (1687–c. 1768), and Luo Ping. Other possible candidates include Zheng Xie (1693–1765) and Li Shan (1686–c. 1756). These "eccentric" artists and their colleagues tended to specialize both in style and subject matter, gravitating away from standard landscapes and inclining instead toward rocks and bamboo, flowers and birds, insects and fish, or human figures (including ghostly forms).

During the nineteenth century, Shanghai emerged as a major center of artistic production. There, rich patrons and wealthy consumers (including the Japanese and merchants from Fujian and Guangdong), together with the relative security offered by foreign administrative and military control over the treaty port after 1842, encouraged an influx of artists from all over China. Among the most distinguished male painters identified with this area and this time are Qian Du (1763–1844), Dai Xi (1801–1860), Gai Qi (1774–1829), Ren Xiong (1820–1857), Zhao Zhiqian (1829–1884), Ren Bonian (1839–1895), Ren Xun (1835–1893), and Wu Changshi (1842–1927). Most of these individuals were born in Zhejiang, but their artistic center of gravity became Shanghai. Further south, in Guangzhou, local artists such as Xie Lansheng (1760–1831), Su Liupeng (1796–1862), and Su Renshan (1814–1850) continued the region's rich tradition of painting epitomized by the earlier work of Li Jian (1747–1798) and Liang Shu (c. 1760–1810).[67]

The Qing period may well have been the heyday of women painters in China. Most of them were the literate wives or concubines of Chinese scholars, and a number made their mark in poetry as well as painting (see chapter 9). Some sold their artwork, while others gave instruction to friends and family or to empresses, princesses, and concubines at court. Among the many distinguished women painters of the Qing period were Fang Weiyi (1585–1668), Liu Yin (1618–1664), Jin Yue (fl. 1665), Cai Han (1647–1686), Chen Shu (1660–1736), Yun Bing (eighteenth century), Yuexiang (eighteenth century), Fang Wanyi (eighteenth century), Qu Bingyun (1767–1810), Ma Quan (c. 1768–1848), Guan Yun (nineteenth century) and Wang Qinyun (nineteenth century).[68]

For the most part, these talented painters were sustainers of inherited male traditions rather than innovators. They have almost never been characterized by art critics as "individualistic" or "eccentric." Although the extremely gifted Chen Shu was once described as surpassing the renowned male painter from Suzhou, Chen Chun (1483–1544), in the "vigor and originality" of her brushstrokes, she painted landscapes and other standard subjects in conventional ways, following the lead of "orthodox" painters such as Wang Shimin and Wang Hui. As Marsh Weidner observes, the inventive potential of women painters "was limited by conventions designed to support the rigorously patriarchal social system of premodern China."[69]

Flowers were the favorite subject matter for women painters in the Qing, although landscapes, bamboo, and figure paintings (including, of course, the Buddhist deity Guanyin) were also popular. Conventionally, male connoisseurs disparagingly referred to women's paintings as "weak and soft." Backhanded compliments took forms such as the following: "[Her] brush strength is not the best, but for a woman it is remarkable." Statements of this kind, which seem to have deterred Western scholars from taking Chinese women painters seriously until recently, seem to reflect deeply held Chinese stereotypes more than artistic reality. We know, for instance, that women sometimes executed "ghost paintings" for talented male artists, and that a number of highly regarded male painters, including Zhang Geng, received valuable instruction from women.[70]

Prejudices of another sort plagued the Jesuit painters who served the Qing court. Among these individuals, Guiseppe Castiglione (Lang Shining, 1688–1766), a personal favorite of the Qianlong emperor, proved to be especially adept at combining the techniques of Western realism with traditional Chinese media and subject matter. Castiglione had numerous Chinese pupils, imitators, and admirers, but he and his Western colleagues exerted no lasting influence on Chinese art. The reason was that most Qing painter-critics saw their use of shading and perspective as mere craftsmanship. In the words of one admirer (Zou Yigui, 1686–1772, a talented court painter in his own right): "The student should learn something of their achievements so as to improve his own method. But their technique of strokes [that is, brushwork] is negligible. Even if they attain [representational] perfection it is merely craftsmanship. Thus, foreign painting cannot be called art."[71]

Far less were foreigners able to master the intricacies of Chinese calligraphy. As a recognized art form, calligraphy predated painting, but by late imperial times the two were inseparably linked. In the words of a common proverb: "Calligraphy and painting have the same source" (*shuhua tong yuan*). Lu Shihua states simply: "Calligraphy and painting are skills [*jineng*], but they embody the great *Dao*. . . . The ancients achieved immortality [*buxiu*] through their calligraphy and painting." These two Chinese arts used the same basic media, utilized many of the same brush strokes and techniques, required the same kind of mental preparation and discipline, and were measured by the same aesthetic standards. Furthermore, both were seen as an index of the artist's morality. Lu Shihua tells us, "If the heart is right, then the brush will be right" (*xinzheng ze bizheng*).[72]

During the Ming and Qing periods, calligraphy often adorned paintings, amplifying in various ways the artist's general philosophical statement and/

or emotional response to the scene, and sometimes piquing the viewer's curiosity. Poetic inscriptions might also be written by subsequent owners and admirers of the work, who were moved to comment on it and self-confident enough to do so. Some paintings boasted a number of different colophons. Perhaps the Qianlong emperor, whose enthusiasm occasionally outstripped his aesthetic judgment, holds the record for inscriptions of this sort by one individual. He is reported to have written over fifty inscriptions on one hand scroll alone and to have placed thirteen of his seals on a single painting. In the main, however, multiple inscriptions and seals of ownership were added tastefully, and they, in turn, enriched both the emotional, artistic, and historical value of the work.

Of course, calligraphy stood solidly on its own as an independent art form, universally admired as the ultimate measure of cultural refinement. In the words of the *Essential Criteria of Antiquities*: "No other art is comparable to that of calligraphy. Saints and sages of past centuries paid a great deal of attention to it, for it always has been and will forever be the means whereby civilization and the orders of government are made intelligible, while things, great or trivial, from the Six Classics to matters of daily routine, are conveyed to people." Calligraphy was ubiquitous in traditional China. It graced private homes, shops, teahouses, restaurants, temples, monasteries, official buildings, and imperial palaces. It was engraved on metal, wood, stone, and even on the face of rocks and mountains in nature. Calligraphers were in demand by all levels of Chinese society, and success in the civil-service examinations could not be achieved without a good hand—regardless of one's mastery of the Classics and the "eight-legged essay."[73]

Chinese critics distinguished six basic styles of calligraphy: (1) big seal script (*dazhuan*), (2) small seal script (*xiaozhuan*), (3) clerical script (*lishu*), (4) regular or standard script (*kaishu* or *zhengshu*), (5) running script (*xingshu*), and (6) cursive script (*caoshu*). Of these, the last two were the most susceptible to individualized interpretation. The regular script may be likened to *gongbi* in painting and the cursive script to *xieyi*, in the sense that the former style demanded precision while the latter style encouraged spontaneity and freedom; but all forms of Chinese calligraphy left a great deal of room for creative potential.

In fact, the eighteenth century witnessed a revival of the *zhuan* and *li* styles, modifying a calligraphic tradition that had been in place for over a thousand years. As early as the fourth century CE, the renowned calligrapher Wang Xizhi (307–365) had developed a masterly synthesis of styles, which became the basis for virtually all Chinese brush writing until the mid-Qing period. The standard works in this tradition employed the regular, running, or cursive styles instead of the more ancient and seemingly overprecise seal

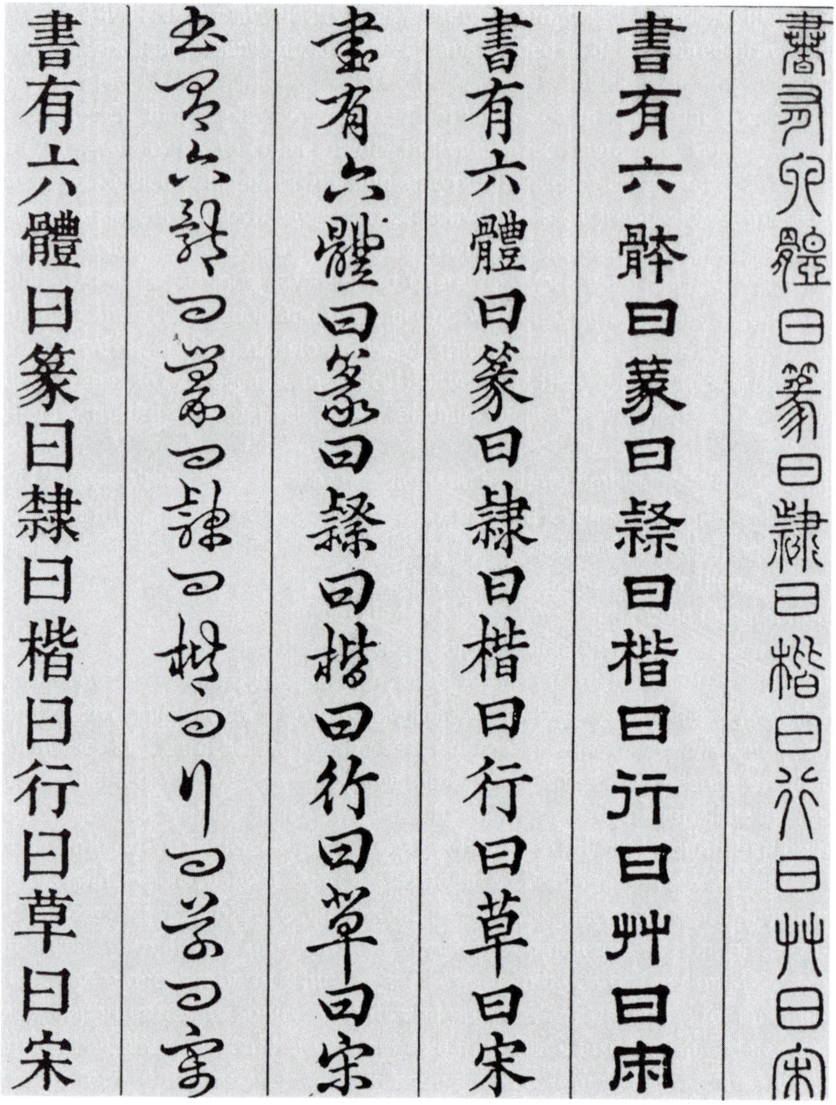

Figure 8.5. Six Styles of Calligraphy

Each column, reading in the Chinese style from right to left and top to bottom, reads: "There are six forms of calligraphy, called *zhuan, li, kai, xing, cao,* and *song.*" This *liushu* system differs from the one described in the text only in that it fails to distinguish between "big" and "small" seal script (*zhuan*) and adds the category *song,* which refers to the Song dynasty style of printed characters. *Source: Chinese Repository* May 1834–April 1835.

and clerical styles. But the *kaozheng* movement of the eighteenth century (see chapter 6), which dovetailed with the Qing dynasty's ongoing artistic effort to "restore antiquity" (*fugu*), encouraged a reemphasis on ancient Han and pre-Han inscriptions based on actual bronze and stone relics. This development led in two major directions. One was toward what Benjamin Elman calls a "craze" for seal designing and carving. The other was toward the reproduction of ancient calligraphic forms with modern brushes. Individualist and "eccentric" painters such as Shitao and Jin Nong got into the act, inscribing paintings with seal script and experimenting with the simulation on paper of characters engraved on bronze and stone.[74]

Of the several outstanding calligraphers of the mid-Qing period, three deserve special mention. One was Deng Shiru (c. 1740–1805), a colorful and unconventional scholar who gravitated toward the kind of calligraphy inscribed on Qin, Han, and Three Kingdoms relics. Another was Bao Shichen (1775–1855), who not only excelled in the *kai* and *xing* styles, but also experimented boldly with the *zhuan* and *li* styles, rejecting "the mechanical precision of earlier seal script styles in favor of an imposing degree of irregularity in his seal and clerical calligraphy." The third individual, Zhang Qi (1765–1833), is significant not only because he was considered the equal of Deng in the *li* style and Bao in the *kai* and *xing* styles, but also because he raised four daughters who achieved literary fame, including one of the best-known woman calligraphers (Zhang Lunying) of the dynasty.[75]

Many Chinese scholars have remarked on the link between calligraphy and other forms of Chinese art. Jiang Yi suggests, for example, that the style and spirit of Chinese calligraphy influenced not only painting, but also sculpture, ceramics, and architecture. Similarly, Lin Yutang argues that the "basic ideas of rhythm, form and atmosphere [in calligraphy] give the different lines of Chinese art, like poetry, painting, architecture, porcelain and house decorations, an essential unity of spirit."[76] Lin's use of poetry as an example of the link between calligraphy and literature is apt enough, but it may be extended; for even vernacular fiction exhibits at least some of the rhythm and "kinesthetic movement" characteristic of Chinese brushwork.

Chapter Nine

Literary Trends

The Chinese literary tradition shared with the Chinese artistic tradition many fundamental assumptions about past models, aesthetics, ethics, and cosmology. Chinese literature was, however, much more wide-ranging in its subject matter and, by Ming-Qing times at least, more obviously the province of women writers that it had been in previous periods. As one indication of this latter point, we can compare the contents of the *Complete Tang Poems* (*Quan Tangshi*) with a 1985 study of Qing dynasty female writers. The former collection contains only about 600 poems by women out of a total of more than 48,900 by men. By contrast, the author of the 1985 study, Hu Wenkai, has identified about four thousand women whose collected works existed at one time or another in the Qing period. Assuming a minimum of one hundred or so poems per collection, one can easily imagine the staggering output. J. D. Schmidt, the architect of this comparison, claims in an article focusing on Yuan Mei's well-known relationship with Qing women writers (see chapter 8) that it is

> probably no exaggeration to say that more poetry was written by women in Yuan Mei's eighteenth century than in the twentieth. . . . [By] the beginning of the Qing dynasty, an emphasis on combining domestic virtue and literature in such seventeenth-century female writers as Shang Jinglan (fl. mid-seventeenth c.) and Wang Duanshu (fl. 1650) brought the writing of gentry women to the fore. . . . In the eighteenth century more and more women of good family were writing classical poetry, and the numbers only grew after Yuan Mei's age, including such distinguished writers as Wang Duan (1793–1839), Wu Zao (1799–1863), and Gu Taiqing (1799–ca. 1875).[1]

As was the case during the Ming, the majority of woman writers in Qing times wrote poetry in classical Chinese. The reason, discussed briefly in chapter 1, is that poetry was viewed as an exalted literary form, deemed appropriate for elite women, whereas vernacular fiction of almost any sort was socially disesteemed. It should be noted, however, that from the seventeenth to the nineteenth centuries a number of talented women writers created popular and influential works of fiction using a special form of rhymed narrative known as *tanci*. Some examples of this genre include Tao Zhenhuai's (fl. 1640s) *Tian yu hua* (Flowers that rained down from heaven; 1651), Chen Duansheng's (1751–c. 1796) *Zaisheng yuan* (Love reincarnate), and Qiu Xinru's (1805–c. 1872) *Bi sheng hua* (The brush that gives birth to flowers).[2]

Although a great stylistic gap separated popular vernacular literature from more orthodox classical-style writings, there were certain affinities. In the first place, both kinds of literature tended to reflect elite values. Second, popular equivalents existed for nearly every kind of elite literature. Third, in truth, the elite enjoyed certain types of popular literature (such as novels) as much as, if not more than, the less privileged masses. Thus, from the standpoint of both content and appeal, vernacular literature provides us with a valuable perspective on life in late imperial China—and not just for the Han people. It is clear that the Manchus and Mongols also enjoyed vernacular Chinese literature in translation—novels in particular. In fact, all major Ming-Qing novels, several major plays, and a large number of more minor fictional works were rendered into Manchu.[3]

Manchu culture found its way into Chinese vernacular literature not only through borrowed terms (see chapter 5) and borrowed historical motifs (see below), but also in the form of a genre known as "youth books" (*zidi shu*), which flourished in the Beijing area from the mid-eighteenth century to the end of the nineteenth. Some of these rhymed works, designed to be performed to the accompaniment of slow-moving music, combined words written in the Manchu script (explained by Chinese glosses on the side) with words written in Chinese. Perhaps the versions of the WBQS that include separate sections on the Manchu language, also with Chinese glosses on the side, are related in some way to this popular genre.[4] In any case, youth books and performances based on them (originally performed by amateur Bannerman actors) spread to several urban areas in the north. These Manchu-themed stories—some of them satirizing Bannermen—along with a great many tales drawn from popular Chinese drama and fiction, delighted their audiences, which numbered as many as a thousand people at a time. One of the most prolific authors of this genre was Yigeng (c. 1770–1850), a high-ranking Manchu noble who went by the pseudonym Helü ("Companion of Cranes").[5]

In literature, as in art, the Qing was a period of considerable vitality, especially in genres such as song lyrics, classical poetry, parallel prose, classical prose, classical tales, and novels. Material prosperity, the expansion of mass printing, and the growth of popular literacy under the Manchus produced an unprecedented demand for, and supply of, books.[6] At the same time, a consuming interest in all aspects of traditional Chinese culture led Qing scholars (including some Manchus and Mongols) to produce great numbers of antiquarian studies, critical essays, histories, biographies, and gazetteers. More ambitious projects, such as encyclopedias, collections of essays, and literary anthologies, were also undertaken, both by the throne and by energetic private individuals. In theory, these works were designed to provide inspired guidance for the present and the future based on a glorious past, but in practice they often betrayed narrow scholarly prejudices and sometimes led to destructive factional rivalries.

Intellectual trends obviously influenced literary fashions. The scholastic controversy between advocates of Han Learning and Song Learning (see chapter 6), for example, had implications for prose style because the former favored the revival of Han dynasty Parallel Prose (*pianwen*) and the latter, especially the Tongcheng School, esteemed so-called Ancient Prose (*guwen*). New Text scholars, for their part, admired Song-style Ancient Prose, but they also took a special interest in "lyric verse" (*ci*), which the influential Ming loyalist Chen Zilong (1608–1647)—himself an accomplished practitioner of the Parallel Prose style—had invested with such power and passion. "Genres," as Benjamin Elman has aptly remarked, "were as much a part of academic debate as Confucian doctrine."[7]

Imperial politics also played a role in Chinese literary life. The Qing emperors, as guardians of official morality, naturally tried to promote certain kinds of literature and to suppress others. Pamela Crossley maintains that no ruler of China surpassed the Qianlong emperor in his ambition to dominate the literary resources of Chinese culture. This ambition took three primary forms: one was to glorify Chinese tradition; one was to eradicate subversive works; and one was to promote the Manchu heritage. During the course of his reign, the Qianlong emperor commissioned over ninety scholarly works, fifteen of which dealt with the Manchu language, Manchu history, or the history of the last years of the Ming.[8]

The fluidity of social statuses in eighteenth-century China, the increasing lack of fit between the theoretical and practical criteria for Chinese political leadership, the Qing elite's passive acceptance of imperial censorship, and the diminishing bureaucratic opportunities for many younger scholars all seem to have encouraged the growth of a certain scholarly cynicism. These circumstances may also have played a role in provoking "a pessimism about the ability to achieve sagehood that hounded intellectuals of this age." Peiyi Wu describes this mood as "a deep awareness of the human proclivity to evil, an urgent need to counter this proclivity, a readiness for self-disclosure, and a deep anguish over one's wrongdoings." The major literary manifestation of this apparent cynicism and pessimism was a great deal of confessional and satirical writing, which continued into the nineteenth century.[9]

CATEGORIES OF CLASSICAL LITERATURE

Of the many great literary compilations of the Qing period, two gigantic government-sponsored projects, both discussed briefly in chapter 2, stand out as worthy of special attention: the *Tushu jicheng* (TSJC) and the *Siku quanshu* (Complete collection of the four treasuries; SKQS). We have encountered the former several times in previous chapters. Commissioned during the Kangxi emperor's reign and published in final form in the early years of the Yong-zheng period, the TSJC has been described as "the largest and most useful encyclopedia that has ever been compiled in China."[10] Orthodox in outlook, often biographical in treatment, and composed almost entirely of selected excerpts from earlier writings of various kinds, the TSJC may be considered a literary anthology as well as a convenient guide to the cultural concerns of the Qing scholarly elite.

The encyclopedia is divided into six main categories, thirty-two subcategories, and 6,109 sections. The writings comprising these sections are arranged in order according to eight major types of literature: (1) orthodox writings, especially the Classics, arranged in chronological order as much as possible and including illustrations (6,740 items); (2) general discussions, considered to be reliable introductions to the subject matter (780 items); (3) biographies, usually from standard sources (2,621 items); (4) literary works, some full length (up to the Tang dynasty) and others (thereafter) abbreviated; (5) selections of felicitous phrases, sentences, and longer quotations (2,248 items); (6) accounts not drawn from standard historical sources (2,400 items); (7) miscellaneous records, of interest but lacking sufficient authority, either because of bias or literary inelegance (2,016 items); and (8) unusual material, such as passages from Buddhist, Daoist, and other "unorthodox" texts (987 items). Not every type of literature is included in every section, but in most cases one can find examples of types 1, 2, 4, 6, and 7.

In all, the TSJC consists of ten thousand *juan* (that is, small bound volumes) and about one hundred million characters. Of the encyclopedia's six major categories, Human Relationships is the largest (2,604 *juan*), followed by Geography (2,144), Political Economy (1,832), Nature (1,656), Literature (1,220), and Celestial Phenomena (544). Of the subcategories, by far the largest is Political Divisions (1,544 *juan*), followed by Arts and Occupations (824), Government Service (800), Clan and Family Names (640), Classical and Non-Canonical Writings (500), Women (376), Foods and Commercial Goods (360), Ritual (348), Religion (320), Plants (320), Mountains and Rivers (320), The Emperor (300), Confucian Conduct (300), and Military Administration (300). The remaining subcategories include Literature (260 *juan*), Manufactures (252), Animal Life (192), Strange Phenomena (188), Law and Punishment (180), The Study of Characters (160), The Earth (140), Foreign States (140), The Imperial Household (140), Astronomy and Mathematics (140), The Examination System (136), Music (136), Officialdom (120), Social Intercourse (120), Family Relationships (126), The Year (116), Human Affairs (112), and The Heavens (100).

The overlapping of these subcategories blurs the focus somewhat, but we can still see in the TSJC the Qing elite's preoccupation with orderly administration, scholarship, Confucian values, and family relations, as well as its abiding interest in both natural and supernatural phenomena. Moreover, we can discern in the overall organization of the encyclopedia the implicit cosmological assumption that Heaven, Earth, and Man are the interrelated elements of all knowledge.

The SKQS ranges almost as broadly in subject matter as the TSJC, but it has a more self-conscious literary emphasis and has been more extensively studied by both Chinese and Western scholars. As discussed briefly in chapter 2, the SKQS project provided the Qianlong emperor with a way to demonstrate his great appreciation for traditional Chinese culture while at the same time offering him an opportunity to conduct a "Literary Inquisition" that resulted in the destruction of more than two thousand threatening titles. In this effort to identify and destroy potentially seditious works, over fifty-thousand printing blocks were burned. Significantly, Chinese officials, not Manchus, were the individuals primarily responsible for ferreting out and prohibiting this material. But viewed from a more positive angle (as it should be, all things considered), the SKQS project resulted in the accumulation, transcription and publication (in seven sets) of about thirty-five hundred priceless literary works in nearly 80,000 *juan* (c. 2.3 million pages per set).

The Commission in charge of the SKQS also compiled a massive catalog known as the *Siku quanshu zongmu tiyao* (Annotated index of the *Complete Collection of the Four Treasuries*), which critically reviewed the 3,500 or so works mentioned above plus an additional 6,793 works of lesser quality. This catalog, the most thorough of its kind in all of Chinese history, provides information on the size and general contents of each work, as well as an overall critical evaluation. Although these evaluations were profoundly affected by *kaozheng* scholarship, they were also influenced by what Kent Guy describes as "Manchu sensitivities and imperial pride."[11]

Of the more than ten thousand works reviewed in the Annotated Index, more than two thousand are included in the first ten-part section on the Classics (*jing*). This section begins with subsections devoted to each of the Five Classics, followed by individual subsections on the *Classic of Filial Piety*, "general works," the Four Books, music, and language. By far the largest of the ten subsections is devoted to the *Yijing* (nearly five hundred works). The second section, on History (*shi*), comprising about two thousand works in the Index, is divided into fifteen subsections. Of these, physical and political geography is the largest category (nearly six hundred works), followed by biographies and "personal accounts" (over two hundred). Other subsections include those on the twenty-four dynastic histories, other kinds of historical records and historical criticism (including a subsection on unofficial histories and one on bronze and stone inscriptions), administrative works, official documents, and memoirs of travels in China and elsewhere.

The section on Philosophers (*zi*), covering about three thousand works in fourteen subsections, ranges widely. Although, as one might suppose, it places heavy emphasis on orthodox neo-Confucian philosophical tracts (over four hundred works), the largest subsection is titled simply "miscellaneous writings" (over 850 works). It includes the writings of non-Confucian philosophers such as Mozi, as well as a great variety of assorted tracts, pamphlets, and collections of anecdotes. Somewhat surprisingly, the editors of the Index give Mozi, who had long been discredited by orthodox Confucian philosophers, high marks for his emphasis on "temperance and the timely utilization of resources." Indeed, they go so far as to blame his lack of influence for over two thousand years on the well-known, but in their view somewhat misguided, attack that Mencius once leveled against him.[12]

The section on philosophers also devotes specific subsections to such diverse topics as military arts, agricultural writings, medicine, astronomy and mathematics, divination, the arts (including calligraphy, painting, seals, music, and games), repertories (including works on hobbies, connoisseurship, culinary art, and natural science), dictionaries and encyclopedias, narrative writings (but no vernacular novels or short stories) and a few Buddhist and Daoist works. Of these subsections, the last is distinguished not only by its nearly total neglect of popular beliefs, but also by its small size and certain inconsistencies in the selection of texts. The final section, *Belles Lettres* (*ji*), consisting of about 3,500 works, is divided into five subsections: the Elegies of Chu (*Chuci*), the collected works of individuals, general anthologies (selections of writings from various authors), critical treatises on literature, and songs and rhymes.

An outstanding feature of many Chinese scholars in late imperial times was their astonishing productivity and literary versatility. Take, for example, Qian Qianyi (1582–1664), a famous Jiangsu literatus "not untypical" of the Ming-Qing transition era, who had a preliminary version of his collected works published in 1643 in 110 *juan*. This collection included poetry (21

juan), prefaces and postfaces (17), biographical and genealogical sketches
(10), obituaries and epitaphs (20), funeral odes and eulogies (2), essays (6),
historical annotations (5), critiques of poetry (5), memorials (2), other official
documents (13), and letters and miscellany (9). To this corpus, Qian eventually added a supplement in 50 *juan*. In addition, he produced an anthology
of Ming poetry in 81 *juan*, a draft history of the Ming dynasty in 100 *juan*,
and annotated editions of several Buddhist texts.[13] The Qing monarchs also
aspired to such productivity and versatility—most notably the prolific, but at
times rather pedestrian, Qianlong emperor.

All such writings, and the vast majority of the works included in both the
TSJC and the SKQS were written in classical Chinese—the language of the
scholarly elite (see chapter 5). Like the most exalted forms of Chinese art,
classical Chinese literature was distinguished by its emphasis on rhythm and
balance; its close relationship with past masters, models, and styles; the assumed link between creative genius and personal morality; and by much of
the same or similar critical terminology. In both art and literature we find an
abiding concern with life (*sheng*), vitality (*qi*), spirit (*shen*), and movement
(*dong*). Even the rules of composition in classical literature suggest equivalents or analogs in Chinese art. Liu Dakui (1698–1780) tells us:

> Literature must, above all, attempt to be strong in vital force, but if there is no
> spirit to control the vital force, it will run wild, not knowing where to settle
> down. The spirit and the vital force are the finest essences of literature; intona-
> tion and rhythm [*yinjie*] are the somewhat coarser elements of literature; [and]
> diction and syntax [*zizhu*] are the coarsest elements of literature.[14]

During the Qing period there were several different conceptions of literature, all deriving from earlier theories or critical approaches. One was the notion of literature as a manifestation of the principle of the universe (the *Dao*,
or Way). The most influential early exponent of this point of view was Liu
Xie, quoted in chapter 8. In Liu's view, "The *Dao* is handed down in writing
through the sages, and the sages make the *Dao* manifest in their literary writings." Yao Nai (1731–1815), a leading figure in the Tongcheng School of the
Qing period (see chapter 6), put the matter this way:

> I have heard that the *Dao* of Heaven and Earth consists of nothing but the *yin*
> and *yang*, the gentle and strong. Literature is the finest essence of Heaven and
> Earth, and the manifestation of the *yin* and the *yang*. . . . From the philosophers
> of the various schools [down to the present] there has been none whose writing
> is not biased [in favor of either *yin* or *yang*]. If one has obtained the beauty of
> the *yang* and strong, then one's writing will be like thunder, like lightning, like
> a long wind emerging from the valley, like lofty mountains and steep cliffs, like
> a great river flooding, like galloping steeds. . . . If one has obtained the beauty

of the *yin* and gentle, then one's writing will be like the sun just beginning to rise, like cool breeze, like clouds, like vapor, like mist, like secluded woods and meandering streams, like ripples, like water gently rocking, like the sheen of pearls or jade, like the cry of a wild goose disappearing into the silent void.[15]

Yao believed that philosophical substance required literary style. Thus, in criticizing the inelegance of Mozi as an index of his philosophical errors, Yao wrote: "If the writing is insufficient, then the truth will not be clear."

Some Qing scholars saw literature as a reflection of political realities. The early Qing critic Wang Wan (1624–1690), for example, discerned a close correspondence between the rise and fall of the Tang dynasty and the history of its poetry. He wrote,

At the height [of the Tang], the ruler above exerted his energies, [and] the ministers and officials below hastened about their tasks and spoke without reserve; the administration was simple and punishments were few; the atmosphere among the people was harmonious and peaceful. Therefore, what issued forth in poetry was generally leisurely and refined. . . . [By the time the dynasty declined] there was factional strife [at court] and in the country military struggle; the administration was complex and punishments were severe; the atmosphere among the people was sorrowful and bitter. Therefore, what issued forth [in poetry] was mostly sad, nostalgic, and urgent. At the very end, [poetry] became superficial and extravagant.[16]

But if there were those who viewed literature as an index of political and social circumstances, there were also those who saw in it a means of rectifying those conditions. Shen Deqian (1673–1769) begins his *Shuoshi zuiyu* (Miscellaneous remarks on poetry) by observing, "The way of poetry is such that it can be used to regulate one's nature and emotions, to improve human relationships, . . . to move the spirits and gods, to spread [moral] teaching in the states, and to deal with feudal lords"; and in his preface to an anthology of Qing verse he maintains that poetry must "concern itself with human relationships, everyday uses, and the causes of the rise and fall [of the state] in ancient and modern times." Gu Yanwu, for his part, states succinctly, "Literature must be beneficial to the world."[17]

Aesthetic theories of literature focused primarily on the patterns of the classical language and their immediate impact on the reader. In critical writings of this sort, analogies were often drawn with other sensual experiences, including viewing art, hearing music, and eating food. But not all aesthetic theories relied on such analogies. The longstanding debate between advocates of Ancient Prose and Parallel Prose, for instance, revolved around concrete questions of style. The former was simple and forceful; the latter, elegant and allusive. Both occupied prominent positions in the Chinese classical literary tradition, but vigorous debate on their respective merits continued well into the twentieth century.

Ruan Yuan (1764–1848) was a particularly powerful proponent of Parallel Prose in the late Qing period. In contrast to Tongcheng advocates of Ancient Prose, such as Liu Dakui and Yao Nai, Ruan argued that only writings employing rhyme and parallelism could be called true literature. He thus revived the old Six Dynasties concept of literature as *belles lettres* rather than "plain writing." In Ruan's words,

> Those engaged in literary composition, who do not concern themselves with harmonizing sounds to form rhymes or polishing words and phrases to make them go far so that what they write should be easy to recite and easy to remember, but merely use single [that is, nonparallel] sentences to write . . . [wildly], do not realize that what they write is what the ancients called "speech" [*yan*], which means "straightforward speech," or "talk" [*yu*], which means "argument," but not . . . what Confucius called *wen* [patterned words, that is, true literature].[18]

Qing scholars often employed Parallel Prose to illustrate stylistic virtuosity, but the supreme test of their literary ability was poetry (generically *shi*). From earliest times, poetry had been a central Chinese cultural concern. In fact, the *Shijing* (Classic of poetry) is considered by some authorities to be the single most important work in China's entire literary history. Confucius once said, "If you do not learn the *Shi* you will not be able to converse"; and again, "[One's character is] elevated by poetry, established by ritual, and completed by music." Virtually every major type of Chinese literature—from the classics and histories to plays and novels—included substantial amounts of poetry, and few self-respecting gentlemen in Qing times lacked the ability to compose elegant verse rapidly, in any social circumstance. Moreover, in poetry as in calligraphy, the Qing period witnessed a revival of several major styles, including regulated verse (*lüshi*) and lyric verse (*ci*). Regulated verse consists of eight lines of the same length (usually five or seven characters, with strict rhyming and tonal patterns), while lyric verse has fixed tones and fixed rhythm, but lines that vary in length (the number of characters in each line and the arrangement of tones is based on several hundred set musical patterns).[19]

Many literary authorities have remarked on how well suited the classical Chinese language was for poetic expression. Even ordinary prose had an evocative, ambiguous, rhythmic quality. Poetry—which as a generic category should include not only the various types of *shi* and lyric verse, but also "song-poems" (*qu*) and rhyme prose or "rhapsody" (*fu*)—gave full scope to the creative potential of the language. The grammatical flexibility of classical Chinese, as well as the multiple meanings and subtle ambiguities of each character, allowed Chinese poets to express a wide range of ideas and emotions with vividness, economy, grace, and power. Grouping elements together in spatial patterns and temporal rhythms, the poet created integrated structures of meaning that, though unified, presented a kaleidoscopic series of impressions. The visual quality of the characters, enhanced by the use of calligraphy as an artistic medium, complemented the tonal and other auditory qualities of the language—all of which were exploited to great advantage in poetry. Furthermore, Chinese poetry never lost its intimate relationship with music. Even when the musical context for lyrics had been forgotten, poems were still written to be chanted, not simply read aloud. Unhappily, the visual and auditory effects that contributed so much to the richness of traditional Chinese poetry are invariably lost in translation.

Although the Qing was not, on the whole, a period of poetic invention, there were a number of talented poet-critics of the era who kept previous traditions alive and well. In the early years of the dynasty, Ming loyalists such as Huang Zongxi, Gu Yanwu, and Wang Fuzhi (see chapter 6) performed this function. Later, during the Kangxi era, individuals such as Zhu Yizun (1629–1709) and Wang Shizhen (1634–1711) exerted enormous influence in Chinese poetic circles. In the High Qing, Shen Deqian, Zheng Xie (1693–1765), Yuan Mei (1716–1798), Chao Yi (1727–1814), Weng Fanggang (1733–1818), and Yao Nai did the same. And in the late Qing period, poets such as Gong Zizhen (1792–1841), Wei Yuan (1794–1857), Gu Taiqing (1799–1875), Jin He (1819–1885), Huang Zunxian (1848–1905), and Kang Youwei (1858–1927) developed substantial reputations.[20] Meanwhile, as will be discussed shortly, women poets in the Jiangnan area were developing their own important poetic traditions and followings.

In addition to the emergence of specific regional traditions,[21] we may identify four main "schools" of Chinese poetry, described by James J. Y. Liu as the Technicians, Moralists, Individualists (or Expressionists), and Intuitionalists. Although these designations do not imply the existence of four distinct and mutually exclusive schools of literary criticism, they do suggest certain tendencies in the thinking of poets and literary critics during the late imperial period of Chinese history, including the Qing. A number of these tendencies stand in sharp contrast to those of Western poets and critics. Pauline Yu has observed, for instance, that Western poets set out to "construct" a fictive world in order to embody an ideal from a higher plane of existence, and in so doing they create "ontological dichotomies," whereas Chinese poets "respond" to the external world, writing in literary conventions and emphasizing "categorical correspondences" that are immanent in the world and expressed in the *Yijing*.[22]

The Technicians, as their name implies, viewed poetry primarily as a literary exercise. Their outlook was traditionalistic and frankly imitative, although rationalized on grounds that the principles of poetry embodied in the work of the great masters were, in effect, natural laws of rhythm and euphony. In the words of the Qing critic Weng Fanggang,

> The fundamental principles of poetic methods do not originate with oneself; they are like rivers flowing into the sea, and one must trace their sources back to the ancients. As for the infinitely varied applications of poetic methods, from such major considerations as the structural principles down to such details as the grammatical nature of a word, the tone of a syllable, and the points of continuation, transition, and development—all these one must learn from the ancients. Only so can one realize that everything is done according to rules and in consonance with the laws of music and that one cannot do as one likes to the slightest degree.[23]

Although the technical view of poetry placed a premium on ancient models, it also encouraged creative stylistic manipulations, such as taking apart the characters in one line of a poem and reconstituting them (*lihe*) to form new characters in another line, or composing verse that could be read from top to bottom or bottom to top with different meaning but equal clarity (*huiwen*). Technicians also enjoyed composing poems consisting of collected lines (*jiju*) taken from past poems by different writers. Zhu Yizun provides an example:

> Lightly colored clouds, concealing the sun.
> Multiple reds and greens, bright flowers blooming in the garden.
> Where could there be a better poetic place?
> Listen to the spring birds,
> After they fly away, the branches in bloom continue to wave.[24]

These lines are taken, respectively, from the Tang poets Wang Wei (699–759), Wang Jian (d. c. 830), Sikong Tu (837–908), Gu Kuang (c. 757–c. 814), and Wei Yingwu (739–792).

Many forms of Chinese verse were highly structured, requiring careful attention to the number of lines, the number of characters in a line, the matching of tones, rhyme, and parallelism or antithesis. Antithesis was, of course, especially admired. It appeared not only in regulated verse (where it was required), four-character verse, and ancient verse (*gushi*), but also in lyric verse and song-poems, which often did not even have lines of equal length. In the best antithetical couplets, each character in the first line contrasted in tone with the corresponding character in the second. At the same time, ideally the contrasted words served the same grammatical function in each line and referred to the same categories of things.[25] A simple example drawn from the novel *Honglou meng* (Dream of the red chamber) should suffice:

When the sun sets, the water whitens;
When the tide rises, all the world is green.[26]

These lines, from the brush of Wang Wei, elicit the following response from an appreciative student of his work in the novel: "'Whitens' and 'green' at first seem like nonsense but when you start thinking about it, you realize that he *had* to use those two words in order to describe the scene exactly as it was. When you read those lines out loud, the flavor of them is so concentrated that it's as though you had an olive weighing several thousand catties [that is, ten thousand pounds] inside your mouth."[27]

Traditional handbooks on Chinese poetry gave detailed lists of categories of objects for use in antithesis, including astronomy, geography, plants, and animals. In the hands of unskilled writers, this technique could degenerate into a mere mechanical pairing of words, but when employed by the masters it became a vivid expression of *yinyang* reconciliation of opposites. In the words of the modern critic James J. Y. Liu,

> At its best [antithesis] can reveal a perception of the underlying contrasting aspects of Nature and simultaneously strengthen the structure of the poem. The perfect antithetical couplet is natural, not forced, and though the two lines form a sharp contrast, they yet somehow seem to possess a strange affinity, like two people of opposite temperaments happily married, so that one might remark of the couplet, as of the couple, "What a contrast, yet what a perfect match!"[28]

The didactic view of poetry shared with the technical view a concern with tradition, and many Qing writers, such as Shen Deqian, could be described as technicians as well as moralists. But the fundamental purpose of poetry in the minds of the Moralists was self-cultivation and, by extension, the betterment of society. Shen wrote, for example, "To use what is poetic in poetry is commonplace; it is only when you quote from the classics, the histories, and the philosophers in poetry that you can make it different from wild and groundless writings." Here is an example from a poem on the *Yijing* that appears in the TSJC along with thirty-three other pieces inspired by the cryptic classic:

> Seeing the *Changes*, it becomes even more necessary to employ the
> *Changes*.
> The sages originally relied on nothing but centrality and commonality.
> When firmness and yielding are manifest, availing of the incipient
> moment brings good fortune.
> When centrality and correctness are lost, action results in misfortune.
> Those who are fearful, from beginning to end, can avoid blame.
> Those who embrace sincerity, whether hidden within [themselves] or openly,
> will become dragons.
> Do not say that divination trivializes [the *Yijing*];

The time-honored principle of the *Changes* is to divine [in
circumstances involving] movement and quiescence.[29]

Here is another example of a moralistically oriented poem, inspired in this
case by a Daoist priest. It is written in the so-called broken line (*jueju*) style
by the famous Qing reformist scholar Gong Zizhen:

> Our country's vital spirit (*shengqi*) depends upon wind and thunder.
> How sad that the myriad horses are now unable to whinny.
> I exhort the Lord of Heaven (*Tiangong*) to become revitalized;
> And to send down human talent of every sort.[30]

Individualist poets were not bereft of such sentiments, but they did not
view poetry primarily as a didactic exercise. Instead, they saw it as an expression of the unfettered self. In the words of the famous Qing poet Yuan Mei:
"Poetry is what expresses one's nature and emotion. It is enough to look no
further than one's self [for the material of poetry]. If its words move the heart,
its colors catch the eye, its taste pleases the mouth, and its sound delights the
ear, then it is good poetry." Such diverse individuals as Yuan, his literary
arch enemy Zhang Xuecheng, and the noted New Text scholar Gong Zizhen
shared these individualist sentiments.[31]

Individualist poetry covered a wide range of emotional territory. Common
topics included friendship and drinking, romantic love, homesickness and
parting, history and nostalgia, leisure and nature. Here, from the brush of the
widowed Manchu aristocrat Nalan Xingde (1655–1685), is an example of
lyric verse (*ci*) that reflects some of these individualist themes:

> Who is replaying the desolate and sorrowful tune of the Music Bureau?
> The wind sighs;
> The rain sighs;
> The lamp flame gets thinner and thinner—another sleepless night!
> I don't know what tangles my mind—
> Awake, I feel lost;
> Drunk, I feel lost;
> Even in dreams, have I ever been able to visit Xie Bridge?[32]

The Qing historian Zhao Yi offers us a very different sort of individualist
sentiment in this poem, titled "Seeking Seclusion":

> Seeking seclusion, I feel no fatigue;
> My intent is to traverse long and unfamiliar paths.
> I roam places where I have never been;
> After a few turns, the terrain looks ever more remote.
> All of a sudden, I arrive at the bank of a wild river;

The path ends, and no human traces can be found.
I want to ask the way, but there are no people anywhere;
Only a white egret standing by the grass.[33]

The Intuitionalists, perhaps best represented by Wang Shizhen and Wang Fuzhi, dealt with many of the themes of the Individualists, but they advocated a more intuitive apprehension of reality (*miaowu*). Their poetry was concerned with the relationship between human emotion (*qing*) and external scene (*jing*). In the words of Wang Fuzhi, who had far greater respect for human emotions than orthodox neo-Confucianism allowed, "Although *qing* and *jing* are two in name, they are inseparable in reality. In the most inspired poetry they subtly join together, with no barrier. Good poets include *jing* in *qing* and *qing* in *jing*." He goes on to say,

> Emotion is the activity of *yin* and *yang*, and things are the products of Heaven and Earth. When the activity between *yin* and *yang* takes place in the mind, there are things produced by Heaven and Earth to respond to it from the outside. Thus, things that exist on the outside can have an internal counterpart in emotion; and where there is emotion on the inside there must be the external object [to match it].[34]

The Intuitionalists attempted, in other words, to identify the self with the object of contemplation in order to establish a form of "spiritual resonance" (*shenyun*). Although criticized by Individualists such as Yuan Mei for lacking genuine emotion, poets such as Wang Shizhen actually sought a deeper spiritual awareness and an appreciation of the interrelatedness of all things, animate and inanimate. They were concerned not simply with self-expression, but with conveying a world view. We get a hint of this attitude in a fragment of Wang's "Moonlit Night at Fragrant Mountain Temple":

> A bright moon rises from the Eastern Cliff,
> where all the peaks are quiet.
> Remnants of snow still lie on the ground,
> Contrasts of light and shadow front the Western Studio.
> The color of the bamboo is peaceful and calm;
> The shadows of the pine trees flirt with the ripples.
> As the pure moonlight shines over it all,
> Ten thousand images are at once clarified and fresh.[35]

But for all that seemed to divide the Technicians, Moralists, Individualists, and Intuitionalists, there was considerable creative overlap. We have mentioned the link between Technicians and Moralists as exemplified in Shen Deqian, but there was other common ground. Individualists such as Gong

Zizhen, for example, could be highly didactic, while Intuitionalists such as Wang Shizhen paid great attention to style. Shen Deqian, for his part, stressed the quality of "spiritual resonance" that was so important to Wang, yet he also recognized the merit of "romantic" poets such as Li E (1692–1752), whose writing was characterized by originality and freedom from the stylistic standards of Wang, Zhu Yizun, and others. In fact, the best Qing poets were masters of a variety of styles and moods, as the numerous poems in Arthur Waley's delightful biography of Yuan Mei attest.

On the whole, Chinese (and Manchu and Mongol) women poets, like their counterparts in art, found it necessary to employ the tools and techniques of the dominant male culture. It has therefore been said that women writers in the Qing dynasty were largely dependent on a language they did not create. But the more we find out about these writing women, the more evident it is that they commanded the language rather than simply submitting to it. They wrote powerfully in a wide variety of genres, including not only verse of all sorts (their principal focus), but also parallel prose, plays, *tanci*, and even novels. Moreover, the subject matter of these writings ranged broadly and had wide appeal. It may be true, as some have claimed, that Chinese women writers found their most important audience in each other. But the biographical material included in works such as Kang-i Sun Chang and Haun Saussy, eds., *Women Writers of Traditional China* (1999) and Wilt Idema and Beata Grant, eds., *The Red Brush: Writing Women of Imperial China* (2004) clearly indicates that many women authors reached a wider appreciative audience.

It would be tedious to identify all of the accomplished women writers of the Qing period, just as it would be to list all of the gifted male writers.[36] But until fairly recently, the men have been abundantly recognized, while the women, with very few exceptions, have not. Now, however, we have several excellent anthologies in which we can find illuminating biographies and annotated excerpts from the writings of more than sixty extraordinarily talented women.[37] Several of them are worth mentioning by name here: Xu Can (c. 1610–c. 1677); Wang Duanshu (1621–c. 1706); Li Yin (1616–1685); Wu Qi (mid-seventeenth century); Lin Yining (1655–c. 1730); Mao Xiuhui (fl. 1735); Wang Yuzhen (late eighteenth century); Wu Guichen (late eighteenth century); Sun Yunhe (late eighteenth–early nineteenth centuries); Wang Duan (1793–1839); Gu Taiqing; and Wu Zao (1799–1863). I have singled out these individuals not only because they were excellent poets, but also because—with the partial exceptions of Wang Duan and Wu Zao, who had particularly spectacular literary gifts—they were well known for their painting and/or calligraphy as well as their poetry, a point to which I shall return at the end of this chapter.

The geographical center of women's writing (and much of men's writing as well), was the highly commercialized area of Jiangnan, where the exchange of verses and cross fertilization of ideas by women writers gained momentum thanks to a concentration of educated women, a core of male supporters, and numerous publication houses, academies, and art markets. We may therefore pause here briefly to examine a couple of books that do an especially good job of conveying the life and work of "writing women" in the Jiangnan region: Susan Mann's *Precious Records: Women in China's Long Eighteenth Century* (1997) and her *The Talented Women of the Zhang Family* (2007). What Mann does in both of these books is to show her readers that upperclass women in the area were active "agents" of the Confucian patriarchy and not simply passive victims and that, comparatively speaking, elite women in the "High Qing" probably enjoyed more substantial educational opportunities than their female counterparts in the West at that time.

Precious Records achieves this object with broad brush strokes, drawing on the poetry of talented women writers, along with the perspectives of their male kinfolk, other male admirers, and some critics in the period from 1683 to 1839—bookended by the suppression of the Three Feudatories Revolt and by the beginning of the first Opium War (see chapters 2 and 11). In the process, Mann maps out the spatial terrain of most Qing woman writers, discussing their common life experiences, and illustrating the importance of poetry and art in their complicated personal lives. We thus see these women not only in their "conventional" roles as wives, daughters, mothers, grandmothers, and household managers, but also as accomplished writers, painters, and teachers.

Mann's book on the extended Zhang family goes deeper than *Precious Records*, but it still illumines broad and important themes, taking certain liberties with the historical materials (I am reminded of Jonathan Spence's masterful *The Death of Woman Wang*), but staying true to her subjects. In *Precious Records* the only woman who emerges as a fully developed individual character is Yun Zhu (1771–1833), the Han Chinese wife of a Manchu Bannerman and the compiler of an important anthology of poetry titled *Guochao guixiu zhengshi ji* (Correct beginnings: Women's poetry of the [Qing] dynasty; 1831). But in *The Talented Women of the Zhang Family*, Mann takes a close look at the lives of three women from successive generations of a distinguished Jiangsu literati family: Tang Yaoqing (1763–1831), her daughter Zhang Qieying (1792–c. 1863), and Tang's granddaughter/Zhang's niece Wang Caipin (1826–1893). The chronological span of this book extends into the late Qing, a time of great social and political turmoil, which has been insightfully examined by a number of other able scholars of women's history in China (see chapter 11).

Zhang Qieying is the only one of the three Qing women to achieve a major poetic reputation, but the three, taken together, speak volumes (literally) about family ties, personal relationships, literati networks, elite values, historical memory, a sense of place, and the nature of "women's work" in elite Chinese households. Zhang's story is particularly interesting not only because of her well-deserved fame as a poet, but also because of the conflict that existed between her burdensome domestic duties (she helped her family by doing household chores and producing embroidery for sale) and her desire to write. Mann's close look at the lives and labors of Ms. Zhang and other historical actors underscores ongoing debates at the time about the proper role of women and the place of poetry in their complicated lives (see also chapter 3).

What, then, did literary women write about? Employing, for the most part, rhymed verses and lyric forms, Qing women poets not only supplied fresh perspectives on conventional literati themes such as nature and travel (their travel accounts are generally more positive than those of men), but they also explored new topical and emotional territory. They wrote movingly of absent parents, friendships with women, and close mother-child relationships.[38] Consider, for example, the following poem by Gu Ruopu (1592–c. 1681) titled "Refurbishing a Boat for My Son to Use as a Study":

> I was always conscience-stricken
> before the zeal of those ancient mothers
> until I found it [the boat], at a scenic spot
> beside a bridge where in other days
> it used to skirt the woods
> following the chaste moon (not like
> those craft that cruise the mist
> in search of frivolous ladies).
> You have long hoped to study
> in Yang Zhu's school, but now
> passers-by will see the scholar Mi Fei's barge.
> Don't mistake it for a pleasure boat
> the way I've fixed it up
> with all those old coverlets
> woven of blue silk.[39]

Here, Gu, inspired (and ostensibly intimidated) by the child-rearing efforts of historical role-models such as the mother of Mencius, good-naturedly chides her oldest son for preferring Daoist self-indulgence (Yang Zhu) to Confucian scholarship—epitomized by Mi Fei, a famous Song dynasty literatus, painter, and connoisseur who maintained a large library of books and paintings on his barge so that they would always be with him, wherever he went.

The most famous Manchu woman writer in Qing times was undoubtedly Gu Taiqinq who, as mentioned previously, was also an accomplished painter. In addition to leaving behind a corpus of more than eight hundred *shi* poems and three hundred *ci* lyrics, she was also a playwright and a novelist, who wrote *Honglou meng ying* (Shadows of the *Dream of the Red Chamber*) as a sequel to the great Qing novel *Honglou meng* (Dream of the red chamber; to be discussed shortly). But Gu Taiqing is best known and most respected as a poet. Like almost all Manchu women writers, she belonged to the Banner upper class, but unlike the majority of them she had direct and extensive contacts with Han Chinese women poets of the Jiangnan area.[40]

Here, however, I have chosen to focus on an elite Banner woman who was not connected in this way—a Mongol poet by the name of Naxun Lanbao (1824–1873).[41] Nanxun Lanbao is one of the very few Mongol women in Qing times to leave a collection of her own poetry in Chinese (a total of ninety-one *shi* pieces, published by her second son, Shengyu). Shengyu's remarks on this collection are worthy of mention. In 1874, he wrote:

> My late mother entered the family school at the age of seven, could write poems at the age of twelve, grasped the Five Classics at the age of fifteen, and married my esteemed late father at the age of seventeen. She not only served her mother-in-law assiduously, but also lived in harmony with her sisters-in-law. In the spare time left by her domestic duties, she continued to practice "chanting and singing." The poems she wrote had been accumulated into one huge tome. But entering upon middle age, she loved to read useful books, and in her final years she busied herself with the Classics and Histories, and she only rarely would write poems. By the year of *bingyin* (1866), when my esteemed late father passed away, she did not write poems anymore, as she was exhausted each day by arranging internal matters and warding off outside worries.[42]

Although Nanxun Lanbao instructed her son not to publish her self-described "idle words," he eventually decided to do so, confessing that if he printed her poems he would be disobeying the direct order of his late mother, which would be "a grave sin," but if he did not print her poems,

> the words of virtue of my late mother would have no means of transmission, and unavoidably end up getting lost, and that sin would even be graver. So I asked the elders of our neighborhood for advice, and they deemed upon inspection the poems of my late mother to be pure and manly, graceful and beautiful works, poems that well merited transmission despite her own dissatisfaction. That's why I have dared [to print her poems,] basing myself on the manuscript she had compiled herself in the year of *dingsi* (1857), to which I added what I collected. In total I obtained ninety-one poems, which I have arranged in two chapters. This I have entrusted to the block-carvers.

Nanxun Lanbao was born in Kulun (modern-day Ulan Bator), but lived most of her life in Beijing, where her father served in the Imperial Guard. She never returned to Mongolia, and forgot entirely how to speak Mongolian.

Nonetheless, the poem below suggests an undeniable romantic connection with her Mongol heritage. It is titled "My Second Elder Brother Yingjun was Appointed to a Position in Kulun, Which is Our Old Hometown. On the Day I Saw Him Off, I Hastily Composed This Poem":

> At the age of four I came to the Capital,
> For thirty years I've been away from home.
> Where is it located?
> North of the passes, obscured by the clouds.
> Our family pedigree began with Chinggis Khan;
> We have left our old fief in Kulun.
> We had a hundred thousand archers then—
> Proud sons of Heaven, strong since ancient times.
> At night we lodged conveniently in felt tents;
> In the morning we happily drank animal milk.
> Fortunately, we have [now] entered a world of Great Unity,
> Where no borders separate China and foreign countries.
> Carrying knives, we have served in the royal guard;
> Installed as nobility, we have inherited rank.
> I laugh at myself as the material of the inner-chamber;
> Long ago I changed to the current fashion.
> I have no dream of riding a saddled horse,
> My only ambition is for a literary life.
> By the green window I apply cosmetics;
> Under the crimson lamp I work hard on my books.
> Chinese and foreigners differ in customs and styles;
> My old country has now become a strange place.
> When someone greets me using that twittering [Mongol] language,
> I have to apologize for forgetting it all!
> Now, my elder brother, you have received the royal charge,
> And you will return home to a hall of splendid glory.
> How could we regard Kulun as an alien region,
> One that filled us all with uneasiness?
> I would like a word in solitude,
> Upon toasting you farewell.
> The Son of Heaven keeps watch over foreigners everywhere,
> Protecting even those areas beyond the pale.
> Recently, I hear about weakness and timidity;
> Once-pure customs are now uncommonly ornate.[43]
> I regret that I am not a man,
> And so I have no way to fulfill my desire to return home.
> I only hope that you, my brother, will try hard
> To restore our ancestral inheritance to its former glory.
> Let us not cry like young children,
> Sadly looking at each other in vain.[44]

In closing this section on poetry I would like to remind readers once again of the close ties between poetry and painting. By Qing times, and in fact well before, these two activities had become inextricably linked as the most exalted forms of elite cultural indulgence for women as well as for men. Poems and paintings were both "written" with brush and ink, both treated a wide variety of subject material, both drew on previous models for inspiration, and both were concerned with simplicity and stylistic balance. Furthermore, poetry and painting often inspired each other. Painters were moved to create art after reading a poem, and poets were moved to create verse after viewing a painting. Thus, we have the "eccentric" painter Zheng Xie writing the following lines to his contemporary Bian Weiqi:

> From your painting of wild geese I can clearly see them crying,
> On this fine silken scroll I hear the sound of reeds in the wind.
> What regrets tangle your brush, sending out a frigid autumn gust?
> Nothing but the sorrow of parting on the mountain passes![45]

In the end, the relationship between painting and poetry is perhaps best expressed in Su Dongpo's (1036–1101) famous tribute to Wang Wei, "There is painting in his poetry and poetry in his painting." Ideally, and very often in fact, the Chinese literatus in Qing times was both poet and painter.

VERNACULAR LITERATURE

Although no major literary figure in China after the first century CE attempted to write his or her principal works in a language consonant with the spoken language, the written vernacular (*baihua wen*) still enjoyed considerable popularity throughout much of the imperial era—especially from the Tang period onward. During the Qing dynasty, a variety of vernacular works circulated widely, reflecting, as well as contributing to, the growth of basic literacy in China—estimated by some to be as high as 45 percent for males and 10 percent for females.[46] Although not as succinct, exalted, or aesthetically pleasing as classical Chinese, the vernacular was comparatively easy to learn, direct, colorful, and often extremely forceful.

Vernacular equivalents existed for most forms of elite literature. Administrative manuals advocated the modification of complex official documents for public consumption through the use of simple rhymed phrases in "nice calligraphy, easy to read." Zhang Boxing (1652–1725), as governor of Fujian in the early eighteenth century, personally wrote three different versions of the famous Sacred Edict of the Kangxi emperor: "one embellished with classical allusions for the literati, one illustrated with popular sayings for those of medium intelligence, and one with memorable jingles for the simple country folk."⁴⁷ Similarly, practical handbooks were produced in several versions to reach different reading audiences throughout the empire. "Books of convenience" (*bianshu*), often illustrated, provided specific guidance on ritual and etiquette drawn from classical sources as well as more recent works, such as Zhu Xi's paradigmatic *Jiali* (Family ritual). Popular vernacular histories paralleled the orthodox histories of the elite, "morality books" and "precious scrolls" were the popular equivalents of religious and philosophical tracts, and colloquial short stories served as the counterparts to Tang-style classical tales (*chuanqi*), a genre that Pu Songling's (1640–1715) *Liaozhai zhiyi* (Records of the strange) brought to such high levels of achievement in the early Qing period.⁴⁸

Illustrated encyclopedias for daily use (*riyong leishu*) represent an interesting middle ground between classical and vernacular literature because they were often written in both styles, depending on the subject matter. To a certain extent, the content of these works overlaps with the major categories of concern in the TSJC. Most Qing editions of the WBQS, for instance, like those produced in the Ming period (see chapter 1 and appendix E), begin with conventional sections on celestial and terrestrial phenomena, human relationships, Chinese history, and foreign peoples. At the same time, however—because these works were clearly intended as a means by which literate commoners such as merchants might gain easy access to important aspects of elite culture—they generally included sections on music, poetic composition, painting, calligraphy, and styles of correspondence. They also contained sections on drinking games and jokes—presumably as a means of impressing people at social gatherings, or at least amusing potential customers and contacts. In addition, *riyong leishu* often provided easy to memorize practical advice on mundane matters such as gestation, childbirth and childrearing, farming and sericulture, the handling of domestic animals, health and medicine, martial arts, and Qing law. And, as with popular almanacs (see chapters 1, 7, and 10), they devoted a great deal of attention to divination, including dream interpretation, physiognomy, fate calculation, and geomancy.

Like the WBQS, the vast majority of popular writings in Qing China reflected conventional elite values, including such widespread Buddhist and Religious Daoist tracts as the *Taishang ganying pian* (Tract of Taishang on action and response), the *Bufeiqian gongde li* (Meritorious deeds at no cost), and the *Guangshan pian gongguo ge* (Ledger of merit and demerit for the spreading of goodness). Although based on the idea of divine retribution and buttressed by other religious notions, these works employed a great deal of elite symbolism and had a decidedly ethical, this-worldly cast. To be sure, they often contained admonitions to spare animal life, to show respect to sacred images, and "not to speak ill of Buddhist and Daoist clergy," but the importance in these tracts of family affairs, filial piety, loyalty to the ruler, obedience to the "principles of Heaven," social harmony, the avoidance of lawsuits, and even respect for paper with written characters on it indicates a decidedly Confucian point of view. Furthermore, although works such as the *Bufeiqian gongde li* classify meritorious deeds according to various social and occupational groupings, the striking feature of these works is their active promotion of the existing Confucian social hierarchy.[49]

For the most part, vernacular fiction also reflected an elite outlook, and despite the fact that dramatic works and popular novels were generally disparaged by the Confucian literati, and sometimes outlawed by the state, they were enjoyed by all sectors of Chinese society. During the late Ming and throughout the Qing, the popular theater eclipsed traditional storytelling in influence, bringing history, legends, and other stories directly to both urban centers and the countryside. Indeed, it seems evident that the bulk of popular knowledge concerning the narrative tradition in China—major heroes and villains, stock scenes, allusions, and so forth—was transmitted more on stage than through the written word. Even the Kangxi emperor's Sacred Edict was popularized most effectively by this medium. Andrea S. Goldman's *Opera and the City: The Politics of Culture in Beijing, 1770–1900* (2012) provides a particularly vivid illustration of the way that the Qing court and commercial playhouses exerted influence on the social and moral order at the capital.

There were several types of drama in Qing times: some of the most widespread were classic Yuan dynasty "variety performances" (*zaju*); southern dramas (*xiwen* or *chuanqi*); various subregional styles such as "Kunshan music" (*Kunqu*); and the late Qing hybrid interregional form known as Beijing opera (*Jingxi*). Although each of these types had its own special features, all shared certain general characteristics. One such feature was a multimedia presentation, combining spoken language (both verse and prose), music (both vocal and instrumental), and acting—including mime, dance, and acrobatics. Another was its nonrepresentational nature, its stress on the expression of emotion rather than the imitation of life. As James J. Y. Liu indicates,

> In nonrepresentational drama, the words spoken or sung by a character do not necessarily represent actual speech or even thought; they are the dramatist's means to make the audience imagine the feelings and thoughts of the characters as well as the situations in which they find themselves. When a character speaks or sings fine poetry, he or she is not usually represented as a poet. . . . The poetry, in most cases, belongs to the dramatist, not the character.[50]

Like music in a play, poetry was extremely important in conveying dramatic mood, and when read, Chinese drama tended to be measured primarily by its verse.

Because Chinese playwrights were not interested in "imitating life," they did not usually try to create highly individualized characters. Instead, they were concerned with portraying human types, a categorical approach to characterization abetted by Chinese stage conventions such as colorful makeup and an extraordinarily elaborate system of hand, sleeve, and facial expressions. Among the most appreciated character types were upright scholars, military men (both good and bad), heroic women, and buffoons. There was not, however, a sharp division between tragedy and comedy as such in Chinese drama, in part because theatrical convention, like much of the vernacular literary tradition, demanded happy endings or at least some sort of poetic justice.

Chinese plays covered all of the thematic territory embraced by traditional Chinese fiction: sex, love, intrigue, supernatural events, religious commitment, historical and pseudo-historical episodes (civil and military), domestic dramas, murder, lawsuits, banditry, and so forth. Many dramatic themes were derived from short stories or novels. At least a few plays of the Qing period explored explicitly lesbian or bisexual themes—notably *Lianxiang ban* (The companion who loved fragrance), written by Li Yu (1611–1680), a colorful and creative playwright who was also an epicure, an inventor, and a designer of houses and gardens. According to a preface to *Lianxiang ban* written by a man named Yu Wei, the phenomenon of a beautiful girl meeting another by chance and "falling in love with her fragrance" was commonplace in Li's time. In fact, Yu indicates that the play is based on the situation in Li's own household, where his wife and concubine loved both Li and each other.[51]

In many ways Li Yu exemplified the tumultuous, uncertain times in which he lived. As indicated previously, the growing commercialization, urbanization, and monetization of China in the seventeenth century not only created new opportunities for social mobility and provided greater scope for the literary and artistic talents of both women and men, but it also introduced new attitudes toward friendship, love, sex, and marriage. Many of Li Yu's writings touch on these and related themes. Although known primarily as a dramatist, Li also wrote a novel (see below), a number of short stories (again, some of which deal explicitly with homosexual themes), and three hundred essays on topics close to his heart—all organized under a few pithy headings such as writing plays, putting on plays, women and beauty, houses and gardens, food and drink, flowers and trees, and health and pleasure. Much of what Li wrote was witty and humorous. Patrick Hanan describes him as "the most whole-hearted and versatile exponent of comedy in the history of Chinese literature—the Chinese comic specialist par excellence." Li himself once confessed: "Broadly speaking, everything I have ever written was intended to make people laugh."[52]

Of the dozen or so plays attributed to Li Yu, most are his own creation, although a few are revisions of earlier works, such as *Mingzhu ji* (Record of an illustrious pearl) by Lu Cai (1497–1537). Significantly, Li produced and directed his own plays, which were then performed for high officials by his own small troupe of concubine-actresses—rather than by male actors as was the usual practice. According to Man-kuei Li, Li Yu's experience as a producer and director "enabled him to understand thoroughly the secret of the stage and to exemplify in practice the principles of acting and playwriting which he formulated . . . [in his essays]."[53]

Among the numerous outstanding plays written during the Qing period, we may single out for special attention the popular drama *Taohua shan* (Peach blossom fan; 1708), a "southern drama" of forty scenes. Written by a descendant of Confucius named Kong Shangren (1648–1718), *Peach Blossom Fan* ranks as one of the greatest plays in the Chinese language by virtue of its historical vision, dramatic construction, and literary quality. It is also noteworthy for its wide-ranging subject material and effective characterization. The name derives from an incident in which the heroine, Li Xiangjun, resists being forced to become a concubine by hitting her head on a wall, spattering her fan with blood. A famous painter then converts the bloodstains into a peach blossom design, which serves as a vibrant visual metaphor for "the mixture of violence and beauty that Kong saw as lying at the heart of late Ming moral and intellectual life."[54]

Carefully structured as a historical romance, *Peach Blossom Fan* touches on many different aspects of Chinese life: personal and private, social and political, military, and even artistic. Its major characters, all actual personalities of the late Ming period, have more individuality than most Chinese dramatic characters. For example, the "hero," Hou Fangyu, is less than perfect, while the "villain," Ruan Dacheng, possesses certain admirable qualities. This attempt at balance is also evident in the dramatic story line, which alternates between scenes of sadness and joy, quiescence and activity. In these and other ways, *Peach Blossom Fan* resembles some of the great novels of the Ming and Qing periods.

The play is a moving romantic story, but it is also a basically accurate historical account, and as such deals with the politically sensitive subject of the fall of the Ming dynasty. It should come as no surprise, therefore, to find that Kong Shangren sometimes distorts the record in an apparent effort not to offend the Manchus. The loyalist minister Shi Kefa, for instance, commits suicide in the play, whereas in real life Qing forces killed him after he refused to surrender. On the other hand, Kong has his hero renounce the world rather than take the examinations under the Manchus (as he did in fact), presumably to provide a more satisfying climax to the play. In all, Kong must have struck an effective balance because we know that *Peach Blossom Fan* was presented at court and was also well received by the Chinese public at large. Hong Sheng's (1645–1704) *Changsheng dian* (Palace of everlasting life), which was created at about the same time as *Taohua shan*, expressed similar sentiments and enjoyed the same sort of popularity.

A significant feature of most Chinese dramas and short stories is their neat resolution of the plot for maximum impact. By contrast, the Chinese novel—the supreme achievement in vernacular fiction during Ming-Qing times—gives very little sense of unilinear plot development and provides no dramatic climax. The reasons for this rest in the aesthetic and philosophical assumptions that underlie such works. A volume of translations titled *How to Read the Chinese Novel* (1990), edited by David Rolston and based on a special genre of Chinese literature known as *dufa* (lit. "how to read") books, brings together a number of valuable commentaries on the great works of Ming and Qing fiction, allowing us to see clearly how they were understood in traditional times.[55]

Western scholars have drawn on such Chinese commentarial traditions and written about them as well. They have also brought "modern" interpretive techniques and sensibilities to their literary criticism. The result has been a proliferation of studies in various Western languages that view Chinese literature—novels in particular—in increasingly sophisticated ways. For instance, a great many books and essays have been written on the relationship between Chinese narrative and topics such as "history and legend," "gender and meaning," "expressions of self," "writing and law," "autobiographical sensibility," "culture and the body," "love and emotion," "desire," "causality and containment," "sexuality," and "male-female relations."[56] Westerners have also studied Chinese illustrated fiction and, naturally enough, issues of translation. As something of a counterpoint to this sort of scholarship, C. T. Hsia, a more or less "traditional" Chinese literary specialist, has offered a stinging critique of various Western scholars in his book *C.T. Hsia on Chinese Literature* (2004).

Hsia is particularly critical of the interpretive stance of Andrew Plaks, whose structural and aesthetic preoccupations Hsia finds annoying (to say the least). But I find the arguments of Plaks interesting, convincing, and valuable. Plaks maintains, for example, that the structure of the best Chinese novels is rooted in a logic of interrelated and overlapping categories—the presentation of experience in terms of *yinyang*-style juxtapositions of images, themes, situations, and personalities. Reflecting the deeply ingrained idea of existence as "ceaseless alternation and cyclical recurrence," Plaks argues effectively that the Chinese novel proceeds along narrative axes of change such as separation and union, prosperity and decline, sorrow and joy, elegance and baseness, and movement and stillness. It also often drifts between the realms of reality and illusion. The salient point made by Plaks is that these dualities are complementary rather than antithetical; they do not take the form of a master dualism and are not resolved in a truly dialectical process. Instead of the kind of resolution or synthesis that might be expected in a Western novel, there is instead infinite overlapping and alternation.[57]

One gains the impression of endlessness in a Chinese novel—much the same quality we have identified in landscape paintings, gardens, and certain kinds of Chinese poetry. But as in art and poetry, endlessness or purposelessness was not tantamount to meaninglessness, for there was always the assumption that the entire ground of existence is intelligible. In Plaks's words,

> Any meaning in the narrative texts will tend to come not in the configurations of the individual event, or its logical relation to other events, but only in the hypothetical totality of all (or at least a good many) events. . . . This sense of meaning in the overview may be partially behind the centrality of historical and pseudohistorical narrative in the Chinese tradition. The idea that an objective recounting of human events will eventually bear out its own pattern of meaning is relatively clear in historiography, and one might even say that the dimension of significance which Western narrative tends to derive from epic models of unique greatness is manifest sooner in the Chinese context in terms of the recurrent cycles, the vast overview of history.[58]

The comparison between fictional narrative and history may also be extended to the treatment of character, which in most of Chinese vernacular literature tends to be categorical. Like the evaluation of historical personalities—not to mention that of artists and writers—the tendency in Chinese narrative is to sum up the individual in vivid, economical brush strokes. Most novelists describe their characters from the outside, focusing primarily on actions rather than ideas, but assuming an integral relationship between the two. Characterization in the best Chinese novels is more complex than in conventional historical writing, however, because in Chinese narrative the emphasis is usually on the momentary and changing attributes of character rather than on abiding or developing attributes. The central figures in novels are seldom "heroic" in the Western sense and often give the impression of inconsistency or ambivalence. Again, these features can be explained in part by the aesthetic and philosophical notion of *yinyang* alternation and complementarity, an outlook that can accommodate change and inconsistency with comparative ease.

Furthermore, in keeping with the traditional Chinese emphasis on relational thinking, the character of any given individual in a novel is seldom as important as the relationship of that person to others—hence the emphasis on groups of people acting in concert or the elaborate interplay of various individuals in a group context. Sometimes fictional characters are even depicted as composites of their acquaintances. Also important to Chinese characterization is the tension created by conflicting social roles within the framework of the Three Bonds and the Five Relationships. In narrative, as in life, a man might well be torn by the conflicting imperatives of being at once a father, a son, a husband, a minister or subject (or emperor), an elder or younger brother, and a friend.

Moral dilemmas are central to the structure of Chinese novels, which, like most other forms of vernacular literature, are marked by a heavy didacticism, a strong emphasis on themes of reward and retribution. This reflects the Confucian idea of an inherent moral order in the universe and the principle of *bao* (requital or recompense), which requires that a fictional tale be morally satisfying. The result is that Chinese narrative, while full of tragic situations, lacks a well-developed concept of tragedy in the Western sense. There is, however, a considerable amount of irony in the best Chinese novels, and so the moral judgments within them are not always either simple or straightforward.

The moral world of the Chinese novel is fundamentally Confucian, but Buddhist and Daoist elements appear prominently in several major works, and many stories have an explicitly supernatural dimension. Although the most esteemed values in Chinese narrative are those of loyalty, duty, filial piety, and chastity, a number of novels exhibit a "syncretic hospitality" to the transcendental doctrines of Buddhism and Daoism, as well as to the universalistic ethic of the knight-errant (*xia*). Moreover, we find that some of the greatest works in the Chinese narrative tradition serve as vehicles for satirizing or otherwise criticizing certain values and practices of traditional Chinese society, despite their Confucian tone. This helps account for the ambivalence of Confucian scholars toward the novel and the periodic efforts by the state in Ming-Qing times to ban a number of "novels and licentious works" (*xiaoshuo yinci*) on grounds that they were "frivolous, vulgar and untrue."[59]

A memorial by the Qing censor Asitan (Chinese: Ashitan; d. 1683), a Manchu scholar and translator, reflects ethical concerns of precisely this sort:

[Books other than classical and historical writings] are not worth considering. Recently I have noticed many obscene passages in fictional works translated into Manchu. These not only have no use, but it is to be feared that their harmful influence will spread everywhere, until the hearts of men turn to rebellion and wickedness. . . . This literature, with its immoral passages, ought to be forbidden and its translation no longer permitted. Such action will . . . support the advancement of education and will create a basis for the development of human capacities."[60]

In a similar vein, Yu Zhi (1809–1874), a Han Chinese official, wrote in the mid-nineteenth century that "the collecting of erotic novels damages natural dispositions, impairs female relationships, is a danger to youth, and spreads terrible diseases."[61] Even China's greatest novel, *Dream of the Red Chamber*, was officially proscribed during a portion of the nineteenth century, although we know that the Qianlong emperor himself read and enjoyed the work in the previous century.

But for all their satirical tendencies and "vulgar" content, the best novels of the Qing period, like those of the Ming, enthusiastically celebrated traditional Chinese culture and provided all sectors of Chinese society with a common repository of heroes and villains—individuals who either inspired emulation or served as negative examples. I have discussed the four most famous Ming novels in chapter 1: *Sanguo zhi yanyi* (Romance of the Three Kingdoms), *Shuihu zhuan* (Water margin), *Jin Ping Mei* (Plum in the golden vase), and *Xiyou ji* (Journey to the west).[62] These books were all immensely popular in the Qing, but three of them were considered subversive by the state and therefore periodically banned. A proverb of the period advised, "Let not the young read *Shuihu*; let not the old read *Sanguo*." For just as the latter novel encouraged deviousness and intrigue, so the former encouraged rebellion against authority. Naturally the overt sexual content of *Jin Ping Mei* offended orthodox sensibilities.

There are no original knight-errant novels in the Qing that match the *Romance of the Three Kingdoms* or *Water Margin* in style or sophistication, but military romances of various sorts—some quite accomplished—flourished throughout the dynasty, especially during the Jiaqing period.[63] On the civil side of the narrative coin, the Qing boasted several outstanding works. From the standpoint of sharp-edged satire, the most impressive of these is *Rulin waishi* (The scholars) by Wu Jingzi (1701–1754). This novel surpasses even *Journey to the West* in this respect, for the latter work merely takes good-natured aim at Buddhism, whereas *The Scholars* focuses sharply and directly on the hypocrisy of the Confucian elite itself.

Through his skilled use of an omniscient narrator, Wu—himself an examination failure—explores the often sordid and corrupt world of the Chinese literati, underscoring both the vital importance of the examination system to the scholarly class and the many abuses that the system encouraged. In all, the novel boasts about two hundred characters, many of whom are very skillfully portrayed—sometimes with conflicting information supplied by different observers. A few scholarly figures are seen as upright and exemplary, but many more appear as imposters and hypocrites. Several critics have emphasized the autobiographical nature of the book and the author's identification with the able but highly individualistic scholar Du Shaoqing; yet even Du is satirized on occasion, as Wu Jingzi projects a consistently moral vision in the midst of vulgarity, hypocrisy, and human folly. Although sometimes criticized for its episodic structure and apparent lack of a cohesive overall design, *The Scholars* illustrates very well the traditional Chinese emphasis on "a mass weaving of many narrative strands" and on vast networks of human relationships.[64]

From the standpoint of erotic literature, the Qing novel *Rou putuan* (Carnal prayer mat), attributed by some to the idiosyncratic dramatist Li Yu, is at least the equal of *Plum in the Golden Vase*.[65] Like the latter work, *Carnal Prayer Mat* is in part a religious allegory revolving around the theme of Buddhist redemption. It is well structured, lively, funny, sympathetic to women, and psychologically realistic. In several respects, *Carnal Prayer Mat* is an even better novel than *Plum in the Golden Vase*. It is tighter and makes more skillful use of character analogies, humor, and irony. The female character Yuxiang ("Jade Scent"), wife of the hero known as Weiyang Sheng ("Before Midnight Scholar"), provides an excellent illustration of the problem of conflicting social roles as a daughter, wife, mistress, and prostitute. She also serves as an interesting example of the interplay of individuals in a group context because she is linked in some way to nearly all of the major male characters in the novel.

The closest Qing equivalent to *Journey to the West*, putting sequels aside, is the nineteenth-century novel *Jinghua yuan* (Flowers in the mirror) by Li Ruzhen (c. 1763–1830). Mark Elvin describes this work as "a microcosm of the educated Chinese mind around the year 1830." If *Journey to the West* can be considered China's *Pilgrim's Progress*, then *Flowers in the Mirror*, also set in the Tang dynasty, is perhaps the Chinese equivalent of *Gulliver's Travels*. Like *Journey to the West*, *Flowers in the Mirror* is a blend of mythology and adventure, fantasy and allegory, and satire and wit. By design, the viewpoints of its characters frequently differ from one another, suggesting "polarities of problems" rather than fixed positions. Although more a reflection of Confucian moral values (loyalty and filial piety) and the Daoist search for immortality than of Buddhist theology or mythology, *Flowers in the Mirror* is far from conventional. It satirizes snobbery, hypocrisy, and social climbing, sharply criticizes certain Chinese social practices—particularly foot binding and concubinage—and celebrates accomplished women such as Tang Guichen (who represents literary talent), Shi Lanyan (the embodiment of morality and wisdom), and Meng Zizhi (who is witty and humorous). At the same time, however, *Flowers in the Mirror* evinces obvious admiration for nearly every other aspect of traditional Chinese culture.[66]

A few additional works of overt social criticism deserve at least passing mention, including the late Qing novels *Lao Can youji* (The travels of Lao Can) by Liu E (1857–1909) and the innovative first-person narrative titled

Ershi nian mudu guai xianzhuang (Bizarre happenings eyewitnessed over two decades) by Wu Woyao (1867–1910).[67] These and other novels of the period not only shed valuable light on the dynasty in decline (and on the unprecedented influence of the West and Japan during the late nineteenth and early twentieth centuries; see chapter 11), they also represent an important transitional stage between "traditional" and "modern" fiction in China. One important work that facilitated this transition was *Haishang hua liezhuan* (Singsong girls of Shanghai), a vivid and realistic account of late Qing "courtesan culture." David Der-Wei Wang considers this work to be "a masterpiece that helped to modernize late imperial Chinese fiction."[68] Ironically, however, the novel was never popular among general readers—in part because the language of the work reflected the Wu (Shanghai) dialect and also because of its unconventional style.

By almost any standard, the greatest of all traditional Chinese novels is *Honglou meng* (Dream of the red chamber; aka Dream of red mansions). The first eighty chapters of this massive and elegant work, commonly known as *Shihtou ji* (Story of the stone), were written by Cao Xueqin (c. 1715–1763), a Chinese bondservant in the Banner organization and a talented painter; the last forty chapters are generally attributed to Gao E (fl. 1791), a full-fledged Bannerman and a degree-holding scholar. Some versions of the full 120-chapter work consist of nearly thirteen hundred pages and about seven hundred thousand words. The novel contains at least thirty major figures and some four hundred minor ones, ranged all along the Chinese social spectrum. Yet as numerous as these characters are, Chao-ying Fang rightly observes that

> they intermingle in a wonderful unity, each individual constituting an integral member of a large family group, sharing its glory and its shame, contributing to its prosperity or its ruin. Some, taking it for granted that the family fortune is irreversible, spend their days in emotional excesses or in sensual pleasures. Some, who are avaricious, contrive to profit by mismanagement of the family estate. Some foresee the dangers and so plan for their own futures; others voice warnings, but their words go unheeded. Such a panorama of complex human emotions, involving tens of masters and hundreds of servants, constitutes source-material of supreme value for a study of the social conditions in affluent households of the early Qing period.[69]

As the above summary suggests, the major story line of the novel revolves around the fortunes of the Jia family and a complex love affair involving various individuals living in the family compound—notably Jia Baoyu, the "hero" (one might say anti-hero) of the book, and his talented female cousins, Lin Daiyu and Xue Baochai. Much of the novel is strongly autobiographical, for like Baoyu, Cao Xueqin was a sensitive, well-educated individual whose

Figure 9.1. Jia Baoyu
Source: Gai Qi (1773–1828) 1916.

Figure 9.2.   Lin Daiyu
Source: Gai Qi 1916.

wealthy and established family experienced financial reverses and other difficulties during his lifetime. The book has several different layers of meaning,
and it is written in several different literary modes—realistic, allegorical, and
narrative. Like *The Scholars*, *Dream of the Red Chamber* is in part a critique
of early Qing political and social life, and like *Flowers in the Mirror*, which
was heavily influenced by Cao's brilliant narrative, it can be seen as a celebration of women.

    The structure of *Dream of the Red Chamber* illustrates especially well the
basic organizing principle of *yinyang* complementarity and the traditional
Chinese philosophical interest in relations, qualities, and states of being. As
Plaks, Lucien Miller, Angelina Yee, Jing Wang, and others have indicated
(see appendix F), much of the appeal of the novel can be found in the interpenetration or overlapping of themes of reality and illusion; the juxtaposition
of Confucian and Buddhist (or Daoist) elements; contrasts between rich and
poor, exalted and base; and the alternation of scenes, moods, and situations.
Antithetical couplets at the beginning of many chapters, and contrasting char-
acterizations such as those of the frail Lin Daiyu and the robust Xue Baochai,
heighten the reader's sense of interpenetration, alternation, and complementary opposition.[70] Early in the novel the structural and thematic tone is set:

> There actually are some happy affairs in the Red Dust [the "real" world], it's just
> that one cannot depend on them forever. Then again, there is "discontent within
> bliss, numerous demons in auspicious affairs," a phrase of eight words all of
> which belong tightly bound together. In the twinkling of an eye, sorrow is born
> of utter happiness, men are no more, and things change. In the last analysis, it's
> all a dream and the myriad realms return to nothingness.[71]

    Predictably, *Dream of the Red Chamber* ends in what Plaks describes
as "narrative lame-duck fashion." Well before the conclusion of the novel,
Baoyu's family secretly arranges for him to marry Baochai rather than his
true love, Daiyu, who dies grief stricken on Baoyu's wedding day. A series
of Jia family disasters follow, but Baoyu eventually passes the examinations,
Baochai bears him a son, and the Jia family fortunes rise again. Baoyu then
decides to renounce the world and become a Buddhist monk, thus seeking
Enlightenment and personal salvation after at least partially fulfilling his
Confucian responsibilities as a son and a husband. As some modern Chinese
scholars have argued, the novel has a genuinely tragic dimension, but the
tragedy is tempered somewhat by larger patterns of existential movement.[72]

    Chinese and Western scholars alike have identified *Dream of the Red
Chamber* as a microcosm of traditional Chinese culture. In both its elaborate
structure and its exquisite detail, the novel evokes a mood of completeness
and authenticity. Furthermore, in a very real sense it represents the culmina-

tion of China's entire pre-modern literary tradition. The novel includes every major type of Chinese literature—including philosophy, history, poetry, and fiction. We find in it quotations from Confucius and Zhuangzi, Tang poets and Yuan dramatists. Throughout the Qing period and up to the present, *Dream of the Red Chamber* has inspired countless plays, poems, games, and sequels, as well as a huge body of critical scholarship.

But while the novel is a supremely accomplished example of traditional Chinese fiction, the author reveals conventional literati prejudices throughout the work. In chapter 42, for example, Baochai lectures Daiyu on the purpose of literature:

> A boy's proper business is to read books in order to gain an understanding of things, so that when he grows up he can play his part in governing the country. . . . As for girls like you and me, . . . since we can read, let us confine ourselves to good, improving books; let us avoid like the plague those pernicious works of fiction, which so undermine the character that in the end it is past reclaiming.[73]

Undoubtedly Cao Xueqin is writing a bit with tongue in cheek, but it is clear that the author's greatest delight lies in displaying his erudition through philosophical discussions, word games, riddles, and especially classical verse. Although his characters quote freely from such popular works as the famous thirteenth-century play *Xixiang ji* (Romance of the western chamber),[74] they spend countless hours composing poetry and discussing it. In fact, *Dream of the Red Chamber* provides the reader with a first-rate education in the refinements of poetic composition and appreciation.

The cultural breadth of the novel is perhaps most evident in its vivid portrayal of Chinese society. In both its psychological realism and encyclopedic scope, it is unparalleled in the history of traditional Chinese literature. As Chao-ying Fang has indicated, *Dream of the Red Chamber* sheds light on virtually every aspect of Chinese life and covers a vast social spectrum. It highlights the importance of popular religion and family ritual, the values of filial piety and respect for age and authority, and the tensions and conflicts of role fulfillment at various levels of society. In addition, it provides a wealth of detail on Chinese aesthetics, housing, clothing, food, amusements, festivals, sexual life, and popular customs. Perhaps most important, it illustrates the gap between social theory and social practice so often neglected or downplayed in official documents and other orthodox sources. With this point in mind, we may now turn our attention to Chinese daily life.

Chapter Ten

Social Life

As with other realms of culture, social customs during the Qing period varied—sometimes dramatically—from region to region, time to time, and class to class. They also differed among the Chinese, the Manchus, the Mongols, and other non-Han peoples. Once again, then, we encounter the sticky issue of generalizing. We also face the difficulty of reconciling theory and practice—negotiating the distance between what people said and what they actually did. These are particular problems when we look at daily life in Qing dynasty China, for every family in the empire was different, just as every person was. Nonetheless, as I have indicated previously, we have to generalize in order to make meaning, so let us see what can comfortably be said.

As noted in previous chapters, a significant gap separated the Manchu, Mongol, and Chinese Bannermen from the non-Banner Han majority in China Proper. The Banners lived in isolated compounds with distinctive architectural features; they often had Manchu-style decorations in their homes (for example, bows and arrows on display); they celebrated their own martial traditions and common legends; they engaged in their own shamanistic religious practices; they socialized primarily among themselves; and, for much of the Qing period, many of them spoke a non-Han language. They observed different forms of greeting, called themselves by their personal names rather than their family names, and wore distinctive clothing. Elite Manchu women were especially unlike their Han counterparts: they did not generally bind their feet, they wore their hair differently, and they had different styles of attire and jewelry. They enjoyed more substantial property rights than Han women, and they had a generally higher status in the Banner world than Han women had in theirs. Manchu policy toward the remarriage of women was also more forgiving than in the dominant Han culture.[1]

Nonetheless, prolonged interaction with the Chinese had an effect on many Manchus, both men and women—particularly after the Qianlong emperor sanctioned the policy of allowing permanent Banner residence in the provinces (1756). By stages, first in Beijing and then later in the provinces, the Manchus succumbed to certain so-called evil Chinese habits. Apparently, Chinese Bannermen often took the lead in these activities, which included an early attraction to Chinese-style entertainments and a growing neglect of their military heritage. The process also involved the increasing use of the Chinese language as opposed to Manchu; by 1800 at the latest, the Qing court had lost its battle to preserve Manchu as the spoken language among the majority of Bannermen. From that time onward, even the "jottings" (*biji*) designed to celebrate Manchu culture "were written, not in workaday Manchu, but in elegant literary Chinese."[2]

In other ways, too, Chinese culture proved alluring. As we have seen, many Manchus, and certainly all of the Qing emperors from Kangxi onward, found Chinese art and literature attractive. In terms of lifecycle rituals, the Manchus at all levels celebrated a number of Han Chinese festivals, including the lunar New Year. Manchu cities, although clearly distinguishable from their Chinese counterparts, had Chinese-style religious temples, such as those for the City God, the God of Literature, the God of War, and the Gods of Wealth and Fire (see chapter 7). Although foot binding was discouraged among Banner women, some engaged in the practice, and a large number surrendered to the idea that a "horse-hoof" extension on their shoes (*mati xie*) might look as if their feet had been bound, or at least produce an apparently attractive foot bound gait (see figure 4.3). An additional problem over time was declining financial support for the Banner garrisons, which encouraged Banner families to interact more substantially with Han Chinese in an effort to enhance their economic prospects—increasingly by investing in Chinese commercial enterprises.[3]

Let us assume, then, that to greater or lesser degrees, Manchu, Mongol, and Chinese Banner families found some aspects of Han culture attractive or at least expedient to adopt. But beyond the generalizations offered above, we still know too little about exactly how, where, when, and why this happened. To be sure, in recent years there has been a surge of Chinese-language scholarship on the beliefs, customs, and institutions of the Manchus, both before and after the Qing conquest of China in 1644.[4] But much more work needs to be done on primary sources such as the *Baqi tongzhi* (Comprehensive history of the Eight Banners; 1796)—not to mention diaries, memoirs, and the observations of "outside" observers—before we can speak confidently about the processes of culture change in individual Banner communities at particular times. Somewhat surprisingly, Chinese provincial and local gazetteers seldom mention the Manchus, and the otherwise invaluable account of Qing customs written by a late eighteenth-century Japanese sojourner named Nakagawa Tadahide says virtually nothing about the Manchus as a distinct ethnic group. In 1900, a decade before the collapse of the dynasty, Dun Li-chen, a Manchu Bannerman, wrote a book in Chinese titled *Yanjing suishi ji* (Record of a year's time in Yanjing [Beijing]), but it reveals very little about Manchu customs. The same is true of M. L. C. Bogan's *Manchu Customs and Superstitions* (1928), which was reportedly compiled with the assistance of a "Manchu scholar" named Zhou Qixian.[5] These latter two works seem to suggest the rapid "sinicization" of the Manchus in the first decades of the twentieth century, but they tell us nothing about earlier periods.

Another feature of Qing social life that has proved vexing to scholars for different reasons is the question of how women were viewed and treated in traditional Chinese society. As we have seen in previous chapters, China had no shortage of talented women. But there is comparatively little recognition of this fact in most official sources. On first glance, the large amount of space devoted to women (*guiyuan*, lit. beauties of the female living quarters) in the TSJC (376 *juan*) might seem encouraging. But in the main, the individuals discussed in this section of the encyclopedia are distinguished less by their personal accomplishments than by their exemplary Confucian virtues—notably female chastity. Of all the various subsections on women in the TSJC, by far the largest is "Widows Who Would Not Remarry" (*guijie*, 210 *juan*). By contrast, only seven *juan* are devoted to women writers (*guizao*), four to wise women (*guizhi*), and only one each to artistic women (*guiqiao*) and witty women (*guihui*).

According to the so-called cult of chastity in Qing China, Chinese women were expected not to remarry upon the death of their husbands, and they were often ritually rewarded if they committed suicide to join their husbands in the afterlife. They were also rewarded if they took their own lives to preserve their "reputation." During the Qianlong period in particular, the Qing government sought to encourage such forms of female chastity by issuing edicts, passing laws, and building monuments to heroines and martyrs. These efforts were part of a combined state-elite attempt to "tighten control in many areas of gender relations: more rigid rape laws, bans on pornography, legislative attacks on homosexuality, statutory support for patriarchal authority, the virtuous widow cult, and so on."[6] But were these attempts to link theory and practice successful? In some respects yes, and in others no. The variables included differences in class as well as differences in time periods, local mores, and the relative strength of families and lineages.

Overall, at least on my reading of the evidence, it appears that imperial policy and social pressures combined to create a situation that placed inordinate burdens on women for most of the Qing period. It has become unfashionable in scholarly circles to dwell on the difficulties that women faced in the late imperial era. In an insightful review article titled "Women in Late Imperial China" (1994), Paul Ropp noted that

> recent scholarship has moved increasingly away from the framework of asking whether "women's status" was rising or falling, and has begun instead to analyze the ambiguities and subtleties of the many ways that gender worked in Ming and Qing society. Recent scholarship has also begun to move away from "victimization" studies, and to emphasize instead that Chinese women's lives have been shaped by many factors, including their own active choices and participation in social, economic, and family life. Finally, many scholars have begun to question the assumption that dominated early twentieth-century analyses (and that still dominates some work in the People's Republic of China), namely that the suffering of women in Chinese society was primarily a function of conservative patriarchal Neo-Confucianism.[7]

More recent work on women in late imperial China by scholars such as Dorothy Ko, Susan Mann, and Harriet Zurndorfer—to name only three of many—also reflects this important scholarly trend.

It is clear, of course, that gender issues in traditional China cannot, or at least should not, be reduced to simple themes of subordination, oppression, and victimization. For example, foot binding was undeniably a painful and debilitating practice, yet it was also a distinctive Chinese marker of status, ethnicity, and personal pride.[8] It is also important to note that even in the Qing dynasty, a period known for the prevalence of "conservative" attitudes toward women, official policy varied over time, and the opinions of individuals—both women and men—varied even more (see below).

Still, it would be misleading in my view to suggest that women in Qing China, like women in most earlier periods (and in most other societies at almost any time), were not disadvantaged in certain significant ways. In fact, a careful reading of Ropp's review article reveals several of them. Women in Qing China generally had few property rights. Chinese men could divorce their wives for seven reasons, including loquaciousness; Chinese women could not divorce their husbands for any reason except severe physical mutilation or the husband's attempt to sell his wife into prostitution. Chastity was expected of women, not of men. Infanticide overwhelmingly involved baby girls, not baby boys. Traditional Chinese rituals underscored at every turn the subordination of women to men. Moreover, demeaning expressions about women could be found everywhere, from the Confucian classics and ritual handbooks to popular proverbs.

The *Classic of Poetry* notes, for example, that when a son is born, he is placed on a bed, clothed in robes, and given a jade scepter because he is destined to be the "lord of the household"; but when a girl is born, she is placed on the floor, wrapped in swaddling clothes, and given a loom weight made of clay, with the hope that she will "neither do wrong nor good, take care of food and drink, and cause no sorrow to her parents." The *Jinsi lu* cites Zhou Dunyi's remark, based on the Kui ("Contrariety" #38) and Jiaren ("Family" #37) hexagrams of the *Yijing*, that "If members of the family are separated, the cause surely lies with women." Popular proverbs from the Qing period include the following: "The absence of virtue in women is manifest in threes: egotism (*du*), envy (*du*) and maliciousness (*du*)"; "The humaneness of women is like a petty person's courage"; and "A woman's mouth is like a measure without limits; truth and lies issue from it [without discrimination]."[9]

Despite such negative stereotypes, there was no general agreement in Qing times about the place and purpose of women in Chinese society. Debates continued throughout the life of the dynasty, often in the context of a larger but closely connected question: the relationship between ancient "ritual teachings" (*lijiao*) and "current social practices" (*shisu*). The most visible participants in the gender debate, overwhelmingly male for most of the Qing era, cut across the intellectual spectrum of the day. They included "libertine aesthetes" like Yuan Mei, *kaozheng* philologists like Qian Daxin, orthodox Cheng-Zhu moralists like Zhang Xuecheng, and practical-minded Confucian activists like Chen Hongmou. Few of them held entirely consistent opinions. Yuan, for instance, argued for (and contributed to) the literary education of women, yet defended concubinage as a reflection of the inherent inferiority of females to males. Zhang believed that men and women had the same innate intellectual gifts (he castigated Yuan for treating women as sex objects), but insisted that literate women should remain at home and have no public voice. Even Chen, for all of his well-intentioned egalitarian impulses, openly defended the so-called female chastity cult as a "civilizing mechanism." But, as we shall see in chapter 11, the parameters of debate would change significantly in the late nineteenth century.

EARLY LIFECYCLE RITUAL

As a general rule, the higher the social class in China, the more rigid the adherence to ritual as a matter of both Confucian responsibility and public prestige. Another factor was financial: most elites had the advantage of indulging in costly ceremonies without undue financial hardship. An ancient Chinese proverb tells us: "Ritual and righteousness are born of adequate wealth." Another states: "When one is wealthy, one loves the rites." Nonetheless, a powerful and persistent feature of ritual life in traditional China was the effort on the part of all classes of society to put on the most impressive ceremonial displays possible, regardless of cost. One mid-nineteenth-century account of rural life in south China explains:

> Poverty and death are haunting spectres of the poor. They roam through the village and inspire fear that is not physical but social. It is not that the villager fears death; his belief in Fate relieves him of that worry. But to think of his parent drawing near to the time of departure without funds for proper rites and burial—this is a real fear. To fail in the provision of rites, feasts, coffin, and funeral would be conduct most unfilial and condemned by social opinion.[10]

Other works, both Western and Chinese, confirm this view. John L. Buck indicates that as late as 1930, nearly 80 percent of rural credit in some areas of China was used for non-economic purposes—primarily birth, marriage, funeral, and other ceremonies. Undoubtedly the costs were at least as high in Qing times, when, according to early Republican-era ceremonial handbooks, ritual requirements were even more rigid and elaborate.[11]

All aspects of Chinese family life were highly structured, at least in principle. Ritual handbooks, encyclopedias for daily use, "family instructions" (*jiaxun*), and other such sources offered meticulous guidance for proper behavior in every domestic situation. Husbands and wives were expected to live in harmony, without jealousy or rancor, and children were socialized at a very early age to be filial and obedient (see below). This was the theory, but what was the practice? Research by Jonathan Ocko, Janet Theiss, and others has shown that despite an "ideological" commitment to harmony at all levels of Chinese society, and notwithstanding a fundamental aversion to the court system on the part of most Chinese subjects, legal cases from the Qing period indicate a great deal of conflict within Chinese families. The quarrels that found their way to the magistrate's yamen generally involved parents and daughters-in-law and widowed or remarried mothers and their sons. Sexual misconduct, jealousy, problems with adopted children, and property disputes were major sources of family disharmony. Women were usually blamed for conflicts, but as Ocko notes, "the fault was not in the women per se, but rather the role assigned to them in Chinese society." The hierarchical nature of the Chinese family system, with its conflicting roles and responsibilities, "shaped the disharmony within it."[12]

In addition to handbooks, encyclopedias, and other forms of guidance, popular almanacs (*huangli, lishu, tongshu*, etc.) were considered essential to the conduct of daily affairs in Qing China. By virtue of their wide distribution and practical utility, almanacs were probably the most frequently used book of any kind in late imperial times. Virtually every household had one. In addition to providing basic calendrical information (like official state calendars), they supplied medical and agricultural advice, educational material for children (in the form of morality tales), and various charms and divination techniques. Virtually all sectors of society employed almanacs in some way, whether for protection against evil spirits, for ethical guidance, or for advice on propitious times to undertake various domestic ritual activities such as sacrifices, prayers, marriages, and funerals. Almanacs (again, like state calendars) even offered information on the best times to undertake such mundane activities as bathing, sewing, sweeping, meeting friends, taking medicine, embarking on journeys, doing business, and entering school.[13]

As indicated briefly in chapter 7, the divinatory systems of Chinese almanacs were based on a set of interrelated cosmic variables: *yinyang/wuxing* correlations, the twenty-four directions of the compass, the twenty-eight asterisms, and so forth. Individuals fit into the cosmic order according to their date of birth, which was always carefully recorded in the form of eight characters (*bazi*), two each for the year, month, day, and hour. In the popular mind—and among many members of the elite as well—birth in a certain year identified an individual with one of twelve symbolic animals associated with the system of "earthly branches." Each of these animals, in turn, was linked with certain character traits, the qualities of *yin* or *yang*, one of the five agents, and certain stars or constellations. Quite naturally, such natal information had to be taken into account by both fortune tellers and matchmakers.

The ceremonies connected with birth in traditional China varied tremendously, but a few common denominators may be identified. Because infant mortality was so high, measures had to be taken to protect newborn children through the use of charms, prayers, and offerings. Many Chinese believed that boy babies were the special prey of evil spirits, but that these spirits might be dissuaded if the child had an unattractive "milk name" (*naiming*). Sometimes the strategy was to give the boy a girl's name. In general, milk names were bestowed at feasts known as "full-month" (*manyue*) ceremonies, which marked the first month of life and underscored the uncertainty surrounding a child's early existence.[14]

Life was especially precarious for newborn girls because the practice of infanticide involved them primarily. A number of astute Western observers in the late Qing period considered infanticide to be no more common in China than in Europe, but other nineteenth-century accounts—both Western and Chinese—indicate that the outlawed practice was often quite widespread, especially in times of economic hardship. Listen to You Zhi, gentry organizer of an infant protection society in his home village near Wuxi, Jiangsu, during the mid-nineteenth century:

> [When] poor families have too many children, they are often forced by practical considerations to drown the newborn infants, a practice which has already become so widespread that no one thinks it unusual. . . . Not only are female

infants drowned, at times even males are; not only do the poor drown their children; even the well-to-do do it. People follow each other's example, and the custom becomes more widespread day by day. There is a case where one family drowned more than ten girls in a row; there are villages where scores of girls are drowned each year. We who dwell in the country witness the crime with our own eyes—a scene too brutal to be described.[15]

Girls were considered a poor social investment in traditional China because after years of nurture the majority of them would simply marry to become members of other households. Hard-pressed families might sell their female children into slavery or prostitution, but infants brought a low price, and many believed that it was better to destroy the child than to doom it to a life of poverty and shame. Hence such common euphemisms for infanticide as "giving [the child] away to be married" and "transmigrating [the soul of the child] to the body of someone else." Furthermore, the demands of Confucian filial piety were such that the death of a baby girl might be morally justifiable if the choice for the future was between providing for one's parents and providing for one's children. A famous story in Chinese popular lore explicitly condoned and rewarded the impulse of a man prepared to sacrifice his child for the sake of a parent (see below).

Filial piety had other dimensions and ramifications. While a girl child was essentially irrelevant to the question of patrilinear kinship, a boy was considered crucial for the continuation of the family line and the maintenance of ancestral sacrifices. Mencius had male children in mind when he remarked, "Of the three most unfilial things, the worst is to have no posterity." In the absence of heirs, matrilocal (uxorilocal) marriage was an option, though not a very attractive one (see below). The other possibility was adoption. As with marriage, intermediaries of various sorts facilitated the process.

Of the several forms of adoption, the most regular and esteemed was kin related. According to the Qing Code, an adopted heir to the family ancestral sacrifices had to have the same surname as the head of the household, and specific stipulations existed regarding preferential succession from various classes of nephews and grandnephews on the paternal side. In practice, however, individuals often purchased and adopted individuals outside their lineage, changing their surnames and acquiring heirs with comparatively few complications. This was particularly common in south China. The ceremony of adoption usually entailed a contract, a feast, and ancestral sacrifices in which the adopted son took part. Such ceremonies stood somewhere in significance between the rituals of birth and those of marriage.[16]

The stages of growth in traditional China were viewed in a variety of ways. As noted in chapter 6, Confucius placed special stress on the ages fifteen, thirty, forty, fifty, sixty, and seventy. The "Family Regulations" chapter of the *Record of Ritual* discusses child-rearing practices for young males, emphasizing the ages six, ten, and thirteen and then the adult years of twenty, thirty, forty, fifty, and seventy. Predictably, females are treated in a much more cursory way, with an emphasis placed on the ages ten, fifteen, and twenty. The subcategory on human affairs in the TSJC includes separate sections for every year of life from birth to age twenty and for each decade thereafter from the twenties, thirties, forties, and so on up to "one hundred and above." But perhaps the most common periodization in traditional times consisted of six major stages: (1) infancy, (2) the juvenile period, (3) young adulthood, (4) adulthood, (5) middle age, and (6) old age.[17]

A number of reference works in late imperial China, including popular encyclopedias such as the WBQS, gave advice to parents on "educating children within the womb" (*taijiao*). This was the pedagogical byproduct of a cosmologically based theory that the senses perceive external phenomena and then transmit them inside the body (*waixiang neigan*). Most editions of the WBQS that I have seen include illustrations of the growth of embryos/fetuses from month to month, providing information in both verse and prose intended to educate parents and to encourage prenatal care. Many almanacs did the same. There were also several widely distributed works on pediatric medicine, such as the *Yingtong baiwen* (One hundred questions on infants and children), the *Yingtong leicui* (Essentials in looking after infants and children), and the *Youyou jicheng* (Complete compendium on the care of children).[18]

Infancy generally lasted from birth to about three or four years old (four or five *sui* in Chinese reckoning), depending on the presence or absence of siblings and/or nursemaids. The first two years of life were a time of great indulgence; babies were fed whenever hungry, day or night, played with by the entire family, especially grandparents, and only gradually toilet trained and weaned. Elementary discipline began at about age three or four, with an effort to teach respect and obedience and a special emphasis on status distinctions and filial devotion. At this time children were exposed to songs and didactic stories, the content of which they would later memorize. The texts of these stories included the *Ershisi xiao* (Twenty-four examples of filial piety), the *Xiaojing* (Classic of filial piety), and the *Sanzi jing* (Three-character classic). Male children were the principal targets for these works, but, as with the Confucian *Analects* and several other foundational documents, there were similar versions of these tracts designed specifically for girls. Such young women also received counsel from Ban Zhao's time-honored *Nüjie* (Admonitions for women).[19]

The anecdotes in the *Twenty Four Examples of Filial Piety*, which commonly appeared in Qing almanacs, illustrate the extremes to which Chinese children were expected to go in the service of their parents. In addition to the story mentioned above, in which a man named Guo Ju demonstrates a willingness to kill his male child in order to have resources enough to feed his aged mother, we hear of a prince (later to become an emperor) who attended his ailing mother relentlessly, day and night, for three years, "during which time his eyelids did not close"; a man who, even at the age of seventy, dressed up and frolicked around like a child in order to amuse his parents; a man who decided to sell himself into slavery so that he might give his father a proper burial; a child who warmed the ice over a river with his own body in order to procure fresh fish for his stepmother; a young boy who invited mosquitoes to feed on his body so that they would not disturb his sleeping parents; and a woman who nourished her toothless mother-in-law with milk from her own breast. In some versions, a young man cuts flesh from his leg to use as medicine for his ailing father.[20] This last story explains the surprisingly common practice known as *gegu* (lit. "cutting the thigh [for one's parents]"), which was institutionally rewarded by the Qing state.[21]

In the *Nü ershisi xiao* (Women's twenty-four examples of filial piety), most of the stories revolve around similar themes of heroism and self-sacrifice. One of the stories, for example, involves a young girl who removes part of her liver to feed her ailing mother-in-law. Another features a woman who emulates Wang Xiang, the young man who warmed an ice-covered river with his body in order to procure fresh fish for his stepmother. Among the several stories in this collection emphasizing the heroism of women is the famous tale of Hua Mulan, who, despite her father's objections, dons men's clothing and takes his place in a twelve-year military campaign against the Turks. In battle, she distinguishes herself as a skilled and brave warrior, winning the admiration of the emperor and the eventual respect of her family.[22]

The *Classic of Filial Piety*, which, like the *Twenty-Four Examples* and other such works might be illustrated, focused for the most part on broad themes—filial piety as the principle of Heaven and Earth; as the "root of virtue and the wellspring of instruction"; as the way to govern all under Heaven; as the foundation of imperial rule; as a means of protecting the state and making the people harmonious; and as a way of honoring the ancestors and avoiding shame to "those who have given you birth." At the same time, however, it mandated particular forms of filial behavior, such as carrying out the proper mourning rituals and, significantly, taking care of one's body (on the grounds that it is the legacy of one's ancestors; see below). Patricia Ebrey offers a revealing side-by-side comparative translation of the "original" version of this work and an early version of the *Nü xiaojing* (Women's classic of filial piety).[23] The major difference between the two is the emphasis placed in the latter on the positive transformative effect women can have on the men in their lives.

The *Three-Character Classic*, rhymed in three-character phrases and designed for easy memorization, repeatedly emphasizes the value of education, the sacrifices necessary to be a successful student, and the terrible consequences of failure (for a translation, see appendix G). It also provides a wealth of information about fundamental cultural concerns, focusing in particular on time-honored numerical categories such as the Three Powers, the Three Bonds, the Four Seasons, the Four Books, the Five Classics, the Five Constant Virtues, the Five Agents, the Five Directions, the Six Grains, the Six Animals, the Seven Emotions, the Eight Musical Sounds, the Nine [Agnatic] Family Relationships, and the Ten Duties. In addition, this work introduces children to a chronological overview of Chinese history, highlighting heroes and villains and patterns of dynastic rise and fall. Most significantly, it identifies various paragons of learning, including two highly accomplished women—Cai Wenji from the Han dynasty and Xie Daoyun from the Eastern Jin (317–420). The text concerning these two women reads: "They were girls [but] they were also intelligent and perceptive (*congmin*). You boys ought to alert yourselves [to this sort of challenge]."

The discipline of Chinese children began in earnest during the juvenile period, which lasted from three or four to about fifteen or sixteen. This was a period of intense formal education for young men in elite households, and less formal instruction for young women. Generally speaking, where schooling was available for peasant children—for example in the so-called charitable schools (*yixue*) of the Ming-Qing period—the emphasis was not on mass literacy but rather on moral education. The same was true of efforts to educate non-Han ethnic groups in southwest China.[24]

Limin Bai's book *Shaping the Ideal Child: Children and Their Primers in Late Imperial China* (2005) places particular emphasis on the role of ritual in Chinese childhood education. In fact, she points out that the primary object of educators in the Ming and Qing periods was to "ritualize the body"—that is, to "control the external" and "nourish the internal." To this end, primers taught children how to hold their bodies, how to walk, how to bow, and how to fix their gaze and speak. They also provided advice on how to dress and even how to breathe. Classrooms were sometimes adorned with pictures that illustrated important rituals. In one school, for example, a series of pictures depicted the protocols for welcoming new babies into a home, the proper posture for youths, the way scholars greet one another, a wedding ceremony, sons serving parents, women serving parents-in-law, and ancestor worship.[25]

In elite households, all males received early training in the recitation of verse and the memorization of Chinese characters, followed by instruction in calligraphy and painting, and finally by schooling in the techniques of chess and the playing of musical instruments. Elite girls might also acquire these

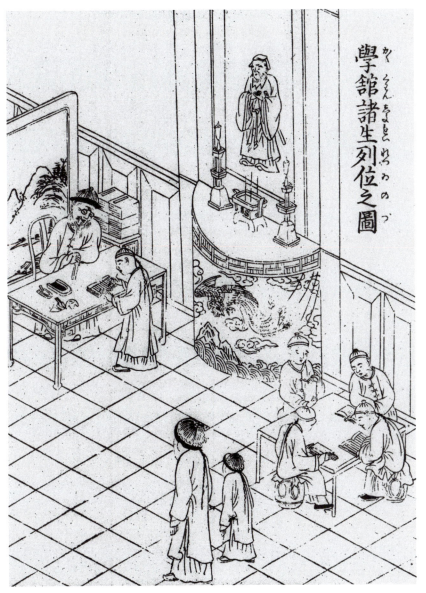

學館諸生列位之圖

Figure 10.1. Students at School
Source: Nakagawa 1799.

書生
禮拜之圖

Figure 10.2.   Student Bowing to the Sage
Here we see a student offering his devotions under the watchful eye of his tutor and another adult. Source: Nakagawa 1799.

skills, but they were usually expected to learn the "womanly" work of embroidery and weaving first.[26] Well-educated women often played a prominent part in the education of both sons and daughters, balancing their domestic chores and their own scholarly and artistic interests with their roles as teachers. Naturally this process was somewhat easier for women in households that could afford to hire servants and maids.

By the age of five or six, the binding of young girls' feet usually began in households that could afford the loss of labor in the fields. This crippling practice—which was far more widespread than generally recognized—brought both status and suffering to Chinese women. Sexual segregation also began at this time, and although never complete, the cultural ideal in China remained the isolation of women in the inner apartments. Young men, for their part, began to experience the disciplinary tyranny of their fathers who, in order to abide by explicit Confucian admonitions in the *Analects* to remain "distant" and "severe," became increasingly aloof and often harsh as they trained their sons in family ritual roles and proper social conduct. By contrast, the relationship between mothers and their daughters (and often their sons as well) was warm and close.[27]

Parental power was nearly absolute in traditional China, depicted graphically in literature by the treatment of Jia Baoyu at the hands of his father in *Dream of the Red Chamber*. In fact, unfilial behavior was a capital crime—one of the "Ten Great Wrongs" in the Qing Code (see chapter 3 and below).[28] At an early age, therefore, Chinese children learned total submission to parents, grandparents, teachers, masters of trades, and other authority figures. This produced what has been described as a strong "dependency orientation" in youths of both sexes.[29] In peasant households, however, there was sometimes greater equality between parents and children (and between males and females) because all members of the family lived in close quarters and worked together in the fields as a single cooperative economic unit.

The stage of development known as young adulthood was by and large an elite phenomenon. It was a time of transition that occurred during the teenage years but before marriage. By the mid-teens, the worst of parental discipline and educational rigor had passed. Chinese males began to experience considerable freedom and to have their first sexual contacts with prostitutes or servant girls. Their sisters, however, remained confined within the home and bound by a double standard of rigid chastity. In some families, the rituals of capping males and binding up the hair of females marked the formal transition to adulthood, but for the most part these ceremonies, if they took place at all, were associated in late imperial times with marriage, which normally occurred from about eighteen to twenty-one years of age in the case of boys and from sixteen to eighteen with girls.

MARRIAGE AND BEYOND

The formal ceremonies of marriage brought adulthood regardless of age. Marriage was expected of every normal man and woman in Chinese society, including slaves. Indeed, the Qing Code stipulated that slave owners were subject to criminal punishment if they neglected to find husbands for their female slaves. The purpose of marriage was explicitly to continue the male line of descent. In the words of the *Record of Ritual*: "The rites of marriage unite two [different] surnames in love, in order to maintain services in the ancestral temple and to ensure the continuation of the family line."[30] Marriage was thus primarily an alliance between two different families, not a matter of individual choice and mutual affection. By law, two people of the same surname could not be married, even if unrelated, and the legal principals in the match were the heads of the respective households, not the individuals to be joined in wedlock. In some cases, the wishes of the prospective bride and groom might be taken into account, but very often the choice of a marriage partner by parents or elders was arbitrary and unilateral. Baoyu's arranged marriage to Xue Baochai rather than to Lin Daiyu in the novel *Dream of the Red Chamber* provides a fine literary example of how family interests could, and often did, override personal feelings.

Marriage was always a contractual affair in Qing China—by far the most important contractual relationship in traditional times. Marriage contracts might be oral or written, general or detailed, but elaborate rituals that enhanced them, gave them public visibility, and symbolized their social and cosmological significance surrounded them all. Contracts were also associated with divorce and adoption procedures. As a rule, the smaller the economic or ritual investment in such contracts, the greater the likelihood that they would be breached.

Several different forms of marriage existed in traditional China, each a product of different social or economic circumstances. The most prestigious was the standard, or major, marriage. It involved the transfer of an "adult" bride from her natal home and her ritual rebirth in the home of her husband. This form of marriage, to be discussed in some detail below, was considered the norm, the social standard. Minor marriages followed the basic ritual pattern of major marriages, except that the bride lived in the home of her prospective husband for ten or fifteen years as a "daughter-in-law reared from childhood" (*tongyang xi* or *miaoxi*) before the actual marriage date. This arrangement was particularly common among the poor in China, but by no means limited to them. Another less common and less esteemed variety of marriage was uxorilocal (matrilocal), involving the transfer of a male into the household of a female as a son-in-law, reversing the pattern of major and minor marriages. The males involved in such matches usually came from families with several sons and entered families in which there were none. The period of residence in the bride's home was variable, from a few years to a lifetime, always carefully spelled out by contract.[31]

The distribution of major, minor, and matrilocal marriages throughout China hinged on several factors: family status, wealth, social organization (especially lineage ties), and geography. Major marriages dominated the social landscape of north China, but in many southern areas the alternative forms predominated. Arthur Wolf and Chieh-shan Huang write:

> Viewing China's marriage and adoption customs as from an earth satellite, we would probably see that minor marriages were concentrated in a continuous area along the South China coast, reaching their highest density in southern Jiangxi southwestern Fujian, and northern Guangdong. Uxorilocal marriages would probably appear common in the same region but would achieve their highest density on the Lower Yangzi Delta and in a second area of concentration on China's Western frontier. But as soon as we moved closer to our subject, we would soon discover that this view from on high concealed a great deal of local variation, variation even more marked than that between the country's major regions.[32]

A distinctive feature of family life in traditional China was the institution of concubinage. Theoretically, this ancient practice was justified by the filial imperative of producing sons to continue the male line. Often concubines (*qie*) were purchased outright from poor families by the more well-to-do, and ordinarily they did not enjoy the same status as the principal wife (*qi*).[33] As a matter of fact, on entering her new family, a concubine usually had to participate in ceremonies designed to show her subservience to the principal wife. Qing law prohibited the degradation of a principal wife to the position of concubine or the elevation of a concubine to the position of principal wife. As further testimony to her inferiority, a concubine was required to observe the same degree of mourning for her master's wife as she was for his parents, his sons (by the principal wife or other concubines), and her own sons. Her sons were expected to treat the principal wife as their own mother, and by custom they were entitled to equal rights of inheritance along with the sons of the wife. Paternity was what mattered in Chinese marriages, and in divorce, the husband almost always received custody of the children.[34]

The practices of concubinage and infanticide, together with the strong social pressure on widows not to remarry as a matter of Confucian propriety, created a large pool of surplus men looking for wives—a situation that matrilocal marriage helped to reduce only in part. From 10 to 20 percent of Chinese men in Qing times probably never married.[35] This was one reason why a major marriage carried with it so much prestige and required so much public display. Although the specific customs surrounding major marriages often differed from place to place, certain practices were nearly universal, at least among elites.[36]

One prominent feature in virtually all Chinese marriages—major, minor, and matrilocal alike—was the employment of a go-between, or matchmaker. Intermediaries of this sort were essential to a great many aspects of Chinese social life, especially those involving delicate matters of prestige or "face." The responsibilities of the matchmaker were extremely weighty. He or she had to take into account not only the relative social positions of the two families involved, but also certain important economic and personal factors such as family wealth and individual character. Ideally, the match was expected to benefit both parties, which generally meant that the families had to be of approximately equal status and means, or that one family might contribute greater status while the other contributed greater wealth. Some Qing officials, notably Chen Hongmou, deplored "viewing women as commodities" (*shi wei qihuo*) in this way, but financial considerations almost always loomed large in marriage calculations.[37]

All stages of marriage ritual were full of elaborate symbolism, either positive or protective. Red—the color of happiness and good fortune—was prominent in dress and decorations, including candles and lanterns, which were used even in the daytime.[38] Firecrackers served as purifiers and signs of joy, and charms were often employed to provide additional protection for the bride. Food played an important role at various stages of the marriage ritual (as it did in most other aspects of Chinese ritual life) in the form of symbolic gifts, offerings, and ceremonial meals. "Longevity noodles," fruits, and other food items denoted marital harmony, happiness, and prosperity. Presents such as paired geese symbolized marital fidelity, and felicitous inscriptions of various sorts appeared everywhere.

The first of the standard six rites of marriage (*liuli*) was the selection of the match (*nacai*), engineered by the go-between after consultation with the families involved. In this and most other matters, the family of the groom normally took the initiative on advice from the matchmaker. After making discreet investigations and compiling preliminary information on all marriageable males and females in a given locality, the matchmaker was in a position to propose a partnership, usually to the male's family. The matchmaker was also responsible for negotiating matters such as the amount of the betrothal gifts (*pinli*) and betrothal money (*pinjin*) to be given by the groom's family to the wife's. The family of the bride, for its part, had to decide on the proper dowry and trousseau (*jiazhuang*) to send along at the time of transfer for exhibition at the groom's home. All these calculations were of tremendous importance to the prestige and material interests of each of the families concerned.

The next step was the formal exchange of astrological information on the bride and groom (*wenming*). The third stage, called *naji*, required the ritual test of the match by means of divination. Fortune tellers were usually employed, but the ancestors and other spirits might also be consulted by means of devices such as "moonblocks" (*beijiao* or *jiaobei*). The fourth and crucial step was the betrothal (*nazheng*), for acceptance of the betrothal gifts (often termed the "bride price") by the family of the bride sealed the match. As with the previous stage, elaborate ceremonies accompanied the transfer of gifts, which were dictated by rank at the higher levels of society. Again, ancestral sacrifices usually accompanied these ceremonies.

The fifth stage, *qingji*, involved the selection of propitious times for the transfer of the bride and related ritual activities. Here, decisions might rest with fortune tellers or other sources of supernatural authority, including temple oracles. Almanacs also provided guidance on the proper times to undertake various marriage-related rituals. The transfer itself, known as "welcoming the bride" (*qinying*), was the final stage of the formal marriage process. On the day preceding this ceremony, the groom was supposed to be "capped" and given an adult name, and the bride's hair was put up in ritual fashion. Meanwhile, the groom's family had arranged to send the brightly decorated wedding chair to the wife's home, and the wife's family had her trousseau sent to his.

On the day of the transfer, the bride paid solemn obeisance to her parents and ancestors, received a brief lecture on her wifely duties, and entered the gaudy red sedan chair that would take her on a noisy, ostentatious, and circuitous journey to her husband's home. There, the bride performed various acts designed to show subservience to her husband and his family, and for the first time, perhaps—at least in most elite matches—the bride and groom actually saw each other's faces. After these ceremonies, the bridal pair reverently worshipped tablets representing Heaven and Earth, the ancestors of the groom, and the major household deities of the groom's family, especially the God of the Hearth. These activities highlighted the cosmological and familial dimensions of the match.

The transfer was, of course, marked by a banquet, which, like the wedding procession and display of dowry and trousseau, might well be a measure of a family's financial status. Often, however, the guests contributed shares (*fenzi*) to help defray costs. Local custom dictated whether or not the bride's family would be invited to the transfer feast, but at some point in almost all major marriages the bride's parents were treated to a banquet and given additional gifts.

When the bride visited her parents after the formal transfer, she generally did so as a guest, not as kin. Although still emotionally tied to her parents and

親
迎

花
轎

Figure 10.3.   Wedding Procession
This picture, only half of a two-part scene, shows the stage of wedding ritual known as "welcoming the bride" (*qinying*). She is transported in a sedan chair with her trousseau (*jiazhuang*) behind her. In the case of a large trousseau, the items would be transported independently. *Source:* Nakagawa 1799.

Figure 10.4. Wedding Guests Listening to Music

This picture—again, only half of a two-part scene—is one of a series showing the various elements of an elite-style wedding banquet. Here the major inscription notes that the guests are enjoying the musical entertainment. Among the several other interesting illustrations in this series we see depictions of the husband and wife worshipping Heaven and Earth and a group of men preparing for the ritual of teasing the bride and groom after the wedding transfer (*nao xinfang*). *Source:* Nakagawa 1799.

relatives, she was now by law and custom a full-fledged member of her husband's family and bound to devote far more ritual attention to that family than to her natal family.[39] It was a difficult existence, especially at first. Except in the case of minor or matrilocal marriages, the new bride found herself in a house full of virtual strangers. In this environment, the mother-in-law wielded tremendous power over her daughter-in-law because a filial son was bound to respect his mother's wishes. Mothers were sometimes known to force sons to divorce their wives. Small wonder, then, that in the period preceding the marriage transfer, brides sometimes wept and sang sad songs together with their friends and family.[40]

There were seven grounds for divorce in traditional China: (1) lack of offspring, (2) adultery, (3) jealousy, (4) thievery, (5) disobedience to the husband's parents, (6) incurable disease, and (7) being too talkative. In principle, a husband could not be divorced by his wife, but this was not the main reason that divorce was comparatively rare in Qing times. In the first place, there were three circumstances under which a woman could not be divorced (except in the case of adultery): (1) if she had mourned as a daughter for her husband's deceased parents, (2) if she had no family to go to, or (3) if her husband had been poor when they were married and was now rich. Often one or more of these conditions prevailed. In addition, the perennial glut of men looking for wives made the task of acquiring another virgin bride rather difficult, especially if the grounds for an earlier divorce were not very substantial. Furthermore, at least to a degree, her biological parents and former kinsmen protected the interests of the wife because marriage was a family affair. Nonetheless, we know that many women found married life intolerable and either ran away or committed suicide. Others made a conscious choice never to marry.[41]

Aside from the domination of mothers-in-law, another common frustration for Chinese wives, at least in elite families, was the introduction of concubines. Unlike principal spouses, concubines were usually chosen by the husband rather than his parents, and often they were selected for their beauty or their artistic, literary, and musical talents rather than their moral character and/or family connections. Although ostensibly brought into the household for the purpose of producing sons to assure continuation of the line, concubines often served as little more than symbols of elite conspicuous consumption. Despite their social inferiority to the principal wife, they were often the primary object of the husband's sexual attention and thus a potential source of jealousy—one of the seven grounds for divorce.

We should not assume, however, that arranged marriages were devoid of romance. There is abundant evidence to indicate that in the Qing, as in earlier periods of Chinese history, companionate love often grew out of arranged marriages. We even know of instances when husbands refused to remarry or committed suicide upon the death of their wives.[42] Such actions on the part of women appear somewhat more problematical, however. As already indicated, devotion to one's husband after his death was not only encouraged by neo-Confucianism, but also ritually rewarded by the state. Thus, powerful social pressures that had nothing to do with conjugal love or mutual affection might influence a wife's decision to "honor" her husband's memory.

On the other hand, there was great countervailing pressure on widows to remarry. For all the orthodox emphasis on women remaining "faithful" to their deceased husbands, many families did not want to provide financial support for the women who returned to them. Some, in effect, callously auctioned their youthful widowed daughters off to the highest bidder. In poor families, the economics of survival, coupled with high mortality rates, often made remarriage a necessity. A good deal of demographic data indicates that many women who were widowed before the age of thirty did, in fact, remarry, and that "chaste wives" (*jiefu*), widowed early in life and honored with plaques, arches, and official biographies, "were clearly a small minority of all widowed women."[43]

Chinese sexual life is seldom discussed but certainly important to an understanding of traditional Chinese culture, including marriage.[44] The pioneering research of R. H. Van Gulik indicates that the Chinese have long had a remarkably "healthy" attitude toward sex. Despite the rigid standards of Confucian propriety—which went so far as to condemn a husband and wife for accidentally touching hands in public (and which naturally eliminated the possibility of a Chinese tradition of social dancing on the part of couples)—Van Gulik argues that on the whole, sexual life in traditional China was full, rich, and remarkably free from the prejudices and "perversions" of the West.[45] At the same time, however, "illicit sex," variously defined by the Qing authorities, was vigorously condemned by intellectuals and the state as a threat to Confucian family values and therefore a mortal danger to China's family-centered social and political order.[46]

The Chinese drew a sharp distinction between inner (*nei*) and outer (*wai*), between what was public and what was private. In public, men were unquestionably superior to their wives, who were expected to be passive, submissive, and satisfied with few rights and privileges. In the privacy of the bedchamber, however, women often seem to have enjoyed relative sexual equality. One of the female characters in Li Yu's popular novel *Carnal Prayer Mat* articulates the idea of a woman's "sexual rights" within the framework of orthodox Confucian values (and Buddhist concepts of reincarnation):

We behaved improperly in our previous existence and now, having been born female, we must spend all our lives in the women's quarters. Unlike men, we can't go out sightseeing or visiting friends. Sex is the one diversion we have in our lives. Surely we can't be forbidden to enjoy that! Still, we are created by Heaven and Earth for marriage, and matched with a husband by our parents; naturally it is right and proper for us to enjoy ourselves with him. . . . [If] a woman does not have sex, fine, but if she is going to have sex, she should at least see that she suits herself.[47]

Detailed handbooks on sex (*fangshu*), dating from at least the Han dynasty, demonstrate a longstanding concern on the part of Chinese men with techniques explicitly designed to satisfy the sexual needs of women. Chinese erotic novels do the same. Even the popular medical tracts of late imperial times seem to have encouraged the sexual satisfaction of women—at least insofar as the aim of intercourse was to produce male children. Some of these works, for instance, emphasize that female orgasm is essential to fertility, and that the party who has an organism last determines the gender of a child. Although men may simply have had their own reproductive or medical interests in mind, some of their beliefs seem to have worked to the sexual advantage of women.[48]

As is well known (although often overemphasized), the bound foot was an object of erotic appeal for many men in traditional China, and even women took pride in their so-called golden lilies. Historically, foot binding began in the Tang-Song period, an ironic outgrowth of the practice of wrapping the feet of dancers with colorful ribbons. During the Yuan dynasty it gradually spread from north China to the south, where it took hold primarily among the upper classes. By Qing times, the crippling practice had become widespread not only among the Chinese gentry class, but also among commoners, who sought the social status that foot binding implied. As we have seen, even the Manchus succumbed in a sense to the fashion by wearing small attachments on the bottoms of their shoes to give the appearance and gait of bound feet. Although foot binding was a painful process, its appeal was neither sadistic nor masochistic. Instead, it was justified by men as a means of keeping women at home and was admired by them for the style of walking it produced and the alleged effect this gait had on female sexual performance. Many passages in Chinese erotic literature dwell on the shape and mystery of the bound foot.[49]

Beyond the psychology of sexual attraction was the idea of sex as a form of physical therapy. This notion can be traced back for centuries in China. The principles were essentially the same as those of Daoist alchemy and traditional Chinese medicine. Harmony between interacting *yin* (female) and *yang* (male) influences brought physical well-being and longevity. Normally, the two essences nourished one another other, except in the case of male intercourse with an older woman, which was commonly thought to take away *yang* essence without benefit to the man. Undoubtedly this was one reason for the traditional preference among Chinese men for youthful wives and concubines. Homosexuality was frowned upon by the state—particularly in Qing times when it was actually outlawed—but often tolerated, perhaps in part because of the medical/sexual assumption that the exchange of the same "essence" entailed no net loss.[50]

The Chinese preoccupation with good health and longevity can be seen not only in sexual practices and related therapeutic techniques (including Daoist "inner alchemy"), but also in medical tracts, encyclopedias, almanacs, popular proverbs, religious practices, and secular symbolism. As one striking indication of this interest, the section on medicine in the TSJC contains 520 *juan*—more than any other single section in this massive work. Popular encyclopedias such as the WBQS also devote a great amount of attention to matters of health and well-being under categories such as "nourishing life" (*yangsheng*), "medicine" (*yixue*), "managing illness" (*fabing*), and "dispelling illness" (*qubing*) (see appendix E).

During the last two decades or so there has been a burst of excellent scholarship on Chinese medical theories and practices, which has both enriched and complicated our understanding of medicine in late imperial China. One productive area of research has focused on women—from the work of female doctors (some scholars prefer the term "medical practitioners" for both men and women) and conceptions of the female body to specific health-related issues such as gynecology, birth control, childbirth, breast maladies (although men also had such problems), and even what came to be described as female "sexual madness." Another emphasis in recent research has been on doctors and learning traditions, including the practice of monastic medicine. Yet a third area of intense scholarly interest has been the evaluation of medical texts, from "classic" works such as the *Shanghan lun* (Treatise on cold damage disorders) and the *Huangdi neijing suwen* (Basic questions on the Yellow Emperor's *Inner Canon* [*of Medicine*]) to the great Qing compilation known as the *Yuzuan yizong jinjian* (Imperially sponsored golden mirror of medical orthodoxy).[51]

The *Yuzuan yizong jinjian* is a particularly revealing object of study because it represents an effort on the part of the Qing Imperial Medical Bureau to assert a unified "orthodox" tradition of Chinese medicine against an eighteenth-century challenge from medical practitioners living in the Jiangnan region. The basic struggle was between two different etiological theories—a monolithic "orthodox" one that had prevailed in China from the Han dynasty through the Ming, emphasizing "harm from the cold" (*shanghan*), and another "revived" theory that emphasized "harm from the heat" (*wenbing*). Despite a growth of interest in the latter theory during the nineteenth century, abbreviated versions of the *Yuzuan yizong jinjian* circulated widely among the Chinese population.[52]

Many different clinical approaches were available to doctors in late imperial China. Some practitioners favored preventive techniques associated with "nourishing life"; others favored herbal medicines; still others preferred techniques such as acupuncture, acupressure, and moxibustion; and some relied on religious traditions of shamanism, magic, and exorcism.[53] But most conventional medical remedies had as their primary therapeutic goal the restoration of *yinyang*/five agents balance in the body. As one version of the *Huangdi neijing suwen* states, *yin* and *yang* and the five agents "are the way of Heaven and Earth, the parents of change, the origin of life and death and the abode of the spiritual and the bright."[54]

Naturally there were professional rivalries—for example, competition between so-called Confucian doctors (*Ruyi*), who tended to emphasize textual traditions in their practice, and hereditary doctors (*shiyi*), who were more inclined to emphasize their own medical lineages. The Qing period boasted a number of famous and able medical practitioners, including such well-known individuals as Ye Gui (1666–1745) and Xu Dachun (1693–1771).[55] But we should remember that the vast majority of individuals who practiced the medical arts in China were low-status individuals, "artisans" who were viewed by Chinese society as mere technicians. To the degree that they were well educated, they might enjoy considerable status, but their occupation itself was not socially esteemed.

In this respect, doctors were like fortune tellers. In fact, there were many similarities between the two professions. A comparison of Florence Bretelle-Establet's study of the biographies of more than four hundred medical practitioners in the Qing dynasty with my own research on approximately 1,200 diviners during the same period reveals that the two groups were represented in much the same way by the compilers of local gazetteers.[56] Moreover, at least 15 percent of the biographies I have examined for the Qing period refer to individuals who knew both medicine and divination (*yibu*). A Qianlong period gazetteer from Shandong explicitly links medicine and divination as arts of prognostication that "understand *yin* and *yang*, investigate *li* and *qi*, know the way of transformation [*bianhua*] and have efficacy in everyday affairs."[57] Doctors and fortune tellers embraced the same cosmological principles and used several of the same evaluative techniques with their clients.

Yet for all this concern with health and medicine, average life expectancy in Qing China was probably not much more than thirty-five. Mark Elvin provides the following estimates based on data from the Lower Yangzi valley during the mid-Qing period. Note that these estimates are not broken down by social class and that they apply to the most prosperous region in China, at the height of the dynasty.

Female expectancy of life at birth: 27.2 years
Female expectancy of life at age ten: 41.1 years
Male expectancy of life at birth: 28.4 years
Male expectancy of life at age ten: 42.2 years.[58]

Small wonder, then, that the last two stages of Chinese life—middle age and old age—were times of special significance and cause for great celebration.

For most members of the Chinese elite, middle age, lasting from about forty to fifty-five, brought many satisfactions: career success, material security, and grandchildren. By the end of this period, the majority of wives had escaped domination by their mothers-in-law, only to become in some cases domineering mothers-in-law themselves. Middle age for the lower classes of Chinese society may have been somewhat less satisfying than for the elite, but a bit of property and a male heir probably provided a sufficient sense of accomplishment and security for aging commoners.

Old age elicited respect and esteem from all sectors of Chinese society. Village elders in rural areas often wielded substantial power, and, as mentioned in chapter 4, some were officially recognized as longevous commoners or longevous officials. The state-sponsored community drinking ritual known as *xiangyin jiu*, although not always regularly or properly performed, also provided a means of officially acknowledging and rewarding old age. According to statute, this ritual was supposed to be performed twice a year in various counties and departments of each province. At a particular point in the proceedings, a local scholar would state: "The object of *xiangyin jiu* is to show proper respect for the aged and consideration for the virtuous, and to keep away the unrighteous and the perverse. Persons of advanced age and outstanding virtue are to occupy seats of honor, and others are to have places proper to their ages." Although this ceremony did not always appeal to the local scholarly elite, it was certainly tempting to "obscure townsmen and villagers who aspired to local eminence."[59]

At home, the elderly were pampered and accorded maximum deference. As *Dream of the Red Chamber* indicates, older women often enjoyed substantial power within the family, despite the pervasive notion of the "three types of womanly obedience" (*sancong*)—first to the father, then to the husband, and eventually to the son. Major birthday celebrations for men and women usually began at about age fifty or so. From this point onward, such celebrations increased in size and significance, especially at the beginning of each new decade. The sixtieth birthday held special meaning because it marked the completion of one full sexegenary cycle (see chapter 6). Naturally enough, the concrete symbolism of birthday ceremonies centered on longevity: longevity candles, the longevity star, longevity noodles, longevity peaches or peach cakes, and the stylized character *shou* (longevity). Ancestral sacrifices were often closely associated with such birthday celebrations.

Longevity was also a prominent theme in funeral ceremonies. Grave clothes were designated longevity clothes, the coffin was composed of longevity boards, and the principal mourner ate longevity noodles. A "longevity portrait" of the deceased might also be displayed near the coffin, serving as an object of worship. As with the use of the auspicious color red in funerals for all that was not white (the color of mourning), the self-conscious employment of the term longevity in the midst of death underscores the themes of "fear-propitiation and hope supplication" that ran through so much of traditional Chinese religious life.[60]

Looking back on these Chinese lifecycle rituals, we see a striking cohesiveness and continuity. Patricia Ebrey's study of family ritual notes, for example, that by the end of the imperial period, ceremonial practices

> across the country bore many general resemblances to the steps described in Confucian texts. Ancestral rites included periodic offerings of food and drink at domestic altars . . . and on death-day anniversaries and major festivals. Continuities in wedding ceremonies included negotiations by matchmakers, exchanges of gifts, the highly ceremonial transfer of the bride to her husband's homes where the new couple consumed wine and food together and the bride was introduced to her husband's parents, relatives, and ancestors. For funerals and burials, major continuities included ritualized wailing, mourning garments that visibly indicated the proximity of kinship to the deceased, setting food and drink near the coffin until burial, postponing burial days, weeks or months to prolong mourning, restrictions on social activities during deepest mourning, use of heavy coffins, ceremonial funeral processions to the graveyard, and post burial sacrifices to the deceased.[61]

According to Ebrey, the narrowing of class distinctions in these ritual performances was "a significant factor in creating cultural cohesion within the enormous expanse of China." It allowed people who "spoke mutually unintelligible dialects and knew very little of each other's daily work lives to see each other as Han Chinese." Throughout the imperial era, then, the performance of lifecycle rituals was a marker not only of family solidarity, but also of ethnic boundaries. As Ebrey puts the matter, "Every time a family hired a sedan chair for a wedding or paraded to the grave in mourning garments, it was acting out of allegiance to both Han Chinese identity and the Confucian moral order."[62]

AMUSEMENTS

Notwithstanding the relentless demands of ritual at all levels of Qing society, there was also time for recreation, ranging from simple domestic games to huge community festivals. Despite the endless variety of Chinese amusements, certain patterns of play seem typical of late imperial China as a whole. Many of these reflect elite values and preoccupations. The general lack of physically demanding sports, for instance, can be attributed both to a concern for maintaining proper decorum and to a real fear of harming the body—an unfilial act, for the physical self was a gift of the ancestors. Far better were games and other diversions that suggested scholarly refinement. Encyclopedias for daily use such as the WBQS provide an especially valuable indication of the leisure activities of Chinese elites, presented in the form of guidelines for people who aspired to be just like them (see appendix E).[63]

On the other hand, the attractiveness of active public exhibitions of acrobatics and martial arts (*wushu*), like the tradition of Chinese knight-errant literature, may be explained as a form of vicarious release in what was predominantly—for the Han people outside the Banners at least—a civil-oriented, "non-military culture" (*wubing di wenhua*). To be sure, even within the gentry class there were some individuals who gravitated to various types of "boxing" as a means of cultivating their "vital force" (*qi*). The category of Military Preparedness (*Wubei men*) in encyclopedias such as the WBQS includes information of precisely this sort. Like the graceful and therapeutic posturing known as *Taiji quan*, these more vigorous martial arts were predicated on the principle of *yinyang* harmonization of body and mind. But the people who displayed their strength and swordsmanship in public places were almost invariably of low social status, more likely to be linked with secret societies than with the literati.[64]

Perhaps the traditional Chinese preference for individual competition over team games reflects a form of recreational escape from the constraints of conventional society, since so much of Chinese social life demanded subordination of the self to the larger group and placed no real premium on individualism. The popularity of raucous festivals and risqué dramatic performances, as well as the widespread practice of teasing the bride and groom after the wedding transfer (*nao xinfang*), also suggests the periodic need to break loose, even if only temporarily, from the rigid constraints of Confucian propriety and social control.

Aside from a general reluctance to engage in roughhouse and team play, there is little remarkable about most traditional Chinese games. Chinese youths ran; skipped; threw rocks; pitched coins; played with balls, shuttlecocks, tops, dolls, and other toys; kept pets (fish, birds, rabbits, kittens, etc.);

and so forth. Older children and adults enjoyed watching activities such as rooster or cricket fights. Gambling of all kinds—from cards and dice to mahjong (*majiang*)—was popular, although often outlawed. More refined pastimes, all nature oriented, included the enjoyment of gardens, leisurely strolls (often with a caged bird), boating, swinging, and flying kites.⁶⁵ Recreational activities for women were restricted somewhat by social isolation and the practice of foot binding, but, as we have seen, in many gentry households the women received a satisfying education in poetry and the arts. In these households, as *Dream of the Red Chamber* indicates, much leisure time was spent on refinements such as the so-called Four Noble Recreations—calligraphy, painting, playing the *qin*, and playing *weiqi*.

Because painting and calligraphy have already been discussed at length in chapter 8, only the latter two recreations need be mentioned here. The *qin* or *guqin* (often translated "zither") had a long and distinguished pedigree in China. For over two thousand years it stood as the most revered Chinese musical instrument, celebrated in verse, art, and popular literature, and inextricably linked with both friendship and moral cultivation. The term *qin* came to be associated etymologically with the similar-sounding word *jin* (to prohibit) because the instrument was believed to check evil passions; and it also served as a general metaphor for marital happiness and social harmony. The rounded top and flat bottom of the *qin* symbolized the unity of Heaven and Earth, and its melodies, which pleased the ear and soothed the mind, were often descriptive of nature.⁶⁶

Originally composed of five strings (according to tradition) and later seven, the *qin* illustrates the tremendous value attached to rhythm in classical Chinese music, as well as the versatility of its five tone core (*wusheng*). The *qin* was, however, only one of a great many sophisticated musical instruments employed for ritual or recreational purposes in traditional China. S. W. Williams, a perceptive long-time resident of the "Middle Kingdom," observed in the nineteenth century that no people on earth made more use of music than the Chinese.⁶⁷

Weiqi, known as *go* in Japanese, was (and is) a popular game played on a board with nineteen vertical and nineteen horizontal lines intersecting to form 361 tactical positions. It remained a favorite pastime of Chinese generals, statesmen, and literati from early Han times through the Qing. Each player had about 180 men or pieces. The object of the game was to control territory and capture, or "kill," enemy men. At first glance one might wonder why *weiqi* was included as one of the Four Noble Recreations of a Confucian gentleman. Painting, calligraphy, and music were, after all, aesthetically satisfying and morally uplifting, while *weiqi* was war on a game board, attack and defense, killing and capture.

Perhaps the appeal of *weiqi* can be explained in part by the Confucian scholar's yearning for identification with ancient China's martial heritage and with the lost tradition of the feudal knight. But another explanation can be found in the structure and assumptions of the game itself. In the first place, like the Chinese scholar, the game of *weiqi* valued both intellect and intuition. Second, in *weiqi*, victory and defeat were relative, not absolute. "Victory" was based on the number of intersections dominated at the end of the game, but "defeat" was never total; a player could always save face. Furthermore, the style of play involved dispersed, yet related, non-geometric configurations rather than a single decisive tactical engagement. This emphasis on a total pattern of seemingly aimless interrelationships has been described as an "efficient, almost aesthetic, balance of forces."[68] As a creative form of competition, *weiqi* held much the same artistic attraction as a landscape painting, garden, poem, musical composition, or even a good novel.

Other board games were also popular in Qing times. One of these, *xiangqi* ("elephant chess"), resembled Western chess in its basic structure. Reputedly invented by King Wu of the Zhou, *xiangqi* had enduring appeal to scholars and commoners alike in China. Qing editions of the WBQS regularly include instructions on playing *xiangqi*, just as they do for playing *weiqi* and the *qin* (see appendix E). Another game, *shengguan tu* (lit. "advancing in official-dom") enjoyed less popularity, but it is somewhat more revealing from a cultural standpoint. Leo Stover has perceptively contrasted it with the famous Parker Brothers game *Monopoly*, observing that the point of the latter is the control of property and services to gain wealth, while the object of the former is to acquire rank and prestige in order to achieve financial advantage.[69] The game "board" (usually a paper chart) approximates the opportunity structure of the Qing bureaucratic hierarchy. It has dozens of separate compartments (from 63 to 117) for positions ranging from lowly student to grand councilor. The higher a player climbs on the official ladder (by throws of six dice), the more money can be collected from those below him. In Qing times, and probably well before, this was a gambling game, and apparently the great Qing scholar Ji Yun (1724–1805) was deeply addicted to it.

Social intercourse in Qing China was almost invariably a status game, played out at all levels of society. In elite circles, extraordinary attention was paid to matters of dress, salutation, demeanor, conversation, written communications (including invitations and responses), the giving of gifts, seating arrangements, food, and so forth. Novels such as *Dream of the Red Chamber* and *Flowers in the Mirror* devote an enormous amount of space to discussions of ritually correct behavior, prompting Mark Elvin to observe, "it is close to impossible for a reader who has not spent years of self-induction into pre-modern ways of [Chinese] thought to share . . . [a concern] for the almost countless specific details [of ritual and ceremony in works of this sort]."[70] The vocabulary of Chinese social relations, like that of kinship and family protocol, was extraordinarily complex, with social distinctions that would not even occur to most non-Chinese. There were, for instance, several different kinds of bowing, each designated by a different name and all dutifully illustrated in ritual handbooks. On formal occasions, the guest of honor always sat on the left (*yang*) side of the host, and his actions dictated the responses of the other guests. At the lower levels of society, and in relatively informal circumstances, less explicit attention was paid to status distinctions, but the distinctions were seldom forgotten. An astute mid-nineteenth-century Western observer remarked, for example, "When a number of individuals are walking together, you may generally infer their age or rank or position by the order in which they naturally and almost unconsciously range themselves."[71]

Many other longtime Western residents in late Qing China have commented on the extraordinary attention given to etiquette in all facets of Chinese social intercourse. J. H. Gray informs us, "A Chinese is seldom at a loss to know what polite observances must regulate his behaviour. Etiquette is an essential part of his education." R. F. Johnston's observations are worth quoting at length:

> [Chinese] rules of ceremony may seem, from the foreigner's point of view, too stiff and artificial, or exasperating in their pedantic minuteness. The European is inclined to laugh at social laws which indicate with preciseness when and how a mourner should wail at a funeral, what expressions a man must use when paying visits of condolence or congratulation, what clothes must be worn on different occasions, how a visitor must be greeted, how farewells are to be said, how modes of salutation are to be differentiated, and how chairs are to be sat on. . . . [These] rules of Chinese etiquette may be stiff, but there is no stiffness about the Chinese gentleman—or about the illiterate Chinese peasant—when he is acting in accordance with these rules.[72]

Chinese social ritual may often have been restrictive, but to most Qing subjects it was also probably reassuring.

Food had enormous social importance in traditional China. Although in all societies food is used to create and maintain interpersonal bonds, the Chinese employed it in a particularly sophisticated way as "a marker and communicator in social transactions." The bigoted but otherwise observant missionary Arthur Smith wrote just before the turn of the century, "If there is anything which the Chinese have reduced to an exact science, it is the business of eating."[73] Elaborate meals were required of all major social occasions, just as sacrificial dishes were essential to the proper performance of all major forms of religious ritual.

Figure 10.5. Greeting Guests
Nakagawa's fascinating illustrated account of Qing customs includes many examples of bowing. Here, the host greets two guests and their retainers. One of the retainers is carrying some tobacco sacks (*yanbao*).
Source: Nakagawa 1799.

The social significance of food can be measured in a variety of ways. As is often noted, a common greeting in traditional China was "Have you eaten?" Food was always a fit topic for genteel conversation, as well as the subject of personal correspondence, poetry, and classical prose. A number of famous Qing scholars wrote essays on food, and much information on it appears in local gazetteers, government documents, and encyclopedias such as the TSJC. Vernacular literature abounds with descriptions of food, and writers such as Li Yu, Wu Jingzi, and Cao Xueqin are acknowledged masters in the use of food to describe characters, develop or define social situations, and even link subplots within their works. *Dream of the Red Chamber* is especially noteworthy for its elaborate descriptions of food and feasts.

Food was always a good index of status in Chinese society for both gods and humans. Qing statutes specified in extraordinary detail the type, amount, and style of food for official sacrifices, just as local custom dictated the requirements for popular offerings to gods, ghosts, and ancestors. Similarly, in the human world, official regulations and popular practice indicated the proper kinds and amounts of dishes appropriate to persons of different rank and station, from the emperor down to commoners. Many Qing emperors had quite simple preferences, but, as Jonathan Spence reminds us, "the personal tastes of the emperor had little to do with the scale of culinary operations or their costs. The regulations were firm about the exact content of all major meals, which were carefully graded in accordance with their level of ritual significance."[74]

On formal occasions at the lower levels of elite society, the type and number of dishes had to be pegged to the status of the participants and the importance of the meal. Clan rules sometimes specified the number of dishes to be offered by lineage members to guests, but most commoners could not indulge in formal and elaborate meals except on special ritual occasions such as births, marriages, and funerals. *Dream of the Red Chamber* provides several indications of the gap between the eating habits of commoners and those of the elite. In discussing the price of certain dishes for a relatively small gentry party, Liu Laolao, an old countrywoman, exclaims, "It couldn't have cost less than twenty taels in all. Bless and save us! That'd keep a farmer and his family for a year."[75] And so it might have in the early or mid-eighteenth century. Naturally enough, most peasant fare was simple and monotonous, but it was still prepared with special care. In the words of a Scottish sojourner to China in the 1850s, "the poorest classes in China seem to understand the art of preparing their food much better than the same classes at home."[76]

Despite the sharp difference between rich and poor in eating habits and the existence of a plethora of regional cooking styles, Chinese attitudes toward food were remarkably similar. The most fundamental distinction was between grains and other starches (*fan*) and vegetable or meat dishes (*cai*). A proper balance between the two was deemed necessary to a good meal—although fragrance, flavor, color, and texture also had to be harmoniously blended. *Fan* was primary; *cai* secondary. This concern with balance had a classical foundation. The *Record of Ritual* states: "In feasting and at the vernal sacrifice in the ancestral temple they had music; but in feeding the aged and at the autumnal sacrifice they had no music: these were based on the *yin* and *yang*. All drinking serves to nourish the *yang*; all eating to nourish the *yin*. . . . The number of *ding* and *zu* [vessels] was odd [*yang*], and that of [the vessels] *bian* and *dou* was even [*yin*]."[77]

Foods and cooking styles were usually designated *yin* or *yang*, cold or hot, "military" or "civil." Given the holistic approach of the Chinese to good health, we should not be surprised to find that eating certain foods affected the balance of *yin* and *yang* in the body. A sore on the skin or an inexplicable fever, for example, might be blamed on overeating "hot" foods (oily, fried, or peppery items, fatty meat, and oily plants), while "cold" foods (water plants, crustaceans, and certain beans) could be blamed for producing or exacerbating a common cold. Complicating matters was the classification of Chinese food according to the five flavors—sweet, sour, bitter, pungent, and salty—which were, in turn, correlated with the five viscera, the five agents, the five seasons, and so forth. As with other aspects of traditional Chinese medicine, the variables were nearly infinite.

Tea had both medicinal and gastronomical appeal. During the Qing dynasty teahouses were popular centers of recreation for males, and a number of individuals considered themselves connoisseurs of the national beverage. Most of the best teas were grown in south China, and although certain types were believed to be especially valuable in digesting some types of foods and ameliorating certain kinds of physical distress, the principal medical benefit of tea seems to have been the fact that it was made with boiling (and therefore sterile) water.

Some alcoholic beverages had explicitly medicinal purposes, but most were valued primarily as social lubricants, closely associated with the joys of good food, friendship, and the composition of verse. The Chinese did not distinguish between true wines and starch-based spirits—both were designated *jiu* ("liquor"). As with tea, there were many different varieties of *jiu*, most of which were identified with locations in south China. The amount of alcohol might vary from as little as 10 percent (twenty proof) to as much as 80 percent (160 proof), and although moderation was encouraged in drinking as well as eating, the Chinese periodically threw caution to the wind. Drinking games were extremely popular at parties (note the category *Youshang* in the WBQS, appendix E), and many members of the elite belonged to drinking clubs. The poet Yu Huai (1616–1696) describes marathon binges that went on in the brothel quarter of Nanjing until "all the guests vomited and fell asleep on the ground." But even in more refined circumstances there were numerous instances of heavy drinking by members of the elite. The lower classes of Chinese society do not seem to have acquired a special fondness for liquor, but they did prove susceptible to the curse of opium in the late eighteenth and early nineteenth centuries.[78]

Parties in traditional China often involved entertainment other than eating and drinking, composing verse, or cavorting with prostitutes. Among the elite, exhibitions of singing and dancing were popular, as were dramatic performances. Plays proved particularly appealing to the women of elite households, as we can see from a reading of *Dream of the Red Chamber*. Performances also might be staged for family and friends on festive occasions such as marriages, birthdays for the elderly, or examination successes. Apparently, the actors engaged by individual households did not always know what play they would be performing until an honored guest made a request. The troupe thus had to have a repertoire of several dozen plays, and some groups were known to have command of nearly a hundred.

Plays were also staged in villages and towns. These performances might be sponsored by the whole community through subscription, by a segment of that community such as merchants, by a local temple, or by a private individual. In contrast to the more frequent dramatic performances of major cities, community plays were usually associated with periodic religious fairs or local festivals, which brought families and friends together for a few days of colorful and exciting entertainment, punctuated by noise and the smell of burning firecrackers and incense. Temples often sponsored plays because they were one of the few places in traditional China that were well equipped to stage them. These performances were often held on the "birthday" of the temple's major deity and intended explicitly for the entertainment of that deity. Sacrifices usually attended the dramatic event. As Barbara Ward and others have emphasized, the cumulative impact of such plays exerted a powerful influence in "the dissemination and standardization of [Chinese] culture, particularly in the sphere of ideas and values."[79]

Like local fairs and community celebrations, pilgrimages proved to be extremely popular in Qing China. The Chinese term for this sort of activity is *chaoshan jinxiang*: literally "to pay respects to a mountain." Most pilgrimage sites were located in mountainous regions, and most pilgrimages involved making contact with a resident deity enshrined in a mountain temple. Pilgrims came from all social classes. In the words of Susan Naquin and Chün-fang Yu, "Differentiated literati, imperial, clerical, and lay traditions existed together with a continuously growing set of shrines to a variety of local, regional, and national deities." With increasing ease of travel and greater political and economic integration, pilgrimage flourished in Qing times. In many parts of China, associations developed that "promoted these journeys and cared for the growing numbers of pilgrims."[80]

Countrywide annual festivals, always highlighted in popular almanacs and liturgical calendars, played an especially important role in unifying traditional Chinese culture and in educating people about their social roles and responsibilities. Almost every month a major festival occurred throughout the land, touching all classes of Chinese society directly and even cutting across ethnic lines. Banner families, for example, celebrated most of these major festivals in garrison cities, as did the Manchu nobility at the capital.[81] Many of these occasions were marked by official sacrifices and/or ancestor worship. They also generally involved feasts, firecrackers, dramatic performances, and music. Unfortunately, the brief descriptions below convey very little of the color and pageantry surrounding such events.[82]

The most important annual festival in traditional China was the month-long celebration of the New Year (*Yuandan*). This observance began in the twelfth lunar month. On about the twentieth day, Qing officials at every level commenced the ritual of "sealing the seals" of their yamens, in effect closing down government for a total of about four weeks. This action paralleled the shutdown of most commercial establishments during the same period. A week or so before the turn of the year, households throughout the country paid obeisance to the God of the Hearth, who, according to popular belief, ascended to Heaven to report to the Jade Emperor on the family's activities during the past year. This ceremony was taken seriously but often celebrated lightly, with sweet substances smeared on the mouth of the god's image to ensure a favorable report.

On New Year's eve, the family again sacrificed to the God of the Hearth, as well as to other household deities and, of course, the ancestors. These ceremonies paralleled aspects of marriage ritual in symbolic significance. A family feast reaffirmed kinship ties, and the ritual of paying respect to the heads of the household in order of precedence through bowing and kowtowing served as a vivid reminder of status relationships within the family. The next day—brought in with fireworks, incense, and bursts of color—entailed visits in proper dress to friends, neighbors, relations, and superiors; gift giving; and general merriment. Auspicious "spring couplets," written by local calligraphers on red paper, adorned residences and other buildings, bringing blessings and prosperity to families and businesses for the coming year.

The first two weeks of the New Year were devoted to various amusements, celebrations, and religious sacrifices. Ancestors and domestic gods were usually worshipped again, along with deities such as the popular God of Wealth.

Officials throughout the country welcomed spring (*yingchun*) in elaborate public ceremonies designed to indicate, through the symbolism of color, what the agricultural prospects were for the coming year and to assure the best results under the circumstances. The Lantern Festival (*Dengjie*) on the fifteenth day of the first month marked the end of the New Year's celebration. It was a happy time, devoted largely to the display of colorful lanterns in homes and businesses and to the entertainment of women and children. About a week later, Qing officials "opened their seals" and resumed government business.

The next major festival, Qingming (lit. "Pure and Bright"), took place in the third month, 106 days after the winter solstice. It was one of three important "ghost festivals" (*guijie*) in traditional China. Qingming was a time of family reunion, celebration, and devoted ancestor worship—including the sweeping of graves and offerings of food for the dead. Large-scale lineage sacrifices might also take place at this time. An important transformation during the Qianlong period was that public ceremonies associated with the ancestral cult began to grow ever more elaborate—at least in the provinces of Guangdong and Fujian, where powerful lineages predominated. During the late Ming and early Qing, the rites of grave worship had been confined to "recent" ancestors (up to twelve generations after death), and involved gatherings of fewer than one hundred people. But by the mid-Qing, entire lineages of hundreds and even thousands of individuals began visiting the graves of even their remote founders (up to thirty generations back).

The *Chinese Repository* of 1832 carried an absorbing account of one such sacrifice, involving more than two thousand clan members. The prayer offered at the tomb of the founding father, taken directly from a famous ritual handbook, illustrates the purposes of the ceremony:

> Revolving years have brought again the season of Spring. Cherishing sentiments of veneration, I look up and sweep your tomb. Prostrate, I pray that you will come and be present; that you will grant to your posterity that they may be prosperous and illustrious; at this season of genial showers and gentle breezes, I desire to recompense the root of my existence, and exert myself sincerely. Always grant your safe protection. My trust is in your divine spirit. Reverently I present the fivefold sacrifice of a pig, a chicken, a duck, a goose, and a fish; also an offering of five plates of fruit; with oblations of spirituous liquors; earnestly entreating that you will come and view them.[83]

The elaborate ceremonies concluded with a massive feast in which the participants in time-honored fashion shared the sacrificial foods. Although most Qingming devotions were far more personal and casual, all had the effect of establishing a close bond between the living and the dead.

The so-called Dragon Boat Festival (*Duanyang jie*, lit. Festival of the Upright Sun) took place early in the fifth month. Although celebrated countrywide, it was especially popular in south China, where colorful and exciting boat races took place on rivers and lakes. These races, and the festival generally, commemorated the death by drowning of the famous but ill-fated Zhou dynasty scholar and poet Qu Yuan, who committed suicide in despair after losing the favor of his ruler through slander. Although a joyous occasion, the Dragon Boat Festival was surrounded by rituals designed to protect the population from evil and unhealthy influences that were believed to be especially prevalent in the fifth month. A late Ming account of the festival in Qu Yuan's home province of Hunan states:

> The current popular belief is that the boat race is held to avert misfortunes. At the end of the race, the boats carry sacrificial animals, wine, and paper coins and row straight downstream, where the animals and wine are cast into the water, the paper coins are burned, and spells are recited. The purpose of these acts is to make pestilence and premature death flow away with the water.[84]

On the seventh day of the seventh month unmarried Chinese women celebrated the Double Seventh festival, an occasion that valorized women in their local communities and beyond. It was, by all accounts, "a central event in women's culture [that cut] across class boundaries throughout China."[85] It commemorated the one time during the year when the Weaving Maiden (Zhinü) of Chinese mythology could join her husband, the Herdsman (Niulang), across the Milky Way. A play based on the Zhinü legend was usually performed and young women made offerings to the patron deity of needlework. Preparations for the festival naturally involved sewing and embroidering. Because the Double Seventh was considered a particularly propitious day to look into the future, young girls tried to predict, through a lighthearted form of divination called "dropping the needle," whether they would be dexterous or clumsy in their work. Needle-threading competitions also took place as part of the festivities.

On the fifteenth day of the seventh month, various ceremonies were undertaken to honor the ancestors and placate "hungry ghosts." Graves were swept and ancestral sacrifices performed. The great Buddhist religious service known as All Soul's Day (*Yulan hui*) also took place at this time. It involved the reading of sutras by the clergy to "lead those [souls] deeply engulfed in the lower world [across the sea of suffering]." Significantly, the theme of these devotions was the filial piety of Mu Lian (Maudgalyayana), a disciple of the Buddha who offered sacrifices to save his deceased mother from the torments of Hell.[86]

Exactly a month later, the Mid-Autumn Festival (*Zhongqiu jie*) occurred. Among the most popular of all Chinese festivals, it involved family gatherings and feasts, the exchange of "mooncakes," offerings to the moon, ancestor worship, and the burning of incense to Heaven and Earth. Like the Lantern Festival, the Mid-Autumn Festival was especially popular with women and children. Men played a marginal role in the ceremonies because, in the words of a popular Beijing proverb, "Men do not worship the moon, [just as] women do not sacrifice to the God of the Hearth."

The Chongyang (Double Yang) Festival on the ninth day of the ninth month was in many parts of the country a relatively minor celebration, with little overt religious significance. It was primarily a day of hill climbing, sight-seeing, kite flying, and feasting. Contemporary Western descriptions of the festival suggest a gala mood, echoed by Chinese accounts: "Reciting poetry and drinking wine, roasting meat and distributing cakes—truly this is a time of joy." In some parts of the country, however, Chongyang was marked by large-scale lineage sacrifices of the sort that occurred during the Qingming festival. Even national celebrations were not carried out with perfect uniformity throughout the country, but the similarities appear far more striking than the differences.

On the first day of the tenth month, Chinese families again worshipped their ancestors in ceremonies paralleling those of the seventh month and the Qingming festival. This celebration was known popularly as the ceremony of Sending Winter Clothes (*Song hanyi*). Concern for the well-being of the ancestors was expressed at this time by inscriptions on colored paper garments or plain paper wrappers enclosing "spirit money." It was also in the tenth month that the Qing officials prepared the ritual calendar for the coming year. From this time until the New Year's preparations began in the twelfth month there were no national festivals of any consequence—only relatively minor celebrations and a few official sacrifices. Perhaps the most widely observed ritual of the period in Chinese households was the preparation of "eighth-day gruel" (*laba zhou*) in the twelfth month, a thanksgiving ceremony designed to show gratitude for good fortune during the year.

Although most Chinese festivals contributed to community solidarity and a shared sense of culture, they were not an unmixed blessing from the standpoint of either Chinese elites or the throne. This was particularly true of local religious festivals, village fairs, and pilgrimages. As crowds gathered in public places to watch entertainers, enjoy food and drink, and do business, men and women mingled more freely, fights sometimes erupted, and social discipline occasionally broke down. Gamblers, thieves, and swindlers naturally exploited the situation. Especially threatening to the government was the possibility that community celebrations would serve as the recruiting grounds for secret societies. An edict of 1724 expresses this fear:

[A] class of loafers, with neither a livelihood nor an abode, . . . has come forth to usurp the name of . . . [Buddhism and Daoism] and to corrupt the practical use of the same. The majority of them use [doctrines about] calamities and felicity, misfortune and happiness, to sell their foolish magic and baseless talk. They begin by cheating on goods and money to fatten themselves. Then they proceed to hold meetings for the burning of incense where males and females mingle promiscuously. Farmers and craftsmen forsake their business and trades, and engage . . . in talking about miracles. Worst of all, rebellious and subversive individuals and heretical miscreants glide in among them, establish parties and form leagues by taking membership oaths. They assemble at night and disperse in daytime. They thus transgress their proper status and sin against their duty, mislead mankind and deceive the people.[87]

For the most part, the Qing authorities relied on social pressures and the vast network of nongovernmental organs of local control to maintain or restore order in towns and villages. But penal law remained a powerful weapon in the state's arsenal, to be used with ruthless severity whenever crimes occurred that threatened the Chinese social or political system. Among these crimes, the worst were the "Ten Great Wrongs," discussed earlier and in chapter 3: (1) rebellion against the emperor and his ritual order; (2) subversion or destruction of imperial temples, tombs, or palaces; (3) desertion or treason; (4) parricide (including the murder of a father, mother, uncle, aunt, grandfather, or grandmother); (5) the murder of three or more persons in one family; (6) lack of respect for, or improper use of, the ritual articles and implements of the emperor; (7) unfilial conduct; (8) maltreatment of relatives; (9) insubordination by inferiors toward their superiors; and (10) incest. All of these crimes were potentially punishable by death from slicing (*lingchi*)—the most severe form of punishment in the Qing code.[88]

In especially serious cases, punishment went well beyond the perpetrator. The statute on rebellion and high treason, for example, not only stipulated death by slicing for the principal offender, but also the decapitation of all males in his household over the age of fifteen (including the offender's father, grandfather, sons, grandsons, brothers, and brothers' sons, as well as his maternal grandfather, father-in-law, and brothers-in-law). Further, the law provided that the rest of the family (all females and all males fifteen years of age and under) would be enslaved in the households of "meritorious ministers." This statute illustrates both the traditional emphasis on ancestral concerns as a deterrent and the pervasive principle of collective responsibility in Chinese society.[89]

Unfortunately, such draconian legal measures did not prevent crimes against the state or crimes within the family. Throughout the Qing period, rebellions repeatedly broke out, despite the harsh treatment received by the leaders of such uprisings and their families. Heterodox ritual specialists found opportunities to usurp the prerogatives of the Qing elite, and secret societies flourished. And although the state dictated severe penalties for domestic crimes, we know that among the most common cases in the Qing dynasty's *Xing'an huilan* (Conspectus of penal cases) were the killing of a wife's paramour; disobedience to parents or grandparents; incest; and assault by either wives or concubines on husbands, slaves or servants on masters, or offspring on parents or grandparents.[90] Clearly, Chinese society was not all harmony and cooperation, even in the best of times.

Yet in all, the fabric of Confucian society wore remarkably well, strengthened by the interwoven strands of religion, law, education, and ritual. For all that divided China, much more united it: a centralized system of administration; shared social attitudes and practices; a similar cosmology and world view; a common repository of ethical principles, artistic symbols, historical heroes, and literary myths; a powerful sense of unparalleled cultural development; and a universal pride in simply being "Chinese." It took the combined impact of unprecedented population pressure and Western imperialism in the nineteenth century to begin to tear this traditional garment apart, and even now it has not been completely destroyed.

Chapter Eleven

The Late Qing and Beyond, 1860–2014

The theme of Chinese history during the last century or so has been revolutionary change.[1] Yet in the midst of China's modern transformation we can see the powerful persistence of tradition. From the late nineteenth century to the present, inherited patterns of language and perception, as well as traditional attitudes toward politics, ritual, social organization, ethics, art, and literature, have unquestionably influenced the course and speed of China's modern development. Although a full and systematic analysis of the complex interplay between the past and the present must await further study, this concluding chapter examines at least some of the modern manifestations and modernizing implications of China's rich, cohesive, and tenacious cultural tradition. It should be emphasized that my preoccupation in this last chapter with the legacy of China's past should not be viewed in any way as a denial of the dramatic revolutionary changes that have taken place.

REFORM, REVOLUTION, AND CHINA'S INHERITED CULTURE

In his path-breaking book on the late Qing reformer Wang Tao (1828–1897), Paul Cohen warns against measuring nineteenth-century China's modernization (meaning primarily technological advancement) by external standards. "Modernization," he maintains, "is not a horse race," and a "much more valid way of measuring change in nineteenth century China is by internal points of reference."[2] Yet one might well argue that a horse race is exactly what modernization is. It involves the notion of competition (usually between nation-states) and assumes some kind of external standard of judgment (political, social, economic, technological, etc.) for "success." Seen in this light, modernization is a cross-cultural phenomenon, distinct from reform, which is essentially intra-cultural. Or, to pursue our racing metaphor, reform pits the horse against the clock (its own "best time"), while modernization stacks the horse up against other horses. In the case of nineteenth-century China, the purse was more than money or pride; it was national survival.

It is true, of course, that this distinction between reform and modernization is somewhat artificial. Even if we define modernization as a special kind of externally motivated, rationally organized, technologically oriented, competitive change, it often bears a close relationship to indigenous reform. The acquisition of Western weapons by Qing officials in the 1860s, for example, was only part of a general reform program that owed its primary inspiration to the demands of the Taiping Rebellion. Qing policymakers recognized that Western guns and ships could be used as foreign policy tools as well as instruments in the suppression of the rebellion, but their priorities were overwhelmingly internal, and the *yongying* armies that used Western weapons and techniques most effectively throughout the entire nineteenth century developed primarily in response to an internal stimulus, within the framework of Chinese tradition and without significant Western influence.[3]

As indicated in previous chapters, "Chinese tradition" encompassed a great deal, to say the least. The intellectual heritage of Confucianism, for example, ran the gamut in the nineteenth century from the obdurate political and social conservatism of the imperial tutor Woren (d. 1871) to the highly creative synthetic philosophy of the brilliant Cantonese scholar Kang Youwei (1858–1927). Buddhism exerted considerable intellectual influence in late Qing times, and there was always a heterodox strain of millenarian thought that held out the promise of a utopian future, a "great leap" into a new age of social justice. The question facing Chinese intellectuals in the late Qing period was whether any of these ideologies had the capacity to transform the Middle Kingdom in the modern era, to effect meaningful change in the midst of unprecedented challenges.

On the whole, I believe that the reformist tradition of China's Confucian heritage provided an adequate intellectual foundation for modernization based on Western standards of economic, scientific, and technological development. Certainly it sanctioned the idea of making adjustments to meet changing conditions (*biantong*), and it did not prevent loyal Confucian scholar-officials in the nineteenth century from sponsoring the establishment of Western-style arsenals, shipyards, foreign-language schools, educational missions, military and naval academies, railroads and telegraphs, mines, and a wide variety of manufacturing industries. Measured solely against the baseline of China's traditional political and economic system, the reforms of the late nineteenth century were in many ways quite impressive, as Cohen, Benjamin Elman, Allen Fung, and many others have pointed out.[4]

But these reforms did not take place in a vacuum, and increasingly their impetus came to be external rather than internal. As foreign imperialism loomed ever larger on China's horizons, Qing policymakers could not avoid viewing their accomplishments in terms of foreign progress, including that of Meiji Japan (1868–1912). Western ideas of science, technology, and economic growth, as well as concepts such as nationalism, democracy, egalitarianism, and individualism, began to emerge as alternatives to inherited Chinese attitudes and values. The modernized West (and Japan) became the twentieth-century standard for China's progress in a world dominated by industrialization, imperialism, international competition, and rapid political and social change.

The process by which the West emerged as a modernizing model for East Asia began with the imposition of the notorious "unequal treaties" on China in the period from 1842 to 1860. According to the terms of these treaties, which were imposed by force and not totally abrogated until 1943, the foreign powers gained the right to establish self-governing treaty port settlements for Western residence and trade, to have access to the Chinese interior, to operate foreign ships between the treaty ports on the coast and on inland waterways, to promulgate Christianity without obstruction, to limit Chinese customs duties, and to establish formal diplomatic relations at the capital and in treaty port areas. Westerners enjoyed immunity from Chinese law (extraterritoriality) and other nonreciprocal privileges. The entire structure was held together by the most-favored-nation clause, which in effect brought to all the treaty powers any benefit extracted from the Chinese by one or another of the powers over time.[5]

From 1860 on, the treaty ports became conduits for the transmission of Western influences of all kinds. Foreign merchants, missionaries, diplomats, and military men collected in the port cities, bringing to China new products, ideas, practices, and skills. At the same time, these Western intruders exerted a disruptive influence on Chinese society, threatening the traditional economic system, elite prerogatives, the Chinese world order, and China's security and sovereignty. The treaty ports were both showcases for the modern West and vivid reminders of the challenge of foreign imperialism.

Contact with foreigners in treaty port areas during the Taiping Rebellion (1851–1864) gave at least some foresighted Chinese provincial officials—notably Li Hongzhang (1823–1901)—the opportunity to observe firsthand the technological and organizational advantages of the West and to employ a number of Westerners in various new modernizing enterprises. Li became the leading figure in China's so-called Self-Strengthening Movement (c. 1860–1895)—a concerted, albeit unsystematic, effort on the part of Qing officials at the capital and in the provinces to build China's military and economic strength in order to contend with both internal disorder and external aggression.

The earliest phase of this attempt at meaningful reform in the midst of dynastic decline became known as the Tongzhi Restoration (1862–1874).[6]

During Li's extraordinarily long tenure as governor-general of Zhili from 1870 to 1895, new ideas penetrated much of the Middle Kingdom. The rise of Western-style Chinese newspapers, together with a growing number of Western works translated into Chinese by missionaries and by foreign employees in arsenals, shipyards, educational institutions, and the Imperial Maritime Customs Service, brought a heightened awareness of the West to China. So did interaction between high Qing officials and Westerners in the Qing foreign affairs office known as the Zongli Yamen (established in 1861).[7] During the first half of the nineteenth century, the majority of translated Western books and pamphlets had been religious, but during the later part of the century, most of the translated works were in the natural, applied, and social sciences, including history and geography. New-style encyclopedias and almanacs and popular magazines such as the *Dianshizhai huabao* (Illustrated review of the Dianshi Studio) portrayed the advantages of Western science and technology, as well as the disruptive influence of foreign activity in China. By the end of the nineteenth century, the rapidly expanding Chinese periodical press had become a potent weapon in the movement for radical reform.

But until the Sino-Japanese War of 1894–1895, change came relatively slowly in China. When Japan's Prime Minister Itō Hirobumi (1841–1909) met Li Hongzhang to sign the Treaty of Shimonoseki after the conclusion of the conflict, Itō asked Li why China had not done more to reform. Li replied: "Affairs in my country have been so confined by tradition that I could not accomplish what I desired."[8] As I have pointed out elsewhere, the outcome of the conflict perhaps causes us to place the modernizing "success" of Japan and the "failure" of China in too sharp relief.[9] Yet it is impossible to avoid asking what went wrong with China's Self-Strengthening Movement after more than three decades of costly effort. This was, after all, precisely the question that Chinese intellectuals themselves were asking after the debacle of 1895, and the answers they produced determined in large measure whether they would become conservative reformers like Zhang Zhidong (1837–1909), radical reformers like Tan Sitong (1865–1898), or revolutionaries like Sun Yat-sen (Sun Zhongshan; 1866–1925).

In retrospect, it is clear that China's modernizing problems in the late Qing period were both internal and external. On the one hand, the aggressiveness of the foreign powers in the realms of diplomacy, commerce, evangelism, and military affairs created a variety of political and economic problems. It encouraged Chinese anti-foreignism and produced a natural suspicion of both Western employees and Western influences. But compounding these difficulties in the nineteenth century were China's pressing and inescapable demographic and environmental problems, the vastness and diversity of the Chinese empire, the turmoil created by the abortive millenarian movements of the Taipings and other rebel groups, and the tenacity and integration of China's traditional culture. For most of the nineteenth century, the Qing dynasty seems to have been too weak militarily and economically to protect itself from imperialism, but too strong culturally to inaugurate the kinds of fundamental educational and institutional reforms that might have produced a different outcome in the Sino-Japanese War.

In the realm of culture, the classical Chinese language remained the standard written medium of the Chinese elite throughout the Qing period, reinforcing longstanding attitudes, values, perceptions, and prejudices, and limiting the audience for reformist sentiments. The preeminent translator of Western thought in the late Qing period, Yan Fu (1853–1921), refused to employ the more flexible and more widely accessible vernacular language in his renderings of Mill, Rousseau, Spencer, and others, arguing that "where language has no refinement [*ya*], the effects will not extend very far." Benjamin Schwartz argues that Yan's elegant translations "succeed on the whole in transmitting the essential thought of the Western sages," but there can be little doubt that Yan's young contemporary Liang Qichao (1873–1929) was correct in asserting that "those who have not read many ancient books . . . [find] his translations most difficult to comprehend."[10]

Schwartz himself points out that Yan resisted the use of most "standard" neologisms created by the Japanese during the early Meiji period in favor of his own renderings, and that he tended to make maximum use of the traditional "allusive categories of ancient philosophic thought" in rendering Western ideas. Yan thus contributed to the general intellectual confusion of the late nineteenth and early twentieth centuries—a confusion reminiscent of the early decades of Buddhist translating activities when

> translators with different backgrounds chose different Chinese equivalents for foreign terms; translators had different degrees of knowledge of the language from which they were translating; communication among translators was infrequent; different versions or editions of foreign works were used by different translators; [and] different stylistic preferences produced different versions of the same work.[11]

Another problem for most of the period between 1860 and 1894 was a widespread reluctance on the part of Qing scholars and officials to recognize that China might need more from the West than mere technology. To accept anything beyond technology, many feared, would compromise the foundations of Chinese culture itself. Thus, the popular *tiyong* formula arose: "Chinese learning for the substance [*ti*], Western learning for the function/

practical application [*yong*]." A similar formulation juxtaposed the Chinese "moral way" (*Dao*) with Western "concrete things" (*qi*)—a polarity derived from the *Yijing*. A third way of justifying change—one that was as common among Chinese intellectuals in the late Qing as it had been during the heyday of the Jesuits—was to emphasize the "Chinese origins of Western learning." By the early 1890s, growing numbers of Chinese scholars and officials had come to see that the West had more to offer China than "concrete things" (*qi*), and that substance and function were more closely related than advocates of the *tiyong* formula were willing to admit. Nonetheless, in the view of Hao Chang, the *tiyong* approach had psychological significance, "for it facilitated China's modernization" without the loss of China's "cultural identity."[12]

The vast repository of Chinese fixed expressions (*chengyu*) provided yet another means of rationalizing Western-inspired change. The traditional phrase "viewing all ['foreigners'] with the same benevolence" (*yishi tongren*), for example, could be used both to justify the most-favored-nation clause of the unequal treaties and to determine policy regarding the treatment of foreign employees in the Chinese service.[13] The problem with such traditional formulations was that they often mitigated an awareness of the need for more fundamental policy changes on the part of the Qing government. Perhaps the most vivid illustration of this problem can be found in the documentary record of China's foreign relations in the Tongzhi period (1862–1874) titled *Chouban yiwu shimo* (A complete record of the management of barbarian affairs), which was presented to the throne in 1880.

Although intended to be a secret rather than a public document, the preface casts all of the humiliations of the Tongzhi reign—Western demands for an audience with the emperor on terms of diplomatic equality; the use of foreign troops to defend the treaty ports from the Taipings; the loss of Chinese territory to the Russians; the failure of the Alcock Convention; the establishment of an Interpreters College to train Chinese in Western languages in order to meet the needs of modern diplomacy; the belated establishment of Chinese legations abroad (related directly to a mission of apology sent by China to Great Britain after the murder of a British consular official in 1875); the limitation of Chinese Customs duties, and the establishment of the Imperial Maritime Customs Administration—in terms of imperial condescension. The preface reads in part:

> We respectfully consider that after the Tongzhi emperor came to the throne and stabilized the policy, . . . the amphibious monsters were quickly driven away and His Majesty's awful dignity vastly overawed everything within the imperial domain. . . . [When the barbarians returned to China] they requested to have an audience, no different from the Xiongnu king coming to the court of the Han dynasty. When they departed they wanted to join up as auxiliaries on the flanks

of the imperial guard, just as the Uighurs assisted the Tang. They relied on the [emperor's] jade axe to mark off the rivers, confer their borders, and settle their boundaries. They presented cinnabar and turned toward civilization. How could they be aware that control-by-light-rein of the imperial pattern was entirely carried out according to the emperor's design? As a means by which speech might penetrate to all countries, the [Interpreters] College began to instruct in common languages. The fame of our classic books was spread everywhere. His Majesty proclaimed his orders to dispatch envoys abroad. . . . the merchants' customs duties were fixed, and . . . with the emperor's grace and rewards extended to them, [the foreigners] became cultivated and learned elegance and etiquette. Inner [Chinese] and outer [foreigners] formed one family.[14]

Even the granting of imperial audiences to Western diplomats on terms of equality could be rationalized by the notion that foreigners were simply too barbaric to be controlled by conventional Chinese rituals. In the opinion of the censor Wu Kedu (1812–1879), Westerners understood only material gain and not Confucian rites; thus, requiring them to observe Chinese ceremonies based on Confucian assumptions was as pointless as "gathering a herd of sheep, dogs, horses, and pigs in a hall and making them dance to music."[15]

Such attitudes were reinforced by the traditional civil service examination system. One of the topics for the metropolitan exams in 1880 was the following quotation from the Four Books: "By indulgent treatment of men from afar they resort to him from all quarters. And by kindly cherishing the princes of states, the whole empire is brought to revere him." Such quotations, dutifully memorized by all examination candidates, perpetuated the myth of the Chinese emperor's universal kingship and encouraged China's deeply entrenched attitude of cultural condescension to foreigners. To be sure, Chinese attitudes toward Western "barbarians" began to change in some circles by the 1870s and 1880s, but they remained remarkably persistent in most others.[16]

The examination system also reinforced neo-Confucian intellectual orthodoxy, with its emphasis on loyalty to the state and its premium on the acquisition of moral over scientific and technological knowledge. Mary Wright is correct in asserting that during the late Qing period the civil service examinations were not always concerned exclusively with literary and scholastic questions, but she admits that at their best the exams were "overloaded with precedent," with a premium placed on knowledge of facts rather than analysis or judgment. Similarly, Benjamin Elman points out that throughout the Qing period the "policy" (*ce*) questions in the examinations were moral and historical in their emphasis. Chung-li Chang, for his part, goes so far as to say that the nineteenth century saw "the complete domination of the Confucian classics in the examination questions."[17] There were, of course, Chinese criticisms of the examination system throughout the Qing period, but the basic cultural assumption remained intact: scholars in China were moral men of broad learning who "need not be specialists" (*bubi zhuanmen mingjia*).

Prior to 1895, neither the court nor most classically trained Qing scholars saw the need for meaningful change in either the examinations or the Chinese educational system. Education remained overwhelmingly private in nineteenth-century China, and the central government gave little support or encouragement to educational reform. The only major innovations in Qing educational policy before the Sino-Japanese War were the establishment of a few Interpreters Colleges and the sending abroad of about two hundred students, most of whom were recalled by the government—in part because they were neglecting their traditional Chinese studies and also because they had begun to acquire Western customs (some went so far as to cut their queues). Meanwhile, the civil service examinations remained essentially unchanged and a powerful lure to the best minds of the empire.

Even the disesteemed military examination system underwent virtually no change in the nineteenth century. One important reason was fear over tampering with inherited institutions and respect for ancestral precedent (*zuzong chengfa*). Time and again in late Qing China we find that concern over the policies of previous emperors played a key role in imperial deliberations. For instance, a major factor in the decision to spend vast amounts of precious revenue on the reestablishment of central government control over Chinese Central Asia in the 1870s instead of devoting the funds to maritime defense was the throne's reluctance to abandon territory conquered by an imperial ancestor (the Qianlong emperor). Even after the Sino-Japanese War, Qing officials and the throne repeatedly expressed a concern for ancestral precedent in deliberations over civil and military reform.[18]

Given such cultural conservatism, it should come as no surprise to find that there was very little enthusiasm for Western art, literature, or social customs in late Qing China outside of certain treaty port enclaves—certainly nothing comparable to the Meiji government-sponsored wave of Westernization that washed over Japan in the 1870s and 1880s. Ironically, the multicultural Manchus, who had been so open to foreign cultural influences in the seventeenth and eighteenth centuries, did nothing to encourage the Westernization of Chinese culture during the nineteenth. Embattled and on the defensive everywhere (including parts of their empire in Inner Asia), the Manchus clung tenaciously to the idea that they were the protectors of China's cultural heritage. It followed, then, that they could scarcely afford to appear neglectful of traditional values, practices, and institutions without compromising their political position.

Complicating China's problems in the late nineteenth century was the fact that the Empress Dowager Cixi had become the country's de facto ruler from 1861 to 1908. As a woman who had executed a coup d'état to gain power and then manipulated the dynastic laws of succession to keep it, Cixi proved to be particularly inclined to use neo-Confucian orthodoxy and the patronage of traditional Chinese culture as a means of serving personal political ends. Her cultural conservatism translated not only into a vigorous defense of orthodoxy, but also into an obsessive concern with internal control. It is true that during and after the Taiping Rebellion (1851–1864), the Qing central government was forced to grant greater power and administrative leeway to certain loyal Chinese "regional" officials as a matter of expediency, but it continually attempted to play these officials off against one another through the powers of appointment and the purse and by the careful manipulation and deployment of their so-called regional military forces. By and large the effort was successful, but in both the civil bureaucracy and the regular military forces of the empire, including the Banners, corruption and costly inefficiency continued.

In China's civil administration, the only major institutional innovations of the nineteenth century were the Zongli Yamen and the Imperial Maritime Customs Administration—both of which resulted from Western pressure. These organizations were relatively successful as ad hoc expedients, but neither was viewed as a permanent institution. Meanwhile, the longstanding Qing system of checks and balances discouraged initiative and often destroyed administrative continuity. Overlapping jurisdictions, dyarchy, the rule of avoidance, and the policy of frequent transfer were particularly detrimental in this regard. The throne, for its part, avoided administrative responsibility whenever possible and seldom initiated modernizing projects except those relating specifically to the Banner armies.[19]

Despite the internally motivated military reforms of the mid-nineteenth century, the Qing army as a whole played no significant role in the modernization of Chinese society, unlike the case in Meiji Japan. The degenerate Banner and Green Standard forces of the empire consumed vast amounts of money but were largely untouched by Western influences, and even in the new-style *yongying* armies that increasingly assumed their military role, modernization went no further than the piecemeal acquisition of Western weapons and a certain amount of Western drill. Locally raised, armed, and trained, these "temporary" forces had little sense of either national identification or political awareness. The great majority of Chinese soldiers remained illiterate and uninformed. Within the military, as in the rest of Chinese society, personal ties of blood, friendship, or local affinity generally counted for more than expertise, thus militating against the introduction of new ideas and influences. The existence of widespread corruption and opium smoking, coupled with the lack of modern medical and other facilities, neither improved the living conditions of the average Chinese soldier nor altered his expectations.

On the more positive side of the ledger, recent research has indicated that China's nineteenth-century economy developed much faster than previously thought; that neither imperialism nor landlordism was as detrimental to Chinese development as was once supposed; and that "daily life in imperial China for commoners as well as elites was permeated with the trappings of commerce."[20] From the standpoint of industry, the period from 1860 to 1895 witnessed the establishment of dozens of modernizing enterprises, including mills, mines, ironworks, and railroad and telegraph lines, as well as arsenals and shipyards. But as with the late Qing economy overall, commercial and industrial development tended to become ever more localized in the late nineteenth century. Industrial enterprises were generally confined to treaty port areas, and large, well-endowed regions like Jiangnan flourished commercially and industrially while the rest of China "lagged further and further behind." Moreover, as James Pomeranz has argued in *The Great Divergence: China, Europe, and the Making of the Modern World Economy* (2000), most Chinese industries lacked easy access to coal resources, limiting their use of steam power.[21]

Most of the modernizing activities of the late Qing were either undertaken by local officials or managed under the traditional formula of "government supervision and merchant operation" (*guandu shangban*). Such enterprises occasionally brought quick returns to certain investors, but because of bureaucratic inefficiency and corruption they discouraged reinvestment and regular growth. Private enterprises in China were generally weak and few in number. Commerce and agriculture developed largely on their own momentum, without the kind of systematic central government attention they received in Meiji Japan. Although a few leaders of the Self-Strengthening Movement recognized the need for government-sponsored reform of public finance, it was not until 1897 that the first Chinese-owned bank based on a Western model was established—and it was a failure. On the whole, as indicated briefly in chapter 3, the Qing government remained an "extraordinarily weak" financial instrument.[22]

Meanwhile, Chinese social attitudes underwent no significant changes, except perhaps for a somewhat greater appreciation of commerce on the part of gentry who engaged in productive relationships with merchants. In the absence of meaningful legal or administrative reform, particularistic ties of kinship, local affinity and other forms of *guanxi* continued to loom large in various spheres of Chinese life. At the same time, conservative family values, social inequalities, and notions of collective responsibility remained firmly in place. Foot binding still received widespread customary sanction, despite its crippling effect on one-half of China's elite class and a great many other women as well. The civil ethos (*wende*) of late imperial China also proved to be an obstacle to modernization. The low prestige of the military made most of the Qing elite disdainful of military affairs and unaware of the need for meaningful reform, unlike the samurai class of Tokugawa Japan. Within the army and navy there was little incentive to acquire Western military knowledge beyond the rudiments of Western drill and tactics, and most officers continued to long for identification with the civil bureaucracy.

Qing ritual practices at all levels discouraged innovation. Despite the time-honored argument that ritual must "change with the times," the state remained wed to costly traditional ceremonial practices out of fear that radical alterations or benign neglect would undermine the central government's authority. At the popular level, local religious observances, community festivals, and lifecycle ritual reinforced traditional values and status relationships, while at the same time consuming great amounts of scarce capital. Meanwhile, of course, the preservation of at least the outward form of the highly ritualized tributary system for most of the nineteenth century blunted the throne's awareness that a new order of foreign relations had begun long ago. Between 1860 and 1894, for instance, Korea presented tribute at least twenty-five times, Liuqiu at least eight times, Annam (Vietnam) at least five times, and Nepal at least four times.[23]

Naturally enough, the lingering sense of the Qing as a universal empire hindered the rise of modern nationalism—the identification of the individual with the nation-state and the general acceptance of a multistate system of other sovereign (and competing) national entities. The Sino-Japanese War of 1894–1895, however, shattered the dynasty's outmoded self-image at a single blow. This event not only marked the total destruction of the traditional Chinese world order, but it also laid bare China's military weakness, exposed the bankruptcy of the Self-Strengthening Movement, and resulted in the loss of Chinese territory and the imposition of a costly and humiliating unequal treaty on China by the Japanese themselves. A surge of Chinese nationalism ensued, and with it a burst of reform sentiment. New print media and new forms of political and social activity helped to spread reformist ideas.

The shock of China's defeat in the Sino-Japanese War produced a variety of reactions on the part of Chinese intellectuals in the late Qing:

For many, the outcome of the conflict was traumatic and humiliating. But the crisis atmosphere that prevailed in the immediate postwar years also provoked a sense of urgency, introspection, wide-ranging cultural exploration, and a variety of reformist and revolutionary proposals and strategies. The sense of possibility at the time was palpable. Under the new circumstances, some intellectuals sought primary inspiration from ideas derived from the West and/or Japan. Others looked mostly to past models and precedents for guidance, an approach epitomized by the now discredited *tiyong* (substance and function) formula of the Self-Strengthening era. . . . Still others sought some sort of creative synthesis involving both the past and the present—a synthesis that went beyond the *tiyong* model, assumed diverse forms, and changed over time, frequently in unanticipated ways.[24]

In the past, male reformers such as Kang Youwei and Liang Qichao have received the bulk of attention from historians of the period from 1895 to 1911. But it is increasingly clear, thanks to a spate of recent books and articles on the subject, that women played an important role in the reform era—not only as reformers but also as revolutionaries.[25] Anarcho-feminists such as He Zhen (1884–c. 1920) and Qiu Jin (1875–1907) have enjoyed relatively high visibility, but there were many other women of their time who also deserve notice. One such person was the writer and reformer Xue Shaohui (1866–1911). Xue provides a particularly instructive example of one kind of reformist response to the trauma of the Sino-Japanese War. For her, China's search for "modernity," however it might have been defined at the time, was not simply a matter of appropriating the new; it was also a matter of finding the proper place for inherited ideas and values. In her view, "traditional" values could have "modern" applications. The challenge was more than simply grafting "Western" things onto a "Chinese" base. In many respects, Xue was a genuinely cosmopolitan internationalist. A new biography by Nanxiu Qian, titled *Politics, Poetics, and Gender in Late Qing China: Xue Shaohui (1866–1911) and the Era of Reform* (2015), provides a vivid account of Xue's colorful life and the remarkable men and women in her social and political networks.

The so-called One Hundred Days of Reform in 1898 resulted directly from the acceleration of foreign imperialism in the wake of the Sino-Japanese War. The "scramble for concessions" on the part of the Western powers during 1897–1898, which threatened to dismember China, prompted the Guangxu emperor (r. 1875–1908) to initiate a reform movement from above with the advice and assistance of radical reformers such as Kang Youwei and Liang Qichao. At this time, the emperor's adoptive mother, the Empress Dowager Cixi, was in "retirement" at the Summer Palace outside of Peking. Although conservative and cautious, the Empress Dowager gave her initial approval to the reform scheme, reportedly stating, "So long as you keep the ancestral tablets and do not burn them, and so long as you do not cut off your queue, I shall not interfere."[26]

But the reform edicts issued in the emperor's name in the period from June 11 to September 20, 1898, proved to be too threatening to Cixi and her supporters. Changes such as the abolition of sinecures and the appointment of progressives in government, the replacement of the "eight-legged essay" in the civil service examinations by essays on current affairs, and the establishment of modern schools with both Western and Chinese curricula appeared too radical, and on September 21, the Empress Dowager executed a coup d'état, claiming that a serious illness had incapacitated the emperor. Reportedly chastising the hapless monarch for sweeping away "ancestral institutions," Cixi rescinded virtually all the reform edicts and put a price on the head of the reformers, several of whom were executed. Kang and Liang escaped to Japan, where they continued to agitate for reform.

The return of the conservatives to power happened to coincide with an upsurge of activity on the part of a secret society in North China known as the Boxers United in Righteousness (*Yihe quan*), or simply the Boxers. This loose coalition of several diverse groups had in common a hostility toward Westerners engendered by foreign imperialism and a belief in the magical efficacy of traditional Chinese martial arts. The Manchus, eager to put the sectarian movement to their own political purposes, encouraged the Boxers to "Support the Qing and exterminate the Westerners" (*Fu Qing mieyang*). Eventually this led to a Boxer siege of the foreign legations in 1900, and the relief of the legations by an eight-nation expeditionary force in the summer of that year. The result was the occupation of Beijing by the Allied armies, the imposition of a huge indemnity on China, and a number of other destructive and demoralizing provisions stipulated in the Boxer Protocol of 1901.

This humiliating event forced the Empress Dowager and her conservative supporters to commit themselves to more fundamental reforms, inspired by Japan's ongoing Meiji Restoration (1868–1912). In the period from 1901 to 1909, a great number of reform edicts were issued by the throne as part of an effort to establish a "New Administration" (*Xinzheng*) in China. Many of these edicts reflected changes proposed in 1898, but a number of others went further. For instance, as early as August of 1901, the Qing court abolished the eight-legged essay format, signaling that examination questions for the *shengyuan* degree would now include Western learning (*Xixue*) as well as Chinese learning (*Zhongxue*). Moreover, it became clear that at the higher examination levels (for the *juren* and *jinshi* degrees) at least one set of policy questions would focus on "world politics."

One such policy question, posed in the metropolitan examinations of 1902, asked *jinshi* candidates to discuss Japan's use of Western models during the Meiji Reforms, which began in 1868. Their answers followed a consistent pattern of defending Chinese moral learning and criticizing Japan's enthusiasm for foreign things. Answers to other such questions reflected similar biases. One reason was that the phrasing of the questions indicated a clear

emphasis on the superiority of Chinese leaning. Here are five of eight examination questions on the "natural sciences":

1. Much of European science originated in China; we need to stress what
   became a lost learning as the basis for wealth and power.
2. In the sciences, China and the West are different; use Chinese learning to
   critique Western learning.
3. Substantiate in detail the theory that Western methods all originated in
   China.
4. Prove in detail that Western science studies were based mainly on the
   theories of China's pre-Han masters.
5. Itemize and demonstrate using scholia that theories from the Mohist Canon
   preceded Western theories of calendrical studies, light and pressure.[27]

In short, the training of both the candidates and the examiners predisposed
them to privilege Chinese tradition.

Increasingly, however, Chinese reformers came to see that the key to
meaningful educational change was the establishment of a system of degrees
granted by "new-style" schools (*xuetang*) with Chinese and Western curriculum rather than degrees gained by success in the examination system. In
the immediate aftermath of the Russo-Japanese War of 1904–1905—which
was fought primarily on Chinese soil (Manchuria) and resulted in Japan's
overwhelming victory—the entire examination system was abolished (1905).

Other important New Administration reforms included the termination of
the military examinations, the establishment of a new, provincially based
Western-style army (the New Army or *Lujun*), and the creation of representative local, provincial, and national assemblies as a prelude to eventual
constitutional government on the Meiji model. Debilitating practices such as
foot binding were outlawed (1902), and the throne even established a School
of Ritual Studies (*Lixue guan*) in 1907, charged with the task of selecting the
best of China's "ancient and modern customs and the everyday habits of the
people" and bringing them to the attention of the throne. "This," an imperial
edict stated, "is proof of Our earnest desire for the preparation of the way
towards the granting of a constitution and parliamentary representation to the
country."[28]

The imperial reforms of the early twentieth century, designed to preserve the
dynasty, had revolutionary consequences. Abolition of the traditional examinations, for example, dealt a staggering blow to the Confucian concept of rule
by virtue and eliminated the institutional reinforcement of orthodox Confucian values. Representative government radicalized the Chinese elite, giving
them a new political awareness and a new base of political power. The New

Army, whose officers and men were increasingly exposed to, and influenced by, nationalistic revolutionary propaganda, became a revolutionary instrument. The establishment of the School of Ritual Studies, although itself of little real importance, symbolized the erosion of the official ritual system that the destruction of the Chinese world order had precipitated. The pathetic effort in 1907 to elevate the worship of Confucius to the first level of state sacrifice—presumably in order to enhance the reputation of the sage (and the Manchus) after the literary examinations that had reinforced his teachings for so many centuries had been abolished—testified to the desperation of the dynasty.

Despite their reform efforts, the Manchus became increasingly scorned and despised for their inability either to resist imperialism or to protect elite interests. Chinese nationalism no longer permitted alien rulers to claim legitimacy as the protectors of China's cultural heritage, for Chinese intellectuals increasingly saw the need to differentiate between politics and culture in order to achieve the modern goals of collective achievement and dynamic growth. Despite Kang Youwei's contention that the faults of the Qing government were those of the inherited culture and not simply those of the Manchus, increasing numbers of Chinese thought otherwise. The cultural conservatism of the throne, its desperate attempt to maintain Manchu political supremacy, and a flurry of anti-Manchu propaganda that revived memories of the atrocities committed by the "barbarian" Manchus during the Qing conquest, all made them a convenient target for nationalistic advocates of republican revolution.[29] The death of the Guangxu emperor in 1908 destroyed China's best chance for a Meiji-style constitutional monarchy, and in 1911–1912, a loose coalition of republican revolutionaries under Sun Yat-sen threw out the imperial baby with the Manchu bathwater. This created a political vacuum and a ritual void that the hastily constructed system of representative institutions could not fill. The Republic of China soon degenerated into warlordism.

The warlord period, from about 1915 to 1928, witnessed the rise of the so-called New Culture Movement—an iconoclastic assault on traditional Chinese culture, and a search for new values and institutions in the midst of political chaos, social unrest, widespread demoralization, and foreign imperialism. Nearly every aspect of the inherited civilization came under attack by Chinese intellectuals, including Confucian ethics and the "teachings of ritual." At the same time, the Chinese women's movement gathered momentum. The period was marked by a tremendous surge of interest in Western ideologies, science, and democracy; by experimentation with new artistic, dramatic, and literary forms; and by the development of a new national literature influenced strongly by Western themes and models. There was also a growing interest in Western fashions and amusements.[30]

The early outlook of the Japanese-educated intellectual Chen Duxiu (1880–1942) exemplifies the vibrantly iconoclastic spirit of the New Culture Movement. Although Chen was born into an elite family and received a thorough grounding in the Confucian classics, his experience abroad and China's deteriorating domestic situation led him to reject Chinese tradition and to embrace Western ideas. As editor of the famous and influential journal *Xin qingnian* (*La Jeunesse*, The New Youth), Chen issued a "Call to Youth" in 1915, declaring passionately that he would "much rather see the past culture of our nation [*guocui*, often translated 'national essence'] disappear than to see our race die out now because of its unfitness for living in the modern world." He urged his readers to be independent, not servile; progressive, not conservative; aggressive, not retiring; cosmopolitan, not isolationist; utilitarian, not formalistic; and scientific, not mystical. He railed against "all traditional ethics, law, scholarship, rites and customs," and scoffed at the use of *yinyang* and five-agents notions to explain natural phenomena.[31] Until his conversion to Marxism around 1920, Chen remained a leading spokesman for Western-style liberalism and a reliance on "Mr. Science" and "Mr. Democracy" for China's salvation.

The thrust of the New Culture Movement was toward what has been described as "totalistic iconoclasm." This widespread disposition to reject the past completely and to seek holistic and all-encompassing solutions to China's complex problems reflected a growing recognition that the very perfection of China's highly integrated cultural tradition now presented the nation with its most formidable modernizing problem. In the words of Chen Duxiu and Hu Shi (1891–1962), "The old literature, old politics, and old ethics have always belonged to one family; we cannot abandon one and preserve the others."[32]

To many radicals of the day, even the Chinese language was an impediment to modernization. For this reason, Hu Shi spearheaded a movement to replace the classical language with the vernacular on the grounds that the old literary language merely reinforced outmoded ideas. By 1920 the vernacular had become the official medium of instruction in China's new-style schools. But Qian Xuantong, another New Culture intellectual, wanted to go further. In a letter to Chen Duxiu he wrote:

> In an earlier essay of yours, you strongly advocated the abolition of Confucianism. Concerning this proposal of yours, I think that it is now the only way to save China. But, upon reading it, I have thought of one thing more: If you want to abolish Confucianism, then you must first abolish the Chinese language; if you want to get rid of the average person's childish, uncivilized, obstinate way of thinking, then it is all the more essential that you first abolish the Chinese language.[33]

Qian's quixotic proposal was for China to adopt Esperanto. Lin Yü-sheng explains the radical character of the New Culture movement in the following terms:

> Iconoclastic intellectuals were hardly capable of differentiating those traditional social norms and political practices that were abhorrent to them from traditional cultural symbols and values. This lack of differentiation and tendency to be monistic and holistic was affected, among other factors, by the long-term historical disposition to interlace the cultural center with a socio-political center in Chinese traditional society and by a traditional Chinese pattern of thinking in terms of association. . . . The intelligentsia in China believed in the necessary priority of cultural and intellectual change over social, political, and economic changes and not vice versa.[34]

Although the scientific spirit of the New Culture Movement attracted growing numbers of Chinese intellectuals, there were still a number of diehard traditionalists among the educated elite, even at Beijing University. In response to the early call for "total Westernization" (*quanban Xihua*), steadfast conservatives such as Gu Hongming (1857–1928) stood solidly in defense of China's cultural tradition. Although educated in the West and able to read several foreign languages (including English, French, German, Latin, and ancient Greek), Gu maintained that Western utilitarian culture was incapable of developing the "inner mind," and that China's "spiritual civilization" was so perfect that it could not only save China but also rescue the West from its materialistic malaise. He strenuously opposed Western science and technology, defended all traditional values, and even continued to wear the Manchu queue as a sign of traditionalistic defiance.[35]

The vast majority of Chinese intellectuals, however, did not take the extremist positions of either totalistic iconoclasm or ultraconservatism. Instead, they tried to find a creative cultural balance between Chinese tradition and Western-inspired modernity. Some gravitated more toward the West, others more toward an emphasis on China's "national essence"; but even the conservatives now viewed the past from new perspectives, using new methodologies borrowed from the West. Then again, if we look at Chinese society as a whole during this period, it is clear that the New Culture Movement was essentially an urban intellectual movement that had very little impact on the rest of China. For every Western-educated radical there remained "hundreds of thousands of local leaders of secret societies, Buddhist abbots, Daoist priests, and leaders of Confucian uplift societies who continued to expound their views almost wholly in terms of categories provided by the culture of the past."[36] Traditional family values and relations of subordination, as well as the lifecycle rituals that reinforced these values and relations, remained deeply entrenched in the countryside, where about 80 percent of the people still resided.

Furthermore, the political imperatives of Chinese nationalism, the success of the newly organized Nationalist party (Guomindang) in its Northern Expedition against the warlords in the period from 1926 to 1928, and the establishment of a new central government at Nanjing under Sun Yat-sen's successor, Chiang Kai-shek (Jiang Jieshi; 1888–1975), narrowed somewhat the parameters of discussion and debate. In politics, even among Chinese liberals, there seems to have been a "widespread tendency to appreciate democracy more as an indispensable functioning part of a modern nation state than as an institution to protect individual rights and liberties."[37] Thus, nationalist impulses and the desire for a strong and rationally organized state became more important than liberal values and individualism in Chinese political and social thought. Although a battle of words still raged between advocates of "total Westernization" and those who advocated "cultural construction on a Chinese base," the Guomindang in this period of "political tutelage" and one-party rule demonstrated a clear concern with the restoration of traditional values. Although committed to rapid economic modernization and the realization of Sun Yat-sen's Three Principles of the People (nationalism, democracy, and the people's livelihood), Chiang Kai-shek's new government moved quickly to reestablish Confucianism as a kind of state-sponsored orthodoxy.

As late as February 1927, the Nationalist government had ordered the abolition of official Confucian rites on the grounds that "the principles of Confucius were despotic. For more than twenty centuries they have served to oppress the people and to enslave thought. . . . As to the cult of Confucius, it is superstitious and out of place in the modern world . . . China is now a Republic. These vestiges of absolutism should be effaced from the memory of citizens." But the vestiges were not effaced for long. On November 6, 1928, Chiang Kai-shek was already urging his officers to spend their leisure time studying the Four Books of Confucianism, and in 1931, the birthday of Confucius became a national holiday. By 1934, Confucius had been recanonized, and an official delegate of the national government was sent to take part in the solemn ceremonies at the Confucian temple at Qufu, birthplace of the Sage. During the same year, Generalissimo Chiang inaugurated the famous New Life Movement, which called for a return to the four ancient Confucian virtues of *li* (ritual), *yi* (right behavior), *lian* (integrity), and *chi* (sense of shame). Chinese politics and culture became reunited.

The New Life Movement has often been ridiculed for its over-attention to minute rules of decorum and for its philosophical superficiality. In Mary Wright's words, "The whole of the neo-Restoration of the Guomindang was a dismal failure, a far sadder spectacle than the Tongzhi Restoration it tried to copy."[38] But the fundamental aims of the two "restorations" were different, and despite the weaknesses of the New Life Movement, it did lay the foundations for a government-sponsored approach to traditional Chinese culture that continues, with varying degrees of enthusiasm, to this day on Taiwan. This approach considers Confucian values to be fully compatible with science and democracy and conducive to modern economic growth as well. At present, traditional forms of art and literature, and even traditional religious and ritual practices, continue to flourish alongside more "modern" aspects of material culture. The result has been a constantly evolving dualistic (some scholars, like Melissa J. Brown, might say triadic) culture that draws on the traditions of both East and West in apparently judicious combination—albeit with a certain amount of political tension created by the Taiwan Independence Movement.[39]

Until relatively recently, the Chinese Communist approach to traditional culture has been very different from that of the Guomindang (and other ruling parties) on Taiwan. From the founding of the Chinese Communist Party (CCP) in 1921 onward, the Chinese Communists promoted a vision of social revolution based on the rejection of Confucianism and the implementation of Marxist-Leninist principles and practices. Although the revolutionary movement of Mao Zedong (1893–1976) grew out of the same deep patriotism and esteem for science, democracy, and social justice that had motivated Sun Yat-sen as a founder of the Guomintang, Mao laid his wager on the Chinese peasantry, developing a kind of populist Marxism-Leninism that stood in sharp contrast to the urban-centered elitism that had characterized the Nationalist era. In both theory and practice, Mao emphasized the importance of ideology, human will, mass political participation, anti-imperialism, egalitarianism, social and economic reform, and, above all, the transformation of consciousness. He assailed Confucian beliefs, as well as the popular religious practices and social rituals that seemed to encourage conservatism, waste time or money, and strengthen the position of the traditional elite.[40]

From 1949 to his death in 1976, Mao succeeded in transforming much of Chinese society. In addition to promoting Marxist-Leninist values nationwide and elevating the social position of traditionally disadvantaged groups (notably workers, peasants, women, and soldiers), Mao brought to the People's Republic a new system of economic organization, which included the nationalization or collectivization of agriculture, industry, and commerce and a host of related changes in health, education, and welfare. Life expectancy nearly doubled, as did population. During the early 1950s Mao received considerable assistance from the Soviet Union, but his militantly self-reliant revolutionary approach can best be seen in the radical (and disastrous) Great Leap Forward (1958–1960) and especially the tumultuous (and also disastrous) Great Proletarian Cultural Revolution of 1966–1976, which hearkened back to the New Culture Movement in its self-conscious effort to "destroy the old and establish the new" (*pojiu lixin*). Yet for all his revolutionary iconoclasm, Mao did not totally reject China's heritage. As early as 1938 he wrote: "Today's China is an outgrowth of historic China. We are Marxist historicists; we must not mutilate history. From Confucius to Sun Yat-sen we must sum it up critically, and we must constitute ourselves the heirs of all that is precious in this past. . . . A communist is a Marxist internationalist, but Marxism must take on a national form before it can be applied." In 1956, Mao attacked both the *tiyong* modernizing formula of the late Qing period and the notion of "total Westernization" prevalent in the New Culture era, arguing: "We must learn good things from foreign countries and also learn good things from China. . . . China's art must not look more and more to the past, nor must it become more and more Western."⁴¹

Mao's deep sense of history and esteem for much of Chinese tradition is evident in his writings and speeches, which bristle with historical allusions and references to traditional Chinese literature. Much of Mao's discourse employs traditional terms, phrases, and metaphors. Moreover, some scholars have suggested that the Maoist concept of the transformative power of the mind resonates strongly with the traditional neo-Confucian emphasis on efficacious moral efforts (*gongfu*), and that the prominent strains of dynamism, activism, and utopianism in Mao's thought seem to be derived at least in part from the tradition of the great Ming Confucian scholar Wang Yang-ming. Mao's distinctive notion of "contradictions" may perhaps owe something to *yinyang* influences, and his "Great Leap" mentality hearkens back to the millenarian tradition of the Taipings and others. Certainly the persistent emphasis on ethics, self-cultivation, and small group ritual in the People's Republic bears the strong imprint of traditional Chinese social thought.⁴²

Like Chiang Kai-shek, Mao ruled in the imperial style, manipulating factions and ritual symbolism for his own political purposes. Furthermore, in practice Mao's administration, like that of his imperial and Nationalist predecessors, displayed the familiar characteristics of authoritarianism: state supervision of political, social, and economic life; an emphasis on political morality over law; a preoccupation with ideological, artistic, and literary orthodoxy; and a clear stress on collective responsibility and mutual surveillance. Many of these tendencies were, of course, encouraged and reinforced by Marxist-Leninist ideology and practice.

As an intellectual system, Maoism differed fundamentally from the ideology of both imperial China and the Guomindang. Yet Mao's system was every bit as holistic as Zhu Xi's neo-Confucianism had been. Although the Marxist dialectic replaced *yinyang* notions of cyclical alternation and complementary opposition as the logical underpinning of Chinese Communist ideology, public discourse continued to exhibit many time-honored features of traditional Chinese philosophical expression. Quite apart from the powerful linguistic tendency to group phrases in neat sets of four characters, and the deeply ingrained moralistic tendency to parcel out praise and blame in categorical either/or fashion, we find in much Chinese writing of the Maoist period a dogmatic formalism expressed in arbitrary groupings of elements, often organized in numerical configurations.

Chinese political rhetoric in particular exhibits this tendency. If we review the various political campaigns of the early Maoist era, we encounter literally dozens of formalized numerical categories embodied in slogans such as the "three antis" (*sanfan*), the "three highs" (*sangao*), the "three red banners" (*sanmian hongqi*), the "three histories" (*sanshi*), the "three reconciliations and one reduction" (*sanhe yishao*), the "three freedoms and one contract" (*sanzi yibao*), the "four olds" (*sijiu*), the "four firsts" (*sige diyi*), the "five histories" (*wushi*), the "five category elements" (*wulei fenzi*), and so forth. Later, we encounter the "four cardinal principles" (*sixiang jiben yuanze*), the "four modernizations" (*sige xiandaihua*), the "gang of four" (*siren bang*), the "five stresses, four beautifications and three ardent loves" (*wujiang simei sanreai*), and the "eight great eminent elders" (*ba da yuanlao*). More recently, we hear of the "three represents" (*sange daibiao*) and so forth.[43] Naturally, in the current more "open" environment in China, the government's approach to this form of propaganda has generated sarcastic counter-slogans, such as "The Four Clears and the Four Unclears," which poke fun at officials and officialdom:

Why hold a meeting?—Unclear
But who sits in what seat?—Very clear
Who brought which gifts?—Unclear
But who brought no gift?—Very clear
Whose work has been good?—Unclear
But who will be promoted?—Very clear
Who went to bed with the leader?—Unclear
But what was done there?—Very clear.[44]

The Great Proletarian Cultural Revolution has generally been viewed as a relentless assault on Chinese tradition, and it was. The "four olds" mentioned above were among Mao's main targets: old thought, old culture, old customs, and old habits. Beginning in 1966 the Chairman's overenthusiastic and sometimes fanatical agents, the Red Guards, ransacked museums, temples, and private homes; they destroyed ancestral tablets, graves, ancient artifacts, old books, and works of art; and they attacked citizens who dressed in the traditional fashion, followed old rituals, or possessed Buddhist and Daoist relics. Confucianism came to be virulently attacked in both word and deed. For instance, Red Guards ransacked the temple at Confucius's birthplace in Qufu and unearthed tombs, including that of the Sage himself. In 1973, the Chinese government launched an especially vigorous campaign to "criticize Confucius" (*pi Kong*), in an effort to link the once-venerated Sage with a stigmatized CCP commander, Lin Biao, who was accused of attempting to overthrow Mao.

But in many respects the Cultural Revolution reflected longstanding Chinese cultural predispositions. Mao himself assumed the position of an imperial-style demigod, whose writings were believed to have mystical, semimagical power. During 1968, the cult of Mao grew to especially extravagant proportions, as Maurice Meisner has indicated:

> The writings of the Chairman were printed and distributed in ever-greater volume. Portraits, statues, and plaster busts of Mao increased both in size and number. . . . In households there were often "tablets of loyalty" to Mao's thought around which family members gathered to pay reverence. Schoolchildren no longer began the day by saying "good morning" but by chanting "May Chairman Mao live ten thousand times ten thousand years." Throughout the land exhibition halls were built to chronicle and commemorate the life and deeds of the Chairman, and people came on organized pilgrimages to pay homage at what the official press termed "sacred shrines." The test of loyalty to Mao was no longer measured by revolutionary acts inspired by his thought but more by the ability to recite his sayings and by the size of portraits that were carried in the streets or hung in homes. In 1966 the Mao cult had stimulated iconoclasts; in 1968 it produced icons.[45]

During the same period on Taiwan the Guomindang government sponsored a "Cultural Renaissance" (*wenhua fuxing*) explicitly designed to preserve and foster traditional Chinese culture. In obvious response to the Cultural Revolution on the Mainland, it called for the republication of the Confucian Classics and encouraged new writings and translations in order to "publicize Chinese culture and build a bridge between Chinese and Western cultures." It also promoted a revival of literature and art "based on ethics, democracy and science," and emphasized the principles and practices of the New Life Movement, including the "four social controls" (*li, yi, lian,* and *chi*) and the "eight virtues" (loyalty, filial piety, benevolence, love, faithfulness, justice, harmony, and peace). Like the New Life Movement of the 1930s, the Cultural Renaissance has been criticized for its stress on outer form over inner substance and for its obviously political character. Nonetheless, it offered a sharp and significant contrast to Mao's brutally destructive effort to exorcise the "ghosts and monsters" of the past on the Mainland.[46]

Since Mao's death in 1976, there has been a sharp reaction to the chaotic excesses of the Cultural Revolution (including Mao's "cult of personality"), and a wholehearted commitment to the Four Modernizations: agriculture, industry, science and technology, and national defense. By stages, and under a succession of essentially pragmatic leaders—Deng Xiaoping (1904–1997), Jiang Zemin (b. 1926), Hu Jintao (b. 1942), and now Xi Jinping (b. 1953)—the PRC has become in many important ways a fully modern nation-state, and one that Mao would have found in most ways utterly unrecognizable. Having adopted a market-based economy (a combination of bureaucratic and free market capitalism) under the thin veneer of socialism ("socialism with Chinese characteristics"), China has emerged as the second-largest economy in the world (it was sixth in 2002). Its rapidly growing cities (more than one hundred of them in excess of one million people) are pulsing centers of commercial activity, and urban cultural life in the PRC is about as vibrant and varied as anywhere on earth.[47]

China's government, although neither democratic nor appreciably restrained by "rule of law," has become ever more responsive to its citizens. David Lampton explains why:

> First, individual Chinese leaders have become progressively weaker in relation to both one another and the rest of society. Second, Chinese society, as well as the economy and the bureaucracy, has fractured, multiplying the number of constituencies China's leaders must respond to, or at least manage. Third, China's leadership must now confront a population with more resources, in terms of money, talent, and information, than ever before.[48]

Despite these changes, Chinese "bureaucratism" (*guanliao zhuyi*)—an outlook associated with both imperial and Nationalist China, and regularly denounced as rigid, dogmatic, autocratic, elitist, and conservative—is still an impediment to effective administration. Official corruption also remains a monumental problem, in part because there is still too little rule of law to offer protection for either bureaucrats or common people; hence, the continued importance of personalistic relationships (*guanxi*).

Ironically, ever since the inauguration of the so-called Open Policy of the PRC in 1978, which was designed primarily to promote the Four Modernizations, there has been a revival of many traditional attitudes and practices. Birth control programs in the countryside have suffered from powerful traditional preferences for male children to continue the line and help support the family. Indeed, the combination of this preference and the availability of new technologies to determine the sex of a child in utero have resulted in severe gender imbalances.[49] Once again, as in Qing times, young men have found it difficult to marry. Meanwhile, the state's effort to curtail costly traditional rituals has also encountered serious obstacles in the rural sector, and many households go deeply in debt in order to provide a proper wedding for the sake of community face. The cost of funerals also remains high, despite official encouragement of simple ceremonies and cremation.

Traditional art and literary forms are no longer stigmatized, and religious institutions of all sorts continue to thrive. Buddhist monasteries and Daoist temples, first reopened in the late 1970s along with some Christian churches, have attracted ever-growing numbers of worshippers—young and old alike. Some attribute this surge of interest in institutional religion to a "spiritual crisis" (*jingshen weiji*) resulting from a loss of faith in the Chinese Communist Party, but whatever the cause, the commitment seems genuine. Meanwhile, domestic ancestral sacrifices and other household religious devotions, severely condemned during the Cultural Revolution, have become more prominent, and reports in the Chinese press indicate the widespread recrudescence of so-called superstitious (*mixin*) practices such as geomancy, fortune telling, and occasionally witchcraft—especially in the countryside. But even in urban centers such practices flourish, despite occasional propaganda campaigns against them. In Beijing, for instance, the streets between the Yonghe Buddhist Temple and the Confucian Temple (*Kongzi miao*) are filled with shops selling incense, charms, and spirit money, as well as several stalls where fortune tellers openly ply their once-suppressed trade. Religion is big business, but there is clearly more to it than that.

Perhaps the most dramatic instance of the recrudescence of Chinese tradition, at least in the realm of intellectual life, is the flourishing on the Mainland of state-supported "National Studies" (*guoxue*), and the related idea of a Chinese "Cultural Renaissance" (*wenhua fuxing*). Neither concept is new, and neither has been precisely defined, but both are clearly oriented strongly toward the celebration of traditional Chinese culture.[50] According to Li Shenming, vice president of the Chinese Academy of Social Sciences:

> The purpose of advocating *guoxue* studies in contemporary China is to carry forward the excellent cultural traditions of the various nationalities in China, to complete the sinicization of Marxism, to facilitate development of a systematic theory of socialism with Chinese characteristics, to accomplish the historic task of rejuvenating China, to further reinforce the integrative unity of Chinese culture, to maintain the ideological basis of the solidarity of Chinese communities all over the world and their inseparable connection, to enhance the cultural exchange and cooperation between the Chinese on both sides of the Taiwan Strait with a view to expediting the reunification of China, to help satisfy the desire of other peoples of the world to understand China, to introduce traditional Chinese culture to the world, and to quicken the process of popularizing outstanding Chinese culture in different parts of the world.[51]

Viewed in this light, *guoxue* can be seen as a manifestation of what has been called "cultural nationalism"—one of many vibrant forms of nationalism that exist in the People's Republic of China today.[52]

From the 1990s onward there has been a "National Studies Fever" (*guoxue re*) in the PRC. Xie Xiaobo wrote in 2011:

> All or at least most of the leading universities in China are running *guoxue* institutes or *guoxue* training classes, some of which are designed particularly for CEOs. There are all kinds of televised *guoxue* lectures forums, and a fairly large horde of emerging *guoxue* "masters," headed by Yu Dan, Yi Zhongtian, Fu Peirong, He Yizhou, Chen Zhaojie, Zhang Qicheng, and Qian Wenzhong, to name only a few, who have become media celebrities with large followings for their televised *guoxue* lectures on the *Zhuangzi*, the *Lunyu*, *Sanguo yanyi* (Romance of the Three Kingdoms), *Sanzi jing* (Three Character Classic), *Honglou meng* (Dream of the Red Chamber), *Xiyou ji* (Journey to the West), and the *Yijing* (Classic of Changes). In large cities such as Chongqing, Chengdu, Wuhan, Beijing, Guangzhou, Shenzhen, Nanning, Jinan, and Xiamen, *guoxue* is becoming a subject for elementary school children. Small kids are made not only to recite the *Three-Character Classic*, the *Analects*, the *Classic of Filial Piety*, and the *Principles and Rules for Children*, but also to practice meditation and *qigong* in Han-style children's clothes.[53]

A significant part of the National Studies agenda has been the promotion of what has been called "New Confucianism" (*Xin Ruxue*). According to John Makeham, by successfully transcending the geographical and political boundaries of "cultural China" (that is, the PRC, Taiwan, and Hong Kong), New Confucianism has increasingly played a leading role in "bridging the cultural and ideological divide separating mainland and overseas Chinese scholars by providing a shared intellectual discourse." Makeham goes on to say:

> The wider influence of this discourse is evident not just in the way it has shaped philosophical research and debate in the region, but also in its contribution to broad cultural and intellectual issues, with some protagonists identifying "exclusive" links between "Confucian values" and East Asian economic prosperity. New Confucianism has also proven to be the most successful form of philosophical appropriation, reinvention, and "creative transformation" of "Confucianism" in contemporary China, Taiwan, and Hong Kong.[54]

Of course, the exact connection between Confucian values and economic development is a matter of much debate, but many observers have focused on the importance of such cultural factors as a strong emphasis on education, a positive attitude toward "the affairs of this world," a lifestyle of discipline and self-cultivation, respect for authority, frugality, and an overriding concern for stability in family life.

At present, the balance between tradition and modernity in Mainland China, as in Taiwan, appears fairly comfortable, although tensions do exist. As one example, a thirty-one-foot bronze statue of Confucius that had been erected in early 2011 on the east side of Tiananmen Square (in front of the Museum of Chinese History) was abruptly removed at night a mere four months later. There was no official comment. Advocates of a Confucian revival in the PRC naturally deplored the removal of the statue, but pro-Maoist "leftists" applauded the move. One wrote on the internet site Maoflag.net: "The witch doctor who has been poisoning people for thousands of years with his slave-master spiritual narcotic has finally been kicked out of Tiananmen Square!"[55] What tomorrow may bring for Taiwan and the Mainland is impossible to say, but it seems evident that for a long time to come in both societies the past will remain, in some form, an integral part of the Chinese future.[56]

Appendix A

A Note on Chinese Names

In transliterating Chinese words, I have employed the pinyin (PY) romanization system, with the exception of a few extremely common spellings, such as Sun Yat-sen (PY: Sun Yixian) and Chiang Kai-shek (PY: Jiang Jieshi). Pinyin is pronounced more or less the way it looks, with a few noteworthy exceptions: "q" sounds like the *ch* in *ch*eek; "z" sounds like the *ds* in bu*ds* (unless followed immediately by an "h," in which case the two letters together sound like the "j" in *j*ump); "x" sounds like the *sh* in *sh*eep; and "c" sounds like the *ts* in i*ts* (unless followed immediately by an "h," in which case the two letters together sound like the *ch* in *ch*eap). Thus, *qing* sounds like "cheeng"; *zu* sounds like "dsoo"; *zhou* sounds like "joe"; *xing* sounds like "sheeng"; *can* sounds like "tsawn"; and *chu* sounds like "chew."

In the text, Chinese names usually appear in their original order, family name first, with the exception of authors who are known primarily for their English-language writings. I have followed this same basic rule in the notes (for details, see "Preliminary Remarks and Abbreviations" at the beginning of the endnotes). Most Chinese family names consist of one character, while most personal names are comprised of two (for example, Gong Zizhen). The reverse is possible, however, as is the use of two characters for both surname and given name (for example, Sima Xiangru). Polysyllabic Manchu and Mongol names are transliterated either by a single word (for example, Nurhaci) or by a string of sounds representing the characters used by the Chinese to render them (for example, Senggelinqin—the Chinese phonetic equivalent for Senggerinchin, a Mongol name).

Emperors in the Qing dynasty are usually referred to by their reign names (*nianhao*) rather than their personal names (which became taboo upon their accession to the throne). All reign names have felicitous meanings, but some, such as Guangxu ("Glorious Succession"), have a certain irony (see chapter 3).

Appendix B

Weights and Measures, Exchange Rates and Costs

WEIGHTS AND MEASURES

Length

1 *cun* (inch)	=	c. 1.4 English inches
10 *cun*	=	1 *chi* (foot, c. 14.1 English inches; c. 35.6 centimeters)
10 *chi*	=	1 *chang* (c. 11.7 English feet; c. 3.56 meters)
180 *chang*	=	1 *li* (c. 0.333 English mile; c. 0.5 kilometer)

Weight

1 *liang* (*tael*)	=	c. 1.333 English ounces
16 *liang*	=	1 *jin* (catty, c. 1.333 pounds; c. 0.6 kilograms)
100 *jin*	=	1 *shi* (picul, c. 133 pounds)

Area

1 *mou*	=	c. 0.166 acre; c. 0.055 hectare

A NOTE ON EXCHANGE

During the Qing period, the "standard" unit of exchange was the *tael* (*liang*), about an ounce (c. 500 grains) of silver, usually in the form of an oval ingot, or "shoe." The paper money experiment of the Xianfeng period (1851–1861)—the first such paper issue since the early Ming dynasty—failed miserably. The value of a silver *tael* varied from time to time and place to place, not only because of changes in market conditions, but also because of different local standards of weight and fineness. Theoretically, 1 *tael* was equal to 1,000 copper cash (*wen* or *li*), but in practice a *tael* might be worth anywhere from 1,000 up to 1,500 cash. The enormous variety in standards of currency, weight, and capacity in traditional China necessitated the employment of a great many money changers and other petty middlemen, complicating both commercial transactions and payment of taxes. For an illuminating discussion of these problems, consult CHC 1980, 11.2: 40 ff.; also H. B. Morse 1908, 145 ff., esp. 149–61.

A NOTE ON PRICES

Yeh-chien Wang 1972 has put together a rough price index for the Qing period. According to his data, the lowest prices were in 1682. Taking this year as a base (100), the following general patterns emerge:

Year	Index number
1646	688
1682	100
1700	130
1800	300
1815	300
1850	150
1864	500
1875	240
1885	240
1895	360
1910	600

Susan Naquin 1976, appendix 3, provides some cost of living figures for North China in the 1810s:

Purchase price of land (cash per *mou*):
Northern Zhili: 6,000
Southern Zhili:
  High-quality land, good year: 10,000
  High-quality land, bad year: 1,000
  Low-quality land, good year: 3,000–4,000
  Low-quality land, bad year: 300–400
Land rents in Henan (annual):
  First-grade land: 500 cash per *mou*
  Second-grade land: 400 cash per *mou*
  Third-grade land: 300 cash per *mou*

Wages:

Bondservant in a prince's household: 4 *taels* in money and grain per month

Regular soldier: 1.8 *taels* per month and two piculs of rice per month

Agricultural laborer during harvest time: 100 cash per day

Agricultural laborer during slack season: 70–80 cash per day

Room and Board:

Room rent: 150–200 cash per month

Militia soldier's food allowance: 50 cash per day

Militia instructor's food allowance: 200 cash per day

Regular soldier's allotment for food: 150 cash per day

Goods:

Knife: 500 cash

One foot of white cotton cloth: 100 cash

Fourteen-year-old boy: 4,000 cash

Eleven-year-old boy: 1,000 cash

Woman: 10,000 cash

According to Sidney Gamble 1943, 43, the wages for unskilled laborers in the area of Beijing ordinarily did not go below 60 cash per day from 1807 to 1856. From 1865 to 1871, the minimum was about 200 cash, and from 1872 to 1902, about 300 cash. Evelyn Rawski's (1979) research indicates that teachers in charitable schools averaged about 24 *taels* per year from 1800 to 1825 and 44 *taels* from 1875 to 1900. On the whole, the cost of a picul of rice seems to have fluctuated between 1.5 and 2.0 *taels* in the early nineteenth century, before dropping to about a *tael* by 1850. During the Taiping Rebellion the cost rose to as high as five or more *taels* per picul. See Yeh-chien Wang 1972, 351–54. According to a report on provisions in the markets of Shanghai during 1849, rice was 24 cash per *jin*; wheat flour, 30 cash per *jin*; mutton and beef, about 100 cash per *jin*, chicken, 80 to 90; and ducks, 90 to 120. *Chinese Repository*, February 1949, 109–10. Cf. Jonathan Spence in Kwang-chih Chang, ed. 1977, 265 ff. See also Beattie 1979, 137 and Chung-li Chang 1962, 143.

In 1864, the exchange value of a "customs" *tael* in Western currency was 80 pence (6s. 8d., about U.S. $1.65). By 1894, the value of the *tael* had declined to 38 pence. For a discussion of late Qing fiscal reform, consult CHC 1980, 11.2: 403 ff.

Appendix C

Regional Differences
and Provincial Stereotypes

Note: This material has been summarized from R. J. Smith 1994, 18–26.

REGIONAL DIFFERENCES

The boundary between north and south China is, of course, transitional; many geographical characteristics overlap or merge gradually from one area to the other. Nonetheless, striking and significant differences separate the regions north and south of the thirty-third parallel—a dividing line roughly marked by the Huai River in the east and the Qinling Mountains in the west.

NORTH-SOUTH DIFFERENCES

North	South
Limited, uncertain rainfall	Abundant rainfall
Frequent floods and droughts	Adequate water year-round
Unleached, calcareous soils	Leached, noncalcareous soils
4–6 month growing season	9–12 month growing season
1–2 crops per year; relatively low yields; frequent famines	2–3 crops per year; relatively high yields; prosperity
Major crops: gaoliang (sorghum), millet, wheat	Major crop: rice and beans
Work animals: donkeys and mules	Work animal: water buffalo
Mud-walled houses with heated brick beds (*kang*)	Woven-bamboo, walled, and thatch-roofed houses
Wide city streets	Narrow city streets

Smooth coastline with poor harbors; little fishing	Rough coastline with many good harbors; much fishing
Foreign intercourse by land	Foreign intercourse by sea
Longtime residence; the "nuclear area" of Chinese culture	Populated mainly by southward migrations since Tang times
Comparatively uniform ethnic makeup	Numerous ethnic groups
Mandarin dialect (*guoyu*)	Many different dialects

Source: Adapted from Cressey 1956.

Such differences help account, in turn, for other contrasts between north and south. The greater strength of the lineage or "clan" system in south China, for example, may be explained at least in part by the requirements of a productive, labor-intensive southern rice economy based on extensive, cooperative waterworks. Similarly, the greater political instability of the south can be attributed not only to the simple fact of distance from the political power center of Beijing, but also to the specific ethnic and other tensions arising out of the unique south China economic and social milieu. Talhelm et al. (2012) argue that "farming rice makes cultures more interdependent, whereas farming wheat makes cultures more independent;" thus, the authors conclude that "rice-growing southern China is more interdependent and holistic-thinking than the wheat-growing north."

REGIONAL CHARACTERISTICS

The regional differences and local identifications that often found their way into dynastic histories, local gazetteers, and private writings were derived from a wide variety of sources. Some reflected concrete geographical circumstances. The richly productive agricultural areas and well-developed commercial activities of south China, for example, encouraged the regional stereotype of southerners as greedy, shrewd, and sometimes unscrupulous. Northerners, by contrast, were viewed as upright and honest. Some regional stereotypes were based on historical and literary associations. Thus, the people of Hunan province were assumed to possess the sentimentality and emotionalism of their poetic countryman Qu Yuan (third century BC); the people of Sichuan, the love of music and adventure of their countryman Sima Xiangru (179–117 BC); and the people of Shandong, the frugality, simplicity, honesty, and sincerity of Confucius himself.

Still other stereotypes were based on cosmological principles. According to the pervasive Chinese theory of the five agents (see chapter 6), the element metal (*jin*) was associated with the direction west. People in west China were therefore believed to enjoy using weapons and to favor "cutting" (that is, spicy) food. Since the south was associated with fire (*huo*), southern Chinese were naturally supposed to be fiery in temperament. Northerners, by contrast, were like water (*shui*)—cold, stern, slow, and straight. The east belonged to the element wood (*mu*), giving easterners the characteristics of growing, flourishing, and constantly changing. The center corresponded to the element earth (*tu*), considered by the Chinese to be stable, well balanced, and harmonious. Thus the people of central China (variously defined) were solid and down to earth, without eccentricities.

Multiple regional stereotypes were common, and occasionally they conflicted. But the striking feature of such stereotypes was their tenacity and widespread acceptance over time. Wolfram Eberhard's 1965 study of contemporary Chinese provincial stereotypes on Taiwan, for instance, indicates a remarkable affinity with Qing dynasty views. According to this study the following major traits can be identified for each of the provinces of China Proper (excluding Xinjiang and Taiwan, which did not become provinces until the mid-1880s):

PROVINCIAL STEREOTYPES

Zhili (Hebei)	Tall and strong in stature; frank, honest, good-mannered, simple
Shandong	Tall and heavyset; frank, honest, straight, simple, upright
Shanxi	Tall; business-minded, simple, honest, resolute
Shaanxi	Strong and medium to tall; honest, sincere, resolute, enduring
Gansu	Tall to medium; enduring, honest, simple
Henan	Tall and strong; honest, straightforward, mannered, violent tempered
Jiangsu	Medium to small and delicate; cunning, crafty, versatile, refined, luxury-loving, good at business
Anhui	Medium size; good in business, simple, frugal, clever
Zhejiang	Medium to small; cunning; obstinate; good in business
Jiangxi	Medium to small; greedy; scheming
Hubei	Medium to small; scheming, unreliable
Hunan	Medium to small; emotional, heroic, military, upright
Sichuan	Medium to small; violent temper, too much talk
Fujian	Small to medium; petty-minded, cunning, risk-taking, clannish
Guangdong	Small; innovative, risk-taking, clannish

Guangxi   Small; enduring, hardy, culturally backward
Guizhou   Medium; frugal, straight, poor, underdeveloped
Yunnan   Medium to small; barbaric, enduring, frugal

By way of comparison, we might consider the Kangxi emperor's observations concerning the personality traits of his subjects:

> Sometimes I have stated that the people of a certain province have certain bad characteristics: thus the men of Fujian are turbulent and love acts of daring . . . while the people of Shaanxi are tough and cruel. . . . Shandong men are stubborn in a bad way; they always have to be first, they nurse their hatreds, they seem to value life lightly, and a lot of them become robbers. . . . The people of Shaanxi are so stingy that they won't even care for the aged in their own families; . . . and since the Jiangsu people are both prosperous and immoral—there's no need to blow their feathers to look for faults. [At another point Kangxi remarked] "The people of the North are strong; they must not copy the fancy diets of the Southerners, who are physically frail, live in a different environment, and have different stomachs and bowels."

County gazetteers (*xianzhi*) promoted more localized stereotypes. In general, the elite compilers of these works distinguished between residents who were comparatively docile and those who were potentially troublesome. Those in the former category (the vast majority of China's counties) tended to be described by stock phrases indicating the "absence of feuds," the avoidance of "involvement in lawsuits," and the habit of "never evading tax payments." Those in the latter category were labeled as "hot tempered," "frequently involved in feuds and lawsuits," and "militant." Such designations did not necessarily apply throughout any given province, however. In Hubei, for example, the residents of Huang'an county came to be described as "tough and daring," whereas in nearby Huanmei the local people were viewed as "soft and timid." Similarly, in Hebei the natives of Xuanhua appeared in county gazetteers to be "militant and adventurous," while in Shunde they were "mild, inactive, and fond of learning the Confucian Classics."

The prevalence of such regional, provincial, and local stereotypes unquestionably affected the outlook and policies of both the throne and local Qing officials, who were prohibited by law from serving in their home areas. They also affected the conduct of Chinese personal and commercial relations—including what G. William Skinner 1971 refers to as the "export" of entrepreneurial talent. Certainly it is no accident that fellow provincials from three neighboring counties in central Shanxi dominated the remittance banking business in China for over a century. Regional and local stereotypes may even have influenced the subconscious self-image of individuals in China. Obviously, they posed an obstacle to nationwide social and political integration.

Appendix D

Glossary of
Some Philosophical Concepts

I. General Philosophical Terms

Note: For a more complete glossary, see Minford 2014, 795–815, esp. 799 ff.

A. *Tian* 天 (Heaven) Often viewed as the equivalent of "Nature"

B. *Dao* 道 (The "Way") Like *Tian*, often equated with "Nature." *Dao* can also refer to "teachings"—for example, the "way" of Confucians, Daoists, or Buddhists

C. *Taiji* 太極 (The "Supreme Ultimate") A relatively late (Song dynasty; 960–1279) philosophical concept—often equated with *Tian* and *Dao*. The Supreme Ultimate refers to a process that generates *yin* and *yang* (see below), which interact to produce all things. It is not, however, any sort of creator deity, external to the cosmos; like *Tian* and *Dao*, it is a term for the self-generating and self-sustaining structure and function of the universe

D. *Yinyang* 陰陽 (Cosmic creative forces; also phases of change and complementary opposites—for example, dark-light; cold-hot; female-male; square-round; etc.)

E. *Li* 理 (Principle) Li is the essential or defining characteristic of a class or category of things; every type of thing that exists, has existed, or will exist has a "principle")

F. *Qi* 氣 (Cosmic breath; material force; the "stuff" of which all things are constituted). *Qi* gives materiality and "life" to all things, seen and unseen, animate and "inanimate"

G. *Wuxing* 五行 (Five Agents) These represent dynamic "qualities" identified with the characteristics and tendencies of wood, fire, earth, metal, and water 木火土金水, respectively. They manifest themselves in various combinations as "material force," thus animating even "inanimate" objects. Also translated elements, phrases, etc.

  H. *Shen* 神 (Spirit) A word with the same basic range of meanings in Chinese as in English

  I. *Xin* 心 (Mind; also rendered Heart-Mind)

  J. *Ti* 體 (Substance; foundation)

  K. *Yong* 用 (Function; application)

II. Some Key Concepts in Confucianism (*Rujia* 儒家)

  A. Core values:

    1. *Xiaodi* 孝悌 (Filial piety and fraternal submission)

    2. *Zhong* 忠 (Devotion or loyalty)

    3. *Shu* 恕 (Reciprocity)

    4. *Cheng* 誠 (Sincerity)

  B. The "Five Constant Virtues":

    1. *Ren* 仁 (Humaneness; humanity; graded love)

    2. *Yi* 義 (Duty; righteousness; moral discrimination)

    3. *Li* 禮 (Ritual; propriety; etiquette; etc.)

    4. *Zhi* 智 (Humane knowledge or wisdom)

    5. *Xin* 信 (Faithfulness; standing by one's word; etc.)

III. Some Key Concepts in Philosophical Daoism (*Daojia* 道家)

  A. Basic concepts:

    1. *Ziran* 自然 (Naturalness; spontaneity)

    2. *Wuwei* 無爲 ("Doing-nothing"; not overdoing)

    3. *Pu* 樸 (An uncarved block of wood; symbol of simplicity)

IV. Some Key Concepts in Religious Daoism (*Daojiao* 道教)

  A. *Neidan* 內丹 ("Inner alchemy"—designed to achieve bodily transformation through meditation, breathing exercises, sexual practices, etc.)

  B. *Waidan* 外丹 ("External alchemy"—designed to achieve bodily transformation through herbs, drugs, etc.)

  C. *Gong* 功 (merits)

  D. *Guo* 過 (demerits)

  E. *Xian* 仙 (An immortal being)

V. Some Key Concepts in Buddhism (*Fojiao* 佛教)

  A. Basic terms:

    1. *Karma* ("Act" in Sanskrit [Chinese: *yeyin* 業因, *yinguo* 因果, etc.]; refers to both deeds and thoughts)

    2. *Bodhi* ("Enlightenment" in Sanskrit [Chinese: *wu* 悟])

    3. *Nirvana* ("Extinction" in Sanskrit [Chinese: *niepan* 涅槃]; likened to the blowing out of a candle)

4. Theravada ("The Way of the Elders" in Sanskrit [Chinese: 小乘];
   a rather restrictive form of Indian Buddhism stressing gradual accumulation of *karma*)
5. Mahayana ("The Great Vehicle" in Sanskrit [Chinese: 大乘]; an
   eclectic and "expedient" form of Indian Buddhism stressing salvation by faith)

B. Other important ideas:
   1. *Jingtu* 淨土 (The "Pure Land"; aka Xitian 西天 or 極樂西天 The
      "Western Paradise") This was the most popular school of Ma-
      hayana Buddhism in Qing China
   2. Amitabha (The "Buddha of Immeasurable Radiance" in Sanskrit
      [Chinese: Amituo Fo 阿彌陀佛]; the Buddha who presides over
      the Western Paradise)
   3. Guanyin *pusa* 觀音菩薩 (The Goddess of Mercy; agent of Am-
      itabha—a bodhisattva ["enlightened one"] who postpones *nirvana*
      to help others achieve enlightenment)
   4. *Diyu* 地獄 (Courts of Judgment; sometimes translated Hells; vari-
      ously numbered—most commonly ten [十殿] or eighteen [十八
      殿]). Here, the "souls" of the deceased are tortured before being
      reborn
   5. *Yanluo wang* 閻羅王 (The "King of the Underworld"—that is,
      Courts of Judgment)

Appendix E

Tables of Contents for Selected Editions of the *Wanbao quanshu* (1612, 1636, 1758, and 1828)

I. *Wanbao quanshu* 萬寶全書 (1612)

Full title: [新板] 全補 [天下便用] 文林紗錦萬寶全書
Volumes: 三十四卷
Editor (putative): Liu Shuangsong 劉雙松
Date: 萬曆四十年 (1612)
Publisher: 書林安正堂

天文門 1 [*Tianwen*; The Heavens]
地理門 2 [*Dili*; Earth]
人紀門 3 [*Renji*; Human Relationships]
外夷門 4 [*Waiyi*; Outer "Barbarians"]
官品門 5 [*Guanpin*; Official Rank]
律法門 6 [*Lüfa*; Law]
武備門 7 [*Wubei*; Military Preparedness]
八譜門 8 [*Bapu*; Eight Amusements]
琴學門 9 [*Qinxue*; The Qin or "Zither"]
棋譜門 10 [*Qipu*; Chess]
書法門 11 [*Shufa*; Calligraphy]
畫譜門 12 [*Huapu*; Painting]
文翰門 13 [*Wenhan*; Correspondence]
啟劄門 14 [*Qizha*; Official Documents]
伉儷門 15 [*Kangli*; Marriage]
喪祭門 16 [*Sangji*; Mourning and Sacrifice]
體式門 17 [*Tishi*; Stylistic Models]
詩對門 18 [*Shidui*; Poetry and Couplets]
涓吉門 19 [*Juanji*; Time Selection]

卜筮門 20 [*Bushi*; Divination with Milfoil]
星命門 21 [*Xingming*; Astrology]
相法門 22 [*Xiangfa*; Physiognomy]
營宅門 23 [*Yingzhai*; Buildings]
修真門 24 [*Xiuzhen*; Immortal Arts]
養生門 25 [*Yangsheng*; Nourishing Life]
醫學門 26 [*Yixue*; Medicine]
全嬰門 27 [*Quanying*; Infants]
訓童門 28 [*Xuntong*; Instructing Children]
算法門 29 [*Suanfa*; Calculations]
農桑門 30 [*Nongsang*; Farming and Sericulture]
勸諭門 31 [*Quanyu*; Exhortation]
侑觴門 32 [*Youshang*; Drinking Games]
笑談門 33 [*Xiaotan*; Jokes]
風月門 34 [*Fengyue*; Erotica/Sexual Adventures]

II. *Wanbao quanshu* 萬寶全書 (1636)

Full title: 新刻天如張先生精選石渠彙要萬寶全書
Volumes: 三十四卷
Editor (putative): Zhang Pu 張溥
Date: 明崇禎九年 (1636)
Publisher: 存仁堂

天文門 1 [*Tianwen*; The Heavens]
地理門 2 [*Dili*; The Earth]
人紀門 3 [*Renji*; Human Relationships]
時令門 4 [*Shiling*; The Seasons]
農桑門 5 [*Nongsang*; Farming and Sericulture]
文翰門 6 [*Wenhan*; Correspondence]
體式門 7 [*Tishi*; Stylistic Models]
勸諭門 8 [*Quanyu*; Exhortation]
爵祿門 9 [*Juelu*; Rank and Emoluments]
茶經門 10 [*Chajing*; Tea Protocols]
外夷門 11 [*Waiyi*; Outer "Barbarians"]
酒令門 12 [*Jiuling*; Drinking Games]
醫學門 13 [*Yixue*; Medicine]
夢解門 14 [*Mengjie*; Dream Interpretation]
狀法門 15 [*Zhuangfa*; Written Complaints]
尅擇門 16 [*Keze*; Selection of Auspicious Dates]
命理門 17 [*Mingli*; Fortune Telling]

相法門 18 [*Xiangfa*; Physiognomy]
秤命門 19 [*Chengming*; Fate Calculations (based on the Eight Characters 八字)]
圍棋局勢門 20 [*Weiqi jushi*; *Weiqi* (Chess) Configurations] and 投壺侑觴門 [*Touhu*; (Arrow Throwing) and *Youshang* (Drinking Games)]
笑談門 21 [*Xiaotan*; Jokes]—also includes an unnumbered section titled 琴法須知 *Qinfa xuzhi* (Essentials for Playing the *Qin* or Zither)]
種子門 22 [*Zhongzi*; Gestation]
營造門 23 [*Yingzao*; Construction]
堪輿門 24 [*Kanyu*; Siting or Geomancy]
字法門 25 [*Zifa*; Calligraphy]
卜筮門 26 [*Bushi*; Divination with Milfoil]
對聯門 27 [*Duilian*; Couplets]
筭法門 28 [*Suanfa*; Calculations]
畫學門 29 [*Huaxue*; Painting]
法病門 30 [*Fabing*; Managing Illness]
養生門 31 [*Yangsheng*; Nourishing Life]
卜筶門 32 [*Bugua/kuo*; Divination with Arrowheads]
牛馬門 33 [*Niuma*; Oxen and Horses]
雜覽門 34 [*Zalan*; Miscellaneous Matters]

III. *Wanbao quanshu* 萬寶全書 (1758)

Full title: *Xinke Tianru Zhang Xiansheng jing xuan Shiqu hui yao Wanbao quanshu* 新刻天如張先生精選石渠彙要萬寶全書
Volumes: 三十二卷
Editor (putative): Zhang Pu 張溥
Date: 乾隆戊寅 (1758)
Publisher: 老會賢堂
A scanned version of this work is available on line at http://digital.staatsbibliothek-berlin.de/dms/werkansicht/?PPN=PPN3303598916&DMDID=DMDLOG_0000.
[NB: The Chinese University of Hong Kong has a photocopied version of this work titled *Zengbu wanbao quanshu* 增補萬寶全書. Although it is also dated 1758 and has exactly the same preface as the above work, the print and formatting are different and there are some discrepancies in the table of contents as well as in the content of some subcategories. My guess is that this is a "pirated" version.]

天文門 1 [*Tianwen*; The Heavens]
地理門 2 [*Dili*; Earth]

人紀門 3 [*Renji*; Human Relationships]
養生門 4 [*Yangsheng*; Nourishing Life]
外夷門 5 [*Waiyi*; Outer "Barbarians"]
民用門 6 [*Minyong*; People's Uses]
詩對門 7 [*Shidui*; Poetic Couplets]
種子門 8 [*Zhongzi*; Seeds [that is, Gestation]
雜用門 9 [*Zayong*; Miscellaneous Uses]
侑觴門 10 [*Youshang*; Drinking Games]
相法門 11 [*Xiangfa*; Physiognomy]
農桑門 12 [*Nongsang*; Farming and Sericulture]
八譜門 13 [*Bapu*; Eight Amusements]
僊術門 14 [*Xian* (仙) *shu*; Immortal Arts]
談笑門 15 [*Tanxiao*; Jokes]
武備門 16 [*Wubei*; Military Preparedness]
數命門 17 [*Shumin*; Calculating Fate]
琴學門 18 [*Qinxue*; The Qin or "Zither"]
营造門 19 [*Yingzao*; Construction]
書柬門 20 [*Shujian*; Correspondence)
算法門 21 [*Suanfa*; Calculations]
堪輿門 22 [*Kanyu*; Siting/Geomancy]
大清法律門 23 [*Da Qing falü*; Qing Code]
爵祿門 24 [*Juelu*; Rank and Emoluments]
勸論門 25 [*Quanlun*; Exhortation]
祛病門 26 [*Qubing*; Dispelling Illness]
時令門 27 [*Shiling*; The Seasons]
畫譜門 28 [*Huapu*; Painting]
字法門 29 [*Zifa*; Calligraphy]
牛馬門 30 [*Niuma*; Oxen and Horses]
狀法門 31 [*Zhuangfa*; Written Statements]
解夢門 32 [*Jiemeng*; Dream Interpretation]

IV. *Wanbao quanshu* 萬寶全書 (1828)

Full title: *Zengbu wanbao quanshu* 增補萬寶全書]
Volumes: 二十九卷
Editor (putative): Chen Jiru 陳繼儒 [Amplified by Mao Huanwen 毛煥文]
Date: 道光八年 (1828) [New version of a 乾隆四年 (1739) edition]
Publisher: 貴文堂

天文門 1 [*Tianwen*; The Heavens]
地理門 2 [*Dili*; Earth]

人紀門 3 [*Renji*; Human Relationships]
品級門 4 [*Pinji*; Official Rank]
外夷門 5 [*Waiyi*; Outer "Barbarians"]
滿漢門 6 [*Man Han men*; Manchu and Chinese (Terms)]
[NB: The subcategories listed in the table of contents for this section do not correspond very closely to the actual subcategories in it.]
字法門 7 [*Zifa*; Calligraphy]
文翰門 8 [*Wenhan*; Correspondence]
對聯門 9 [*Duilian*; Couplets]
算法門 10 [*Suanfa*; Calculations]
談笑門 11 [*Tanxiao*; Jokes]
[NB: 琴學門 (Learning the Qin or "Zither") is included as a subcategory under *Tanxiao* rather than as a separate category as it often is.]
畫譜門 12 [*Huapu*; Painting]
博奕門 13 [*Boyi*; Playing Chess (Xiangqi 象棋 and Weiqi 圍棋)]
酒令門 14 [*Jiuling*; Drinking Games]
茶經門 15 [*Chajing*; Tea]
勸論門 16 [*Quanlun*; Exhortation]
占時門 17 [*Zhanshi*; Determining Times]
農桑門 Not listed in the TOC [*Nongsang*; Farming and Sericulture]
解夢門 18 [*Jiemeng*; Dream Interpretation]
相法門 19 [*Xiangfa*; Physiognomy]
醫學門 20 [*Yixue*; Medicine]
種子門 21 [*Zhongzi*; Seeds [that is, Gestation]
牛馬門 22 [*Niuma*; Oxen and Horses]
通書門 23 [*Tongshu*; Almanac (Information)]
命理門 24 [*Mingli*; Fortune Telling]
稱命門 25 [*Chengming*; Naming Fate]
卜筮門 26 [*Bushi*; Divination with Milfoil]
宅經門 27 [*Zhaijing*; Home Construction]
堪輿門 28 [*Kanyu*; Siting/Geomancy]
祛病門 29 [*Qubing*; Dispelling Illness]

Appendix F

Some English-Language Writings on *Honglou Meng* (Dream of the Red Chamber)

Preliminary note: The works listed below are just a few of the many English-language studies on the *Dream of the Red Chamber*. In Chinese, the novel has generated an enormous amount of attention as part of a scholarly enterprise known as "Red [Chamber] Studies" (*Hongxue*).

ARTICLES

Bech, Lene 2004. "Fiction that Leads to Truth: The Story of the Stone as Skillful Means." *CLEAR* 26: 1–21.

Brightwell, Erin 2005. "Analyzing Gender: Wang Xi-feng and the Shrew." *Tamkang Review* 36.1–2: 67–87.

Brown, Tristan Gerard 2011. "The Metaphorical Dimensions of Symbolic Prices and Real-World Values in *Hong Lou Meng*." *Tsing Hua Journal of Chinese Studies*, new series 41.4 (December): 795–812. Available at http://thjcs.web.nthu.edu.tw/ ezfiles/662/1662/img/1294/THJCS414–6.pdf.

Cooper, Eugene and Meng Zhang 1993. "Patterns of Cousin Marriage in Rural Zhejiang and in *Dream of the Red Chamber*." *Journal of Asian Studies* 52.1 (February): 90–106.

Eber, Irene 1996. "Riddles in The Dream of the Red Chamber." In Hasan-Rokem and David Shulman, eds. 1996: 237–51.

Edwards, Louise 1988–1989. "Jia Baoyu and Essential Feminine Purity." *The Journal of the Oriental Society of Australia* 20–21: 36–47.

Edwards, Louise 1990a. "Gender Imperatives in *Honglou meng*: Baoyu's Bisexuality." *CLEAR* 12: 69–81.

Edwards, Louise 1990b. "Women in *Honglou meng*: Prescriptions of Purity in the Femininity of Qing Dynasty China." *Modern China* 16.4: 407–29.

Edwards, Louise 1993. "Representations of Women and Social Power in Eighteenth Century China: The Case of Wang Xifeng." *Late Imperial China* 14.1 (June): 34–59.

Edwards, Louise 1995. "Women Warriors and Amazons of the Mid Qing Texts *Jinghua yuan* and *Honglou meng*." *Modern Asian Studies* 29.2: 225–55.

Edwards, Louise 2001. "New Hongxue and the 'Birth of the Author:' Yu Pingbo's 'On Qin Keqing's Death.'" *CLEAR* 23: 31–54.

Edwards, Louise 2013. "Painting Boundaries of Sex Segregation in Qing China: Representing the Family in *The Red Chamber Dream*." In Silbergeld and Ching, eds. 2013: 339–71.

Ferrara, Mark 2005a. "True Matters Concealed: Utopia, Desire, and Enlightenment in *Honglou meng*." *Mosaic* 38.4: 191–204.

Ferrara, Mark 2005b. "'Emptying Emptiness': Kongkong daoren in *Honglou meng*." *Tamkang Review* 36.1–2: 105–16.

Ferrara, Mark 2011. "'Rustic Fiction Indeed!: Reading Jia Yu-cun in *Dream of the Red Chamber*." *New Zealand Journal of Asian Studies* 13: 87–99.

Gao, George 1974. "Lin Yutang's Appreciation of the 'Red Chamber Dream.'" *Renditions* 2 (Spring): 23–30.

Ge, Liangyan 2002. "The Mythic Stone in *Honglou meng* and an Intertext of Ming-Qing Fiction Criticism." *Journal of Asian Studies* 61.1: 57–82.

Gray, R. 2005. "Returning to the Unpolished: Jia Bao-yu and Zhuang-zi in *Honglou meng*." *Tamkang Review* 36.1–2: 177–94.

Hawkes, David 1980. "The Translator, the Mirror and the Dream—Some Observations on a New Theory." *Renditions* 13 (Spring): 5–20.

Hawkes, David 1986. "*The Story of the Stone*: A Symbolist Novel." *Renditions* 25 (Spring): 6–17.

Kao, Yu-kung 1977. "Lyric Vision in Chinese Narrative: A Reading of *Hung-lou Meng* and *Ju-lin Wai-shih*." In Plaks, ed. 1977: 227–43.

Lee, Haiyin 1997. "Love or Lust? The Sentimental Self in *Honglou meng*." *CLEAR* 19: 85–111.

Levy, Dore J. "Embedded Texts: How to Read Poetry in the *Story of the Stone*." *Tamkang Review* 36.1–2: 195–228.

Li, Qiancheng 2005. "Jia Zheng: Self, Family, and Religion in *Honglou meng*." *Tamkang Review* 36.1–2: 3–34.

Liao, Chaoyang 1992–1993. "Mutant Texts and Minor Literature: *Honglou meng* as National Narrative." *Tamkang Review* 23: 143–63.

Lin, Shuen-fu 1992. "Chia Pao-yu's First Visit to the Land of Illusion: An Analysis of a Literary Dream in an Interdisciplinary Perspective." *CLEAR* 14 (December): 77–106.

McMahon, Keith 2004. "Eliminating Traumatic Antinomies: Sequels to *Honglou meng*." In M. W. Huang, ed. 2004: 98–115.

Miller, Lucien 1995. "Children of the Dreams: The Adolescent World in Cao Xueqin's *Honglou meng*." In Kinney, ed. 1995: 219–50.

Plaks, Andrew 1990. "Chang Hsin-chih on How to Read the *Hung-lou meng* (Dream of the Red Chamber)." In Rolston, ed. 1990: 316–22.

Plaks, Andrew 2005. "Completeness and Partiality in Traditional Commentaries on *Honglou meng.*" *Tamkang Review* 36.1–2 (Fall–Winter): 117–35.

Plaks, Andrew 1977. "Allegory in *Hsi-yu Chi* and *Hung-lou Meng.*" In Plaks, ed. 1977: 163–202.

Saussey, Haun 1987. "Reading and Folly in *Dream of the Red Chamber.*" *CLEAR* 9.1–2 (July): 23–47.

Saussey, Haun 2003. "The Age of Attribution: Or, How the *Honglou meng* Finally Acquired an Author." *CLEAR* 25: 119–32.

Saussy, Haun 1997. "Women's Writing Before and Within the *Hong lou meng.*" In Widmer and Chang 1997: 285–305.

Schonebaum, A. "The Medical Casebook of *Hong lou meng.*" *Tamkang Review* 36.1–2: 229–50.

Soong, Stephen 1977. "Two Types of Misinterpretation—Some Poems from 'Red Chamber Dream.'" *Renditions* 7 (Spring): 73–92.

Sychov, L. and V. Sychov 1981. "The Role of Costume in Cao Xueqin's Novel *The Dream of the Red Chamber.*" *Tamkang Review* 11.3: 287–305.

Wagner, Marsha 1985. "Maids and Servants in Dream of the Red Chamber: Individuality and the Social Order." In Hegel and Hessney, eds. 1985: 251–81.

Waltner, Ann 1989. "On Not Becoming a Heroine: Lin Daiyu and Cui Ying-ying." *Signs* 15.1: 63–89.

Wang, John C. Y. 1978. "The Chih-yen-chai Commentary and the *Dream of the Red Chamber*: A Literary Study." In Rickett, ed. 1978: 189–200.

Wang, Ying 2003. "Imitation as Dialogue: The Mongolian Writer Yinzhan naxi (1837–1892) and His Imitations of *The Dream of the Red Chamber.*" *Tamkang Review* 34.2: 23–61.

Wang, Ying 2005. "The Disappearing of the Simulated Oral Context and the Use of the Supernatural Realm in *Honglou meng.*" *CLEAR* 27 (2005): 137–50.

Wang, Ying 2006. "The Supernatural as the Author's Sphere: Jinghua Yuan's Reprise of the Rhetorical Strategies of *Honglou meng.*" *T'oung Pao* 92: 129–61.

Widmer, Ellen 1997. "Ming Loyalism and the Woman's Voice in Fiction After *Hong lou meng.*" In Widmer and Chang, eds. 1997: 366–96.

Widmer, Ellen 2004. "*Honglou meng* Sequels and Their Female Readers in Nineteenth-Century China." In M. W. Huang, ed. 2004: 116–42.

Widmer, Ellen. "Extreme Makeover: Daiyu and Baochai in Two Early Sequels to *Honglou Meng.*" *Nan Nü* 8.2 (2006): 290–315.

Wo, Karen Hoi-kwan 2008. Language and Culture in 'Hongloumeng.'" LCOM Papers 1: 53–63.

Wong, Kam-ming 1977. "Point of View, Norms, and Structure: *Hung-lou Meng* and Lyrical Fiction." In Plaks, ed. 203–226.

Wong, Kam-ming 2005. "Anatomy of The Stone: Dotting the 'I' of the Lichee and the Monkey." *Tamkang Review* 36.1–2: 147–76.

Wu, Hung 1997. "Beyond Stereotypes: The Twelve Beauties in Qing Court Art and the *Dream of the Red Chamber.*" In Widmer and Chang, eds. 1997: 306–65.

Yang, Michael 1996. "Naming in *Honglou meng*," *Chinese Literature: Essays, Articles, and Reviews* 18: 69–100.

Yau, Ka-Fai 2005. "Realistic Paradoxes: The Story of the *Story of the Stone.*" *Comparative Literature* 57.2: 117–34.

Yee, Angelina 1995. "Self, Sexuality, and Writing in *Honglou meng*" *Harvard Journal of Asiatic Studies* 55.2 (December): 373–407.

Yee, Angelina 1990. "Counterpoise in *Honglou meng,*" *Harvard Journal of Asiatic Studies* 50.2 (December): 613–50.

Yim, Chi-hung 2000. "The 'Deficiency of Yin in the Liver'—Dai yu's Malady and Fubi in *Dream of the Red Chamber.*" *CLEAR* 22: 85–111.

Yü, Anthony 1980. "Self and Family in the *Hung-lou meng*: A New Look at Lin Tai-yü as Tragic Heroine." *Chinese Literature: Essays, Articles, and Reviews* 2.2 (July): 199–223.

Yü, Ying-shih 1974. "The Two Worlds of *Hung-lou meng.*" *Renditions* 2 (Spring): 5–21.

Zhao, Xiaohuan 2011. "Court Trials and Miscarriage of Justice in *Dream of the Red Chamber.*" *Law and Literature* 23.1: 129–56.

Zhou, Ruchang 2005. "None The Red Chamber Message Hears: Art as Living Philosophy." *Tamkang Review* 36.1–2: 89–104.

Zhou, Yiqun 2013. "*Honglou Meng* and Agrarian Values." *Late Imperial China* 34.1 (June): 28–66.

BOOKS

Edwards, Louise 1994. *Men and Women in Qing China: Gender in "The Red Chamber Dream."* New York: E.J. Brill.

Hasan-Rokem, Galit and David Shulman, eds. 1996. *On Riddles and Other Enigmatic Modes.* Oxford: Oxford University Press.

Knoerle, Jeanne 1972. *The Dream of the Red Chamber: A Critical Study.* Bloomington: Indiana University Press.

Levy, Dore J. 1999. *Ideal and Actual in the Story of the Stone.* New York: Columbia University Press.

Li, Qiancheng 2004. *Fictions of Enlightenment: Journey to the West, Tower of Myriad Mirrors, and Dream of the Red Chamber.* Honolulu: University of Hawaii Press.

Li, Wai-yee 1988. "Rhetoric of Fantasy and Irony: Studies in the *Liao-chai Chih-i* and *Hungloumeng.*" Unpublished Ph.D. dissertation, Princeton University, 1988.

Liu, Zaifu 2008. *Reflections on Dream of the Red Chamber.* Amherst, N.Y.: Cambria Press.

Miller, Lucien 1975. *Masks of Fiction in Dream of the Red Chamber: Myth, Mimesis, and Persona.* Tucson: University of Arizona Press.

Plaks, Andrew H. 1976. *Archetype and Allegory in the "Dream of the Red Chamber."* Princeton, N.J.: Princeton University Press (reprinted by UMI Books on Demand, 1993).

Schonebaum, Andrew and Tina Lu, eds. 2012. *Approaches to Teaching The Story of the Stone (Dream of the Red Chamber).* Chicago: Modern Language Association of America.

Wang, Jing 1992. *The Story of Stone: Intertextuality, Ancient Chinese Stone Lore, and the Stone Symbolism in Dream of the Red Chamber*. Durham: Duke University Press.

Wu, Shichang 1961. *On the Red Chamber Dream: A Critical Study of Two Annotated Manuscripts of the Eighteenth Century*. Oxford: Clarendon Press.

Xiao, Chi 2001. *The Chinese Garden as Lyric Enclave: A Generic Study of the Story of the Stone*. Ann Arbor: University of Michigan.

Yi, Jeannie Jinsheng 2004. *The Dream of the Red Chamber: An Allegory of Love*. Paramus, N.J.: Homa and Sekey Books.

Yu, Anthony 1997. *Rereading the Stone: Desire and the Making of Fiction in Dream of the Red Chamber*. Princeton: Princeton University Press.

Yu, Yingshi 1981. *Honglou meng de liangge shijie* (The Two Worlds of the *Dream of the Red Chamber*). Taipei: Lianjin chuban she (includes English translation).

Zhou, Ruchang 2009. *Between Noble and Humble: Cao Xueqin and Dream of the Red Chamber*. New York: Peter Lang Academic Press. Edited by Ronald Gray and Mark Ferrara.

Appendix G

The Three Character Classic (*Sanzi Jing;* 三字經)

Note: This work is often attributed to Wang Yinglin 王應麟 (1223–1296) with later elaborations by various authors. During the Ming and Qing dynasties the *Three Character Classic* became one of three major primers (the other two were known as the *Thousand Character Classic* [*Qianzi wen*] and the *Hundred Family Names* [*Bai jia xing*]) which young students invariably memorized at the outset of their classical education. The assumed readers were males, although young girls in elite households might also begin their education with these basic texts. For a discussion of the controversies surrounding the authorship of the *Sanzi jing*, see James T. C. Liu 1985.

[Lines 1–4]
Humans at birth 人之初
are [all] fundamentally good. 性本善
[Their] natures are close to one another; 性相近
[but] in habit/practice they are far apart from one another. 習相遠

[Mencius (line 9) held the position that Man's nature is basically good; cf. Xunzi (line 172): Man's nature is basically evil (not, however, in the sense of "original sin"); cf. Yang Xiong (line 172): Man's nature is neither good nor bad—also the position of Gaozi.]

[Lines 5–8]
If there is no education, 苟不教
[a person's good] nature will decline. 性乃遷
The way of education 教之道
is to value thoroughness. 貴以專

[A standard commentary to these lines emphasizes that education begins even before birth. The prospective mother should see no evil sights, nor hear evil sounds. She must not indulge in strong language or eat unusual dishes, and should cultivate the values of loyalty, filial piety, etc. After the child is born it should be taught to eat with the right hand, to be deferential, unselfish, etc. Formal schooling should begin about eight *sui* (seven years old in Western reckoning).]

[Lines 9–12]
In the past, the mother of Mencius 昔孟母
chose a [proper] district in which to reside. 擇鄰處
When her child would not learn, 子不學
she broke [the thread on her] loom shuttle. 斷機杼

[After several unsatisfactory moves—first near a cemetery, then near a marketplace—the mother of Mencius found a location near a school, where her son finally acquired scholarly habits. The breaking of the thread on the shuttle symbolized the bad effect of not continuing to learn.]

[Lines 13–16]
Dou, [the scholar from] Swallow Hills 竇燕山
had a method for righteousness. 有義方
He taught five sons 教五子
who all elevated the family name. 名俱揚

[Dou Yujun lived in the Song dynasty in the tenth century. All of his sons achieved high office.]

[Lines 17–20]
If children are fed but not taught, 養不教
it is the father's fault. 父之過
To teach without severity 教不嚴
is the lazy thing for a teacher [to do]. 師之惰
[Lines 21–24]
If a child does not learn, 子不學
[that is] not proper. 非所宜
If in one's youth there is no learning, 幼不學
what will [a person] be [like] in old age? 老何為
[Lines 25–28]
[If] jade is not polished 玉不琢
it cannot become a useful implement. 不成器
[If] a person does not learn, 人不學
[he or she] cannot know righteousness. 不知義

[Lines 29–32]
The child of a man, 為人子
in the period of its youth, 方少時
should become close to teachers and friends, 親師友
and practice ritual and etiquette. 習禮儀
[Lines 33–36]
[Huang 黃] Xiang, at nine years of age 香九齡
could warm [his parents'] bed. 能溫席
Filial piety towards parents 孝于親
is what should be grasped. 所當執

[Huang Xiang, of the Han dynasty (second century CE), was one of the famous Twenty-Four Examples of Filial Piety (*Ershisi xiao* 二十四孝).]

[Lines 37–40]
[Kong 孔] Rong, at four years of age 融四歲
was able to leave [the biggest] pears [for others to eat]. 能讓梨
To subordinate oneself to elders 弟于長
should be the first [thing to be] known. 宜先知

[Kong Rong was a twentieth-generation descendent of Confucius. He died in 208 CE. Reportedly, he explained his unselfish behavior by saying: "I am a small boy, so I take the small pears." Four *sui* would be three years old according to Western reckoning.]

[Lines 41–44]
Begin with filial piety and fraternal submission; 首孝弟
then acquire knowledge (lit. see and hear [things]). 次見聞
Know how to count 知某數
and know how to read. 識某文
[Lines 45–48]
One to ten; 一而十
tens to hundreds. 十而百
Hundreds to thousands; 百而千
thousands to ten thousands. 千而萬
[Lines 49–52]
The Three Powers 三才者
are Heaven, Earth, and Man. 天地人
The Three Luminaries 三光者
are the sun, the moon, and stars. 日月星
[Lines 53–56]
The Three Bonds are: 三綱者
the duty of ruler and subject; 君臣義
the closeness of father and child; 父子親
the agreement of husbands and wives. 夫婦順

[Lines 57–60]
[We] speak of spring and summer; 曰春夏
[we] speak of autumn and winter. 曰秋冬
These four seasons 此四時
revolve without ceasing. 運不窮
[Lines 61–64]
[We] speak of south and north; 曰南北
[we] speak of west and east. 曰西東
These four directions 此四方
respond to the middle. 應乎中
[Lines 65–68]
[We] speak of water and fire 曰水火
and wood, metal and earth. 木金土
These five agents [activities, qualities, etc.] 此五行
originate in numbers. 本乎數

[This last reference is to the numerology of the *Zhouyi/Yijing*. The *wuxing* were considered to be not only the constituent "elements" of all things, but also cosmic forces that produced or overcame one another in various sequences. For an example of the five agents as cosmological symbols, see the commentary after line 254 below.]

[Lines 69–72]
[We] speak of humaneness and righteousness, 曰仁義
propriety, wisdom, and faithfulness. 禮智信
These Five Constant [Virtues] 此五常
cannot accommodate confusion. 不容紊
[Lines 73–76]
Rice, spiked millet, and pulse; 稻粱菽
wheat, glutinous millet and common millet; 麥黍稷
these six grains 此六谷
are what humans eat. 人所食
[Lines 77–80]
Horses, oxen and sheep; 馬牛羊
chicken, dogs and pigs; 雞犬豕
these six animals 此六畜
are what humans provide feed for. 人所飼
[Lines 81–84]
[We] speak of joy and anger; 曰喜怒
[we] speak of pity and fear. 曰哀懼
[and] love, hate and desire. 愛惡欲
Together, [these are the] seven emotions. 七情具
[Lines 85–88]
Gourds, earthenware and leather; 匏土革
wood, stone and metal; 木石金

silk and bamboo: 絲與竹
[These yield] the eight [musical] sounds. 乃八音
[Lines 89–96]
Great-great grandfather, great-grandfather, and grandfather 高曾祖
father and self; 父而身
self and son; 身而子
son and grandson; 子而孫
from son and grandson 自子孫
to great-grandson and great-great grandson: 至元曾
[These are] the nine agnates [that constitute] 乃九族
human relationships. 人之倫
[Lines 97–106]
The affection of fathers and children; 父子恩
the compliance of husbands and wives; 夫婦從
fraternal affection [lit. friendship] on the part of elder bothers; 兄則友
respectfulness on the part of younger brothers; 弟則恭
proper order between old and young, 長幼序
friendliness among friends; 友與朋
respect on the part of the sovereign; 君則敬
loyalty on the part of subjects: 臣則忠
These ten duties 此十義
are common to all humans. 人所同

[According to one well-known commentary, the ten duties are conceived of as: 2 in line 97, 2 in line 98, 1 in line 99, 1 in line 100, 2 in lines 101 and 102 combined, 1 in line 103, and 1 in line 104.]

[Lines 107–110]
In educating the young 凡訓蒙
there must be explanation and investigation [meticulousness], 須講究
detailed instructions from written commentaries, 詳訓詁
and clear punctuation of sentences. 名句讀
[Lines 111–114]
Those who learn 為學者
must have a beginning. 必有初
When [Zhu Xi's 朱熹] *Learning for the Young* is finished 小學終
[one] comes to the Four Books. 至四書
[Lines 115–122]
The *Analects* 論語者
consists of twenty sections 二十篇
in which [Confucius'] disciples 群弟子
have recorded [his] good words. 記善言
The *Mencius* 孟子者
is in seven sections. 七篇止
[These two works] explain the Way and its power, 講道德
speaking of benevolence and duty. 說仁義

[Lines 123–126]
The *Doctrine of the Mean* 作中庸
was created by the brush of Zisi. 子思筆
The middle does not lean to one side 中不偏
and the course does not change 庸不易

[Zisi's original name was Kong Ji. He was the grandson of Confucius.]

[Lines 127–130]
The *Great Learning* 作大學
was created by Zengzi. 乃曾子
It begins with [self] cultivation and ordering [of the family] 自修齊
and ends with pacifying [the empire] and governing [the state]. 至平治

[Zengzi's name was Zeng Can (also pronounced Zeng Shen). He is one of the most famous disciples of Confucius. He also supposedly wrote the *Xiaojing*; see line 131 below.

[Lines 131–134]
When the *Classic of Filial Piety* is understood [completely] 孝經通
and the Four Books have been mastered, 四書熟
Then the Six Classics 如六經
can begin to be read. 始可讀

[Lines 135–138]
The [works of] *Poetry, History* and the *Changes* 詩書易
and the [*Record of*] *Ritual* and the *Spring and Autumn* [*Annals*] 禮春秋
are called the Six Classics, 號六經
which should be explained and explored. 當講求

[The number of the Six Classics is usually calculated either by dividing the *Liji* into the *Record of Ritual* and the (now lost) *Classic of Music* (*Yuejing*), or by considering *Li* as a reference to both the *Rites of Zhou* (*Zhouli*) and the *Liji*.]

[Lines 139–142]
There are [also] the *Linked Mountains*, 有連山
the *Return to the Hidden* 有歸藏
and the *Zhou Changes*], 有周易
[which together] detail the three [forms of the] *Changes*. 三易詳

[By late imperial times the *Linked Mountains* and the *Return to the Hidden* no longer existed as complete texts.]

[Lines 143–146]
There are the Regulations and Counsels 有典謨
and the Instructions and Announcements, 有訓誥
and the Oaths and Charges, 有誓命
which are the profundities of the *Classic of History.* 書之奧

[The Regulations refer to the words and deeds of the great sage emperors, Yao and Shun; the Counsels refer to the advice of great ministers (for example, Yu); the Instructions are admonitions to the ruler upon ascending the throne; the Announcements are proclamations by the ruler; the Oaths refer to the ruler's requests for assistance from officials; and the Charges refer to orders given to officials at important moments.]

[Lines 147–150]
Our Duke of Zhou 我周公
created the *Rites of Zhou* 作周禮
[in which] he wrote about the six [classes of] officials, 著六官
[thus] preserving governing forms. 存治體

[The Duke of Zhou was the younger brother of King Wen. He served as the regent for King Wen's son, King Wu, the primary founder of the Zhou dynasty.]

[Lines 151–154]
The Elder and Younger Dai 大小戴
annotated the *Record of Ritual.* 注禮記
They transmitted the sacred words, 述聖言
[which] provided the rules of ritual and music. 禮樂備

[Of the two main editions of the *Record of Ritual*; the one compiled by the Younger Dai was considered orthodox in Qing times.]

[Lines 155–158]
[We] speak of the Customs of the States; 曰國風
we speak of the Odes and Hymns. 曰雅頌
[These are] the names of the four [sections] of the *Classic of Poetry* 號四詩
[which] should be recited and chanted [over and over]. 當諷詠

[The Customs of the States refers to ballads that were commonly sung by the people of the various feudal kingdoms; the Odes, which were sung at entertainments, were divided into lesser and greater, depending on the importance of the occasion; the Hymns were used to express wishes or prayers.]

[Lines 159–166]
After poetry writing declined 詩既亡
the *Spring and Autumn* [*Annals*] were created. 春秋作
[In these *Annals*] dwell praise and blame 寓褒貶
and the distinction between good and bad [deeds]. 別善惡
The three [*Annals*] commentaries 三傳者
[are:] the *Gongyang* [*Commentary*], 有公羊
Mr. Zuo's [*Commentary*] 有左氏
and the *Guliang* [*Commentary*]. 有穀梁

[Of these commentaries, the *Zuozhuan*, ascribed to Zuo Qiuming (a contemporary of Confucius), was considered orthodox in late imperial times.]

[Lines 167–170]
When the Classics are understood, 經既明
then the philosophers should be read. 方讀子
Select the important [points] 撮其要
and record the [facts of] events. 記其事
[Lines 171–174]
The five [supplementary] philosophers 五子者
are Xunzi, Yang [Xiong 雄], 有荀楊
Wen Zhongzi [Wang Tong 王通], 文中子
Laozi and Zhuangzi. 及老莊

[The implication here is that the works of these individuals should be read after one masters the writings of Confucius, Mencius, Zhu Xi, and the authors of the Confucian classics. Yang Xiong (53 BCE–18 CE), author of the *Taixuan jing* (Classic of great mystery) and Wang Tong (584–617; courtesy name, Wen Zhongzi), a founding figure in the neo-Confucian revival, are the only two thinkers of the five who lived in imperial times.]

[Lines 175–178]
When the Classics and Philosophers have been mastered, 經子通
all the Histories [should] be read, 讀諸史
and generational connections should be examined 考世系
so that one may know the endings and beginnings [of things]. 知終始

[The Histories refers primarily to the orthodox dynastic histories, of which there were twenty-two by early Qing times. The first and most famous of these works was the *Historical Records* (*Shiji*) of Sima Qian (Han dynasty).]

[Lines 179–182]
From [Fu 伏] Xi and [Shen 神] Nong 自羲農
to the Yellow Emperor 至黃帝

[these] are called the Three Sovereigns 號三皇
who lived in the early ages. 居上世

[The reign for Fu Xi (aka Fuxi) was traditionally believed to be from 2953–2838 BCE; for Shen Nong (aka Shennong), from 2838–2698 BCE; for the Yellow Emperor, from 2698–2598 BCE.]

[Lines 183–186]
Tang [Yao 堯] and Youyu [Shun 舜] 唐有虞
are called the Two Emperors. 號二帝
They abdicated one after the other, 相揖遜
[and theirs was] called the Prosperous Age. 稱盛世

[The reign for Yao was traditionally believed to be from 2357–2255 BCE; for Shun, from 2255–2205 BCE. Both men were considered exemplary because they passed the throne to an especially worthy minister rather than to their own sons. Yao abdicated to Shun, and Shun, to the Great Yu—see immediately below.]

[Lines 187–190]
The Xia [dynasty] had Yu. 夏有禹
The Shang [dynasty] had Tang. 商有湯
The Zhou [dynasty had Kings] Wen and Wu [together]. 周文武
[These are] called the Three Kings. 稱三王

[Here, King Wen and King Wu are treated as if they were one person; see the commentary after line 150 above.]

[Lines 191–194]
[In the] Xia [dynasty the throne] was transmitted [from father] to son, 夏傳子
[making] the empire a family. 家天下
[After] four hundred years 四百載
the sacrificial altar passed from the Xia [dynasty]. 遷夏社
[Lines 195–198]
Tang attacked the Xia (dynasty) 湯伐夏
and the state [he founded] was called Shang. 國號商
[After] six hundred years 六百載
it ended with Zhou [Xin 辛]. 至紂亡

[Zhou Xin was the epitome of the "evil last emperor" in the Chinese historiographical tradition.]

[Lines 199–202]
King Wu of the Zhou [dynasty] 周武王

started [his reign] by killing [the tyrant] Zhou [Xin], 始誅紂
and the eight hundred years [of his family's rule] 八百載
made it the longest lasting [of all the dynasties]. 最長久
[Lines 203–208]
When Zhou carts went eastward, 周轍東
the kingly bonds collapsed. 王綱墜
The favored [means of achieving things were] shields and spears, 逞干戈
and traveling advisers were held in high esteem. 尚游說
[This period] began with the Spring and Autumn [era] 始春秋
and ended with the Warring States [era]. 終戰國

[The reference to carts moving eastward indicates the fall to "barbarians" in 771 BCE of the Zhou capital at Hao (in modern-day Shaanxi) and its movement to Luoyi (in modern-day Henan).]

[Lines 209–212]
The Five Hegemons dominated [in the Spring and Autumn period] 五霸強
and the Seven Powerful States emerged [during the Warring States period]. 七雄出
[Then] the Qin family [descended from the Ying [lineage] 嬴秦氏
and it was the first to unite together [all of the states]. 始兼并

[The five hegemons were Dukes Huan, Wen, Xiang, Mu, and Zhuang; the seven states were Qin, Chu, Qi, Yan, Han, Zhao, and Wei.]

[Lines 213–216]
[The throne] was transmitted to the second generation, 傳二世
[after which the state of] Chu struggled with Han. 楚漢爭
[Emperor] Gaozu arose 高祖興
and the Han house was established. 漢業建
[Lines 217–220]
[During the] Xiaoping [reign] 至孝平
Wang Mang usurped the throne. 王莽篡
[Then] the Guangwu [emperor] arose 光武興
and established the Eastern Han. 為東漢

[The Xiaoping reign began in 1 CE; the Wang Mang usurpation lasted from 9–23 CE.]

[Lines 221–222]
[The Han lasted] four hundred years 四百年
and ended with [Emperor] Xian. 終於獻
[Lines 223–226]
[The states of] Wei, Shu and Wu 魏蜀吳
fought for the Han tripod. 爭漢鼎

[They were called the Three Kingdoms 號三國
[and lasted] until the Two Jin [dynasties]. 迄兩晉
[Lines 227–230]
[Then] followed the Song and Qi [dynasties] 宋齊繼
[and then] the Liang and Chen [dynasties] 梁陳承
[These are considered] the Southern Dynasties. 為南朝
[all with their] capital at Jinling [modern-day Nanjing]. 都金陵

[The "Chinese" dynasties in the south, with their capitals at present-day Nanjing, were considered "legitimate" by subsequent dynastic chroniclers—as opposed to the "illegitimate" "barbarian" dynasties of the north.]

[Lines 231–234]
The Northern [Dynasties] are the Wei of the Yuan [family], 北元魏
which split into the Eastern and Western [Wei]; 分東西
the Zhou [dynasty] of the Yuwen 宇文周
and the Qi [dynasty] of the Gao [family]. 與高齊
[Lines 235–238]
[We then] arrive at the Sui [dynasty], 迨至隋
[which] united [the Chinese territory [once more]. 一土宇
[But the throne] was not again transmitted 不再傳
and the [Sui] succession was lost. 失統緒
[Lines 239–242]
[Emperor] Gaozu of the Tang 唐高祖
raised righteous forces, 起義師
eliminating the Sui disorder 除隋亂
and establishing the foundations of the dynasty. 創國基
[Lines 243–246]
Twenty times [the throne was] transmitted 二十傳
[in a period of] three hundred years. 三百載
The Liang [state] destroyed it 梁滅之
and the dynasty then changed. 國乃改
[Lines 247–250]
The Liang, Tang and Jin 梁唐晉
and the Han and Zhou 及漢周
are called the Five Dynasties. 稱五代
[They] all arose [out of their own special circumstances]. 皆有由
[Lines 251–254]
[Then] the fire[-dominated] Song [dynasty] arose, 炎宋興
receiving the abdication of the house of Zhou. 受周禪
Eighteen [times] the throne was transmitted 十八傳
including [both] the Southern and Northern [regimes]. 南北混

[The reference to fire in line 251 indicates that this was the dynasty's designated "ruling agent"—see line 67 above. Fire, in other words, overcame the "metal" agent of the previous regime, just as metal had destroyed wood before it, wood had triumphed over earth, earth had absorbed water, water had extinguished fire, and so forth in repetitive cycles. The Song period is usually divided into the Northern Song, with its capital at Kaifeng, which lasted from 960 to 1122, and the Southern Song, with its capital at Hangzhou, which lasted from 1126 to 1279. The alien Nüzhen (Jurchen) people, who founded the Jin dynasty in north China, forced the Song to retreat southward in 1126.]

[Lines 255–260]
The seventeen dynastic histories
are all [represented] here [in the above account].
[They] contain [examples] of order and disorder 載治亂
[from which we can] know [the circumstances of] rise and fall. 知興衰

[See the appendix after line 359 below for an "updated" historical account.]

[Lines 261–268]
Those who read history 讀史者
[must] study the Veritable Records 考實錄
[in order to] understand ancient and modern [events] 通古今
as if they had been witnessed personally. 若親目
Recite them out loud 口而誦
and take them to heart. 心而惟
[Do] this in the morning; 朝於斯
and [do] this in the evening. 夕於斯

[The Veritable Records were written as an official account of the major activities during the reign of each individual ruler.]

[Lines 269–273]
In the past Confucius 昔仲尼
took Xiang Tuo as his teacher. 師項橐
The ancient sages and worthies 古聖賢
valued diligent study. 尚勤學

[According to a well-known story in Chinese folklore, Xiang Tuo was a precocious young boy of seven who is said to have instructed Confucius.]

[Lines 274–277]
Zhao, High Minister [of the Song] 趙中令
studied the Lu [text] of the *Analects*. 讀魯論
He was already an official 彼既仕
[but] he studied diligently. 學且勤

[The reference here is to Zhao Pu (916–992 CE), a statesman who assisted in the establishment of the Song dynasty.]

[Lines 278–281]
[One man] spread out rushes and plaited them [to make a book]. 披蒲編
[Another] scraped bamboo tablets [for this purpose]. 削竹簡
They had no books, 彼無書
but they knew how to strive. 且知勉

[The first reference is to a shepherd in the Han dynasty named Lu Wenshu, who copied portions of the *Classic of History* on a sheet of plaited reeds because he was too poor to buy books. The second reference is to a poor swineherd named Gongsun Hong, also of the Han, who, at the age of fifty, copied the *Spring and Autumn Annals* on slips of bamboo.]

[Lines 282–285]
[One man] tied his head to a rafter [so as not to nod off], 頭懸梁
[and another] pricked his thigh with an awl [to stay awake]. 錐刺股
They were not taught [by others] 彼不教
[but] worked hard on their own. 自勤苦

[The respective references here are to: (1) Sun Qing of the Later Han dynasty, and (2) Su Qin, who died in 317 BCE.]

[Lines 286–289]
Then [there is the case of the young man who put] fireflies in a bag, 如囊螢
[and another who studied by reflected] moonlight on the snow. 如映雪
Although their families were poor, 家雖貧
they studied unceasingly. 學不綴

[These references are to Che Yin in the fourth century, who was too poor to afford candles, and Sun Kang, also of the fourth century, who was similarly disadvantaged.]

[Lines 290–293]
[And again we have one who] carried fuel, 如負薪
[and another who] hung [books] on the horns [of a water buffalo]. 如掛角
Although they toiled with their bodies 身雖勞
they still distinguished themselves [as] hardworking [students]. 猶苦卓

[Here the references are to (1) the woodcutter Zhu Maichen, (d. 116 BCE), who studied diligently, despite his time-consuming labors, and (2) the farmer Li Mi of the third century CE who did the same.]

[Lines 294–301]
Su Laoquan 蘇老泉
[at the age of] twenty-seven 二十七
began [at last] to put forth effort 始發憤
and read books and records. 讀書籍
[Because he] was already past the age [of the most productive learning], 彼既老
[he] especially regretted his delay. 猶悔遲
You, young students, 爾小生
ought to think about [such things] early [in your lives]. 宜早思

[Su Laoquan was one of the alternative names of Su Xun (1009–1066), father of the renowned Song dynasty scholar Su Shi (aka Su Dongpo; 1037–1101).]

[Lines 302–307]
[Consider also the case of] Liang Hao, 若梁灝
[who, at the age of] eighty-two 八十二
responded [to the emperor] in the great [audience] hall 對大廷
[and came out] first among the many scholars [in the examinations]. 魁多士
He succeeded late [in life] 彼晚成
and the masses called him a prodigy. 眾稱異

[Liang Hao, born in 913 CE, did not receive the highest examination degree until he was seventy-two years old. The above account adds ten years to the time it took him to succeed.]

[Lines 308–317]
You, young students, 爾小生
should set your minds [on learning]. 宜立志
[Zu 祖] Rong, at eight years of age 瑩八歲
could [compose and] recite poetry. 能詠詩
[Li 李] Mi at seven years of age 泌七歲
could write a narrative verse on chess. 能賦棋
These [youths] were clever and perceptive, 彼穎悟
and people called them prodigies. 人稱奇
You, young learners, 爾幼學
ought to imitate them. 當效之

[Zu Rong (Rong is also pronounced Yong), who lived in the sixth century CE, reportedly mastered (memorized) the *Classic of Poetry* and the *Classic of History* by the age of eight *sui* (seven years old in Western reckoning). Li Mi (722–789 CE) was a famous scholar and bibliophile. His *fu* at the age of seven *sui* was apparently a clever four-line epigram on the squareness of the board, the roundness of the pieces, the activity of the pieces when in play, and their quiescence when "dead" (removed from play).]

[Lines 318–325]
Cai Wenji 蔡文姬
was able to evaluate *qin* [music]. 能辨琴
Xie Daoyun 謝道韞
could [compose and] chant verse. 能詠吟
They were girls, 彼女子
[but they] were also intelligent and perceptive. 且聰敏
You boys 爾男子
ought to alert yourselves [to this sort of challenge]. 當自警

[Cai Wenji was the daughter of a famous Han dynasty official; Xie Daoyun was the niece of a well-known fourth century CE statesman. Both women were extraordinarily accomplished.]

[Lines 326–333]
Liu Yan of the Tang [dynasty] 唐劉晏
when [he was only] seven years old 方七歲
was elevated as a "spiritual child" [precocious], 舉神童
and appointed a Corrector of Texts. 作正字
Although [only] a child, 彼雖幼
he already held office. 身己仕
You, young learners, 爾幼學
[should] strive to do [the same]. 勉而致

[Liu Yan, a famous Tang dynasty scholar (d. 780 CE), was reportedly identified as a precocious "spiritual child" by the eighth-century Emperor Minghuang.]

[Lines 334–335]
Those who strive 有為者
will also [be successful] like this. 亦若是
[Lines 336–339]
The dog guards the night. 犬守夜
The rooster rules the dawn. 雞司晨
If you do not study, 苟不學
how can you become a [genuine] person? 曷為人
[Lines 340–343]
The silkworm produces silk. 蠶吐絲
The bee makes honey. 蜂釀蜜
A person who isn't devoted to learning 人不學
can't even measure up to a beast. 不如物

[*Wu* literally means "thing"—any object alive or dead; here, however, the idea is clearly a lowly animal, like an insect.]

[Lines 344–347]
Learn while [you are] young 幼而學
and act [on it as a] grownup, 壯而行
influencing the ruler above 上致君
and benefitting the people below. 下澤民
[Lines 348–351]
Make a name for yourself 揚名聲
and bring distinction to your parents. 顯父母
Glorify your ancestors 光於前
and enrich your posterity. 裕於后
[Lines 352–355]
People bequeath to their children 人遺子
strong-boxes full of gold. 金滿籯
I teach [you] children 我教子
only [this] one book. 惟一經

[The reference here is to a traditional Chinese aphorism attributed to a scholar named Wei Xian (first century BCE): "To teach your children one book [lit. classic] is better than [giving them] a strong-box full of gold" (黃金滿籯不如教子一經).]

[Lines 356–359]
There is merit in diligence; 勤有功
[and] there is no benefit from play. 戲無益
Oh, beware! 戒之哉
You must devote your strength [to study]. 宜勉力

Appendix: The following twenty-four lines appear in one standard Qing dynasty version of the *Sanzi jing* reportedly edited by a man named He Xingsi. They are normally added after line 254 in the version usually attributed to Wang Yinglin.

The Liao and Jin [rulers] 遼與金
all called [themselves] emperors. 皆稱帝
The Yuan destroyed the Jin 元滅金
and ended the Song line. 絕宋世
[The Mongols] ruled the Middle Kingdom, 蒞中國
including the Rong and Di [people], 兼戎狄
[but after] ninety years 九十年
the dynasty fell. 國祚廢
[Emperor] Taizu [then] arose 太祖興
and the dynasty was [known as] the great Ming. 國大明
His reign-title was Vast Military [Accomplishment] 號洪武
and his capital was Jinling [modern-day Nanjing]. 都金陵

Eventually [under the] Chengzu [emperor] 逮成祖
the capital was shifted to Yanjing [present-day Beijing]. 遷燕京
[There were] seventeen reigns 十七世
down to [and including] Chongzhen. 至崇禎
[By then,] powerful eunuchs behaved recklessly, 權閹肆
and] rebels [emerged] like [trees in] a forest. 寇如林
[The rebel] Li Chuang [Li Zicheng 李自成] arrived, 至李闖
and the divine utensils [of the Ming dynasty] were destroyed. 神器焚

[Li Zicheng (1606–1644), who toppled the Ming dynasty, called himself "The Dashing Prince" (Chuangwang) and briefly established the Shun dynasty. He was soon driven out of Beijing by the invading Manchus, assisted by the Ming general Wu Sangui (1612–1678).]

[Emperor Taizu] of the Qing [dynasty] 清太祖
responded to the bright [auspicious] Mandate [of Heaven] 應景命
and pacified the four directions, 靖四方
[thus] achieving a great settlement. 克大定

Notes

First, in the interest of space, I have generally used endnotes only for direct citations and occasional explanations or amplifications. Readers seeking additional sources related to a given topic are encouraged to word search the extensive online bibliography at www.rowman.com/ISBN/9781442221925/ The-Qing-Dynasty-and-traditional-chinese-culture.

Second, I have cited comparatively few Chinese- or Japanese-language materials in these notes, despite many years of work on both primary and secondary sources. The main purpose of the notes is to guide nonspecialists toward available Western sources (including Chinese and Japanese works in translation) that illustrate or amplify the point I am making, or lead the reader into areas of Qing culture that cannot be discussed more fully in the body of the book for lack of space (see also the bibliographical note at the beginning of the online bibliography). Translations from Chinese sources (other than my own) have been modified for consistency and clarity. In particular, I have rendered all Wade-Giles and other transliterations of Chinese names into the pinyin system, even when quoting directly from older Western-language publications.

Third, I have adhered to the following conventions in the notes: (A) Rather than including complete references to books and articles, I cite only the name of the author, the date of the publication, and the page number. If an author has produced more than one publication in a given year, lower case letters will indicate the item in question. (B) In citing the author of a work written in Chinese or Japanese, I have observed the East Asian practice of placing the family name first, followed by the entire personal name (for example, He Bingdi or Nakagawa Tadahide). (C) In citing the author of a Western-

446

language work, even if he or she is of East Asian descent, I give only the family name, unless two or more authors have the same surname (for example, Kidder Smith and Richard Smith or Peng-Yoke Ho [He Bingyu] and Ping-ti Ho [He Bingdi]). In these instances I add the first initial of the personal name (and sometimes, if there is still ambiguity, the second initial or full personal name); hence K. Smith, P. T. Ho, and so on. In the case of individuals who write in both Asian and Western languages, I have followed the rules indicated, depending on the language in which a given work was written. (D) In most cases, I have cited only the page numbers of articles included in collections. At times, however, if the citation is a general one in an anthology, I have included the name of the author as well as the editor(s). Also, in order to keep endnotes to a minimum, I have in many cases combined several sources into a single citation. Sources for all quoted material in any one paragraph (or successive paragraphs) are listed in order, separated by a semicolon, and ending with a period. If such citations give a span of relevant pages, the quoted material appears within that span.

ABBREVIATIONS

CC Legge, James, trans. 1893–1895. *The Chinese Classics*. London and Oxford: Clarendon Press. Reprinted by the Hong Kong University Press in 1979. 5 volumes.

CHC Twitchett, Denis et al., eds. 1978–2009. *The Cambridge History of China*. Cambridge, Eng.: Cambridge University Press. Eight volumes, several divided into more than one part.

CHCL Chang, Kang-i Sun and Stephen Owen, eds. 2010. *The Cambridge History of Chinese Literature*. Volume 2. Cambridge, Eng.: Cambridge University Press.

CLEAR Chinese Literature Essays Articles Reviews.

MHY McGill-Harvard-Yenching Library, Ming-Qing Women's Writings Digitization Project. http://digital.library.mcgill.ca/mingqing/english/proj ect.htm.

MIT Massachusetts Institute of Technology. "Visualizing Cultures." http://ocw.mit.edu/ans7870/21f/21f.027/home/index.html.

QS Zhang, Qiyun et al., eds. 1961. *Qingshi* (History of the Qing dynasty). Taibei: Guofang yanjiu yuan. Six volumes.

SCC Needham, Joseph et al. 1956–present. *Science and Civilisation in China*. Cambridge, Eng.: Cambridge University Press. Seven volumes, some (such as chapter 5) divided into several separately published parts.

SCT de Bary, William T. et al., eds. 1999–2000. *Sources of Chinese Tradition*. New York: Columbia University Press, 1999 (second edition, volume 1) and 2000 (second edition, volume 2).

SKQS Ji, Yun et al., eds. 1983–1986. *Qinding Siku quanshu* (Imperial edition of the *Complete Collection of the Four Treasuries*). Reprint Taibei: Shangwu yinshu guan, under the title *Yingyin Wenyuange Siku quanshu*.

TSJC Chen, Menglei et al., eds. 1977. *Qinding gujin tushu jicheng* (Imperial edition of the complete collection of illustrations and writings, past and present). Taibei: Dingwen shuju.

WBQS *Wanbao quanshu* (Complete collection of myriad treasures). Various editions and various publishers.

WWTC Chang, Kang-i Sun and Haun Saussy, eds. 1999. *Women Writers of Traditional China: An Anthology of Poetry and Criticism*. Stanford: Stanford University Press.

INTRODUCTION

1. Cited in Lynch 2013, 641.

2. See P. T. Ho 1967.

3. For other Western scholars who have explored one or another facet of the complex Qing cultural terrain with particular insight see the selected bibliography. A recent work in Chinese that gives systematic attention to both sides of the complex Manchu–Chinese political, social, and cultural interaction in the Qing period is Zhongguo shehui kexue yuan, ed. 2011. See also Dai Yinghua 2010; Diao Shuren 2002; Ding Yichuang 1992; Li Li 2012; Li Yanguang and Guan Jie 1991; Liu Xiaomeng 2001; Manzu jianshi bianxie zu, ed. 2009; Wang Zhonghan, ed. 1996; Yang Xichun 1991; Zhang Jie 2007; and Zhou Yuanlian 1981.

4. For a discussion of the origins and development of discourses and debates regarding "sinicization," see R. J. Smith 2013, 12–14.

5. E. Rawski 1996, 131; cf. Millward et al., eds. 2004, 1–2 and 15–21.

6. See Waley-Cohen 2004, 200; cf. Elliott 2012a.

7. See Crossley 1990 and the introduction to Crossley, Siu, and Sutton, eds. 2006.

8. "China Proper" (often designated *neidi* in Chinese) refers to the core eighteen provinces of the Qing dynasty. From a Manchu perspective, however, the concept of "China" (Chinese: *Zhongguo*; Manchu: *Dulimbai Gurun*) embraced the entire empire, including Manchuria, Mongolia, Xinjiang, and Tibet. See G. Zhao 2006.

9. See my discussion of some of the most recent of these works at the beginning of the online bibliography.

10. Cohen 2003, 13–14.

11. R. J. Smith 2013, 9–10

12. Hevia 1995, 5–7 and 18–20.

13. See, for example, Judith Farquhar and James Hevia cited in R. J. Smith 2013, 49.

14. Sahlins 1993, 15. Ian Morris argues persuasively that culture "is less a voice in our heads telling us what to do than a town hall meeting where we argue about our options." Cited in Katzenstein 2012, 211.

15. See R. J. Smith 2013, 1–14.

16. Qian, Fong, and Smith, eds. 2008, 1–2.

17. Significantly, even before the Qing conquest of China in 1644, one of the first books the Manchus translated into their own language was a widely circulated Ming version of the WBQS.

18. Cited in R. J. Smith 1994, 3 (modified slightly). Cf. D. Kang 2010, 29 ff.

19. Wei Zhengtong 1981, 23–63.

20. See, for example, Rowe 2006 and Meyer-Fong 2013.

21. Wei Zhengtong 1981, 33–36.

22. See Rowe 2001, esp. chapter 12; also R. J. Smith 2013, esp. 3–9.

23. See P. T. Ho 1967 and 1998 and Pei Huang 2011.

24. Cited in R. J. Smith 2013, 90.

25. Cited in R. J. Smith 1991, 7–8.

26. See Brook 2005, 129.

27. Guldin 1984, esp. 140–43.

28. Cited in R. J. Smith 1994, 8.

29. All cited in ibid.

30. D. Johnson in D. Johnson, ed. 1985, 45 ff.

31. See the discussion in R. J. Smith 1991, 8–10.

32. See, for example, the many recent books on women cited in the online bibliography of this book.

33. See in particular the work by Kang-i Sun Chang, Patricia Ebrey, Grace Fong, Dorothy Ko, Joan Judge, Wai-yee Li, Susan Mann, Nanxiu Qian, Paul Ropp, Haun Saussy, Ellen Widmer, and Harriet Zurndorfer.

34. R. J. Smith 1991, 9–10.

35. This novel was written by a Chinese member of the Manchu Banner system and it describes a Banner household. See Hawkes, trans. 1973–1979, 1: 15–46.

36. Hawkes, trans. 1973–1979, 1: 122–24. Slightly modified.

37. See D. W. Y. Kwok in Smith and Kwok, eds. 1993 and Chung-ying Cheng 1991, 1–58.

38. Sangren 1987, 132–40 and 166–86.

39. Y. Fung 1948, 355 and 406.

40. It should be emphasized that while Confucian ethics were secular in origin, they had a decidedly sacred quality because they were inextricably linked to cosmology throughout the imperial era. See K. C. Liu in K. C. Liu, ed. 1990, 7–12.

41. C. K. Yang 1961, 175–76.

42. Geertz 1973, 112–13.

43. See R. J. Smith 2013, esp. 89–110 and 112–13.

44. Williams 1883, 1:424; A. Smith 1899, 193; Nevius 1869, 239. See also Gray 1878, 1: 347 and Wieger 1913, 110.

45. Geertz 1973, 89.

46. See, for example, Kang Youwei cited in SCT 2: 269–70.

47. Spence 2013.

CHAPTER ONE: THE MING DYNASTY LEGACY

1. See esp. Atwell 1986 and CHC 8: 376–416 and 692–99.
2. Wills 2012, 440.
3. D. Robinson 2008, 1.
4. CHC 7: 2–4. Cf. I. Clark 2014, 31–37 and 41–42.
5. CHC 7: 3.
6. Brook 2005, 189–90.
7. Dardess 2010, 67.
8. CHC 7: 181.
9. The discussion that follows is based primarily on CHC 7: 107–81.
10. A lasting change in Chinese ritual life dating from this time was the Hongwu emperor's replacement of bronze vessels by color-coded ceramic ones. See I. Clark 2014, 33.
11. CHC 7: 109.
12. Cited in CHC 7: 109–11, slightly modified.
13. Chan 1982, 41–42. A *mou* was equivalent to about 800 square yards, 660 square meters, or 0.160 of an acre.
14. See T. Wilson, ed. 2003.
15. Y. L. Jiang 2010 and 2014. Cf. Bodde and Morris 1967 and W. C. Jones 1994.
16. See Brook 2005, esp. 21–24.
17. Elman 2000, 38–40, 66–157, 173–95, 213–20, and 380–99.
18. Brook 2005, esp. 182.
19. Cited in CHC 7: 181, slightly modified.
20. Cited in Mair, Steinhardt, and Goldin eds. 2005, 490–93, slightly modified.
21. I have relied heavily on S. S. Tsai 2001 and CHC 8: 182–304 in the writing of this section.
22. Quoted in S. S. Tsai 2001, 79–80, slightly modified.
23. Elman 2000, 108–15.
24. See G. Wade 2004.
25. For a discussion of Nanjing's continued importance as the Ming dynasty's southern capital, see J. Fang 2014.
26. CHC 8: 108–9.
27. Ibid.
28. CHC 8: 109. The following summary of Ming policy is based primarily on CHC 7: 272 ff.
29. CHC 8: 580–81.
30. See Waldron 1990.
31. See Swope 2002 and 2009, esp. 123, 142–43, and 285–97.
32. Crawford 1961, 8. For details on the late Ming, see H. S. Tsai 1996.
33. Spence 2013, 79.
34. Elman 2005, 5–20.
35. CHC 8: 579–707. The quotation is from ibid., 580.
36. Cited in Brook 1998, 238 (slightly modified).
37. Cited in CHC 8: 636.

38. See K. W. Chow 2004, esp. 57–148 and 241–53; cf. CHCL 2: 63–73.

39. See Sakai Tadao 2011; Wu Huifang 1996 and 2005; and Zhong Shaohua 1996. Most of the following discussion is drawn from Wu 2005, esp. 44–47 and 56 ff. See also W. Shang 2005, 67 ff.

40. On Zhang's publications and politics see K. W. Chow 2004, esp. 231–32, 212–13, and 231–36.

41. See R. J. Smith 2014.

42. CHCL 2: 51–56 and 99–116.

43. Plaks 1989.

44. Plaks 1989 and C. T. Hsia 1968 both discuss all four of these novels at length.

45. See the translation by Roberts 1999. For an overview, consult CHCL 2: 51–54.

46. See the translation of this work by Dent-Young 1994–2003. For an overview, consult CHCL 2: 51–54.

47. See the translation by A. Yu 1977–1979. For an overview, consult CHCL 2: 51–54.

48. W. Shang 2005, 64–65. For an excellent translation, see Roy 1993–2013. For an overview, consult CHCL 2: 104–11.

49. For an overview, see CHCL 2: 47ff.

50. Chang and Saussy 1999, 4.

51. D. Berg 2013.

52. See Y. Tseng 1993 and Weidner 1988 and 1990.

53. On Lu, see Chang and Saussy eds. 1999, 239 ff.; on Xue, see Chang and Saussy eds. 1999, 227 ff.; on Huang, see Chang and Saussy eds. 1999, 172 ff.; on Meng, see Chang and Saussy eds. 1999, 161 ff. CHCL 2: 145–49 discusses the vibrant and creative "courtesan culture" of the Ming.

54. The following several paragraphs draw heavily upon CHCL 2: 3–82.

55. For a discussion of the so-called Seven Late Masters of the Ming, which included such notable writers as Wang Shizhen (1526–1590), Xie Zhen (1495–1575), and Zong Chen (1525–1560), see CHCL 2: 58–62.

56. For translations, see Birch 1980 and Rongpei Wang 2000.

57. For a recent study of these societies and their influence, see H. Miller 2009.

58. Cited in CHCL 2: 79–82. Cf. Ray Huang 1981, 189–221.

59. Handler-Spitz 2008, 27–28 documents Li's high opinion of Ricci and Ricci's high opinion of Li.

60. See, for example, Hart 2013, Elman 2005, and Zurndorfer 2004.

61. D. Schafer 2011, 233.

62. Elman 2005, 34–46.

63. See R. J. Smith 2008, 240; see also D. Schafer 2011, 230.

64. Elman 2005, Hart 2013, and Zurndorfer 2004 and 2009 discuss the limitations of Jesuit influence. See also R. J. Smith 2013, 173–92.

CHAPTER TWO: CONQUEST AND CONSOLIDATION

1. Quoted in CHC 8: 413, slightly modified.

2. CHC 8: 414; Spence 2013, 23.

3. See Albert Chan 1982, 330–33; Wakeman 1985, 8: 15–18.

4. Parsons 1970.

5. Cited in Albert Chan 1982, 333, slightly modified.

6. Parsons 1957, 393–98; cf. Albert Chan 1982, 350–53.

7. This paragraph and the next several are based primarily on Wakeman 1985, 1: 227–301.

8. Crossley 1990a, 8.

9. Ibid., 34.

10. For details, see Udry 2000 and Zhao and Jiang 1997.

11. Crossley 1999, 141. Pei Huang 2011, 31–171 offers a detailed narrative of the rise of the Manchus.

12. Crossley 2002, 39 ff.

13. Elliott 2001a, 83.

14. Perdue 2005, 117; Pei Huang 2011, 113–19.

15. The following discussion of the Banners is based primarily on the work of Mark Elliott, Pamela Crossley, and Peter Purdue. For details, see the dated but still useful dissertations by Wei-p'ing Wu 1969 and Im 1981.

16. On Jurchen/Manchu relations with foreigners prior to the Qing conquest of China, see Di Cosmo and Bao 2003; Pei Huang 2011, 174–203; Purdue 2005, 109–29; and Zhongguo shehui kexue yuan, ed. 2011, esp. 3–88.

17. On the confusing category of bondservants, see Elliott 2001a, 81–84.

18. For details, see Wakeman 1985, 164–66 and esp. 170–94.

19. For details see Elliott 2001a, 79 ff. and CHC 9: 311 ff.

20. Elliott 2001a, 71.

21. E. Rawski 1998, 231 ff.

22. Udry 2000, esp. 26–32.

23. Crossley and Rawski 1993, 63–69.

24. On these dynastic names, see Elliott 2001a, 402 n.118.

25. See Evelskog 2006, 14 ff., esp. 24–39.

26. Elliott 2001a, 77–78. Cf. CHC 9: 311 ff., esp. 321–22 and 342–45.

27. Quoted in Wakeman 1985, 300, slightly modified.

28. Ibid., 311–12.

29. Ibid., 316–18, esp n. 283.

30. Rowe 2009, 22–24; cf. Feng Erkang 1990, 170–80.

31. See, for example, Dennerline 1981.

32. Jay 1990, 261–63.

33. Wakeman 1985, 848–62.

34. Wakeman 1985, 848–93.

35. Pei Huang 2011, 83–84.

36. Spence 2013, 39. Cf. Crossley 2002, 81; CHC 9: 310–311 and 339; Ding Yizhuang 1992, 11–31.

37. Elliott 2001a, 93–94 and 105–32.

38. Ibid., 98–101.

39. Bonk 2014. See also Luo Ergang 1984; Xu Xueji 1987; M. G. Chang 2007, 167–70.

40. Hummel, ed. 1943–1944, 1: 168–69. For details on the Qing political and military policies discussed above and below, see Wakeman 1985, 1: 414–508 and 2: 848–1127.

41. CHC 9: 73–119 provides a useful overview of the Shunzhi reign.

42. H. Miller 2013, 47–77.

43. CHC 9: 120–82 provides an able overview of the Kangxi reign.

44. Di Cosmo 2006.

45. CHC 9: 167–68 and 175–76.

46. M. G. Chang 2007, esp. 72–74.

47. Crossley 1990a.

48. Spence 1988; Silas Wu 1970a and 1979. See also Spence 1966 and 1968.

49. See, for example, Zurndorfer 1988b and 2004; Jami 2011. See also CHC 9: 156–60 and R. J. Smith 2013, 173–81.

50. On the so-called Rites Controversy, see Mungello, ed. 1995.

51. Mote 2003, 877.

52. CHC 9: 183–229 provides an able overview of the Yongzheng reign. See also Pei Huang 1974 and Spence 2001.

53. See Bartlett 1991, 258–59 and 271; see also Zelin 1984, passim.

54. On the Kangxi emperor's Sacred Edict and its amplification, see R. J. Smith 2013, 113–16.

55. For details, see CHC 9: 221–28, esp. 223. Rowe 2001, esp. 406–26, provides a particularly useful discussion of the joint Manchu–Chinese "civilizing" project.

56. See Dunstan 2006.

57. CHC 9: 208; cf. Spence 2012, 72–83. For additional details on the economic policies of the Yongzheng period, as summarized below, see CHC 9: 209–21.

58. National Palace Museum 2010.

59. See H. C. Lo 2010. Cf. Hung Wu 1995.

60. Crossley 1999, 223–336 provides an illuminating overview of the Qianlong emperor's reign. See also CHC 9: 230–309. For a short but excellent biography of the Qianlong emperor, see Elliott 2009.

61. CHC 9: 230.

62. Bartlett 1991, 264.

63. See P. Kuhn 1990.

64. CHC 9: 239–42. See also Y. C. Dai 2005.

65. See Kristina Kleutghen forthcoming; also Rawski and Rawson, eds. 2005.

66. For detailed accounts of Qing "colonial" campaigns and their consequences, see esp. Di Cosmo 1998, 2003, 2006, and 2010; Elliott 2009, 86–106; Lary, ed. 2007; Millward 1998; Perdue 2005; and Waley-Cohen 2006.

67. CHC 9: 242–43. "Overwhelmed" may be too strong a word here, since a large proportion of top Qing officials were Bannermen and as such had no need of the examinations.

68. Millward et al., eds. 2004, 2.

69. CHC 9: 191–93; see also Spence 2001.

70. Crossley 2012, 9.

71. Guy 1987 and Elliott 2009 117–24.

72. See Crossley 1987; Elliott 2001a, 46–47; Elliott 2009, 55 ff.
73. Elliott 2009, 58–60. For some examples of Manchu shamanic songs, see Mair and Bender, eds. 2011, 184–89.
74. Elliott 2009, 58.
75. Elverskog 2006, 1–4; Patricia Berger 2003, 33 ff. Cf. Milward et al., eds. 2004, 188–98.
76. Farquhar 1978, 33; E. T. Williams 1913, 12.
77. Alexander Woodside in CHC 9: 237.
78. CHC 9: 232, citing Kahn 1971, 136. Cf. Elliott 2009, 107–17.
79. Cited in Bartlett 1991, 371.
80. R. J. Smith 1974, 145 ff. Cf. Bonk 2014.
81. Daniel McMahon 2015.
82. Zelin 1984, 301. See also Dodgen 1991, 52–53.
83. See L. L. Zhang 2010 and Kaske 2012.
84. See Leonard and Watt, eds. 1984, 67; also Antony and Leonard, eds. 2002, esp. 1–26. Cf. Daniel McMahon 2015.
85. Mosca 2013, 232–33. cf. Isett, 2007.
86. CHC 10: 36.

CHAPTER THREE: THE QING POLITICAL ORDER

1. Guy 2010, 352.
2. CHC 9: 571. See also Lee and Wang 2001.
3. For a summary discussion of the differences between Qing colonial policy in south China and Taiwan on the one hand and in Inner Asia on the other, see Di Cosmo 1998. Details on these policies can be found in Lary, ed. 2007, Millward 1998, Millward et al., eds. 2006, Mosca 2013, Perdue 2005, Power and Standen, eds. 1999, Souza 1986, and Waley-Cohen 2006.
4. See, for example, Di Cosmo and Wyatt, eds. 2003; Du and Kyong-McClain, eds. 2013; Leeming 1993; and Tan Qixiang 1993.
5. See Skinner 1971 and 1993. Cf. Crissman 2010 and Henderson, Skinner, and Crissman 1999.
6. See Herman 1997.
7. See Rowe 2001, esp. 406 ff.; also CHC 11: 211–43.
8. Cited in Feuerwerker, ed. 1967, 15.
9. Crossley 1992; see also E. Rawski 1998, 247–48.
10. Spence 1988, 29–59.
11. See E. Rawski 1998, esp. 197–294; R. J. Smith 2013, 89–110, esp. 91–96; and Zito 1997.
12. Meyer 1978 and 1991; see also Barmé 2008.
13. See James Watson in Baker and Feuchtwang, eds. 1991.
14. *Chinese Repository*, October 1832, 236–38, slightly modified.
15. Bartlett 1991, 270.
16. See Guilin Liu in Er et al. 1986, 60 ff.; also M. G. Chang 2007, esp. 98–103.

17. Yipu Xu in Er et al. 1986, 142 ff. Cf. J. Chang 2013, 145–55.

18. For a systematic discussion of Manchu privilege, see Elliott 2001a, 175–209; cf. Rhoads 2000, 42–48. On Qing intermarriage policies, see Elliott 2001a, 254–55, 339, and 473 note 91 and Rhoads 2000, 41–42. On Qing official dress, consult Garrett 2007, 10 ff.

19. See Perdue 2005, esp. 338.

20. E. Rawski 1998, 179.

21. Spence 1988, 45–46, slightly modified.

22. On eunuchs in the Qing, see Dale 2000; also E. Rawski 1998, esp. 160–66, 181–89, 191–93.

23. Bartlett 1985 and 1991; Crossley and Rawski 1993. For detail on Banner military institutions, see Feng Erkang 1990, Im 1981, and Wei-ping Wu 1969.

24. See Bartlett 1991 and Elliott 2001b. For Robert Hart's firsthand observations concerning the grand councilors who served in the Zongli Yamen, see R. J. Smith et al., eds. 1991, passim.

25. Lui 1990, 33–45.

26. Metzger 1973, chapter 4; cf. Kuhn 1990, 191 ff.

27. E-tu Zen Sun 1962–1963.

28. See Lisha Li 1993; Ben Wu 1998; Yung, Rawski, and Watson, eds. 1996, esp. 164–75.

29. R. J. Smith 1974, 127–30.

30. Q. Zheng 1995, 311–14.

31. W. Jones 1994, 6.

32. Ibid., 34–36. Descriptions of these crimes figure prominently in Qing editions of the WBQS.

33. W. Jones 1994, 7–28. As an indication of the magistrate's discretion, article 386 of the Qing Code provided for up to eighty strokes with the heavy bamboo as punishment for individuals who did "that which ought not to be done [*bu ying wei*]." W. Jones 1994, 359. But this article was seldom invoked. In criminal cases, magistrates were always required to cite a specific substatute.

34. Elliott 2001a, 225–33. See also ibid., 175–209 and X. Hu 2011.

35. On Qing prisons, see Bodde 1982.

36. Ocko 1988, 311; Alford 1984, 1242. See also Poling 2012 on the Autumn Case Reviews, also known as the Autumn Assizes.

37. Lillian Li 1982, 689. See also Lillian Li 2007; Will 1990; Will and Wong 1990; and Antony and Leonard, eds. 2002.

38. See Adam Lui 1978.

39. See Rudolph 2008.

40. Bartlett 1991, 49–64, 264, and 270.

41. Silas Wu 1970, 132–39.

42. The quotation is from Zito 1989, 12; see also Zito 1997.

43. Ocko 1973. The quotation is from S. W. Williams 1883, 1: 420.

44. Guy 2010, 47.

45. See Elman 2000, esp. 136 ff. and Elman 2013, 103–5 and 235–36.

46. Leung 1990.

47. Djang 1984.

48. Wei-jen Chang summarizes these points in Elman and Woodside, eds. 1994, 310–13. See also Philip Huang 1998, 207–12. As Chang's essay indicates clearly, the legal questions (*panyu*) that were part of the Qing civil service examination system until 1756 required no real detailed knowledge.

49. L. Chen 2012.

50. See B. Reed 2000.

51. G. Zhou 1995, 3.

52. Macauley 1998, 1–17, esp. 14.

53. See B. Reed 2000.

54. See esp. Kuhn 1980.

55. Elman 1991, 8. See also Elman 2000 and 2013 and Man-Cheong 2004.

56. Lawrence Zhang 2010 and 2013; Elman 2000, 687 and 2013, 241–49.

57. Pamela Crossley in Elman and Woodside, eds. 1994, 349–65; see also Elliott 2001a, esp. 299.

58. For examples of eight-legged essays, see C. Tu 1974–1975 and Elman 2013, 57–59.

59. For changes in the format of the exams during the Qing, see Elman 2000, 521–626 and 735–37. In all, Elman 2000 offers more than eighty separate tables relating to the examination system over time, including information on quotas, success ratios, examination officials, social origins of candidates, geographic distribution of candidates, importance of topics, topic specializations, etc.

60. Ibid., 173–213, esp. 179–88.

61. See Elman 2013, 81–92; also Plaks 2004.

62. Kuhn 1990, 231.

63. Chu and Saywell 1984; cf. Guy 2010.

64. Chu and Saywell 1984, 84 ff. Cf. R. J. Smith 1974, 131–45.

65. Metzger 1977, 207.

66. See Nathan 1976, 47–58.

67. See Zhang Dechang 1970.

68. Cited in CHC 9: 194. See also Kaske 2012.

69. Perkins 1967, 487 and 491–92.

70. Metzger 1973, 23 ff. Cf. Bourgon 2002.

71. Cited in Balazs 1965, 65. See also Guy 2010, esp. 109–10.

72. Chu and Saywell 1984, 12 ff. and 81 ff.; Watt 1972, 174–76; Ch'ü 1962, 34–35.

73. Kahn 1971, 10.

CHAPTER FOUR: SOCIAL AND ECONOMIC INSTITUTIONS

1. Elliott 2001a, 89–132 and 175–209 provides a well-illustrated description of life in Manchu cities at the capital and in the provinces. See also ibid., 210–33 on Manchu–Chinese interactions. Rhoads 2000, 11–69 ably describes the situation of the Banners in the late Qing period. For Chinese-language sources see below, 474 n1.

2. See Waley-Cohen 2006, 13–17 and Elliott 2001a, 294–95.

3. Rhoads 2000, 38.

4. Fei 1992, 71; cf. Feng Erkang 1990, 54–67. Some other important works on *guanxi* in China include Gold, Guthrie, and Wank, eds. 2002, G. Hamilton 2007, King 1991, Kipness 1996 and 1997, Nathan 1976 and 1993, Y. Yan 1996, M. Yang 1994, and J. Zhao 2000.

5. Fei 1992, 70.

6. Cited in L. Yang 1969, 3, modified.

7. L. Yang 1969, 4.

8. CHC 8: 579–707 and 9: 563–645. For studies on social and economic change in late imperial China see the online bibliography under the relevant search categories.

9. Rowe 1992, 8. See also Goodman and Larson, eds. 2005.

10. Rowe 1992, 8, citing Susan Mann in R. Watson and Ebrey, eds. 1991.

11. Elliott 2001a and E. Rawski 1998 provide excellent discussions of Manchu privilege; see also Feng Erkang 1990, 3–7, 47–49, and 390–99.

12. Elliott 2001a, 305–44, esp. 311–22. See also Crossley 1990 and T. Brown 2013.

13. See Brunnert and Hagelstrom 1911, 490–514. On clothing, consult Garrett 1990 and 2007.

14. Frederic Wakeman Jr. in Crowley, ed. 1970, 13–15.

15. C. L. Chang 1962, 372–78; Rozman et al. 1981, 122; Madeleine Zelin in Lieberthal et al., eds. 1991, 46 and 55.

16. Judge 2001, 768–69.

17. On He Shuangqing see Choy 2000 and Ropp 2001. For examples of poems attributed to her, see Chang and Saussy, eds., 1999, 453–65.

18. Rozman et al. 1981, 151; Rowe 1989, 29–38.

19. P. T. Ho 1962, 20–21, 80. On the cultural life of commoners (*shumin wenhua*), see Wang Ermin 1996.

20. For some general descriptions of the rural environment in Qing dynasty China, see CHC 9: 612–16 and 632–36; I. Hsü 2000, 63–69; Spence 2012, 12–16 and 76–78; Rowe 2009, 96–99. Xu Hao 1999 offers a Chinese-language comparative perspective on rural life in China and the West.

21. Spence 1978, 10–11 and 14.

22. For a great many studies on agricultural life in late imperial China see the online bibliography.

23. See, for example, Bray 1997, Bell 1999, Feng Erkang 1990, 153 ff., and Zurndorfer 2011b.

24. See David Arkush's revealing study of peasant proverbs in K. C. Liu, ed. 1990. Also Feng Erkang 1990, 10–19.

25. M. Cohen 1991, esp. 117–19.

26. Gu is quoted in Beattie 1979, 180 n. 12.

27. Moll-Murata, Song, and Vogel, eds. 2005, 9. Cf. Feng Erkang 1990, 291–306.

28. For a sense of the wide range of commercial activity in Qing China, see G. Hamilton 2007; Kwan 2001; Lufrano 1997; Mann 1987; Metzger 1970; Rowe 1984 and 1989; CHC 9: 576–77, 585–85, and 588–91.

29. See Mann 1987; also Madeleine Zelin in Lieberthal et al. eds. 1991, 53 ff.

30. Rankin 1986, 7; P. T. Ho 1962, 81–86.

31. Cited in Y. Yü 1993, 142–43.

32. Wakeman 1975, 51. See also Rowe 1989, 56 ff.

33. P. T. Ho 1962, 90–91 and 107–11; cf. Elman 2000, 240–56.

34. On educational opportunities in the Qing period, see the essays in Elman and Woodside, eds. 1994; also Elman 1991, 2000, and 2013; M. Gu 2005; Rawski 1979; Ridley 1977; Woodside 1983; L. Yu 2003; and Zurndorfer 1992. For some studies focusing on women's education, see C. W. Ho 1995 and 1999; Ko 1994b; F. W. Liu 2004; Mann 1994; Martin-Liao 1985; N. Qian 2005, 2010, 2013, and 2015; and Zhang and Bradshaw 1996.

35. Frederick Mote in Buxbaum and Mote, eds. 1972, 13–14; cf. CHC 9: 488–91. Feng Erkang 1990, 43–47 provides numerous examples of individuals from humble origins who attained civil service degrees and high bureaucratic status in the Qing period.

36. For information on Qing patronage of Tibetan-style Buddhism, see A. Campbell 2011; Elverskog 2006, esp. 1–4, 47–48, 75–78, 103–23, and 134–46; Grupper 1984; D. Liu 2010; E. Rawski 1998, 244–47, 251–58, 261–63, 267–68, and 271–72.

37. Cited in Kenneth Chen 1964, 453; cf. C. K. Yang 1961, 189 ff.

38. Li and Naquin 1988.

39. See R. J. Smith 1974; also Liu and Smith 1980.

40. On slavery in Banner garrisons, where the ratio of slaves to Banner males might be as low as eight to one, see Elliott 2001a, 227–30. See also E. Rawski 1998, 166–78 on the role of bondservants, state slaves, Banner servants, and other servile people in the Qing service.

41. On these groups, see Feng Erkang 1990, 28–40. CHC 9: 493–502 offers a highly nuanced view of the many forms of servitude in the Qing, suggesting the incompleteness of the Yongzheng era's "liberation."

42. See W. Jones 1994, 133, 297, 311, 352. The punishments for these crimes were often severe. For instance, a slave who cursed the head of the household was punished by strangulation, and one who struck the head of the household, even if there was no bodily harm, was decapitated.

43. M. Cohen 1991, 116. Cf. Feng Erkang 1990, 135–70.

44. Bourgon, 2002. Cf. Huang 1998 and 2001, L. Liang 2007, and Zelin, Ocko, and Gardella, eds. 2004.

45. Cited by Charlotte Furth in K. C. Liu, ed. 1990, 187.

46. Bodde and Morris 1967, 37–38 and 40–41. See also Jones 1994, 66 ff., 123 ff., 268 ff., and 278 ff.

47. Spence 1978, 138.

48. On kinship terminology, see Ebrey and Watson, eds. 1986, 4–10; also H. Feng 1967.

49. Feng Erkang 1990, 95–170 provides a valuable overview of Chinese family and clan life. For English-language works on this subject, see the online bibliography.

50. Hui-chen Wang Liu 1959.

51. C. K. Yang 1961, 40–43 and 52–53. See also Rowe 1998.

52. Cohen is cited by Madeleine Zelin in Lieberthal et al., eds. 1991, 40. See also Naquin and Rawski 1987, 230. On the use of contracts by the Manchus, see T. Brown 2013.

53. Cited in K. Hsiao 1960, 354–55.

54. CHC 9: 512–22. CHC 9: 614–15 provides an example of a landlord-tenant contract in which 15 percent of the yield would go to the landlord and 85 percent would go to the multiple cultivators.

55. See Skinner 1971. For the growth of absentee landlordism in the late Qing see CHC 11: 11–13.

56. Skinner 1993; cf. CHC 9: 581–83.

57. CHC 9: 582.

58. Skinner 1993.

59. Skinner 1971, 272–77. On village administration, see Hayes 1977; cf. Knapp, ed. 1992.

60. See Elliott 2001a, chapter 2, esp. 219–25.

61. Elliott 2001a, 222, slightly modified. On Han-Manchu commercial interactions more generally, see Zhongguo shehui kexue yuan, ed. 2011, passim, esp. 168–98; also T. Brown 2013.

62. Elliott 2001a, 224.

63. Rankin 1986, 242–43. See also Skinner, ed. 1977, esp. 103–19, 258–61, 508–10, and 609.

64. Rowe 1989; 15–18, 83–87, 176, and 345 ff. For recent studies that emphasize the vibrancy of Chinese urban life, see Wu Renshu 2013 and S. Zhao 2014.

65. See F. W. Mote in Skinner, ed. 1977, esp. 114–17.

66. Wakeman and Grant, eds. 1975, 4.

67. Skinner, ed. 1977 contains a wealth of information on these and related organizations. The discussion that follows is based primarily on this source.

68. For an overview of Qing-era philanthropy, see CHC 9: 546–50. For case studies, see J. H. Smith, 1987 and 1998.

69. Fairbank 1992, 181.

70. R. J. Smith 2013, 103–5. See also the essays in Liu and Shek, eds. 2004. Cf. Feng Erkang, 49–95.

71. Kuhn 1980, 165; and 176; Wakeman 1977, 207.

72. See Hung 2011.

73. Skinner 1971.

74. Lamley 1977, 34 reminds us, however, that the rise of social tensions and even violence did not always coincide with dynastic decline. For at least partial corroboration of this point, see Hung 2011.

CHAPTER FIVE: LANGUAGE AND SYMBOLIC REFERENCE

1. See, for example, Elliott 2001a, 167–71 and 210 ff. Cf. Spence 1988, 44.

2. See Pamela Crossley in Elman and Woodside, eds. 1994, esp. 340–48; also Gimm 1988, P. Schmidt 1932, and Söderblom Saarela 2013 and 2014.

3. Millward c. 2010.

4. Norman 1988, esp. 113 and 218 ff; Ramsey 1987, 217. See also Bartlett 1985; Crossley and Rawski 1993; and Wadley 1996.

5. Elliott 2001a, 241–45.

6. Elman and Woodside, eds. 1994, 341; P. Schmidt 1932; Söderblom Saarela 2013 and 2014.

7. See Hess 1993, 403; cf. Pei Huang 2011, 240–42.

8. Crossley and Rawski 1993, 82–83.

9. CHCL 2: 397–99 summarizes the themes of these ballads. See also Gao Yin-xian et al. 1991; Idema, trans. 2009; McLaren 1998; and Silber 1994.

10. See the British Library collection titled "Shui archives in Libo, Guizhou" at http://eap.bl.uk/database/results.a4d?projID=EAP143. For examples of other ethnic scripts in China, see Cindy Ho 1997.

11. See Crossley 1991.

12. R. J. Smith 2013, 173–83.

13. Cited in De Francis 1984, 63.

14. See the discussion in Bol 1992, 84–107; also Hanan 1981, 15. Cf. Wei Shang 2014b.

15. Bodde 1991, 21–22.

16. W. A. P. Martin 1881, 196. See also De Forges 2006.

17. Hummel 1943–1944, 1: 22.

18. R. J. Smith 1991, 202.

19. R. Wilhelm 1967, 335. See also Lewis 1999, esp. chapters 5 and 6.

20. Creel 1936, 97.

21. See C.Y. Cheng 1973, 92–93; also Elman 1984, 213 ff.

22. See the analysis in T'sou 1981.

23. R. J. Smith 1991, 202–4, 216–18, 226–29, and 250–52.

24. Rolston, ed. 1990, 338.

25. Wang Anshi cited in Bol 1992, 232.

26. Bodde 1991, 31–42, esp. 34; Rosemont 1974, 81.

27. Y. R. Chao 1976, 289. See also Bodde 1991, 42–55 and Granet 1934, 56–82, 115–48.

28. Tung-sun Chang 1952, 214–15 and 222–23. Cf. A. Graham 1989, 397–99.

29. See Rosemont 1974 and Black 1989, esp. 141–59.

30. TSJC, *dian* 13, 15, and 22. See also R. J. Smith 2014.

31. Wing-tsit Chan 1967, 27, 39, and 195. See also Bodde 1991, 42 ff.

32. V. Shih 1983, xlix and 368–69.

33. Ibid., 373.

34. A. C. Graham in Dawson, ed. 1964, 54–55.

35. Bodde 1957, 65.

36. T. S. Chang 1952; Y. Fung 1948, 16; K. C. Chang 1976, chapter 7. See also Hansen 1992, 14 ff., esp. 30–32; M. Sung 1979; and T'sou 1981.

37. For convenient Chinese-language studies, see Guo Jinfu 1993 and Shen Xilun 2004.

38. See C. Hansen 1992, 33 ff., esp. 53–54.

39. See Bloom 1981; also Elman 1983 and SCC 7.2: 108–9.

40. Arthur Wright in A. Wright, ed. 1953, esp. 287; cf. Nakamura 1971, 177–90.

41. Bloom 1981; C. Y. Cheng 1971 and 1973; Elman 1983; C. Hansen 1992, esp. 52; and Graham 1989, esp. 395–98.

42. Yu-kuang Chu in Meskill ed. 1973, 600; Tung-sun Chang 1952, 211–17; Graham 1986, passim; SCC, esp. 2: 279 ff.

43. See A. C. Graham 1989, 75–105, 137–70, 389–401, and 406–28.

44. See Mayers 1874, 293–360; cf. Bodde 1991, 64 ff.

45. Rosemont 1974, 87.

46. Tat 1977, xxx.

47. C. Y. Cheng 1977 draws substantially on Whitehead; see also Jullien 1989 on the "process logic" of both classical Chinese and the *Yijing*.

48. W. Chan 1967, 108.

49. Cited in Smith 2008, 3–4.

50. Cited in R. J. Smith 2008, 40. The following few paragraphs have been drawn primarily from material in R. J. Smith 1991, 2008, and 2012.

51. R. J. Smith 2013, 15–17.

52. For a more complete inventory, see R. J. Smith 2008, 41–43; also R. J. Smith 2012a, 64–70.

53. Y. Fung 1948, 168.

54. Spence 1988, 59, slightly modified.

55. R. J. Smith 2008, 220–21. Much of the following discussion has been drawn from chapter 9 of this source. See also R. J. Smith 2012a, "Concluding Remarks."

56. D. N. Zhang, passim, esp. 178–219.

57. R. J. Smith 1991, 122–26, slightly modified. Trigrams were ubiquitous as decorative motifs on all sorts of craft productions.

58. Cited in R. J. Smith 2008, 222.

59. Quoted R. J. Smith 2008, 226, slightly modified.

60. I have translated several of these poems in R. J. Smith 2008, 223 ff.

61. P. Y. Ho 1972, 26–29; cf. SCC, 2: 315–21.

62. W. Chan 1967, 111.

63. R. J. Smith 2008, 234–35.

64. R. Lynn 1994, 85.

65. Cited in Ruan 1991, 16–17.

66. SCC 2: 336.

67. P. Y. Ho 1972.

68. See, for instance, SCC, 2: 292, 304–40; 3: 56–59, 119–20, 140–41, 464, 625; 4.1: 14, 16; 4.2: 143, 530; 4.3: 125; 5.3: 51–53, 60–66, 69–74, 128, 201, 217, etc.

69. R. J. Smith 2012a, 220.

70. SCC, 2: 329–35; also Li Yang 1998, 322 ff.

71. SCC, 2: 322–26.

72. Cited in R. J. Smith 1991, 56 (slightly modified).

73. Li Yang 1998, passim, esp. 21–35 and 197–214; also R. J. Smith 2008, 107, 185–86, and 235–37.

74. Sivin 2005, 57 (hardcopy).

75. Sivin 2005, 12 (online version).

76. Sivin 2005, 57 (hardcopy).

77. Sivin 2005, 13 (online version).
78. Sivin 2005, 62–65 (hardcopy).
79. Schafer 2011, 263.
80. See Elman 2005 and 2009, Hostetler 2001, Nappi 2009, and D. Schafer 2011; also R. J. Smith 2008, 235–40, Waley Cohen 1999, and Zurndorfer 2004.
81. See R. J. Smith 2008, 239–41; also R. J. Smith 2013, 44–46.
82. Elman 2006, 3.
83. R. J. Smith 2008, 141 and esp. 240.
84. Nathan Sivin in Ropp, ed. 1990, 169–70.
85. Y. Kim 2000, passim, esp. 295–309.
86. See Elman 2009, chapter 9. See also the argument in On-cho Ng 2003.
87. Yang and Tang are cited in R. J. Smith 2012a, 222–23.
88. See R. J. Smith 2013, esp. 183 ff.
89. See Hart 2013, 12–20, 57–60, and 68–75.
90. Discussed in Bodde 1991, esp. 88–93. In his "General Conclusions and Reflections," Needham refers to the "profoundly logical structure" of the Chinese language. SCC 7.2: 89.
91. Bodde 1991, 82–88. See also Sivin in Daojing Hu, ed. 1982, 91–93.
92. Cited in Bodde 1991, 88. See also SCC 7.2: 108–9.
93. See Arthur Wright in A. Wright, ed. 1953, 286–301. Cf. Hart 2013.

CHAPTER SIX: PATTERNS OF THOUGHT

1. Some Western scholars prefer to describe "Confucianism" as "Ru Learning" (*Ruxue*)—a term that the Chinese have long used in identifying a scholarly preference for the ideas and values of Confucius and his early disciples. I think, however, that this usage is unnecessarily confusing to nonspecialists.
2. Elman 1981, 4–5; also CHCL 2: 157–62, 220–29, and 247–56. For some overviews of Qing thought in Chinese, see Lu Baoqian 2009, Luo Guang 1996, and Wang Ermin 2005.
3. O. Ng 2001, esp. 6–12. Cf. Elman 2000, 163–72, 481–625.
4. CHCL 2: 257, 336–42, and 422–27.
5. Elman 1981. See also CHCL 2: 336 and Guy 1987, esp. 201–7.
6. See McMahon 2005. Cf. Zurndorfer 1992. Hummel 1943–1944 discusses all of these individuals at length.
7. On Kang and Liang, see H. Chang 1971. The description of Kang's approach comes from H. Chang 1971, 23.
8. See H. Wilhelm 1951; also K. Chow 1994.
9. W. Tu 1989, Y. Yü 1975. See also Elman 1991 and Metzger 1977, esp. 13–15 and 50 ff.
10. W. T. de Bary in de Bary 1975, 11.
11. W. Chan 1963, 140; Mote 1990, 400–1.
12. W. Chan 1967, 11 (modified) and W. Chan 1963, 151–52 and 169 (modified).
13. SCT 2: 57–60 and Mann 1992.

14. CHC: 9: 148–49.
15. Arthur Wright in Gottschalk, ed. 1963, 38.
16. Y. Han 1955, 196–203.
17. See T. Wilson 1994.
18. On Chinese terms for the "other," see W. Fang 2001, Fiskesjö 1999, and Smith 2013, 202 n. 42.
19. Mosca 2013, 26.
20. See Hostetler 2001.
21. For examples, see R. J. Smith 2012b and R. J. Smith 2013.
22. Benjamin Schwartz in Fairbank, ed. 1968, 277–78.
23. See esp. R. J. Smith 2012b. For a summary of the debate about the tributary system, see R. J. Smith 2013, 10–11 and 78–81.
24. For details, see Fairbank and Teng 1941 and R. J. Smith 2012b. For some Chinese-language perspectives on the system, see Cao Wen 2010, Gan Huaizhen, ed. 2007, Huang Yilong 2007, and Li Yunquan 2004.
25. See Wills 1984 and Hevia 1989. Cf. Huang Yilong 2007 and R. J. Smith 2012b, 78–84.
26. Cited by Benjamin Schwartz in Fairbank, ed. 1968, 277–78.
27. P. T. Ho 1967, 193; Kessler 1976, 169.
28. Frederick Mote in Buxbaum and Mote, eds. 1972, 15.
29. CC, *Analects*, 146; CC, *Great Learning*, 364.
30. See the online bibliography for English-language translations of many of these important works.
31. For these and other such views, see R. J. Smith 2008 and 2012.
32. C. Y. Cheng 1973, esp. 97. The works of Makeham 2003, Slingerland 2006, and Van Norden, ed. 2002 reveal the wide variety of views expressed in commentaries on the *Analects*.
33. Y. Fung 1948, 196–97, slightly modified.
34. CC, *Mencius*, 125; R. Wilhelm 1967, 540.
35. CC, *Mencius*, 346. For an analysis of the place of women in Confucian thought, see Rosenlee 2006, Mann 1997, 2007, 2011b, and the many other works on women noted in the online bibliography.
36. See Rowe 1992, 17; H. Chang 1987, 5–7, 99–100, and esp. 184–87.
37. CC, *Mencius*, 264–65, 309; CC, *Great Learning*, 370. SCT 1: 325–28 provides a translation of the *Xiaojing*. For a few of many studies on the importance of filial piety in traditional China, see Cahn and Tan, eds. 2004, Y. Hu 2009, Kutcher 1999, and W. Y. Li 2008.
38. W. Chan 1955, 297–98 and 305.
39. W. Chan 1955, 300; CC, *Analects*, 194. In these and subsequent quotations from CC I have occasionally modified the text somewhat in the interest of clarity and consistency.
40. CC, *Mencius*, 150–51, 195, 241, and 313–14; Chai and Chai 1967, 1: 63, 2: 92 ff., 257–60. See also CC, *Analects*, 143, 147, 161, 169, 193, 208, 211, 250, 323, and 354.
41. Chai and Chai 1967, part 4, sections 12–14 (modified). See also CC, *Analects*, 299 and CC, *Mencius*, 307.

42. Watt 1972, 96–97.

43. These quotations have been taken from R. J. Smith 2013, 93.

44. CC, *Mencius*, 356; CC, *Analects*, 250; CC, *Great Learning*, 422. See also Du cited in R. J. Smith 2013, chapter 3.

45. See C. Y. Li 2004.

46. CC, *Mencius*, 150–51, 195, 241, and 313–14; Chai and Chai 1967, 1: 63, 2: 92 ff., 257–60. See also CC, *Analects*, 143, 147, 161, 169, 193, 208, 211, 250, 323, and 354.

47. CC, *Analects*, 299; CC, *Mencius*, 307.

48. See C. Y. Cheng 1972; also CC, *Mencius*, 202. Despite the general Confucian disdain for "profit," Richard Lufano 1997 has shown how "middle merchants" in late imperial China appropriated Confucian values for their own purposes, using them in ways that orthodox Confucians did not approve of.

49. CC, *Analects*, 318. See also CC, *Mencius*, 204–5, 402, and 459; CC, *Analects*, 151, 204–5, 212, 225, 260, and 313–14; CC, *Mencius*, 303.

50. CC, *Doctrine of the Mean*, 395, and 412–19; also CC, *Analects*, 139, 141, 153, 202, 224, 256, 265, 267, 295–96, 319, and 331; CC, *Mencius*, 303.

51. CC, *Great Learning*, 257–59.

52. See W. Chan 1963, 19, 84–85, 659, and 707–8; Kai-wing Chow in Smith and Kwok, eds. 1993, 190–91.

53. CC, *Analects*, 146–47; also 179, 251, 253, 259, 271, 273, 274, 279, and 292; CC, *Mencius*, 185, 265, 455, and 458–59; CC, *Doctrine of the Mean*, 388 and 428.

54. CC, *Doctrine of the Mean*, 383–84, 386, 388, 390, 391, 393, and 395–96.

55. Zhu Xi is cited in Y. Fung 1948, 301; see also CC, *Analects*, 318; CC, *Mencius*, 465.

56. See On-cho Ng in Smith and Kwok, eds. 1993, 41 and 48; also Benjamin Elman in Smith and Kwok, eds. 1993, 63 and W. Chan 1963, 714.

57. For these and other examples, see C. K. Yang in Nivison, ed. 1959, 142–43; W. Chan 1963, 14, 141, 159, 267, 323, 344, 358, 368–69, 401, 403–4, and 414–15; Y. Fung 1952, 2: 363, 366, 369, 375, and 619; Black 1989, 94 ff.

58. CC, *Mencius*, 357; CC, *Doctrine of the Mean*, 383; also Needham 1956, 2: 562–64.

59. CC, *Doctrine of the Mean*, 416; CC, *Mencius*, 119, 208–9, 359, 362, and 448; R. Wilhelm 1967, 295 and 351.

60. R. J. Smith 1991, 95. See also R. J. Smith 1991, 10, 14, 33, 35–36, 42, 173–74, and 177 ff. for discussions of fate and R. J. Smith 2013, chapters 1 and 5.

61. Levenson 1964 p. 511.

62. See the online bibliography for a great many works on Chinese Daoism, including Hansen's. W. Chan 1963, 136–210 and SCT 1: 77–111, 263–68, and 381–90 offer excellent translations of Daoist writings.

63. See, for example, Kirkland 2004, esp. 1–19. Zhang Chengquan 2012 reflects the prevailing Chinese distinction.

64. W. Chan 1963, 102.

65. Ibid., 167, modified. See also ibid., 162.

66. Ibid., 141, modified.

67. de Bary et al., eds. 1964, 1: 70, modified. Cf. W. Chan 1963, 185–86.
68. W. Chan 1963, 190–91.
69. de Bary et al., eds., 1964, 1: 69, modified.
70. Ibid., 1: 69, modified.
71. de Bary et al., eds. 1964, 1: 69–70, modified. Cf. W. Chan 1963, 182–83.
72. W. Chan 1963, 141–42.
73. Ibid., 177–78.
74. Ibid., 117. Mote 1990, 399 discusses Wang's views.
75. Cited in R. J. Smith 1994, 152; cf. W. Chan 1963, 189.
76. W. Chan 1963, 148–49.
77. See, for example, the essay on Daoism by Kwang-Ching Liu and Richard Shek in Liu and Shek, eds. 2004, 29–72.
78. W. Chan 1967, 274; W. Chan 1963, 196.
79. W. T. de Bary in de Bary, ed. 1975, 10 and 94.

CHAPTER SEVEN: RELIGIOUS LIFE

1. E. Rawski 1998, chapters 6–8. The quotations come from 264. See also de Harlez 1887.
2. For details, see E. Rawski 1998, 234–44. Rawski 269 notes that "As the shamanistic rites faded from the court, sacrifices to the ancestors took their place."
3. E. Rawski 1998, 231 and 270 ff.; Grupper 1984.
4. Maspero is cited in Thompson 1979, 55. See also Freedman in Wolf, ed. 1974, 37 ff. and D. Johnson 2009, esp. 9–11.
5. James Watson in Lieberthal et al., eds. 1991, 74.
6. See the essays in Sutton, ed. 2007; also Snyder-Reinke 2007, 177 ff.
7. See E. T. Williams 1913, 15–17 and 21–23; cf. the essays by Edward Farmer and Romeyn Taylor in K. C. Liu, ed. 1990. See also I. Clark 2014.
8. On Islam in China, see Atwill 2005, Israeli 1980, K. Kim 2008, and Leslie 1986; on Judaism in China, see Goldstein 1999–2000 and Pollak 1980.
9. See Brook 1989 and Sutton 1989.
10. Brokaw 1991, 157 ff., esp. 162 and 232–33, and S. W. Chan 1985.
11. Arthur Wolf in Wolf, ed. 1974, 145; E. Rawski 1998, 197 ff.
12. Stephan Feuchtwang in Skinner, ed. 1977, 607. Much of the following discussion of official religion is drawn from Feuchtwang. Also R. J. Smith 2013, chapter 3; Rawski 1998, chapter 6; and Zito 1997 passim.
13. Stephan Feuchtwang in Skinner, ed. 1977, 591–93.
14. See, for example, Townley 1904, 93–97.
15. Quoted in Stephan Feuchtwang in Skinner, ed. 1977, 601. See also Zito 1987.
16. C. K. Yang 1961, 156–57.
17. Cited in Spence 1978, 49–50.
18. On gender issues in Chinese religion, see X. Kang 2006, Snyder-Reinke 2007, esp. chapters 3 and 4, and Sangren 1987, 74, 135–36, 148–56, 183–84, and 198.
19. C. K. Yang 1961, 98–99.

20. See Arthur Wolf in Wolf, ed. 1974 and Thompson, ed. 1973, 196–201.

21. T. Ch'ü 1962, 165; Balazs 1965, 63–64; Johnston 1910, 134–35.

22. Snyder-Reinke 2007, 81 and 184. Compare Katz 2009.

23. Katz 2009.

24. E. Rawski 1998, 252–54.

25. For details, see ibid., 244–63. On Chengde/Rehe, see Cary Liu 2010 and Whiteman 2011.

26. K. Greenblatt in de Bary, ed. 1975, 131–32. On Qing efforts to control the Buddhist and Daoist religious establishment, see C. K. Yang 1961, 187–192.

27. W. Chan 1967, 283.

28. See Richard Shek's excellent article on Peng in Smith and Kwok, eds. 1993.

29. Nivison 1966, 76 and 126–27.

30. Cited by Hui-chen Wang Liu in Nivison and Wright, eds. 1959, 71–72.

31. For details on these and other points of Buddhist doctrine, see SCT 1: 413–20 and note 32 below. For excellent translations of other Chinese Buddhist texts, see SCT 1: 421–536, and W. Chan 1963, 336–449.

32. For details on these and other Buddhist schools and teachings, including the Three Treatise School (*Sanlun*), the Consciousness-Only School (*Weishi*), and the Meditation School (*Chan*), see SCT 1: 433–536. See also the online bibliography under search categories such as Buddhism, Buddhist, etc.

33. SCT 1: 436.

34. W. Chan 1963, 407, slightly modified.

35. B. Grant 1996 and 2008b. On *gong'an*, see in particular Sharf in Furth, Zeitlin, and Hsiung, eds. 2007.

36. The Pure Land School did, however, generate its own corpus of specialized literature. See, for example, the material in SCT 1: 481–91.

37. For descriptions and illustrations of the Ten Courts of Hell and the Western Paradise, see Wieger 1913, 345–91 and 397–98; also http://academic.reed.edu/hellscrolls/.

38. See Y. H. Li 2012. On Guanyin, consult Barbara Reed in Cabezon, ed. 1985.

39. For details, see Reichelt 1934, 174–99.

40. Welch 1967, 398 ff., slightly modified.

41. SCT 436–40 and E. Rawski 1998, 244 ff. Mādhyamika teachings in China formed the foundation of the so-called Three Treatise School (*Sanlun*). See SCT 1: 436–40.

42. Cozort 1998, esp. 429.

43. See Hopkins 1980.

44. E. Rawski 1998, 259.

45. W. Chan 1969, 419. For excellent translations of Religious Daoist and related texts, see SCT 1: 392–414 and 899–916. For works on various kinds of Daoism, consult the online bibliography using search terms such as "Daoist" or "Taoist."

46. Saso 1978, 52 ff.; Kirkland 2004, 168.

47. Kirkland 2004, 169–71.

48. On the *Zhouyi chanzhen*, see R. J. Smith 2008, 186–87; on the *Xiuzhen houbian*, see Pregadio 2013.

49. Idema 2008. See also Brokaw 1991 and CHCL 2: 399–412.

50. C. K. Yang 1961, 25.

51. C. K. Yang 1961, 7–10.

52. B. Schwartz 1985, 379.

53. See Saso 1989 and 1991. The proverb comes from Plopper 1926, 78.

54. Doré 1914–1933, 3: iii–vi. A wealth of information on Chinese popular religion can be found in De Groot 1892–1910, 1903, and 1912.

55. For details on *fengshui* theories and the pervasiveness of *fengshui* practices, see Feuchtwang 2002, Meyer 1978 and 1991, and R. J. Smith 1991, chapter 4. See also Aylward 2007; D. McMahon 2012; Paton 2013; and Yi Ding et al. 1996.

56. Eitel 1873, 18, slightly modified.

57. Meyer 1978, 148–55. Cf. the description in Feuchtwang 2002, 37–49.

58. E. Rawski 1998, 265. On Chinese homes, see Knapp 1986, 1989, 1990, and 1999.

59. E. Rawski 1998, 285–90. Rawski points out that some imperial ancestors were favored over others, which was often the case in Chinese ancestor worship as well.

60. James Watson in Watson and Rawski, eds. 1988, 12–15; Evelyn Rawski discusses imperial death rituals in ibid., 228–53.

61. See Evelyn Rawski in Watson and Rawski, eds. 1988, 234–35.

62. C. K. Yang in Fairbank, ed. 1957, 227. See also Welch 1967, 181–85.

63. On these and other heterodox sects and teachings, see the essays in Liu and Shek, eds. 2005; also Atwill 2005; CHC 11: 202–44; Esherick 1987; Murray 1994; Naquin and Rawski 1987, 134–37, 166–67, 185–86, and 191–93; Seiwert and Ma 2003, esp. 209–484; and ter Haar 1992.

64. On the Taipings, see Richard Bohr in Liu and Shek, eds. 2005; also Meyer-Fong 2013 and S. Platt 2012.

65. R. J. Smith 2013, 105–6.

66. Allen Chun 1992.

CHAPTER EIGHT: ARTS AND CRAFTS

1. See Greenwood 2013, Fong and Watt, eds. 1996, and E. Rawski 1998, esp. 51–55 and 175–78; also Berger 2003; Cahill 1996 and 2010; Cahill et al. 2013; Findlay 2011; Cary Liu 2010; H. C. Lo 2009; T. Miller 2007; Nie Chongzheng 1996; Stuart and Rawski 2001; Vinograd 1992; H. Wu 1995 and 1996; Wu and Tsiang, eds. 2005; and H. X. Zhang 2000.

2. On Qing maps, see Cams 2012, Elman 2003, Hostetler 2001, and esp. R. J. Smith 2013, chapter 2. The archives of the Grand Council include a category for visual documents, that is divided into seven sections: (1) atlases of administrative divisions, maps of individual regions, and city plans; (2) maps of the Yangzi River, the Yellow River, and coastlines; (3) the Grand Canal; (4) battles and battlefields; (5) royal tours and visits; (6) religious sites; (7) imperial mausolea. See H. X. Zhang 2000.

3. On the arts of the brush, see Luo Zhongfeng 2001; for popular art, see Berliner 1989; Liang 2002; Xiao Hongfa 2009; Zhu and Ren, eds. 2010.

4. See also Clunas 1991, esp. 169. David 1971 offers a translation of the *Gegu yaolun*.

5. See E. Rawski 53–54; Cahill 1996 and 2010; and Cahill et al. 2013. See also Hong Wu 1996 and Hong Wu in Widmer and Chang, eds. 1997.

6. Kleutghen 2014 and forthcoming; also Cahill 2010; Cahill 1994 and 1996; Cahill et al. 2013; and Clunas 2006. Cf. Nie Chongzheng 1996.

7. Sullivan 1979, 140. On patronage, see the sources cited in note 1.

8. Cahill 2010, 3. Cahill 2010, 150 ff. emphasizes the sexual content of *meiren hua*, and tentatively links the theme of sexual longing to social trends in the Ming-Qing period, including the commercialization of courtesan culture.

9. Sullivan 1977, 216–19 and 233–36.

10. See Jun Zhang 2008, esp. 195–206, for a discussion of the link between Duan-fang's political and social networking and his connoisseurship.

11. V. Shih 1983, 13, modified. Cf. Yu-kung Kao in Murck and Fong, eds. 1991, esp. 64 ff.

12. Cited in Mungello 1969, 379.

13. Michael Sullivan in Dawson, ed. 1964, 178.

14. See Chai and Chai 1967, 2: 98–100. On the link between music, aesthetics, and ritual, see Bell, Rawski, and Watson, eds. 1996; DeWoskin 1982; Yu-kung Kao in Murck and Fong, eds. 1991; V. Shih 1983, 353–59; and B. Wu 1998.

15. Frederick Mote in Murck, ed. 1976, 6.

16. See the essays by Wei-ming Tu and Wen Fong in Murck, ed. 1976.

17. Wen Fong in Murck, ed. 1976, 93.

18. Michael Sullivan in Dawson, ed. 1964, 206.

19. Van Gulik, trans. 1958, 59–60.

20. Michael Sullivan in Dawson, ed. 1964, 207–10.

21. On Chinese symbolism, see Berlinger 1989; Burling and Burling 1953; Cammann 1990; David, trans. 1971; Dutu shidai xiangmuzu, ed. 2012; Eberhard 1986; Garrett 1990 and 2007; Knapp 1990 and 1999; H. M. Sung 2009; Ting 1998; Y. H. Tseng 1977; C. A. S. Williams 1941; and Yetts 1912. The following several paragraphs are based primarily on these sources.

22. For discussions of various kinds of Chinese craft productions, including silk, see Berlinger 1986; Garrett 1990 and 2007; R. S. Johnston 1991; Knapp 1990 and 1999; Ellen Huang 2008; Keswick 1978; Kuwayama, ed. 1992; Legeza 1980; Moll-Murata, Song, and Vogel, eds. 2005; T. C. Liu 1993; Schafer 2011; V. Siu 2013; Steinhardt 2002; and Vainker 2004.

23. See E. Rawski 1998, 175–78.

24. See, in particular, Hui-chun Yu 2007.

25. W. Watson 1962, 15; David 1971, 12.

26. Wen Fong 1980, esp. 30–31. Cf. Clark 2004.

27. Van Gulik 1958, 50, 76 n. 20.

28. Chai and Chai 1967, 2: 464.

29. Hansford 1969, 24. Jade "carving" is a misnomer because jade is much too hard and brittle to be carved like soapstone. Instead, it had to be laboriously ground into shape using a drill or wheel mechanism coated with abrasive.

30. Hansford 1969, 16.

31. I. Clark 2014. See also Vainker 2005.

32. Jenyns 1965, 2, modified. For more recent scholarship on ceramics, see Ellen Huang 2008, Huwayama, ed. 1992, and Li and Cheng 1996.

33. Legeza 1980.

34. On the Yuanming yuan, see Finlay 2011 and the images and commentary available at MIT, "The Garden of Perfect Brightness." For other useful discussions of Chinese gardens, see Keswick 1978, T. C. Liu 1993, and V. Siu 2013.

35. Cited in Keswick 1978, 60.

36. See McDowell 2001; Riegel 2010; and Schmidt 2008. Riegel's article is of special interest because it creatively combines discussions of gender, gardens, and painting.

37. Cited in Keswick 1978, 196–97.

38. Wing-tsit Chan in Inn and Lee, eds. 1940, esp. 31–32. See also Yu-kung Kao in Murck and Fong, eds. 1991.

39. On the aesthetics of *fengshui*, see R. J. Smith 1991, chapter 4.

40. Keswick 1978, 12–14. On the Chinese household module, see Knapp 1986, 1989, 1990, and 1999.

41. Cited in Keswick 1978, 198–99.

42. On erotic art in China, see Beurdeley et al. eds., 1969 and Douglas and Slinger 1994; also Van Gulik 2003 passim.

43. On Luo Ping, see Karlsson, Murck, and Matteini, eds. 2010.

44. David 1971, 14–15. See also James Cahill in A. Wright, ed. 1960a, 117–18 and 130.

45. James Cahill in A. Wright, ed. 1960a, 117–18.

46. Siren 1937, 195 and 209; see also Mungello 1969.

47. Siren 1937, 215.

48. Siren 1937, 209.

49. David, trans. 1971, 14–15.

50. M. Sze 1959, 115, 130–31, and 133–53. See also Rowley 1970, Silbergeld 1982, and S. K. Ng 1992.

51. Zhang Geng is quoted in Siren 1937, 217. On Wang Hui's "clear and radiant" painting, see Hearn, ed. 2008.

52. Loehr 1970, 35–36.

53. Y. T. Lin 1967, 198.

54. Y. T. Lin 1967, 200; Loehr 1970, 36.

55. Loehr 1970, 36. On lines of transmission, see Wen Fong 1971.

56. Siren 1937, 210.

57. Y. T. Lin 1967, 165; see also Siren 1937, 206–7.

58. Wen Fong 1971, 283. See also Silbergeld 1982 and S. K. Ng 1992.

59. Siren 1937, 208–9.

60. Y. T. Lin 1967, 169.

61. Y. T. Lin 1967, 175–76.

62. M. Sze 1959, 157 and 325–28; Rowley 1970, 8, 13–14, 17, 42, 47, 51–55, and 93; Silbergeld 1982, esp. 56–57.

63. M. Sze 1959, 107; Yu-kung Kao and Tsu-lin Mei in Murck, ed. 1976, esp. 132. See also Andrew Plaks in Plaks, ed. 1977, 338; Wen Fong 1971, 282–83; Rowley 1970, 64–67.

64. See, for example, Ginger Hsu 2002; Cahill 1994; Li, Cahill, and Ho, eds. 1991.

65. Sherman Lee in Rogers and Lee, eds. 1988, 28. On Shitao, see J. Hay 2001; on Zhu Da, see Wang and Barnhart 1990.

66. M. Sze 1959, 5, modified.

67. See the essays by Ginger Tong, Ginger Cheng-hsi Hsu, and Stella Yu Lee in Chu-tsing Li, ed. 1989; also Brown and Chou 1992, 17–21, 40–42, 102–9, 240–47, and 282–84.

68. See esp. Weidner 1988, Weidner et al., eds. 1988, and Weidner, ed. 1990; also Hummel 1943–1944, 99, 278, 324, 386, 431, 566, 685–86, and 841.

69. Marsha Weidner in Weidner, ed. 1988, 13 and 130–33. See also Ellen Johnston Laing in Weidner, ed. 1990, 93–94.

70. Marsha Weidner in Weidner, ed. 1988, 26, 94, and 148.

71. Cited in Sullivan 1979, 142. On Castiglione, see Beurdeley and Beurdeley 1972.

72. Van Gulik 1958, 34, modified.

73. David, trans. 1971, 201. On the cultural importance of calligraphy, see, for example, Y. Chiang 1973, esp. 225–39.

74. Elman 1984, 28 and 191–99.

75. Hummel 1943–1944, 25–26, 610–11, and 715–16. See also ibid., 278, on Wang Zhaoyuan 1763–1851, another talented woman calligrapher and writer of the Qing period.

76. Y. Chiang 1973, chapter 1; Y. T. Lin, 1935, 290–97.

CHAPTER NINE: LITERARY TRENDS

1. Schmidt 2008, 129–30. As indicated in the introduction and in chapters 1, 2, 8, and 10, over the past two decades or so there has been an enormous amount of excellent scholarship on women in late imperial China, including women writers. See the online bibliography for a great many such works.

2. See Hu Xiaozhen 2008 and S. C. Hu 2005. Aside from *tansi* and a few quite exceptional works (particularly Gu Taiqing's sequel to the great Qing novel *Honglou meng*), women writers only began producing full-fledged novels in the late Qing period. For examples, see the essays by Jing Tsu and Ellen Widmer in Qian, Fong, and Smith, eds. 2008. Cf. Y. L. Guo 2003, 114.

3. Among the most well known of these works are: *Sanguo yanyi* (Romance of the Three Kingdoms), *Shuihu zhuan* (Water margin), *Xiyou ji* (Journey to the west), *Jin Ping Mei* (Plum in the golden vase), *Fengshen yanyi* (Investiture of the gods), *Hou Xiyouji* (Continuation of *Journey to the West*), *Honglou meng* (Dream of the red

chamber), *Rou putuan* (Carnal prayer mat), and *Liaozhai zhiyi* (Strange stories from the Liao Studio). See Gimm 1988, passim.

4. See R. J. Smith 2014 for visual examples taken from a nineteenth-century edition of the WBQS.

5. See CHCL 2: 370–72. For the related literary forms of "drum ballads" and "string ballads," see CHCL 2: 368–88. Many of the latter works were produced by talented women in the Jiangnan area.

6. See Brokaw 2005 and 2007; Brokaw and Chow, eds. 2005; L. Chia 2002; K. Chow 2004; McDermott 2006; and Meyer-Fong 2007.

7. Elman 1981, 13. On Ming loyalist writing, see Widmer 1987.

8. Crossley 1987, 1999, passim, esp. 296 ff. and 2002, esp. 122–29; cf. Guy 1987, 163.

9. Naquin and Rawski 1987, 67; P. Wu 1990. See also Vinograd 1992 and Dryburgh and Dauncey, eds. 2013. An excellent example of Qing autobiographical writing is Shen Fu's (1763–1825) *Fusheng liuji* (Six records of a floating life). See Pratt and Chiang 1983 and Sanders 2011.

10. Teng and Biggerstaff 1971, 95. See also Wilkinson 2013, esp. 959–60. R. J. Smith 2014 provides a more complete breakdown of the contents of the TSCC.

11. Guy 1987, 201. See also Wilkinson 2013, 945–50.

12. Guy 1987, 150–52; also Elman 1984, 76–78.

13. Hucker 1975, 386–87. On Qian Qianyi as a major literary figure of the Ming-Qing transition, see CHCL 2: 146 ff. and 175 ff.

14. J. Y. Liu 1975, 44 and 96–97.

15. J. Y. Liu 1975, 45. Liu Xie is quoted in V. Shih 1983, 19.

16. J. Y. Liu 1975, 66.

17. Quoted in J. Y. Liu 1975, 113 and 136.

18. J. Y. Liu 1975, 21, 26–27, 82, 88, and 104. On the debate, see ibid., 99–105.

19. CC, *Analects*, 211. The best collection of translated Qing poetry is Lo and Schultz, eds. 1986. Other useful collections of translated poetry that have selections from the Qing period include: Chang and Saussy, eds. 1999; Chaves, ed. 1986; Idema and Grant, eds. 2004; Liu and Lo, eds. 1975; Panda Books 1986; and W. Yip 1976.

20. Lo and Schultz 1986, 3–29.

21. See CHCL 2: 162–68 and Lo and Schultz 1986, 11–26.

22. Pauline Yu 1987, 17 ff., esp. 24–25.

23. J. Y. Liu 1966, 80.

24. Liu and Lo, eds. 1976, 214.

25. Y. K. Wong 1990, 157 ff., esp. 160; see also T. C. Lai 1969 and J. Y. Liu 1966, 149–50.

26. Hawkes 1973–1979, 2: 459. Used with the permission of Penguin Publishers.

27. Hawkes 1973–1979, 2: 459.

28. J. Y. Liu 1966, 149–50.

29. Quoted in R. J. Smith 2008, slightly modified.

30. Liu and Lo, eds. 1976, 220. The reference to "wind and thunder" (*fenglei*) suggests the notion of great possibility after the correction of errors—based on the Commentary on the Judgment and the Commentary on the Images of the Yi hexagram (#42).

31. J. Y. Liu 1975, 70–76.

32. Xie Bridge is a common poetic reference to the imagined residence of a beloved woman. The premature death of Nalan Xingde's wife during childbirth seems to account for his pessimism, although he later remarried and had several sons and daughters. For details on Nalan Xingde's life and poetry, see Carpenter 1983. A Chinese version of this poem can be found at www.xys.org/xys/classics/poetry/Qing/Nalan-Xingde.txt.

33. Liu and Lo, eds. 1976, 220. The grammatical emphasis in this last line is on the "whiteness" of the bird, which seems to accentuate the theme of isolation.

34. Siu–kit Wong in Rickett 1978, 130–31 and 140. See also Black 1989, 242 ff.

35. Liu and Lo, eds. 1976, 215.

36. Male poets are inordinately represented in most pre-1995 collections of late imperial poetry. See, for example, the otherwise excellent anthology of Qing poetry by Lo and Schultz 1986. See also Panda Books 1986.

37. In addition to Chang and Saussy, eds. 1999 and Idema and Grant, eds. 2004, see Mann and Cheng, eds. 2001. See also the many other monographs on women writers listed in the online bibliography.

38. For a wide variety of examples, see Chang and Saussy, eds. 1999; Idema and Grant, eds. 2004; Robertson 1992 and 2010; also Irving Yucheng Lo in Weidner, ed. 1988; and Widmer 2009.

39. Robertson 1992, 86–87. Used with permission from the author and from *Late Imperial China*.

40. Idema and Grant, eds. 2004, 652. See also Q. Huang 2004 and Widmer 2002 for details on Gu Taiqing's literary life.

41. For background, see Idema and Grant, eds. 2004, 653 and 679 ff. This magnificent anthology contains an entire chapter on Manchu women writers, with biographical information as well as translations.

42. Idema and Grant, eds. 2004, 679–81, slightly modified.

43. The grammar here seems to suggest that Naxun Lanbao is speaking of the notoriously weak-willed Daoguang emperor, although the reference could also be to the decline in Mongol traditions of military rigor. I am grateful to Nanxiu Qian for bringing this interesting ambiguity to my attention.

44. The Chinese version of this poem appears in MHY at http://digital .library.mcgill.ca/mingqing/search/details-poem.php?poemID=18573&language =eng.

45. Liu and Lo, eds. 1976, 218.

46. E. Rawski 1979, 140; cf. De Francis 1984, 204–5. Other estimates range from a low of 20 to 25 percent male literacy to a high of 40 to 50 percent. On hierarchies of literacy, see David Johnson in Johnson, et al., eds. 1985, 36–38, 42–43, and 55–57; see also L. Bai 2005, xiv–xx and passim.

47. Spence 1968, 5. For a full discussion of "folk literature" in the Ming-Qing era, see CHCL 2: 343–412.

48. On Pu, see Chang and Chang 1992 and Zeitlin 1993 and 2007. Another talented and famous writer of "strange tales," Ji Yun (aka Ji Xiaolan; 1724–1805) was a high-ranking Qing official, a co-editor of the SKQS, and a gifted poet. He was also

a sharp critic of Pu. See CHCL 2: 253–56. For examples of Ji's stories, see Pollard 2014.

49. See, for example, Brokaw 1991; Tadeo Sakai in de Bary 1970, 341–62; Eberhard 1967, esp. 117–25. For translations of some popular religious tracts, see SCT 1: 899–919.

50. James J. Y. Liu 1979, 86. For useful works on Chinese drama, see Liao Ben 1997, A. Goldman 2012, and Q. Ma 2005; also T. C. Hsu 1985, D. Johnson 2009, Wichmann 1991, and B. Yung 1989.

51. Hanan 1988, 15–16. See also CHCL 2: 203–10.

52. Hanan 1988, 1. For an analysis of Li's essays, see Hanan 1988, chapter 8, esp. 196–97.

53. CHCL 2: 203–10.

54. Spence 2013, 61. See also CHCL 2: 239–44 and Struve 1977. Chen and Acton 1976 translate the play.

55. See Rolston 1997; also Plaks 2005.

56. A word search of the online bibliography will yield the authors and titles of such works.

57. See Plaks 1976, 1977, and 1987; also Plaks in Rolston, ed. 1990. For Hsia's critique, see C. T. Hsia 2004, 31–42 and esp. 171–87.

58. Plaks 1977, 42. For a useful discussion and analysis of lesser known Chinese novels of the Qing period, see CHCL 2: 291–98.

59. Gimm 1988, 81 notes that "Proscriptions or actions taken against Chinese fictional works can be attested for the following years: 1642, 1652, 1663, 1687, 1701, 1709, 1711, 1714, 1724, 1736, 1738, 1753, 1754, 1774, 1802, 1810, 1813, 1834, 1844, 1851, 1868, and 1871."

60. Cited in Gimm 1988, 81 (slightly modified).

61. Cited in ibid.

62. On sequels, see the essays in M. W. Huang, ed. 2006; also CHCL 2: 212 ff.

63. On "military romances" see C. T. Hsia 2004, 135–70, esp. 166 ff. and CHCL 2: 432–35.

64. Shuen-fu Lin in Plaks, ed. 1977. For an able English-language translation of *The Scholars*, see Yang and Yang 1957. On Wu Jingzi, consult Ropp 1981. For an excellent summary and analysis of the novel, see CHCL 2: 274–82; also W. Shang 1998.

65. Hanan 1988 assumes Li Yu to be the author; Chang and Chang 1992 argue otherwise. The standard English-language translation of this novel is Hanan 1990.

66. Elvin 1991, reproduced in Elvin 1997; see also C. T. Hsia in Plaks, ed. 1977; Brandauer 1977. For an English-language translation see T. Y. Lin 1966. CHCL 2: 296–98 provides an excellent summary and analysis.

67. The best English-language translation of *Travels of Laocan* is still Shadick 1952; the best English-language translation of *Bizzare Happenings* is S. S. Liu 1975. On the *Travels of Laocan*, see C. T. Hsia 2004, 247–68.

68. CHCL 2: 430–31. For an excellent discussion of late Qing fiction and its sociopolitical context, see CHCL 2: 413–22, 427–35, and 440–56. See also Dloezelova-Velingerova, ed. 1980; T. Y. Liu 1984; Qian, Fong, and Smith eds. 2008; and Starr 2007.

69. Hummel 1943–1944, 738. The best English-language translation of this work is Hawkes 1973–1979 and Minford 1979–1987. See also Yang and Yang 1978–1980. For an excellent summary and analysis, see CHCL 2: 282–91.

70. For a critique of traditional concepts of "binary schematicization," see Yu 1997, 238. See also the rather harsh critique of Plaks by C. T. Hsia 2004, 31–42 and 171–87.

71. Miller 1975, 56.

72. Andrew Plaks in Plaks, ed. 1977, 334–39, esp. 338.

73. Hawkes 1973–1979, 2: 334.

74. For an excellent summary and analysis of this play, see CHCL 2: 22–23 and 358–91.

CHAPTER TEN: SOCIAL LIFE

1. On these and other distinctions, see Crossley 1990, Elliott 2001a, and Rhoads 2000, esp. 18–63. For some detailed Chinese-language descriptions of Manchu culture, see Dai Yinghua 2010; Diao Shuren 2002; Ding Yizhuang 1992; Li Li 2012; Li Yanguang and Guan Jie 1991; Liu Xiaomeng 2001; Manzu jianshi bianxie zu, ed. 2009; Wang Zhonghan, ed. 1996; Yang Xichun 1991; Zhang Jie 2007; Zhongguo shehui kexue yuan, ed. 2011; and Zhou Yuanlian 1981.

2. Elliott 2001a, 346. See also the Chinese-language sources noted in n. 1 above, esp. Dai Yinghua 2010, Diao Shuren 2002, Li Li 2012, Liu Xiaomeng 2001 and Yang Xichun 1991. For a discussion of the criticisms heaped on the Chinese Bannermen for departing from the "Manchu Way," see Elliott 2001a, 333–42.

3. See Elliott 2001a, 305–44, esp. 311–22; also Zhongguo shehui kexue yuan, ed. 2011, esp. 168–98 and Rhoads 2000, esp. 49–51 and 259–63.

4. See the Chinese-language sources cited in n. 1 above.

5. For Dun's account, originally published in 1936, see Bodde, trans. 1977. Bogan's work, originally published in 1928, was reprinted together with Bodde's translation in 1977.

6. See Ropp 1976, esp. 20–21. For useful perspectives on the Qing dynasty's chastity cult, see Elvin 1984; Paderni 1999; Ropp et al., eds. 2001; Sommer 2000, esp. 10–11, 67–73, 78–79, 168–70, 177–83, 277–78, and 312–13; and C. Tao 1991.

7. Ropp 1994, 355.

8. See Blake 1994; Ebrey 1999; Ko 1997, 2001, 2005; P. Wang 2000; and Zito 2006.

9. The quotations from the *Classic of Poetry* and the *Jinsi lu* are from Waley 1987, 283–84 and R. J. Smith 2008, 233, respectively—both modified after consulting the original. For the proverbs, see A. H. Smith 1914, 69 and R. J. Smith 2013, 114. David Arkush's article on peasant proverbs in K. C. Liu, ed. 1990, esp. 327–28, gives several examples of sayings comparing women to animals.

10. Cited in Baker 1979, 39. For the proverbs, see A. Smith 1899, 191 and Walshe 1906, 212–13.

11. Buck 1937, 462 ff; see also James Hayes in Johnson et al., eds. 1985; M. Cohen 1991, 117–19.

12. Ocko 1990, 228–30. See also the legal cases described by Melissa Macauley 1998, Matthew Sommer 2000, and Janet Theiss 2009. These cases generally concerned non-elites—not only because elites were a statistical minority, but also because they often had the power to influence the behavior of family members without recourse to the justice system.

13. See R. J. Smith 1992 and R. J. Smith forthcoming.

14. On infant mortality, see Elvin and Fox 2012 and 2014. Cf. Pomeranz 2000, 37. Of the Kangxi emperor's more than fifty children, twenty-two died before the age of four. See Naquin and Rawski 1987, 107.

15. Ebrey, ed. 1993, 313–17, slightly modified. Pomeranz 2000, 38–39, drawing on the research of James Li and Feng Wang, notes that even within the imperial family perhaps as many as 25 percent of female newborns were killed, with the rate peaking in the eighteenth century. See also Naquin and Rawski 1987, 108 and 110 and Rowe 2009, 9.

16. Waltner 1990. See also L. Bai 2005, 16–18, 44, and 207–8.

17. See M. Levy 1949.

18. See L. Bai 2005, 8–11, 19, and 175–76. For illustrations of prenatal growth and texts on prenatal education, see WBQS 1758, *zhongzi men*, 171–84. Cf. R. J. Smith 2014.

19. For excerpts from these works designed for young women, see SCT 1: 819–27. Susan Mann in Elman and Woodside, eds. 1994 provides an excellent essay on the education of daughters in the mid-Qing period.

20. For a full translation of one version of these stories, see Jordan 2014, item 7; cf. the excerpts in SCT 2: 139–41. See also Mo and Shen 1999; P. Hsiung 2005, 21–23, 111–12, and 208; and L. Bai 2005, 104–5, and 107–8.

21. See the appendix to T'ien 1988; also K. Chong 1990, 93–94, 115–20, and 164–66.

22. For these and other such stories, see Yu Zhi 1872, 1–50.

23. An abridged version appears in SCT 1: 325–29. For Ebrey's comparison, see Mann and Cheng, eds. 2001, 47–70.

24. For excerpts from school codes, instructions for students, a primer on "human nature and principle" and Zhu Xi's famous *Dushu fa* (How to read books), see SCT 1: 807–16. On charitable schools and the education of non-Han ethnic people, consult Elman and Woodside, eds. 1994, esp. 9–10, 384–91, 417–57, 419–46, and 527–29.

25. See L. Bai 2005, esp. chapter 4.

26. See the schedule in Dorothy Ko 1992, 24. Cf. SCT 1: 807–16.

27. See Dorothy Ko 1992, 25–28. Mothers also tried to establish close relationships with their sons (see P. Hsiung 1994 and 2005, 129–30, 149, 151–53), and were often accused of "spoiling" them. Rowe 1992, 25; also Eastman 1988, 28–29.

28. "Lack of filial piety," the seventh of the Ten Great Wrongs, included cursing one's parents or paternal grandparents or cursing one's husband's paternal grandparents. W. Jones 1994, 35.

29. See Metzger 1977, 19–20; cf. Pye 1981, 137.

30. Chai and Chai 1967, 2: 248–434. For information on Chinese marriage customs, see Bao Zhonghao 2006, Holmgren 1995, Watson and Ebrey, eds. 1991, and Wolf and Huang 1980. The following discussion is based primarily on these sources.

31. For variations, see James Watson in Ebrey and Watson, eds. 1986, 284–85; also Diana Martin in Baker and Feuchtwang, eds. 1991.

32. Wolf and Huang 1980, chapter 21, esp. 335.

33. For a valuable discussion of marriage terminology, see R. Watson and Ebrey 1991, 7–8. E. Rawski 1998, 130–59 discusses the institution of concubinage as practiced by the Qing nobility.

34. David Buxbaum in Buxbaum and Mote, eds. 1972, esp. 216–17; also Baker 1979, 35–36.

35. H. H. Zhang et al., eds. 2013, 103.

36. For details, see Baker 1979, Bao Zhonghao 2006, Holmgren 1995, Watson and Ebrey, eds. 1991, and Wolf and Huang 1980. For contemporary Western accounts, consult Doolittle 1865, 1: 65 ff.; Gray 1878, 1: 191 ff.; Walshe 1906, 108 ff.; and S. W. Williams 1883, 1: 785 ff. For the surprisingly similar rituals of marriage *resistance*, see Marjorie Topley in Wolf, ed. 1978.

37. Rowe 1992, 16. On matchmaking, see R. J. Smith 1991, 184–88; on dowries and inheritance, consult Chung-min Chen in Hsieh and Chuang, eds. 2002, 117–27.

38. On Qing dynasty wedding attire, see Garrett 2007, 49–50, 98–100, and 120–23. E. Rawski 1998, 274–76 discusses the ways that Chinese-style rituals, including marriage ceremonies, were modified at court in accordance with Manchu beliefs and practices.

39. An exception was the extremely localized marriage practice known as *buluojia*. See Helen Siu 1990.

40. Baker 1979, 46–47 and 125 ff.

41. See Spence 1978. On divorce and its limitations, consult Wolf and Huang 1980, chapter 13 and Baker 1979, 129–30. For various kinds of marriage resistance, consult Marjorie Topley in Wolf, ed. 1978; Helen Siu 1990; and Stockard 1989.

42. See Barr 2013, Ropp 1981, 146–47, and Rowe 2009, 104–5. For Western perspectives, see R. F. Johnston 1910, 219, 243–45; Macgowan 1912, 249 and 255–56. N. Qian 2015 provides a splendid example of a companionate marriage in the late Qing.

43. Telford 1986, 126. See also the cases cited in Theiss 2009.

44. Jin Wenxue 2004.

45. See especially Paul Goldin's long and illuminating introduction to the new edition of Van Gulik 2003. The literature on Chinese sexuality is abundant. For a small sample, see Cabezon 1985; N. Ding 2002; Finnane and McLaren 1998; Hinsch 1990; Jin Wenxue 2004; Mann 2011b; McMahon 1988, 1995, and 2009; Meijer 1985 and 1991; V. Ng 1987; F. Ruan 1991; Sommer 2000, 2005, and 2013; G. Song 2004; Wile, ed. 1992.

46. See esp. Sommer 2000.

47. Cited in Hanan 1988, 121.

48. See Furth 1992, esp. 33–34; also Harper 1987; Wile, ed. 1992; F. Ruan 1991; MacMahon 1995, esp. 127–28 and 33.

49. See H. Levy 1967 and M. Cohen 1991, 120–21. Cf. Ebrey 1999; Ko 1997, 2001, and 2005; and Zito 2006.

50. On the history of homosexuality in China, consult Hinsch 1990. On the Qing state's changing attitudes toward homosexuality, see Sommer 2000, esp. 10, 28–29, 114–18, 121–32, 130–32, 148–58, and 353–54.

51. For a number of such works, search the online bibliography under categories such as "medicine" and "medical." See also SCC 6 (2000).

52. See Brokaw 2007, 428–49; also Elman 2005, 227–36.

53. See, for example, Katz 1995, Strickmann 2002, and Y. L. Chao 2009.

54. Cited in E. Hsu 1999, 107, slightly modified. On theories of Chinese medicine, in addition to the sources cited above and below, consult Unschuld 1985, 1986, 1988 and Porkert 1988.

55. See the discussion of Ye Gui by Charlotte Furth in Furth and Hsiung, eds. 2007 and of Xu Dachun by Unschuld 1989; see also Y. L. Chao 2009; Hummel 1943–1944, 322–24, 902–3; Wong and Wu 1936.

56. See Bretelle-Establet 2009 and R. J. Smith 1991, esp. 26–27, 51, 82, 87, 189–200, 222–25, 229–32, 240–42, and 248–49.

57. Cited in R. J. Smith 1991, 194.

58. Elvin 2014. Cf. the demographic statistics in Naquin and Rawski 1987, 106–14 and those in Pomeranz 2001, 326.

59. K. Hsiao 1960, 205–20.

60. Thompson, ed. 1979, 50.

61. Ebrey 1991a, 204.

62. Ibid., 229. As indicated previously, Manchu mourning requirements were far less demanding than those of the Han majority, although in the case of a deceased parent they did mandate cutting the queue and remaining at home for one hundred days. See Elliott 2001a, 206.

63. For an illuminating Chinese-language history of "game culture" in China, see Song and Miao 2010. See also Wang Ermin 1996 on the "culture of commoners" (*shumin wenhua*).

64. On China's "a-military culture," see R. J. Smith 1974, 124–25. On "boxing," see Burkhardt 1953–1958, 2: 88–94; M. C. Cheng 1996; Esherick 1987, 38, 45–66, 209–14, and 333–40; Naquin 1976, 30–32 and 106–7; and esp. Wile 1996.

65. For some Western perspectives on Chinese amusements in Qing times, see Bryson 1886; Doolittle 1865; Gray 1878; Headland 1901; R. F. Johnson 1910; Macgowan 1912; and Nevius 1869.

66. See Guo Ping 2006; also W. Y. Hsu 1978; Van Gulik 2010; and Watt 1981.

67. S. W. Williams 1883, 2: 104. On Chinese (and Manchu) music, see DeWoskin 1982; A. Goldman 2012; Kaufman 1976; L. S. Li 1993; Wichmann 1991; B. Wu 1998; Yung 1989; and Yung, Watson, and Rawski, eds. 1996.

68. S. Boorman 1969, chapter 1. On noted Qing players, consult Hummel 1943–1944, 63, 70, and 528.

69. See Stover 1974, 215–25. Carole Morgan 2004 offers the most detailed description in English of the origins, development, and structure of the game.

70. Elvin 1991, 43. See also W. Shang 1998 and 2006 and R. J. Smith 2013, chapters 3 and 4. For Western-language perspectives on late Qing ritual, see Gray 1878, esp. 1: 342 ff.; Kiong 1906; and Walshe 1906, passim.

71. Nevius 1869, 239–40.

72. R. F. Johnston 1910, 170–71; Gray 1878, 1: 347 ff.

73. See in particular the essay by Jonathan Spence in K. C. Chang, ed. 1977. Other useful sources include E. Anderson 1988; F. T. Cheng 1954; Hauf 2011; and Simoons 1991.

74. Spence in K. C. Chang, ed. 1977, 282 and Rawski 1998, 46–49. See also Stuart Thompson in Watson and Rawski, eds. 1988 and Arthur Wolf in Wolf, ed. 1974, 176 ff.

75. Hawkes, trans. 1973–1979, 2: 265.

76. See the discussion by Jonathan Spence in K. C. Chang, ed. 1977.

77. Cited in K. C. Chang, ed. 1977, 48; see also 7–8, 10, 227–34, and 272–75.

78. You Huai is quoted in K. C. Chang, ed. 1977, 278. On opium smoking in the Qing, see Jonathan Spence in Wakeman and Grant, eds. 1975.

79. Ward 1987, 22; see also Ward in Jain 1977, Ward in Johnson et al., eds. 1985, and Naquin and Rawski 1987, 60–62. For more complex urban and rural perspectives on the role of drama in China, see respectively A. Goldman 2012 and D. Johnson 2009.

80. Naquin and Yu, eds. 1992, 19. See also Brian Dott's excellent 2004 study of pilgrimage in late imperial China.

81. See E. Rawski 1998, chapter 8, esp. 265–70, 272 ff.

82. For convenient overviews of Chinese festivals, consult Bodde 1977; Bogan 1977; Stepanchuk and Wong 1991; and Wieger 1913, 405–41. For evidence of cultural similarities and differences, see D. Johnson 2009. Unless otherwise noted, the following general descriptions have been drawn from Bodde 1977 and/or Bogan 1977.

83. *Chinese Repository*, July 1849, 378. On the prayer, see Stover 1974, 207–9 (slightly modified).

84. Cited in Ebrey 1993, 208–9.

85. Dorothy Ko 1992, 21 n. 8; see also Susan Mann in Elman and Woodside, eds. 1994, 28–30.

86. Bodde 1977, 61. Cf. D. Johnson 2009, 3, 122, and 171–72.

87. Cited in C. K. Yang 1961, 195. See also C. K. Yang 1961, 84–85 and Esherick 1987, esp. 63 ff.

88. W. Jones 1997, 34–36; Bodde and Morris 1967, 76–112. On the punishment of death by slicing, see Brook, Bourgon, and Blue 2008. Bodde 1969 provides a fascinating firsthand account of prison life by the well-known scholar-official Fang Bao (1668–1749).

89. Bodde and Morris 1967, 286.

90. Ibid., 162–63, 271–75; see also Meijer 1991 and Jonathan Ocko in K. C. Liu, ed. 1990.

CHAPTER ELEVEN: THE LATE QING AND BEYOND, 1860–2014

1. For up-to-date and reliable overviews of modern Chinese history in English, see Spence 2013 and Rowe 2009. For a few of the many works in Chinese that grapple with the issue of "modernity" in China, see my bibliographical note at the beginning of the online bibliography.

2. Cohen 1974, 4.

3. I am happy to have made this point rather early in my career; see R. J. Smith 1974. For more recent and detailed evidence, see Elman 2005, esp. 281–395 and 2009, esp. 100–97.

4. See, for example, Cohen 2003, 48–84, Elman 2006, 158–97, and Fung 1996.

5. John Fairbank in CHC, 10: 213–63 provides an instructive overview of the unequal treaty system, emphasizing (overemphasizing, in the view of some scholars) continuities with traditional Qing practice in foreign relations. For different perspectives, see Mosca 2013, esp. 237–304 and Rudolph 2008, passim.

6. On Li, see the essays in Chu and Liu, eds. 1993. There were, of course, a number of other "Confucian reformers" during the late Qing. Many of their writings have been translated in SCT 2: 233–53.

7. Rudolph 2008 argues persuasively for the most part that the Zongli Yamen was a late Qing success story.

8. Cited in Teng and Fairbank 1979, 126.

9. R. J. Smith 1974, 1975, 1976a, 1976b, 1978a, 1978b, and 1993.

10. Schwartz 1964, 94–95.

11. Arthur Wright in A. Wright, ed. 1953, 293. On the complicated issues of translation in the late Qing period, see in particular Lydia Liu 2004; Lackner 2008; Lacker, Amelung, and Kurtz, eds. 2001; Lackner and Vittunghoff, eds. 2010; and Svarverud 2007.

12. CHC 11: 201.

13. R. J. Smith 1978b, 162–63 and 194.

14. Cited by John K. Fairbank in Fairbank, ed. 1968, 265 (slightly modified).

15. Cited in R. J. Smith 1981a, 102. CHC 10: 250 ff. documents the resistence to Western diplomatic representation at the capital as a fundamental threat to "the proper order of things" (*tizhi*). See also CHC 11: 70 ff.

16. CHC 11: 142–201 provides a convenient overview of changing Chinese attitudes toward "barbarians" in the late Qing. See also W. Fang 2001.

17. M. Wright 1967, 83–84; Elman 2000, 488; C. L. Chang 1967, 176 ff.

18. R. J. Smith 1978c, 19.

19. The following discussion of the late Qing military is based primarily on R. J. Smith 1976a, 1976b, and 1978b and K. C. Liu and R. J. Smith in CHC 11: 244–50 and 266–29. Cf. Elman 2004 and A. Fung 1996.

20. T. Rawski 2011, 43–44. See also Brandt, Ma, and Rawski 2013, esp. 17–20.

21. See Pomeranz 2000 and esp. 2001, 337–38; also CHC 11: 50 and 60–61. For an interesting case study of local production, see L. S. Bell 1999.

22. See CHC 11: 32–34, 39, 422–36, and 454–60; T. Rawski 2011, 49–50; and Zurndorfer 2004b.

23. CHC, 10: 260.

24. Introduction to Qian, Fong, and Smith, eds. 2008, 1.

25. See, for example, K. R. Chow 1991; C. W. Ho 1999; Y. Hu 2004; Judge 1997, 2001, 2008, and 2011; W. Y. Li 2005; X. R. Li 2012; Ono 1989; N. Qian 2008, 2010, 2013, 2014, and 2015; Ropp 2002; Waltner 1996; Widner 2006; and Zurndorfer 2014. See also the essays on or by late Qing women in collections such as C. W. Ho, ed.

1998, 2009, 2012a, and 2012b; Gilmartin et al., eds. 1994; Fong and Widmer, eds. 2010; Judge and Hu, eds. 2011; Liu, Karl, and Ko, eds. 2013; Qian, Fong, and Smith, eds. 2008; SCT 2: 389–94; Widmer and Chang, eds. 1997; WWTC; and Zurndorfer, ed. 1999.

26. Cited in I. Hsu 2000, 377.

27. Elman 2000, 594–605, esp. 601–2 (slightly modified).

28. Cited in the *North-China Herald*, July 19, 1907. On the *Xinzheng* reforms as a whole, see D. Reynolds 1993.

29. See in particular Rhoads 2000. For other useful discussions of anti-Manchuism, consult Crossley 1990; Dikotter 1992; Laitinen 1990; Shimada 1990; Y. T. Wong 1989 and 2010; and Zarrow 2004.

30. On the New Culture era, see the stimulating essays in Kai-wing Chow et al., eds. 2008. See also works such as J. T. Chen 1997; Cong 2007; D. Lin 2005; W. Yeh 1990, 1996, and 2008, and the articles by Evelyn Rawski, Leo Lee, Michael Hunt, and Lloyd Eastman in Lieberthal et al., eds. 1991. For a few different perspectives on the women's movement in China, see T. Barlow 2004; K. R. Chow 1991; X. Cong 2007; Gilmartin et al., eds. 1994; K. Johnson 1983; H. Siu 1989; Ono 1989; and T. Kennedy, trans. 1993. SCT 2: 351–95 includes a number of translations from the New Culture era.

31. Teng and Fairbank 1979, 239–45. Cf. SCT 2: 352–56, 360–61, and 366–68. On Chen's activities and networks in the New Culture era, see Anne Chao 2009.

32. T. T. Chow 1960, 289. On the theme of totalistic iconoclasm, see Y. S. Lin 1979.

33. Cited in Ramsey 1987, 3.

34. Y. S. Lin 1979, 29.

35. H. M. Ku 1956. On conservatism in the New Culture era, see also Alitto 1986, Dongen 2009, Furth, ed. 1976, and SCT 2: 377–92 passim.

36. Benjamin Schwartz in Schwartz, ed. 1972, 4.

37. Hao Chang 1971, 305.

38. M. Wright 1967, 304. R. J. Smith 2013, chapter 4 discusses the New Life Movement in comparative perspective.

39. For some useful perspectives on contemporary Taiwan, see Bosco 1992; M. Brown 2004; Fetzer and Soper 2007; Makeham and Hsiau, eds. 2005; and Nathan and Chen 2004. On the Taiwan Independence Movement, see Ross 2006 and Nathan and Chen 2004; also Fetzer and Soper 2007

40. The works on Mao are innumerable and of extremely uneven quality. For a variety of perspectives, see Boorman 1966; Chang and Halliday 2005; Dirlik 1989; Dirlik, Healy, and Knight, eds. 1997; Jing Li 2010; MacFarquhar 2012; Meisner 1986; Roux 2009; Schram 1969, 1974, and 1989; Soloman 1971; Wakeman 1973; Wasserstrom 1996; and Womack 1982 and 1986.

41. Schram 1969, 172; Schram 1974, 88. For a Chinese-language evaluation of Mao and his complex relationship with traditional Chinese culture, see Nie Yaodong 1992.

42. See Wakeman 1973; Tian 2005; Whyte 1974; also R. J. Smith 1981b, 1989, and 1997.

43. On Chinese political rhetoric in general, see Dittmer and Chen 1982; Lu and Simons 2006; Schoenals 1992; and K. Zhan 1992. On the "five stresses, four beautifications and three ardent loves" in particular, see R. J. Smith 2013, 124–31.

44. Reported in the *Washington Post*, July 27, 2008.

45. Meisner 1986, 363–64.

46. Tozer 1970. See also R. J. Smith 2013, 131–32.

47. For these and other dramatic changes, see Spence 2013, 587–707. Gunde 2001 provides a somewhat dated but still useful overview of contemporary Chinese culture in the light of the past.

48. See Lampton 2014b, a summary of the themes in Lampton 2014a.

49. See "China Faces Growing Gender Imbalance," *BBC News*, January 11, 2010. Available at http://news.bbc.co.uk/2/hi/asia-pacific/8451289.stm.

50. For a sampling of writings in Chinese and English on National Studies and the idea of a Cultural Renaissance, see Dirlik 2011, Gan and Zhou 2012–2013, S. H. Hu 2007, Huang Zhao 2001, X. Kang 2012–2013, Z. H. Liu 2013–2014, Tang Wenming 2010, X. Xie 2011, and Yuan Xingpei 1993.

51. X. Xie 2011, 42 (slightly modified).

52. See Dirlik 2001 and Makeham 2008, esp. 333 ff. Cf. Harris 1997.

53. X. Xie 2011, 42 (slightly modified).

54. Makeham, ed. 2003, 3.

55. *New York Times*, April 22, 2011. Available at www.nytimes.com/2011/04/23/world/asia/23confucius.html?_r=0.

56. See Nathan and Chen 2004; also Fetzer and Soper 2007.

Selected Bibliography
of Western-Language Works

Bibliographical Note: For a much more extensive list of relevant works in Western and Asian languages, see the online bibliography at www.rowman.com/ISBN/9781442221925/The-Qing-Dynasty-and-traditional-chinese-culture. The works included below consist of Western-language studies on the Qing period published since the late 1990s, with an emphasis on art, literature, education, gender, sexuality, politics, law, medicine, science and technology, and military affairs. By far the best English-language reference work on China is Endymion Wilkinson's *Chinese History: A New Manual* (Cambridge, Mass., and London: Harvard-Yenching Institute Monograph Series 84, second, revised printing, 2013).

Bai, Limin 2005. *Shaping the Child: Children and Their Primers in Late Imperial China*. Hong Kong: Chinese University Press.

Berger, Patricia Ann 2003. *Empire of Emptiness: Buddhist Art and Political Authority in Qing China*. Honolulu: University of Hawaii Press.

Bernhardt, Kathryn 1999. *Women and Property in China, 960–1949*. Stanford: Stanford University Press.

Bray, Francesca 1997. *Technology and Gender: Fabrics of Power in Late Imperial China*. Berkeley: University of California Press.

Brokaw, Cynthia and Kai-wing Chow, eds. 2005. *Printing and Book Culture in Late Imperial China*. Berkeley: University of California Press.

Cahill, James 2010. *Pictures for Use and Pleasure: Vernacular Painting in High Qing China*. Berkeley: University of California Press.

Cahill, James et al. 2013. *Beauty Revealed: Images of Women in Qing Dynasty Chinese Painting*. Berkeley: University of California Press.

Chang, Chun-shu and Shelley Hsueh-lun Chang 1999. *Redefining History: Ghosts, Spirits, and Human Society in P'u Sung-ling's World, 1640–1715*. Ann Arbor: University of Michigan Press.

Chang, Kang-i Sun and Haun Saussy, eds. 1999. *Women Writers of Traditional China: An Anthology of Poetry and Criticism.* Stanford: Stanford University Press.

Chang, Michael G. 2007. *A Court on Horseback: Imperial Touring and the Construction of Qing Rule, 1680–1785.* Cambridge, Mass.: Harvard University Press.

Chao, Yuan-ling 2009. *Medicine and Society in Late Imperial China: A Study of Physicians in Suzhou, 1600–1850.* New York: Peter Lang.

Chow, Kai-Wing 2004. *Publishing, Culture and Power in Early Modern China.* Stanford: Stanford University Press.

Crossley, Pamela K. 1999. *A Translucent Mirror: History and Identity in Qing Imperial Ideology.* Berkeley: University of California Press.

Crossley, Pamela Kyle, Helen Siu, and Donald Sutton, eds. 2006. *Empire at the Margins: Culture, Ethnicity and Frontier in Early Modern China.* Berkeley: University of California Press.

Dai, Yi et al. 2011. *A Concise History of the Qing Dynasty.* Singapore Silk Road Press. Four volumes.

Di Cosmo, Nicola and Dalizhabu Bao, eds. 2003. *Manchu-Mongol Relations on the Eve of the Qing Conquest: A Documentary History.* Leiden: Brill.

Dolezelova-Velingerova, Milena and Rudolf G. Wagner, eds. 2014. *Chinese Encyclopedias of New Global Knowledge (1870–1930): Changing Ways of Thought.* Heidelberg: Springer.

Dunstan, Helen 2006. *State or Merchant? Political Economy and Political Process in 1740s China.* Cambridge, Mass.: Harvard University Press.

Elliott, Mark C. 2001. *The Manchu Way: The Eight Banners and Ethnic Identity in Late Imperial China.* Stanford: Stanford University Press.

Elliott, Mark C. 2009. *Emperor Qianlong: Son of Heaven, Man of the World.* New York: Longman/Pearson.

Elman, Benjamin A. 2000. *A Cultural History of the Civil Examinations in Late Imperial China.* Berkeley: University of California Press.

Elman, Benjamin A. 2005. *On Their Own Terms: Science in China, 1550–1900.* Cambridge, Mass.: Harvard University Press.

Elman, Benjamin A. 2013. *Civil Examinations and Meritocracy in Late Imperial China.* Cambridge, Mass.: Harvard University Press.

Fong, Grace 2008. *Herself an Author: Gender, Agency, and Writing in Late Imperial China.* Honolulu: University of Hawaii Press.

Fong, Grace and Ellen Widmer, eds. 2010. *Inner Quarters and Beyond: Women Writers from Ming through Qing.* Leiden: Brill.

Foret, Philippe 2000. *Mapping Chengde: The Qing Landscape Enterprise.* Honolulu: University of Hawaii Press.

Guy, R. Kent 2010. *Qing Governors and Their Provinces: The Evolution of Territorial Administration in China, 1644–1796.* Seattle and London: University of Washington Press, 2010.

Hanson, Marta 2011. *Speaking of Epidemics in Chinese Medicine: Disease and the Geographic Imagination in Late Imperial China.* London: Routledge.

Hay, Jonathan S. 2001. *Shitao: Painting and Modernity in Early Qing China.* Cambridge, Eng.: Cambridge University Press.

Hearn, Maxwell K. 2008. *Landscapes Clear and Radiant: The Art of Wang Hui (1632–1717)*. New York: Metropolitan Museum of Art.

Hegel, Robert E. and Katherine Carlitz, eds. 2007. *Writing and Law in Late Imperial China: Crime, Conflict, and Judgment*. Seattle: University of Washington Press.

Ho, Ping-ti 1998. "In Defense of Sinicization: A Rebuttal of Evelyn Rawski's 'Reenvisioning the Qing.'" *Journal of Asian Studies* 57.1 (February): 123–55.

Hostetler, Laura 2001. *Qing Colonial Enterprise: Ethnography and Cartography in Early Modern China*. Chicago: University of Chicago Press.

Hsiung, Ping-chen 2005. *A Tender Voyage: Children and Childhood in Late Imperial China*. Stanford: Stanford University Press.

Huang, Pei 2011. *Reorienting the Manchus: A Study of Sinicization, 1583–1795*. Ithaca: East Asia Program, Cornell University.

Huang, Philip C. 1998. *Civil Justice in China: Representation and Practice in the Qing*. Stanford: Stanford University Press.

Huang, Philip C. 2001. *Code, Custom and and Legal Practice in China: The Qing and the Republic Compared*. Stanford: Stanford University Press.

Hung, Ho-fung 2011. *Protest with Chinese Characteristics: Demonstrations, Riots, and Petitions in the Mid-Qing Dynasty*. New York: Columbia University Press.

Idema, Wilt and Beata Grant, eds. 2004. *The Red Brush: Writing Women of Imperial China*. Cambridge, Mass.: Harvard East Asian Monographs.

Im, Kaye Soon 1981. "The Rise and Decline of the Eight Banner Garrisons in the Ch'ing Period (1644–1911): A Study of the Kuang-chou, Hang-chou and Ching-chou Garrions." PhD dissertation, University of Illinois at Urbana-Champaign.

Jones, William C., trans. 1994. *The Great Qing Code*. Oxford: Clarendon Press.

Ko, Dorothy 2005. *Cinderella's Sisters: A Revisionist History of Footbinding*. Berkeley and Los Angeles: University of California Press.

Kutcher, Norman 1999. *Mourning in Late Imperial China: Filial Piety and the State*. Cambridge, Eng.: Cambridge University Press.

Laamann, Lars, ed. 2013. *Critical Readings on the Manchus in Modern China (1616–2012)*. Leiden: Brill. Four volumes.

Lee, James Z. and Feng Wang 2001. *One Quarter of Humanity: Malthusian Mythology and Chinese Realities, 1700–2000*. Cambridge, Mass.: Harvard University Press.

Li, Lillian 2007. *Fighting Famine in North China: State, Market, and Environmental Decline, 1690s–1990s*. Stanford: Stanford University Press.

Li, Xiaorong 2012. *Women's Poetry of Late Imperial China: Transforming the Inner Chambers*. Seattle and London: University of Washington Press.

Liang, Linxia 2007. *Delivering Justice in Qing China: Civil Trials in the Magistrate's Court*. Oxford: Oxford University Press.

Lu, Weijing 2008. *True to Her Word: The Faithful Maiden Cult in Late Imperial China*. Stanford: Stanford University Press.

Macauley, Melissa A. 1998. *Social Power and Legal Culture: Litigation Masters in Late Imperial China*. Stanford: Stanford University Press.

Man-Cheong, Iona D. 2004. *The Class of 1761: Examinations, State and Elite in Eighteenth Century China.* Stanford: Stanford University Press.

Mann, Susan L. 1997. *Precious Records: Women in China's Long Eighteenth Century.* Stanford: Stanford University Press.

Mann, Susan L. 2007. *The Talented Women of the Zhang Family.* Berkeley: University of California Press.

McMahon, Daniel 2015. *Rethinking the Decline of China's Qing Dynasty: Imperial Activism and Borderland Management at the Turn of the Nineteenth Century.* London: Routledge.

Millward, James A. 1998. *Beyond the Pass: Economy, Ethnicity and Empire in Qing Xinjiang, 1759–1864.* Stanford: Stanford University Press.

Millward, James A. et al., eds. 2006. *New Qing Imperial History: The Making of Inner Asian Empire at Qing Chengde.* London: Routledge.

Mosca, Matthew W. 2013. *From Frontier Policy to Foreign Policy: The Question of India and the Transformation of Geopolitics in Qing China.* Stanford: Stanford University Press.

Mungello, David E. 2008. *Drowning Girls in China: Female Infanticide Since 1650.* Lanham, Md.: Rowman and Littlefield.

Mungello, David E. 2009. *The Great Encounter of China and the West, 1500–1800.* Lanham, Md.: Rowman and Littlefield. Third edition.

Ng, On-cho 2001. *Cheng-Zhu Confucianism in the Early Qing: Li Guangdi (1642–1718) and Qing Learning.* Albany: State University of New York Press.

Perdue, Peter 2005. *China Marches West: The Qing Conquest of Central Asia.* Cambridge, Mass.: Harvard University Press.

Rawski, Evelyn S. 1996. "Reenvisioning the Qing: The Significance of the Qing Period in Chinese History." *Journal of Asian Studies* 55.4 (November): 829–50.

Rawski, Evelyn S. 1998. *The Last Emperors: A Social History of Qing Imperial Institutions.* Berkeley: University of California Press.

Rawski, Evelyn S. 2015. *Early Modern China and Northeast Asia.* Cambridge, England: Cambridge University Press.

Rawski, Evelyn S. and Jessica Rawson, eds. 2005. *China: The Three Emperors 1662–1795.* London: Royal Academy Books.

Reed, Bradly W. 2000. *Talons and Teeth: County Clerks and Runners in the Qing Dynasty.* Stanford: Stanford University Press.

Rhoads, Edward 2000. *Manchus and Han: Ethnic Relations and Political Power in Late Qing and Early Republican China, 1861–1928.* Seattle: University of Washington Press.

Ropp, Paul S. 2002. "Chinese Women in the Imperial Past: New Perspectives." *China Review International* 9.1 (Spring): 41–51.

Ropp, Paul S. et al., eds. 2001. *Passionate Women: Female Suicide in Late Imperial China.* Leiden: Brill.

Rowe, William T. 2001. *Saving the World: Chen Hongmou and Elite Consciousness in Eighteenth-Century China.* Stanford: Stanford University Press.

Rowe, William T. 2009. *China's Last Empire: The Great Qing.* Cambridge, Mass.: Harvard University Press.

Siu, Victoria M. 2013. *Gardens of a Chinese Emperor: Imperial Creations of the Qianlong Era, 1736–1796.* Lanham, Md.: Rowman and Littlefield.

Smith, Richard J. 2013. *Mapping China and Managing the World: Culture, Cartography and Cosmology in Late Imperial Times.* Oxfordshire, Eng.: Routledge.

Snyder-Reinke, Jeffrey 2009. *Dry Spells: State Rainmaking and Local Governance in Late Imperial China.* Cambridge, Mass.: Harvard University Press.

Sommer, Matthew H. 2000. *Sex, Law and Society in Late Imperial China.* Stanford: Stanford University Press.

Struve, Lynn 2004. *The Qing Formation in World-Historical Time.* Cambridge, Mass.: Harvard University Press.

Theiss, Janet M. 2005. *Disgraceful Matters: The Politics of Chastity in Eighteenth-Century China.* Berkeley: University of California Press.

Waley-Cohen, Joanna 2004. "The New Qing History." *Radical History Review* 88 (Winter): 193–206.

Waley-Cohen, Joanna 2006. *The Culture of War in China: Empire and the Military under the Qing Dynasty.* New York: I. B. Tauris.

Wang, Fangyu and Barnhart Richard. 1990. *Master of the Lotus Garden: The Life and Art of Bada Shanren 1626–1705.* New Haven: Yale University Press.

Widmer, Ellen 2006. *The Beauty and the Book: Women and Fiction in Nineteenth-Century China.* Cambridge, Mass.: Harvard University Press.

Widmer, Ellen and Kang-i Sun Chang, eds. 1997. *Writing Women in Late Imperial China.* Stanford: Stanford University Press.

Wills, John E., Jr. et al., eds. 2011. *China and Maritime Europe, 1500–1800: Trade, Settlement, Diplomacy, and Missions.* Cambridge, Eng.: Cambridge University Press.

Wu, Yi-li 2010. *Reproducing Women: Medicine, Metaphor, and Childbirth in Late Imperial China.* Berkeley: University of California Press.

Zhao, Shiyu 2014. *The Urban Life of the Qing Dynasty.* Reading, Eng.: Paths International. Translated by Wang Hong and Zhang Linlin.

Zito, Angela 1997. *Of Body and Brush: Grand Sacrifice as Text/Performance in 18th Century China.* Chicago: University of Chicago Press.

Zurndorfer, Harriet T. 1997. *Change and Continuity in Chinese Local History: The Development of Hui-Chou Prefecture, 800 to 1800.* Leiden: Brill.

Zurndorfer, Harriet T., ed. 1999. *Chinese Women in the Imperial Past: New Perspectives.* Leiden: Brill.

Online Bibliography

Online Bibliography (URL: www.rowman.com/ISBN/9781442221925/The
-Qing-Dynasty-and-traditional-chinese-culture)

Bibliographical Note: In the hope that this book will be of value not only as an interpretive synthesis but also as a research tool, I have included a number of references in Chinese and Japanese as well as Western languages in both the bibliography and the notes. Still, these citations represent only a small percentage of the huge amount of available material.

Since the last version of this book appeared in 1994, a number of extremely useful English-language reference works on China have become available, including encyclopedias such as Linsun Cheng, ed. 2009; Dillon, ed. 2013; and Wilkinson 2013. Wilkinson's meticulously annotated *Chinese History: A New Manual* is a particularly impressive scholarly achievement (be prepared for more than 1,000 pages of small but high-quality print). Another recent reference work of great value is Haihui Zhang et al., eds. 2013 *A Scholarly Review of Chinese Studies in North America*, available online at no cost. It provides generally high-quality essays on the following broad topics: Early China, Early Medieval China; Song Studies; Yuan Studies; Ming History; Qing Historical Studies; Qing Legal History; the History of Science; Social History and the Great Divergence Debate in Qing and World History; Studies of China's Economy; Chinese Organizations; Chinese Social Stratification and Social Mobility; Chinese Politics; Literature: Early China; Song, Jin, and Yuan Dynasties Literature; Ming and Qing Literature; Modern Chinese Literature; Chinese Linguistics; Chinese Music; and Art History.

A great many other China-related reference works have become available online. Two of the most substantial are subscription based. One is the word searchable "Bibliography of Asian Studies," produced by the Association for Asian Studies. The other, also word searchable, and much more detailed in its annotations, is T. Wright, ed. 2014 "*Oxford Bibliographies* in Chinese Studies." Among the currently available categories in this latter publication are: Ancient Chinese Religion; Buddhist Monasticism; Calligraphy; Central-Local Relations; Ceramics; Children's Culture and Social Studies; China and the World, 1900–1949; China's Agricultural Regions; Chinese Architecture; Classical Confucianism; Dialect Groups of the Chinese Language; Ethnicity and Minority Nationalities Since 1949; Landscape Painting; Language Varia-tion in China; Late Imperial Economy, 960–1895; Legalism; Local Elites in Ming-Qing China; Macroregions; Mencius; Ming Dynasty; Ming-Qing Fic-tion; Mohism; Population Dynamics in Pre-Modern China; Printing and Book Culture; Qing Dynasty up to 1840; School of Names; The Chinese Script; The Examination System; The Fall of the Qing, 1840–1912; The Marketing System in Pre-Modern China; The Needham Question (concerning Chinese Science); The Tribute System; Traditional Chinese Law; Traditional Chinese Medicine; Traditional Chinese Poetry; and Traditional Prose. Forthcoming bibliographies include: Bronzes; Buddhism; Christianity in China; Five Classics; Folk Reli-gions; Folklore and Popular Culture; Gardens; History of Chinese Philosophy; Imperialism and China; Islam in China; Kinship and the Family in Pre-modern China; Li Bai and Du Fu (Poets); Material Culture; Missionaries in China; Neo-Confucianism; New Confucianism; Russian Studies of Pre-modern China; The Great Divergence (Sino-Western economic comparisons); Traditional Chinese Drama and Theatre Arts; and Traditional Criticism.

Two other particularly useful online bibliographies, both in English and free to all users, are Elman 2014 ("Classical Historiography for Chinese History") and Lecher 2008 ("Online Bibliographies for Chinese Studies"). Another valuable online reference work is the Society for Qing Studies' "Research Resources." Yet another, also free, is the word-searchable McGill-Harvard-Yenching Library Ming-Qing Women's Writings Digitization Project. In addi-tion, it is worth noting that most major university libraries, and many national and local libraries as well, have made their online catalogs available to outside users. Since these catalogs can all be searched electronically using the conven-tional transliterations for authors and titles that I have employed in this book, it is easy to find the corresponding Chinese and Japanese characters/scripts.

As indicated in the bibliographical introduction to the 1994 edition of *China's Cultural Heritage*, the 1980s produced a flood of Mainland publica-tions on traditional Chinese culture as a result of what the Chinese described at the time as "culture fever" (*wenhua re*). During this period, for example, Fudan University in Shanghai published a series of volumes under the general title *Zhongguo wenhua yanjiu jikan* (Collected papers on research into Chinese culture) and at about the same time the Chinese People's University of Beijing sponsored a number of publications under the general heading *Chuantong wen-*

hua yu xiandai wenhua congshu (A collection of works on traditional and modern culture). Meanwhile, on Taiwan, Taibei's *Shibao* (The Times) produced a great many books on traditional Chinese culture under the general series title *Wenhua Zhongguo congshu* (A collection of works on cultural China). Since then, a torrent of other such collections and series have either appeared or continued to thrive, bearing titles such as (in alphabetical order): *Beijing daxue Zhongguo chuantong wenhua yanjiu zhongxin guoxue yanjiu congkan* (Series on National Learning research from Beijing University's center for the study of China's traditional culture); *Da shi yan zhong de guoxue* (National Learning in the eyes of great scholars); *Zhongguo chuantong wenhua xinlun* (New essays on China's traditional culture); *Zhongguo chuantong wenhua yu Jiangnan diyu wenhua yanjiu congshu* (Collection of research on China's traditional culture and Jiangnan regional culture); *Zhongguo chuangtong wenhua jingdian* (Classics of China's traditional culture); *Zhongguo chuantong wenhua biecai* (Selected writings on China's traditional culture); *Zhongguo chuantong wenhua congshu* (A collection on China's traditional culture); *Zhongguo chuantong wenhua duben* (Readings on China's traditional culture); *Zhongguo chuantong wenhua gushi huicui* (A select collection of stories from China's traditional culture); *Zhongguo chuantong wenhua jingcui shuxi* (Series on the essentials of China's traditional culture); *Zhongguo chuantong wenhua jingdian wenku* (Treasury of classic writings about China's traditional culture); *Zhongguo chuantong wenhua manbi congshu* (A collection of essays on China's traditional culture); *Zhongguo chuantong wenhua qingshaonian wenku* (Treasury of China's traditional culture for young people); *Zhongguo chuantong wenhua toushi* (Perspectives on China's traditional culture); *Zhongguo chuantong wenhua xilie jiaocai* (A set of instructional materials on China's traditional culture); *Zhongguo chuantong wenhua yanjiu congshu* (A collection of research on China's traditional culture); *Zhongguo chuantong wenhua yishu congshu* (A collection of the artistic productions of China's traditional culture); *Zhongguo chuantong wenhua zhi gen* (The foundations of China's traditional culture); *Zhongguo chuantong wenhua zhuanti yanjiu congshu* (A collection of research on special topics pertaining to China's traditional culture); and *Zhonghua wenhua jiangzuo congshu* (A collection of lectures on Chinese culture).

A representative sample of some relatively recent overviews of traditional Chinese culture that are written in Chinese and organized alphabetically (by author) would include: Bao Zhonghao 2006; Cai Dongzhou, ed. 2003; Cai Hairong and Huang Yinfu, eds. 2005; Cai Yi, trans. 2002; Chen Ming, ed. 1996; Chen Zhanguo 2004, Dai Zheng and Wang Yang 2013; Du Xiulin 2007; Dutu shidai xiangmuzu, ed. 2012; Feng Erkang 1990; Feng Xi 2012; Ge Chenhong 2001; Ge Jianxiong 2004; Gong Pengcheng 2009; Li Baolong and Yang Shuqin, eds. 2006; Liu Jiemin 1997; Lü Simian 2007; Qian Wenzhong 2010; Qiu Ren and Lin Xianghua 1995; Takeuchi Minoru 2006; Tang Yijie, ed. 1993; Wang Jianhui and Yi Xuejin, eds. 1998; Wang Qiang and Bao Xiaoguang, eds. 2004; Wang Xinting et al. 1997; Xu Guanghua 2002; Yu Yingshi 2010; Zhang Yinghang et al., eds. 2000; Zheng Xinsen, ed. 2005; Zhong Mingshan, Zhu Zhengwei, and Han Pengjie, eds. 2001; Zhou Xiao-guang and Qiu Shijing, eds. 2006; Zhu Chengru and Ren Wanping, eds. 2010; and Zhu Yaoting, ed. 1998.

For a similar but more limited sample of Chinese-language studies focus-ing specifically on Manchu culture, see Dai Yinghua 2010; Diao Shuren 2002; Ding Yizhuang 1992; Li Li 2012; Li Yanguang and Guan Jie 1991; Liu Xiaomeng 2001; Manzu jianshi bianxie zu, ed. 2009; Wang Zhonghan, ed. 1996; Yang Xichun 1991; Zhang Jie 2007; and Zhou Yuanlian 1981.

There are several recent studies that explore the "psychology" of the Chi-nese, following in the wake of the extremely controversial 1980s book by Sun Longji (aka Sun Lung-kee) titled *Zhongguo wenhua di shenceng jiegou* (The deep structure of Chinese culture). Among these more recent Chinese-language works are Xiao Taitao 1998 and Zhu Jianjun 2008. Sun Longji, for his part, published a collection of writings on history and psychology in 2004. The Chinese-language work that probably comes closest to the volume in hand in terms of chronological focus, content, and structure is Feng Erkang 1990.

Relatively recent Chinese-language reference works that focus specifically on traditional Chinese culture—such as dictionaries, handbooks, and encyclo-pedias—include Gan Chunsong and Zhang Xiaomang, eds. 2008; Hu Jingjun and Dai Qihou, eds. 1992; Liu Jun, ed. 2011; Qian Yulin and Huang Lili, eds. 1996; Xu Yi et al., eds. 1996; Zhuang Fulin and Zhang Ruichang, eds. 1990. A particularly useful reference work is Wang Shuliang and Li Yu, eds. 1992–. The twenty volumes in this collection cover philosophy (three volumes), religion (three volumes), history (three volumes), literature (three volumes), the arts (one volume), nationalities (one volume), geography (one volume), economics (one volume), science and technology (one volume), law and military affairs (one volume), medicine (one volume), and language (one volume). A full table of contents can be found at www.columbia.edu/cgi–bin/cul/toc.pl?3722275.

An even more substantial compendium, compiled by the Zhongguo chuan-tong wenhua daguan bianzuan weiyuan hui, bears the title *Zhongguo chuan-tong wenhua daguan* (A grand view of China's traditional culture). It was produced in the period from 1997 to 2001 and published in Beijing by the Zhongguo dabaike quanshu chubanshe. This collection has 66 categories, more than 80,000 individual entries, and more than 50,000 illustrations in 74 volumes. It is also available in CD-ROM and via subscription. A more concise version was published in 2009.

Other especially rich sources of images relating to Chinese culture in late imperial times are Ebrey 2010; Guojia tushuguan, ed. 2006; Hearn 1996;

Nakagawa 1799; E. Rawski and Rawson, eds. 2006; Yang and Zhu 1999; Zheng Xinsen, ed. 2005; Zhu Chengru and Ren Wanping, eds. 2010. Many of the line drawings in this book are taken from the extraordinary Nakagawa volume.

Some publications in Chinese that pay particular attention to the relationship between "tradition" and "modernity" include Ding Qing 1991; Dong Ping, ed. 2001; Duanmu Cixiang 2005; Gong Shufeng 1997; Hou Yangxing 2000; Huang Aiping and Huang Xingtao, eds. 2008; Jia Qingjun 2009; Nie Yaodong 1992; Song Zhenghai and Sun Guanlong, eds. 1999; Yang Zhenning and Rao Zongyi, eds. 2003; Yu Zuhua 2012; Zhang Li 2005; Zhang Ying et al., eds. 2000; Zheng Dahua and Zou Xiaozhan, eds. 2011; and Zhou Changzhong 2002.

A few of many Chinese works focusing on regional, local, and/or "minority" culture are: Fei Junqing, ed. 2004; Huang Haiyun 2009; Lin Jiashu 1995; Tai Zhenlin, ed. 1991; Wang Lijian 2013; Wu Renshu 2013; and Lou Yiqun 1993. See also the previous discussion of Chinese-language works on the Manchus.

Finally, among the most informative contemporary accounts of the late Qing period by Western observers are: Bryson 1886; J. F. Davis 1836; De Groot 1903, 1892–1910, and 1912; Doolittle 1865; Doré 1914–1933; R. Douglas 1882; J. Gray 1878; Headland 1901; R. F. Johnston 1910; Macgowan 1912; W. Martin 1897; Meadows 1856; W. H. Medhurst 1838; Milne 1857; Nevius 1869; Parker 1899; A. Smith 1899; Walshe 1906; Wieger 1913; and S. W. Williams 1883. Unfortunately, but predictably, these and other such accounts by Westerners are generally biased strongly in favor of Western culture.

ABBREVIATIONS

CC Legge, James, trans. 1893–1895. *The Chinese Classics*. London and Oxford: Clarendon Press. Reprinted by the Hong Kong University Press in 1979.

CLEAR Chinese Literature Essays Articles Reviews.

CHC Twitchett, Denis et al., eds. 1978–2009. *The Cambridge History of China*. Cambridge, Eng.: Cambridge University Press. Eight volumes, several divided into more than one part.

CHCL Chang, Kang-i Sun and Stephen Owen, eds. 2010. *The Cambridge History of Chinese Literature*. Volume 2. Cambridge, Eng.: Cambridge University Press.

MHY McGill-Harvard-Yenching Library Ming-Qing Women's Writings Digitization Project. http://digital.library.mcgill.ca/mingqing/english/project.htm.

MIT Massachusetts Institute of Technology. "Visualizing Cultures." http://ocw.mit.edu/ans7870/21f/21f.027/home/index.html.

QS Zhang, Qiyun et al., eds. 1961. *Qingshi* (History of the Qing dynasty). Taibei: Guofang yanjiu yuan. Six volumes.

SCC Needham, Joseph et al. 1956–present. *Science and Civilisation in China*, Cambridge, Eng.: Cambridge University Press. Seven volumes, some (such as chapter 5) divided into several separately published parts.

SCT de Bary, William T. et al., eds. 1999–2000. *Sources of Chinese Tradition*. New York: Columbia University Press, 1999 (second edition, volume 1) and 2000 (second edition, volume 2).

SKQS Ji, Yun et al., eds. 1983–1986. *Qinding Siku quanshu* (Imperial edition of the *Complete Collection of the Four Treasuries*). Reprint Taibei: Shangwu yinshu guan, under the title *Yingyin Wenyuange Siku quanshu*.

TSJC Chen, Menglei et al., eds. 1977. *Qinding gujin tushu jicheng* (Imperial edition of the complete collection of illustrations and writings, past and present). Taibei: Dingwen shuju.

WBQS *Wanbao quanshu* (Complete collection of myriad treasures). Various editions and various publishers.

WWTC Chang, Kang-i Sun and Haun Saussy, eds. 1999. *Women Writers of Traditional China: An Anthology of Poetry and Criticism*. Stanford: Stanford University Press.

Adas, Michael 1998. "Imperialism and Colonialism in Comparative Perspective." *The International History Review* 20.2 (June): 371–88.

Adkins, Curtis and Winston Yang, eds. 1980. *Critical Essays on Chinese Fiction*. Hong Kong: Chinese University Press.

Aque, Stuart 2004. "Pi Xirui and Jingxue lishi." Ph.D. dissertation, University of Washington, Seattle.

Ahern, Emily 1982. *Chinese Ritual and Politics*. Cambridge, Eng.: Cambridge University Press.

Ahern, Emily and Hill Gates, eds. 1981. *The Anthropology of Taiwanese Society*. Stanford: Stanford University Press.

Alford, William P. 1984. "Of Arsenic and Old Laws: Looking Anew at Criminal Justice in Late Imperial China." *California Law Review* 72: 1180–256.

Alitto, Guy 1984. "Ch'ing Local History Projects." *Ch'ing-shih wen't'i* 5.1 (June): 56–79.

Alitto, Guy 1986. *The Last Confucian: Liang Shuming and the Chinese Dilemma of Modernity*. Berkeley: University of California Press. Second edition.

Allee, Mark A. 1994. *Law and Local Society in Late Imperial China: Northern Taiwan in the Nineteenth Century*. Stanford: Stanford University Press.

Allinson, Robert E. 1989. *Chuang-Tzu for Spiritual Transformation*. Albany: State University of New York Press.

Allinson, Robert E., ed. 1989. *Understanding the Chinese Mind*. Oxford: Oxford University Press.

Ames, Roger and David Hall, trans. 2003. *The Dao De Jing: A Philosophical Translation*. New York: Ballantine Books.

Ames, Roger and Henry Rosemont, Jr., trans. 1999. *The Analects of Confucius: A Philosophical Translation*. New York: Ballantine Books.

Amelung, Iwo 2007. "New Maps for the Modernizing State: Western Cartographic Knowledge and Its Application in 19th and 20th Century China." In Bray, Lichtman and Metailie, eds. 2007: 685–72.

An, Pingqiu and Zhang Peiheng 1990. *Zhongguo jinshu daguan* (An overview of book-banning in China). Shanghai: Shanghai wenhua chubanshe.

An, Shuangcheng 1993. *Man-Han da cidian* (Great Manchu-Chinese dictionary). Shenyang: Liaoning chubanshe

Anderson, E. N. 1988. *The Food of China*. New Haven: Yale University Press.

Anderson, Mary 1990. *Hidden Power: The Palace Eunuchs of Imperial China*. Buffalo: Prometheus.

Andrade, Tonio 2007. *How Taiwan Became Chinese: Dutch, Spanish, and Han Colonization in the Seventeenth Century*. New York: Columbia University Press.

Antony, Robert J. and Jane Kate Leonard, eds. 2002. *Dragons, Tigers and Dogs: Qing Crisis Management and the Boundaries of State Power in Late Imperial China*. Ithaca: Cornell University East Asia Program.

Arrault, Alain 2002. *Shao Yong (1012–1077): Poète et cosmologue*. Paris: Collège de France.

Atwell, William S. 1986. "Some Observations on the 'Seventeenth-Century Crisis' in China and Japan." *Journal of Asian Studies* 45.2 (February): 223–44.

Atwill, David 2005. *The Chinese Sultinate: Islam, Ethnicity, and the Panthay Rebellion in Southwest China, 1856–1873*. Stanford: Stanford University Press.

Atwill, David and Yurong Y. Atwill, eds. 2010. *Sources in Chinese History: Diverse Perspectives from 1644 to the Present*. London: Prentice Hall.

Atwood, Christopher P. 2000. "'Worshipping Grace': The Language of Loyalty in Qing Mongolia." *Late Imperial China* 21.2 (December): 86–139.

Aylward, Thomas F. 2007. *The Complete Guide to Chinese Astrology and Feng Shui*. London: Watkins Publishing.

Bai, Limin 2005. *Shaping the Child: Children and Their Primers in Late Imperial China*. Hong Kong: Chinese University Press.

Baker, Hugh 1979. *Chinese Family and Kinship*. London: Macmillan.

Baker, Hugh and Stephan Feuchtwang, eds. 1991. *An Old State in a New Setting: Studies in the Social Anthropology of China*. Oxford: Oxford University Press.

Balazs, Etienne 1964. *Chinese Civilization and Bureaucracy*. New Haven: Yale University Press.

Balazs, Etienne 1965. *Political Theory and Administrative Reality*. London: School of Oriental and African Studies, University of London.

Bantly, Francisca Cho 1989. "Buddhist Allegory in the *Journey to the West*." *Journal of Asian Studies* 48.3 (August): 512–24.

Bao, Zhonghao 2006. *Hunsu yu Zhongguo chuantong wenhua* (Marriage customs and China's traditional culture). Guilin: Guangxi shifan daxue chubanshe.

Baptandier, Brigitte 2008. *The Lady of Linshui: A Chinese Female Cult*. Stanford: Stanford University Press. Translated by Kristin Ingrid Fryklund.

Baqi tongzhi (Comprehensive history of the Eight Banners), published in 1796 and reprinted in the SKQS, volumes 664–71. Available online at http://ctext.org/library. pl?if=gb&file=76676&page=3&remap=gb.

Barfield, Thomas J. 1989. *The Perilous Frontier: Nomadic Empires and China*. Oxford: Oxford University Press.

Barlow, Tani 2004: *The Question of Women in Chinese Feminism*. Durham: Duke University Press.

Barmé, Geremie R. 2008. *The Forbidden City*. London: Profile Books.

Barr, Allan H. 2013. "Marriage and Mourning in Early-Qing Tributes to Wives." *Nan Nü* 15.1: 137–78.

Bartlett, Beatrice S. 1985. "Books of Revelations: The Importance of the Manchu Language Archival Record Books for Research on Ch'ing History." *Late Imperial China* 6.2: 25–36.

Bartlett, Beatrice S. 1991. *Monarchs and Ministers: The Grand Council in Mid-Ch'ing China 1723–1820*. Berkeley: University of California Press.

Bauer, Wolfgang 1996. "The Encyclopedia in China." *Cahiers d'Histoire Mondiale* 9.3: 665–91.

Beattie, Hilary 1979. *Land and Lineage in China*. Cambridge, Eng.: Cambridge University Press.

Behr, Wolfgang 2010. "Role of Language in Early Chinese Constructions of Ethnic Identity." *Journal of Chinese Philosophy* 37.4: 567–87.

Bell, Catherine 1989. "Religion and Chinese Culture: Toward an Assessment of 'Popular Religion.'" *History of Religions* 29.1: 35–57.

Bell, Catherine 1997. *Ritual: Perspectives and Dimensions*. New York: Oxford University Press.

Bell, Catherine, ed. 2007. *Teaching Ritual*. New York: Oxford University Press.

Bell, Daniel A. 2008. *China's New Confucianism: Politics and Everyday Life in a Changing Society*. Princeton: Princeton University Press.

Bell, Lynda S. 1999. *One Industry, Two Chinas: Silk Filatures and Peasant-Family Production in Wuxi County, 1865–1937*. Stanford: Stanford University Press.

Bentley, Tamara H. 2012. *The Figurative Works of Chen Hongshou (1599–1652): Authentic Voices/Expanding Markets*. Brookfield, Vt.: Ashgate.

Berg, Daria 2013. *Women Writers and the Literary World in Early Modern China, 1580–1700*. New York: Routledge.

Berg, Daria and Chloë Starr, eds. 2007. *The Quest for Gentility in China: Negotiations beyond Gender and Class*. New York: Routledge.

Berger, Patricia Ann 2003. *Empire of Emptiness: Buddhist Art and Political Authority in Qing China*. Honolulu: University of Hawaii Press.

Berger, Peter and Thomas Luckmann 1967. *The Social Construction of Reality*. London: Penguin Books.

Bergere, Marie-Claire 1989. *The Golden Age of the Chinese Bourgeoisie*. Cambridge, Eng.: Cambridge University Press.

Berliner, Nancy 1989. *Chinese Folk Art: The Small Skills of Carving Insects*. Boston: Little, Brown.

Berliner, Nancy, ed. 2010. *The Emperor's Private Paradise: Treasures from the Forbidden City*. New Haven: Yale University Press.

Berling, Judith 1980. *The Syncretic Religion of Lin Chao-en*. New York: Columbia University Press.

Bernhardt, Kathryn 1992. *Rents, Taxes and Peasant Resistance: The Lower Yangzi Region 1840–1850*. Stanford: Stanford University Press.

Bernhardt, Kathryn 1999. *Women and Property in China, 960–1949.* Stanford: Stanford University Press.

Beurdeley, Cécile and Michel Beurdeley 1972. *Giuseppe Castiglione: A Jesuit Painter at the Court of the Chinese Emperors.* London: Lund Humphrey. Translation of Beurdeley and Beurdeley, *Castiglione, peintre jesuite a la cour de Chine.* Fribourg: Office du livre, 1971.

Beurdeley, Michel et al., eds. 1969. *Chinese Erotic Art.* Rutland, Vt.: Charles E. Tuttle. Translated by Diana Imber.

Biggerstaff, Knight 1961. *The Earliest Modern Government Schools in China.* Ithaca: Cornell University Press.

Billioud, Sébastien 2011. "Confucian Revival and the Emergence of 'Jiaohua Organizations': A Case Study of the Yidan Xuetang." *Modern China* 37: 286–314.

Bingenheimer, M. 2011. *Manchu Bibliography.* Available at http://buddhistinformatics.ddbc.edu.tw/manchu/manchuBibl.php.

Birch, Cyril, ed. 1974. *Studies of Chinese Literary Genres.* Berkeley: University of California Press.

Birdwhistell, Anne 1989. *Transition to Neo-Confucianism: Shao Yung on Knowledge and Symbols of Reality.* Stanford: Stanford University Press.

Birdwhistell, Anne 1996. *Li Yong (1627–1705) and Epistemological Dimensions of Confucian Philosophy.* Stanford: Stanford University Press.

Bischoff, Friedrich Alexander 2005. *San tzu ching Explicated: The Classical Initiation to Classic Chinese, Couplet I to XI.* Vienna: Austrian Academy of Sciences Press.

Bisetto, Barbara 2010. "Memorie di mondi amorosi: Raccolta letteraria ed enciclopedismo nel Qingshi leilüe." In Paolo De Troia, ed. 2010: 519–30.

Black, Alison H. 1986. "Gender and Cosmology in Chinese Correlative Thinking." In Bynum et al., eds. 1986: 166–95.

Black, Alison H. 1989. *Man and Nature in the Philosophical Thought of Wang Fu-chih.* Seattle: University of Washington Press.

Blake, Fred 1994. "Foot-binding in Neo-Confucian China and the Appropriation of Female Labor." *Signs* 19.3: 676–712.

Bloom, Alfred 1981. *The Linguistic Shaping of Thought: A Study in the Impact of Language on Thinking in China and the West.* Hillsdale, N.J.: Erlbaum Associates.

Bloom, Irene, ed. and trans. 1987. *Knowledge Painfully Acquired: The K'un-chih chi of Lo Ch'in-shun.* New York: Columbia University Press.

Bodde, Derk 1957. *China's Cultural Tradition: What and Whither?* New York: Holt, Rinehart and Winston.

Bodde, Derk 1982. "Prison Life in Eighteenth-Century Peking." In LeBlanc and Blader, eds. 1982: 195–215.

Bodde, Derk 1991. *Chinese Thought Society and Science: The Intellectual and Social Background of Science and Technology in Pre-Modern China.* Honolulu: University of Hawaii Press.

Bodde, Derk and Clarence Morris 1967. *Law in Imperial China.* Cambridge, Mass.: Harvard University Press.

Bodde, Derk, trans. 1977. *Annual Customs and Festivals in Peking as Recorded in the Yen-ching Sui-shih-chi by Tun Li-ch'en.* Peiping: Henri Vetch. Originally published in 1936. Reprinted in Taipei by the Southern Materials Center, Inc.

Bogan, M. L. C. 1977. *Manchu Customs and Superstitions.* Tientsin: China Booksellers. Originally published in 1928. Reprinted in Taipei by the Southern Materials Center Inc.

Bol, Peter K. 1992. *"This Culture of Ours": Intellectual Transition in T'ang and Sung China.* Stanford: Stanford University Press.

Boltz, Judith M. 1987. *A Survey of Taoist Literature: Tenth to Seventeenth Centuries.* Ann Arbor: University of Michigan Center for Chinese Studies.

Boltz, Judith M. 2009. "On the Legacy of Zigu and a Manual on Spirit-Writing in Her Name." In Clart and Crowe, eds. 2009: 349–88.

Bond, M. H. 1991. *Beyond the Chinese Face: Insights from Psychology.* Hong Kong: Oxford University Press.

Bond, M. H., ed. 1989. *The Psychology of the Chinese People.* Oxford: Oxford University Press.

Bonk, James Bruce 2014. "Chinese Military Men and Cultural Practice in the Early Nineteenth Century Qing Empire." Ph.D. dissertation, Princeton University.

Boorman, Howard 1966. "Mao Tse-tung as Historian" *China Quarterly* 28 (October–December): 82–105.

Boorman, Scott 1969. *The Protracted Game.* New York: Oxford University Press.

Bosco, Joseph 1992. "Taiwan Factions: Guanxi, Patronage, and the State in Local Politics." *Ethnology* 31.2 (April): 157–83.

Bossler, Beverly 2013. *Courtesans, Concubines, and the Cult of Female Fidelity.* Cambridge, Mass.: Harvard-Yenching Institute Monograph Series 83.

Bourgon, Jerome 2002. "Uncivil Dialogue: Law and Custom Did Not Merge into Civil Law under the Qing." *Late Imperial China* 23.1 (June): 50–90.

Brandauer, Frederick 1977. "Women in the *Ching-hua yüan.*" *Journal of Asian Studies* 36.4 (August): 647–60.

Brandauer, Frederick P. and Chün-Chieh Huang, eds. 1994. *Imperial Rulership and Cultural Change in Traditional China.* Seattle: University of Washington Press.

Brandt, Loren 1989. *Commercialization and Agricultural Development: Central and Eastern China 1870–1937.* Cambridge, Eng.: Cambridge University Press.

Brandt, Loren, Debin Ma, and Thomas G. Rawski 2013. "From Divergence to Convergence: Re-evaluating the History Behind China's Economic Boom." Hitotsubashi University Global COE Hi-Stat Discussion Paper Series 217: 1–132. Available at gcoe.ier.hit-u.ac.jp/research/discussion/2008/pdf/gd11-217.pdf.

Brasier, Ken. E. N.d. "Taizong's Hell: A Study Collection of Chinese Hell Scrolls." Available at http://academic.reed.edu/hellscrolls/.

Bray, Francesca 1997. *Technology and Gender: Fabrics of Power in Late Imperial China.* Berkeley: University of California Press.

Bray, Francesca, Vera Lichtman, and Georges Metailie, eds. 2007. *Graphics and Text in the Production of Technical Knowledge in China, The Warp and the Weft.* Leiden: Brill.

Brenner, Robert and Christopher Isett 2002. "England's Divergence from China's Yangzi Delta: Property Relations, Microeconomics, and Patterns of Economic Development." *Journal of Asian Studies* 61.2 (May): 609–62.

Bretelle-Establet, Florence 2009. "Chinese Biographies of Experts in Medicine: What Uses Can We Make of Them?" *East Asian Science, Technology and Society: An International Journal* 3.4: 421–51.

British Library. N.d. "Shui archives in Libo, Guizhou." Available at http://eap.bl.uk/database/results.a4d?projid=EAP143.

Brokaw, Cynthia 1991. *The Ledgers of Merit and Demerit: Social Change and Moral Order in Late Imperial China*. Princeton: Princeton University Press.

Brokaw, Cynthia 2005. "On the History of the Book in China." In Brokaw and Chow, eds. 2005: 3–54.

Brokaw, Cynthia 2007. *Commerce in Culture: The Sibao Book Trade in the Qing and Republican Periods*. Cambridge, Mass.: Harvard University Press.

Brokaw, Cynthia and Kai-wing Chow, eds. 2005. *Printing and Book Culture in Late Imperial China*. Berkeley: University of California Press.

Brook, Timothy 1988. *Geographical Sources of Ming-Qing History*. Ann Arbor: University of Michigan Press.

Brook, Timothy 1989. "Funerary Ritual and the Building of Lineages in Late Imperial China." *Harvard Journal of Asiatic Studies* 49: 465–99.

Brook, Timothy 2005. *The Chinese State in Ming Society*. New York: Routledge.

Brook, Timothy 2010. *The Troubled Empire: China in the Yuan and Ming Dynasties*. Cambridge, Mass.: Harvard University Press.

Brook, Timothy, Jérome Bourgon, and Gregory Blue 2008. *Death by a Thousand Cuts*. Cambridge, Mass. and London: Harvard University Press.

Brooks, E. Bruce and Taeko Brooks, trans. 2001. *The Original Analects*. New York: Columbia University Press.

Brown, Claudia and Ju-hsi Chou 1992. *Transcending Turmoil: Painting at the Close of China's Empire 1796–1911*. Phoenix: Phoenix Art Museum.

Brown, Melissa J. 2004. *Is Taiwan Chinese? The Impact of Culture, Power, and Migration on Changing Identities*. Berkeley: University of California Press.

Brown, Melissa J. 2007. "Ethnic Identity, Cultural Variation, and Processes of Change: Rethinking the Insights of Standardization and Orthopraxy." *Modern China* 33.1 (January): 91–124.

Brown, Tristan G. 2013. "Illuminating the Shadow Economy of the Banner Garrison: Manchu Language Contracts as Sources for Qing Social History." Manchu Studies Group. Available at www.manchustudiesgroup.org/2013/09/17/1101/.

Brunero, Donna 2006. *Britain's Imperial Cornerstone in China: The Chinese Maritime Customs Service, 1854–1949*. New York: Routledge.

Brunnert, H. S. and V. V. Hagelstrom 1911. *Present Day Political Organization of China*. Foochow: Kelly and Walsh. Taipei reprint, Ch'eng-wen 1978.

Bryson, M. I. 1886. *Home Life in China*. New York: American Tract Society.

Buck, John L. 1937. *Land Utilization in China*. Nanking: Nanking University.

Burkhardt, V. R. 1953–1958. *Chinese Creeds and Customs*. Hong Kong: South China Morning Post. Three volumes.

Burling, Judith and Arthur Burling 1953. *Chinese Art.* New York: Studio Publishers.

Bush, Susan and Christian Murck, eds. 1983. *Theories of the Arts in China.* Princeton: University Press.

Busswell, Robert E. 1990. *Chinese Buddhist Apocrypha.* Honolulu: University of Hawaii Press.

Buxbaum, David, ed. 1967. *Traditional and Modern Legal Institutions in Asia and Africa.* Leiden: Brill.

Buxbaum, David and Frederick Mote, eds. 1972. *Transition and Permanence: Chinese History and Culture: A Festschrift in Honor of Dr. Hsiao Kung-ch'üan.* Hong Kong: Cathay Press.

Bynum, Caroline Walker et al., eds. 1986. *Gender and Religion: On the Complexity of Symbols.* Boston: Beacon.

Cabezon, José, ed. 1985. *Buddhism, Sexuality and Gender.* Albany: State University of New York Press.

Cahill, James 1982. *The Compelling Image: Nature and Style in Seventeenth Century Chinese Painting.* Cambridge, Mass.: Harvard University Press.

Cahill, James 1994. *The Painter's Practice: How Artists Lived and Worked in Traditional China.* New York: Columbia University Press.

Cahill, James 1996. "The Three Zhangs, Yangzhou Beauties, and the Manchu Court." *Orientations* (October): 59–68.

Cahill, James 2010. *Pictures for Use and Pleasure: Vernacular Painting in High Qing China.* Berkeley: University of California Press.

Cahill, James et al. 2013. *Beauty Revealed: Images of Women in Qing Dynasty Chinese Painting.* Berkeley: University of California Press.

Cai, Ce 1968. *Shuo Shengguan tu* (On [the game] *Shengguan tu*). Taibei: Laogu chubanshe.

Cai, Dongzhou, ed. 2003. *Zhongguo chuantong wenhua yaolue* (Essentials of China's traditional culture). Chengdu: Ba Shu shushe.

Cai, Hairong and Huang Yinfu, eds. 2005. *Zhongguo chuantong wenhua gailun* (Introduction to China's traditional culture). Hangzhou: Zhejiang daxue chubanshe.

Cai, Yi, trans. 2002. *Zhongguo chuantong wenhua zai Riben* (China's traditional culture in Japan). Beijing: Zhonghua shuju.

Campbell, Aurelia 2011. "The Impact of Imperial and Local Patronage on Early Ming Temples in the Sino-Tibetan Frontier." Ph.D. dissertation, University of Pennsylvania.

Campbell, Cameron and James Z. Lee 2000. "Connections Within and Between Households in Rural Liaoning, 1789–1909." Los Angeles: California Center for Population Research: 1–27. Available at http://escholarship.org/uc/item/0bt032g6.

Campbell, Cameron and James Z. Lee 2005. "Deliberate Fertility Control in Late Imperial China: Spacing and Stopping in the Qing Imperial Lineage." Los Angeles: California Center for Population Research: 1–39. Available at http://escholarship.org/uc/item/7f05s2n4.

Campbell, Cameron and James Z. Lee 2006. "Kinship, Employment and Marriage: The Importance of Kin Networks for Young Adult Males in Qing Liaoning." *Social Science History* 32.2: 175–214.

Campbell, Cameron and James Z. Lee 2008. "Was There a Revolution? Kinship and Inequality over the Very Long Term in Liaoning, China, 1749–2005." Los Angeles: California Center for Population Research: 1–39. Available at http://escholarship .org/uc/item/8wj993rq.

Cams, Mario 2012. "The Early Qing Geographical Surveys (1708–1716) as a Case of Collaboration between the Jesuits and the Kangxi Court." *Sino-Western Cultural Relations Journal* 34: 1–20.

Cantoniensis [pseud.] 1868. "Cost of Living Among the Chinese" *Notes and Queries on China and Japan* 1 (January 1868): 4–11.

Cao, Huimin and Chen Kang, eds. 2010. *Yangzhou baguai quanshu* (A complete collection of the Eight Eccentrics of Yangzhou). Beijing: Zhongguo yanshi chubanshe.

Cao, Shuji, Yushang Li, and Bin Yang 2012. "Mt. Tambora, Climatic Changes, and China's Decline in the Nineteenth Century." *Journal of World History* 23.3: 587–607.

Cao, Wen 2010. *Qing chao dui wai tizhi yanjiu* (Research on the Qing dynasty's approach to outsiders). Beijing: Shehui kexue wenxian chubanshe.

Carletti, S. M. et al., eds. 1996. *Studi in onore di Lionello Lanciotti*. Naples: Instituto Universitario Orientale, Dipartimento di Studi Asiatici, Series minor 51. Three volumes.

Carlitz, Katherine 1986. *The Rhetoric of Chin P'ing Mei*. Bloomington: University of Indiana Press.

Carpenter, Bruce 1983. "Drinking Water; Lyric Songs of the Seventeenth Century Manchu Poet Na-lan Hsing-te." *Bulletin of Tezukayama University* 20: 100–137.

Chaffee, John W. *The Thorny Gates of Learning in Sung China*. Cambridge, Eng.: Cambridge University Press, 1985.

Chai Ch'u, and Winberg Chai 1967. *Li-chi*. New Hyde Park, N.Y.: University Books. Reprint of James Legge's translation of the *Liji* originally printed in *The Sacred Books of the East*, Oxford, Eng. 1885. Two volumes.

Chan, Alan and Sor-Hoon Tan, eds. 2004. *Filial Piety in Chinese Thought and History*. London: Routledge Curzon.

Chan, Albert 1982. *The Glory and Fall of the Ming Dynasty*. Norman, Okla.: University of Oklahoma Press.

Chan, Hok-lam 2011. *Ming Taizu (r. 1368–98) and the Foundation of the Ming Dynasty in China*. Brookfield, Vt.: Ashgate.

Chan, Sin-Wai 1985. *Buddhism in Late Ch'ing Political Thought*. Hong Kong: Chinese University Press.

Chan, Wing-tsit 1955. "The Evolution of the Confucian Concept *Jen*." *Philosophy East and West* 4: 295–319.

Chan, Wing-tsit 1969. *Neo-Confucianism Etc.* Hanover, N.H.: Oriental Society, 1969.

Chan, Wing-tsit, ed. 1989. *Chu Hsi: New Studies*. Honolulu: University of Hawaii Press.

Chan, Wing-tsit, ed. and trans. 1963. *A Source Book in Chinese Philosophy*. Princeton: Princeton University Press.

Chan, Wing-tsit., trans. 1967. *Reflections on Things at Hand: The Neo-Confucian Anthology*. New York: Columbia University Press.

Chan, Wing-tsit, trans. 1986. *Neo-Confucian Terms Explained: The Pei-hsi tzu-i*. New York: Columbia University Press.

Chang, Che-chia 1998. "The Therapeutic Tug of War: The Imperial Physician-Patient Relationship in the Era of Empress Dowager Cixi (1874–1908)." Ph.D. dissertation, University of Pennsylvania.

Chang, Chihyun 2013. *Government, Imperialism and Nationalism in China: The Maritime Customs Service and Its Chinese Staff*. New York: Routledge.

Chang, Chun-shu and Shelley Hsueh-lun Chang 1999. *Redefining History: Ghosts, Spirits, and Human Society in P'u Sung-ling's World, 1640–1715*. Ann Arbor: University of Michigan Press.

Chang, Chun-shu and Shelly Hsueh-lun Chang 1992. *Crisis and Transformation in Seventeenth-Century China*. Ann Arbor: University of Michigan Press.

Chang, Chung-li 1962. *The Income of the Chinese Gentry*. Seattle: University of Washington Press.

Chang, Chung-li 1967. *The Chinese Gentry*. Seattle: University of Washington Press.

Chang, Chung-yuan 1963. *Creativity and Taoism*. New York: Julian Press, 1963.

Chang, Hao 1971. *Liang Ch'i-ch'ao and Intellectual Transition in China 1890–1907*. Cambridge, Mass.: Harvard University Press.

Chang, Hao 1987. *Chinese Intellectuals in Crisis: Search for Order and Meaning 1890–1911*. Berkeley: University of California Press.

Chang, Jung 2013. *Empress Dowager Cixi: The Concubine Who Launched Modern China*. New York: Knopf.

Chang, Jung and Jon Halliday 2005. *Mao: The Inknown Story*. London: Jonathan Cape.

Chang, Kang-i Sun and Stephen Owen, eds. 2010. *The Cambridge History of Chinese Literature*, Volume 2, From 1375. Cambridge, Eng.: Cambridge University Press. Abbreviation: CHCL.

Chang, Kang-i Sun and Haun Saussy, eds. 1999. *Women Writers of Traditional China: An Anthology of Poetry and Criticism*. Stanford: Stanford University Press. Abbreviation: WWTC.

Chang, Kwang-chih, ed. 1977. *Food in Chinese Culture*. New Haven: Yale University Press.

Chang, Michael G. 2007. *A Court on Horseback: Imperial Touring and the Construction of Qing Rule, 1680–1785*. Cambridge, Mass.: Harvard University Press.

Chang, Shelly Hsueh-lun 1990. *History and Legend: Ideas and Images in the Ming Historical Novels*. Ann Arbor: University of Michigan Press.

Chang, Tung-sun [Zhang Dongsun] 1952. "A Chinese Philosopher's Theory of Knowledge." *Etc.: A Review of General Semantics* 9. 3 (Spring): 203–26.

Chao, Anne Shen 2009. *Chen Duxiu's Early Years: The Importance of Personal Connections in the Social and Intellectual Transformation of China 1895–1920*. Ph.D. dissertation, Rice University.

Chao, Kang 1986. *Man and Land in Chinese History: An Economic Analysis*. Stanford: Stanford University Press.

Chao, Yuan-ling 2009. *Medicine and Society in Late Imperial China. A Study of Physicians in Suzhou, 1600–1850*. New York: Peter Lang.

Chao, Yuen Ren 1976. *Aspects of Chinese Sociolinguistics*. Stanford: Stanford University Press.

Chaves, Jonathan 1993. *Singing of the Source: Nature and God in the Poetry of the Chinese Painter Wu Li*. Honolulu: University of Hawaii Press.

Chaves, Jonathan, ed. 1986. *The Columbia Book of Later Chinese Poetry: Yuan, Ming and Ch'ing Dynasties 1279–1911*. New York: Columbia University Press.

Chemla, Karine, Donald Harper, and Marc Kalinowski, eds. 1999. *Divination et rationalité en Chine ancienne*. Saint-Denis: Presses Universitaires de Vincennes.

Chen, Dengyuan 1989. *Zhongguo wenhua shi* (History of Chinese culture). Shanghai: Shanghai shudian.

Chen, Gaoyong 1992. *Zhongguo wenhua wenti yanjiu* (Research on problems of Chinese culture). Shanghai: Shanghai shudian.

Chen, Guofu and Qiu Peihao 1950. *Tongli xinbian* (A new study of [Chinese] ritual). Taibei: Zhengzhong shuju.

Chen, Hsiu-fen 2011. "Between Passion and Repression: Medical Views of Demon Dreams, Demonic Fetuses, and Female Sexual Madness in Late Imperial China." *Late Imperial China* 32.1 (June): 51–82.

Chen, Jack W. and David Schaberg, eds. 2013. *Gossip and Anecdote in Traditional China*. Berkeley: University of California Press.

Chen, Jiujin 1999. *Zhongguo gudai di tianwen yu lifa* (Ancient Chinese astronomy and calendrical methods). Taibei: Taiwan shangwu yinshu guan.

Chen, Joseph T. 1997. *The May Fourth Movement in Shanghai: The Making of a Social Movement in Modern China*. Leiden: Brill.

Chen, Li 2012. "Legal Specialists and Judicial Administration in Late Imperial China, 1651–1911." *Late Imperial China* 33.1 (June): 1–54.

Chen, Menglei et al., eds. 1977. *Qinding gujin tushu jicheng* (Imperial edition of the complete collection of illustrations and writings, past and present). Taibei: Dingwen shuju. Abbreviation: TSJC.

Chen, Ming, ed. 1996. *Zhongguo chuantong wenhua zhong di rendao zhuyi* (The humanitarianism in China's traditional culture). Beijing: Huaxia chubanshe.

Chen, Mingsheng 1842. *Jiali tieshi jicheng* (Collection of family rituals and writing models). N.p.

Chen, Shih-hsiang and Harold Acton, trans. 1976. *The Peach Blossom Fan*. Berkeley: University of California Press.

Chen, Zhanguo 2004. *Chaoyue shengsi: Zhongguo chuantong wenhua zhong di shengsi zhihui* (Transcending life and death: The wisdom of life and death in China's traditional culture). Kaifeng: Henan daxue chubanshe.

Ch'en, Kenneth 1964. *Buddhism in China*. Princeton: Princeton University Press.

Ch'en, Kenneth 1973. *The Chinese Transformation of Buddhism*. Princeton: Princeton University Press.

Cheng, Chi-pao, ed. 1964. *Symposium on Chinese Culture*. New York: China Institute.

Cheng, Chongde 1999. *Shiba shiji di Zhongguo yu shijie: Bianjiang minzu juan* (China and the world in the eighteenth century: Frontiers and border peoples). Shenyang: Liaohai chubanshe.

Cheng, Chung-ying 1971. "Aspects of Classical Chinese Logic." *International Philosophical Quarterly* 11.2 (June): 213–35.

Cheng, Chung-ying 1971. *Tai Chen's Inquiry into Goodness*. Honolulu: University of Hawaii Press.

Cheng, Chung-ying 1972. "On *Yi* as a Universal Principle of Specific Application in Confucian Morality." *Philosophy East and West* 22.3 (July): 269–80.

Cheng, Chung-ying 1973. "A Generative Unity: Chinese Language and Chinese Philosophy" *Tsing Hua Journal* n.s. 10.1 (June): 1–17.

Cheng, Chung-ying 1991. *New Dimensions of Confucian and Neo-Confucian Philosophy*. Albany: State University of New York Press.

Cheng, Chung-ying 1997. "Chinese Philosophy and Symbolic Reference." *Philosophy East and West* 27.3 (July): 307–22.

Cheng, F. T. 1954. *Musings of a Chinese Gourmet*. London: Hutchinson.

Cheng, François 1982. *Chinese Poetic Writing*. Bloomington: University of Indiana Press. Translated by Donald Riggs and Jerome Seaton.

Cheng, Linsun, ed. 2009. *Berkshire Encyclopedia of China*. Great Barrington, Mass.: Berkshire Publishing Group. Five volumes.

Cheng, Lucie et al., eds. 1984. *Women in China: Bibliography of Available English Language Materials*. Berkeley: Institute of East Asian Studies, University of California.

Cheng, Man Ch'ing 1993. *Cheng Tzu's Thirteen Treatises on T'ai Chi Ch'uan*. Berkeley: North Atlantic Books. Translated by Benjamin Pang Jeng Lo.

Cheng, Pei-kai, Michael Lestz, and Jonathan Spence, eds. 1999. *The Search for Modern China: A Documentary Collection*. New York: Norton.

Chengyu da cidian bianwei hui, ed. 2004. *Chengyu da cidian* (Great dictionary of fixed expressions). Beijing: Shangwu yinshu guan guoji youxian gongsi.

Chesneaux, Jean 1971. "The Modern Relevance of *Shui-hu chuan*." *Papers on Far Eastern History* 3 (March): 1–25.

Chesneaux, Jean 1972. *Popular Movements and Secret Societies in China 1840–1950*. Stanford: Stanford University Press.

Chia, Lucille 2002. *Printing for Profit: The Commercial Publishers of Jianyang, Fujian (11th–17th Centuries)*. Cambridge, Mass.: Harvard University Asia Center.

Chia, Ning 2009. "Manchu Language Resources in the People's Republic of China: A Comprehensive Review." *China Review International* 16.3: 308–22.

Chia, Ning 2012. "Lifanyuan and the Management of Population Diversity in Early Qing (1636–1795)." *Max Planck Institute for Social Anthropology Working Paper* 139: 1–21.

Chiang, Michael H. 2007. "Lessons in Bureaucracy: The Politics of Crisis Management and the Pedagogy of Reform in Qing China, 1724–1730." Ph.D. dissertation, University of Michigan.

Chiang, Yee 1973. *Chinese Calligraphy*. Cambridge, Mass.: Harvard University Press.

Ch'ien, Edward T. 1986. *Chiao Hung and the Restructuring of Neo-Confucianism in the Late Ming*. New York: Columbia University Press.

Ch'ien, Mu. *Traditional Government in Imperial China: A Critical Analysis*. Hong Kong: Chinese University Press, 1982. Translated by Chün–tu Hsüeh and George O. Totten.

Chin, Ann-ping 2007. *The Authentic Confucius: A Life of Thought and Politics*. New York and London: Scribner.

Chin, Ann-ping and Mansfield Freeman, trans. 1990. *Tai Chen on Mencius: Explorations in Words and Meaning: A Translation of the Meng Tzu tzu-i shu-cheng*. New Haven and London: Yale University Press.

Ching, Julia 1976. *To Acquire Wisdom*. New York: Columbia University Press.

Ching, Julia, ed. and trans. 1987. *The Records of Ming Scholars*. Honolulu: University of Hawaii Press.

Chiu, Martha Li 1986. *Mind, Body, and Illness in a Chinese Medical Tradition*. Ph.D. dissertation, Harvard University.

Chong, Key Ray 1990. *Cannibalism in China*. Wakefield, N.H.: Longwood Academic.

Chou, Ju-hsi and Claudia Brown 1985. *The Elegant Brush: Chinese Painting Under the Qianlong Emperor 1735–1795*. Phoenix: Phoenix Art Museum.

Chow, Kai-Wing 1994. *The Rise of Confucian Ritualism in Late Imperial China: Ethics, Classics, and Lineage Discourse*. Stanford: Stanford University Press.

Chow, Kai-Wing 2004. *Publishing, Culture and Power in Early Modern China*. Stanford: Stanford University Press.

Chow, Kai-Wing et al., eds. 2008. *Beyond the May Fourth Paradigm: In Search of Chinese Modernity*. Lanham, Md.: Lexington Books.

Chow, Key Rey 1991. *Woman and Chinese Modernity: The Politics of Reading Between East and West*. Minneapolis: University of Minnesota Press.

Chow, Tse-tsung 1960. *The May Fourth Movement*. Stanford: Stanford University Press.

Choy, Elsie 2000. *Leaves of Prayer: The Life and Poetry of He Shuangqing, a Farmwife in Eighteenth-Century China*. Hong Kong: Chinese University Press. Second edition.

Chu, Pingyi 1995. "Ch'eng-Chu Orthodoxy, Evidential Studies and Correlative Cosmology: Chiang Yung and Western Astronomy." *Philosophy and the History of Science* 4.2 (October): 71–108.

Chu, Raymond and William Saywell William. 1984. *Career Patterns in the Ch'ing Dynasty: The Office of Governor-general*. Ann Arbor: University of Michigan Press.

Chu, Samuel and Kwang-Ching Liu, eds. 1993. *Li Hung–chang and China's Early Modernization* Armonk, N.Y.: M. E. Sharpe.

Chü, T'ung-tsu 1962. *Local Government in China under the Ch'ing*. Cambridge, Mass.: Harvard University Press.

Chun, Allen. 1992. "The Practice of Tradition in the Writing of Custom, or Chinese Marriage from *Li* to *Su*." *Late Imperial China* 13.2 (December): 82–122.

Clark, Iain M. 2014. "Legitimacy from Antiquity: Qing Imperial Ceramic Vessels for State Ritual." Ph.D. thesis, Macquarie University, Australia.

Clart, Philip and Paul Crowe, eds. 2009. *The People and the Dao: New Studies in Chinese Religions in Honour of Daniel L. Overmyer*. Sankt Augustin: Institut Monumenta Serica.

Clunas, Craig 1991. *Superfluous Things: Material Culture and Social Status in Early Modern China*. Cambridge, Eng.: Cambridge University Press.

Clunas, Craig 1997. *Art in China*. Oxford: Oxford University Press.

Clunas, Craig 2006. "Wuzhi wenhua—zai Dong Xi eryuanlun zhi wai (Material culture—Beyond the East/West binary). *Xin shixue* 17.4: 195–215.

Clunas, Craig 2012. *Empire of Great Brightness: Visual and Material Cultures of Ming China, 1368–1644*. London: Reaktion Books.

Coclanis, Peter A. 2011. "Ten Years After: Reflections on Kenneth Pomeranz's *The Great Divergence*." *Historically Speaking* 12.4 (September): 10–12.

Cohen, Joan Lebold 1987. *The New Chinese Painting: 1949–1986*. New York: Harry N. Abrams.

Cohen, Myron 1990. "Lineage Organization in North China." *Journal of Asian Studies* 49.3 (August): 509–34.

Cohen, Myron 1991. "Being Chinese: The Peripheralization of Traditional Identity." *Daedalus* 120.2 (Spring): 113–34.

Cohen, Paul A. 1974. *Between Tradition and Modernity: Wang T'ao and Reform in Late Ch'ing China*. Cambridge, Mass.: Harvard University Press.

Cohen, Paul A. 1984. *Discovering History in China: American Historical Writing on the Recent Chinese Past*. New York: Columbia University Press, 1984.

Cohen, Paul A. 1997. *History in Three Keys: The Boxers as Event, Experience and Myth*. New York: Columbia University Press.

Cohen, Paul A. 2003. *China Unbound: Evolving Perspectives on the Chinese Past*. New York: Routledge.

Cohen, Paul A. and John Schrecker, eds. 1976. *Reform in Nineteenth Century China*. Cambridge, Mass.: Harvard University Press.

Cohen, Paul A. and Merle Goldman, eds. 1990. *Ideas Across Cultures: Essays on Chinese Thought in Honor of Benjamin I. Schwartz*. Cambridge, Mass.: Harvard University Press.

Cole, Alan 1998. *Mothers and Sons in Chinese Buddhism*. Stanford: Stanford University Press.

Cole, James H. 1986. *Shaohsing: Competition and Cooperation in Nineteenth-Century China*. Tucson: University of Arizona Press.

Cong, Xiaoping 2007. *Teachers' Schools and the Making of the Modern Chinese Nation-State, 1897–1937*. Vancouver: University of British Columbia Press.

Council for Cultural Planning and Development 1986. *The Traditional Art of Chinese Woodblock Prints*. Taipei: Executive Yuan.

Council of the Chinese Cultural Renaissance 1977. *An Introduction to Chinese Culture*. Taipei: Council for Cultural Planning and Development.

Covell, Ralph 1986. *Confucius, the Buddha and Christ: A History of the Gospel in Chinese*. Maryknoll, N.Y.: Orbis.

Cowden, Charlotte 2011. "Balancing Rites and Rights: The Social and Cultural Politics of New-Style Weddings in Republican Shanghai, 1898–1953." Ph.D. dissertation, University of California, Berkeley.

Cozort, Daniel 1998. *Unique Tenets of the Middle Way Consequence School.* Ithaca: Snow Lion Publications.

Crawford, Robert B. 1961. "Eunuch Power in the Ming Dynasty." *T'oung Pao* 49.1: 115–48.

Creel, H. G. 1936. "On the Nature of Chinese Ideography." *T'oung Pao* 32 (1936): 85–161.

Cressey, George 1956. *Land of the Five Hundred Million: A Geography of China.* New York: McGraw Hill.

Crissman, Lawrence W. 2010. "G. William Skinner's Spatial Analysis of Complex Societies: Its Importance for Anthropology." *Taiwan Journal of Anthropology* 8.1: 27–45.

Croll, Elizabeth 1980. *Feminism and Socialism in China.* New York: Routledge and Kegan Paul.

Crossley, Pamela K. 1978. "The Conquest Elite of the Ch'ing Empire." *CHC* 9: 310–59.

Crossley, Pamela K. 1987. "*Manzhou yuanliu kao* and the Formalization of the Manchu Heritage." *Journal of Asian Studies* 46.4 (November): 761–90.

Crossley, Pamela K. 1990a. *Orphan Warriors: Three Manchu Generations and the End of the Qing World.* Princeton: Princeton University Press.

Crossley, Pamela K. 1990b. "Thinking about Ethnicity in Early Modern China." *Late Imperial China* 10.1 (June): 1–35.

Crossley, Pamela K. 1991. "Structure and Symbol in the Ming-Ch'ing Translator's Bureaus (*ssu-i kuan*)." *Central and Inner Asian Studies* 5: 38–70.

Crossley, Pamela K. 1992. "The Rulerships of China." *American Historical Review* 97.5 (December): 1468–83.

Crossley, Pamela K. 1994. "Manchu Education." In Elman and Woodside, eds. 1994: 340–78.

Crossley, Pamela K. 1997. *The Manchus.* Oxford: Blackwell Publishers.

Crossley, Pamela K. 1999. *A Translucent Mirror: History and Identity in Qing Imperial Ideology.* Berkeley: University of California Press.

Crossley, Pamela K. 2010. *The Wobbling Pivot, China Since 1800: An Interpretive History.* Oxford: Wiley-Blackwell.

Crossley, Pamela K. 2012. "The *Dayi juemi lu* and the Lost Yongzheng Philosophy of Identity." *Crossroads: Studies on the History of Exchange Relations in the East Asian World* 5: 1–12. Available at www.eacrh.net/ojs/index.php/crossroads/article/view/27/Vol5_Crossley_html.

Crossley, Pamela K. and Evelyn Rawski 1993. "A Profile of the Manchu Language in Ch'ing History." *Harvard Journal of Asiatic Studies* 53.1 (June): 63–102.

Crossley, Pamela K., Helen Siu, and Donald Sutton, eds. 2006. *Empire at the Margins: Culture, Ethnicity and Frontier in Early Modern China.* Berkeley: University of California Press.

Crowley, James ed. 1970. *Modern East Asia.* New York: Harcourt Brace Jovanovich.

Cua, Antonio S. 1979. "Dimensions of Li Propriety." *Philosophy East and West* 29.4 (October): 373–94.

Cua, Antonio S. 1985. *Ethical Argumentation: A Study in Hsun Tzu's Moral Epistemology*. Honolulu: University of Hawaii Press.

Cua, Antonio S., ed. 2003. *Encyclopedia of Chinese Philosophy*. New York: Routledge.

Cui Deli and Liao Douxing 1968. *Zhongguo wenhua gailun* (Introduction to Chinese culture). Taibei: Taiwan Zhonghua shuju.

Culin, Stewart 1972. *Chinese Games with Dice and Dominoes*. Seattle: Shorey Book Store.

Cutter, Robert 1989. *The Brush and the Spur: Chinese Culture and the Cockfight*. Hong Kong: Chinese University Press.

Da Qing huidian (Collected statutes of the Qing dynasty). Reprinted in the SKQS. Available at http://ctext.org/library.pl?if=gb&res=5542.

Da Qing huidian shili (Collected statutes of the Qing dynasty with precedents and regulations). Reprinted in the SKQS. Available at http://ctext.org/library.pl?if=en&res=2299.

Dabringhaus, Sabine and Roderich Ptak, eds. 1997. *China and Her Neighbors: Borders, Visions of the Other, Foreign Policy 10th–19th Century*. Wiesbaden: Harrassowitz.

Dai, Yi et al. 2011. *A Concise History of the Qing Dynasty*. Singapore: Silk Road Press. Four volumes.

Dai, Yingcong 2005. "Yingyun Shengxi: Military Entrepreneurship in the High Qing Period, 1700–1800." *Late Imperial China* 26.2 (December): 1–67.

Dai, Yinghua 2010. *Qingmo Minchu qimin shengcun zhuangtai yanjiu* (Research on the living conditions of the Manchu Bannermen at the end of the Qing and the beginning of the Republic). Beijing: Renmin chubanshe.

Dai, Zheng and Wang Yang 2013. *Zhongguo chuantong yilun shuping* (A critical interpretation of Chinese tradition). Lanzhou: Gansu renmin chubanshe.

Dale, Melissa S. 2000. "With the Cut of a Knife: A Social History of Eunuchs during the Qing Dynasty (1644–1911) and Republican periods (1912–1949)." Ph.D. dissertation, Georgetown University.

Dardess, John W. 2010. *Governing China: 150–1850*. Indianapolis: Hackett Publishing.

Dardess, John W. 2011. *Ming China, 1368–1644: A Concise History of a Resilient Empire*. Lanham, Md.: Rowman and Littlefield.

David, Percival 1971. *Chinese Connoisseurship*. New York: Faber.

Davis, J. F. 1836. *The Chinese: A General Description of the Empire and Its Inhabitants*. London: C. Knight. Two volumes.

Dawson, Raymond, ed. 1964. *The Legacy of China*. Oxford: Oxford University Press.

Dawson, Raymond 1978. *The Chinese Experience*. London: Weidenfeld and Nicolson.

de Bary, William T. 1983. *The Liberal Tradition in China*. New York: Columbia University Press.

de Bary, William T. 1989. *The Message of the Mind in Neo-Confucian Thought*. New York: Columbia University Press.

de Bary, William T. 1991a. *Learning for One's Self: Essays on the Individual in Neo–Confucian Thought*. New York: Columbia University Press.

de Bary, William T. 1991b. *The Trouble with Confucianism*. Cambridge, Mass.: Harvard University Press.

de Bary, William T. 1993. "The Uses of Neo-Confucianism: A Response to Professor Tillman." *Philosophy East and West* 43.3 (July): 541–55.

de Bary, William T. et. al., eds. 1964. *Sources of Chinese Tradition*. New York: Columbia University Press. Two volumes.

de Bary, William T., ed. 1970. *Self and Society in Ming Thought*. New York: Columbia University Press.

de Bary, William T., ed. 1975. *The Unfolding of Neo-Confucianism*. New York: Columbia University Press.

de Bary, William T., ed. 1981. *Neo-Confucian Orthodoxy and the Learning of the Mind–and-Heart*. New York: Columbia University Press.

de Bary, William T., ed. 2011. *Finding Wisdom in East Asian Classics*. New York: Columbia University Press.

de Bary, William T. and Irene Bloom, eds. 1979. *Principle and Practicality*. New York: Columbia University Press.

de Bary, William T. and John W. Chaffee, eds. 1989. *Neo-Confucian Education: The Formative Stage*. Berkeley: University of California Press.

de Bary, William T. et al., eds. 1999–2000. *Sources of Chinese Tradition*. New York: Columbia University Press, 1999 (second edition, volume 1) and 2000 (second edition, volume 2). Abbreviation: SCT.

De Forges, Alexander 2006. "Burning with Reverence: The Economics and Aesthetics of Words in Qing China." *PMLA* 121.1 (January): 139–55.

De Francis, John 1950. *Nationalism and Language Reform in China*. Princeton: Princeton University Press.

De Francis, John 1984. *The Chinese Language: Fact and Fantasy*. Honolulu: University of Hawaii Press.

De Groot, J. J. M. 1892–1910. *The Religious System of China*. Leiden: Brill. Six volumes.

De Groot, J. J. M. 1903. *Sectarianism and Religious Persecution in China*. Amsterdam: J. Miller. Two volumes.

De Groot, J. J. M. 1912. *The Religion of the Chinese*. New York: Macmillan.

de Harlez, Charles Joseph 1887. "La religion des Tartares orientaux, comparée à la religion des anciens Chinois, d'après les textes indigènes, avec le rituel tartare de l'emperor K'ien-Long." Académie royale des sciences, des lettres et des beaux-arts de Belgique, Brussels. *Mémoires couronnés et autres mémoires* 40: 61–172.

De Troia, Paolo, ed. 2010. *La Cina e il Mondo: Atti dell'XI Convegno dell'Associazione Italiana Studi Cinesi*. Rome: Edizione Nuova Cultura.

Dean, Kenneth 1993. *Taoist Ritual and Popular Cults of Southeast China*. Princeton: Princeton University Press.

Dennerline, Jerry 1981. *The Chia-ting Loyalists: Confucian Leadership and Social Change in Seventeeth Century China*. New Haven: Yale University Press.

Dennerline, Jerry 1988. *Qian Mu and the World of Seven Mansions*. New Haven: Yale University Press.

Dent-Young, John and Alex Dent-Young, trans. 1994–2003. *The Marshes of Mount Liang*. Hong Kong: Chinese University Press. Five volumes.

Desnoyers, Charles, trans. 2004. *A Journey to the East: Li Gui's A New Account of a Trip Around the Globe*. Ann Arbor: University of Michigan Press.

Despeux, Catherine 1987. *Prescriptions d'acuponcture valant mille onces d'or. Traité d'acuponcture de Sun Simiao du VIIe siècle*. Paris: Guy Trédaniel.

Despeux, Catherine and Livia Kohn 2005. *Women in Daoism*. Honolulu: University of Hawaii Press.

DeWoskin, Kenneth 1982. *A Song for One or Two: Music and the Concept of Art in Early China*. Ann Arbor: University of Michigan Press.

Di Cosmo, Nicola 1998. "Qing Colonial Administration in Inner Asia." *The International History Review* 20.2 (June): 287–309.

Di Cosmo, Nicola 2003. "Kirghiz Nomads on the Qing Frontier: Tribute, Trade, or Gift-Exchange?" In Di Cosmo and Wyatt 2003: 351–72.

Di Cosmo, Nicola 2006. *The Diary of a Manchu Soldier in Seventeenth-Century China*. New York: Routledge.

Di Cosmo, Nicola and Dalizhabu Bao, eds. 2003. *Manchu-Mongol Relations on the Eve of the Qing Conquest: A Documentary History*. Leiden: Brill.

Di Cosmo, Nicola and Don J. Wyatt, eds. 2003. *Political Frontiers, Ethnic Boundaries, and Human Geographies in Chinese History*. New York: Routledge.

Di Cosmo, Nicola, ed. 2009. *Military Culture in Imperial China*. Cambridge, Mass.: Harvard University Press.

Diao, Shuren 2002. *Manzu shenghuo lueying* (A glimpse of Manchu life). Shenyang: Shenyang chubanshe.

Dikotter, Frank 1992. *The Discourse of Race in Modern China*. Stanford: Stanford University Press.

Dikötter, Frank 2010. *Mao's Great Famine: The History of China's Most Devastating Catastrophe, 1958–1962*. New York: Walker and Co.

Dillon, Michael, ed. 2013. *China: A Cultural and Historical Dictionary*. New York: Routledge.

Ding, Naifei 2002. *Obscene Things: Sexual Politics in Jin Ping Mei*. Durham: Duke University Press.

Ding, Qing 1991. *Huahun gaoyang: Zhongguo chuantong wenhua di xiandai zhuanhuan* (Developing the soul of China: The transformation of China's traditional culture). Chengdu: Sichuan renmin chubanshe.

Ding, Yizhuang 1992. *Qingdai baqi zhufang zhidu yanjiu* (Research into the Eight Banner garrison system of the Qing dynasty). Tianjin: Tianjin guji chubanshe.

Dirlik, Arif 1989. *The Origins of Chinese Communism*. Oxford, Eng.: Oxford University Press.

Dirlik, Arif 2011. "Guoxue/National Learning in the Age of Global Modernity." *China Perspectives*, special issue: 4–13.

Dirlik, Arif, Paul Healy, and Nick Knight, eds. 1997. *Critical Perspectives on Mao Zedong's Thought*. Atlantic Highlands, N.J.: Humanities Press.

Dittmer, Lowell and Chen Ruoxi 1982. *Ethics and Rhetoric of the Chinese Cultural Revolution*. Berkeley: University of California Press.

Djang, Chu, trans. 1984. *A Complete Book Concerning Happiness and Benevolence: Fu-hui ch'üan-shu: A Manual for Local Magistrates in Seventeenth-Century China by Huang Liu-hung*. Tucson: University of Arizona Press.

Dodgen, Randall A. "Hydraulic Evolution and Dynastic Decline: The Yellow River Conservancy 1796–1855." *Late Imperial China* 12.2 (December 1991): 36–63.

Dolezelova-Velingerova, Milena, ed. 1980. *The Chinese Novel at the Turn of the Century*. Toronto: University of Toronto Press.

Dolezelova-Velingerova, Milena and Rudolf G. Wagner, eds. 2014. *Chinese Encyclopedias of New Global Knowledge (1870-1930): Changing Ways of Thought*. Heidelberg: Springer.

Dong, Jianzhong, ed. *Qianlong yupi* (The vermillion rescripts of the Qianlong emperor). Beijing: Zhongguo Huaqiao chubanshe. Two volumes.

Dong, Ping, ed. 2001. *Zhongguo chuantong wenhua yu xiandaihua* (China's traditional culture and modernization). Beijing: Zhongguo zhengfa daxue chubanshe.

Dongen, Els Van, 2009. "'Goodbye Radicalism!': Conceptions of Conservatism among Chinese Intellectuals during the Early 1990s." Ph.D. dissertation, University of Leiden.

Dongfang zazhishe, ed. 1923. *Mixin yu kexue* (Superstition and science). Shanghai: Dongfang zazhishe.

Dongfang zazhishe, ed. 1925. *Zhongguo wenhua shehui* (Chinese society and culture). Shanghai: Dongfang zazhishe.

Doolittle, Justus 1865. *Social Life of the Chinese*. New York: Harper and Brothers.

Doré, Henri 1914–1933. *Researches into Chinese Superstitions*. Shanghai: T'usewei Press. Translated by M. Kennelly and D. J. Finn. Six volumes. Originally published as *Recherches sur les superstitions en Chine*. Shanghai: La Mission catholique, 1911–1919.

Dott, Brian R. 2004. *Identity Reflections: Pilgrimages to Mount Tai in Late Imperial China*. Cambridge, Mass.: Harvard University Press.

Douglas, Nik and Penny Slinger 1994. *The Erotic Sentiment in the Paintings of China and Japan*. Rochester, Vt.: Park Street Press.

Douglas, Robert K. 1882. *China*. New York: E. and J. B. Young and Company.

Drake, Fred W. 1975. *China Charts the World: Hsu Chi-yu and His Geography of 1848*. Cambridge, Mass.: Harvard University Press.

Dray-Novey, Alison 1981. "Policing Imperial Peking: The Ch'ing Gendarmerie, 1650–1850. Ph.D. dissertation, Harvard University.

Dreyer, June Teufel 1976. *China's Forty Millions*. Cambridge, Mass.: Harvard University Press.

Dryburgh, Marjorie and Sarah Dauncey, eds. 2013. *Writing Lives in China, 1600–2010: Histories of the Elusive Self*. New York: Palgrave Macmillan.

Du, Fangqin and Cai Yiping 2012. "Localizing the Study of Women's History in China." *Chinese Studies in History* 45.4: 7–23. Translated by Michelle LeSourd.

Du, Xiulin 2007. *Gudian yishu shilue* (A brief history of the classical arts). Shenyang: Liaohai chubanshe.

Du, Yongtao and Jeff Kyong-McClain, eds. 2013. *Chinese History in Geographical Perspective.* Lanham, Md.: Lexington Books.

Duara, Prasenjit 1988. *Culture, Power and the State: Rural North China 1900–1942.* Stanford: Stanford University Press.

Dunmu, Cixiang 2005. *Zhongguo chuantong wenhua de xianjing* (The trap of China's traditional culture). Beijing: Changzheng cubanshe.

Dunstan, Helen 2006. *State or Merchant? Political Economy and Political Process in 1740s China.* Cambridge, Mass.: Harvard University Press.

Durand, Pierre-Henri 1992. *Lettrés et Pouvoirs: Un Proces Littéraire dans la Chine Impériale.* Paris: École des Hautes Études en Sciences Sociales.

Durrant, Stephen 1977. "Manchu Translations of Chou Dynasty Texts." *Early China* 3: 52–54.

Durrant, Stephen 1979. "Sino-Manchu Translations at the Mukden Court." *Journal of the American Oriental Society* 99: 653–61.

Dutu shidai xiangmuzu, ed. 2012. *Fuhao Zhongguo: Zhongguo chuantong wenhua jingyao tujian* (Symbolic China: An illustrated handbook of the essence of China's traditional culture). Changsha: Hunan meishu chubanshe.

Eastman, Lloyd 1988. *Family Fields and Ancestors: Constancy and Change in China's Social and Economic History 1550–1949.* Oxford: Oxford University Press.

Eastman, Lloyd. 1974. *The Abortive Revolution.* Cambridge, Mass.: Harvard University Press.

Eber, Irene 1985. "Weakness and Power: Women in *Water Margin.*" In Gerstlacher et al., eds. 1985: 3–28.

Eber, Irene, ed. 1986. *Confucianism: The Dynamics of Tradition.* New York: Columbia University Press.

Eberhard, Wolfram 1965. "Chinese Regional Stereotypes." *Asian Survey* 5.12 (December): 596–608.

Eberhard, Wolfram 1967. *Guilt and Sin in Traditional China.* Berkeley: University of California Press.

Eberhard, Wolfram 1971. *Moral and Social Values of the Chinese.* Taipei: Chengwen.

Eberhard, Wolfram 1982. *China's Minorities: Yesterday and Today.* Belmont, Calif.: Wadsworth.

Eberhard, Wolfram 1986. *A Dictionary of Chinese Symbols.* London: Routledge and Kegan.

Ebrey, Patricia B. 1983. "Types of Lineages in Ch'ing China: A Re-examination of the Chang Lineage of T'ung–ch'eng." *Ch'ing-shih wen-t'i* 4.9 (June): 1–20.

Ebrey, Patricia B. 1991a. *Confucianism and Family Rituals in Imperial China.* Princeton: Princeton University Press.

Ebrey, Patricia B. 1991b. *Chu Hsi's Family Rituals.* Princeton: Princeton University Press.

Ebrey, Patricia B. 1995. "The Liturgies for Sacrifices to Ancestors in Successive Versions of the Family Rituals." In David Johnson, ed. 1995: 104–36.

Ebrey, Patricia B. 1999. "Gender and Sinology: Shifting Western Interpretations of Footbinding, 1300–1898." *Late Imperial China* 20.2 (December): 1–34.

Ebrey, Patricia B. 2002. *Women and the Family in Chinese History*. New York: Routledge.

Ebrey, Patricia B. 2010. *The Cambridge Illustrated History of China*. Cambridge, Eng.: Cambridge University Press. Second edition.

Ebrey, Patricia B. and James Watson, eds. 1986. *Kinship Organization in Late Imperial China 1000–1940*. Berkeley: University of California Press.

Ebrey, Patricia B., ed. 1993. *Chinese Civilization and Society*. New York: Free Press.

Ebrey, Patricia B., trans. 1984. *Family and Property in Sung China: Yuan Tsai's Precepts for Social Life*. Princeton: Princeton University Press.

Edwards, Louise 2010. "Transformations of the Woman Warrior Hua Mulan: From Defender of the Family to Servant of the State." *Nan Nü* 12.2: 175–214.

Egerod, Soren and Else Glahn, eds. 1959. *Studia Serica Karlgren Dedicata*. Copenhagen: Munksgaard.

Eifring, Halvor, ed. 2004. *Love and Emotions in Traditional Chinese Literature*. Leiden: Brill.

Eitel, Ernest J. 1873. *Feng-Shui: The Science of Sacred Landscape in Old China*. London: Tuber and Company. Reprinted by Synergetic Press, 1993.

Elliot, Mark C. 1990. "Bannerman and Townsman: Ethnic Tension in Nineteenth-Century Jiangnan." *Late Imperial China* 11.2 (June): 36–74.

Elliott, Mark C. 1996. "Manchu (Re)Definitions of the Nation in the Early Qing." *Indiana East Asian Working Papers Series on Language and Politics in Modern China* 7: 47–78.

Elliott, Mark C. 2000. "The Limits of Tartary: Manchuria in Imperial and National Geographies." *The Journal of Asian Studies* 59.3 (August): 603–46.

Elliott, Mark C. 2001a. *The Manchu Way: The Eight Banners and Ethnic Identity in Late Imperial China*. Stanford: Stanford University Press.

Elliott, Mark C. 2001b. "The Manchu-language Archives of the Qing Dynasty and the Origins of the Palace Memorial System." *Late Imperial China* 22.1 (June): 1–70.

Elliott, Mark C. 2006. "The Manchus as Ethnographic Subject in the Qing." In Esherick, Zelin, and Yeh, eds. 2006: 17–37.

Elliott, Mark C. 2009. *Emperor Qianlong: Son of Heaven, Man of the World*. New York: Longman/Pearson.

Elliott, Mark C. 2010. "The Qianlong Emperor and His Age." In Berliner, ed. 2010: 32–50.

Elliott, Mark C. 2012a. "Guanyu Xin Qingshi de jige wenti" (Some questions regarding the New Qing History). In Liu Fengyun et al., eds. 2012.

Elliott, Mark C. 2012b. "*Hushuo*: The Northern Other and the Naming of the Han Chinese." In T. Mullaney et al., eds. 2012: 173–90. Excerpt available at www .chinaheritagequarterly.org/scholarship.php?searchterm=019_han_studies_elliott .incandissue=019.

Elman, Benjamin A. 1979. "The Hsueh-hai T'ang and the Rise of New Text Scholarship in Canton." *Ch'ing-shih wen-t'i* 4.2 (December): 51–82.

Elman, Benjamin A. 1981–1983. "Geographical Research in the Ming-Ch'ing Period." *Monumenta Serica* 35: 1–18.

Elman, Benjamin A. 1981. "Ch'ing Dynasty 'Schools' of Scholarship." *Ch'ing-shih wen-t'i* 4.6: 1–44.

Elman, Benjamin A. 1983. Review of Bloom 1981 in the *Journal of Asian Studies* 42.3 (May): 611–14.

Elman, Benjamin A. 1984. *From Philosophy to Philology: Intellectual and Social Aspects of Change in Late Imperial China.* Cambridge, Mass.: Harvard University Press.

Elman, Benjamin A. 1990. *Classicism, Politics and Kinship: The Ch'ang-chou School of New Text Confucianism in Late Imperial China.* Berkeley: University of California Press.

Elman, Benjamin A. 1991. "Political, Social and Cultural Reproduction via Civil Service Examinations in Late Imperial China." *Journal of Asian Studies* 50.1 (February): 7–28.

Elman, Benjamin A. 1999–2000. "Classical Reasoning in Late Imperial Chinese Civil Examination Essays." *Journal of Humanities East/West* 20–21: 361–420.

Elman, Benjamin A. 2000. *A Cultural History of the Civil Examinations in Late Imperial China.* Berkeley: University of California Press.

Elman, Benjamin A. 2003. "The Jesuit Role as 'Experts' in High Qing Cartography and Technology." *Taida lishi xuebao* 31 (June): 223–50.

Elman, Benjamin A. 2004. "Naval Warfare and the Refraction of China's Self-Strengthening Reforms into Scientific and Technological Failure, 1865–1895." *Modern Asian Studies* 38.2 (May): 283–326.

Elman, Benjamin A. 2005. *On Their Own Terms: Science in China, 1550–1900.* Cambridge, Mass.: Harvard University Press.

Elman, Benjamin A. 2007. "Collecting and Classifying: Ming Dynasty Compendia and Encyclopedias (*Leishu*)." *Extrême-Orient, Extrême-Occident* 1 (2007): 131–57.

Elman, Benjamin A. 2009. *A Cultural History of Modern Science in China.* Cambridge, Mass.: Harvard University Press.

Elman, Benjamin A. 2013. *Civil Examinations and Meritocracy in Late Imperial China.* Cambridge, Mass.: Harvard University Press.

Elman, Benjamin A. 2014. "Classical Historiography for Chinese History." Available at www.princeton.edu/chinese-historiography/.

Elman, Benjamin A., ed. 2014. *Rethinking East Asian Languages, Vernaculars, and Literacies, 1000–1919.* Leiden: Brill.

Elman, Benjamin A. and Alexander Woodside, eds. 1994. *Education and Society in Late Imperial China, 1600–1900.* Berkeley: University of California Press.

Elvin, Mark 1973. *The Pattern of the Chinese Past.* Stanford: Stanford University Press.

Elvin, Mark 1984. "Female Virtue and the State in China." *Past and Present* 104: 111–52.

Elvin, Mark 1997. *Changing Stories in the Chinese World.* Stanford: Stanford University Press.

Elvin, Mark 2014. "Qing Demographic History: Lower Yangzi Valley in the Mid Qing." Available at http://gis.rchss.sinica.edu.tw/QingDemography/data.htm.

Elvin, Mark and Josephine Fox 2012. "Marriages, Births, and Deaths in the Lower Yangzi Valley during the Later Eighteenth Century." In C. Ho, ed. 2012: 1–28. Available at http://gis.rchss.sinica.edu.tw/QingDemography/Paper/Marriage.Births.Deaths/Marriages.%20births.and%20deaths.pdf.

Elvin, Mark and Josephine Fox 2014. "Local Demographic Variations in the Lower Yangzi Valley during Mid-Qing Times." Academia Sinica website: 1–33. Available at http://gis.rchss.sinica.edu.tw/QingDemography/Paper/Local/Local_Demographic_Variation.pdf.

Eno, Robert 1990. *The Confucian Creation of Heaven: Philosophy and the Defense of Ritual Mastery*. Albany: State University of New York Press.

Eno, Robert 2012. *The Analects of Confucius: A Teaching Guide*. Available at www.indiana.edu/~p374/Analects_of_Confucius_%28Eno-2012%29.pdf

Entwisle, Barbara and Gail E. Henderson, eds. 2000. *Re-Drawing Boundaries: Work, Households, and Gender in China*. Berkeley: University of California Press.

Epstein, Maram 1996. "Engendering Order: Structure, Gender, and Meaning in the Qing Novel *Jinghua yuan*." *CLEAR* 18: 105–31.

Epstein, Maram 1999. "Inscribing the Essentials: Culture and Body in Ming-Qing Fiction." *Ming Studies* 41: 6–36.

Epstein, Maram 2001. *Competing Discourses: Orthodoxy, Authenticity, and Engendered Meanings in Late Imperial Chinese Fiction*. Cambridge, Mass.: Harvard University Press.

Epstein, Maram 2009. "Writing Emotions: Ritual Innovation as Emotional Expression." *Nan Nü* 11.2: 155–96.

Er, Si et al. 1986. *Inside Stories from the Forbidden City*. Beijing: New World Press. Translated by Zhao Shuhan.

Esherick, Joseph 1981. "Number Games: A Note on Land Distribution in Prerevolutionary China." *Modern China* 7.4 (October): 387–411.

Esherick, Joseph 1987. *The Origins of the Boxer Uprising*. Berkeley: University of California Press.

Esherick, Joseph and Mary Rankin, eds. 1990. *Chinese Local Elites and Patterns of Dominance*. Berkeley: University of California Press.

Esherick, Joseph, Hasan Kayali, and Eric Van Young, eds. 2006. *Empire to Nation: Historical Perspectives on the Making of the Modern World*. Lanham, Md.: Rowman and Littlefield.

Esherick, Joseph, Madelein Zelin, and Wen-hsin Yeh, eds. 2006. *Empire, Nation, and Beyond: Chinese History in Late Imperial and Modern Times*. Berkeley: Institute of East Asian Studies.

Eto, Shinkichi and Harold Schiffrin, eds. 1984. *The 1911 Revolution: Interpretive Essays*. Tokyo: University of Tokyo Press.

Evans, John C. 1992. *Tea in China: The History of China's National Drink*. New York: Greenwood Press.

Fairbank, John K. 1942. "Tributary Trade and China's Relations with the West." *The Far Eastern Quarterly* 1.2 (February): 129–49.

Fairbank, John K. 1992. *China: A New History*. Cambridge, Mass.: Harvard University Press.

Fairbank, John K. and Ssu-yü Teng 1940. "On the Types and Uses of Ch'ing Documents." *Harvard Journal of Asiatic Studies* 5: 1–71.

Fairbank, John K. and Ssu-yü Teng 1941. "On the Ch'ing Tributary System." *Harvard Journal of Asiatic Studies* 6.2 (June): 135–246.

Fairbank, John K., ed. 1957. *Chinese Thought and Institutions*. Chicago: University of Chicago Press.

Fairbank, John K., ed. 1968. *The Chinese World Order*. Cambridge, Mass.: Harvard Universty Press.

Fang, Chao-ying 1950. "A Technique for Estimating the Numerical Strength of the Early Manchu Military Forces." *Harvard Journal of Asiatic Studies* 13.1–2 (June): 192–215.

Fang, Jun 2014. *China's Second Capital: Nanjing under the Ming, 1368–1644*. New York: Routledge.

Fang, Ke and Sun Xuanling, eds. 2006. *Qingsu jiwen* (A record of Qing dynasty customs). Beijing: Zhinghua shuju. Chinese edition of Nakagawa 1799.

Fang, Weigui 2001. "Yi, Yang, Xi, Wai and Other Terms: The Transition from 'Barbarian' to 'Foreigner' in Nineteenth-Century China." In Lackner, Amelung, and Kurtz, eds. 2001: 95–124.

Fang, Zhao-hui 2002. "A Critical Reflection on the Systematics of Traditional Chinese Learning." *Philosophy East and West* 52.1 (January): 36–49. Edited by David R. Schiller.

Farmer, Edward L. 1995. *Zhu Yuanzhang and Early Ming Legislation: The Reordering of Chinese Society Following the Era of Mongol Rule*. Leiden: Brill.

Farquhar, David 1978. "Emperor as Bodhisattva in the Governance of the Ch'ing Dynasty." *Harvard Journal of Asiatic Studies* 38.1 (June): 5–34.

Faure, Bernard 1991. *The Rhetoric of Immediacy: A Cultural Critique of Chan/Zen Buddhism*. Princeton: Princeton University Press.

Faure, Bernard 1993. *Chan Insights and Oversights: An Epistemological Critique of the Chan Tradition*. Princeton: Princeton University Press.

Faure, David 1976. "Land Tax Collection in Kiangsu Province in the Late Ch'ing Period." *Ch'ing-shih wen-t'i* 3.6 (December): 49–75.

Faure, David 1989. *The Rural Economy of Pre-Liberation China: Trade Expansion and Peasant Livelihood in Jiangsu and Guangdong 1870–1937*. Oxford, Eng.: Oxford University Press.

Faure, David 1990. "What Made Foshan a Town? The Evolution of Rural-Urban Identities in Ming-Qing China." *Late Imperial China* 11.2 (December): 1–31.

Fei, Junqing, ed. 2004. *Zhongguo chuantong wenhua yu Yue wenhua yanjiu* (Research on China's traditional culture and Yue culture). Beijing: Renmin chubanshe.

Fei, Xiaotong 1992. *From the Soil: The Foundations of Chinese Society*. Berkeley: University of California Press. Translated by Gary Hamilton and Wang Zheng.

Feng, Erkang 1990. *Qingren shehui shenghuo* (The social life of people in the Qing). Tianjin: Tianjin renmin chubanshe.

Feng, Han-yi 1967. *The Chinese Kinship System*. Cambridge, Mass.: Harvard University Press.

Feng, Xi 2012. *Zhongguo wenhua gaiyao* (An introduction to the essentials of Chinese culture). Beijing: Zhongguo renmin daxue chubanshe.

Fetzer, Joel S. and J. Christopher Soper 2007. "The Effect of Confucian Values on Support for Democracy and Human Rights in Taiwan." *Taiwan Journal of Democracy* 3.1 (July): 143–54.

Feuchtwang, Stephan 1992. *The Imperial Metaphor: Popular Religion in China*. London: Routledge.

Feuchtwang, Stephan 2002. *An Anthropological Analysis of Chinese Geomancy*. Bangkok: White Lotus.

Feuchtwang, Stephan 2010. *The Anthropology of Religion, Charisma and Ghosts*. New York: De Gruyter.

Feuerwerker, Albert 1976. *State and Society in Eighteenth Century China*. Ann Arbor: University of Michigan Press.

Feuerwerker, Albert 1984. "The State and the Economy in Late Imperial China." *Theory and Society* 13.3 (May): 297–326.

Feuerwerker, Albert, ed. 1967. *Approaches to Modern Chinese History*. Berkeley: University of California Press.

Fewsmith, Joseph 1985. *Party, State and Local Elites in Republican China: Merchant Organizations and Politics in Shanghai 1890–1930*. Honolulu: University of Hawaii Press.

Finlay, John R. 2011. "40 Views of the Yuanming yuan": Image and Ideology in a Qianlong Imperial Album of Poetry and Painting." Ph.D. dissertation, Yale University.

Finnane, Antonia and Anne McLaren, eds. 1998. *Dress, Sex and Text in Chinese Culture*. Clayton, Victoria: Monash Asia Institute.

Fisac, Taciana 1996. "Chinese Women Represented: On Gender and Literature in a Male Dominant Culture." In Carletti et al., eds. 1996, 2: 579–99.

Fiskesjö, Magnus. 1999. "The Raw and the Cooked: China and Its Barbarians." Paper for the conference on "Constructed Histories along China's Western Frontiers," UCLA Center for Chinese Studies, February 5–6. Published in modified form as "On the 'Raw' and 'Cooked' Barbarians of Imperial China." *Inner Asia* 1.2 (1999): 135–68.

Fong, Grace 2008. *Herself an Author: Gender, Agency, and Writing in Late Imperial China*. Honolulu: University of Hawaii Press.

Fong, Grace, Nanxiu Qian, and Harriett Zurndorfer, eds. 2004. *Beyond Tradition and Modernity: Gender, Genre and Cosmopolitanism in Late Qing China*. Leiden: Brill.

Fong, Grace and Ellen Widmer, eds. 2010. *Inner Quarters and Beyond: Women Writers from Ming through Qing*. Leiden: Brill.

Fong, Wen C. 1969. "Towards a Structuralist Analysis of Chinese Landscape Painting." *Art Journal* 28.4 (Summer): 388–97.

Fong, Wen C. 1971. "How to Understand Chinese Painting." *Transactions of the American Philosophical Society* 115.4 (August): 282–92.

Fong, Wen C. and James C. Y. Watt, eds. 1996. *Possessing the Past: Treasures from the National Palace Museum*. New York: Metropolitan Museum of Art.

Foret, Philippe 2000. *Mapping Chengde: The Qing Landscape Enterprise*. Honolulu: University of Hawaii Press.

Forke, Alfred 1925. *The World Conception of the Chinese*. London: A. Probsthain.

Fraser, J. T. et al., eds. 1986. *Time, Science and Society in China and the West*. Amherst Mass.: University of Massachusetts Press.

Freedman, Maurice 1966. *Chinese Lineage and Society*. London: Athlone Press.

Freedman, Maurice 1975. "Sinology and the Social Sciences." *Ethnos* 40: 194–211.

Freedman, Maurice 1979. *The Study of Chinese Society*. Stanford: Stanford University Press.

Fu, Marilyn and Fu Shen 1973. *Studies in Connoisseurship*. Princeton: Princeton University Press.

Fu, Sima [Richard J. Smith] 2013. "Qingdai di zhanbu" (Divination in the Qing dynasty). In Zhang and Yao, eds. 2013: 245–75.

Fung, Allen 1996. "Testing Self-Strengthing: The Chinese Army in the Sino-Japanese War of 1894–95." *Modern Asian Studies* 30.4 (October): 1007–31.

Fung, Yu-lan 1948. *A Short History of Chinese Philosophy*. New York: Macmillan. Translated and edited by Derk Bodde.

Fung, Yu-lan 1952. *A History of Chinese Philosophy*. Princeton: Princeton University Press. Translated and edited by Derk Bodde. Two volumes.

Furth, Charlotte 1986. "Blood, Body and Gender: Medical Images of the Female Condition in China." *Chinese Science* 7: 53–65.

Furth, Charlotte 1987. "Concepts of Pregnancy, Childbirth and Infancy in Ch'ing Dynasty China." *Journal of Asian Studies* 46.1 (February): 7–35.

Furth, Charlotte 1988. "Androgynous Males and Deficient Females: Biology and Gender Boundaries in Sixteenth- and Seventeenth-Century China." *Late Imperial China* 9.2 (December): 1–31.

Furth, Charlotte 1990. "The Patriarch's Legacy: Household Instructions and the Transmission of Orthodox Values." In Kwang-Ching Liu, ed. 1990: 187–211.

Furth, Charlotte 1999. *A Flourishing Yin: Gender in China's Medical History, 960–1665*. Berkeley: University of California Press.

Furth, Charlotte 2005. "Rethinking Van Gulik Again." *Nan Nü* 7.1: 71–78.

Furth, Charlotte, ed. 1976. *The Limits of Change*. Cambridge, Mass.: Harvard University Press.

Furth, Charlotte, ed. 1992. "Symposium on Poetry and Women's Culture in Late Imperial China." *Late Imperial China* 13.1 (June): 1–9.

Furth, Charlotte, Judith T. Zeitlin, and Ping-chen Hsiung, eds. 2007. *Thinking with Cases: Specialist Knowledge in Chinese Cultural History*. Honolulu: University of Hawaii Press.

Gai, Qi 1916. *Honglou meng tuyong* (Illustrations from the *Dream of the Red Chamber*). Tokyo: Fengsu huijuan tuhua kanxing hui.

Galambos, Imre. "The Myth of the Qin Unification of Writing in Han Sources." *Acta Orientalia* 57.2 (2004): 181–203.

Gamble, Sidney 1943. "Daily Wages of Unskilled Chinese Laborers 1807–1902." *Far Eastern Quarterly* 3.1 (November): 41–73.

Gan, Chunsong and Zhang Xiaomang, eds. 2008. *Zhongguo chuantong wenhua baike quanshu* (Complete encyclopedia of China's traditional culture). Beijing: Jingji kexue chubanshe.

Gan, Chunsong and Zhou Yiqun 2012–2013. "The Religious Nature of Confucianism in Contemporary China's 'Cultural Renaissance Movement.'" *Contemporary Chinese Thought* 44.2 (Winter): 3–15.

Gan Huaizhen [Kan Huai-chen], ed. 2007. *Dongya lishi shang de tianxia yu zhongguo gainian* (Rethinking the East Asian historical concepts of all under Heaven and the Middle Kingdom). Taipei: Guoli Taiwan daxue chuban zhongxin.

Gao, Yinxian et al. 1991. *Nüshu—shijie weiyi di nuxing wenzi* (Women's writing—the only female script in the world). Taipei: Funü xinzhi jijinhui chubanbu.

Gardner, Daniel 1986. *Chu Hsi and the Ta-hsueh: Neo-Confucian Reflection on the Confucian Canon*. Cambridge, Mass.: Harvard University Press.

Gardner, Daniel K. 1998. "Confucian Commentary and Chinese Intellectual History." *Journal of Asian Studies* 57.2 (May): 397–422.

Gardner, Daniel K. 2007. *The Four Books: The Basic Teachings of the Later Confucian Tradition*. Cambridge, Eng.: Hackett Publishing.

Gardner, Daniel, trans. 1990. *Learning to Be a Sage: Selections from the Conversations of Master Chu Arranged Topically*. Berkeley: University of California Press.

Garrett, Valery M. 1990. *Mandarin Squares*. Hong Kong: Oxford University Press.

Garrett, Valery M. 2007. *Chinese Dress: From the Qing Dynasty to the Present*. Rutland, Vt.: Tuttle Publishing.

Ge, Chenhong 2001. *Zhongguo gudai di fengsu liyi* (Ancient Chinese customs and rituals). Taibei: Wenjin chubanshe.

Ge, Jianxiong 2004. *Sihai tonggen: Yimin yu Zhongguo chuantong wenhua* (The common origin of All within the Four Seas: Immigrants and China's traditional culture). Taiyuan: Shanxi renmin chubanshe.

Gedalecia, David 1974. "Excursion into Substance and Function." *Philosophy East and West* 24. 4 (October): 443–51.

Geertz, Clifford 1973. *The Interpretation of Cultures*. New York: Basic Books.

Gernet, Jacques 1985. *China and the Christian Impact: A Conflict of Cultures*. Cambridge, Eng.: Cambridge University Press.

Gerstlacher, Anna et al., eds. 1985. *Woman and Literature in China*. Bochum, Germany: N. Brockmeyer.

Giles, Lionel. 1913. "The Life of Ch'iu Chin." *T'oung Pao* second series 14.2: 211–26.

Gilmartin, Christina K. et al., eds. 1994. *Engendering China: Women, Culture, and the State*. Cambridge, Mass.: Harvard Contemporary China Series.

Gimm, Martin 1988. "'Bibliographic Survey': Manchu Translations of Chinese Novels and Short Stories: An Attempt at an Inventory." *Asia Major*, third series, 1.2: 77–114.

Girardot, N. J. 1983. *Myth and Meaning in Early Taoism*. Berkeley: University of California Press.

Gold, Thomas B. 1986. *State and Society in the Taiwan Miracle*. Armonk, N.Y.: M. E. Sharpe.

Gold, Thomas B., Doug Guthrie, and David Wank, eds. 2002. *Social Connections in China: Institutions, Culture, and the Changing Nature of Guanxi*. Cambridge, Eng.: Cambridge University Press.

Golden, Peter B. 2011. *Central Asia in World History*. Oxford: Oxford University Press.

Goldman, Andrea S. 2012. *Opera and the City: The Politics of Culture in Beijing, 1770–1900*. Stanford: Stanford University Press.

Goldstein, Jonathan, ed. 1999–2000. *The Jews of China: Historical and Comparative Perspectives*. Armonk, N.Y.: M. E. Sharpe. Two volumes.

Goldstone, Jack A. 1998. "The Problem of the 'Early Modern' World." *Journal of the Economic and Social History of the Orient* 41.3: 249–84.

Gong, Pengcheng 2009. *Zhongguo chuantong wenhua shiwu jiang* (Fifteen lectures on China's traditional culture). Taibei: Wunan tushu chuban gufen youxian gongsi.

Gong, Shufeng 1997. *Zhongguo jindai wenhua gailun* (An introduction to modern Chinese culture). Beijing: Zhonghua shuju.

Goodman, Bryna and Wendy Larson, eds. 2005. *Gender in Motion: Divisions of Labor and Cultural Change in Late Imperial and Modern China*. Lanham, Md.: Rowman and Littlefield.

Goodman, David, ed. 1990. *China and the West: Ideas and Activists*. Manchester, Eng.: Manchester University Press.

Goodrich, L. Carrington 1975. *Fifteenth Century Illustrated Chinese Primer*. Hong Kong: Hong Kong University Press.

Goossaert, Vincent 2008. "Irrepressible Female Piety: Late Imperial Bans on Women Visiting Temples." *Nan Nü* 10.2: 212–41.

Gottschalk, Louis, ed. 1963. *Generalization in the Writing of History*. Chicago: University of Chicago Press.

Graff, David A. and Robin Higham, eds. 2012. *A Military History of China*. Lexington, Ky.: University Press of Kentucky.

Graham, A. C. 1986. *Yin-Yang and the Nature of Correlative Thinking*. Singapore: Institute of East Asian Philosophies.

Graham, A. C. 1989. *Disputers of the Tao: Philosophical Argument in Ancient China*. LaSalle, Ill.: Open Court.

Granet, Marcel 1934. *La pensée chinoise*. Paris: La Renaissance du Livre.

Grant, Beata 1994. "Who Is This I? Who Is That Other? The Poetry of an Eighteenth-Century Buddhist Laywoman." *Late Imperial China* 15: 47–86.

Grant, Beata 1995. "Patterns of Female Religious Experience in Qing-Dynasty Popular Literature." *Journal of Chinese Religions* 23: 29–58.

Grant, Beata 1996. "Female Holder of the Lineage: Linji Chan Master Zhiyuan Xinggang." *Late Imperial China* 17.2: 51–76.

Grant, Beata 2008a. "Women, Gender, and Religion in Premodern China: A Selected Bibliography of Secondary Sources in Chinese and Western Languages." *Nan Nü* 10.1: 152–75.

Grant, Beata 2008b. *Eminent Nuns: Women Chan Masters of Seventeenth-Century China*. Honolulu: University of Hawaii Press.

Grant, Joanna 2003. *A Chinese Physician. Wang Ji and the "Stone Mountain Medical Case Histories."* London: Routledge.

Gray, John H. 1878. *China: A History of the Laws, Manners and Customs of the People*. London: Macmillan. Two volumes.

Greenwood, Kevin R. E. 2013. "Yonghegong: Imperial Universalism and the Art and Architecture of Beijing's 'Lama Temple.'" Ph.D. dissertation, University of Kansas.

Gregory, Peter, ed. 1987. *Sudden and Gradual: Approaches to Enlightenment in Chinese Thought*. Honolulu: University of Hawaii Press.

Gregory, Peter 1991. *Tsung-mi and the Sinification of Buddhism*. Princeton: Princeton University Press.

Grove, Linda and Christian Daniels, eds. 1984. *State and Society in China: Japanese Perspectives on Ming-Qing Social and Economic History*. Tokyo: Tokyo University Press.

Grupper, Samuel M. 1984. "Manchu Patronage and Tibetan Buddhism during the First Half of the Ch'ing Dynasty: A Review Article." *Journal of the Tibet Society* 4: 47–75.

Gu, Ming Dong 2005. *Chinese Theories of Reading and Writing: A Route to Hermeneutics and Open Poetics*. Albany: State University of New York Press.

Gu, Tai et al. 1990. *Zhongguo chuantong wenhua qiguan* (The wonders of traditional Chinese culture). Changchun: Jilin wenshi chubanshe.

Gu, Yue 2010. *Zhongguo chuantong wenyang tujian* (Illustrations of traditional Chinese decorations). Beijing: Dongfang chubanshe.

Guan, Xiaolian and Qu Liusheng, eds. 1996. *Kangxi chao Manwen zhupi zhouzhe quanyi* (Complete translation of the Manchu language vermillion rescripts on memorials of the Kangxi reign). Beijing: Zhongguo shehui kexue chubanshe.

Guildin, Gregory 1984. "Seven-Veiled Ethnicity: A Hong Kong Chinese Folk Model." *Journal of Chinese Studies* 1.2: 139–56.

Gunde, Richard 2001. *Culture and Customs of China*. London: Greenwood Press.

Guo, Jinfu 1993. *Hanyu yu Zhongguo chuantong wenhua* (The Chinese language and China's traditional culture). Beijing: Zhongguo renmin daxue chubanshe.

Guo, Licheng 1983. *Zhongguo minsu shihua* (Historical discussions of Chinese customs). Taibei: Hanguang wenhua shiye gufen youxian gongsi.

Guo, Ping 2006. *Guqin congtan* (A discussion of the *guqin* [zither]). Shandong huabao chubanshe.

Guo, Yanli 2003. "An Introduction to Modern Chinese Female Literature." *Sungkyun Journal of East Asian Studies* 3.2: 109–22.

Guojia tushuguan, ed. 2006. *Wenming di cunwang: Guji baohu di lishi yu tansuo* (Bastions of civilization: A history and exploration of ancient book conservation). Beijing: Beijing tushuguan chubanshe.

Gurung, Kalsang Norbu 2013. "The Role of Ambans in the Dalai Lama Government according to the Ten-Point Edict of 1795." In Charles Ramble, Peter Schweiger, and Alice Travers, eds. 2013. *Tibetans Who Escaped the Historian's Net: Studies in the Social History of Tibetan Societies*. Kathmandu: Vajra Books: 27–39.

Guy, R. Kent 1987. *The Emperor's Four Treasuries: Scholars and the State in the Late Ch'ien-lung Era*. Cambridge, Mass.: Harvard University Press.

Guy, R. Kent 2002. "Who Were the Manchus? A Review Essay." *Journal of Asian Studies* 61.1 (February): 151–64.

Guy, R. Kent 2010a. "Ideology and Organization in the Qing Empire." *Journal of Early Modern History* 14.4: 355–77.

Guy, R. Kent 2010b. *Qing Governors and Their Provinces: The Evolution of Territorial Administration in China, 1644–1796*. Seattle: University of Washington Press.

Hall, David L. and Ames Roger T. 1987. *Thinking Through Confucius*. Albany: State University of New York Press.

Hall, David L. and Roger T. Ames 1998. *Thinking from the Han: Self, Truth, and Transcendence in Chinese and Western Culture*. Albany: State University of New York Press.

Hall, David L. and Roger T. Ames. 2000. "Sexism, with Chinese Characteristics." In C. Li, ed. 2000: 75–95.

Hamashita, Takeshi 2008. *China, East Asia and the Global Economy: Regional And Historical Perspectives*. New York: Routledge. Edited by Linda Grove and Mark Selden.

Hamilton, Gary C. 2007. *Commerce and Capitalism in Chinese Society*. New York: Routledge.

Hamilton, Robyn 1997. "The Pursuit of Fame: Luo Qilan (1755–1813?) and the Debates about Women and Talent in Eighteenth-Century Jiangnan." *Late Imperial China* 18: 39–71.

Han, Jingtai 1997. *Lixue wenhua yu wenxue sichao* (The culture of the School of Principle and literary trends). Beijing: Zhonghua shuju.

Han, Yu-shan 1956. *Elements of Chinese Historiography*. Hollywood, Calif.: W. M. Hawley.

Hanan, Patrick 1981. *The Chinese Vernacular Story*. Cambridge, Mass.: Harvard University Press.

Hanan, Patrick 1988. *The Invention of Li Yu*. Cambridge, Mass.: Harvard University Press.

Hanan, Patrick, trans. 1990. *The Carnal Prayer Mat*. Honolulu: University of Hawaii Press.

Handler-Spitz, Rivi 2008. "Li Zhi's Relativism and Skepticism in the Multicultural Late Ming." *Concentric: Literary and Cultural Studies* 34.2 (September): 13–35.

Hansen, Chad 1983. *Language and Logic in Ancient China*. Ann Arbor: University of Michigan.

Hansen, Chad 1992. *A Daoist Theory of Chinese Thought: A Philosophical Interpretation*. Oxford, Eng.: Oxford University Press.

Hansen, Chad 1993. "Chinese Ideographs and Western Ideas." *Journal of Asian Studies* 52.2 (May): 373–93.

Hansford, Howard 1950. *Chinese Jade Carving* London: Lund Humphries.

Hansford, Howard 1961. *A Glossary of Chinese Art and Archaeology*. London: China Society.

Hansford, Howard 1969. *Jade: Essence of Hills and Streams*. New York: American Elsevier Co.

Hanson, Marta 2011. *Speaking of Epidemics in Chinese Medicine: Disease and the Geographic Imagination in Late Imperial China*. London: Routledge.

Hanyu dacidian bianzuan chu 2008. *Kangxi zidian* (The Kangxi dictionary). Shanghai: Shanghai cishu chubanshe.

Hao, Yen-ping 1970. *The Comprador in Nineteenth Century China*. Cambridge, Mass.: Harvard University Press.

Hao, Yen-ping 1986. *The Commercial Revolution in Nineteenth-Century China.* Berkeley: University of California Press.

Harper, Donald 1987. "The Sexual Arts of Ancient China as Described in a Manuscript of the Second Century B.C." *Harvard Journal of Asiatic Studies* 47.2: 539–93.

Harrell, Stevan 1982. *Ploughshare Village: Culture and Context in Taiwan.* Seattle: University of Washington Press.

Harrell, Stevan et al. 1985. "Lineage Genealogy: The Genealogical Records of the Qing Imperial Lineage" *Late Imperial China* 6.2 (December): 37–47.

Harrell, Stevan, ed. 1995. *Cultural Encounters on China's Ethnic Frontiers.* Seattle: University of Washington Press.

Harrell, Stevan 2003. Untitled review of Lee and Wang 2001. *China Quarterly* 174 (June): 541–44.

Harris, Peter 1997. "Chinese Nationalism: The State of the Nation." *The China Journal* 38 (July): 121–37.

Hart, Roger 2013. *Imagined Civilizations: China, the West, and Their First Encounter.* Baltimore: Johns Hopkins University Press.

Harvard University 2010. "China Historical GIS." Available at www.fas.harvard. edu/~chgis/.

Hasan-Rokem, Galit and David Shulman, eds. 1996. *On Riddles and Other Enigmatic Modes.* Oxford: Oxford University Press.

Hauf, Candice 2011. "Using Food to Teach about Chinese Culture." *Education about Asia* 16.3 (Winter): 1–7.

Hawkes, David 1980. "The Translator, the Mirror and the Dream—Some Observations on a New Theory." *Renditions* 13 (Spring): 5–20.

Hawkes, David, trans. 1973–1979. *The Story of the Stone.* Harmondsworth, Eng.: Penguin Classics. Three volumes. See also Minford 1979–1987.

Hay, John, ed., 1994. *Boundaries in China: Critical Views.* London: Reaktion.

Hay, Jonathan S. 2001. *Shitao: Painting and Modernity in Early Qing China.* Cambridge, Eng.: Cambridge University Press.

Hay, Jonathan S. 2010. *Sensuous Surfaces: The Decorative Object in Early Modern China.* Honolulu: University of Hawaii Press.

Hayes, James 1977. *The Hong Kong Region 1850–1911.* Hamden, Conn.: Archon Books.

Hayes, James 1985. "Specialists and Written Materials in the Village World." In Johnson, Nathan, and Rawski, eds.

Hayes, James 2013. "Purchase of Degrees, Rank, and Appointment in Late Qing China: Some Impressions from Contemporary Sources." *Journal of the Hong Kong Branch of the Royal Asiatic Society* 53: 31–88.

He, Changling 1964. *Huangchao jingshi wenbian.* (The Qing dynasty's writings on statecraft). Taibei: Shijie shuju.

He, Lin 1988. *Wenhua yu rensheng* (Culture and life). Beijing: Shangwu yinshu guan. Revision of 1947 edition.

Headland, Isaac Taylor 1901. *The Chinese Boy and Girl.* New York: Fleming H. Revell.

Hearn, Maxwell K. 1996. *Splendors of Imperial China: Treasures from the National Palace Museum, Taipei.* New York: Metropolitan Museum of Art.

Hearn, Maxwell K. 2008. *Landscapes Clear and Radiant: The Art of Wang Hui (1632–1717)*. New York: Metropolitan Museum of Art.

Heberer, Thomas 1989. *China and Its National Minorities: Autonomy or Assimilation?* Armonk, N.Y.: M. E. Sharpe. Translated by Michael Vale.

Hegel, Robert 1981. *The Novel in Seventeenth Century China*. New York: Columbia University Press.

Hegel, Robert and Richard C. Hessney, eds. 1985. *Expressions of Self in Chinese Literature*. New York: Columbia University Press.

Hegel, Robert 1998. *Reading Illustrated Fiction in China*. Stanford: Stanford University Press.

Hegel, Robert and Katherine Carlitz, eds. 2007. *Writing and Law in Late Imperial China: Crime, Conflict, and Judgment*. Seattle: University of Washington Press.

Henderson, John B. 1984. *The Development and Decline of Chinese Cosmology*. New York: Columbia University Press.

Henderson, John B. 1991. *Scripture, Canon and Commentary: A Comparison of Confucian and Western Exegesis*. Princeton: Princeton University Press.

Henderson, Mark, G. William Skinner, and Lawrence W. Crissman 1999. "A Hierarchical Regional Space Model for Contemporary China." Paper for the Geoinformatics Conference, China Data Center, University of Michigan, Ann Arbor: 1–11.

Herman, John E. 1997. "Empire in the Southwest: Early Qing Reforms to the Native Chieftain System." *Journal of Asian Studies* 56.1 (February): 47–74.

Herman, John E. 2007. *Amid the Clouds and Mist: China's Colonization of Guizhou, 1200–1700*. Cambridge, Mass.: Harvard University Asia Center.

Hershatter, Gail 2004. "State of the Field: Women in China's Long Twentieth Century." *Journal of Asian Studies* 63.4 (November): 991–1065.

Hess, Laura E. 1993. "Manchu Exegesis of the *Lunyü*." *Journal of the American Oriental Society* 113.3 (July–September): 402–17.

Hevia, James 1993. "Postpolemical Historiography: A Response to Joseph W. Esherick." *Modern China* 23.3 (July): 319–27.

Hevia, James 1995. *Cherishing Men from Afar: Qing Guest Ritual and the Macartney Embassy of 1793*. Durham: Duke University Press.

Hevia, James 2003. *English Lessons: The Pedagogy of Imperialism in Nineteenth-Century China*. Durham: Duke University Press.

Hihara, Toshikuni, ed. 1984. *Chugoku shiso jiten* (Dictionary of Chinese thought). Tōkyō: Kenbun shuppan.

Hinsch, Bret 1990. *Passions of the Cut Sleeve: The Male Homosexual Tradition in China*. Berkeley: University of California Press.

Hinsch, Bret 2007. "The Emotional Underpinnings of Male Fidelity in Imperial China." *Journal of Family History* 32.4: 392–412.

Hinsch, Bret 2011. "Male Honor and Female Chastity in China." *Nan Nü* 13.2: 169–204.

Ho, Chuimei and Cheri A. Jones, eds. 1998. *Life in the Imperial Court of Qing Dynasty China*. Proceedings of the Denver Museum of Natural History, series 3.15 (November 1).

Ho, Cindy 1997. *Trailing the Written Word: The Art of Writing among China's Ethnic Minorities*. New York: John Jay College, City University of New York.

Ho, Clara Wing-chung [Liu Yongcong] 1995. "The Cultivation of Female Talent: Views on Women's Education during the Early and Late Qing Periods." *Journal of the Economic and Social History of the Orient* 38: 191–223.

Ho, Clara Wing-chung 1999. "Encouragement from the Opposite Gender: Male Scholars and Women's Publications in Ch'ing China, A Bibliographic Study." In Zurndorfer, ed. 1999: 308–53.

Ho, Clara Wing-chung, ed. 1998. *Biographical Dictionary of Chinese Women: The Qing Period, 1644–1911.* Armonk, N.Y.: M. E. Sharpe.

Ho, Clara Wing-chung, ed. 2009. *Windows on the Chinese World: Reflections by Five Historians.* Lanham, Md.: Lexington Books.

Ho, Clara Wing-chung, ed. 2012a. *Overt and Covert Treasures: Essays on the Sources for Chinese Women's History.* Hong Kong: Chinese University Press.

Ho, Clara Wing-chung, ed. 2012b. *A New Look at Chinese History through the Lens of Gender.* Beijing: Social Sciences Academic Press.

Ho, Dahpon David 2008. "The Men Who Would Not Be Amban and the One Who Would." *Modern China* 34.2 (April): 210–46.

Ho, Dahpon David 2011. "Sealords Live in Vain: Fujian and the Making of a Maritime Frontier in Seventeenth-century China." Ph.D. dissertation, University of California, San Diego.

Ho, David Yau-fai et al., eds. 1989. *Chinese Patterns of Behavior: A Sourcebook of Psychological and Psychiatric Studies.* New York: Praeger.

Ho, Peng Yoke 1972. "The System of the *Book of Changes* and Chinese Science." *Japanese Studies in the History of Science* 11: 23–39.

Ho, Peng Yoke 1986. *Li Qi and Shu: An Introduction to Science and Civilization in China.* Hong Kong: Hong Kong University Press.

Ho, Peng Yoke 2003. *Chinese Mathematical Astrology: Reaching Out to the Stars.* London: Routledge.

Ho, Ping-ti 1954. "The Salt Merchants of Yang-chou: A Study of Commercial Capitalism in Eighteenth-century China." *Harvard Journal of Asiatic Studies* 17: 130–68.

Ho, Ping-ti 1959. *Studies on the Population of China 1368–1953.* Cambridge, Mass.: Harvard University Press.

Ho, Ping-ti 1962. *The Ladder of Success in Imperial China.* New York: Columbia University Press.

Ho, Ping-ti 1967. "The Significance of the Ch'ing Period in Chinese History." *Journal of Asian Studies* 26.2 (February): 189–95.

Ho, Ping-ti 1998. "In Defense of Sinicization: A Rebuttal of Evelyn Rawski's 'Reenvisioning the Qing.'" *Journal of Asian Studies* 57.1 (February): 123–55.

Holmgren, Jennifer 1981. "Myth, Fantasy or Scholarship: Images of the Status of Women in Traditional China." *Australian Journal of Chinese Affairs* 6: 147–70.

Holmgren, Jennifer 1984. "The Economic Foundations of Virtue." *Australian Journal of Chinese Affairs* 13: 1–27.

Holmgren, Jennifer 1995. *Marriage, Kinship and Power in Northern China.* Brookfield, Vt.: Ashgate.

Hong Kong Museum of History 1986. *Local Traditional Chinese Wedding.* Hong Kong: Hong Kong Museum of History.

Honig, Emily 1992. *Creating Chinese Ethnicity: Subei People in Shanghai 1850–1980*. New Haven: Yale University Press.

Hopkins, Jeffrey 1980. *Tantra in Tibet: The Great Exposition of Secret Mantra*. London: Allen and Unwin.

Hosoya, Yoshio 2010. "Chinese Bannermen in the Late Qing: The Shang Family." *Memoirs of the Research Department of the Toyo Bunko* 67: 49–57.

Hostetler, Laura 2001. *Qing Colonial Enterprise: Ethnography and Cartography in Early Modern China*. Chicago: University of Chicago Press.

Hou, Yangxing 2000. *Chuantong yu chaoyue: Kexue yu Zhongguo chuantong wenhua de duihua* (Tradition and beyond: The dialogue between science and China's traditional culture). Nanjing: Jiangsu renmin chubanshe.

Howland, Douglas R. 1996. *Borders of Chinese Civilization: Geography and History at Empire's End*. Durham: Duke University Press.

Hsia, C. T. 1968. *The Classic Chinese Novel*. New York: Columbia University Press. Reprinted by the Cornell University Press in 1996.

Hsia, C. T. 2004. *C. T. Hsia on Chinese Literature*. New York: Columbia University Press.

Hsiao, Kung-ch'üan 1960. *Rural China: Imperial Control in the Nineteenth Century*. Seattle: University of Washington Press.

Hsiao, Kung-ch'üan 1975. *A Modern China and a New World*. Seattle: University of Washington Press.

Hsiao, Kung-ch'üan 1979. *A History of Chinese Political Thought*. Princeton: Princeton University Press. Translated by Frederick Mote.

Hsiao, Kung-ch'üan 1979. *Compromise in Imperial China*. Seattle: University of Washington Press.

Hsieh Pao-chao 1925. *The Government of China 1644–1911*. Baltimore: Johns Hopkins University Press.

Hsieh, Bao Hua 2014. *Concubinage and Servitude in Late Imperial China*. Lanham, Md.: Lexington Books.

Hsieh, Jih-chiang and Ying-chang Chuang, eds. 2002. *The Chinese Family and Its Ritual Behavior*. Taipei: Institute of Ethnology, Academia Sinica. Third printing.

Hsiung, Ping-chen 1994. "Constructed Emotions: The Bond Between Mothers and Sons in Late Imperial China." *Late Imperial China* 15.1 (June): 87–117.

Hsiung, Ping-chen 2005. *A Tender Voyage: Children and Childhood in Late Imperial China*. Stanford: Stanford University Press.

Hsu, Dau-lin 1970–1971. "The Myth of the Five Human Relationships of Confucius." *Monumenta Serica* 29: 27–37.

Hsu, Elisabeth 1999. *The Transmission of Chinese Medicine*. Cambridge, Eng.: Cambridge University Press.

Hsu, Elisabeth, ed. 2001. *Innovation in Chinese Medicine*. Cambridge, Eng.: Cambridge University Press.

Hsu, Francis L. K. 1971. "Filial Piety in Japan and China: Borrowing, Variations and Significance." *Journal of Comparative Family Studies* 2.1 (Spring): 57–74.

Hsu, Francis L. K. 1981 *Americans and Chinese: Passage to Differences*. Honolulu: University of Hawaii Press.

Hsu, Ginger 2002. *A Bushel of Pearls: Painting for Sale in Eighteenth-Century Yangchou*. Stanford: Stanford University Press.

Hsü, Immanuel C. Y. 1959. *Intellectual Trends in the Ch'ing Period*. Cambridge, Mass.: Harvard University Press. This is a condensed version of a much earlier edition of Liang Qichao 2011.

Hsü, Immanuel C. Y. 2000. *The Rise of Modern China*. New York: Oxford University Press. Sixth edition.

Hsu, Tao-Ching 1985. *The Chinese Conception of the Theatre*. Seattle and London: University of Washington Press.

Hsu, Wen-ying 1978. *The Ku-Ch'in*. Los Angeles: Wen Ying Studios.

Hu, Daojing, ed. 1982. *Explorations in the History of Science and Technology in China*. Shanghai: Shanghai Chinese Classics Publishing House.

Hu, Jingjun and Dai Qihou, eds. 1992. *Zhongguo gudai wenhua shiyong shouce* (Practical handbook of ancient Chinese culture). Changsha: Hunan wenyi chubanshe.

Hu, Shaohua 2007. "Confucianism and Contemporary Politics." *Politics and Policy* 35.1: 136–53.

Hu, Shiu-ying 1999. *An Enumeration of Chinese Materia Medica*. Hong Kong: Chinese University Press. Second edition.

Hu, Siao-chen [Hu Xiaozhen] 2005. "The Daughter's Vision of National Crisis: Tianyuhua and the Woman Writer's Construction of the Late Ming." In Wang and Wei, eds. 2005: 200–231.

Hu, Xiaozhen [Hu Siao-chen] 2008. *Cainü cheye weimian: Jindai zhongguo nüxing xushi wenxue de xingqi* (Talented women burning the midnight oil: The rise of female narrative in early modern China). Beijing: Beijing daxue chubanshe.

Hu, Wenkai 2008. *Lidai funü zhuzuo kao* (An examination of women's writings by dynasty). Shanghai: Shanghai guji chubanshe. Second edition, revised and expanded by Zhang Hongsheng.

Hu, Xiangyu 2011. "The Juridical System of the Qing Dynasty in Beijing (1644–1900)." Ph.D. dissertation, University of Minnesota.

Hu, Xiangyu 2013. "Reinstating the Authority of the Five Punishments: A New Perspective on Legal Privilege for Bannermen." *Late Imperial China* 34.2 (December): 28–51.

Hu, Xianzhong, comp. Undated [Ming dynasty]. *Datong huangli jingshi* (General almanac for managing the affairs of the world).

Hu, Xiaoming 1996. *Honglou meng yu Zhongguo chuantong wenhua* (*Dream of the Red Chamber* and China's traditional culture). Wuhan: Wuhan cehui keji chubanshe.

Hu, Ying 1993. "Angling with Beauty: Women as Narrative Bait in the *Romance of the Three Kingdoms*." *CLEAR* 15: 99–112.

Hu, Ying 2004. "Writing Qiu Jin's Life: Wu Zhiying and Her Family Learning." *Late Imperial China* 25.2 (December): 119–60.

Hu, Ying 2009. "'How Can a Daughter Glorify the Family Name?': Filiality and Women's Rights in the Late Qing." *Nan Nü* 11: 234–69.

Hua, Shiping 2001. *Chinese Political Culture, 1989–2000*. Armonk, N.Y.: M. E. Sharpe.

Hua, Shiping 2013. "Shen Jiaben and the Late Qing Legal Reform (1901–1911)." *East Asia* 30.2 (June): 121–38.

Huang Aiping and Huang Xingtao, eds. 2008. *Xixue yu Qingdai wenhua* (Western learning and Qing culture). Beijing: Zhonghua shuju.

Huang, Chin-shing 1995. *Philosophy, Philology, and Politics in Eighteenth Century China: Li Fu and the Lu-Wang School under the Ch'ing.* Cambridge, Eng.: Cambridge University Press.

Huang, Ellen 2008. "China's China: Jingdezhen Porcelain and the Production of Art in the Nineteenth Century." Ph.D. dissertation, University of California, San Diego. Available at http://escholarship.org/uc/item/43w755pg.

Huang, Haiyun 2009. *Qingdai Guangxi Han wenhua chuanbo yanjiu* (Research on the dissemination of Han culture in Guangxi province during the Qing dynasty). Beijing: Minzu chubanshe.

Huang, Huaibo, ed. 2007. *Zhongguo chuantong wenhua yu Zhong yi* (China's traditional culture and Chinese medicine). Beijing: Renmin weisheng chubanshe.

Huang, Jih-chang and Ying-chang Chuang, eds. 1985. *The Chinese Family and Its Ritual Behavior.* Taipei: Institute of Ethnology, Academia Sinica.

Huang, Martin W. 1995. *Literati and Self-Re/Presentation: Autobiographical Sensibility in the Eighteenth-Century Chinese Novel.* Stanford: Stanford University Press.

Huang, Martin W. 2001. *Desire and Fictional Narrative in Late Imperial China.* Cambridge, Mass.: Harvard University Press.

Huang, Martin W. 2006. *Negotiating Masculinities in Late Imperial China.* Honolulu: University of Hawaii Press.

Huang, Martin W., ed. 2004. *Snake's Legs: Sequels, Continuations, Rewritings, and Chinese Fiction.* Honolulu: University of Hawaii Press.

Huang, Pei 1974. *Autocracy at Work: A Study of the Yung-cheng Period, 1723–1735.* Bloomington: University of Indiana Press.

Huang, Pei 2011. *Reorienting the Manchus: A Study of Sinicization, 1583–1795.* Ithaca: East Asia Program, Cornell University.

Huang, Philip C. 1985. *The Peasant Economy and Social Change in North China.* Stanford: Stanford University Press.

Huang, Philip C. 1990. *The Peasant Family and Rural Development in the Yangzi Delta 1350–1988.* Stanford: Stanford University Press.

Huang, Philip C. 1998. *Civil Justice in China: Representation and Practice in the Qing.* Stanford: Stanford University Press.

Huang, Philip C. 2001. *Code, Custom and and Legal Practice in China: The Qing and the Republic Compared.* Stanford: Stanford University Press.

Huang, Philip C. 2003. "Development or Involution in Eighteenth-Century Britain and China?" *Journal of Asian Studies* 61.2 (2002): 501–38. See also his exchange with Kenneth Pomeranz in *Journal of Asian Studies* 62.1: 157–87.

Huang, Qiaole 2004. "Writing from within a Women's Community: Gu Taiqing (1799–1877) and Her Poetry." M.A. thesis, McGill University.

Huang, Ray 1981. *1587 A Year of No Significance: The Ming Dynasty in Decline.* New Haven: Yale University Press.

Huang, Ray 1988. *China: A Macro History.* Armonk, N.Y.: M. E. Sharpe.

Huang, Yinong [aka Huang Yi-Long] 2007. "Yinxiang yu zhenxiang: Qingchao Zhong Ying liangguo jinli zhi zheng" (Impression and reality: The guest-ritual controversy between Qing China and Great Britain). *Zhongyang yanjiuyuan lishi yuyan yanjiusuo jikan* 78.1: 35–106.

Huang, Yinong [Huang Yi-Long] 1996. "Tongshu—Zhongguo chuantong tianwen yu shehui di jiaorong" (Almanacs—the interaction between traditional Chinese astronomy and Chinese society). *Hanxue yanjiu* 14.2: 159–86.

Huang, Zhao 2011. *Guoxue yu Ru Dao Shi wenhua fawei* (National Learning and the subtleties of Confucianism, Daoism and Buddhism). Beijing: Zhongguo shehui kexue chubanshe, 2011.

Huangfu, Zhengzheng 2012. "Internalizing the West: Qing Envoys and Ministers in Europe, 1866–1893." Ph.D. dissertation, University of California, San Diego.

Hucker, Charles 1966. *The Censorial System of Ming China.* Stanford: Stanford University Press.

Hucker, Charles 1975. *China's Imperial Past: An Introduction to Chinese History and Culture.* Stanford: Stanford University Press.

Hucker, Charles 1985. *A Dictionary of Official Titles in Imperial China.* Stanford: Stanford University Press.

Hummel, Arthur, ed. 1943–1944. *Eminent Chinese of the Ch'ing Period.* Washington, D.C.: Library of Congress. Two volumes. Reprinted by SMC Publishing in 2002. Available at www.dartmouth.edu/~qing/portal.shtml.

Hung, Ho-fung 2011. *Protest with Chinese Characteristics: Demonstrations, Riots, and Petitions in the Mid-Qing Dynasty.* New York: Columbia University Press.

Huters, Theodore 2005. *Bringing the World Home: Appropriating the West in Late Qing and Early Republican China.* Honolulu: University of Hawaii Press.

Huters, Theodore, ed. 1997. *Culture and State in Chinese History: Conventions, Accommodations, and Critiques.* Stanford: Stanford University Press.

Idema, Wilt, trans. 2008. *Personal Salvation and Filial Piety: Two Precious Scroll Narratives of Guanyin and Her Acolytes.* Honolulu: University of Hawaii Press.

Idema, Wilt and Beata Grant, eds. 2004. *The Red Brush: Writing Women of Imperial China.* Cambridge, Mass.: Harvard East Asian Monographs.

Idema, Wilt, trans. 2009. *Heroines of Jiangyong: Narrative Ballads in Women's Script.* Seattle: University of Washington Press.

Im, Kaye Soon 1981. "The Rise and Decline of the Eight Banner Garrisons in the Ch'ing Period: A Study of the Kuang-chou, Hang-chou and Ching-chou Garrisons." Ph.D. dissertation, University of Illinois at Urbana-Champaign.

Inn, Henry and S. C. Lee, eds. 1940. *Chinese Homes and Gardens.* Honolulu: University of Hawaii Press.

Israeli, Raphael 1980. *Muslims in China: A Study in Cultural Confrontation.* Atlantic Highlands, N.J.: Humanities Press.

Isett, Christopher 2007. *State, Peasant, and Merchant on the Manchurian Frontier, 1644–1862.* Stanford: Stanford University Press.

Ivanhoe, Philip J. 1990. *Ethics in the Confucian Tradition: The Thought of Mencius and Wang Yang-ming.* Atlanta: Scholars Press.

Ivanhoe, Philip J., ed. 1996. *Chinese Language, Thought, and Culture: Nivison and His Critics.* Chicago: Open Court.

Ivanhoe, Philip J. and Bryan Van Norden, eds. 2001. *Readings in Classical Chinese Philosophy.* Cambridge, Eng.: Hackett Publishing. Second edition.

Jagchild, Sechin and Van Jay Symons 1989. *Peace, War and Trade along the Great Wall: Nomadic Chinese Interaction through Two Millennia.* Bloomington: University of Indiana Press.

Jansen, Marius 1969. *Changing Japanese Attitudes toward Modernization.* Princeton: Princeton University Press.

Jaschok, Maria and Suzanne Miers, eds. 1994. *Women and Chinese Patriarchy: Submission, Servitude, and Escape.* London: Zed.

Jay, Jennifer W. 1990. *A Change in Dynasties: Loyalism in Thirteenth-Century China.* Bellingham, Wash.: Western Washington University Press.

Jen, Yu-wen 1973. *The Taiping Revolutionary Movement.* New Haven: Yale University Press.

Jenyns, Soame 1965. *Later Chinese Porcelains.* London: Faber and Faber.

Ji, Yun 1983. *Qinding siku quanshu zongmu* (Reviews from the *Complete Collection of the Four Treasuries*). Reprint Taibei: Shangwu yinshu guan.

Ji, Yun et al., eds. 1983–1986. *Qinding Siku quanshu* (Imperial edition of the *Complete Collection of the Four Treasuries*). Reprint Taibei: Shangwu yinshu guan, under the title *Yingyin Wenyuan ge Siku quanshu*. Abbreviation: SKQS.

Jia, Qingjun 2009. *Chongtu yihuo ronghe: Ming Qing zhi ji xixue dongjian yu Zhejiang xueren* (Conflict or convergence: Zhejiang scholars and the dissemination of Western learning to the east during the Ming-Qing period). Beijing: Haiyang chubanshe.

Jiang, Xinyan 2009. "Confucianism, Women, and Social Contexts." *Journal of Chinese Philosophy* 36.2: 228–42.

Jiang, Yong 1774. *He Luo jingyun* (Quintessence of the Hetu and the Luoshu). Liangyi tang.

Jiang, Yonglin 2010. *The Mandate of Heaven and the Great Ming Code.* Seattle: University of Washington Press.

Jiang, Yonglin 2014. *The Great Ming Code.* Seattle: University of Washington Press.

Jiao, Guocheng 2006. *Dui Zhongguo chuantong wenhua fansi de fansi* (Reflections on Reflection in China's traditional culture). Shanghai: Shanghai renmin chubanshe.

Jiaoyu bu wenhua ju, ed. 1969. *Zhonghua wenhua zhi tezhi* (The special characteristics of Chinese culture). Taibei: Youshi shudian.

Jin, Guantao and Liu Qingfeng 2006. "Cong 'tianxia,' 'wanguo' dao 'shijie': Wan Qing minzuzhuyi xingcheng de zhongjian huanjie" (From "all under heaven" and "myriad nations" to "world": Intermediate stages in the development of late Qing nationalism). *Ershiyi shiji shuangyuekan* 94: 40–53.

Jin, Kaicheng 1980. "Artistic Recreation of the Unique Characteristics of Things." *Social Science in China* 1.3: 215–29.

Jin, Qiu 2006. *Zhongguo chuantong wenhua yu wudao* (China's traditional culture and dance). Beijing: Zhongguo shehui kexue chubanshe.

Jin, Wenxue 2004. *Kōshoku to Chūgoku bunka: Chūgoku no rekishi wa yoru ni tsukurareta* (Lust and Chinese culture: Chinese history was created at night). Kawaguchi-shi: Nihon kyōhōsha.

Jin, Yi 1995. *Zhongguo wenhua gailun* (Introduction to Chinese culture). Beijing: Zhongguo guangbo dianshi chubanshe.

Jing, Su and Lun Luo 1978. *Landlord and Labor in Late Imperial China*. Cambridge, Mass.; Harvard University Press. Translated by Endymion Wilkinson.

Jochim, Christian 1979. "The Imperial Audience Ceremonies of the Ch'ing Dynasty." *Bulletin of the Society for the Study of Chinese Religions* 7 (Fall): 88–103.

Jochim, Christian 1980. "Imperial Audience Ceremonies of the Ch'ing Dynasty: A Study of the Ethico-Religious Dimension of the Confucian State." Ph.D. dissertation, University of Southern California.

Jochim, Christian 1986. *Chinese Religions: A Cultural Perspective*. Englewood Cliffs, N.J.: Prentice-Hall.

Jochim, Christian 1988. "'Great' and 'Little' 'Grid' and 'Group': Defining the Poles of the Elite-Popular Continuum in Chinese Religion." *Journal of Chinese Religions* 16: 18–42.

Johnson, David 2009. *Spectacle and Sacrifice: The Ritual Foundations of Village Life in North China*. Cambridge, Mass.: Harvard University Asia Center.

Johnson, David, Andrew J. Nathan, and Evelyn Rawski, eds. 1985. *Popular Culture in Late Imperial China*. Berkeley: University of California Press.

Johnson, David, ed. 1995. *Ritual and Scripture in Chinese Popular Religion: Five Studies*. Berkeley: Institute of East Asian Studies.

Johnson, Kay Ann 1983. *Women, the Family and Peasant Revolution in China*. Chicago: University of Chicago Press.

Johnson, Linda Cooke, ed. 1993. *Cities of Jiangnan in Late Imperial China*. Ithaca: Cornell University Press.

Johnston, R. F. 1910. *Lion and Dragon in Northern China*. London: John Murray.

Johnston, R. Stewart 1991. *Scholar Garden of China: A Study and Analysis of the Spatial Design of the Chinese Private Garden*. Cambridge, Eng.: Cambridge University Press.

Jones, William 1974. "Studying the Ch'ing Code—The *Ta Ch'ing Lü Li.*" *The American Journal of Comparative Law* 22: 330–35.

Jones, William C., trans. 1994. *The Great Qing Code*. Oxford: Clarendon Press.

Jordan, David K. 1972. *Gods, Ghosts and Ancestors: The Folk Religion of a Taiwanese Village* Berkeley: University of California Press. A revised version is available online at Jordan 2014.

Jordan, David K. 2014. "Teachers' and Students' Resources (China-Related)." Available at http://pages.ucsd.edu/~dkjordan/chin/china.html. Among the many useful materials available on this site are (in no particular order):

1. *Gods, Ghosts, & Ancestors: Folk Religion in a Taiwanese Village* (1999; full text)
2. "The Traditional Chinese Family & Lineage (Illustrated Background Essay)"
3. "Chinese Administrative Units (Brief Table)"

4. "Chinese Civil Service Exams (Brief Table)"
5. "Folk Filial Piety in Taiwan: The 'Twenty-Four Filial Exemplars'" (1986)
6. "Syncretism & Sectarian Behavior in Taiwan" (1988)
7. "Twenty-Four Filial Exemplars" (a translation)
8. "Master Zhu's Maxims for Managing the Home" (a translation)
9. "Full Table of Chinese Imperial Reigns"

Jordan, David K. and Overmyer Daniel L. 1986. *The Flying Phoenix: Aspects of Chinese Sectarianism in Taiwan*. Princeton: Princeton University Press.

Judge, Joan 1997. *Print and Politics: "Shibao" and the Culture of Reform in Late Qing China*. Stanford: Stanford University Press.

Judge, Joan 2001. "Talent, Virtue, and the Nation: Chinese Nationalisms and Female Subjectivities in the Early Twentieth Century." *The American Historical Review* 106.3 (June): 765–803.

Judge, Joan 2008. *The Precious Raft of History: The Past, the West, and the Woman Question in China*. Stanford: Stanford University Press.

Judge, Joan 2011. "Exemplary Time and Secular Times: Wei Xiyuan's Illustrated Biographies of Exceptional Women and the Late Qing Moment." In Judge and Hu, eds. 2011: 104–20.

Judge, Joan and Ying Hu, eds. 2011. *Beyond Exemplar Tales: Women's Biography in Chinese History*. Berkeley: University of California Press.

Jullien, François 1989. *Procès ou création: une introduction à la pensée des lettrés chinois: essai de problématique interculturelle*. Paris: Éditions du Seuil.

Kaderas, Christoph 1998. *Die Leishu der imperialen Bibliothek des Kaisers Qianlong (reg. 1736–1796): Untersuchungen zur chinesische Enzyklopädie*. Wiesbaden: Harrassowitz.

Kaderas, Christoph n.d. "Why Sparrows and Dragons belong to the Same Species— On the Taxonomic Method in Old Chinese Encyclopedias." Available at www. kaderas.de/abstracts.html#eastandwest.

Kahn, Harold 1967. "The Politics of Filiality" *Journal of Asian Studies* 26.2 (February): 197–203.

Kahn, Harold 1971. *Monarchy in the Emperor's Eyes*. Cambridge, Mass.: Harvard University Press.

Kalinowski, Marc. 2004. "Technical Traditions in Ancient China and *Shushu* Culture in Chinese Religion." In Lagerwey, ed. 2004: 223–48.

Kalinowski, Mark and Donald Harper, eds. forthcoming. *Popular Culture and Books of Fate in Early China: The Daybook Manuscripts (rishu) of the Warring States, Qin, and Han*.

Kamachi, Noriko et al., eds. 1975. *Japanese Studies of Modern China since 1953*. Cambridge, Mass.: Harvard University Press.

Kang, Chao 1981. "New Data on Land Ownership Patterns in Ming-Ch'ing China." *Journal of Asian Studies* 40.4 (August): 719–34.

Kang, David C. 2010. *East Asia Before the West: Five Centuries of Trade and Tribute*. New York: Columbia University Press.

Kang, Xiaofei 2006. *The Cult of the Fox: Power, Gender, and Popular Religion in Late Imperial and Modern China*. New York: Columbia University Press.

Kang, Xiaoguang 2012–2013. "Confucianism and Conceiving a Cultural Renaissance in the New Century." *Contemporary Chinese Thought* 44.2 (Winter): 61–75.

Kao, Mayching, ed. 1988. *Twentieth-Century Chinese Painting*. Hong Kong: Oxford University Press.

Karlsson, Kim, Alfreda Murck, and Michele Matteini, eds. 2010. *Eccentric Visions: The Worlds of Luo Ping (1733–1799)*. Zürich: Museum Rietberg.

Kaske, Elizabeth 2012. "Metropolitan Clerks and Venality in Qing China: The Great 1830 Forgery Case." *T'oung Pao* 98: 217–69.

Katz, Paul R. 1995. *Demon Hordes and Burning Boats. The Cult of Marshal Wen in Late Imperial Chekiang*. Albany: State University of New York Press.

Katz, Paul R. 2009. *Divine Justice: Religion and the Development of Chinese Legal Culture*. New York: Routledge.

Katzenstein, Peter J., ed. 2012. *Sinicization and the Rise of China: Civilizational Processes beyond East and West*. London: Routledge.

Kaufmann, Walter 1976. *Musical References in the Chinese Classics*. Detroit: Information Coordinators.

Keenan, Barry C. 2011. *Neo-Confucian Self-Cultivation*. Honolulu: University of Hawaii Press.

Kelleher, M. Theresa, trans. 2013. *The Journal of Wu Yubi: The Path to Sagehood*. Cambridge, Eng.: Hackett Publishing.

Kennedy, Thomas 1974. "Self-Strengthening." *Ch'ing-shih wen-t'i* 3.1 (November): 3–35.

Kennedy, Thomas, trans. 1993. *Testimony of a Confucian Woman: The Autobiography of Mrs. Nie Zeng Jifen 1852–1942*. Athens, Ga.: University of Georgia Press.

Kessler, Lawrence 1981. *K'ang-hsi and the Consolidation of Ch'ing Rule 1661–1684*. Chicago: University of Chicago Press.

Keswick, Maggie 1978. *The Chinese Garden*. New York: Rizzoli International Publications.

Kim, Kwangmin 2008. "Saintly Brokers: Uyghur Muslims, Trade, and the Making of Qing Central Asia, 1696–1814." Ph.D. dissertation, University of California, Berkeley.

Kim, Yung Sik 1992. "Chu Hsi (1130–1200) on Calendar Specialists and Their Knowledge: A Scholar's Attitude toward Technical Scientific Knowledge in Traditional China." *T'oung Pao*, second series 78: 94–115.

Kim, Yung Sik 2000. *The Natural Philosophy of Chu Hsi (1130–1200)*. Philadelphia: American Philosophical Society.

King, Ambrose 1991. "*Kuan-hsi* and Network Building: A Sociological Interpretation." *Daedalus* 120.2 (Spring): 63–84.

Kinney, Anne Behnke 2004. *Representations of Childhood and Youth in Early China*. Stanford: Stanford University Press.

Kinney, Anne Behnke, ed. 1995. *Chinese Views of Childhood*. Honolulu: University of Hawaii Press.

Kiong, Simon [Gong Guyu] 1906. *Quelques mots sur la politesse chinoise*. Shanghai: Catholic Mission Press.

Kipness, Andrew B. 1996. "The Language of Gifts: Managing *Guanxi* in a North China Village." *Modern China* 22: 285–314.

Kipness, Andrew B. 1997. *Producing Guanxi: Sentiment, Self, and Subculture in a North China Village*. Durham: Duke University Press.

Kirby, William C., ed. 2003. *Realms of Freedom in Modern China*. Stanford: Stanford University Press.

Kirkland, Russell 2004. *Taoism: The Enduring Tradition*. New York: Routledge.

Kleeman, Terry F. 1994. *A God's Own Tale: The Book of Transformations of Wenchang, the Divine Lord of Zitong*. Albany: State University of New York Press.

Kleinman, Arthur and T. Y. Lin, eds. 1981. *Normal and Abnormal Behavior in Chinese Culture*. Dordrecht: D. Reidel.

Kleutghen, Kristina 2014. "Chinese Occidenterie: The Diversity of 'Western' Objects in Eighteenth-Century China." *Eighteenth-Century Studies* 47.2 (Winter 2014): 117–35.

Kleutghen, Kristina forthcoming. *Imperial Illusions: Crossing Pictorial Boundaries in Eighteenth-Century China*. Seattle: University of Washington Press.

Knapp, Ronald G. 1986. *China's Traditional Rural Architecture: A Cultural Geography of the Common House*. Honolulu: University of Hawaii Press.

Knapp, Ronald G. 1989. *China's Vernacular Architecture: House Form and Culture*. Honolulu: University of Hawaii Press.

Knapp, Ronald G. 1990. *The Chinese House: Craft, Symbol and the Folk Tradition*. Hong Kong: Oxford University Press.

Knapp, Ronald G. 1999. *China's Living Houses: Folk Beliefs, Symbols, and Household Ornamentation*. Honolulu: University of Hawaii Press.

Knapp, Ronald G., ed. 1992. *Chinese Landscapes: The Village as Place*. Honolulu: University of Hawaii Press.

Knapp, Ronald G. and Kai-yin Lo, eds. 2005. *House Home Family: Living and Being Chinese*. Honolulu: University of Hawaii Press.

Knapp, Ronald G., ed. 1980. *China's Island Frontier: Studies in the Historical Geography of Taiwan*. Honolulu: University of Hawaii Press.

Knoblock, John, trans. 1988–1994. *Xunzi: A Translation and Study of the Complete Works*. Stanford: Stanford University Press. Three volumes.

Knoerle, Jeanne 1972. *"The Dream of the Red Chamber": A Critical Study*. Bloomington: Indiana University Press.

Ko, Dorothy 1992. "Pursuing Talent and Virtue: Education and Women's Culture in Seventeenth- and Eighteenth-Century China." *Late Imperial China* 13.1 (June): 9–39.

Ko, Dorothy 1994a. "Lady-Scholars at the Door: The Practice of Gender Relations in Eighteenth-Century Suzhou." In John Hay, ed. 1994: 198–216.

Ko, Dorothy 1994b. *Teachers of the Inner Chambers: Women and Culture in Seventeenth-Century China*. Stanford: Stanford University Press.

Ko, Dorothy 1996. "Thinking about Copulating: An Early-Qing Confucian Thinker's Problem with Emotion and Words." In Hershatter et al. 1996: 59–76.

Ko, Dorothy 1997. "The Body as Attire: The Shifting Meanings of Footbinding in Seventeenth-Century China." *Journal of Women's History* 8.4: 1–27.

Ko, Dorothy 2001. *Every Step a Lotus: Shoes for Bound Feet.* Berkeley: University of California Press.

Ko, Dorothy 2005. *Cinderella's Sisters: A Revisionist History of Footbinding.* Berkeley: University of California Press.

Ko, Dorothy et al., eds. 2003. *Women and Confucian Cultures in Premodern China, Korea, and Japan.* Berkeley: University of California Press.

Kohn, Livia 2001. *Daoism and Chinese Culture.* Magdelena, N.M.: Three Pines Press.

Kohn, Livia 2009. *Introducing Daoism.* New York: Routledge.

Kohn, Livia, ed. 1989. *Taoist Meditation and Longevity Techniques.* Ann Arbor: University of Michigan Press.

Kohn, Livia, ed. 1993. *The Taoist Experience: An Anthology.* Ithaca: Cornell University Press.

Kohn, Livia, ed. 2000. *Daoism Handbook.* Leiden: E.J. Brill.

Kohn, Livia, ed. 2008. *Laughing at the Dao: Debates among Buddhists and Daoists in Medieval China.* Magdelena, N.M.: Three Pines Press.

Kohn, Livia and Michael La Fargue, eds. 1998. *Lao-tzu and the Tao-te-ching.* Albany: State University of New York Press.

Kolmaš, Joseph 1967. "Tibet and Imperial China: A Survey of Sino-Tibetan Relations Up to the End of the Manchu Dynasty in 1912. *Occasional Paper 7.* Canberra: Australian National University, Centre of Oriental Studies.

Kolmaš, Joseph 1994. "The Ambans and Assistant Ambans of Tibet (A Chronological Study)." *Archiv Orientalni,* supplement 7. Prague: Oriental Institute.

Komjathy, Louis 2002. *Title Index to Daoist Collections.* Cambridge, Mass.: Three Pines Press.

Ku, Hung-ming 1956. *The Spirit of the Chinese People.* New York: Macmillan.

Ku, Yangjie 1980. "The Feudal Clan System Inherited from the Song and Ming Periods." *Social Science in China* 3: 29–82.

Kuhn, Philip 1980. *Rebellion and Its Enemies in Late Imperial China: Militarization and Social Structure, 1796–1864.* Cambridge, Mass.: Harvard University Press.

Kuhn, Philip 1990. *Soulstealers: The Chinese Sorcery Scare of 1768.* Cambridge, Mass.: Harvard University Press.

Kuhn, Philip. 1977. "Origins of the Taiping Vision." *Comparative Studies in Society and History* 19.3 (July): 350–66.

Kulp, Daniel H. 1925. *Country Life in South China.* New York: Columbia University Press.

Kuo, Jason, ed. 2006. *Discovering Chinese Painting: Dialogues with Art Historians.* Dubuque, Iowa: Kendall/Hunt.

Kuriyama, Shigehisa, ed. 2001. *The Imagination of the Body and the History of Bodily Experience.* International symposium, 15. Kyoto: International Research Center for Japanese Studies.

Kutcher, Norman 1997. "The Death of the Xiaoxian Empress: Bureaucratic Betrayals and the Crises of Eighteenth-Century Chinese Rule." *Journal of Asian Studies* 56.3: 708–25.

Kutcher, Norman 1999. *Mourning in Late Imperial China: Filial Piety and the State.* Cambridge, Eng.: Cambridge University Press.

Kuwayama, George, ed. 1992. *New Perspectives on the Art of Ceramics in China.* Honolulu: University of Hawaii Press.

Kwan, Man Bun 2001. *The Salt Merchants of Tianjin: State-making and Civil Society in Late Imperial China.* Honolulu: University of Hawai'i Press.

Kwong, Luke S. K. 1984. *A Mosaic of the Hundred Days: Personalities, Politics and Ideas of 1898.* Cambridge, Mass.: Harvard University Press.

Laaman, Lars, ed. 2013. *Critical Readings on the Manchus in Modern China (1616–2012).* Leiden: Brill. Four volumes.

Lackner, Michael 2008. "'Ex Oriente Scientia?' Reconsidering the Ideology of a Chinese Origin of Western Knowledge." *Asia Major,* third series 21.1: 183–200.

Lackner, Michael, Iwo Amelung, and Joachim Kurtz, eds. 2001. *New Terms for New Ideas: Western Knowledge and Lexical Change in Late Imperial China.* Leiden: Brill.

Lackner, Michael and Natascha Vittinghoff, eds. 1999. *Mapping Meanings: The Field of New Learning in Late Qing China.* Leiden: Brill.

Lagerwey, John 1987. *Taoist Ritual in Chinese Society and History.* New York: Macmillan.

Lagerwey, John and Pengzhi Lü, eds. 2010. *Early Chinese Religion: Part Two, The Period of Division (220–589).* Leiden: Brill. Two volumes.

Lagerwey, John, ed. 2004. *Chinese Religion and Society.* Hong Kong: Chinese University Press. Two volumes.

Lai, Bao 1759. *Qinding Da Qing tongli* (Imperially endorsed comprehensive rituals of the Qing dynasty). Taibei reprint, Shijie shuju, 1988.

Lai, Karyn L. 2008. *An Introduction to Chinese Philosophy.* Cambridge, Eng.: Cambridge University Press.

Lai, T. C. 1969. *Chinese Couplets.* Hong Kong: Kelly and Walsh.

Lai, T. C. 1970. *A Scholar in Imperial China.* Hong Kong: Kelly and Walsh.

Lai, Yu-chih 2013. "Images, Knowledge and Empire: Depicting Cassowaries in the Qing court." *Transcultural Studies* 1: 7–100. Translated by Philip Hand.

Laing, Ellen 2002. *Art and Aesthetics in Chinese Popular Prints: Selections from the Muban Foundation Collection.* Ann Arbor: University of Michigan Center for Chinese Studies.

Laitinen, Kauko 1990. *Chinese Nationalism in the Late Qing Dynasty: Zhang Binglin as an Anti-Manchu Propagandist.* London: Curzon Press.

Lamley, Harry 1977. "*Hsieh-tou*: The Pathology of Violence in South-east China." *Ch'ing-shih wen-t'i* 3.7 (November): 1–39.

Lampton, David M. 2014a. *Following the Leader: Ruling China, from Deng Xiaoping to Xi Jinping.* Berkeley: University of California Press.

Lampton, David M. 2014b. "How China Is Ruled." *Foreign Affairs* (January–February). Available at ww.cfr.org/china/china-ruled/p32500.

Lancashire, David, ed. 1982. *Chinese Essays on Religion and Faith.* Cambridge, Mass.: Harvard University Press.

Lau, D. C. 1963. "On Mencius' Use of the Method of Analogy in Argument." *Asia Major,* new series 10.2: 173–94.

Lau, D. C., trans. 1992. *Confucius: The Analects*. Hong Kong: Chinese University Press. Second edition.

Laufer, Berthold 1916. "Loan-Words in Tibetan." *T'oung Pao*, second series 17.4–5 (October–December): 403–552.

Lavely, William 1989. "The Spatial Approach to Chinese History: Illustrations from North China and the Upper Yangzi." *Journal of Asian Studies* 48.1 (February): 100–113.

Lavely, William et al. 1990. "Chinese Demography: The State of the Field." *Journal of Asian Studies* 49.4 (November): 807–34.

Le Blanc, Charles 1985. *Huai-nan Tzu: Philosophical Synthesis in Early Han Thought*. Hong Kong: Hong Kong University Press.

Le Blanc, Charles and Dorothy Borei, eds. 1982. *Essays on Chinese Civilization*. Princeton: Princeton University Press.

LeBlanc, Charles and Susan Blader, eds. 1987. *Chinese Ideas About Nature and Society*. Hong Kong: Hong Kong University Press.

Lecher, Hanno 2008. "Online Bibliographies for Chinese Studies." Available at http://sun.sino.uni–heidelberg.de/igcs/igbiblio.htm.

Ledderose, Lothar 2000. *Ten Thousand Things: Module and Mass Production in Chinese Art*. Princeton: Princeton University Press.

Lee, Byung Ho 2011. "Forging the Imperial Nation: Imperialism, Nationalism, and Ethnic Boundaries in China's Longue Durée." Ph.D. dissertation, University of Michigan.

Lee, James Z. and Feng Wang 2001. *One Quarter of Humanity: Malthusian Mythology and Chinese Realities, 1700–2000*. Cambridge, Mass.: Harvard University Press.

Lee, Lily Xiao Hong 1994. *The Virtue of Yin: Studies of Chinese Women*. Sydney: Wild Peony.

Lee, Thomas H. C. 2000. *Education in Traditional China: A History*. Leiden: Brill.

Leeming, Frank 1993. *The Changing Geography of China*. Oxford: Blackwell.

Legeza, Laszlo 1980. "Ming and Ch'ing Imperial *Tou-ts'ai* and *Wu-Ts'ai* Porcelains." *Arts of Asia* 10.1 (January–February): 100–107.

Legge, James, trans. 1893–1895. *The Chinese Classics*. London and Oxford: Clarendon Press. Reprinted by the Hong Kong University Press in 1979. Abbreviation: CC.

Lenk, Hans and Paul Gregor, eds. 1993. *Epistemological Issues in Classical Chinese Philosophy*. Albany: State University of New York Press.

Leonard, Jane Kate 1984. *Wei Yuan and China's Rediscovery of the Maritime World*. Cambridge, Mass.: Harvard University Press.

Leonard, Jane Kate and John Watt, eds. 1992. *To Achieve Security and Wealth: The Qing Imperial State and the Economy 1644–1911*. Ithaca: Cornell University Press.

Leslie, Donald D. 1986. *Islam in Traditional China: A Short History to 1800*. Canberra: Canberra College of Advanced Education.

Leung, Angela Ki Che 1987. "Organized Medicine in Ming-Qing China: State and Private Medical Institutions in the Lower Yangzi Region." *Late Imperial China* 8.1 (June): 134–66.

Leung, Angela Ki Che 1999. "Women Practicing Medicine in Premodern China." In Zurndorfer, ed. 1999: 101–34.

Leung, Angela Ki Che 2009. *Leprosy in China: A History.* New York: Columbia University Press.

Leung, Angela Ki Che, ed. 2006. *Medicine for Women in Imperial China.* Leiden: Brill.

Leung, Yuen-sang 1990. *The Shanghai Taotai: Linkage Man in a Changing Society 1843–1890.* Honolulu: University of Hawaii Press.

Levenson, Joseph. 1964. "The Humanistic Disciplines: Will Sinology Do?" *Journal of Asian Studies* 23.4 (August): 507–12.

Levius, John 1936. *The Foundations of Chinese Musical Art.* Peiping: Henry Vetch.

Levy, Dore 1999. *Ideal and Actual in The Story of the Stone.* New York: Columbia University Press.

Levy, Howard S. 1967. *Chinese Footbinding: The History of a Curious Erotic Custom.* New York: Bell Publishing.

Levy, Howard 1974. *Chinese Sex Jokes in Traditional Times.* Taipei: Chinese Association for Folklore.

Levy, Marion 1949. *The Family Revolution in Modern China.* New York: Octagon Books.

Levy, Marion 1953. "Contrasting Factors in the Modernization of China and Japan." *Economic Development and Cultural Change* 2 (October 1953): 161–97.

Levy, Marion 1962. "Some Aspects of 'Individualism' and the Problem of Modernization in China and Japan." *Economic Development and Cultural Change* 10.3 (April): 225–40.

Lewis, Mark E. 1990. *Sanctioned Violence in Early China.* Albany: State University of New York Press.

Lewis, Mark E. 1999. *Writing and Authority in Early China.* Albany: State University of New York Press.

Li, Baolong and Yang Shuqin, eds. 2006. *Zhongguo chuantong wenhua* (China's traditional culture). Beijing: Zhongguo renmin gongan daxue chubanshe.

Li, Changhao 1987. *Zhongguo Tianwenxue shi* (History of Chinese astronomy). Beijing: Kexue chubanshe.

Li, Chenyang, ed. 2000. *The Sage and the Second Sex: Confucianism, Ethics, and Gender.* Chicago and La Salle, Ill.: Open Court.

Li, Chu-tsing and James C. Y. Watt, eds. 1987. *The Chinese Scholar's Studio.* New York: The Asia Society Galleries.

Li, Chu-tsing, James Cahill, and Wai-Kam Ho, eds. 1991. *Artists and Patrons: Some Social and Economic Aspects of Chinese Painting.* Seattle: University of Washington Press.

Li, Cunyang 2004. "Qin Huitian and His General Study on the Five Rites." *Sungkyun Journal of East Asian Studies* 4.1: 156–83.

Li, Dun J. 1978. *The Ageless Chinese: A History.* New York: Pearson.

Li, Jing 2010. "Was Mao Really a Monster? The Academic Response to Chang and Halliday's *Mao: The Unknown Story*." *China Review International* 17.4: 408–12.

Li, Li 2012. *Baishan heishui Manzhou feng: Manzu minsu yanjiu* (Manchurian culture in the northeast: Research on Manchu folklore). Taibei: Guoli lishi bowuguan.

Li, Lillian 1982. "Introduction: Food, Famine and the Chinese State." *Journal of Asian Studies* 41.4 August: 687–707.

Li, Lillian 2007. *Fighting Famine in North China: State, Market, and Environmental Decline, 1690s–1990s.* Stanford: Stanford University Press.

Li, Lisha 1993. "Mystical Numbers and Manchu Traditional Music: A Consideration of the Relationship between Shamanic Thought and Musical Ideas." *British Journal of Ethnomusicology* 2: 99–115.

Li, San-pao 1978. "K'ang Yu-wei's Iconoclasm." Ph.D. dissertation, University of California, Davis.

Li, Thomas Shiyu and Naquin Susan. 1988. "The Baoming Temple: Religion and the Throne in Ming and Qing China." *Harvard Journal of Asiatic Studies* 48.1: 131–88.

Li, Wai-yee 1993. *Enchantment and Disenchantment: Love and Illusion in Chinese Literature.* Princeton: Princeton University Press.

Li, Wai-yee 1999. "Heroic Transformations: Women and National Trauma in Early Qing Literature." *Harvard Journal of Asiatic Studies* 59.2: 363–443.

Li, Wai-yee 2004. "Languages of Love and Parameters of Culture in 'Peony Pavilion' and *The Story of the Stone.*" In Eifring, ed. 2004: 237–70.

Li, Wai-yee 2005. "Women as Emblems of Dynastic Fall from Late Ming to Late Qing." In D. Wang and W. Shang, eds. 2005: 93–150.

Li, Wai-yee 2008. "The Filial Woman of Jiangdu." *Renditions* 70: 89–100.

Li, Wai-yee 2010a. "Early Qing to 1723." In Chang and Owen, eds. 2010: 152–244.

Li, Wai-yee 2010b. "Women Writers and Gender Boundaries during the Ming-Qing Transition." In Fong and Widmer 2010: 179–213.

Li, Xiaorong 2012. *Women's Poetry of Late Imperial China: Transforming the Inner Chambers.* Seattle: University of Washington Press.

Li, Yanguang and Guan Jie. 1991. *Manzu tongshi* (A general history of the Manchus). Shenyang: Liaoning minzu chubanshe.

Li, Yinghua 2006. *Ru Dao Fo yu Zhongguo chuantong wenhua jiaoyu* (Confucianism, Daoism and Buddhism and traditional Chinese cultural education). Wuchang: Wuhan daxue chubanshe.

Li, Yiyuan and Yang Guoshu, eds. 2005. *Zhongguo ren di xingge* (The character of the Chinese). Nanjing: Jiangsu jiaoyu chubanshe.

Li, Youzheng 2000–2001. "Modern Theory and Traditional Chinese Historiography. NOAG 167–70: 181–204. Available at www.uni–hamburg.de/oag/noag/noag2001_8.pdf.

Li, Yu 2012. "Character Recognition: A New Method of Learning to Read in Late Imperial China." *Late Imperial China* 33.2 (December): 1–39.

Li, Yu-ning, ed. 1992. *Chinese Women through Chinese Eyes.* Armonk, N.Y.: M. E. Sharpe.

Li, Yuhuang 2012. "Oneself as a Female Deity: Representations of Empress Dowager Cixi as Guanyin." *Nan Nü* 14: 75–118.

Li, Yunquan 2004. *Chaogong zhidu shilun: Zhongguo gudai duiwai guanxi tizhi yanjiu* (A history of the tributary system: Research on China's ancient institutions for [the conduct of] foreign relations). Beijing: Xinhua chubanshe.

Li, Zehou 1988. *Li Zehou ji* (The collected works of Li Zehou). Harbin: Heilongjiang jiaoyu chubanshe.

Li, Zhiyan and Cheng Wen 1996. *Zhongguo taoci jianshi* (A concise history of Chinese ceramics). Beijing: Waiwen chubanshe.

Liang, Congjie 1986. "Bu chonghe de quan—cong baike quanshu kan Zhong Xi wenhua (Non-congruent circles—The organization of encyclopedic knowledge in Chinese and Western cultures). *Zouxiang weilai* 4.

Liang, Jie, ed. 1895. *Jiali quanji* (A complete collection of guides to family rituals). Shanghai: n.p.

Liang, Linxia 2007. *Delivering Justice in Qing China: Civil Trials in the Magistrate's Court*. Oxford: Oxford University Press.

Liang, Qichao 2011. *Zhongguo jin sanbai nian xueshu shi* (A history of Chinese scholarship over the past three hundred years). Edited and annotated by Xia Xiaohong and Lu Yin.

Liao, Ben 1997. *Zhongguo gudai juchang shi* (History of the theater in ancient China). Zhengzhou: Zhongzhou guji chubanshe.

Library of Congress. "Prints and Photographs Online Catalogue." Available at www.loc.gov/pictures/index/subjects/.

Lieberthal, Kenneth et al., eds. 1991. *Perspectives on Modern China: Four Anniversaries*. Armonk, N.Y.: M. E. Sharpe.

Lin, Jiashu 1995. *Tulou yu Zhongguo quantong wenhua* (Earthen houses [of the Hakka people] and China's traditional culture). Shanghai: Shanghai renmin chubanshe.

Lin, Man-houng 1991. "Two Social Theories Revealed: Statecraft Controversies Over China's Monetary Crisis 1808–1854." *Ch'ing-shih wen-t'i* 12.2 (December): 1–35.

Lin, Diana Xiaoqing 2005. *Peking University: Chinese Scholarship and Intellectuals, 1898–1937*. Albany: State University of New York Press.

Lin, Tai-yi, trans. 1966. *Flowers in the Mirror*. Berkeley: University of California Press.

Lin, Yü-sheng 1979. *The Crisis of Chinese Consciousness*. Madison, Wisc.: Wisconsin University Press.

Lin, Yutang 1935. *My Country and My People*. New York: John Day.

Lin, Yutang 1967. *The Chinese Theory of Art*. London: G. P. Putnam's Sons.

Linduff, Katheryn M. and Karen S. Rubinson, eds. 2008. *Are All Warriors Male? Gender Roles on the Ancient Eurasian Steppe*. Lanham, Md.: Rowman and Littlefield.

Linqing 1877. *Hongxue yinyuan tuji* (Illustrated record of vast-snow destiny). Shanghai: Zhuyi tang. Compiled by Wang Xiqi.

Lipman, Jonathan and Stevan Harrell, eds. 1990. *Violence in China: Essays in Culture and Counterculture*. Ithaca: Cornell University Press.

Little, Daniel 1985. *Understanding Peasant China: Case Studies in the Philosophy of Social Science*. New Haven: Yale University Press.

Little, Daniel and Esherick Joseph. 1989. "Testing the Testers" *Journal of Asian Studies* 48.1 (February): 91–99.

Liu, Cary Y. 2010. "Archive of Power: The Qing Dynasty Imperial Garden-Palace at Rehe." *Guoli Taiwan daxue meishu shi yanjiu jikan* 28 (March): 6–82.

Liu, Dan 2010. "Patronage and Meaning of Tibetan Buddhist Temples Decreed by the Qing Emperors in Central China in the Early and Middle Qing Dynasty." Ph.D. dissertation, Chinese University of Hong Kong.

Liu, Fei-wen 2004. "Literacy, Gender, and Class: *Nüshu* and Sisterhood Communities in Southern Rural Hunan." *Nan Nü* 6.2: 241–82.

Liu, Fengyun, Dong Jianzhong, and Liu Wenpeng, eds. 2012. *Qingdai zhengzhi yu guojia rentong* (Politics and national identity in the Qing). Beijing: Shehui kexue wenxian chubanshe.

Liu, Guang'an 1990. "A Short Treatise on the Ethnic Legislation of the Qing Dynasty" *Social Sciences in China* 4 (Winter): 97–117.

Liu, Hui-chen Wang 1959. *The Traditional Chinese Clan Rules*. Locust Valley, N.Y.: J. J. Augustin.

Liu, James J. Y. 1966. *The Art of Chinese Poetry*. Chicago: University of Chicago Press.

Liu, James J. Y. 1975. *Chinese Theories of Literature*. Chicago: University of Chicago Press.

Liu, James J. Y. 1979. *Essentials of Chinese Literary Art*. Stanford: Stanford University Press.

Liu, James J. Y. 1988. *Language—Paradox—Poetics: A Chinese Perspective*. Princeton: Princeton University Press.

Liu, James T. C. 1985. "The Classical Chinese Primer: Its Three-Character Style and Authorship." *Journal of the American Oriental Society* 105.2 (April–June): 191–96.

Liu, Jiemin 1997. *Zhongguo chuantong wenhua jingshen* (The spirit of China's traditional culture). Guangzhou: Jinan daxue chubanshe.

Liu, Jinzao. 1935. *Huangchao xu wenxian tongkao* (Supplement to the encyclopedic examination of the historical records of the Qing dynasty). Shanghai: Shangwu yinshu guan.

Liu, Jun, ed. 2011. *Zhongguo suwen ku* (Treasury of [Chinese] folk literature). Beijing: Renmin chubanshe.

Liu, Kwang-Ching 1981. "World View and Peasant Rebellion." *Journal of Asian Studies* 40.2 (February): 295–326.

Liu, Kwang-Ching 1988. "Chinese Merchant Guilds: An Historical Inquiry." *Pacific Historical Review* 57.1 (February): 1–23.

Liu, Kwang-Ching and Richard J. Smith 1980. "The Military Challenge: The Northwest and the Coast." *CHC* 11.2: 202–73.

Liu, Kwang-Ching, ed. 1990. *Orthodoxy in Late Imperial China*. Berkeley: University of California Press.

Liu, Kwang-Ching and Richard Shek, eds. *Heterodoxy in Late Imperial China*. Honolulu: University of Hawaii Press, 2004.

Liu, Lexian, ed. 1997. *Wenxin diaolong* (The literary mind and the carving of dragons). Beijing: Zhongguo youyi chuban gongsi.

Liu, Lydia 2004. *The Clash of Empires: The Invention of China in Modern World Making*. Cambridge, Mass.: Harvard University Press.

Liu, Lydia, Rebecca E. Karl, and Dorothy Ko, eds. 2013. *The Birth of Chinese Feminism: Essential Texts in Transnational Theory.* New York: Columbia University Press.

Liu, Shih-shun 1975. *Vignettes from the Late Ch'ing.* Hong Kong: Chinese University Press.

Liu, Ts'un-yan, ed. 1984. *Chinese Middlebrow Fiction from the Ch'ing and Early Republican Eras.* Hong Kong: The Chinese University Press.

Liu, Tun-chen 1993. *Chinese Classical Gardens of Suzhou.* New York: McGraw-Hill. Translated by Lixian Chen.

Liu, Wu-chi and Irving Yucheng Lo, eds. 1975. *Sunflower Splendor: Three Thousand Years of Chinese Poetry.* Bloomington: Indiana University Press.

Liu, Wu-chi and Irving Yucheng Lo, eds. 1976. *K'uei Yeh Chi.* Bloomington: Indiana University Press, 1976. Chinese-language text for Liu and Lo, eds. 1975.

Liu, Xiaomeng 2001. *Manzu cong buluo dao guojia di fazhan* (The development of the Manchus from tribe to country) Shenyang: Liaoning minzu chubanshe.

Liu, Yizheng 2008. *Zhongguo wenhua shi* (History of Chinese culture). Shanghai: Shanghai kexue jishu wenxian chubanshe. Three volumes (originally published in 1964).

Liu, Zehua 2013–2014. "A Few Questions Regarding the Promotion of National Studies." *Contemporary Chinese Thought* 45.2–3 (Spring): 128–43.

Liu, Zhiwan 1983. *Zhongguo minjian xinyang lunji* (A collection of essays on Chinese folk beliefs). Taibei: Lianjing chuban shiye gongsi.

Lo, Hui-Chi 2009. "Political Advancement and Religious Transcendence: The Yongzheng Emperor's (1678–1735) Deployment of Portraiture." Ph.D. dissertation, Stanford University.

Lo, Irving Yucheng and William Schultz, eds. 1986. *Waiting for the Unicorn: Poems and Lyrics of China's Last Dynasty 1644–1911.* University of Indiana Press.

Loehr, Max 1970. "Art-Historical Art." *Oriental Art* 16 (Spring): 35–37.

Louie, Kam 2002. *Theorising Chinese Masculinity: Society and Gender in China.* Cambridge, Eng.: Cambridge University Press.

Louis, François 2003. "The Genesis of an Icon: The 'Taiji' Diagram's Early History." *Harvard Journal of Asiatic Studies* 63.1 (June): 145–96.

Lovin, Robin and Frank Reynolds, eds. 1985. *Cosmogony and Ethical Order: New Studies in Comparative Ethics.* Chicago and London: University of Chicago Press.

Lowe, H. Y. [Lu Xingyuan] 1983. *The Adventures of Wu.* Princeton: Princeton University Press.

Lu, Baoqian 2009. *Qingdai sixiang shi* (History of Qing thought). Shanghai: Huadong shifan daxue chubanshe.

Lu, Shendon Hsiao-Peng 1994. *From Historicity to Fictionality: The Chinese Poetics of Narrative.* Stanford: Stanford University Press.

Lü, Simian 2007. *Zhongguo wenhua shiliu jiang* (Sixteen lectures on Chinese culture). Tianjin: Tianjin guji chubanshe.

Lu, Weijing 2008. *True to Her Word: The Faithful Maiden Cult in Late Imperial China.* Stanford: Stanford University Press.

Lü, Zizhen 1975. *Jiali dacheng* (Great collection of family rituals). Taibei: Xibei chubanshe. Reprint of 1842 edition.

Lu, Xing and Herbert W. Simons 2006. "Transitional Rhetoric of Chinese Communist Party Leaders in the Post-Mao Reform Period: Dilemmas and Strategies." *Quarterly Journal of Speech* 92.3: 262–86.

Lufrano, Richard 1997. *Honorable Merchants: Commerce and Self-Cultivation in Late Imperial China.* Honolulu: University of Hawaii Press.

Lui, Adam Y. C. 1970. "The Ch'ing Civil Service: Promotions, Demotions, Transfers, Leaves, Dismissals and Retirements." *Journal of Oriental Studies* 8: 333–56.

Lui, Adam Y. C. 1971. "The Education of the Manchus: China's Ruling Race (1644–1911)." *Journal of Asian and African Studies* 6.2: 125–33.

Lui, Adam Y. C. 1981. *The Hanlin Academy.* Hamden, Conn.: Archon Books.

Lui, Adam Y. C. 1974a. "Syllabus of the Provincial Examination (*hsiang-shih*) under the Early Ch'ing 1644–1795." *Modern Asian Studies* 8: 391–96.

Lui, Adam Y. C. 1974b. "The Imperial College *Kuo-tzu-chien* in the Early Ch'ing 1644–1795." *Papers on Far Eastern History* 10: 147–66.

Lui, Adam Y. C. 1978. *Chinese Censors and the Alien Emperor 1644–1660.* Hong Kong.

Lui, Adam Y. C. 1990. *Ch'ing Institutions and Society.* Hong Kong: Centre of Asian Studies, University of Hong Kong.

Luo, Ergang 1984. *Lüying bing zhi* (History of the Green Standard Army). Beijing: Zhonghua shuju. Second edition.

Luo, Guang 1996. *Zhongguo zhexue sixiang shi: Qingdai* (History of Chinese philosophical thought: The Qing dynasty). Taibei: Taiwan xuesheng shuju.

Luo, Ming 1984. "The General State of Qing Historical Research in Recent Years [in the People's Republic of China]." *Ch'ing-shih wen-t'i* 5.2 (December): 116–34. Translated by Lynn Struve.

Luo, Yiqun 1993. *Zhongguo Miaozu wushu toushi* (A perspective on the magical arts of the Miao people). Beijing: Zhongyang minzu xueyuan chubanshe.

Luo, Zhongfeng 2001. *Zhongguo chuantong wenren shenmei shenghuo fangshi zhi yanjiu* (Research on the aesthetic lifestyle of traditional Chinese scholars). Taibei: Hongye wenhua shiye youxian gongsi.

Lynch, Daniel C. 2013. "Securitizing Culture in Chinese Foreign Policy Debates: Implications for Interpreting China's Rise." *Asian Survey* 53.4 (July–August): 629–52.

Lynn, Richard John 1994. *The Classic of Changes: A New Translation of the I Ching as Interpreted by Wang Bi.* New York: Columbia University Press.

Ma, Fengchen 1935. *Qingdai xingzheng zhidu yanjiu cankao shumu* (Annotated bibliography for research into the administrative system of the Qing dynasty). Beijing: Guoli Beijing daxue zhengzhi xi yanjiu shi.

Ma, Qian 2005. *Women in Traditional Chinese Theater: The Heroine's Play.* Lanham, Md.: University Press of America.

Ma, Xisha and Han Bingfang 1992. *Zhongguo minjian zongjiao shi* (A history of Chinese popular religion). Shanghai: Shanghai renmin chubanshe.

Ma, Yin, ed. 1989. *China's Minority Nationalities.* Beijing: Foreign Language Press.

Ma, Yong et al., eds. 1988. *Zhong Xi wenhua xin renshi* (New understandings of Chinese and Western culture). Shanghai: Fudan daxue chubanshe.

Macauley, Melissa A. 1998. *Social Power and Legal Culture: Litigation Masters in Late Imperial China*. Stanford: Stanford University Press.

MacCormack, Geoffrey 1990. *Traditional Chinese Penal Law*. Edinburgh: Edinburgh University Press.

MacFarquhar, Roderick 2012. "Who Was Mao Zedong?" *New York Review of Books* (October 25): 1–14.

MacFarquhar, Roderick and Michael Schoenhals, eds. 2006. *Mao's Last Revolution*. Cambridge, Mass.: Harvard University Press.

Macgowan, John 1912. *Men and Manners of Modern China*. London: T. F. Unwin.

Machle, Edward 1993. *Nature and Heaven in the Xunzi*. Albany: State University of New York Press.

Mackerras, Colin 1972. *The Rise of Peking Opera 1770–1870*. Oxford: Clarendon Press.

Madsen, Richard, et al., eds. 1989. *Unofficial China: Essays in Popular Culture and Thought*. Boulder, Colo.: Westview.

Mair, Victor H. 1989. *T'ang Transformation Texts: A Study of the Buddhist Contribution to the Rise of Vernacular Fiction and Drama in China*. Cambridge, Mass.: Harvard University Press.

Mair, Victor H., ed. 1991. *Schriftfestschrift: Essays on Writing and Language in Honor of John DeFrancis on His Eightieth Birthday*. Sino-Platonic Papers 27.

Mair, Victor H., ed. 1994. *The Columbia Anthology of Traditional Chinese Literature*. New York: Columbia University Press.

Mair, Victor H., Nancy C. Steinhardt, and Paul Golden, eds. 2005. *Hawai'i Reader in Traditional Chinese Culture*. Honolulu: University of Hawaii Press.

Mair, Victor and Mark Bender, eds. 2011. *The Columbia Anthology of Chinese Folk and Popular Literature*. New York: Columbia University Press.

Makeham, John 2003. *Transmitters and Creators: Chinese Commentators and Comentaries on the Analects*. Cambridge, Mass.: Harvard University Press.

Makeham, John 2008. *Lost Soul: "Confucianism" in Contemporary Chinese Academic Discourse*. Cambridge, Mass.: Harvard University Press.

Makeham, John, ed. 2003. *New Confucianism: A Critical Examination*. New York: Palgrave.

Makeham, John, ed. 2010. *Dao Companion to Neo-Confucian Philosophy*. Dordrecht: Springer.

Makeham, John and A-chin Hsiau, eds. 2005. *Cultural, Ethnic, and Political Nationalism in Contemporary Taiwan: Bentuhua*. New York: Palgrave.

Malek, Roman, ed. 1998. *Western Learning and Christianity in China: The Contribution and Impact of Johann Adam Schall von Bell, S.J. (1592–1666)*. Sankt Augustin, Germany: Jointly published by China-Zentrum and the Monumenta Serica Institute.

Mancall, Mark 1984. *China at the Center: Three Hundred Years of Foreign Policy*. New York: The Free Press.

Man-Cheong, Iona D. 2004. *The Class of 1761: Examinations, State and Elite in Eighteenth Century China*. Stanford: Stanford University Press.

Mane, Perrine, Jacques Le Goff, and Jean Lefort, eds. 2002. *Les calendriers: Leurs enjeux dans l'espace et dans le temps*. Paris: Somogy.

Mann, Susan L. 1987a. *Local Merchants and the Chinese Bureacracy 1750–1950.* Stanford: Stanford University Press.

Mann, Susan L. 1987b. "Widows in the Kinship, Class, and Community Structures of Qing Dynasty China." *Journal of Asian Studies* 46: 37–56.

Mann, Susan L. 1991. "Grooming a Daughter for Marriage: Brides and Wives in the Mid-Ch'ing Period." In Watson and Ebrey 1991: 204–30.

Mann, Susan L. 1992. "*Fuxue* Women's Learning by Zhang Xuecheng 1738–1801: China's First History of Women's Culture." *Late Imperial China* 13.1 (June): 40–62.

Mann, Susan L. 1994. "The Education of Daughters in the Mid-Ch'ing Period." In Elman and Woodside, eds. 1994: 19–49.

Mann, Susan L. 1996. "Women in the Life and Thought of Zhang Xuecheng." In Ivanhoe, ed. 1996: 94–120.

Mann, Susan L. 1997. *Precious Records: Women in China's Long Eighteenth Century.* Stanford: Stanford University Press.

Mann, Susan L. 1999. *East Asia (China, Japan, Korea): Women's and Gender History in Global Perspective.* Washington, D.C.: American Historical Association.

Mann, Susan L. 2000a. "Myths of Asian Womanhood." *Journal of Asian Studies* 59.4: 835–62.

Mann, Susan L. 2000b. "The Male Bond in Chinese History and Culture." *American Historical Review* 105.5: 1600–14.

Mann, Susan L. 2000c. "Work and Household in Chinese Culture: Historical Perspectives." In Entwisle and Henderson, eds. 2000: 15–32.

Mann, Susan L. 2005a. Untitled review of Theiss 2004. *Harvard Journal of Asiatic Studies.* 65.2 (December): 522–30.

Mann, Susan L. 2005b. "The Virtue of Travel for Women in the Late Empire." In Goodman and Larson 2005: 55–74.

Mann, Susan L. 2007. *The Talented Women of the Zhang Family.* Berkeley: University of California Press.

Mann, Susan L. 2011a. "Biographical Sources and Silences." In Judge and Hu, eds. 2011: 17–35.

Mann, Susan L. 2011b. *Gender and Sexuality in Modern Chinese History.* Cambridge, Eng.: Cambridge University Press.

Mann, Susan L. and Yu-yin Cheng, eds. 2001. *Under Confucian Eyes: Documents on Gender in East Asian History.* Berkeley and Los Angeles: University of California Press.

Manzu jianshi bianxie zu, ed. 2009. *Manzu jianshi* (A concise history of the Manchus). Beijing: Minzu chubanshe.

Mao, Zengyin, ed. 2005. *Sanzi jing yu Zhongguo minsu hua* (The Three Character Classic and Chinese popular illustrations). Beijing: Wuzhou chuanbo chubanshe.

March, Andrew 1974. *The Idea of China: Myth and Theory in Geographic Thought.* London and Vancouver: Praeger.

March, Benjamin. 1935. *Some Technical Terms of Chinese Painting.* Baltimore: Waverly Press, Inc.

March, Tamar, ed. 1987. *Interpreting the Humanities 1986.* Princeton: Princeton University Press.

Marks, Robert B. 1991. "Rice Prices, Food Supply and Market Structure in Eighteenth–Century South China." *Late Imperial China* 12.2 (December): 64–116.

Marks, Robert B. 2002. *The Origins of the Modern World: A Global and Ecological Narrative*. Lanham, Md.: Rowman and Littlefield.

Marsh, Robert M. 1996. *The Great Transformation: Social Change in Taipei, Taiwan since the 1960s*. Armonk, N.Y.: M. E. Sharpe.

Martin-Liao, Tienchi 1985. "Traditional Handbooks of Women's Education." In Gerstlacher et al. eds. 1985: 165–89.

Martin, W. A. P. 1881. *The Chinese: Their Education, Philosophy, and Letters*. New York: Harper and Brothers.

Martin, W. A. P. 1897. *A Cycle of Cathay*. Edinburgh and London: Oliphant, Anderson and Ferrier.

Martzloff, Jean-Claude 2000. "Le calendrier chinois: cadre historique général, structure, typologie et calcul." In Mane, Perrine, and Lefort, eds. 2002: 155–67.

Maspero, Henri 1981. *Taoism and Chinese Religion* Amherst, Mass.: University of Massachusetts Press. Translated by Frank Kierman Jr.

Massachusetts Institute of Technology. "Visualizing Cultures." Available at http:// ocw.mit.edu/ans7870/21f/21f.027/home/index.html. Abbreviation: MIT. This site provides a wealth of China-related (and Japan-related) images. Among the units of this project most relevant to this book are: "Rise and Fall of the Canton Trade System" by Peter C. Perdue; "The Garden of Perfect Brightness" by Lilian M. Li; "The First Opium War" by Peter C. Perdue; "John Thomson's China" by Allen Hockley; "'Pictures to Draw Tears from Iron': The North China Famine of 1876–1879" by Kathryn Edgerton-Tarpley; "Shanghai's Lens on the New(s)" by Jeffrey Wasserstrom and Rebecca Nedostup; "Throwing Off Asia" by John W. Dower; "The Cause of the Riots in the Yangtse Valley" by Peter C. Perdue; "Visualizing the Boxer Uprising" by Peter C. Perdue and Ellen Sebring; "The Empress Dowager and the Camera" by David Hogge; "China's Modern Sketch" by John A. Crespi. I am grateful to John Dower for permission to use several images from this website in my book.

Matthews, Barbara M. 2000. "The Chinese Value Survey: An Interpretation of Value Scales and Consideration of Some Preliminary Results." *International Education Journal* 1.2: 117–26.

Mayers, William 1874. *The Chinese Reader's Manual*. Shanghai: American Presbyterian Mission Press.

Mayers, William 1897. *The Chinese Government*. Shanghai: Kelly and Walsh.

McDermott, Joseph P. 2006. *A Social History of the Chinese Book: Books and Literati Culture in Late Imperial China*. Hong Kong: Hong Kong University Press.

McDowell, Stephen. 2001. "In Lieu of Flowers: The Transformation of Space and Self in Yuan Mei's (1716–1798) Garden Records." *New Zealand Journal of Asian Studies* 3.2 (December): 136–49.

McGill-Harvard-Yenching Library Ming-Qing Women's Writings Digitization Project. Available at http://digital.library.mcgill.ca/mingqing/english/project.htm. Abbreviation: MHY

McKnight, Brian 1992. *Law and Order in Sung China*. Cambridge, Eng.: Cambridge University Press.

McLaren, Anne 1998. "Crossing Gender Boundaries in China: *Nüshu* Narratives." Available at wwwsshe.murdoch.edu.au/intersections/back_issues/nushu2.html.

McMahon, Daniel 2012. "Geomancy and Walled Fortifications in Late Eighteenth Century China." *Journal of Military History* 76.2 (April): 373–93.

McMahon, Daniel 2015. *Rethinking the Decline of China's Qing Dynasty: Imperial Activism and Borderland Management at the Turn of the Nineteenth Century.* London: Routledge.

McMahon, R. Keith 1988. *Causality and Containment in Seventeenth-Century Chinese Fiction.* Leiden: Brill.

McMahon, R. Keith 1988. "A Case for Confucian Sexuality: The Eighteenth-Century Novel *Yesou puyan.*" *Late Imperial China* 9.2: 32–55.

McMahon, R. Keith 1995. *Misers, Shrews, and Polygamists: Sexuality and Male-Female Relations in Eighteenth-Century Chinese Fiction.* Durham: Duke University Press.

McMahon, R. Keith 2009. *Polygamy and Sublime Passion: Sexuality in China on the Verge of Modernity.* Honolulu: University of Hawaii Press.

McMahon, R. Keith 2013. *Women Shall Not Rule: Imperial Wives and Concubines in China from Han to Liao.* Lanham, Md.: Rowman and Littlefield.

McMullen, David 1988. *State and Scholars in T'ang China.* Cambridge, Eng.: Cambridge University Press.

McRae, John R. 1987. *The Northern School and the Formation of Early Ch'an Buddhism* Honolulu: University of Hawaii Press.

Meadows, Thomas Taylor 1849. *Translations from the Manchu with the Original Texts, Prefaced by an Essay on the Language.* Canton: S. W. Williams Press.

Meadows, Thomas Taylor 1856. *The Chinese and Their Rebellions.* London: Smith, Elder and Company.

Medhurst, W. H. 1838. *China: Its State and Prospects.* Boston: Crocker and Brewster.

Meijer, M. J. 1981. "The Price of a P'ai-lou." *T'oung Pao* 67: 288–304.

Meijer, M. J. 1985. "Homosexual Offenses in Ch'ing Law." *T'oung Pao* 71: 109–33.

Meijer, M. J. 1991. *Murder and Adultery in Late Imperial China: A Study of Law and Morality.* Leiden: Brill.

Meisner, Maurice 1986. *Mao's China and After.* New York: Free Press.

Meng Sen 1960. *Qingdai shi* (A history of the Qing dynasty). Taibei: Zhengzhong shuju.

Meng, Liuxi [Louis] 2007. *Poetry as Power: Yuan Mei's Female Disciple Qu Bingyun (1767–1810).* Lanham, Md.: Lexington Books.

Metzger Thomas 1970. "The State and Commerce in Imperial China." *Journal of Asian and African Studies* 6: 23–46.

Metzger Thomas 1973. *The Internal Organization of Ch'ing Bureaucracy.* Cambridge, Mass.: Harvard University Press.

Metzger, Thomas 1977. *Escape from Predicament: Neo-Confucianism and China's Evolving Political Culture.* New York: Columbia University Press.

Meyer, Jeffrey 1978. "*Feng-shui* of the Chinese City." *History of Religions* 18.2 (November): 138–55.

Meyer, Jeffrey 1991. *The Dragons of Tiananmen.* Columbia, S.C.: University of South Carolina Press.

Meyer-Fong, Tobie 2003. *Building Culture in Early Qing Yangzhou.* Stanford: Stanford University Press, 2003.

Meyer-Fong, Tobie 2007. "Books, Publishing Culture, and Society in Late Imperial China." *Journal of Asian Studies* 66.3 (August): 787–817.

Meyer-Fong, Tobie 2013. *What Remains: Coming to Terms with Civil War in 19th Century China.* Stanford: Stanford University Press.

Michael, Franz 1966 and 1972. *The Taiping Rebellion.* Seattle: University of Washington Press. Three volumes.

Miller, Harry 2009. *State versus Gentry in Late Ming Dynasty China, 1572–1644.* New York: Palgrave Macmillan.

Miller, Harry 2013. *State versus Gentry in Early Qing Dynasty China, 1644–1699.* New York: Palgrave Macmillan.

Miller, Lucien 1975. *Masks of Fiction in Dream of the Red Chamber.* Tucson: University of Arizona Press.

Miller, Tracy 2007. *The Divine Nature of Power: Chinese Ritual Architecture at the Sacred Site of Jinci.* Cambridge, Mass.: Harvard-Yenching Institute Monograph Series.

Millward, James A. 1998. *Beyond the Pass: Economy, Ethnicity and Empire in Qing Xinjiang, 1759–1864.* Stanford: Stanford University Press.

Millward, James A. Undated [c. 2010]. "What did the Qianlong court mean by "huairou yuanren"?: An examination of Manchu, Mongol, and Tibetan translations of the term as it appears in Chengde steles." Unpublished manuscript, available at: www.georgetown.edu/faculty/millwarj/website%20images/Cherishing%20Ambiguity.doc.

Millward, James A. et al., eds. 2006. *New Qing Imperial History: The Making of Inner Asian Empire at Qing Chengde.* London: Routledge.

Milward, James A., Yashushi Shinmen, and Jun Sugawara, eds. 2010. *Studies on Xinjiang Historical Sources in 17–20th Centuries.* Tokyo: Toyo Bunko.

Milne, William. 1857. *Life in China.* London: Routledge. Available at https://play.google.com/books/reader?id=81wBAAAAQAAJ&printsec=frontcover&output=reader&authuser=0&hl=en&pg=GBS.PR1.

Min, Jiayin, ed. 1995. *The Chalice and the Blade in Chinese Culture: Gender Relations and Social Models.* Beijing: China Social Sciences Publishing House.

Min, Tu-ki 1989. *National Polity and Local Power: The Transformation of Late Imperial China.* Cambridge, Mass.: Harvard Univesity Press. Edited by Philip Kuhn and Timothy Brook.

Minford, John, trans. 1979–1987. *The Story of the Stone.* Harmondsworth, Eng.: Penguin. Two volumes, 4 and 5. See also Hawkes 1973–1979.

Minford, John, trans. 2014. *I Ching (Yijing): The Book of Change.* New York: Viking Penguin.

Ming-Qing yanjiu tuidong weiyuanhui (Committee for the Promotion of Ming-Qing Studies). Available at http://mingching.sinica.edu.tw/.

Mittler, Barbara 2004. *A Newspaper for China? Power, Identity, and Change in Shanghai's News Media, 1872–1912.* Cambridge, Mass.: Harvard University Asia Center.

Miyazaki, Ichisada 1976. *China's Examination Hell*. New York: Weatherhill. Translated by Conrad Schirokauer.

Mo, Weimin and Wenju Shen 1999. "The Twenty-Four Paragons of Filial Piety: Their Didactic Role and Impact on Children's Lives." *Children's Literature Association Quarterly* 24.1 (Spring): 15–23.

Moll-Murata, Christine, Jianze Song, and Hans Ulrich Vogel, eds. 2005. *Chinese Handicraft Regulations of the Qing Dynasty: Theory and Application*. Munich: Iudicium Verlag.

Moore, Charles, ed. 1967. *The Chinese Mind*. Honolulu: University of Hawaii Press.

Morgan, Carole 2004. "The Chinese Game of *Shengguan tu*." *Journal of the American Oriental Society* 124.3 (July–September): 517–32.

Morse, H. B. 1908. *The Trade and Administration of the Chinese Empire*. New York and London: Longmans, Green and Co.

Mosca, Matthew W. 2013. *From Frontier Policy to Foreign Policy: The Question of India and the Transformation of Geopolitics in Qing China*. Stanford: Stanford University Press.

Moser, Leo 1985. *The Chinese Mosaic: The Peoples and Provinces of China*. Boulder, Colo.: Westview Press.

Mote, Frederick 1989. *Intellectual Foundations of China*. New York: McGraw-Hill.

Mote, Frederick 2003. *Imperial China 900–1800*. Cambridge, Mass.: Harvard University Press.

Mote, Frederick and Chu Hung-lam, eds. 1988. *Calligraphy and the East Asian Book*. Princeton: Trustees of Princeton University.

Mou, Sherry J. 2002. *Gentlemen's Prescriptions for Women's Lives: A Thousand Years of Biographies of Chinese Women*. Armonk, N.Y.: M. E. Sharpe.

Mou, Sherry J., ed. 1999. *Presence and Presentation: Women in the Chinese Literati Tradition*. New York: St. Martin's.

Mühlhahn, Klaus 2009. *Criminal Justice in China: A History*. Cambridge, Mass.: Harvard University Press.

Mullaney, Thomas 2011. *Coming to Terms with the Nation: Ethnic Classification in Modern China*. Stanford: Stanford University Press.

Mullaney, Thomas et al., eds. 2012. *Critical Han Studies*. Berkeley: University of California Press.

Muller, A. Charles, trans. 2013. *The Analects of Confucius*. Available at www.acmuller.net/con-dao/analects.html.

Mungello, David E. 1969. "Neo-Confucianism and *Wen-jen* Aesthetic Theory." *Philosophy East and West* 19.4 (October 1969): 367–83.

Mungello, David E. 1977. *Leibniz and Confucianism*. Honolulu: University of Hawaii Press.

Mungello, David E. 1989. *Curious Land: Jesuit Accomodation and the Origins of Sinology*. Honolulu: University of Hawaii Press.

Mungello, David E. 2008. *Drowning Girls in China: Female Infanticide Since 1650*. Lanham, Md.: Rowman and Littlefield.

Mungello, David E. 2009. *The Great Encounter of China and the West, 1500–1800*. Lanham, Md.: Rowman and Littlefield. Third edition.

Muramatsu, Yuji 1966. "A Documentary Study of Chinese Landlordism in the Late Ch'ing and Early Republican Kiangnan." *Bulletin of the American Oriental Society* 29.3: 566–99.

Murck, Alfreda and Wen C. Fong, eds. 1991. *Words and Images: Chinese Poetry, Calligraphy and Painting*. Princeton: Princeton University Press.

Murck, Christian, ed. 1976. *Artists and Traditions*. Princeton: Princeton University Press.

Murray, Dian H. 1987. *Pirates of the South China Coast 1790–1810*. Stanford: Stanford University Press.

Murray, Dian H. 1994. *The Origins of the Tiandihui: The Chinese Triads in Legend and History*. Stanford: Stanford University Press. In collaboration with Qin Baoqi.

Myers, Ramon 1980. *The Chinese Economy Past and Present*. Belmont, Calif.: Wadsworth.

Myers, Ramon 1991. "How Did the Modern Chinese Economy Develop?: A Review Article." *Journal of Asian Studies* 50.3 (August): 604–28.

Nakagawa, Tadahide 1799. *Shinzoku kibun* (A record of Qing dynasty customs). Tokyo: Setsuonkan zōhan. Reprinted in 1966 by Heibonsha (Tokyo). See also Fang Ke and Sun Xuanling, eds. 2006.

Nakamura, Hajime 1971. *Ways of Thinking of Eastern Peoples*. Honolulu: University of Hawaii Press. Translated by Philip Wiener.

Nakayama, Shigeru and Nathan Sivin, eds. 1973. *Chinese Science*. Cambridge, Mass.: Harvard University Press.

Nalan, Xingde 1995. *Nalan ci* (The song-lyrics of Nanlan Xingde). Shanghai: Shanghai guji chubanshe. Commentary by Zhang Caoren.

Nappi, Carla 2009. *The Monkey and the Inkpot: Natural History and Its Transformations in Early Modern China*. Cambridge, Mass.: Harvard University Press.

Naquin, Susan 1976. *Millenarian Rebellion in China: The Eight Trigrams Uprising of 1813*. New Haven: Yale University Press.

Naquin, Susan and Chün-fang Yü, eds. 1992. *Pilgrims and Sacred Sites in China*. Berkeley: University of California Press.

Naquin, Susan and Evelyn Rawski 1987. *Chinese Society in the Eighteenth Century*. New Haven: Yale University Press.

Nathan, Andrew 1976. *Peking Politics 1918–1923: Factionalism and the Failure of Constitutionalism*. Berkeley: University of California Press.

Nathan, Andrew 1985. *Chinese Democracy*. New York: Knopf.

Nathan, Andrew 1993. "Is Chinese Culture Distinctive?" *Journal of Asian Studies* 52.4 (November): 923–36.

Nathan, Andrew and Tse-hsin Chen 2004. "Traditional Social Values, Democratic Values, and Political Participation." *Asian Barometer Working Paper* 23: 1–27. Available at http://asianbarometer.org/newenglish/publications/workingpapers/no.23.pdf

National Palace Museum 2010. "Harmony and Integrity: The Yongzheng Emperor and His Times." Available at www.npm.gov.tw/exh98/yongzheng/en0201.htm.

Nedostup, Rebecca 2010. *Superstitious Regimes: Religion and the Politics of Chinese Modernity*. Cambridge, Mass.: Harvard East Asian Monographs.

Needham, Joseph 1965. *Time and Eastern Man.* London: Royal Anthropological Institute of Great Britain and Ireland.

Needham, Joseph 1976. *Moulds of Understanding.* London: Allen and Unwin.

Needham, Joseph and Ray Huang 1974. "The Nature of Chinese Society—A Technical Interpretation." *Journal of Oriental Studies* 12.1–2: 1–16.

Needham, Joseph et al. 1956–present. *Science and Civilisation in China.* Cambridge, Eng.: Cambridge University Press. Seven volumes, some (such as chapter 5) divided into several separately published parts. Abbreviation: SCC.

Needham, Rodney, ed. 1973. *The Right and the Left: Essays on Dual Symbolic Classification.* Chicago: University of Chicago Press.

Nevius, John. 1869. *China and the Chinese.* New York: Harper and Brothers.

Ng, Chin-keong 1983. *Trade and Society: The Amoy Network on the China Coast 1683–1735.* Singapore: Singapore University Press.

Ng, On-cho 2001. *Cheng-Zhu Confucianism in the Early Qing: Li Guangdi (1642–1718) and Qing Learning.* Albany: State University of New York Press.

Ng, On-cho 2003. "The Epochal Concept of 'Early Modernity' and the Intellectual History of Late Imperial China." *Journal of World History* 14.1: 37–61.

Ng, On-cho, ed. 2008. *The Imperative of Understanding: Chinese Philosophy, Comparative Philosophy, and Onto-Hermeneutics.* New York: Global Scholarly Publications.

Ng, On-cho and Q. Edward Wang, eds. 2005. *Mirroring the Past: The Writing and Use of History in Imperial China.* Honolulu: University of Hawaii Press.

Ng, So Kam 1992. *Styles and Techniques of Chinese Painting.* Seattle: University of Washington Press.

Ng, Vivien W. 1987. "Ideology and Sexuality: Rape Laws in Qing China." *Journal of Asian Studies* 46.1 (February): 57–70.

Ng, Vivien W. 1990. *Madness in Late Imperial China: From Illness to Deviance.* Norman: University of Oklahama Press.

Nie Chongzheng 1996. *Gongting yishu de guanghui: Qingdai gongting huihua luncong* (The glories of Qing court art: essays on Qing courtly painting). Taipei: Dongda tushu gongsi.

Nie, Yaodong 1992. *Mao Zedong yu Zhongguo chuantong wenhua* (Mao Zedong and China's traditional culture). Fuzhou: Fujian renmin chubanshe.

Nivison, David 1956. "Communist Ethics and Chinese Tradition." *Far Eastern Quarterly* 16.1 (November): 51–74.

Nivison, David 1966. *The Life and Thought of Chang Hsüeh-ch'eng 1738–1801.* Stanford: Stanford University Press.

Nivison, David and Arthur Wright, eds. 1959. *Confucianism in Action.* Stanford: Stanford University Press.

Noda, Jin and Takahiro Onuma, eds. 2010. *A Collection of Documents from the Kazakh Sultans to the Qing Dynasty.* Tokyo: University of Tokyo Research Center for Islamic Area Studies, TIAS Central Eurasian Research Series, Special Issue 1.

Norman, Jerry 1988. *Chinese.* Cambridge, Eng.: Cambridge University Press.

Norman, Jerry 2003. "The Manchus and Their Language." *Journal of the American Oriental Society* 123.3 (July–September 2003): 483–91.

Nylan, Michael and Thomas Wilson, eds. 2010. *Lives of Confucius*. New York: Doubleday.

O'Brien, Patrick 2010. "Ten Years of Debate on the Origins of the Great Divergence." *Reviews in History* 1008: N.p. Available at www.history.ac.uk/reviews/review/1008.

Obringer, Frédéric 1997. *L'aconit et l'orpiment. Drogues et poisons in Chine ancienne et médiévale*. Paris: Fayard.

Ocko, Jonathan 1973. "The British Museum's Peking Gazette." *Ch'ing-shih wen-t'i* 2.9 (January 1973): 35–49.

Ocko, Jonathan 1983. *Bureaucratic Reform in Provincial China: Ting Jih-ch'ang in Restoration Kiangsu, 1867–1870*. Cambridge, Mass.: Harvard University Press.

Ocko, Jonathan 1988. "I'll Take It All the Way to Beijing: Capital Appeals in the Qing." *Journal of Asian Studies* 47.2 (May): 293–98.

Ocko, Jonathan 1990. "Hierarchy and Harmony: Family Conflict as Seen in Ch'ing Legal Cases." In K. C. Liu, ed. 1990: 212–30.

Odin, Steve 1982. *Process Metaphysics and Hua-yen Buddhism*. Albany: State University of New York Press.

O'Malley, John W., S. J. et al., eds. 1999. *The Jesuits: Cultures, Sciences, and the Arts 1540–1773*. Toronto: University of Toronto Press.

Ono, Kazuko 1989. *Chinese Women in a Century of Revolution 1850–1950*. Stanford: Stanford University Press. Translated by Joshua Fogel.

Overmyer, Daniel 1976. *Folk Buddhist Religion*. Cambridge, Mass.: Harvard University Press.

Overmyer, Daniel 1986. *Religions of China: The World as a Living System*. New York: Macmillan Publishing Company.

Owen, Stephen 1985. *Traditional Chinese Poetry and Poetics: Omens of the World*. Madison: University of Wisconsin Press.

Owen, Stephen 1986. *Remembrances: The Experience of the Past in Classical Chinese Literature*. Cambridge, Mass.: Harvard University Press.

Owen, Stephen, ed. and trans. 1996. *An Anthology of Chinese Literature: Beginnings to 1911*. New York: Norton.

Oxnam, Robert 1975. *Ruling from Horseback: Manchu Politics in the Oboi Regency, 1661–1669*. Chicago: University of Chicago Press.

Paderni, Paola 1995. "I Thought I Would Have Some Happy Days: Women Eloping in Eighteenth-Century China." *Late Imperial China* 16.1: 1–32.

Paderni, Paola 1999. "Between Constraints and Opportunities: Widows, Witches, and Shrews in Eighteenth Century China." In Zurndorfer, ed. 1999: 258–85.

Palandri, Andrea Jung 1991. "Gender and Sexism in Chinese Language and Literature." In Victor H. Mair, ed. 1991: 167–70.

Panda Books 1986. *Poetry and Prose of the Ming and Qing*. Beijing: Panda Books.

Pang, Tatjana A. 2001. *Descriptive Catalogue of Manchu Manuscripts and Blockprints in the St. Petersburg Branch of the Institute of Oriental Studies Russian Academy of Sciences* 2. Wiesbaden: Harrassowitz.

Paper, Jordan 1985. "'Riding on a White Cloud': Aesthetics as Religion in China." *Religion* 15: 3–27.

Paper, Jordan et al., eds. 1997. *Through the Earth Darkly: Female Spirituality in Comparative Perspective*. New York: Continuum.

Parish, William and Martin K. Whyte 1978. *Village and Family in Contemporary China*. Chicago: University of Chicago Press.

Parker, E. H. 1899. *Chinese Customs*. Shanghai: Kelly and Walsh.

Parsons, James B. 1957. "The Culmination of a Chinese Peasant Rebellion: Chang Hsien-chung in Szechwan, 1644–46." *Journal of Asian Studies* 16.3 (May): 387–400.

Parsons, James B. 1970. *Peasant Rebellions in the Late Ming Dynasty*. Tucson: University of Arizona Press.

Pas, Julian F., ed. 1989. *The Turning of the Tide: Religion in China Today*. Oxford, Eng.: Oxford University Press.

Paton, Michael J. 2013. *Five Classics of Fengshui: Chinese Spiritual Geography in Historical and Environmental Perspective*. Leiden: Brill.

Percival, David, trans. 1971. *Chinese Connoiseurship: The Essential Criteria of Antiquities, Being a Translation of the Ko Ku Yao Lun*. New York: Praeger.

Perdue, Peter 1987. *Exhausting the Earth: State and Peasant in Hunan 1500–1850*. Cambridge, Mass.: Harvard University Press.

Perdue, Peter 2000. Review of Pomeranz 2000. H-World, H-Net Reviews. Available at www.h-net.org/reviews/showrev.php?id=4476.

Perdue, Peter 2005. *China Marches West: The Qing Conquest of Central Asia*. Cambridge, Mass.: Harvard University Press.

Perkins, Dwight H. 1967. "Government as an Obstacle to Industrialization." *Journal of Economic History* 27.4 (December): 478–92.

Perkins, Dwight H. 2006. "Stagnation and Growth in China over the Millennium: A Comment on Angus Maddison's 'China in the World Economy, 1300–2030.'" *International Journal of Business* 11.3: 255–64.

Perry, Elizabeth J. and Stevan Harrell, eds. 1982. "Symposium: Syncretic Sects in Chinese Society." *Modern China* 8.3 (July and October): 283–305.

Peterson, Barbara Bennett et al., eds. 2000. *Notable Women of China: Shang Dynasty to the Early Twentieth Century*. Armonk, N.Y.: M. E. Sharpe.

Peterson, Willard, et al. eds. 1994. *The Power of Culture: Studies in Chinese Cultural History*. Hong Kong: Chinese University Press.

Plaks, Andrew 1976. *Archetype and Allegory in the Dream of the Red Chamber*. Princeton: Princeton University Press.

Plaks, Andrew 1987. *The Four Masterworks of the Ming Novel*. Princeton: Princeton University Press.

Plaks, Andrew 1988. "Where the Lines Meet: Parallelism in Chinese and Western Literatures." *CLEAR* 10.1/2 (July): 43–60.

Plaks, Andrew 1997. Conceptual Models in Chinese Narrative Theory." *Journal of Chinese Philosophy* 4: 25–47.

Plaks, Andrew 2004. "Research on the Gest Library Cribbing Garment." *East Asian Library Journal* 11.2 (Autumn): 1–39.

Plaks, Andrew, ed. 1977. *Chinese Narrative*. Princeton: Princeton University Press.

Platt, Stephen R. 2012. *Autumn in the Heavenly Kingdom: China, the West, and the Epic Story of the Taiping Civil War*. New York: Knopf.

Plopper, Clifford 1926. *Chinese Religion Seen Through the Proverb*. Shanghai: The China Press.

Po, Sung-nien and David Johnson 1992. *Domesticated Deities and Auspicious Emblems: The Iconography of Everyday Life in Village China*. Berkeley: University of California Press.

Polachek, James M. 1992. *The Inner Opium War*. Cambridge, Mass.: Harvard University Press.

Pollak, Michael 1980. *Mandarins, Jews and Missionaries: The Jewish Experience in the Chinese Empire*. Philadelphia: Jewish Publication Society of America.

Pollard, David E., ed. and trans. 2014. *Real Life in China at the Height of Empire Revealed by the Ghosts of Ji Xiaolan*. Hong Kong: The Chinese University Press.

Poling, Kathleen Margaret 2012. "The Performance of Power and the Administration of Justice: Capital Punishment and the Case Review System in Late Imperial China." Ph.D. dissertation, University of California, Berkeley.

Pomeranz, Kenneth 1997. "Power, Gender, and Pluralism in the Cult of the Goddess of Taishan." In Huters, ed. 1997: 182–204.

Pomeranz, Kenneth 2000. *The Great Divergence: China, Europe, and the Making of the Modern World Economy*. Princeton: Princeton University Press.

Pomeranz, Kenneth 2001. "Is There an East Asian Development Path? Long-Term Comparisons, Constraints, and Continuities." *Journal of the Economic and Social History of the Orient* 44.3: 322–62.

Pomeranz, Kenneth 2002. "Beyond the East-West Binary: Resituating Development Paths in the Eighteenth Century World." *Journal of Asian Studies* 61.2: 539–90. See also his exchange with Philip Huang in *Journal of Asian Studies* 62.1 (2003): 157–87.

Pomeranz, Kenneth and Steven Topik 1999. *The World That Trade Created: Society, Culture, and the World Economy 1400 to the Present*. Armonk, N.Y.: M. E. Sharpe.

Pong, David 2003. *Shen Pao-chen and China's Modernization in the Nineteenth Century*. Cambridge, Eng.: Cambridge University Press.

Porkert, Manfred 1988. *Chinese Medicine*. New York: Holt. Translated by Mark Howson.

Porter, David 2010. "Sinicizing Early Modernity: The Imperatives of Historical Cosmopolitanism." *Eighteenth Century Studies* 43.3 (Spring): 299–306.

Pratt, Leonard and Su-Hui Chiang, trans. 1983. *Six Records of a Floating Life*. New York: Viking Press.

Pregadio, Fabrizio 2006. *Great Clarity: Daoism and Alchemy in Early Medieval China*. Stanford: Stanford University Press.

Pregadio, Fabrizio, ed. 2008. *The Encyclopedia of Taoism*. New York: Routledge. Two volumes.

Pregadio, Fabrizio, trans. 2009. *Awakening to Reality: The "Regulated Verses" of the Wuzhen pian, a Taoist Classic of Internal Chemistry*. Mountainview, Calif.: Golden Elixir Press.

Pregadio, Fabrizio, trans. 2011. *The Seal of the Unity of the Three: A Study and Translation of the Cantong qi, the Source of the Taoist Way of the Golden Elixir*. Mountainview, Calif.: Golden Elixir Press.

Pregadio, Fabrizio, trans. 2013. *Cultivating the Tao: Taoism and Internal Alchemy.* Mountainview, Calif.: Golden Elixir Press.

Pye, Lucian 1981. *The Dynamics of Chinese Politics.* Cambridge, Mass.: Oelgeschlager, Gunn and Hain.

Pye, Lucian 1988. *The Mandarin and the Cadre: China's Political Cultures.* Ann Arbor: University of Michigan Press.

Qian, Mu 1964. *Zhongguo jin sanbai nian xueshu shi* (History of the past three hundred years of Chinese scholarship). Taibei: Taiwan shangwu yinshu guan.

Qian, Mu 1971. *Zhongguo wenhua jingshen* (The spirit of Chinese culture). Taibei: Sanmin shuju.

Qian, Mu 1994. *Zhongguo lishi jingshen* (The spirit of Chinese history). Taibei: Lianjing chuban shiye gongsi.

Qian, Mu 2011. *Zhongguo sixiang shi* (History of Chinese thought). Revised edition. Taibei: Lantai chubanshe.

Qian, Nanxiu 2004. "'Borrowing Foreign Mirrors and Candles to Illuminate Chinese Civilization': Xue Shaohui's Moral Vision in the Biographies of Foreign Women." *Nan Nü* 6.1: 60–102.

Qian, Nanxiu 2005. "Poetic Reform amidst Political Reform: The Late Qing Woman Poet Xue Shaohui (1866–1911)." *Hsiang Lectures on Chinese Poetry*, Center for East Asian Research, McGill University: 1–48.

Qian, Nanxiu 2008. "The Mother *Nü Xuebao* versus the Daughter *Nü Xuebao*: Generational Differences between 1898 and 1902 Women Reformers." In Qian, Fong, and Smith, eds. 2008: 257–92.

Qian, Nanxiu 2010. "Xue Shaohui and Her Poetic Chronicle of Late Qing Reforms." In Fong and Widmer, eds. 2010: 339–72.

Qian, Nanxiu 2013. "Transformation of the Min (Fujian) *Cainü* Culture in the Late Qing Reform Era." *Ming-Qing Studies* (November): 285–311.

Qian, Nanxiu 2014. "Shen Queying: A Reform Martyr's Widow or a Reform Martyr Herself?" Unpublished paper for the European Association for Chinese Studies Annual Meeting, Frankfurt (July 4–5).

Qian, Nanxiu 2015. *Politics, Poetics, and Gender in Late Qing China: Xue Shaohui (1866–1911) and the Era of Reform.* Stanford: Stanford University Press.

Qian, Nanxiu, Grace Fong, and Richard J. Smith, eds. 2008. *Different Worlds of Discourse: New Views of Gender and Genre in Late Qing and Early Republican China.* Leiden: Brill.

Qian, Wenzhong 2010. *Chuantong de zaisheng: Qian Wenzhong yanjiang ji* (The regeneration of tradition: The collected lectures of Qian Wenzhong). Beijing: Xinxing chubanshe.

Qian, Xuan 1996. *Sanli tonglun* (A general discussion of the three ritual [classics]). Nanjing: Nanjing shifan daxue chubanshe.

Qian, Yulin and Huang Lili, eds. 1996. *Zhonghua gudai wenhua cidian* (Dictionary of ancient Chinese culture). Jinan: Qi Lu shushe.

Qin, Huidian 1880. *Wuli tongkao* (A comprehesive analysis of the five categories of ritual). Shanghai: Jiangsu shuju.

Qinding Da Qing huidian (Imperially approved collected statutes of the Qing dynasty, 1899). Available at http://archive.org/details/02088170.cn.

Qinding Libu 1966. *Qinding Libu zeli* (Imperially endorsed regulations of the Board of Ritual). Taibei: Chengwen chubanshe. Originally printed in 1844.

Qing, Xitai, ed. 1990. *Daojiao yu Zhongguo chuantong wenhua* (Religious Daoism and China's traditional culture). Fuzhou: Fujian renmin chubanshe.

Qingshi bianzuan weiyuanhui, ed. 1961. *Qingshi* (History of the Qing dynasty). Taibei: Guofang yanjiu yuan.

Qiu, Ren and Lin Xianghua 1995. *Zhongguo chuantong wenhua jinghua* (The essence of China's traditional culture). Shanghai: Fudan daxue.

Qiu, Xinli 2010. *Li Zhaoluo pingzhuan* (A critical biography of Li Zhaoluo). Nanjing: Jiangsu renmin chubanshe.

Ramsey, S. Robert. 1987. *The Languages of China*. Princeton: Princeton University Press.

Rankin, Mary 1986. *Elite Activism and Political Transformation in China: Zhejiang Province 1865–1911*. Stanford: Stanford University Press.

Rankin, Mary 1994. "Managed by the People: Officials, Gentry and the Foshan Charitable Granary, 1795–1845." *Late Imperial China* 15.2 (December): 1–52.

Rapp, John A. 2009. "Continuing the Reevaluation: Four Studies of the Cultural Revolution." *China Review International* 16.2: 160–65.

Rawski, Evelyn S. 1979. *Education and Popular Literacy in Ch'ing China*. Ann Arbor: University of Michigan Press.

Rawski, Evelyn S. 1991a. "Research Themes in Ming-Qing Socioeconomic History—The State of the Field." *Journal of Asian Studies* 50.1 (February): 84–111.

Rawski, Evelyn S. 1991b. "Ch'ing Imperial Marriage and Problems of Rulership." In Watson and Ebrey 1991: 170–203.

Rawski, Evelyn S. 1996. "Reenvisioning the Qing: The Significance of the Qing Period in Chinese History." *Journal of Asian Studies*, 55.4 (November): 829–50.

Rawski, Evelyn S. 1998. *The Last Emperors: A Social History of Qing Imperial Institutions*. Berkeley: University of California Press.

Rawski, Evelyn S. *Early Modern China and Northeast Asia*. Cambridge, England: Cambridge University Press.

Rawski, Evelyn S. and Jessica Rawson, eds. 2005. *China: The Three Emperors 1662–1795*. London: Royal Academy Books.

Rawski, Thomas G. 2011. "Human Resources and China's Long Economic Boom." *Asia Policy* 12 (July): 33–78.

Rawski, Thomas G. and Lillian Li, eds. 1992. *Chinese History in Economic Perspective*. Berkeley: University of California Press.

Redwood French, Rebecca and Mark A. Nathan, eds. 2014. *Buddhism and Law: An Introduction*. New York: Cambridge University Press.

Reed, Bradly W. 2000. *Talons and Teeth: County Clerks and Runners in the Qing Dynasty*. Stanford: Stanford University Press.

Reed, Christopher A. 2004. *Gutenberg in Shanghai: Chinese Print Capitalism, 1876–1937*. Honolulu: University of Hawaii Press.

Reichelt, Karl. 1934. *Truth and Tradition in Chinese Buddhism*. Shanghai: Commercial Press. Translated by Katrina Bugge.

Ren, Cheng. 1991. *Zhongguo minjian jinji* (Popular taboos in China). Beijing: Zuojia.

Reynolds, Douglas R. 1993. *China, 1898–1912: The Xinzheng Revolution and Japan.* Cambridge, Mass.: Harvard Council on East Asian Studies.

Reynolds, Frank and Theodore Ludwig, eds. 1980. *Transitions and Transformations in the History of Religions.* Leiden: Brill.

Rhoads, Edward 2000. *Manchus and Han: Ethnic Relations and Political Power in Late Qing and Early Republican China, 1861–1928.* Seattle: University of Washington Press.

Rhoads, Edward 2011. *Stepping Forth into the World: The Chinese Educational Mission to the United States, 1872–81.* Hong Kong: Hong Kong University Press.

Richard, L. 1908. *Comprehensive Geography of the Chinese Empire and Dependencies.* Shanghai: T'usewei Press. Translated by M. Kennelly.

Rickert, Adele, ed. 1978. *Chinese Approaches to Literature from Confucius to Liang Ch'i-ch'ao.* Princeton: Princeton University Press.

Rickett, W. Allyn 1985. *Guanzi: Political, Economic and Philosophical Essays from Early China.* Princeton: Princeton University Press.

Ridley, Charles P. 1977. "Theories of Education in the Ch'ing Period." *Ch'ing-shih wen-t'i* 3.8 (December): 34–49.

Riegel, Jeffrey 2010. "Yuan Mei (1716–1798) and a Different 'Elegant Gathering.'" *CLEAR* 32: 95–112.

Roberts, Moss, trans. 1999. *Three Kingdoms: A Historical Novel.* Berkeley: University of California Press. A two-volume version was published by the same press in 2004.

Robertson, Maureen 1992. "Voicing the Feminine: Constructions of the Gendered Subject in Lyric Poetry by Women of Medieval and late Imperial China." *Late Imperial China* 13.1 (June): 63–110.

Robertson, Maureen 2010. "Literary Authorship by Late Imperial Governing-Class Chinese Women and the Emergence of a 'Minor Literature.'" In Fong and Widmer, eds. 2010: 375–86.

Robinet, Isabelle and Fabrizio Pregadio 2011. *The World Upside Down: Essays on Taoist Internal Chemistry.* Golden Elixir Press. Available at www.goldenelixir.com/goldenelixir_press.html.

Robinson, David M., ed. 2008. *Culture, Courtiers, and Competition: The Ming Court (1368–1644).* Cambridge, Mass.: Harvard University Press.

Rogers, Howard and Sherman E. Lee 1988. *Masterworks of Ming and Qing Painting from the Forbidden City.* Lansdale, Penn.: International Arts Council.

Rolston, David L. 1997. *Traditional Chinese Fiction and Fiction Commentary: Reading and Writing Between the Lines.* Stanford: Stanford University Press.

Rolston, David L., ed. 1990. *How to Read the Chinese Novel.* Princeton: Princeton University Press.

Ronan, Charles and Bonnie B. C. Oh, eds. 1988. *East Meets West: The Jesuits in China 1582–1773.* Chicago: Loyola University Press.

Ropp, Paul S. 1976. "Seeds of Change: Reflections on the Condition of Women in the Early and Mid Ch'ing." *Signs* 2.1 (Autumn): 5–23.

Ropp, Paul S. 1981. *Dissent in Early Modern China.* Ann Arbor: University of Michigan Press.

Ropp, Paul S. 1994. "Women in Late Imperial China: A Review of Recent English-Language Scholarship." *Women's History* 3: 347–83.

Ropp, Paul S. 2001. *Banished Immortal: Searching for Shuangqing, China's Peasant Woman Poet*. Ann Arbor: University of Michigan Press.

Ropp, Paul S. 2002. "Chinese Women in the Imperial Past: New Perspectives." *China Review International* 9.1 (Spring): 41–51.

Ropp, Paul S. et al., eds. 2001. *Passionate Women: Female Suicide in Late Imperial China*. Leiden: Brill.

Ropp, Paul S., ed. 1990. *Heritage of China: Contemporary Perspectives on Chinese Civilization*. Berkeley: University of California Press.

Rosemont, Henry Jr. 1974. "On Representing Abstractions in Archaic Chinese." *Philosophy East and West* 24.1 (January): 71–88.

Rosemont, Henry Jr. and Roger T. Ames, trans. 2009. *The Chinese Classic of Family Reverence: A Philosophical Translation of the Xiaojing*. Honolulu: University of Hawai'i Press.

Rosemont, Henry Jr. ed. 1984. *Explorations in Early Chinese Cosmology*. Chico, Calif.: Scholars Press.

Rosemont, Henry Jr., ed. 1991. *Chinese Texts and Philosophical Contexts*. La Salle, Ill.: Open Court Press.

Rosenlee, Li-Hsiang Lisa 2006. *Confucianism and Women: A Philosophical Interpretation*. Albany: State University of New York Press.

Ross, Robert S. 2006. "Taiwan's Fading Independence Movement." *Foreign Affairs* (March/April). Available at www.foreignaffairs.com/articles/61516/robert-s-ross/taiwans-fading-independence-movement.

Rossabi, Morris, ed. 1983. *China Among Equals*. Berkeley: University of California Press.

Roux, Alain 2009. *Le singe et le tigre: Mao, un destin chinois*. Paris: Larousse.

Rowe, William T. 1984. *Hankow: Commerce and Society in a Chinese City 1796–1889*. Stanford: Stanford University Press.

Rowe, William T. 1989. *Hankow: Conflict and Community in a Chinese City 1796–1895*. Stanford: Stanford University Press.

Rowe, William T. 1992. "Women and the Family in Mid-Qing Social Thought: The Case of Ch'en Hung-mou." *Late Imperial China* 13.2: 1–41.

Rowe, William T. 1998. "Ancestral Rites and Political Authority in Late Imperial China: Chen Hongmou in Jiangxi." *Modern China* 24: 378–407.

Rowe, William T. 2001. *Saving the World: Chen Hongmou and Elite Consciousness in Eighteenth-Century China*. Stanford: Stanford University Press.

Rowe, William T. 2009. *China's Last Empire: The Great Qing*. Cambridge, Mass.: Harvard University Press.

Rowley, George 1970. *Principles of Chinese Painting*. Princeton: Princeton University Press.

Roy, David Todd, trans. 1993–2013. *Plum in the Golden Vase or Chin P'ing Mei*. Princeton: Princeton University Press. Five volumes.

Rozman, Gilbert. 1982. *Population and Marketing Settlements in Ch'ing China*. Cambridge, Eng.: Cambridge University Press.

Rozman, Gilbert et al. 1982. *The Modernization of China.* New York: The Free Press.

Rozman, Gilbert, ed. 1991. *The East Asian Region: Confucian Heritage and Its Modern Adaptation.* Princeton: Princeton University Press.

Ruan, Fang Fu. 1991. *Sex in China: Studies in Sexology in Chinese Culture.* New York: Plenum Press.

Rudolph, Jennifer 2008. *Negotiated Power in Late Imperial China: The Zongli Yamen and the Politics of Reform.* Ithaca: Cornell University East Asia Program.

Ruitenbeek, Klaus 1993. *Carpentry and Building in Late Imperial China: A Study of the Fifteenth-Century Carpenter's Manual Lu Ban Jing.* Leiden: Brill.

Saari, Jon 1990. *Legacies of Childhood: Growing up Chinese in a Time of Crisis 1890–1920.* Cambridge, Mass.: Harvard University Press.

Sakai, Tadao 2011. *Chūgoku nichiyō ruishoshi no kenkyū* (Research on Chinese encyclopedias for daily use). Tōkyō: Kokusho Kankōkai.

Sander, Graham, trans. 2011. *Six Records of a Life Adrift.* Indianapolis: Hackett Publishing.

Sands, Barbara and Ramon Myers 1990. "Economics and Macroregions: A Reply to Our Critics." *Journal of Asian Studies* 49.2 (May): 344–46.

Sangren, P. Steven 1987. *History and Magical Power in a Chinese Community.* Stanford: Stanford University Press.

Santangelo, Paolo 2013. *Zibuyu, "What The Master Would Not Discuss," according to Yuan Mei (1716–1798): A Collection of Supernatural Stories.* Leiden: Brill. Two volumes.

Santangelo, Paolo and Donatella Guida, eds. 2006. *Love, Hatred, and Other Passions: Questions and Themes on Emotions in Chinese Civilization.* Leiden: Brill.

Santangelo, Paolo, ed. *Ming Qing Studies 2013.* Rome: Aracne editrice.

Saso, Michael 1978. "What is the *Ho-t'u?*" 17.3 (February–May): 399–416.

Saso, Michael 1978. *The Teachings of Taoist Master Chuang.* New Haven: Yale University Press, 1978.

Saso, Michael 1989. *Taoism and the Rite of Cosmic Renewal.* Pullman: Washington State University Press.

Saso, Michael 1991. *Blue Dragon White Tiger: Taoist Rites of Passage.* Honolulu: University of Hawaii Press.

Saussy, Haun. 1993. *The Problem of a Chinese Aesthetic.* Stanford: Stanford University Press.

Schaeffer, Kurtis R., Matthew T. Kapstein, and Gray Tuttle. eds. 2013. *Sources of Tibetan Tradition.* New York: Columbia University Press.

Schafer, Dagmar 2011. *The Crafting of the 10,000 Things: Knowledge and Technology in Seventeenth Century China.* Chicago: University of Chicago Press.

Scheid, Volker 2007. *Currents of Tradition in Chinese Medicine 1626–2006.* Seattle: Eastland.

Schmidt, J. D. 2003. *Harmony Garden: The Life, Literary Criticism, and Poetry of Yuan Mei (1716–1798).* London: Routledge.

Schmidt, J. D. 2008. "Yuan Mei (1716–98) on Women." *Late Imperial China* 29.2 (December): 129–85.

Schmidt, P. 1932. "Chinesische Elemente im Mandschu. Mit Wörterverzeichnis." *Asia Major* 7: 573–628.

Schmidt-Glintzer, Helwig, Achim Mittag, and Jörn Rüsen, eds. 2005. *Historical Truth, Historical Criticism, and Ideology: Chinese Historiography and Historical Culture from a New Comparative Perspective.* Leiden: Brill.

Schoppa, R. Keith 1982. *Chinese Elites and Political Change: Zhejiang Province in the Early Twentieth Century.* Cambridge, Mass.: Harvard University Press.

Schram, Stuart 1969. *The Political Thought of Mao Tse-tung.* New York: Praeger.

Schram, Stuart 1974. *Chairman Mao Talks to the People.* New York: Pantheon.

Schram, Stuart 1989. *The Thought of Mao Tse-tung* Cambridge, Eng.: Cambridge University Press.

Schram, Stuart, ed. 1987. *Foundations and Limits of State Power in China.* London: School of Oriental and African Studies.

Schran, Peter 1978. "A Reassessment of Inland Communications in Late Ch'ing China" *Ch'ing-shih wen-t'i* 3.10 (November): 28–48.

Schwarcz, Vera 1986. *The Chinese Enlightenment: Intellectuals and the Legacy of the May Fourth Movement of 1919.* Berkeley: University of California Press.

Schwarcz, Vera 1991. "No Solace from Lethe: History Memory and Cultural Identity in Twentieth–Century China." *Daedalus* 120.2 (Spring): 85–112.

Schwartz, Benjamin 1964. *In Search of Wealth and Power: Yen Fu and the West.* Cambridge, Mass.: Harvard University Press.

Schwartz, Benjamin 1985. *The World of Thought in Ancient China.* Cambridge, Mass.: Harvard University Press.

Schwartz, Benjamin, ed. 1972. *Reflections on the May Fourth Movement.* Cambridge, Mass.: Harvard University Press.

Seidel, Anna and Holmes Welch, eds. 1979. *Facets of Taoism: Essays in Chinese Religion.* New Haven: Yale University Press.

Seiwert, Hubert and Xisha Ma 2003. *Popular Religious Movements and Heterodox Sects in Chinese History.* Leiden: Brill.

Shadick, Harold, trans. 1952. *The Travels of Lao Ts'an.* Ithaca: Cornell University Press.

Shambaugh, David, ed. 2000. *The Modern Chinese State.* Cambridge, Eng.: Cambridge University Press.

Shang, Wei 1998. "Ritual, Ritual Manuals, and the Crisis of the Confucian World: An Interpretation of *Rulin waishi*." *Harvard Journal of Asiatic Studies* 58.2 (December): 373–424.

Shang, Wei 2003. "'Jin Ping Mei' and Late Ming Print Culture." In Zeitlin and Liu, eds. 2003: 187–238.

Shang, Wei 2006. "The Making of the Everyday World: *Jin Ping Mei* and Encyclopedias for Daily Use." In Wang and Shang, eds. 2006: 63–92.

Shang, Wei 2010. "The Literary Culture and Its Demise (1723–1840)." In Chang and Shang, eds. 2010: 245–342.

Shang, Wei, 2014a. *"The Story of the Stone and the Art of Deceiving in the Manchu Court, 1723–1796."* Paper delivered at the University of Washington, March 6.

Shang, Wei 2014b. "Writing and Speech: Rethinking the Issue of Vernaculars in Early Modern China." In Elman, ed. 2014: 254–302.

Shanghai guji chubanshe, ed. 1987. *Zhongguo wenhua shi sanbai ti* (Three hundred questions concerning China's cultural history). Shanghai: Shanghai guji chubanshe.

Shapiro, Sidney, trans. 1981. *Outlaws of the Marsh*. Bloomington: Indiana University Press.

Shaughnessy, Edward 2014. *Unearthing the Changes: Recently Discovered Manuscripts of the Yi Jing (I Ching) and Related Texts*. New York: Columbia University Press.

Shen, Fuwei 1985. *Zhong Xi wenhua jiaoliu shi* (A History of Sino-Western cultural interaction). Shanghai: Shanghai ren min chu ban she.

Shen, Vincent 1993. "Creativity as Synthesis of Contrasting Wisdoms: An Interpretation of Chinese Philosophy in Taiwan Since 1949." *Philosophy East and West* 43.2 (April): 179–287.

Shen, Xilun 2004. *Zhongguo chuantong wenhua he yuyan* (China's traditional culture and language). Shanghai: Shanghai jiaoyu chubanshe.

Shi Xijiang 2001. *Zhongguo gudai di jiaoyu* (Ancient Chinese education). Taibei: Wenjin chubanshe.

Shiga, Shuzo. 1974. "Criminal Procedure in the Ch'ing Dynasty." *Memoirs of the Research Department of the Toyo Bunko* 32.1: 1–45.

Shih, Vincent 1967. *The Taiping Ideology*. Seattle: University of Washington Press.

Shih, Vincent, trans. 1983. *The Literary Mind and the Carving of Dragons*. Hong Kong: The Chinese University Press.

Shimada, Kenji 1990. *Pioneer of the Chinese Revolution: Zhang Binglin and Confucianism*. Stanford: Stanford University Press. Translated by Joshua Fogel.

Schoenhals, Michael 1992. *Doing Things with Words in Chinese Politics: Five Studies*. Berkeley: University of California, Institute of East Asian Studies.

Silber, Cathy 1994. "From Daughter to Daughter-in-Law in the Women's Script of Southern Hunan." Gilmartin et al., eds. 1994: 47–68.

Silbergeld, Jerome 1982. *Chinese Painting Style*. Seattle and London: University of Washington Press.

Silbergeld, Jerome 1987. "Chinese Painting Studies in the West: A State-of-the-Field Article." *Journal of Asian Studies* 46.4 (November): 849–97.

Silbergeld, Jerome, and Dora C. Y. Ching, eds. 2013. *The Family Model in Chinese Art and Culture*. Princeton: Princeton University Press.

Simoons, Frederick 1991. *Food in China: A Cultural and Historical Inquiry*. Boca Raton: CRC Press.

Siren, Oswald 1937. *The Chinese on the Art of Painting*. Peiping: H. Vetch.

Siu, Helen 1989. *Agents and Victims in South China: Accomplices in Rural Revolution*. New Haven: Yale University Press.

Siu, Helen 1990. "Where Were the Women? Rethinking Marriage Resistance and Regional Culture in South China." *Late Imperial China* 11.2: 32–62.

Siu, Victoria M. 2013. *Gardens of a Chinese Emperor: Imperial Creations of the Qianlong Era, 1736–1796*. Lanham, Md.: Rowman and Littlefield.

Sivin, Nathan 1966. "Chinese Conceptions of Time." *Earlham Review* 1: 82–92.

Sivin, Nathan 1987. *Traditional Medicine in Contemporary China*. Ann Arbor: University of Michigan Press.

Sivin, Nathan 1988. "Science and Medicine in Imperial China: The State of the Field." *Journal of Asian Studies* 47.1 (February): 41–90.

Sivin, Nathan 1995a. *Science in Ancient China: Researches and Reflections*. Brookfield, Vt.: Ashgate Variorum.

Sivin, Nathan 1995b. *Medicine, Philosophy, and Religion in Ancient China: Researches and Reflections*. Brookfield, Vt.: Ashgate Variorum.

Sivin, Nathan 2005. "Why the Scientific Revolution Did Not Take Place in China—Or Did It?" PDF version available at ccat.sas.upenn.edu/~nsivin/scirev.pdf. Originally published in *Chinese Science* 5 (1982): 45–66.

Sivin, Nathan n.d. "Selected, Annotated Bibliography of the History of Chinese Science and Medicine: Sources in Western Languages." Available at http://ccat.sas. upenn.edu/~nsivin/nakbib.html.

Skinner, G. William 1971. "Chinese Peasants and the Closed Community: An Open and Shut Case." *Comparative Studies in Society and History* 13.3 (July): 270–81.

Skinner, G. William 1985. "The Structure of Chinese History." *Journal of Asian Studies* 44.2 (February): 271–92.

Skinner, G. William 1993. *Marketing and Social Structure in Rural China*. Ann Arbor: Association for Asian Studies.

Skinner, G. William, ed. 1977. *The City in Late Imperial China*. Stanford: Stanford University Press.

Skinner, G. William, ed. 1979. *The Study of Chinese Society*. Stanford: Stanford University Press.

Slingerland, Edward 2006. *The Essential Analects: Selected Passages with Traditional Commentary*. Indianapolis: Hackett.

Slote, Michael 2013. "Updating Yin and Yang." *Dao* 12: 271–81.

Smith, Arthur 1899. *Village Life in China*. New York: Fleming H. Revell Company.

Smith, Arthur 1914. *Proverbs and Common Sayings from the Chinese*. Shanghai: American Presbyterian Mission Press.

Smith, Joanna Handlin 1987. "Benevolent Societies: The Reshaping of Charity during the Late Ming and Early Ch'ing." *Journal of Asian Studies* 46.2 (May): 309–37.

Smith, Joanna Handlin 1998. "Social Hierarchy and Merchant Philanthropy as Perceived in Several Late-Ming and Early-Qing Texts." *Journal of the Economic and Social History of the Orient* 41.3: 417–51.

Smith, Richard J. 1974. "Chinese Military Institutions in the Mid-Nineteenth Century 1850–1860." *Journal of Asian History* 8.2: 122–61.

Smith, Richard J. 1975. "The Employment of Foreign Military Talent." *Journal of the Hong Kong Branch of the Royal Asiatic Society* 15: 113–38.

Smith, Richard J. 1976a. "Foreign Training and China's Self-Strengthening: The Case of Feng-huang-shan, 1864–1873." *Modern Asian Studies* 10.2: 195–223.

Smith, Richard J. 1976b. "Reflections on the Comparative Study of Modernization in China and Japan." *Journal of the Hong Kong Branch of the Royal Asiatic Society* 16: 11–23.

Smith, Richard J. 1978a. *Mercenaries and Mandarins: The Ever-Victorious Army in Nineteenth Century China*. Millwood, N.Y.: Kraus-Thomson Ltd.

Smith, Richard J. 1978b. "The Reform of Military Education in Late Ch'ing China 1842–1895." *Journal of the Hong Kong Branch of the Royal Asiatic Society* 18: 15–40.

Smith, Richard J. 1988. "A Note on Qing Dynasty Calendars." *Late Imperial China* 9.1 (June): 123–45.

Smith, Richard J. 1989. "The Future of Chinese Culture." *Futures* (October): 431–46.

Smith, Richard J. 1991. *Fortune-tellers and Philosophers: Divination in Traditional Chinese Society*. Boulder, Colo. and Oxford, Eng.: Westview Press. Slightly revised paperback edition with a new preface issued in 1993.

Smith, Richard J. 1992. *Chinese Almanacs*. Hong Kong: Oxford University Press.

Smith, Richard J. 1993. "Li Hung-chang's Use of Foreign Military Talent: The Formative Period, 1862–1874." In Chu and Liu, eds. 1993: 119–42.

Smith, Richard J. 1994. *China's Cultural Heritage: The Qing Dynasty, 1644–1912*. Boulder, Colo.: Westview Press.

Smith, Richard J. 1996. *Chinese Maps: Images of "All Under Heaven."* New York and Hong Kong: Oxford University Press.

Smith, Richard J. 1997. "Flies and Fresh Air: Culture and Consumerism in Contemporary China." *Problems in Post-Communism* (March–April): 3–13.

Smith, Richard J. 2006a. "Knowing the Self and Knowing the 'Other': The Epistemological and Heuristic Value of the *Yijing* (Classic of Changes)." *Journal of Chinese Philosophy* 33.4 (December): 465–77.

Smith, Richard J. 2006b. "Meditation, Divination and Dream Interpretation: Chan/ Zen Buddhism, the *I Ching* (Book of Changes), and Other Chinese Devices for Jungian Self Realization." Unpublished paper available at history.rice.edu/faculty/ richard-j-smith/.

Smith, Richard J. 2008. *Fathoming the Cosmos and Ordering the World: The Yijing (I Ching or Classic of Changes) and Its Evolution in China*. Charlottesville: University of Virginia Press.

Smith, Richard J. 2012a. *The I Ching: A Biography*. Princeton: Princeton University Press.

Smith, Richard J. 2012b. "Mapping China and the Question of a China-Centered Tributary System." *The Asia-Pacific Journal*, 11.3 (January 28). Available at www.japanfocus.org/-Richard_J_-Smith/3888.

Smith, Richard J. 2013. *Mapping China and Managing the World: Culture, Cartography and Cosmology in Late Imperial Times*. New York: Routledge.

Smith, Richard J. 2014. "The Cultural Role of Popular Encyclopedias in Late Imperial China." Available at history.rice.edu/faculty/richard-j-smith/ and www.slideshare.net/smithrj/encyclopedias-in-late-imperial-china-2014-36080622.

Smith, Richard J. 2015. "Fathoming the *Changes*: The Evolution of Some Technical Terms and Interpretive Strategies in *Yijing* Exegesis." *Journal of Chinese Philosophy* 40 (supplement): 146–70. First published online September 23, 2014.

Smith, Richard J. forthcoming. "The Legacy of *Rishu* in Chinese Civilization." In Kalinowski and Harper, eds.

Smith, Richard J. n.d. "*Yijing* Website" Available at http://history.rice.edu/smith/.

Smith, Richard J. and D. W. Y. Kwok, eds. 1993. *Cosmology, Ontology and Human Efficacy: Essays in Chinese Thought.* Honolulu: University of Hawaii Press.

Smith, Richard J., John K. Fairbank, and Katherine Bruner, eds. 1991. *Robert Hart and China's Early Modernization: His Journals, 1863–1866.* Cambridge, Mass.: Harvard University Press.

Smith, Richard J., Kunio Miura, and Chie Kato 1998. *Tsūsho no sekai: Chūgokujin no hierabi* (The world of almanacs: Day-selection of the Chinese people). Tokyo: Gaifu Publishers. Substantially revised and expanded Japanese-language edition of R. J. Smith 1992.

Smits, Gregory 1999. *Visions of Ryukyu: Identity and Ideology in Early-Modern Thought and Politics.* Honolulu: University of Hawaii Press.

Smolen, Elwyn 1980. "Chinese Bronzes of the Ming Dynasty." *Arts of Asia* 10.1 (January–February): 71–85.

Snyder-Reinke, Jeffrey 2009. *Dry Spells: State Rainmaking and Local Governance in Late Imperial China.* Cambridge, Mass.: Harvard University Press.

Society for Qing Studies. "Research Resources." Available at http://qing_studies .press.jhu.edu/research/index.html.

Söderblom Saarela, Mårten 2013. "Thoughts on the Rise and Fall of the Manchu Language." Manchu Studies Group (April 29). Available at www.manchustudies group.org/2013/04/29/thoughts-on-the-rise-and-fall-of-the-manchu-language/.

Söderblom Saarela, Mårten 2014. "The Manchu Script and Information Management: Some Aspects of Qing China's Great Encounter with Alphabetic Literacy." In Elman, ed. 2014: 169–97.

Solomon, Richard 1971. *Mao's Revolution and the Chinese Political Culture.* Berkeley: University of California Press.

Sommer, Matthew H. 2000. *Sex, Law and Society in Late Imperial China.* Stanford: Stanford University Press.

Sommer, Matthew H. 2005. "Making Sex Work: Polyandry as a Survival Strategy in Qing Dynasty China." In Goodman and Larson, eds. 2005: 29–54.

Sommer, Matthew H. 2013. "The Gendered Body in the Qing Courtroom." *Journal of the History of Sexuality* 22.2: 281–311.

Song, Geng 2004. *The Fragile Scholar: Power and Masculinity in Chinese Culture.* Hong Kong: Hong Kong University Press.

Song, Huiqun and Miao Xuelan 2010. *Zhongguo boyi wenhua shi* (A history of Chinese game culture). Beijing: Shehui kexue wenxian chubanshe.

Song, Yuanqiang 1991. "The Study of Regional Socio-Economic History in China: Retrospect and Prospects." *Late Imperial China* 12.1 (June): 115–31.

Song, Zhenghai and Sun Guanlong, eds. 1999. *Zhongguo chuantong wenhua yu xiandai kexue jishu* (China's traditional culture and modern science and technology). Hangzhou: Zhejiang jiaoyu chubanshe.

Souza, George B. 1986. *The Survival of Empire: Portuguese Trade and Society in China and the South China Sea 1630–1754.* Cambridge, Eng.: Cambridge University Press.

Spence, Jonathan D. 1966. *Ts'ao Yin and the K'ang-hsi Emperor.* New Haven: Yale University Press.

Spence, Jonathan D. 1968. "Chang Po-hsing and the K'ang-hsi Emperor." *Ch'ing-shih wen-t'i* 1. 8 (May): 3–9.

Spence, Jonathan D. 1978. *The Death of Woman Wang.* New York: Viking.

Spence, Jonathan D. 1980. *To Change China: Western Advisers in China.* New York: Penguin.

Spence, Jonathan D. 1986. *The Memory Palace of Matteo Ricci.* New York: Viking.

Spence, Jonathan D. 1988. *Emperor of China: Self-Portrait of K'ang-hsi.* New York: Vintage.

Spence, Jonathan D. 1996. *God's Chinese Son: The Taiping Heavenly Kingdom of Hong Xiuquan.* New York: Norton.

Spence, Jonathan D. 2001. *Treason by the Book.* New York: Viking.

Spence, Jonathan D. 2007. *Return to Dragon Mountain: Memories of a Late Ming Man.* New York and London: Viking.

Spence, Jonathan D. 2013. *The Search for Modern China.* New York: Norton. Third edition.

Spence, Jonathan D. and John Wills, eds. 1980. *From Ming to Ch'ing.* New Haven: Yale University Press.

Standaert, Nicholas 1988. *Yang Tingyun: Confucian and Christian in Late Ming China: His Life and Thought.* Leiden: Brill.

Starr, Chloë F. 2007. *Red-Light Novels of the Late Qing.* Leiden, Brill.

Steinhardt, Nancy Shatzman 1990. *Chinese Imperial City Planning.* Honolulu: University of Hawaii Press.

Steinhardt, Nancy Shatzman 2002. *Chinese Architecture.* New Haven: Yale University Press.

Stepanchuk, Carol and Charles Wong 1991. *Mooncakes and Hungry Ghosts: Festivals of China.* San Francisco: China Books and Periodicals.

Stevenson, Mark and Wu Cuncun, eds. 2013. *Homoeroticism in Imperial China: A Sourcebook.* New York: Routledge.

Stockard, Janice 1989. *Daughters of the Canton Delta: Marriage Patterns and Economic Strategies in South China 1860–1930.* Stanford: Stanford University Press.

Stover, Leon 1974. *The Cultural Ecology of Chinese Civilization.* New York: Mentor Books.

Stover, Leon and Takeko Stover 1976. *China: An Anthropological Perspective.* Pacific Palisades, Calif.: Goodyear Publishing Company, Inc.

Strassberg, Richard E. 1983. *The World of K'ung Shang-jen: A Man of Letters in Early Ch'ing China.* New York: Columbia University Press.

Strassberg, Richard E. 1994. *Inscribed Landscapes: Travel Writing from Imperial China.* Berkeley: University of California Press.

Strassberg, Richard E. 2008. *Wandering Spirits: Chen Shiyuan's Encyclopedia of Dreams.* Berkeley: University of California Press.

Strickmann, Michel 2002. *Chinese Magical Medicine.* Stanford: Stanford University Press. Edited by Bernard Faure.

Strickmann, Michel 2005. *Chinese Poetry and Prophecy.* Stanford: Stanford University Press. Edited by Bernard Faure.

Struve, Lynn 1977. "The Peach Blossom Fan' as Historical Drama." *Renditions* 8 (Autumn): 99–114.

Struve, Lynn 1984. *The Southern Ming 1644–1662*. New Haven: Yale University Press.

Struve, Lynn 1988. "Huang Zongxi in Context: A Reappraisal of His Major Writings." *Journal of Asian Studies* 47.3 (August): 474–502.

Struve, Lynn 1993. *Voices from the Ming-Qing Cataclysm*. New Haven: Yale University Press.

Struve, Lynn 2004. *The Qing Formation in World-Historical Time*. Cambridge, Mass.: Harvard University Press.

Struve, Lynn, ed. 2005. *Time and Temporality in the Ming-Qing Transition*. Honolulu: University of Hawaii Press.

Stuart, Jan and Evelyn S. Rawski 2001. *Worshiping the Ancestors: Chinese Commemorative Portraits*. Stanford: Stanford University Press.

Sullivan, Michael 1977. *The Arts of China*. Berkeley: University of California Press.

Sullivan, Michael 1979. *Symbols of Eternity: The Art of Landscape Painting in China*. Stanford: Stanford University Press.

Sullivan, Michael et al. 1965. *The Arts of the Ch'ing Dynasty*. London: Arts Council of Great Britain.

Sun, E-tu Zen 1961. *Ch'ing Administrative Terms*. Cambridge, Mass.: Harvard University Press.

Sun, E-tu Zen 1962–1963. "The Board of Revenue in Nineteenth Century China." *Harvard Journal of Asiatic Studies* 24: 175–228.

Sun, E-tu Zen and Shiou-Chuan Sun 1966. *Chinese Technology in the Seventeeth Century*. University Park: Pennsylvania State University Press.

Sun, Longji [Sun Lung-kee] 1985. *Zhongguo wenhua di shenceng jiegou* (The deep structure of Chinese culture). Hong Kong: Jixian she. Second edition.

Sun, Longji [Sun Lung-kee] 2004. *Lishi xuejia di jingxian: Lishi xinli wenji* (The warp of historians: Collected writings on history and psychology). Guilin: Guangxi shifan daxue chubanshe.

Sung, Hou-Mei 2009. *Decoded Messages: The Symbolic Language of Chinese Animal Painting*. New Haven: Yale University Press.

Sung, Margaret 1979. "Chinese Language and Culture: A Study of Homonyms, Lucky Words, and Taboos." *Journal of Chinese Linguistics* 7: 416–36.

Sutter, Robert G. 1988. *Taiwan: Entering the 21st Century*. New York: University Press of America.

Sutton, Donald 1981. "Pilot Surveys of Chinese Shamans 1875–1945: A Spatial Approach to Social History." *Journal of Social History* 15.1: 109–15.

Sutton, Donald 1989. A Case of Literati Piety: The Ma Yuan Cult from High-Tang to High-Qing." *CLEAR* 11: 79–114.

Sutton, Donald 2007a. "Introduction." In Sutton, ed. 2007: 3–21.

Sutton, Donald 2007b. "Death Rites and Chinese Culture: Standardization and Variation in Ming and Qing Times." In Sutton, ed. 2007: 125–53.

Sutton, Donald, ed. 2007. "Ritual, Cultural Standardization, and Orthopraxy in China: Reconsidering James J. Watson's Ideas." Special edition of *Modern China* 33.1 (January): 3–158.

Svarverud, Rune 2007. *International Law as World Order in Late Imperial China: Translation, Reception and Discourse, 1847–1911*. Leiden: Brill.

Swanson, Paul 1989. *Foundations of T'ien-t'ai Philosophy: The Flowering of the Two Truths Theory in Chinese Buddhism.* Berkeley: University of California Press.

Sweeten, Alan 1976. "The Ti-pao's Role in Local Government as Seen in Fukien Christian 'Cases' 1863–1869." *Ch'ing-shih wen-t'i* 3.6 (December): 1–27.

Swope, Kenneth M. 2002. "Deceit, Disguise, and Dependence: China, Japan, and the Future of the Tributary System, 1592–1596." *International History Review* 24.4: (December): 757–82.

Swope, Kenneth M. 2009. *A Dragon's Head and a Serpent's Tail: Ming China and the First Great East Asian War, 1592–1598.* Norman, Okla.: University of Oklahoma Press.

Swope, Kenneth M. 2014. *The Military Collapse of China's Ming Dynasty, 1618–44.* New York: Routledge.

Sze, Mai-mai 1959. *The Way of Chinese Painting.* New York: Vintage.

Sze, Mai-mai 1978. *The Mustard Seed Garden Manual of Painting.* Princeton: Princeton University Press.

Szonyi, Michael 2002. *Practicing Kinship: Lineage and Descent in Late Imperial China.* Stanford: Stanford University Press.

Szonyi, Michael 2007. "Making Claims about Standardization and Orthopraxy in Late Imperial China: Rituals and Cults in the Fuzhou Region in Light of Watson's Theories." In Sutton, ed. 2007: 47–71.

Tai, Zhenlin, ed. 1991. *Yuzhou quanxi tongyi lun yu Zhongguo chuantong wenhua* (The theory of holographic unity in the cosmos and China's traditional culture). Jinan: Shandong renmin chubanshe.

Takeuchi, Minoru 2006. *Zhongguo wenhua chuantong tanjiu* (Investigations into China's cultural traditions). Beijing Zhongguo wenlian chubanshe. Translated by Cheng Ma.

Talhelm, T. et al. 2012. "Large-Scale Psychological Difference Within China Explained by Rice Versus Wheat Agriculture." *Science* 344: 603–7.

Tan, Qixiang 1993. *Qingren wenji: Dili lei huibian* (Collected writings by Qing authors: A compilation of geographical works). Volume 3 (Ming-Qing). Jinan: Shandong jiaoyu chubanshe. Originally compiled by Wang Zhongmin.

Tang, Junyi 1981. *Zhongguo wenhua zhi jingshen jiazhi* (The spiritual value of Chinese culture). Taibei: Zhengzhong shuju.

Tang, Yijie, ed. 1993. *Guogu xinzhi: Zhongguo quantong wenhua di zaiquanshi* (Old country, new knowledge: A reinterpretation of China's traditional culture). Beijing: Beijing daxue chubanshe.

Tang, Yijie, ed. 2013. *Ru Shi Dao yu Zhongguo chuantong wenhua* (Confucianism, Buddhism and Daoism and China's traditional culture). Beijing: Zhongguo da baike quanshu chubanshe.

Tanigawa, Michio 1985. *Medieval Chinese Society and the Local "Community."* Berkeley: University of California Press. Translated by Joshua A. Fogel.

Tao, Chia-lien Pao 1991. "Chaste Widows and Institutions to Support Them in Late Qing China." *Asia Major*, third series 4: 101–19.

Tao, Jing-shen 1988. *Two Sons of Heaven: Studies in Sung-Liao Relations.* Tucson: University of Arizona Press.

Tao, Tang 1969. *Zhongguo wenhua gailun* (Introduction to Chinese culture). Taibei: Fuxing shuju.

Taylor, Rodney 1982. "Proposition and Praxis: The Dilemma of Neo-Confucian Syncretism." *Philosophy East and West* 32.2 (April): 187–99.

Taylor, Rodney 1990. *The Religious Dimensions of Confucianism*. Albany: State University of New York Press.

Telford, Ted A. 1986. "Survey of Social Demographic Data in Chinese Genealogies." *Late Imperial China* 7.2 (December): 118–48.

Teng, Emma Jinhua 1996. "The Construction of the 'Traditional Chinese Woman' in the Western Academy: A Critical Review." *Signs* 22.1: 115–51.

Teng, Emma Jinhua 2004. *Taiwan's Imagined Geography: Chinese Colonial Travel Writing and Pictures, 1683–1895*. Cambridge, Mass.: Harvard University Press.

Teng, Ssu-yü and Knight Biggerstaff 1971. *An Annotated Bibliography of Selected Chinese Reference Works*. Cambridge, Mass.: Harvard University Press. Third edition.

Teng, Ssu-yü and John K. Fairbank 1979. *China's Response to the West: A Documentary Survey, 1839–1923*. Cambridge, Mass.: Harvard University Press.

ter Haar, B. J. 1992. *The White Lotus Teachings in Chinese Religious History*. Leiden: Brill.

Theiss, Janet 2009. "Love in a Confucian Climate: The Perils of Intimacy in Eighteenth-Century China." *Nan Nü* 11.2: 197–233.

Theiss, Janet M. 2005. *Disgraceful Matters: The Politics of Chastity in Eighteenth-Century China*. Berkeley: University of California Press.

Thompson, Laurence 1979. *Chinese Religion*. Belmont, Calif.: Wadsworth.

Thompson, Laurence 1980. "Taiwanese Temple Arts and Cultural Integrity." *Bulletin of the Society for the Study of Chinese Religions* 8 (Fall): 70–78.

Thompson, Laurence 1981. "Popular and Classical Modes of Ritual in a Taiwanese Temple." *Bulletin of the Society for the Study of Chinese Religions* 9 (Fall): 106–22.

Thompson, Laurence ed. 1973. *The Chinese Way in Religion*. Belmont, Calif.: Dickenson Publishing Company.

Thomsen, Rudi 1988. *Ambition and Confucianism*. Aarhus, Denmark: Aarhus University Press.

Tian, Chenshan 2005. *Chinese Dialectics: From Yijing to Marxism*. Lanham, Md.: Lexington Books

Tien, Hung-mao 1989. *The Great Transition: Political and Social Change in the Republic of China*. Stanford: Hoover Institution Press.

T'ien, Ju-k'ang 1988. *Male Anxiety and Female Chastity: A Comparative Study of Chinese Ethical Values in Ming-Ch'ing Times*. Leiden: Brill.

Tikhvinsky, S. L. 1983. *Manzhou Rule in China*. Moscow: Progress Publishers. Translated by David Skvirsky.

Tillman, Hoyt 1982. *Utilitarian Confucianism: Ch'en Liang's Challenge to Chu Hsi*. Cambridge, Mass.: Harvard University Press.

Ting, Joseph Sun-pao 1990. *Children of the Gods: Dress and Symbolism in China*. Hong Kong: Urban Council.

Toh, Hoong Teik 2004–2005. "The Taoist Tract *Ganying Pian* in Manchu." *Saksaha: A Review of Manchu Studies* 9: 1–24.

Topley, Marjorie, ed. 1967. *Some Traditional Chinese Ideas and Conceptions in Hong Kong Social Life Today*. Hong Kong: Royal Asiatic Society.

Torbert, Preston 1978. *The Ch'ing Imperial Household Department*. Cambridge, Mass.: Harvard University Press.

Townley, Susan Mary 1904. *My Chinese Note Book*. New York: E. P. Dutton and Company.

Tozer, Warren 1970. "Taiwan's 'Cultural Renaissance.'" *China Quarterly* 43 (July–September): 61–99.

Tregear, T. R. 1965. *A Geography of China*. Chicago: Aldine.

Tsai, Shih-shan Henry 1995. *The Eunuchs in the Ming Dynasty*. Albany: State University of New York Press.

Tsai, Shih-shan Henry 2001. *Perpetual Happiness: The Ming Emperor Yongle*. Seattle: University of Washington Press.

Tseng, Yuho 1993. "Women Painters of the Ming Dynasty." *Artibus Asiae* 53.1–2: 249–59.

Tseng, Yu-ho Ecke 1977. *Chinese Folk Art*. Honolulu: University of Hawaii Press.

Tsien, Tsuen-hsuin 2011. *Collected Writings on Chinese Culture*. Hong Kong: Chinese University Press.

T'sou, B. K. Y. 1981. "A Sociolinguistic Analysis of the Logographic Writing System of the Chinese." *Journal of Chinese Linguistics* 9.1 (January): 1–19.

Tsuya, Prudence et al. 2009. *Pressure: Reproduction and Human Agency in Europe and Asia, 1700–1900*. Cambridge, Mass.: MIT Press.

Tu, Ching-i 1974–1975. "The Chinese Examination Essay: Some Literary Considerations." *Monumenta Serica* 31: 393–406.

Tu, Wei-ming 1976. *Neo-Confucian Thought in Action*. Berkeley: University of California Press.

Tu, Wei-ming 1989. *Way Learning and Politics: Essays on the Confucian Intellectual*. Singapore: Institute of Asian Philosophies.

Tu, Wei-ming. 1991. "Cultural China: The Periphery as the Center." *Daedalus* 120.2 (Spring): 1–32.

Twitchett, Denis et al., eds. 1978–2009. *The Cambridge History of China*. Cambridge, Eng.: Cambridge University Press. Eight volumes, several divided into more than one part. Abbreviation: CHC.

Udry, Stephen Potter 2000. "Muttering Mystics: A Preliminary Examination of Manchu Shamanism in the Qing Dynasty." Ph.D. dissertation, University of Washington, Seattle.

University of Washington, Seattle. "G.W. Skinner Map Archive." Available at http://content.lib.washington.edu/skinnerweb/.

Umekawa, Sumiyo 2003. "Transmission of Sexual Positioning in Relationship with Female Orgasm." Paper for the Asian Society for History of Medicine; Symposium on the History of Medicine in Asia: 1–20.

Unschuld, Paul U. 1985. *Medicine in China: A History of Ideas*. Berkeley: University of California Press.

Unschuld, Paul U. 1986. *Medicine in China: A History of Pharmaceutics*. Berkeley: University of California Press.

Unschuld, Paul U. 1988. *Introductory Readings in Classical Chinese Medicine*. Dordrecht: Kluwer Academic Publishers.

Unschuld, Paul U. 1989. *Forgotten Traditions in Ancient Chinese Medicine. The I-hsueh Yüan Liu Lun of 1757 by Hsü Ta-Ch'un*. Brookline, Mass.: Paradigm Publications.

Unschuld, Paul U. 2003. *Huang Di Nei Jing Su Wen. Nature, Knowledge, Imagery in an Ancient Chinese Medical Text*. Berkeley: University of California Press.

Vainker, Shelagh 2004. *Chinese Silk: A History*. New Brunswick, N.J.: Rutgers University Press.

Vainker, Shelagh 2005. *Chinese Pottery and Porcelain*. London: British Museum Press.

van der Sprenkel, Sybille 2004. *Legal Institutions in Manchu China: A Sociological Analysis*. Oxford: Berg. Originally published in 1962.

Van Ess, Hans 2010. "Cheng Yi and His Ideas about Women as Revealed in His Commentary to the *Yijing*." *Oriens Extremus* 49: 63–77.

Van Gulik, Robert H. 2003. *Sexual Life in Ancient China: A Preliminary Survey of Chinese Sex and Society from ca. 1500 B.C. till 1644 A.D.* Leiden: Brill. Edited, with a new Introduction and Bibliography by Paul Goldin. Originally published in 1961.

Van Gulik, Robert H. 2010. *The Lore of the Chinese Lute: An Essay on the Ideology of the Ch'in*. Bangkok: Orchid Press.

Van Gulik, Robert H. trans. 1958. *Scrapbook for Chinese Collectors*. Beirut: Imprimerie Catholique.

Van Lieu, Joshua 2009. "The Politics of Condolence: Contested Representations of Tribute in late Nineteenth-Century Choson-Qing Relations." *Journal of Korean Studies* 14.1 (Fall): 83–115.

Van Norden, Brian, ed. 2002. *Confucius and the Analects: New Essays*. Oxford, Eng.: Oxford University Press.

Van Slyke, Lyman 1988. *Yangtze: Nature, History and the River*. Reading, Mass.: Addison-Wesley Publishing Company.

Van Zoeren, Steven 1991. *Poetry and Personality: Reading, Exegesis and Hermeneutics in Traditional China*. Stanford: Stanford University Press.

Vande Walle, W. F. and Noël Golvers, eds. 2003. *The History of the Relations between the Low Countries and China in the Qing Era (1644–1911)*. Leuven: Leuven University Press.

Vandermeersch, Léon, ed. 1994. *La société civile face à l'état dans les traditions chinoise, japonaise, coréenne, et vietnamienne*. Paris: École Française d'Extrême-Orient.

Verellen, Franciscus 1989. *Du Guangting (850–933). Taoiste de cour a la fin de la Chine médiévale*. Paris: De Boccard.

Vinograd, Richard 1992. *Boundaries of the Self: Chinese Portraits 1600–1900*. Cambridge, Eng.: Cambridge University Press.

Viraphol, Sarasin 1977. *Tribute and Profit: Sino–Siamese Trade 1652–1853*. Cambridge, Mass.: Harvard University Press.

Vogel, Ezra 2011. *Deng Xiaoping and the Transformation of China*. Cambridge, Mass.: Harvard University Press.

Von Glahn, Richard J. 1996. *Fountain of Fortune: Money and Monetary Policy in China, 1000–1700*. Berkeley: University of California Press.

Wade, Geoff 2004. "The Zheng He Voyages: A Reassessment." *Asia Research Center (ARC) of the National University of Singapore Working Paper 31* (October): 1–27.

Wadley, Stephen A. 1996. "Altaic Influences on Beijing Dialect: The Manchu Case." *Journal of the American Oriental Society* 116.1 (January–March): 99–104.

Wakeman, Frederic Jr. 1972. "The Price of Autonomy: Intellectuals in Ming and Ch'ing Politics." *Daedalus* 101.2 (Spring): 35–70.

Wakeman, Frederic Jr. 1973. *History and Will: Philosophical Perspectives on the Thought of Mao Tse-tung*. Berkeley: University of California Press.

Wakeman, Frederic Jr. 1975. *The Fall of Imperial China*. New York: The Free Press.

Wakeman, Frederic Jr. 1977. "Rebellion and Revolution: The Study of Popular Movements in Chinese History." *Journal of Asian Studies* 36.2 (February): 201–37.

Wakeman, Frederic Jr. 1985. *The Great Enterprise: The Manchu Restoration of Imperial Order in Seventeenth-Century China*. Berkeley: University of California Press. Two volumes.

Wakeman, Frederic Jr. and Carolyn Grant, eds. 1975. *Conflict and Control in Late Imperial China*. Berkeley: University of California Press.

Wakeman, Frederic Jr. and Wang Xi, eds. 1997. *China's Quest for Modernization: A Historical Perspective*. Berkeley: Institute of East Asian Studies.

Waldron Andrew 1990. *The Great Wall of China: From History to Myth*. Cambridge, Eng.: Cambridge University Press.

Waley, Arthur, trans. 1944. *Monkey*. London: Allen and Unwin.

Waley, Arthur 1970. *Yüan Mei*. Stanford: Stanford University Press.

Waley, Arthur 1987. *The Book of Songs*. New York: Penguin.

Waley-Cohen, Joanna 1991. *Exile in Mid-Qing China: Banishment to Xinjiang 1758–1820*. New Haven: Yale University Press.

Waley-Cohen, Joanna 2004. "The New Qing History." *Radical History Review* 88 (Winter): 193–206.

Waley-Cohen, Joanna 2006. *The Culture of War in China: Empire and the Military under the Qing Dynasty*. New York: I. B. Tauris.

Walshe, Gilbert. 1906. *Ways That Are Dark: Some Chapters on Chinese Etiquette and Social Procedure*. Shanghai: Kelly and Walsh.

Walthall, Anne, ed. 2008. *Servants of the Dynasty: Palace Women in World History*. Berkeley: California World History Library.

Waltner, Ann 1986. "The Moral Status of the Child in Late Imperial China: Childhood in Ritual and Law." *Social Research* 53.4 (Winter): 667–87.

Waltner, Ann 1990. *Getting an Heir: Adoption and Construction of Kinship in Late Imperial China*. Honolulu: University of Hawaii Press.

Waltner, Ann 1996. "Recent Scholarship on Chinese Women." *Signs* 21.2: 410–28.

Wang, Bin 1999. *Qingdai jinshu zongshu* (A complete account of book-banning in the Qing dynasty). Beijing: Zhongguo shudian chubanshe.

Wang, Chuanman 2012. "On Variations in Huizhou Women's Chastity Behaviors During the Ming and Qing Dynasties." *Chinese Studies in History* 45.4: 43–57.

Wang, David and Wei Shang, eds. 2006. *Dynastic Decline and Cultural Innovation: From the Late Ming to the Late Qing and Beyond*. Cambridge, Mass.: Harvard University Press.

Wang, Di 2008. *The Teahouse: Small Business, Everyday Culture, and Public Politics in Chengdu, 1900–1950*. Stanford: Stanford University Press.

Wang, Ermin 1995. *Zhongguo jindai sixiang shilun* (Historical discussion of recent Chinese thought). Taibei: Taiwan Shang wu yin shu guan.

Wang, Ermin 1996. *Ming-Qing shidai shumin wenhua shenghuo* (The cultural life of commoners in the Ming and Qing dynasties). Taipei: Zhongyang yanjiuyuan jindaishi yanjiusuo.

Wang, Ermin 2005. *Wan Qing zhengzhi sixiang shilun* (Historical discussion of late Qing political thought). Guilin: Guangxi shifan daxue chubanshe.

Wang, Fangyu and Richard Barnhart 1990. *Master of the Lotus Garden: The Life and Art of Bada Shanren 1626–1705*. New Haven: Yale University Press.

Wang, Gai 1888. *Jiezi yuan huazhuan* (Mustard seed garden painting manual). Shanghai: Fawen xin shuju shiyin.

Wang, Georgette et al. 1991. "Cultural Value Survey in Taiwan." *Journal of Communication Arts* 12.2 (Spring): 71–80.

Wang, Gung-wu 1991. *The Chineseness of China: Selected Essays*. Hong Kong: Oxford University Press.

Wang, Hongsheng 2001. *Zhongguo gudai di kexue jishu* (Ancient Chinese science and technology). Taibei: Wenjin chubanshe.

Wang, Hui 1995. "The Fate of 'Mr. Science' in China: The Concept of Science and Its Application in Modern Chinese Thought." *positions* 3.1 (Spring): 1–67.

Wang, Jianhui and Yi Xuejin, eds. 1998. *Zhongguo wenhua zhishi jinghua* (The essence of Chinese cultural knowledge). Wuhan: Hubei renmin chubanshe.

Wang, Jing 1992. *The Story of Stone: Intertextuality, Ancient Chinese Stone Lore and the Stone Symbolism in Dream of the Red Chamber*. Durham: Duke University Press.

Wang, Junlin et al., eds. 2006. *Si wen zai zi: Ruxue yu Zhongguo chuantong wenhua* (This culture of ours: Confucianism and China's traditional culture). Ji'nan: Qi Lu shushe.

Wang, Lijian 2013. *Qingdai wenxue kuayu yanjiu* (Research on the spread of literature across boundaries in the Qing period). Taibei: Wenjin chubanshe.

Wang, Liping and Julia Adams 2011. "Interlocking Patrimonialisms and State Formation in Qing China and Early Modern Europe." *Annals of the American Academy of Political and Social Science* 636 (July): 164–81.

Wang, Mao et al., eds. 1992. *Qingdai zhexue* (Qing dynasty philosophy). Hefei: Anhui renmin chubanshe.

Wang, Ping 2000. *Aching for Beauty: Footbinding in China*. Minneapolis: University of Minnesota Press.

Wang, Qiang and Bao Xiaoguang, eds. 2004. *Zhongguo chuantong wenhua jingsheng* (The spirit of China's traditional culture). Beijing: Kunlun chubanshe.

Wang, Qunying 2001. *Zhongguo gudai di falü* (Ancient Chinese law). Taibei: Wenjin chubanshe.

Wang, Robin R. 2012. *Yinyang: The Way of Heaven and Earth in Chinese Thought and Culture.* Cambridge, Eng.: Cambridge University Press.

Wang, Shuliang and Li Yu, eds. 1992. *Zhongguo wenhua jinghua quanji* (Complete collection of the essence of Chinese culture). Beijing: Zhongguo guoji guangbo chubanshe. Twenty volumes, covering philosophy (three volumes), religion (three volumes), history (three volumes), literature (three volumes), the arts (one volume), nationalities (one volume), geography (one volume), economics (one volume), science and technology (one volume), law and military affairs (one volume), medicine (one volume), and language (one volume). Full table of contents available at www.columbia.edu/cgi–bin/cul/toc.pl?3722275.

Wang, Shuo 2004. "The Selection of Women for the Qing Imperial Harem." *Chinese Historical Review* 11.2: 212–22.

Wang, Shuo 2008. "Qing Imperial Women: Empresses, Concubines, and Aisin Gioro Daughters." In Walthall, ed. 2008: 137–58.

Wang, Xiafei 2005. *Zhongguo chuantong wenfang sibao* (The Four Treasures of the traditional Chinese study). Beijing: Renmin meishu chubanshe.

Wang, Xinting et al. 1997. *Zhongguo chuantong wenhua gailun* (Introduction to China's traditional culture). Beijing: Zhongguo linye chubanshe.

Wang, Yanping 2004. *Law Codes in Dynastic China: A Synopsis of Chinese Legal History in the Thirty Centuries from Zhou to Qing.* Durham: North Carolina Academic Press.

Wang, Yeh-chien 1972. "The Secular Trend of Prices during the Ch'ing Period 1644–1911. *Journal of the Institute of Chinese Studies* (December): 347–72.

Wang, Yeh-chien 1974. *Land Taxation in Imperial China 1750–1911.* Cambridge, Mass.: Harvard University Press.

Wang, Yeh-chien 1990. Review of Kang Chao 1981 in *Harvard Journal of Asiatic Studies* 50.1: 407–11.

Wang, Ying 2003. "Imitation as Dialogue: The Mongolian Writer Yinzhan naxi (1837–1892) and His Imitations of *The Dream of the Red Chamber.*" *Tamkang Review* 34.2: 23–61.

Wang, Yungkuan 1991. *Zhongguo gudai kuxing* (Torture in ancient China). Zhengzhou: Zhongzhou guji chubanshe.

Wang, Yunwu 1969. *Qingdai zhengzhi sixiang* (Political thought in the Qing dynasty). Taibei: Taiwan shangwu yinshu guan.

Wang Zhonghan, ed. 1996. *Manzu lishi yu wenhua: jinian Manzu mingming 360 zhounian lunji.* (Manchu history and culture: Collected essays commemorating the 360th anniversary of the naming of the Manchus). Beijing : Zhongyang minzu daxue chubanshe.

Ward, Barbara 1979. "Not Merely Players: Drama, Art and Ritual in Traditional China." *Man* new series 14 (March): 18–39.

Wasserstrom, Jeffrey 1996. "Mao Matters: A Review Essay. *China Review International* 3.1 (Spring): 1–21.

Wasserstrom, Jeffrey and Elizabeth Perry, eds. 1992. *Popular Protest and Political Culture in Modern China*. Boulder. Westview.

Watson, Burton. 1962. *Early Chinese Literature*. New York: Columbia University Press.

Watson, Burton. 1989. *The Tso Chuan: Selections from China's Oldest Narrative History*. New York: Columbia University Press.

Watson, James 2007. "Orthopraxy Revisited." In Sutton, ed. 2007: 154–58.

Watson, James and Evelyn Rawski, eds. 1988. *Death Ritual in Late Imperial and Modern China*. Berkeley: University of California Press.

Watson, Rubie S. and Patricia B. Ebrey, eds. 1991. *Marriage and Inequality in Chinese Society*. Berkeley: University of California Press.

Watson, William 1962. *Ancient Chinese Bronzes*. London: Faber and Faber.

Watt, James 1981. "The Qin and the Chinese Literati." *Orientations* (November): 38–49. Available at www.silkqin.com/10ideo/wattart.htm.

Watt, John 1972. *The District Magistrate in Late Imperial China*. New York and London.

Wei, Betty Peh-t'i 2006. *Ruan Yuan, 1764–1849: The Life and Work of a Major Scholar-Official in Nineteenth-Century China before the Opium War*. Hong Kong: Hong Kong University Press.

Wei, Tat 1977. *An Exposition of the I-Ching or Book of Changes*. Hong Kong: Dai Nippon Printing Co.

Wei, Zhengtong 1981. *Zhongguo wenhua gailun* (An introduction to Chinese culture). Taibei: Shuiniu chubanshe.

Weidner, Marsha 1988. "Women in the History of Chinese Painting." In Weidner et al. 1988: 13–29.

Weidner, Marsha 1990. "The Conventional Success of Ch'en Shu." In Weidner, ed. 1990: 123–56.

Weidner, Marsha et al., eds. 1988. *Views from Jade Terrace: Chinese Women Artists, 1300–1912*. Indianapolis: Indianapolis Museum of Art.

Weidner, Marsha, ed. 1990. *Flowering in the Shadows: Women in the History of Chinese and Japanese Painting*. Honolulu: University of Hawaii Press.

Welch, Holmes 1967. *The Practice of Chinese Buddhism 1900–1950*. Cambridge, Mass.: Harvard University Press.

Weller, Robert 1987. *Unities and Diversities in Chinese Religion*. Seattle: University of Washington Press.

Welskopf, Elizabeth, ed. 1964. *Neue Betrage zur Geschichte der alten Welt*. Berlin.

Weng, Wan-go 1978. *Chinese Painting and Calligraphy*. New York: Akademie-Verlag.

Werner E. T. C. 1961. *A Dictionary of Chinese Mythology*. New York: Julian Press.

Whiteman, Stephen Hart 2011. "*Bishu Shanzhuang* and the Mediation of Qing Imperial Identity." Ph.D. dissertation, Stanford University.

Whyte, Martin K. 1974. *Small Groups and Political Rituals in China*. Berkeley: University of California Press.

Wiant, Bliss 1965. *The Music of China*. Hong Kong: Chinese University of Hong Kong.

Wichmann, Elizabeth 1991. *Listening to Theatre: The Aural Dimension of Beijing Opera.* Honolulu: University of Hawaii Press.

Widmer, Ellen 1987. *The Margins of Utopia: Shui-hu hou-chuan and the Literature of Ming Loyalism.* Cambridge, Mass.: Harvard University Press.

Widmer, Ellen 1989. "The Epistolary World of Female Talent in Seventeenth-Century China." *Late Imperial China* 10.2 (December): 1–43.

Widmer, Ellen 2002. "*Honglou Meng Ying* and Its Publisher, Juzhen Tang of Beijing." *Late Imperial China* 23.2: 33–52.

Widmer, Ellen 2006. *The Beauty and the Book: Women and Fiction in Nineteenth-Century China.* Cambridge, Mass. and London: Harvard University Press.

Widmer, Ellen 2009. "Guangdong's Talented Women of the Eighteenth Century." In Van Crevel et al. 2009: 293–309.

Widmer, Ellen 2010. "Retrieving the Past: Women Editors and Women's Poetry, 1636–1941." In Fong and Widmer 2010: 81–105.

Widmer, Ellen 2011. "Women as Biographers in Mid-Qing Jiangnan." In Judge and Hu 2011: 246–61.

Widmer, Ellen 2012. "Gazetteers and the Talented Woman." In Ho, ed. 2012: 261–78.

Widmer, Ellen and Kang-i Sun Chang, eds. 1997. *Writing Women in Late Imperial China.* Stanford: Stanford University Press.

Wieger, L. 1913. *Moral Tenets and Customs in China.* Hokien: Catholic Mission Press.

Wieger, L. 1927. *A History of the Religious Beliefs and Philosophical Opinions in China.* Peking: Hsien-hsien Press.

Wile, Douglas 1992. *Art of the Bedchamber: The Chinese Sexual Yoga Classics Including Women's Solo Meditation Texts.* Albany: State University of New York Press.

Wile, Douglas 1996. *Lost T'ai-Chi Classics from the Late Ch'ing Dynasty.* Albany: State University of New York Press.

Wilhelm, Hellmut 1951. "The Problem of Within and Without: A Confucian Attempt in Syncretism." *Journal of the History of Ideas* 12.1 (January): 48–60.

Wilhelm, Richard, trans. 1967. *The I Ching or Book of Changes.* Princeton: Princeton University Press. Translated from the German by C. F. Baynes.

Wilkinson, Endymion 2013. *Chinese History: A New Manual.* Cambridge, Mass. and London: Harvard-Yenching Institute Monograph Series 84, second, revised printing.

Will, Pierre-Etienne 1990. *Bureacracy and Famine in Eighteenth-Century China.* Stanford: Stanford University Press.

Will, Pierre-Étienne and Wong R. Bin 1991. *Nourish the People: The State Civilian Granary System in China 1650–1850.* Ann Arbor: University of Michigan Press.

Williams, C.A.S. 1941. *Outlines of Chinese Symbolism and Art Motives.* Shanghai: Kelly and Walsh.

Williams, E. T. 1913. "The State Religion of China during the Manchu Dynasty." *Journal of the North China Branch of the Royal Asiatic Society* 46: 111–145.

Williams, Samuel W. 1883. *The Middle Kingdom.* New York.

Wills, John E. 1974. *Peppers, Guns, and Parleys: The Dutch East India Company and China 1622–1681.* Cambridge, Mass.: Harvard University Press.

Wills, John E. 1979. "State Ceremonial in Late Imperial China." *Bulletin of the Society for the Study of Chinese Religions* 7 (Fall): 71–87.

Wills, John E. 1984. *Embassies and Illusions: Dutch and Portuguese Envoys to K'ang-hsi 1666–1687.* Cambridge, Mass.: Harvard University Press.

Wills, John E., Jr. 1995. "How We Got Obsessed with the 'Tribute System' and Why It's Time to Get Over It." Paper for the Association for Asian Studies Annual Meeting, Washington, D.C.

Wills, John E., Jr. 2009. *The World from 1450 to 1700.* Oxford, Eng.: Oxford University Press.

Wills, John E. 2012a. *Mountain of Fame: Portraits in Chinese History.* Princeton: Princeton University Press.

Wills, John E. 2012b. "Functional, Not Fossilized: Qing Tribute Relations with Dai Viet (Vietnam) and Siam (Thailand), 1700–1820." *T'oung Pao* 98: 439–78.

Wills, John E., Jr. et al., eds. 2011. *China and Maritime Europe, 1500–1800: Trade, Settlement, Diplomacy, and Missions.* Cambridge, Eng.: Cambridge University Press.

Wilson, Richard et al., eds. *Moral Behavior in Chinese Society* New York: Praeger.

Wilson, Thomas A., ed. 2003. *On Sacred Grounds: Culture, Society, Politics, and the Formation of the Cult of Confucius.* Cambridge. Mass.: Harvard University Press.

Wilson, Thomas A. 1994. "Confucian Sectarianism and the Compilation of the Ming History." *Late Imperial China* 152 (December): 53–84.

Wo, Karen Hoi-kwan 2008. "What Gets Lost in Translation: Language and Culture in 'Hongloumeng.'" LCOM Papers 1: 53–63.

Wolf, Arthur and Huang Chieh-shan 1980. *Marriage and Adoption in China 1843–1945.* Stanford: Stanford University Press.

Wolf, Arthur ed. 1974. *Religion and Ritual in Chinese Society.* Stanford: Stanford University Press.

Wolf, Arthur, ed. 1978. *Studies in Chinese Society.* Stanford: Stanford University Press.

Wolf, Margery 1985. *Revolution Postponed: Women in Contemporary China.* Stanford: Stanford University Press

Womack, Brantly 1982. *The Foundations of Mao Zedong's Political Thought, 1917–1935.* Honolulu: University of Hawaii Press.

Womack, Brantly 1986. "Where Mao Went Wrong: Epistemology and Ideology in Mao's Leftist Politics." *The Australian Journal of Chinese Affairs* 16 (July): 23–40.

Women of China (website). Available at www.womenofchina.cn/html/folder/504-1.htm.

Wong, David. "Chinese Ethics." In Edward N. Zalta, ed. *The Stanford Encyclopedia of Philosophy* (Spring 2013 edition). Available at http://plato.stanford.edu/archives/spr2013/entries/ethics–chinese/.

Wong, K. Chimin and Wu Lien-teh 1936. *A History of Chinese Medicine.* Shanghai: National Quarantine Service. Reprinted by the AMS Press in 1973.

Wong, Kam-ming 1985. "Point of View and Feminism: Images of Women in *Honglou meng.*" In Gerstlacher et al. 1985: 29–97.

Wong, R. Bin 1992. "Chinese Economic History and Development: A Note on the Myers-Huang Exchange." *Journal of Asian Studies* 51.3 (August): 600–612.

Wong, Shirleen 1975. *Kung Tzu-chen.* Boston: Twayne.

Wong, Young-tsu 1989. *The Search for Modern Nationalism: Zhang Binglin and Revolutionary China 1869–1936.* New York: Oxford University Press.

Wong, Young-tsu 2000. *A Paradise Lost: The Imperial Garden Yuanming Yuan.* Honolulu: University of Hawaii Press.

Wong, Young-tsu 2010. *Beyond Confucian China: The Rival Discourses of Kang Youwei and Zhang Binglin.* London: Routledge.

Woo, Terry Tak-ling. "Emotions and Self-Cultivation in *Nü Lunyu* (Woman's Analects)." *Journal of Chinese Philosophy* 36.2 (2009): 334–47.

Woodside, Alexander 1983. "Some Mid-Qing Theorists of Popular Schools: Their Innovations, Inhibitions and Attitudes Toward the Poor." *Modern China* 9: 3–35.

Wright, Arthur, ed. 1953. *Studies in Chinese Thought.* Chicago: University of Chicago Press.

Wright, Arthur, ed. 1960a. *The Confucian Persuasion.* Stanford: Stanford University Press.

Wright, Arthur 1960b. "The Study of Chinese Civilization." *Journal of the History of Ideas* 21.2 (April–June): 233–55.

Wright, Arthur, ed. 1964. *Confucianism and Chinese Civilization.* New York: Atheneum.

Wright, Mary C. 1967. *The Last Stand of Chinese Conservatism.* New York: Atheneum.

Wright, Mary C., ed. 1968. *China in Revolution: The First Phase, 1900–1913.* New Haven, Conn. and London: Yale University Press.

Wright, Timothy. "*Oxford Bibliographies* in Chinese Studies." Available at www.oxfordbibliographies.com/obo/page/chinese-studies.

Wu, Ben 1998. "Ritual Music in the Court and Rulership of the Qing Dynasty (1644–1911)." Ph.D. dissertation, University of Pittsburgh.

Wu, Chu-Hsia 1995. "On the Cultural Traits of Chinese Idioms." *Intercultural Communication Studies* 5.1: 61–84.

Wu, Cuncun 2004. *Homoerotic Sensibilities in Late Imperial China.* London: Routledge.

Wu, Huifang 1996. *Ming Qing yilai minjian shenghuo zhishi di jiangou yu chuandi* (The construction and transmission of guidance in daily affairs for commoners from Ming and Qing times). Taiwan: Xuesheng shuju.

Wu, Huifang 2005. *Wanbao chuanshu: Ming-Qing shiqi di minjian shenghuo shilu* (The complete collection of myriad treasures: A true record of the life of commoners in the Ming and Qing periods). Taipei: Hua Mulan wenhua gongzuofang. Two volumes.

Wu, Hung 1995. "Emperor's Masquerade: Costume Portraits of Yongzheng and Qianlong." *Orientations* (July and August): 25–41.

Wu, Hung 1996. *The Double Screen: Medium and Representation in Chinese Painting*. Chicago: University of Chicago Press.

Wu, Hung and Katherine R. Tsiang, eds. 2005. *Body and Face in Chinese Visual Culture*. Cambridge, Mass. and London: Harvard East Asian Monographs 239.

Wu, Joseph S. Undated. "Basic Characteristics of Chinese Culture." Available at www.thomehfang.com/suncrates3/1wu.html.

Wu, Pei-yi 1990. *The Confucian's Progress: Autobiographical Writings in Traditional China*. Princeton: Princeton University Press.

Wu, Renshu 2013. *Youyou fangxiang: Ming Qing Jiangnan chengshi de xiuxian xiaofei yu kong jian bianqian* (Urban pleasures: Leisure consumption and spatial transformation in Jiangnan cities during the Ming-Qing period). Taibei: Zhongyang yanjiu yuan jindai shi yanjiu suo.

Wu, Rongguang 1832. *Wuxue lu* (Record of my studies). Minting huijing tang.

Wu, Shanzhong 2005. *Taiping tianguo lifa yanjiu shuping* (A review of research on the Taiping calendar). *Yangzhou daxue xuebao* 9.3 (May): 76–81. Available at http://wenku.baidu.com/view/df8d55d5195f312b3169a590.html.

Wu, Silas 1970a. *Communication and Imperial Control in China*. Cambridge, Mass.: Harvard University Press.

Wu, Silas 1970b. "Emperors at Work: The Daily Schedules of the K'ang-hsi and Yung-cheng Emperors, 1661–1735." *Tsing Hua Journal of Chinese Studies* new series 8.1–2 (August): 210–27.

Wu, Silas 1979. *Passage to Power: K'ang-hsi and his Heir Apparent, 1661–1722*. Cambridge, Mass. and London: Harvard University Press.

Wu, Wei-p'ing 1969. "The Development and Decline of the Eight Banners." Ph.D. dissertation, University of Pennsylvania.

Wu, Xinying 2012. *Ruxue yu Zhongguo chuantong wenhua* (Confucianism and China's traditional culture). Beijing: Zhongyang minzu daxue chubanshe.

Wu, Yenna 1995. *The Lioness Roars: Shrew Stories from Late Imperial China*. Ithaca, N.Y.: Cornell East Asia Series 81.

Wu, Yi-li 2000. "The Bamboo Grove Monastery and Popular Gynecology in Qing China." *Late Imperial China* 21.1 (June): 41–76.

Wu, Yi-li 2010. *Reproducing Women: Medicine, Metaphor, and Childbirth in Late Imperial China*. Berkeley: University of California Press.

Wuhan daxue Zhongguo chuantong wenhua yanjiu zhongxin, ed. 2001. *Xiong Shili yu Zhongguo chuantong wenhua guoji xueshu yantao hui* (A collection of scholarly papers from an international conference on Xiong Shili and China's traditional culture). Wuhan: Hubei jiaoyu chubanshe.

Wylie, Alexander 1897. *Notes on Chinese Literature*. Shanghai: No publisher indicated.

Xi, Yufu, ed. 1969. *Huangchao zhengdian leizuan* (Classified compendium of Qing government statutes). Taibei: Chengwen chubanshe. Reprint of 1903 edition.

Xiao, Hongfa 2009. *Zhongguo chuantong wenhua yishu ji qi yanbian* (The arts of China's traditional culture and their evolution). Nanning: Guangxi minzu chubanshe.

Xiao, Taitao 1998. *Quanwei yifu: Zhongguo chuantong wenhua: Xinli zhong di quanwei yishi yanjiu* (Authority dependency: China's traditional culture: Research on the psychology of authority-awareness). Nanjing: Jiangsu jiaoyu chubanshe.

Xiao, Yishan 1962. *Qingdai tongshi* (Comprehensive History of the Qing Dynasty). Taibei: Taiwan shangwu yinshu guan. Five volumes.

Xie, Xiaobo 2011. "Guoxue Re and the Ambiguity of Chinese Modernity." *China Perspectives* special issue: 39–45. Available at http://chinaperspectives.revues.org/5378?file=1.

Xu, Guanghua 2002. *Zhongguo wenhua gaiyao* (An introduction to the essentials of Chinese culture). Shanghai: Hanyu dacidian chubanshe.

Xu, Hao 1999. *Shiba shiji di Zhongguo yu shijie: Nongmin juan* (China and the world in the eighteenth century: Peasants). Shenyang: Liaohai chubanshe.

Xu, Hua'an 1999. *Qingdai zongzu zuzhi yanjiu* (Research on clan organization in the Qing dynasty). Beijing: Zhongggo renmin gongan daxue chubanshe.

Xu, Ke 1916. *Qingbai leichao* (Classified collection of anecdotes from the Qing dynasty). Shanghai: Shangwu.

Xu, Pingfan et al. 2004. *Zhongguo wenming di xingcheng* (The shape of Chinese civilization). Beijing: Xin shijie chubanshe.

Xu, Shichang, comp. 1938. *Qingru xuean* (Records of Qing Scholars). Tianjin: Xushijia.

Xu, Sufeng 2013. "Domesticating Romantic Love during the High Qing Classical Revival: The Poetic Exchanges between Wang Zhaoyuan (1763–1851) and Her Husband Hao Yixing (1757–1829)." *Nan Nü* 15.2: 219–64.

Xu, Xueji 1987. *Qingdai Taiwan di lüying* (The Green Standard Army of Taiwan in the Qing dynasty). Nangang: Zhongyang yanjiu yuan jindai shi yanjiu suo.

Xu, Yi et al., eds. 1996. *Zhongguo chuantong wenhua cidian* (Dictionary of China's traditional culture). Changchun: Jilin daxue chubanshe).

Yabuuchi, Kiyoshi 1990. *Chūgoku no temmon rekihō* (Astronomical calendar systems of China). Tōkyō: Heibonsha. Amplified and revised edition.

Yamagiwa, Joseph, ed. 1969. *Papers of the CIC. Far Eastern Language Institute.* Ann Arbor, Mich.: CIC Far Eastern Language Institute.

Yan, Susen and Xu Changda, comp. 1871. *Huangchao jiqi yuewu lu* (Record of the Qing dynasty's sacrificial implements, music and dances). Chubei: Chongwen shuju.

Yan, Yunxiang 1996. *The Flow of Gifts: Reciprocity and Social Networks in a Chinese Village.* Stanford: Stanford University Press.

Yang, C. K. 1961. *Religion in Chinese Society.* Berkeley: University of California Press.

Yang, Cengwen 2009. *Fojiao yu Zhongguo chuantong wenhua* (Buddhism and China's traditional culture). Beijing: Zhongguo shehui kexue chubanshe.

Yang, Fujun 2010a. *Zhongguo jizu shi* (History of Chinese ancestor worship). Shanghai: Shanghai daxue chubanshe.

Yang, Fujun 2010b. *Zhongguo xingshi shi* (History of Chinese family names). Shanghai: Shanghai daxue chubanshe.

Yang, Hsien-yi and Gladys Yang, trans. 1957. *The Scholars.* Peking: Foreign Languages Press.

Yang, Hsien-yi and Gladys Yang, trans. 1978–1980. *A Dream of Red Mansions*. Peking: Foreign Languages Press.

Yang, Li 1998. *Book of Changes and Traditional Chinese Medicine*. Beijing: Beijing Science and Technology Press.

Yang, Lien-sheng 1969. *Excursions in Sinology*. Cambridge, Mass.: Harvard University Press.

Yang, Mayfair Mei-hui 1994. *Gifts, Favors and Banquets: The Art of Social Relationships in China*. Ithaca and London: Cornell University Press.

Yang, Winston et al., eds. 1981. *Classical Chinese Fiction: A Guide to Its Study and Appreciation*. Boston: G. K. Hall.

Yang, Xichun 1991. *Manzu fengsu kao* (An examination of Manchu customs). Harbin: Heilongjiang renmin chubanshe.

Yang, Xin and Chengru Zhu 1999. *Secret World of the Forbidden City: Splendors from China's Imperial Palace*. Beijing: National Palace Museum.

Yang, Youjiong 1968. *Zhongguo wenhua shi* (History of Chinese culture). Taibei: Taiwan shudian.

Yang, Zhenning and Rao Zongyi, eds. 2003. *Zhongguo wenhua yu kexue* (Chinese culture and science). Nanjing: Jiaoyu chubanshe.

Yang, Zongyuan 2001. *Zhongguo gudai di wenzi* (Ancient Chinese writing). Taibei: Wenjin chubanshe.

Yao, Jizhong 2010. *Yuanshi wuyu yu Zhongguo chuantong wenhua* (The *Tale of Genji* and China's traditional culture). Beijing: Zhongyang bianyi chubanshe.

Yates, Robin D. S., trans. 1997. *Five Lost Classics: Tao, Huang-Lao, and Yin-Yang in Han China*. New York: Ballantine.

Yates, Robin D. S. 2009. *Women in China from Earliest Times to the Present: A Bibliography of Studies in Western Languages*. Leiden and Boston: Brill.

Ye, Xiaoqing 2003. *The Dianshizhai Pictorial: Shanghai Urban Life 1884–1898*. Ann Arbor: University of Michigan Center for Chinese Studies.

Yee, Angelina C. 1990. "Counterpoise in *Honglou meng*." *Harvard Journal of Asiatic Studies* 50.2: 613–50.

Yeh, Wen-hsin 1990. *The Alienated Academy: Culture and Politics in Republican China 1919–1937*. Cambridge, Mass.: Harvard University Press.

Yeh, Wen-hsin 1996. *Provincial Passages: Culture, Space, and the Origins of Chinese Communism, 1919–1927*. Berkeley: University of California Press.

Yeh, Wen-hsin 2008. *Shanghai Splendor: Economic Sentiments and the Making of Modern China, 1843–1949*. Berkeley: University of California Press.

Yeh, Wen-hsin, ed. 2000. *Becoming Chinese: Passages to Modernity and Beyond*. Berkeley: University of California Press.

Yetts, W. Percival 1912. *Symbolism in Chinese Art*. Leiden: Brill.

Yi, Ding et al. 1996. *Zhongguo gudai fengshui yu jianzhu xuanzhi* (Geomancy and architectural site selection in ancient China). Shijiazhuang: Hebei kexue jishu chubanshe.

Yi, Wen 2010. *Zhongguo chuangta yishu shi* (History of the craft of Chinese beds). Nanjing: Dongnan daxue chubanshe.

Yin, Haiguang 2009. *Zhongguo wenhua de zhanwang* (The outlook for Chinese culture). Shanghai: Shanghai sanlian shudian.

Ying, Demin 1997. *Dongfang di zhihui: Zhongguo chuantong wenhua xieyao* (The wisdom of the East: Selected essentials of China's traditional culture). Beijing: Jingguan jiaoyu chubanshe.

Yip, Evelyn 1992. *Chinese Numbers*. Singapore: Times Books International.

Yip, Wai-lim 1976. *Chinese Poetry*. Berkeley and Los Angeles: University of California Press.

Young, John D. 1983. *Confucianism and Christianity: The First Encounter*. Hong Kong: Hong Kong University Press.

Young, Lung-chang 1988. "Regional Stereotypes in China." *Chinese Studies in History* 21.4 (Summer): 32–57.

Yu, Anthony, trans. 1977–1979. *The Journey to the West*. Chicago: University of Chicago Press. Four volumes.

Yu, Huaming 2008. *Zhong Xi jiaotong shi* (A history of exchanges between China and the West). Shanghai: Shanghai renmin chubanshe.

Yu, Hui-chun 2007. "The Intersection of Past and Present: The Qianlong Emperor and His Ancient Bronzes." Ph.D. dissertation, Princeton University.

Yu, Li 2003. "A History of Reading in Late Imperial China, 1000–1800." Ph.D. dissertation, Ohio State University.

Yu, Pauline 1987. *The Reading of Imagery in the Chinese Poetic Tradition*. Princeton: Princeton University Press.

Yu, Xueming and Chen Hong 2001. *Zhongguo gudai di zhexue yu zongjiao* (Ancient Chinese philosophy and religion). Taibei: Wenjin chubanshe.

Yü, Ying-shih 1975. "Some Preliminary Observations on the Rise of Ch'ing Confucian Intellectualism." *Tsing Hua Journal of Chinese Studies* new series 11.1–2 (December): 104–46.

Yu, Yingshi [Yü Ying-shih] 2010. *Zhongguo wenhua shi tongshi* (A comprehensive elucidation of the history of Chinese culture). Hong Kong: Oxford University Press.

Yü, Ying-shih 1993. "The Radicalization of China in the Twentieth Century." *Daedalus* 122.2 (Spring): 125–50.

Yu, Yuhe 2001. *Zhongguo chuantong wenhua gailun* (Introduction to China's traditional culture). Tianjin: Tianjin daxue chubanshe.

Yu, Zhi, ed. 1872. *Nü ershisi xiao tushuo* (illustrated version of the *Women's Twenty-Four Examples of Filial Piety*). Wujin: Shuangbaiyan tang.

Yu, Zuhua 2012. *Minzuzhuyi yu Zhonghua minzu jingshen di xiandai zhuanxing* (Nationalism and the modern transformation of the Chinese people's national spirit). Beijing: Shehui kexue wenxian chubanshe.

Yuan, Shushan 1948. *Zhongguo lidai buren zhuan* (Biographies of diviners in China by dynastic periods). Shanghai: Rude shuju, 1948. A new 1998 edition was published in Taibei by the Xingwenfeng chuban gongsi with consecutive pagination.

Yuan, Xingpei 1993. *Guoxue yanjiu* (Research on [China's] National Learning). Beijing: Beijing daxue chubanshe.

Yuan, Xingpei 2010. *Zhonghua wenming zhi guang* (The glory of Chinese civilization). New York: Cambridge University Press. Four volumes.

Yue Aiguo 2006. *Zhongguo chuantong wenhua yu keji* (China's traditional culture, science and technology). Guilin: Guangxi shifan daxue chubanshe.

Yue, Shanyue 2008. *Liushu yu Zhongguo chuantong wenhua* (The six [categories of Chinese] characters and China's traditional culture). Shanghai: Shanghai sanlian shudian.

Yung, Bell 1989. *Cantonese Opera: Performance as Creative Process.* Cambridge Eng.: Cambridge University Press.

Yung, Bell, Evelyn Rawski, and Rubie Watson, eds. 1996. *Harmony and Counterpoint: Ritual Music in Chinese Context.* Stanford: Stanford University Press.

Zarrow, Peter 1988. "He Zhen and Anarcho-Feminism in China." *Journal of Asian Studies* 47.4 (November): 796–813.

Zarrow, Peter 2004. "Historical Trauma, Anti-Manchuism and Memories of Atrocity in Late Qing China." *History and Memory* 16.2 (Fall/Winter): 67–107.

Zeitlin, Judith T. 1993. *Historian of the Strange: Pu Songling and the Chinese Classical Tale.* Stanford: Stanford University Press.

Zeitlin, Judith T. 2007. *The Phantom Heroine: Ghosts and Gender in Seventeenth-Century Chinese Literature.* Honolulu: University of Hawaii Press.

Zeitlin, Judith T. et al., eds. 2003. *Writing and Materiality in China: Essays in Honor of Patrick Hanan.* Cambridge, Mass. and London: Harvard-Yenching Institute Monograph Series 58.

Zelin, Madeleine 1984. *The Magistrate's Tael: Rationalizing Fiscal Reform in Eighteenth Century Ch'ing China.* Berkeley: University of California Press.

Zelin, Madeleine, Jonathan K. Ocko, and Robert Gardella, eds. 2004. *Contract and Property in Early Modern China.* Stanford, Calif.: Stanford University Press.

Zen, Sophia, ed. 1969. *Symposium on Chinese Culture.* New York.

Zhan, Heying Jenny and Roger W. Bradshaw 1996. "Texts and Contexts: The Book of *Analects* for Women." *Journal of Historical Sociology* 9.3: 261–68.

Zhan, Kaidi 1992. *The Strategies of Politeness in the Chinese Language.* Berkeley: University of California Press.

Zhang Zhongmou 1997. *Qingdai wenhua yu Zhepai shi* (Qing dynasty culture and the Zhejiang School of poetry). Beijing: Dongfang chubanshe.

Zhang, Bing 2013. *Wenhua shiyu zhong di Qingdai wenxue yanjiu* (Research on Qing dynasty literature from a cultural field of vision). Beijing: Renmin chubanshe.

Zhang, Chengquan 2012. *Daojia daojiao yu Zhongguo wenxue* (Philosophical Daoism, Religious Daoism and Chinese Literature). Hefei: Anhui daxue chubanshe.

Zhang, Cong and Yao Ping, eds. 2013. *Dangdai Xifang Hanxue yanjiu jicui: Sixiang wenhua shijuan* (Collection of the best contemporary Western scholarship on China: Thought, culture and history). Shanghai: Shanghai guji chubanshe.

Zhang, Dainian 2002. *Key Concepts in Chinese Philosophy.* New Haven: Yale University Press. Translated and edited by Edmund Ryden.

Zhang, Dainian 2014. *Zhongguo zhexue da cidian* (Dictionary of Chinese philosophy). Shanghai: Shanghai cishu chubanshe.

Zhang, Dainian and Jiang Guanghui, eds. 1990. *Zhongguo wenhua chuantong duihua* (Dialogues on China's cultural tradition). Beijing: Zhongguo guangbo dianshi chubanshe.

Zhang, Dechang 1970. *Qingji yige jingguan di shenghuo* (The life of a metropolitan official in the late Qing period). Hong Kong: Xianggang Zhongwen daxue.

Zhang, Haihui et al., eds. 2013. *A Scholarly Review of Chinese Studies in North America*. Ann Arbor: Association for Asian Studies. Available at www.asian-studies.org/publications/A_Scholarly_Review_epPDF.pdf.

Zhang, Jiasheng 1997. "Lun 'Baqi wenxue' ji qi xingcheng jichu" (On Banner literature and its formative foundations). *Saksaha: A Review of Manchu Studies* 2 (Spring): 12–18.

Zhang, Jie 2007. *Manzu yaolun* (Essentials of the Manchus). Zhongguo shehui kexue chubanshe.

Zhang, Jun 2008. "Spider Manchu: Duanfang as networker and spindoctor of the late Qing new policies, 1901–1911." Ph.D. dissertation, University of California, San Diego. Available at http://escholarship.org/uc/item/3vq813c4.

Zhang, Lawrence Lok Cheung 2010. "Power for a Price: Office Purchase, Elite Families and Status Maintenance in Qing China." Ph.D. dissertation, Harvard University.

Zhang, Lawrence [Lok Cheung] 2013. "Legacy of Success: Office Purchase and State-Elite Relations in Qing China." *Harvard Journal of Asiatic Studies* 73.2 (December): 259–97.

Zhang, Li 2005. *Cong chuantong zouxiang jindai: Zhongguo kexue wenhua shi shang di Ruan Yuan* (From tradition toward modernity: Ruan Yuan in the history of Chinese scientific culture). Hefei: Anhui jiaoyu chubanshe.

Zhang, Min 1998. "A Brief Discussion of the Banquets of the Qing Court." In Ho and Jones, eds.: n.p. [1–5].

Zhang, Pu 1758. *Wanbao quanshu* (Encyclopedia of myriad treasures). [Full title: *Xinke Tianru Zhang Xiansheng jing xuan Shiqu hui yao Wanbao quanshu*]. Foshan: Laohui xiantang. Available at http://digital.staatsbibliothekberlin. de/dms/werkansi cht/?PPN=PPN3303598916&DMDID=DMDLOG_0000.

Zhang, Qiyun et al., eds. 1961. *Qingshi* (History of the Qing dynasty). Taibei: Guofang yanjiu yuan. Six volumes. Abbreviation: QS.

Zhang, Qiyun, ed. 1973. *Zhongwen da cidian* (Great dictionary of the Chinese language). Taibei [Yangming shan]: Zhonghua xueshu yuan.

Zhang, Rongming 2000. *Fangshu yu Zhongguo chuantong wenhua* (The arts of calculation and China's traditional culture). Shanghai: Xuelin chubanshe.

Zhang, Rongming, ed. 1994. *Dao Fo Ru sixiang yu Zhongguo chuantong wenhua* (Daoist, Buddhist and Confucian thought and China's traditional culture). Shanghai: Shanghai renmin chubanshe.

Zhang, Rucheng 1723. *Jiali huitong* (Compendium on family ritual). Changzhou: Jixin tang.

Zhang, Shaokang 2010. *Liu Xie ji qi Wenxin diaolong yanjiu* (Research on Liu Xie and his *Literary Mind and the Carving of Dragons*). Beijing: Beijing daxue chubanshe.

Zhang, Ying 2010. "Politics and Morality during the Ming-Qing Dynastic Transition (1570–1670)." Ph.D. dissertation, University of Michigan.

Zhang, Zichen. 1985. *Zhongguo minsu yu minsu xue* (Chinese folklore and folklore studies). Hangzhou: Zhejiang renmin chubanshe.

Zhao, Aping and Li Jiang 1997. "On Elements of Saman Culture in Manchu Words." *Saksaha: A Review of Manchu Studies* 2 (Spring): 39–46.

Zhao, Shiyu 2014. *The Urban Life of the Qing Dynasty*. Reading, Eng. and Singapore: Paths International. Translated by Wang Hong and Zhang Linlin.

Zheng, Jixiong 2001. *Qing Ru mingzhu shuping* (A review of the famous writings of Qing Confucians). Taibei: Da'an chubanshe.

Zhong, Fulan 1989. *Zhongguo minsu liubian* (Changes in Chinese popular customs). Hong Kong: Zhonghua shuju.

Zhong, Fulan 2012. *Fengsu yu xinyang* (Customs and beliefs). Shanghai: Fudan daxue chubanshe.

Zhong, Shaohua 1996. *Renlei zhishi de xin gongju: Zhong Ri jindai baike quanshu yanjiu* (New tools of human knowledge: Research on Chinese and Japanese encyclopedias). Beijing: Beijing tushuguan chubanshe.

Zhongguo ge minzu zongjiao yu shenhua da cidian bianshen weiyuan hui, ed. 1990. *Zhongguo ge minzu zongjiao yu shenhua da cidian* (A dictionary of the religions and myths of the various nationalities of China). Beijing: Xueyuan chubanshe.

Zhongguo shehui kexue yuan, ed. 2011. *Qingdai Man-Han guanxi yanjiu* (Research on Manchu-Han relations in the Qing dynasty). Beijing: Shehui kexue wenxiuan chubanshe.

Zhonghua wenhua fuxing yundong tuixing weiyuan hui, ed. 1974. *Zhonghua wenhua gaishu* (Chinese culture: A general narration). Taibei: Shangwu yinshu guan.

Zhou, Guangyuan 1995. "Beneath the Law: Chinese Local Legal Culture during the Qing Dynasty." Ph.D. dissertation, University of California, Los Angeles.

Zhou, Liang 1911. *Liyi bianlan* (A guide to ritual and etiquette). N.p. Personal copy.

Zhou, Yuanlian 1981. *Qingchao kaiguo shi yanjiu* (Research on the history of the founding of the Qing dynasty). Shenyang: Liaoning renmin chubanshe.

Zhu, Xi 1893. *Zhouyi benyi* (The basic meaning of the *Zhou Changes*). Shanghai: N.p.

Zi, Etienne 1894a. *Pratique des examens littéraires en China*. Shanghai: Imprimerie de la Mission Catholique.

Zi, Etienne 1894b. *Pratique des examens militaires en China*. Shanghai: Imprimerie de la Mission Catholique.

Zito, Angela 1984. "Re-presenting Sacrifice: Cosmology and the Editing of Texts." *Ch'ing-shih wen-t'i* 5.2 (December): 47–78.

Zito, Angela 1987. "City Gods, Filiality and Hegemony in Late Imperial China." *Modern China* 13.3: 333–71.

Zito, Angela 1989. "Grand Sacrifice as Text/Performance: Ritual Writing in Eighteenth Century China." Ph.D. dissertation, University of Chicago.

Zito, Angela 1997. *Of Body and Brush: Grand Sacrifice as Text/Performance in 18th Century China*. Chicago: University of Chicago Press.

Zito, Angela 2006. "Bound to Be Represented: Fetishizing/Theorizing Footbinding." In Larissa Heinrich and Fran Martin, eds., *Embodied Modernities: Corporeality, Representation, and Chinese Cultures*. Honolulu: University of Hawaii Press: 29–41.

Zunz, Oliver, ed. 1985. *Reliving the Past: The Worlds of Social History*. Chapel Hill: University of North Carolina Press.

Zurndorfer, Harriet T. 1988a. "A Guide to the 'New' Chinese History: Recent Publications Concerning Chinese Social and Economic Development Before 1800." *International Review of Social History* 33: 148–201.

Zurndorfer, Harriet T. 1988b. "Comment la science et la technologie se vendaient à la Chine au XVIIIe siècle Essai d'analyse interne." *Études chinoises* 7.2 (Autumn): 59–90.

Zurndorfer, Harriet T. 1992. "Learning, Lineages, and Locality in Late Imperial China: A Comparative Study of Education in Huichow (Anhwei) and Foochow (Fukien) 1600–1800." *Journal of the Economic and Social History of the Orient* 35.2: 109–44 and 35.3: 209–38.

Zurndorfer, Harriet T. 1994. "How to Be a Good Wife and a Good Scholar at the Same Time: 18th Century Prescriptions on Chinese Female Behavior—A Preliminary Investigation." In Vandermeersch, ed. 1994: 249–70.

Zurndorfer, Harriet T. 1997. *Change and Continuity in Chinese Local History: The Development of Hui-Chou Prefecture, 800 to 1800*. Leiden: Brill.

Zurndorfer, Harriet T. 1999. "Women in the Epistemological Strategy of Chinese Encyclopedia: Preliminary Observations from Some Sung, Ming, and Ch'ing Works." In Zurndorfer, ed. 1999: 354–95.

Zurndorfer, Harriet T. 2002. "Old and New Visions of Ming Society and Culture." *T'oung Pao*, second series 88.1–3: 151–69.

Zurndorfer, Harriet T. 2004a. "Science Without Modernization: China's First Encounter with Useful and Reliable Knowledge from Europe." Paper for the Fourth Global Economic History Network Workshop. Available at www.lse.ac.uk/eco nomicHistory/Research/GEHN/Conferences/conference9.aspx.

Zurndorfer, Harriet T. 2004b. "Imperialism, Globalization, and Public Finance: The Case of Late Qing China." Paper for the Second Global Economic History Network Conference, Irvine, California (January 15–17). Available at www.lse.ac.uk/ economichistory/research/gehn/gehnpdf/workingpaper06hz.pdf.

Zurndorfer, Harriet T. 2008. "Wang Zhaoyuan (1763–1851) and the Erasure of 'Talented Women' by Liang Qichao." In Qian, Wong, and Smith, eds. 2008: 29–56.

Zurndorfer, Harriet T. 2009. "China and Science on the Eve of the 'Great Divergence' 1600–1800: A Review of Recent Revisionist Scholarship in Western Languages." *The History of Technology* 29: 81–101.

Zurndorfer, Harriet T. 2011a. "The *Lienü zhuan* Tradition and Wang Zhaoyuan's (1763–1851) Production of the *Lienü zhuan buzhu* (1812)." In Judge and Hu 2011: 55–69.

Zurndorfer, Harriet T. 2011b. "Cotton Textile Manufacture and Marketing in Late Imperial China and the 'Great Divergence.'" *Journal of the Economic and Social History of the Orient* 54.5: 701–38.

Zurndorfer, Harriet T. 2012. "Women in Chinese Encyclopedias." In Clara Ho, ed. 2012b: 279–305.

Zurndorfer, Harriet T. 2013. "Chinese Encyclopaedism: A Postscript." In Konig and Woolf, eds. 2013: 505–28.

Zurndorfer, Harriet T. 2014a. "Women in Chinese Learned Culture: Complexities, Exclusivities and Connecting Narratives." *Gender and History* 26.1 (2014): 23–35.

Zurndorfer, Harriet T. 2014b. "Gender Issues in Traditional China." Oxford Bibliographies Online. Oxford: Oxford University Press: 1–45.

Zurndorfer, Harriet T., ed. 1999. *Chinese Women in the Imperial Past: New Perspectives*. Leiden: Brill.

Index

academies, 108, 114, 136, 144, 210,
321, 382
aesthetics, 1, 5, 6, 14, 17, 77, 127,
183, 188, 194, 210, 237, 273, 275,
276, 277, 278, 280–84, 286–288,
290, 302, 303, 306, 313, 325, 330,
331, 339, 344, 368, 369, 468n.14,
469n.39. *See also* art, divination,
music, ritual, *Yijing*
adoption, 94, 150, 345, 347, 354–55
agriculture, 2, 6, 9, 25, 55, 59, 67,
71, 92, 140, 158, 159, 244, 311,
345, 376, 390, 399, 403, 411, 413,
457n.22
alchemy, 199, 201, 233, 261, 362, 363
alcohol, 259, 260, 373–74
aliens. *See* foreigners
almanacs (*huangli, tongshu*), xi, 6, 39,
52, 193, 214, 218, 266, 326, 345,
346, 348, 357, 363, 375, 384. *See
also* calendars
amusements, 6, 40, 326, 339, 349, 367,
375, 395. *See also* chess, drinking
games, festivals, gambling, games,
music, zither
analysis of written characters (*chaizi,
cezi*), 141, 176–80, 265. *See also*
Chinese writing, word magic

ancestor worship (aka ancestor
veneration), 1, 6, 14, 23, 24, 52,
70, 72, 91, 131, 145, 151–54, 157,
158, 159, 166, 176, 211, 232, 244,
267–71, 347, 349, 350, 354, 357,
366, 367, 372, 373, 375–79 passim,
392, 401, 404, 444, 467n.59
ancestral precedent (*zuzong chengfa*),
56, 80, 83, 94, 131, 154, 157, 159,
243, 253, 354, 357, 366, 376, 388,
393
animals. *See* state sacrifice, symbolism
Annam. *See* Vietnam
anti-Manchuism, 62, 66, 96, 167, 395.
See also Manchus
Army of the Green Standard (*Lüying*),
65, 70, 82, 100, 101, 119, 146, 147,
387
art. *See* aesthetics, calligraphy,
connoisseurship, crafts, painting,
vernacular art
artisans (*gong*), 33, 39, 128, 137, 140,
141, 142, 144, 159, 180, 282, 283,
364
astrology, 203, 265, 267, 270. *See also*
astronomy, divination
astronomy, 46, 47, 71, 92, 101, 201–04,
216, 242, 310, 311, 317. *See also*

585

About the Author

Richard J. Smith received his Ph.D. from the University of California, Davis. He is currently George and Nancy Rupp Professor of Humanities, Professor of History, a James A. Baker III Institute for Public Policy Scholar, and Director of Asian and Global Outreach (Center for Education) at Rice University in Houston, Texas. He is also an adjunct professor at the Center for Asian Studies, University of Texas, Austin and a member of the National Committee on U.S.-China Relations. Smith co-founded the Transnational China Project at the Baker Institute (www.ruf.rice.edu/~tnchina/) and served for fifteen years as the Director of Asian Studies at Rice (http://chaocenter .rice.edu/).

A specialist in modern Chinese history and traditional Chinese culture, Smith also has strong interests in transnational, global, and comparative studies. He has websites devoted to the *Yijing* (Classic of Changes) and Chinese encyclopedias (see http://history.rice.edu/faculty/richard-j-smith).

Smith has won twelve teaching awards while at Rice, including the Phi Beta Kappa award (1978), several George R. Brown Superior Teaching awards (1980, 1982, 1983, and 1990), the Piper Professorship award (1987), the George R. Brown Certificate of Highest Merit (1992), the Sarofim Distinguished Teaching Professorship (1994), the Nicholas Salgo Distinguished Teaching Award (1996), and the Carnegie Foundation for the Advancement of Teaching "Texas Professor of the Year" Award (1998).

Smith's nine single-authored books include *Mercenaries and Mandarins: The Ever-Victorious Army in Nineteenth Century China* (1978); *Traditional Chinese Culture: A Brief Introduction* (1978); *Fortune-tellers and Philosophers: Divination in Traditional Chinese Society* (1991); *Chinese Almanacs* (1992); *China's Cultural Heritage: The Qing Dynasty, 1644–1912* (1994); *Chinese Maps: Images of "All Under Heaven"* (1996); *Fathoming the Cos-*

mos and Ordering the World: The Yijing (I Ching or Book of Changes) and Its Evolution in China (2008); *The I Ching: A Biography* (2012); and *Mapping China and Managing the World: Cosmology, Cartography and Culture in Late Imperial Times* (2013).

He has also co-edited or co-authored six volumes: *Chinese Walled Cities* (1979); *Entering China's Service* (1986); *Robert Hart and China's Early Modernization* (1991); *Cosmology, Ontology, and Human Efficacy: Essays in Chinese Thought* (1993); *H. B. Morse, Customs Commissioner and Historian of China* (1995); and *Different Worlds of Discourse: Transformations of Gender and Genre in Late Qing and Early Republican China* (2008).

Smith is presently working on several articles and book chapters, as well as a monograph on encyclopedias and popular science in Qing dynasty China.

Born in Sacramento, California, in 1944, Smith had a brief flirtation with professional baseball before coming to his senses. He has been married to his gifted and charming wife, Lisa, for forty-eight years, and they have a delightful and accomplished son named Tyler.